THE
LONGEST RAID
OF THE CIVIL WAR

Little-Known & Untold Stories of
Morgan's Raid into Kentucky, Indiana & Ohio

By Lester V. Horwitz

"He lives twice who enjoys both the past and present."

—Martial

Dedication

Dedicated to my wife, Florence, whose patience, understanding and encouragement were my constant companion on this thousand mile journey. This book might never have been started except for my beloved children, Reid, Stuart, Leah, Joan and Robin, who challenged me to "get it all down on paper."

Brigadier-General John Hunt Morgan, CSA

General Morgan is shown in the "uniform" he wore on his "Great Raid" into Kentucky, Indiana and Ohio in July 1863. Instead of a traditional general's uniform, he wore a dark linen jacket, gray pants, white shirt, knee-high leather boots with spurs and a wide-brimmed felt hat. There were no decorations or signs of rank visible.

Table of Contents

Foreword... **James A. Ramage,**
Regents Professor of History,
Northern Kentucky University, ... **v**
Author of *Rebel Raider*
PREFACE .... **viii**
Chapter 1: **Why the Raid?** **1**
Chapter 2: **Getting Ready for Battle** **6**

KENTUCKY
Chapter 3: **Crossing the Cumberland Twice** **13**

CUMBERLAND COUNTY
Chapter 4: **"Naked as Jay-Birds!"** **19**

ADAIR COUNTY **21**
TAYLOR COUNTY
Chapter 5: **An Ominous Sign** **22**

MARION, WASHINGTON & NELSON COUNTIES **27**
Chapter 6: **"Twenty-Five Damned Yankees"** **29**
Chapter 7: **Treachery Within the Ranks** **34**

BULLITT, JEFFERSON, HARDIN & MEADE COUNTIES
Chapter 8: **A Feint Toward Louisville** **37**
Chapter 9: **To the River** **40**
Chapter 10: **Get Across the Ohio and Burn the Boats!** **47**
Military Study of Brandenburg Crossing **53**

INDIANA
CLARK & FLOYD COUNTIES
Chapter 11: **Confederate Thunderbolt Strikes Indiana and Ohio** .. **55**

HARRISON COUNTY
Chapter 12: **The Battle of Corydon** **60**
Military Study of Battle of Corydon **71**

WASHINGTON COUNTY
Chapter 13: **The Hoosier Zigzag** 80
JACKSON & SCOTT COUNTIES 84
JENNINGS & JEFFERSON COUNTIES 86
Chapter 14: **Dupont Pays the Price** 92

RIPLEY COUNTY 96
DEARBORN COUNTY
Chapter 15: **Last Day in Indiana** 98

OHIO
HAMILTON COUNTY
Chapter 16: **Harrison Shopping Spree** 106
Chapter 17: **Let's Split!** 110
Chapter 18: **Waiting for Morgan** 113
Chapter 19: **"Veiled" Threat in Glendale** 120
Chapter 20: **While Sherman Slept** 123
Chapter 21: **Camp Dennison's 600-Gun Salute** 126
Chapter 22: **Thoroughbreds in Trade** 131

CLERMONT COUNTY
Chapter 23: **An Unscheduled Train Stop** 137
Chapter 24: **A Romance of Morgan's Rough Riders** 140
Chapter 25: **Williamsburg, the First Good Rest in Weeks!** 145
Chapter 26: **Mayor Leads Cincinnati Cavalry** 149

BROWN COUNTY
Chapter 27: **Colonel Morgan Visits Georgetown** 154
Chapter 28: **Beeline for Buffington** 159

ADAMS COUNTY
Chapter 29: **Winchester's "Fenced In"** 164

PIKE COUNTY
Chapter 30: **"Axes to the Front!"** 169
Chapter 31: **McDougal's Fatal Encounter** 174
Chapter 32: **A Bridge Beyond** 177

JACKSON COUNTY
Chapter 33: **Newspaper Wars** 182

VINTON COUNTY
Chapter 34: **"Our Last Night in the North"** 188
Chapter 35: **The U.S. Navy, the Union's Secret Weapon** 191

GALLIA COUNTY
Chapter 36: **Vinton Loses Its Bridge** 195

MEIGS COUNTY
Chapter 37: **Last Lap to Freedom** 196
Chapter 38: **The Pomeroy-Middleport Gauntlet** 201
Chapter 39: **The Net Tightens** 207
Chapter 40: **In a Fog** 211
Chapter 41: **The Battle at Buffington Island** 214
Chapter 42: **Morgan Escapes, Duke Captured** 220
Chapter 43: **Mopping Up** 225
Chapter 44: **Capture and Surrender. A Partial Victory** 229
Military Study of Battle of Buffington Island 234
Chapter 45: **"Go On. Save Yourself!"** 237
Chapter 46: **The Chase to Cheshire** 243
Chapter 47: **Steamboatin' to Prison** 247

ATHENS COUNTY
Chapter 48: **Riding the Athens-Meigs County Line** 253

GALLIA & VINTON COUNTIES
Chapter 49: **Give Us Your Guns and Go Home** 255

HOCKING & ATHENS COUNTIES
Chapter 50: **Starr's & Stripes** 258

PERRY & MORGAN COUNTIES
Chapter 51: **Heading for the Muskingum** 262
Chapter 52: **The Eagleport Crossing** 267
Chapter 53: **Zanesville Responds** 274

MUSKINGUM COUNTY
Chapter 54: **The Sign of the Freemason** 277

GUERNSEY COUNTY
Chapter 55: **The Bonnie Blink Ride of Mary McClelland** 280

Chapter 56: **"The Most Exciting Day in the History of (Old) Washington"** 284

HARRISON COUNTY
Chapter 57: **Lincoln's Concern About Morgan** 291

JEFFERSON COUNTY
Chapter 58: **"I'll Be Damned if I Will Ever Surrender to a Farmer!"** 299
Chapter 59: **Escape or Capture Tomorrow** 308

CARROLL COUNTY
Chapter 60: **Last Shots Fired in Anger** 317

COLUMBIANA COUNTY
Chapter 61: **"Who the Hell Is Captain Burbick?"** 323
Chapter 62: **"General Morgan Demands Your Surrender!"** 331
Chapter 63: **Be My Guest** 340

PRISON & ESCAPE
Chapter 64: **Welcome to the Pen** 344
Chapter 65: **A Letter to Mattie** 350
Chapter 66: **Breakout from "Castle Merion!"** 356

FIGHT TO THE FINISH
Chapter 67: **A Hero's Welcome** 365
Chapter 68: **End of the Glory Road** 368

EPILOGUE 377

Appendix
Battles & Skirmishes of the Ohio-Indiana Raid 379
Ohio & Indiana Raid Claims 383
Morgan's Men Reunite 384
Battle of Corydon Battlefield 385
Buffington Island Battlefield 386
Ohio & Indiana Civilians Killed During Raid 387
American Presidents Participate in Chase 388
The Morgan Family 389

Acknowledgments 392

End Notes 398

Index 442

Foreword

Grounded on meticulous research in primary sources, this is the first book-length study of John Hunt Morgan's Great Raid, and it reads like a novel. What is so remarkable is how the suspense builds and the reader hastens to turn the page to relive the next encounter between Rebel Raiders, home guards, and women and children in the villages and on the farms in Indiana and Ohio. Lester V. Horwitz, president of Horwitz Advertising, Inc., in Cincinnati, and his wife, Florence, several years ago purchased a historic home in a Cincinnati suburb near Loveland, Ohio. They learned that they were living in the path of the raid and Lester became interested in the fact that their house was raided by Morgan's men.

I first met Lester and Florence on February 16, 1995 at the Loveland Historical Museum when they were serving as co-chairs of an exhibit on the raid. He said he was researching the route of Morgan's men around Cincinnati by studying the state claims made by citizens who lost property. I congratulated him for basing his work on a solid foundation of primary documents and encouraged him to continue. Lester enlarged county engineers' office maps from the time and pinpointed each claim, including his house, and when the exhibit opened on March 11, 1995, he presented the first complete depiction of the raid route in Hamilton and Clermont Counties. The exhibit was an overwhelming success and people came from near and far to hear Lester explain his research and describe the raid: what was astounding was that he discovered that he was unleashing a flood of emotions on the part of descendants of families who experienced the raid. They came eager to tell their stories, many of them never told before outside a small circle of family and friends. The exhibit was extended from May into July, and word spread and Lester began lecturing in the community and attracting crowds that came in buses, overflowing the auditoriums with people standing in the back and around the room.

The Civil War was one of the most significant events in the history of the United States, and down through the generations family members told about when Morgan's raid brought the great war to the front door of their home. On a personal level in July 1863 the war seemed far away in Tennessee or Virginia, but now they heard the cry: "Rebels! The Rebels are coming!" Terrified, they rushed to hide their horses and conceal their valuables, but when the Confederates came, sun-tanned, self-confident and well-armed, the people's fear gave way to surprise and relief, for these were not ten-foot-tall outlaws but polite and gentle young men who were very hungry and asking for something to eat. It was the high moment of adventure in the lives of the people of that generation and they would never forget. An eight-year-old boy standing in a crowd watching the raiders pass through Antrim, Ohio, pushed his way to the front and Morgan stopped and asked him for a drink of water. Recalling years later, he said that as far as he was concerned there were only two people in town that day, him and the General.

Lester published his valuable map, Morgan's Raid TimeLine, in 1995 and extended his study to the entire raid. He read the Official Records, newspapers, diaries, and contemporary letters, and he and Florence traveled and made photographs and continued to draw from the rich, unexplored resource of family records and oral history among the families along the raid route. In this book he provides a great deal of new, previously unpublished information from the view of the citizens, home guards, Confederates and Union cavalry in pursuit. Day by day the action unfolds and the suspense is multi-faceted as the reader anticipates learning how each of these groups will react and what they will say when the raiders reach the next county or township. And meanwhile, the Union Army and Navy are closing in on the rebels, two times: first in the battle of Buffington Island and once again a week later in Morgan's final capture.

Horwitz provides the most detailed account of the battle of Buffington Island in print and provides valuable maps of that battle as well as the battle of Corydon. He reveals that both Morgan and Lieutenant Commander Leroy Fitch directing the Union Navy pursuit relied on newspapers for intelligence on enemy movements. He points out that Morgan's guerrilla strategy of taking nearly all the horses was effective in denying remounts for the Union cavalry in pursuit. One Union officer became so desperate for fresh horses that he ordered his men to open fire on a twelve-year-old Ohio lad who was attempting to escape to the woods with his father's horses. It was amusing the extent to which the farmers went to save their animals. One man brought his horse inside the house, closed the windows and told the raiders that his children were sick inside with smallpox.

Through eyewitness accounts, the book brings Morgan alive, and he moves, speaks and displays his warm, sprightly sense of humor. Throughout the raid he was extremely gentle and mannerly toward women and children, speaking softly and assuring them that they would come to no harm. Perhaps of greatest value is Horwitz's pathbreaking account of the last week of the raid and Morgan's capture and first night in captivity in Wellsville, in a private room in the Whitacre House, guarded all night by a double rank of Union soldiers encircling the hotel.

The book is a significant contribution to historiography and will have enduring value because Lester Horwitz captured the moment when the descendants of the civilians involved came forth to share their Civil War heritage.

James A. Ramage
Regents Professor of History
Northern Kentucky University

Preface

The stories you about to read are all true. Most of them happened 136 years ago. As James Ramage said in his Foreword, "It was the high moment of adventure in the lives of the people of that generation and they would never forget." What I found was that succeeding generations haven't forgotten either. Let me tell you about one incident, which is representative of the experiences I encountered as I went about uncovering stories.

On a field research trip, I was accompanied by a friend, Jack Kindell. We were trying to locate a farmhouse where General John Hunt Morgan had stopped for breakfast on the morning of July 14, 1863. It had been the home of John Schenck (pronounce with hard c as "Skaink."), a breeder of prize cattle and a Cincinnati pharmacist. I had found his home on an 1869 map of Hamilton County, Ohio. I read in the *Daily Cincinnati Enquirer,* dated July 15, 1863, that Morgan had "partaken of breakfast" at John Schenck's home. Today, his residence is in Deer Park, a Cincinnati suburb. The street has been named Schenck Avenue. Driving up and down the road, we studied the homes to see if any appeared to be old enough to date to the 1860s. Selecting the one that fit that criteria, we rang the doorbell.

An alert, elderly woman by the name of Helen Ward answered the door. We explained that I was writing a book about the raid and asked if this had been the home of John Schenck. Her face of puzzlement changed immediately to a smile and she opened the door wide and invited us in. She led us into her living room and seated us on the sofa. She excused herself and returned in a few moments carrying a cardboard box large enough to hold a pillow. Mrs. Ward pulled up a cushioned chair for herself and placed the box on a cocktail table in front of the couch.

As she opened it, she said, "I've been waiting for you for many years." With that, she began handing us yellowed newspaper articles and photographs about Morgan's raid and John Schenck's encounter with the raiders. Although she was not a descendant of Mr. Schenck, she gave us the name of Eileen Schenck, who was residing in California. Between Mrs. Ward's box of memorabilia and the California Schenck source, I was able to piece together the full story of what had happened. A year later, Helen Ward died, but not before she was able to pass her stories and documentation on to be part of this book and an important piece of this historical panorama.

But that was just one story on one street in one town. On this raid, General Morgan and his men rode an unbelievable distance. To get the whole story, I knew there was a lot of traveling ahead. For the next four years,

I drove and walked most of that historic route, taking photos, many times accompanied by my wife, Florence, making notes, talking to local residents and digging into old files for more of those Helen Ward-type treasured tales.

In the annals of Civil War history, this was the longest raid behind enemy lines. More than one thousand miles! Think of it. Morgan's men covered this distance on horseback. They had to fight their way through large groups of militia men in both Indiana and Ohio, while a force larger than theirs of regular Union cavalry were just hours behind in a relentless pursuit. Additional Union cavalry were being shipped by boats and trains paralleling their path. Morgan's men covered well over nine hundred miles through Kentucky, Indiana and Ohio in twenty-four days, less than one month! On horses, that's moving fast!

Staying in the saddle constantly for more than a month under the most stressful conditions was unprecedented hard riding. The rigors of what these men had to face behind enemy lines tested their stamina, dedication and faith in their leaders. General Morgan had quite a task on his hands to feed and care for more than 2,500 men on horseback. They had no supply lines, no quartermaster corps and no reserves. No AAA maps, no radios, no observation planes, no lights at night. When they ran out of ammunition, they had to "borrow." When they got hungry, they had to scavenge. To feed their horses, they had to forage. Two thousand men, at least twice a day, had to enter farmhouses as uninvited guests for meals. And, in almost every case, they had "take-out" orders. When their horse power failed, they had to confiscate what they could get. If it had four legs, they mounted it! They did a lot of "horse-trading." They couldn't stop because they were being relentlessly pursued by a larger force of Union cavalry. They received no mail from home. No USO. No one throwing flowers on them, unless they were dead. They were alone. On their own. And they weren't sure they were ever going back home.

General Morgan led a force of 2,500 ("effectives") Confederate cavalry[1] on the longest raid, starting at McMinnville, Tennessee, through Kentucky, Indiana and Ohio. It ended two miles west of West Point, Ohio, on S.R. 518, nine miles from the Pennsylvania border, twenty-five miles south of Youngstown, and just seventy miles (a one day's ride) from Lake Erie. This raid represented the <u>northernmost penetration</u> of the Confederacy. This was not the first nor would it be the last raid Morgan and his men would make. Col. Basil Wilson Duke, Morgan's second-in-command in his book, *History of Morgan's Cavalry,* said that there were fourteen hundred and sixty men in the First Brigade and one thousand in the Second Brigade, not including the thirty-six men in the four-piece artillery battery.[2] Thus, we will surmise that there were 2,500 men in all.

My wife, Florence, and I first came across Morgan's name when we bought a home in the suburbs of Cincinnati in October 1979. It was an old farmhouse built in 1849 on an eighty-eight acre farm originally owned by Nathaniel and Elizabeth Humphrey. When the farm was developed into a residential subdivision 116 years later, it was named "Morgan's Trace." Wisely, the developer spared the farmhouse and offered it for sale. We fell in love with the charm of this yellow-brick Federal farmhouse with its four wood-burning fireplaces and historic engravings on the root cellar walls. In the dim light, we could read the bold scrawl "Ella Humphrey 1870." As a teenager, Ella had etched her name into history in the basement's mortar walls just a few years after the end of the Civil War.

We were both fascinated with history. We set about researching the Humphrey family who had built the home and why the subdivision had been named Morgan's Trace. Our research uncovered the famous raid Morgan's Cavalry made into Ohio in July 1863. We learned that not only had Morgan's men traversed Humphrey's farm, they had also stolen two horses, a saddle and bridle.[3] Records showed that Humphrey was compensated $155 by the State of Ohio for his raid losses. We didn't know it at the time, but this home in Morgan's Trace was to inspire the interest that eventually led to an award-winning museum exhibit and the writing of this book.

In our early research, we learned that Morgan was reared in Lexington, Kentucky and his home in that city, the Hunt-Morgan House (Hopemont), was a museum open to the public. It is owned and operated by the Blue Grass Trust for Historic Preservation. Located in Lexington's historic Gratz Park District at 201 North Mill Street (40508), it has been beautifully restored to various periods of splendor enjoyed by the Hunt and Morgan families. On the second floor is the Alexander T. Hunt Civil War Museum, (606) 253-0362.

Spring of 1980 was our first visit to Morgan's ancestral home. There would be many other trips to that bluegrass community to learn more about Morgan and his men. For the past two decades, every time I visited a bookstore, I searched the shelves in the Civil War section for additional books and magazine articles about John Hunt Morgan. I have personally researched many state, municipal and private libraries in Cincinnati, Columbus, Indianapolis, Lexington, Frankfort, Louisville, Pomeroy and the Library of Congress in Washington, to name a few, looking for more information about Morgan's raid into Indiana and Ohio. Libraries and historical societies in many counties and towns all along Morgan's raid route have sent me copies of their local histories to augment the source material I needed to prepare this book.

In studying the raid, I did not find a detailed account of the raid in the Cincinnati area and I set out to fill in the blank spaces. To begin with, I decided to construct a TimeLine™ to record Morgan's Raiders' whereabouts, hour-by-hour and day-by-day. As the writing of the book progressed, I determined, whenever possible, to maintain the chronological order of events so that readers could follow the actions in the order they occurred. Throughout the book, you will find day, date and time preceding many events and incidents.

In tracing Morgan's path, I identified the roads he took and the citizens who lost horses and other valuables. Of the three states, Ohio, Indiana and Kentucky, the path through Ohio was the easiest to reconstruct even though it was the longest leg of the 1,000-mile journey. Several sources were used to determine the path Morgan took through southern and eastern Ohio. The primary source referenced were the thousands of claims published in the *Report of the Commissioners of Morgan Raid Claims to the Governor of the State of Ohio*. The hundreds of pages listing property taken, destroyed or injured by "the Rebels" is divided into the twenty-five Ohio counties through which Morgan rode. In addition to this valuable reference, I reviewed reports written by both Confederate and Union officers published in books, as well as the *Official Records of the Union and Confederate Armies*. Another key source were letters written by eyewitnesses shortly after the raid.

Finally, my wife and I attempted to drive much of the route and see with our own eyes the terrain, the battlefields, the towns, the twists and turns of the roads, the hills, the rivers and creeks that Morgan and his men had to negotiate. Along the way, we stopped to talk to local residents, area historians and others who were knowledgeable about events in their town when Morgan came "visiting." Taken all together, the maps in this book are a fairly accurate reconstruction of Morgan's main and secondary routes through Ohio. For Indiana and Kentucky, previous historical maps were referenced as well as Army and civilian reports, and letters helped in the reconstruction of the Confederates' path through those states.

Close to ninety percent of property taken in Indiana and Ohio were horses. Despite the best efforts of citizens to hide them, Morgan's men succeeded in stealing great numbers. In the North, General Morgan and his army were viewed as "terrible men." Their actions even crept into the school curriculum when northern children were obliged to recite one of the twenty-nine paragraphs in the poem, "Kentucky Belle," written by Constance Fenimore Woolson. These four lines describe the fear and tension that gripped the residents in Morgan's path:

> "I'm sent to warn the neighbors. He isn't a mile behind;
> He sweeps up all the horses—every horse that he can find;
> Morgan, Morgan the raider, and Morgan's terrible men,
> With bowie knives and pistols, are galloping up the glen." [4]

Of course, down South, Morgan's adventures were viewed in a much more positive light. Children of Confederate families recited this poem with pride and fervor:

> "I want to be a cavalryman, and with John Hunt Morgan ride,
> A Colt revolver in my belt, a saber by my side.
> I want a pair of epaulets to match my suit of gray,
> The uniform my mother made and lettered C.S.A."[5]

In the entire raid, Morgan was most apprehensive about passing safely around Cincinnati, the largest northern city he would threaten in this military mission. In 1863, Cincinnati was regarded as being in the "Western Theater of Operations." In fact, it was referred to as "The Queen City of the West." The thousands of Union soldiers barracked in Cincinnati could quickly end his raid if they were properly deployed to thwart his advance. How he neutralized this superior force and rode virtually unchallenged through Cincinnati's suburbs, demonstrated Morgan's mastery at guerrilla tactics and lightning bold thrusts that confounded his enemies. The South called him the "Thunderbolt of the Confederacy."

I have been asked, "Did Morgan have a plan to attack and destroy specific military or civilian targets in the North?" My answer is, "No." I explain the true purpose of the raid in more detail in Chapter One. I believe Morgan never planned to attack Indianapolis, Dayton, Columbus or Cleveland. The only major population center he would come close to was Cincinnati. At the time of the raid, Cincinnati was the mean center of population in the United States.[6] In 1860, Columbus had that distinction. By 1900, Louisville held that title and Indianapolis took that honor in 1905. In 1863, Cincinnati was the eighth largest city in the nation, a sprawling metropolis with almost a quarter of a million residents. It had more people than San Francisco (100,000), Cleveland (92,000), Columbus (31,000) and Louisville (90,000). Cincinnati was ten times larger than Atlanta (20,000).[7] And that was before General William T. Sherman burned it. Even Dayton (30,000) was more populous than Atlanta. Morgan felt if he could get safely past Cincinnati, he would no longer be in great danger.[8] His plan was to remain fairly close to the Ohio River so he could effect a crossing if real danger were to threaten his force.

After all the effort, blood, sweat and tears that went into this raid, or all of Morgan's raids combined, did they really change the outcome of the war? No. But the same can be said of Robert E. Lee's sacrificial effort at Gettysburg, Pennsylvania, Braxton Bragg's uncharacteristic "stand and fight" effort at Chickamauga, Georgia, or "Stonewall" Jackson's bittersweet victory at Chancellorsville, Virginia. No matter what the outcome, you can never accuse these men of not having tried. They did their best with the limited resources they had. The Confederacy was an army of shortages . . . in everything except heart.

John Hunt Morgan was a guerrilla leader. He was an accomplished actor who could wear a costume, be it a Union officer's uniform[9] or a businessman's suit[10] and play the part with great conviction. He was a man who could think on his feet, a successful businessman, captain of the fire department, city council member and an entrepreneur among generals. His persona attracted great multitudes of followers. After his escape from the Ohio Penitentiary, when he was given a new command, more than 14,000 men[11] answered his call to join him, although he had but 800 horses for his new cavalry. On his epic raid through Indiana and Ohio, he would leave, in his wake, countless legends and stories that would be told for generations to come. Even a half-century after his death, in 1911, over 10,000 people would gather in Lexington, Kentucky, to unveil his statue. [12] Men who had ridden with him would join together under his name to carry on his memory.[13] He placed the well-being of his men above his own. He was a natural-born leader—dashing, daring and disarming. His exploits were unique, his methods were unconventional, and his moves were unpredictable. He was a man among men. An idol among women. He was faithful and attentive to his invalid wife until her death. He was a model for his brothers and a pride to his parents. He was a treasure to the Confederacy and a beloved son of Kentucky.

No, he wasn't perfect by any stretch of the imagination. His brother-in-law, Basil Duke, admitted that Morgan was no saint.[14] He had his virtues and his flaws. His worst fault was his support of slavery. He not only espoused this degradation of humankind, he bought, sold and leased slaves. You can somewhat attribute his actions to the way he was brought up and educated. Born June 1, 1825, in the slave state of Alabama and then, at an early age, brought to Kentucky where slavery was condoned, he was taught to believe that slavery was an acceptable and desirable practice. His wealthy and respected grandfather and his loving father used slaves. There was no one in his family circle to sit down and convince him that slavery was wrong. Before the war, he did employ and pay freed slaves to work in his mills and other business enterprises. Even on his raid into the North, he brought along black body servants who drove his command van, cooked his meals, acted as his valet and served him with great respect. Except for one known exception, his black servants remained loyal to him throughout the raid and made no attempt to seek freedom while they were in the North. John Morgan flaunted his support of Confederate sympathies by flying the Confederate flag above his mill.

He was considered an undisciplined youth at Transylvania College in Lexington, Kentucky and expelled from its student body.[15] In the army, his commander, Braxton Bragg, didn't like him. But then, Bragg didn't like any of his subordinate generals, and the feeling was mutual.[16] Morgan could be very brash and, at other times, cool-headed. His personality could fluctuate to extremes. Deeply depressed, one day, full of hope and happiness on another. He had a great ego that gloried in praise shown to heroes. And to the South, he was one of their greatest, their Robin Hood. Northern papers called him "The King of Horse Thieves, a bandit, a freebooter, no better than a thug."[17]

He had his good side and his bad. But who is perfect? Had he been born in the North, he might never had been the same person. He flourished in the culture of the South. They molded his attitudes and values. He found his niche in the militaristic life, which attracted Southern gentry seeking their honor. He was reared among fast horses and aristocratic women.

True, none of the war's battlefield atlases shows Morgan's 1,000-mile raid through four states. The longest raid of the Civil War has simply been ignored by respected authors of this all-American conflict. But to the tens of thousands of people who lived in Kentucky, southern Indiana, southern and eastern Ohio, John Hunt Morgan's raid was the Civil War. The people who lived along the 1,000-mile route through Tennessee, Kentucky, Indiana and Ohio, and their descendants, have personal stories of that event that have been passed down in hundreds of family histories and dozens of state and county historical record books. There probably isn't one town of a thousand or more inhabitants, through which Morgan passed, that hasn't had at least one booklet written about Morgan's raid through their village. In just about every one, you'll find "The War came to our town on one day in July, 1863."

To the millions who live in the large cities and small towns through which Morgan passed, the battles of Gettysburg and Vicksburg are almost as remote as Omaha and Utah Beaches (Normandy) and Saigon.

On the other hand, Morgan fought in their back yard and brought the war home in a very personal way. The descendants even speak today about Morgan's men coming into their home, forcing their great-grandmother to cook for them, raiding their neighbors or their great-grandfathers chasing after Morgan. People who have moved out of the area along the raid route come back to visit or transplant their family experiences by joining Civil War Round Tables or participating in reenactments in communities far from their ancestral homes.

With this publication, I hope to pass on this gift of history to future generations and rescue the hundreds of personal stories that might have been lost in the infinite sea of forgotten times. In this book, I have carefully preserved the events that embody Morgan's Great Raid because memories are fragile.

In writing this book, my goal was to tell the many personal stories I uncovered, most never published before, about both sides of the conflict. Previous books have dwelled mostly on the activities of the Confederate raiders and their personal feelings and observations. I wanted this book to be more balanced, presenting the perspective of those who were raided as well as the raiders. My goal was to collect and document the most comprehensive record of this historical event and to give future generations an opportunity to learn what really happened.

Some of these stories have never been told outside of county lines or beyond the family circle. Stories about chivalry and theft. Capture and escape. Pardons and death. These are true stories that reflect courage, kindness and character. Some sad, some senseless, some humorous. Many would affect generations to come. Among most citizens north of the Mason-Dixon Line, Morgan, the "Thunderbolt of the Confederacy," was considered nothing more than a common horse thief or worse. For the Ohio and Indiana citizens who lived in the path of the raiders, it was a frightening experience. The closer Morgan's men came, the greater the panic. Some left town, hoping to avoid contact. Those who stayed behind tried to hide their horses, their money, their food and other valuables.

As you read these stories, you'll sense the emotional stress that drove some to take desperate actions in the face of imminent danger. Where possible, I have repeated the oral conversations descendants have passed down through the generations. Some of the events have been carefully presented in dialogue form based on the author's several decades' study of General Morgan's character, attitudes and actions with the intent of representing the emotions of the moment. For this author, history is where everything has happened: the thrills, the joy, the stress and conflict, the challenges, victories and defeats. This story, in particular, includes one of the most stimulating components of any adventure—the chase! Add to that, the escape! No novel could have the credibility or complexity of this true story; this raid is one of the most adventurous events in the Civil War.

My original focus was on a fifty-mile segment of Morgan's trail through Hamilton and Clermont counties in Ohio. But as my research progressed, I began to uncover stories beyond the Greater Cincinnati area. In my mail, I found letters from people in towns along Morgan's route across the southern and eastern sections of the state. Word had been circulated that I was writing a book about Morgan's raid. People were eager to tell me stories about their relatives who had either chased Morgan or had been raided by his men. Some were relatives of Kentucky men who rode with Morgan, but today, many descendants of Morgan's men live in Ohio, Indiana, Kentucky, all across the United States and around the world.

My view was expanded. I became very interested in what happened to Morgan both <u>before</u> and <u>after</u> he rode across Cincinnati. Morgan's most calamitous battle and gravest threat to his forces occurred, not in Cincinnati, but in a small agrarian community along the banks of the Ohio River, two-hundred miles upstream. There at Portland, Ohio near Buffington Island, 8,000 to 10,000 soldiers, almost 2,000 Confederates and 5,000 to 8,000 Union cavalry engaged in a fierce battle that began early Sunday morning, July 19, and continued for several hours. Hundreds of the Confederate officers and men stood their ground in a holding action to give General Morgan an opportunity to escape with as many men as possible. Even as they withdrew, they hoped that they, too, would escape the Union juggernaut. Morgan's military pursuers respected his skill, daring and unpredictability.

Facing Morgan's Confederate "mounted infantry" were cavalry and artillery regiments of the Army of the Ohio. Even the U.S. Navy participated, fighting from gunboats on the Ohio River. On that fateful day in 1863, Ohio soil shook from the thunder of U.S. naval guns, artillery barrages, "rebel yells," screams from hundreds of dying and wounded and the thump of charging hoof beats descending into the valley to violently clash in the most awesome battle in Ohio's history.

The other battle occurred ten days earlier in Indiana, in Corydon, Indiana's first state capital (1816-1825). In this engagement, the odds where heavily in the Confederates' favor in training, discipline, horses and equipment. Morgan had 2,200 men against an Indiana home guard of four-hundred and fifty. The site of the battle is one mile south of Corydon on a ridge that overlooks the town. The brunt of the battle started around one o'clock in the afternoon of July 9. Against overwhelming odds and deadly cannonade, the Indiana Legion withdrew into the town and raised the white flag.

I realized that there was so much more to this Indiana-Ohio raid than Morgan's record-breaking ride around Cincinnati. In the words of Paul Harvey, I set out to uncover "the rest of the story." As with the first fifty miles through Ohio, I wanted to know where Morgan's men were each day. What date and time did they ride into and exit each county? What unusual obstacles did they face? Who were the interesting men and women whose unique personalities confronted Morgan's men?

To help stir the century-old dust and peer back several generations, I sought out local historians, authors, genealogists, historical societies, county libraries, large and small town newspapers and residents whose attics and chests held old photos, family letters and stories that were known only within the privacy of close family circles. In my intensive research, I came across unpublished family photos, pictures of homes and buildings, letters, documents and accounts of events, written and oral, that helped to reveal what was happening before, during and after the raiders passed through the first fifty-mile leg of Morgan's Ohio venture. At times, I felt like a police detective getting tips from informants about a case I was trying to solve. I had to deal with the many myths and legends that had grown over a century and more. After years of extensive research, I am able to sort out what is credible and what is not. For most of these stories, this will be the first time these oral histories have been shared publicly. Many are the personal accounts of individuals who were directly involved in the course of events. Their tales humanize the raid story so we can understand the attitudes and deep feelings that prevailed at the time.

Some of the stories I relate are of isolated incidents that happened when a few of Morgan's men detached themselves from the main column and went searching for food and fresh horses. Morgan's two brigades moved along at a slow pace to allow individual troopers to stray from the column and forage several miles laterally from their regiments. Some found fresh horses. Some were welcomed into homes, most were not. Some found terror and death. A few found love. Some got lost. Some deserted. Some didn't care to go any farther. Some sacrificed themselves for their General's well-being. As a group, they were a fascinating parade of personalities. If you stood by the road and watched them troop by on their odd assortment of horses and conveyances, it would take two to three hours for the nine regiments to pass.

The extensive list of credits and acknowledgments demonstrates that this work could only have been accomplished because of the unselfish generosity of others to share, assist and contribute. There are many fine people, in both the North and South, who love history and I was fortunate to have been the recipient of their enthusiastic and valuable assistance.

When Col. [later General] Basil Duke, Morgan's second-in-command on this raid, wrote *History of Morgan's Cavalry,* published just two years after the raid, he bemoaned the fact that he received very little assistance in the preparation of his book from those who rode with him on the raid. In the book's Preface he says, "He [Duke] regrets, too, that many of his old comrades have altogether failed to render him aid, confidently expected, and which would have been very valuable." A few must have answered his request for stories because Duke says, "To the friends whose contributions assisted the work, the author returns his warmest thanks." But Duke named only one man publicly when he wrote, "To Mr. Meade Woodson, to whom he [Duke] is indebted for the maps, which so perfectly illustrate his narrative, he is especially grateful."

One hundred thirty-two years later, as I was writing about the Great Raid, Clarence R. Sterling, a great-great-grandson of Meade Woodson, wrote to me offering stories about his ancestor's participation in this historical event. Unlike the meager response Duke received when he requested stories for his book, Woodson's descendant was only one of several hundred who graciously responded to this author's solicitation.

It has been said that "People's memories are short." But the people who helped me were determined *never to forget!* They had heard these stories from their parents, grandparents, great grandparents, uncles and aunts. Tales of the raid had been passed down through the generations, told and retold, waiting for someone, like myself, to collect and fit them together into a historical mosaic so readers could follow along with the columns of blue and gray horsemen down the dusty roads of rural America.

There is a great amount of interest in the Civil War. "In the South," William Faulkner wrote, "the past is not dead; it is not even past." "What's happening in the U.S.," says historian Frank Vandiver, "is that the Civil War keeps coming back the further we get away from it."[18] In addition to the many store shelves of new books about this conflict, there are tens of thousands of reenactors (some even overseas in Europe and Asia), hundreds of web sites on the Internet, numerous Civil War Round Tables, innumerable collectors and sutlers, newsletters, social and historical organizations, museums dedicated to this period and armies of men and women searching to uncover buried bullets, balls, buckles, and USA and CSA weapons that lie just beneath the soil.

To give you a sense of the times, I've tried to retain some of the language, spellings and expressions as they were originally written by early historians and eyewitnesses. Many stories told to me, had many similarities. Yet, each was unique unto itself. Descriptions of several identical events came to me from a number of different family members, now scattered across the nation. Each was unaware that distant relatives had sent me the same story a few days or months earlier. And each had a slight variation of the account, revealing a detail that the others hadn't mentioned. Even after the publication of this book, I am sure that people will continue to send me stories. Depending on the volume of new material received after publication, it may warrant a supplemental reprinting at some later date.

Morgan's hard-riding Southerners were seasoned guerrilla fighters, "alligator soldiers,"[19] who made many raids behind enemy lines in his home state of Kentucky. He was compared to the "Swamp Fox," Colonel Francis Marion, whose guerrilla band, operating in the Carolina swamps, kept alive the resistance against the British in America's Revolutionary War. Morgan was the eminent role model for the Confederacy's Partisan Ranger Act of April 21, 1862, which gave President Jefferson Davis the authority to commission units of Partisan Rangers for detached guerrilla activities.

Another successful Civil War guerrilla fighter was John Singleton Mosby. "Mosby's Rangers" operated mostly in northern Virginia. Unlike Morgan, Mosby's men would disband after an attack behind enemy lines and then regroup at a prearranged location. Morgan, Mosby and Marion's guerrilla tactics are not new, but the word *guerrilla* has been used to describe this form of warfare only since the nineteenth century. It was used when the Duke of Wellington employed Portuguese irregulars, called "guerrillos," to fight the French in Spain. Guerrilla itself means "little war" and is derived from "guerra," the Spanish word for "war."

Guerrilla tactics are as old as the bible.[20] In biblical times, in the Book of Maccabees, the Hebrews launched a guerrilla campaign against the Syrians. These tactics have been used throughout history, from Europe to Asia, and in North and South America. Customarily, guerrillas do not wear military uniforms and are indistinguishable from the general population. Usually in small groups, they make brief, devastating attacks, causing terror and confusion. Guerrillas depend on the local inhabitants for recruits, as well as for food, shelter, concealment and information.

Morgan's raid into Indiana and Ohio does not fit the classic example of guerrillas. They could not seek recruits or support from local inhabitants, because most were unsympathetic enemies. There were rumors that northern sympathizers of the Confederacy (Knights of the Golden Circle, Copperheads, Vallandigham's Peace Democrats, Butternuts and other "Fifth Column" groups) would join, support or materially aid Morgan. One of Morgan's officers commented, "We had information that, upon our arrival in Southern Indiana, the 'Knights of the Golden Circle,' and other organizations opposed to the war of coercion, would come to our assistance, and attract to them, in addition, a large element of northern citizens who were sick of war, and wanted peace at any cost. We hoped to produce a revolution in feeling among the people of Ohio and Indiana, and excite a demand upon the National powers that would force them to entertain propositions for peace." But these promises did not materialize. Their sympathies had no real substance and the threat of their danger to the Union was but lip service. Morgan despised them because they didn't have the guts to leave their homes, as he did, and come south to join the fight. In many cases, he treated these "sympathizers" worse than loyal Unionists. Morgan and his men most despised abolitionists.

Food, shelter, concealment and information were rarely volunteered. Many times, they could only be obtained at the point of a gun. On this raid, Morgan's columns were not small groups that could strike and disperse, as Mosby's men did, melting into the Virginian population. His men numbered in the thousands and they were operating in unfriendly Union territory where it seemed every civilian was a hostile bystander, or worse, a "bushwhacker."

The Civil War was the bloodiest episode in American history. Twenty-five percent of the men in uniform were either killed or wounded. In World War II, only seven percent of our troops suffered the same fate despite the fact that the latter conflict was fought with more sophisticated weaponry. In World War II, of the sixteen million Americans in uniform, about one million men were killed or wounded (1,078,162). The Civil War involved less than four million fighting men, yet the casualties were almost as great (970,227). Actually more American men died in the Civil War (558,052) than in World War II (407,316).[21]

ONE

Why the Raid?

The definition of a raid according to Army doctrine is a swift penetration of hostile territory to secure information, to confuse the enemy and
destroy his installations and support functions. It is a limited-objective
attack for a specific purpose other than gaining and holding ground. It ends
with a planned withdrawal after the completion of the assigned mission.[1]
For John Hunt Morgan, it was, plain and simple, a <u>diversionary raid</u>.[2] The
purpose for this strategy was to allow Morgan's superior, General Braxton
Bragg, commander of the Army of Tennessee, to fall back to a new position
without being attacked or threatened by larger forces.

Pillaging farms, homes and stores in Ohio and Indiana was not the
objective of the raid, rather it was a means to the end. Stealing food, horses,
clothing, weapons and ammunition were necessary acts to sustain Morgan's troops for more than a month while cut off from Confederate sources
of resupply. Pilfering merchandise from shops was rationalized as wartime
booty. Tying bolts of cloth to saddles and dragging the unraveling rolls
behind their horses were mischievous, playful acts of young men, and most
of Morgan's troops were in their early twenties or teenagers.

After the battle of Stones River (December 31, 1862, through January
2, 1863), General Bragg had retreated to Tullahoma, Tennessee. He wanted
to fall back farther through the Sequatchie valley to Chattanooga. He feared
an attack from Union Generals Henry M. Judah and William S. Rosecrans.
There was also the possibility of a flanking attack through eastern Tennessee by General Ambrose E. Burnside's forces headquartered in Cincinnati. In East Tennessee, Confederate General Simon Bolivar Buckner was
defending that important region with an inadequate force. Buckner could
not weaken his small force should Bragg need help. Burnside had from
15,000 to 30,000 men available to invade Tennessee. With this force, he
could easily drive out Buckner.

General Rosecrans had been concerning himself with the construction
of a huge earthen fort and supply depot on the outskirts of Murfreesboro,
Tennessee. The Confederate cavalry outnumbered the Union cavalry by
more than 7,000 men. Despite urgings from his superiors, he was in no
hurry to attack Confederate strong positions, using the excuse of inadequate cavalry and the need for reinforcements.[3]

1

In June 1863, at the insistence of General-in-Chief Henry W. Halleck in Washington, DC, Rosecrans' forces in Tennessee finally prepared to move toward Bragg's forces.[4] Bragg needed a diversion[5] to occupy the Federal forces' attention and to harass supplies and reinforcements being sent to aid Rosecrans. General Morgan, in Bragg's command, proposed a daring answer to prevent the Federals from molesting and endangering Bragg's retreat.

Morgan got his idea from a Union colonel, Benjamin H. Grierson.[6] On April 17, 1863, Grierson led 1,700 Union Cavalry for sixteen days over 450 miles behind Confederate lines and only twenty-six men were killed, wounded, captured or missing. His orders were to ride south from LaGrange, Tennessee, into Mississippi, following a route between the state's two north-south railroads: the Mississippi Central and the Mobile & Ohio.

En route, he was to cut both of those lines and sever the even more important Southern Mississippi Railroad, which ran from Vicksburg through Jackson and on east, tying together the eastern and western halves of the Confederacy. Grierson was also instructed to disrupt enemy communications and destroy any military supplies he might come upon, and make as much mischief as possible while trying to avoid being captured by Confederate forces. He started out April 17, 1863, and by April 21, he detached a third of his force under Col. Edward Hatch and told them to move toward the Confederate base near Columbus, Mississippi and from there to head back to LaGrange.

He ordered this maneuver to deceive pursuing Confederate cavalry into thinking his entire force was returning to LaGrange. He continued his southward journey with his remaining men, accomplished his mission and concluded his march at Union-held Baton Rouge, Louisiana on May 2, 1863. General William T. Sherman praised Grierson's raid as "the most brilliant expedition of the war." A few months later, General Morgan would conduct a raid behind enemy lines that would exceed Grierson's by taking almost a thousand more men more than 500 miles farther. Morgan's men would come within yards of capturing General Sherman's daughter in the northern suburbs of Cincinnati.

Grierson's daring raid captured the attention of Morgan. He proposed to Bragg that he be permitted to lead a substantial force of cavalry through Kentucky, threaten Louisville, raid and destroy the L&N Railroad lines carrying military supplies to Union forces in the South. Like Grierson, he would go behind enemy lines and cross the Ohio River. Once in Indiana, he would make a feint toward Indianapolis, turn east to Ohio, bypass Cincinnati and recross the Ohio River, reenter Kentucky or West Virginia and return to Bragg's headquarters in Tennessee. General Morgan contended that he could do it better than that Union Colonel could. He had better cavalry, better horses and his men had more experience fighting behind enemy lines. He was sure he could keep those Yankees so busy chasing him, they wouldn't have time to come after Bragg. He further assured that by invading the northern states, there would be such a scare and clamor, the Union military leaders and the Lincoln administration would be compelled to furnish troops to capture him. This would draw reinforcements away from Rosecrans and might even prevent or delay an attack on Buckner in eastern Tennessee.[7]

Bragg responded, "I like everything you said, except crossing the Ohio River into the north. Go ahead and raid Kentucky. Capture Louisville if you can. But do not, I repeat, do not cross the river. Stay in Kentucky. Go anywhere you want in your home state, but I command you to stay south of the river." Bragg had given him *carte blanche* to go where he pleased in the Bluegrass State and stay as long as events permitted him, so he could divert the attention of Generals Judah and Rosecrans.[8]

There was another, very personal reason Morgan wanted to lead this raid. While Bragg was in Tullahoma, Morgan's division was nearby in McMinnville, protecting Bragg's flank against a surprise attack. As winter turned to spring in 1863, his troops were idle. There was a scarcity of supplies and horses. Basil Duke was in Georgia recuperating from an injury sustained when crossing the Rolling Fork River en route to Bardstown in December 1862. Many trusted stalwarts like the fifty-four-year-old soldier of fortune, George St. Leger Grenfell, had become bored.

Grenfell, born in London, England, in 1808, was a colorful character. When first introduced to Col. Morgan in the last week of May 1862, he told him he had battled pirates on the Barbary Coast, served as a British officer in the Crimean War, fought in the Sepoy Rebellion in India, and was involved in upheavals in several South American republics. He had first told these stories to General Robert E. Lee in Richmond, Virginia. Lee was impressed enough to recommend him to General P.G.T. Beauregard in Corinth. On his way there, he suffered a severe attack of dysentery. Weak from the illness, he decided not to risk the trip to Corinth but chose instead to recuperate in Mobile, where he met Morgan. The two men took an immediate liking to each other and Grenfell, there and then, put away General Lee's letter.[9] Morgan appointed him assistant adjutant general of the 2nd KY Cavalry. But a year had passed since that initial meeting and Grenfell had left.[10]

On May 27, 1863, General Bragg ordered Col. Grenfell, inspector of cavalry, to report to Major-General Joseph Wheeler, commander of all cavalry for the Army of Tennessee.[11] With Grenfell's departure and no action planned, his troops had become lax. They chafed at the inactivity of winter quarters. Spring of 1863 brought no assignments to relieve the tedium. Morale dropped. During this low ebb, Federal troops, based nearby in Murfreesboro, made a surprise attack.[12] Morgan's force was scattered in every direction. The Federal scouts almost captured him. He escaped only by the swiftness of his steed. Even his wife, Mattie, who had been living with him in camp, had been stopped as she tried to flee. When the Federal officer, in charge, discovered who she was, he gallantly set her free to continue her flight.[13] Morgan was afraid his division was coming apart at the seams. Bragg's approval of raiding to Louisville was the answer to strengthening and energizing his command.

Morgan also needed the approval of Major-General Joseph Wheeler, who commanded the Confederate cavalry. By mid-June, Wheeler sent the following telegram to Morgan authorizing him to conduct the raid into Kentucky.

(Telegram)   Headquarters Cavalry Corps,Shelbyville, Tenn., *June* 14, 1863.
General: Your dispatch was received last night, and the facts communicated to General Bragg, and I visited him to-day in the subject. He directs you to proceed to Kentucky with a sufficient number of regiments to make up 1,500 men, and that you use your own discretion regarding the amount of artillery you take. He directs that you take Kentucky troops and those, which will be most likely to get recruits. The remainder of your command will be left under command of the senior officer. Should you hear that the enemy is advancing for a general engagement, General Bragg wishes you to turn rapidly and fall upon his rear.

I regret exceedingly the circumstances which render it impossible for General Bragg to detach your entire division, but the probability of an advance upon the part of the enemy makes it necessary for him [Bragg] to retain enough force to enable him to hold his position should a general engagement take place, and he hopes, since the enemy's forces in Kentucky are so reduced, you may be able to accomplish much good with the proposed detachment. General Bragg wishes the movement to take place as soon as possible. With great respect, your obedient servant,

JOS. WHEELER, *Major-General.*

Note that Bragg wanted Morgan to take only 1,500 men on the raid. He felt he needed part of Morgan's cavalry division to remain behind to help screen his anticipated withdrawal. To placate Bragg, Morgan left behind the 9th KY under the command of Col. W.C.P. Breckinridge.[14] But there were several dozen members in 9ᵗʰ KY companies who wanted to accompany the Morgan raid and they detached themselves from Breckinridge. Conspicuous among the members of the 9ᵗʰ KY that went on the raid are Captain Thomas Henry Hines and Sgt. Henry Lane Stone. At the time that the raid was planned in June, Morgan had 2,743 ("effectives").[15] By leaving Breckinridge's 9ᵗʰ KY behind, he had about 2,500 men to take with him on the raid, a thousand more than Bragg had authorized.

Preceding this raid, Captain Hines, Co. E, 9ᵗʰ KY, one of Morgan's most trusted scouts, had detached himself and several dozen men from his regiment. They had been sent on an intelligence-gathering mission into Indiana by General Morgan. The General had also ordered Col. Duke to examine fords of the upper Ohio, including Buffington.[16]

Two

Getting Ready for Battle

When preparing for battle, Morgan was not the typical general. He did not sit in a distant office behind the lines and order his men into action. Instead, you could always find Morgan in the thick of conflict, leading his men, tirelessly riding from front to back urging his men on. After his participation in the Battle of Shiloh (Tennessee), he dispensed with the traditional cavalry weapon, the saber,[1] commenting, "The charges at Shiloh were haphazard and chaotic."[2] He could see that the sword was inadequate against Federal firepower and, thereafter, fought instead with carbines and revolvers. Every fourth man was appointed a horse-holder, while the other three could take advantage of ground cover and improve their shooting accuracy.[3] Then, they would remount and advance or retreat as the situation presented itself, which allowed Morgan's men to become mounted infantry. Morgan could be heard shouting, "Horses to the rear!" The General's brother, Calvin, even referred to himself as a "Mounted Rifleman."[4]

The Battle of Shiloh (April 6-7, 1862) was definitely not the type of fighting that Morgan preferred. The careful manipulation of cavalry, infantry and artillery did not appeal to him. For someone who loved the action of confronting the enemy, he was frustrated when told to hold a position until he was ordered to move. Morgan's squadron of Kentucky cavalry was one of 170 Confederate regiments in General Albert Sidney Johnston's army of 43,968 men.[5] After Shiloh, he convinced General Beauregard to allow him to make raids into Tennessee and Kentucky as a detached unit. He didn't want to wait for orders to attack. He wanted to give the orders. Make surprise attacks. That was his forte. There was no one better at this game in the Confederate army. Operating behind enemy lines, Morgan found himself free of interference from Confederate generals and bureaucrats. His informal, swashbuckling style exemplified to Southerners everything that was noble and distinctive about themselves and their cause. Quite apart from his romantic reputation, Morgan was a great tactician.[6] There are some historians who say the "brains" behind Morgan was his brother-in-law, Basil Duke.[7] Even if it was true that Duke was the strategist, there can be no doubt that it was Morgan who had the guts and intuition to carry it off with amazing flair and determination. After Duke was captured at the Battle of Buffington Island (July 19, 1863) and was no longer available to advise the

6

General, Morgan was able to elude hundreds of traps and thousands of pursuers for another full week of "catch me if you can" cat and mouse pursuits. Morgan's cavalry tactics of mounted infantry were used in the War of 1812 by another Kentuckian, Richard Mentor Johnson (1780-1850). He was a colonel of a Kentucky regiment of mounted riflemen, serving under General William Henry Harrison. After the war, he was elected to several high political offices including that of vice-president in 1836 under Martin Van Buren.[8]

John Morgan had a devil-may-care attitude. He looked danger square in the eyes and danger blinked. His bravado attracted adventurous soldiers from Kentucky, Tennessee, Alabama, Virginia, Georgia, Mississippi and even as far away as Texas. Of the 223 men in Companies A and B of the 7th KY Cav., 156 were from Texas towns (Witts Mills, Dallas, Breckinridge, Fort Worth, Jefferson, Grand Junction, Monticello, Sherman, Houston and Hartsville). Company A had sixty-seven Texans, which was 61% of the company.[9] Company B had eighty-nine men from the Lone Star state representing 78% of the company. There were also Texans in Ward's 9th TN regiment.[10] They all wanted to ride with Morgan, to share in the glory and the booty that followed each of Morgan's successful raids. The South sung the praises of Morgan and his men.

After he had made his escape from another surprise Union attack, this one in Lebanon, Tennessee, May 1862, he set about reorganizing his command. The original three companies were reconstituted with recruits from Kentucky and those who had escaped from Lebanon. Two or three companies of Texas cavalry were given permission to join him. Three hundred members of the 1st KY (Confederate) Infantry, having completed their original term of enlistment, decided to do their fighting as cavalry thereafter and reenlisted under Morgan. A cavalry company from Mississippi joined, another from Alabama, and later a Partisan Ranger unit from Georgia. Morgan now had a full regiment, which was officially designated as the 2nd KY Cavalry.[11] The regiment moved to Knoxville, and under the inspiration of the scholarly and thoughtful Lt. Col. Basil Duke, began to drill in the battle tactics that Morgan and he had devised. By the time of the "Great Raid," Morgan's division had grown and was composed of the following nine regiments[12] and the commanders who led each:

First Brigade (Col. Basil W. Duke)
2nd KY Cav., Maj. T.B. Webber
5th KY Cav., Col. D.H. Smith
6th KY Cav., Col. J.W. Grigsby
9th TN Cav., Col. W.W. Ward

Second Brigade (Col. A.R. Johnson)
7th KY Cav., Lt. Col. J.M. Huffman
8th KY Cav., Col. R.S. Cluke
10th KY Cav., Maj. W.G. Owen
11th KY Cav., Lt. Col. J. Tucker
  (Chenault's regiment)
14th KY Cav., Col. R.C. Morgan

Artillery
Kentucky Battery, Capt. E.P. Byrne

There was another regiment, the 9th KY Cav. commanded by Col. W.C.P. Breckinridge, but because General Bragg's orders were to leave behind some of his command, the 9th KY remained in McMinnville. Bragg wanted some of Morgan's cavalry to protect his rear when he withdrew to Chattanooga. In the latter part of February 1863, Richard Morgan had transferred from General A.P. Hill's command in Virginia to join his brother's division for the diversionary raid into Kentucky and beyond. Richard had been a major under A.P. Hill who was part of Robert E. Lee's army.[13] When he transferred to Tennessee, he was given a colonel's rank and he hastily formed the 14th KY Cavalry, not much larger than a company. It included Major Hamilton's battalion and some loose companies that had long been unattached and some that had recently been recruited. Maj. Hamilton became a lieutenant colonel.

More than one Confederate commander wrote to military headquarters in Richmond, Virginia, voicing concern that when their troops' enlistment periods were up, "half of them will desert my command and go join up with Morgan."[14]

As an example, here is a letter written by Captain Wm. O. Jordan, Co. G, 4th VA Heavy Artillery to Morgan six weeks after he had escaped from the Ohio Penitentiary and rejoined the Confederate Army.

Charleston, S.C., January 5th, 1864
(to) Genrl. Jno. H. Morgan, Richmond, Va.
Dear Sir—My company is desirous with the consent of the Secretary of War to change their present arm of service to that of cavalry to go under your command and have requested me to make you a tender of the Company if the Secretary of War will permit it to be detached from I am now in to report to you— It numbers one hundred and twenty men in a high state of efficiency. The Company is peculiarly suited for Cavalry service most of the men are under thirty and trained in the use of

horses from their youth. A majority of men can furnish their own horses and equipments—The Regt. I am in will number 900 men without my company, and if my Company is detached it will not impair its organization, I respectfully refer you to the Hon. Jno. Goode Jr. member of Congress or in his absence to Messrs. Wm. Burwell & Alex Jordan of the House of Delegates Richmond for any information on the subject of this commission.

Very Respectfully,   Wm. O. Jordan Capt.

John Hunt Morgan, at the time of this raid, was thirty-eight years old. The rank and file of Morgan's command yearned for adventure and audacious enterprise. They were filled with the fire of youth, for there were few men in the division older than twenty-five years of age.[15] They were imbued with the spirit of their commander and were confident in his skill and fortune; no endeavor was deemed impossible or even hazardous when he led. Morgan was, beyond all men, adept to independent command of this nature. His energy never flagged, and his invention was always equal to the emergency. Boldness and caution were united in all he undertook. Southern society looked up to men on horseback. When Jeff Davis, President of the Confederacy, was on his deathbed, he was asked by his wife what he would have done differently. He replied, "I would like to have been a cavalryman."[16] As a cavalry leader, Morgan was larger than life. In the Confederacy, there was but a handful of such flamboyant men. And now, in his prime, no other Southern warrior was more respected or loved than John Hunt Morgan.

He was an incurable romantic, unstable, moody, erratic and unpredictable. He operated as if he were a solitary knight-errant looking for adventure. He lacked the single-minded ruthlessness of Nathan Bedford Forrest who claimed to have killed thirty enemies by his own hands.[17] He had not a particle of the killer instinct. He indulged his men. His kindness toward his troopers was well known. And in return, he had the affection of his men. He was far too lenient and easygoing to try to raise the state of discipline of his command to the modest Confederate norm. He failed to make a real effort to control the depredations committed by his undisciplined troopers in Kentucky and Tennessee. Operating normally at a distance from their base, Morgan's men lived off the country. Food for themselves, feed for their mounts, supplies of all kinds, in fact, whatever they needed, they took from the civilian population. They took from friend and foe alike.

The soldiers on both sides went off to war in a disorganized diversity of uniforms.[18] Northerners wore either blue or gray, Southerners either gray or blue, and volunteer units wore almost any color they pleased. The styles varied, with the influence of French military dress showing the strongest. Many units called themselves Zouaves after the colorfully garbed Algerian units in French service. But as the war went on, the uniforms became standardized: blue for the North, because it had been traditional since the Revolution; gray for the South, as a mark of opposition.

By 1863, the typical Confederate soldier wore a uniform that was wearing out and his government could not readily replace. There was little standardization in what Confederate troops wore, since some were supplied by the states and others by the Confederate government. This was especially apparent in the 2nd KY Cavalry. Uniforms were practically nonexistent. Most wore what they had on when they left home to enlist, or what was left of it. When that wore out, it was replaced by more clothing sent from their families or pilfered from stores and homes along the raid route. Ensembles included parts of Federal uniforms taken from prisoners or Union dead. Shoes and socks were a scarce commodity. Northern shoe, boot and dry goods stores were cleaned out as the raiders past through their towns. In some of the letters written by eyewitnesses who observed Morgan's men passing by their homes, it was written that some of the men were riding barefoot.

More serious was the shortage and the lack of uniformity of weapons. Duke wrote in his *History of Morgan's Cavalry* that Morgan's men preferred the medium Enfield and that he considered the Sharps and Spencer rifles the best two of the breech loaders. But he personally believed muzzle loaders were better than breech loaders.[19] Those of Morgan's men who were equipped with the 1852 Sharps' percussion carbine, caliber .52, carried it attached to a shoulder strap and it hung at their side. The most popular pistol was the Navy Colt revolver, which was smaller and lighter than the Army version. But most of his men made do with a miscellany of shotguns, sporting rifles and relics of the Mexican War.

On one of his earlier raids, 200 of 826 men had no firearms at all and carried clubs in lieu of more effective weapons. The supply of blankets and camp gear was totally inadequate. But to compensate for these shortages, the men wore the largest, noisiest spurs and broad-brimmed hats pinned up on one side with a crescent or a star. Morgan often wore such a hat. The reason the brim was pinned up was not a fashionable affectation, but rather it had a utilitarian purpose. It allowed a soldier to raise his arm when he sighted on a rifle or swung his sword without knocking against his hat's brim.[20]

The one article essential to a cavalryman that Morgan's troopers did have was horses. And because of the rich supply of fine Kentucky stock, they usually had good ones. At the beginning, every man brought his own horse from home, or bought one with money borrowed from friends. Some sold their watches to buy a horse. The Confederate Army did not usually provide horses to their cavalrymen. You had to bring your own or find one yourself.

A poster for the 9th Tennessee Cavalry (Col. W.W. Ward's regiment) said:

RECRUITS WANTED
for the
9th TENNESSEE CAVALRY

Now men! Rally to the defense of your liberties,
your homes, and your firesides! Come on boys,
if you want a heap of fun and to shoot at yankees.
Join Now! Must furnish your own arms and mounts.

General Morgan made preparations for this extended raid into unknown hostile territory. He knew Kentucky very well, having been reared in Lexington. He had many friends in the state who would help him feed his troops and pass along military information vital to the safe passage of his men through Union forces occupying his home state. Early in the war, even before he led cavalry groups on raids, he went by himself behind lines to conduct damaging hit-and-run forays.

Now, he was to lead his largest guerrilla raid on an epic ride into military history. He wanted to show the South what a superior force his men represented. Morgan's heroics were legendary in the South. On May 1, 1863, he and his command were given a vote of thanks by the Confederate Congress, which said that Morgan and his men were "entitled to the love and gratitude of their countrymen for the magnificent feat of preserving Middle Tennessee for the [CSA] Government."[21]

Morgan decided to ignore Bragg's order, because he considered Bragg a timid leader unwilling to challenge the enemy. To prepare for his march through the North, he requested of Captain Thomas Hines and Colonel Basil Duke to have their scouts reconnoiter possible fords over the Ohio River that would allow his force to cross safely from Ohio back into Kentucky or West Virginia. Unfortunately, when the raid was launched several weeks later, many of these fords were no longer passable because heavy rains in the West Virginia mountains had caused the river to rise to much higher levels. Most of the 9th KY Cav. men who detached themselves to accompany Hines on his scouting trips were captured in Indiana trying to recross the Ohio River.[22]

The timing of this raid had an emotional effect on General Morgan. He had been married to Martha Ready for only six months when he embarked on this most dangerous mission, which would keep them apart for an unusually long period of separation, especially for newlyweds. Some of his officers didn't look kindly upon his marriage because they thought it would take the edge off his daring leadership, making him less of a risk-taker. In the weeks to come, there would be times when he would have to choose between honor and loyalty to his men or love for his wife.

KENTUCKY

THREE

Crossing the Cumberland Twice

The raid was originally scheduled to start early in June. Morgan had been planning it for well over a month.[1] The success of this raid hinged on nine elements: (1) constant replacement of fresh horses, (2) adequate food supply, (3) obtaining additional weapons and ammunition, (4) procuring local guides for directions, (5) acquiring intelligence about the enemy's presence and diseminating false information, (6) avoiding major confrontations with large groups of enemy forces, (7) the weather, (8) the river and (9) leadership.

Saturday, June 6, 1863

Major-General Joseph Wheeler, the CSA's cavalry commander, sent a telegram to General Morgan to "move all your force from Kentucky to Liberty [Tennessee] by steady but not rapid marches."[2]

Sunday, June 7

Morgan was in Sparta, Tennessee. The Second Brigade was closest to Liberty. Morgan advised General Wheeler, "Orders have also been sent to the First Brigade to move in the direction indicated. The distance, however, being so great, it will necessarily be several days before the entire command [both brigades] can reach Liberty."[3]

Thursday, June 11

They rode out of Alexandria, Tennessee, and headed for the Cumberland River. The men joined in a spirited chorus of My Old Kentucky Home.[4] They crossed not far from Rome. General Morgan had been ordered to attack the Federal force stationed at Carthage. Bragg had authorized this raid on the strongly fortified town.[5] Morgan's division encamped two miles from the northern banks of the river, not far from the turnpike connecting Carthage to Hartsville. But before he could launch his attack, a staff officer from Bragg's headquarters arrived in the evening carrying a dispatch ordering Morgan to

13

cancel his assault on Carthage and delay his raid deep into Kentucky.[6] Instead, he was told to march as rapidly as possible to Monticello in the southern part of Kentucky to intercept a Federal raiding party under Colonel William P. Sanders that was threatening General Buckner at Knoxville.

Sunday, June 14

Even while he was being diverted from his primary mission, Morgan was trying to get permission from the Confederacy's cavalry commander, Major-General Joseph Wheeler, to take a large force into Kentucky. Bragg authorized only 1,500 men. Morgan asked Wheeler if he could take 2,000, which he said he needed to do the job properly. Wheeler gave his approval but warned that if Bragg needed his help, Morgan was to return promptly from Kentucky and help protect Bragg's withdrawal.

Monday, June 15

From his headquarters in McMinnville, Morgan sent General Wheeler the following.

(Telegram)   McMinnville, *June* 15, 1863.
Maj. Gen. Joseph Wheeler:
Your dispatch is just received. Can accomplish everything with 2,000 men and four guns. To make the attempt with less, might prove disastrous, as large details will be required at Louisville to destroy the transportation, shipping, and Government property. Can I go?
The result is certain.

JOHN H. MORGAN,
Brigadier-General.[7]

Now that he had the authority to take 2,000 men, he still had Sanders' incursion to deal with before he could launch his diversionary raid. Morgan crossed the Tennessee border into Kentucky. His troops searched for the elusive enemy but his advance was slowed by tremendously heavy rains that turned the roads into muddy quagmires, rendering them almost impassable for his artillery.

When he learned that the enemy had left and were no longer a threat, he turned and headed northwest to cross the Cumberland River once again.[8] Morgan would cross paths with Sanders again in Ohio later in this raid. The Confederates had spent precious time in an unsuccessful search that had expended carefully hoarded supplies for the raid, taxed the energies of both men and horses and delayed a vital mission. It was a two-week delay that could have dire consequences with Lady Luck spurning Morgan's trust in her and posing the question, "What if?"

<u>Sunday, June 28</u>

Col. Adam R. "Stovepipe" Johnson's Second Brigade was encamped in Turkey-Neck Bend of the Cumberland River, some fifteen miles in a direct line from Burkesville.[9] Duke's First Brigade was encamped along the river, from a point opposite Burkesville to Irish Bottom. To replenish supplies and ammunition expended on the fruitless mission searching for the Union raiding party, General Morgan returned to McMinnville. Six wagons laden with these supplies had to traverse swollen Tennessee streams and quagmire conditions. One stream was so deep that Morgan ordered the wagons dismantled and the wagon parts, ammunition and supplies placed in canoes and carried across the swollen stream.[10] These canoes would be used again when they encountered even more threatening conditions at the Cumberland River. This round trip for supplies delayed Morgan's raid for almost another week. He left behind, at his Tennessee camp, men who were too ill to accompany him, as well as the 9th KY Cav. who remained in camp to protect Bragg's withdrawal to Chattanooga.

Officially, his most famous raid began Thursday, July 2, 1863, if you don't count the twenty-one days he was delayed in Tennessee looking for the elusive Federal raiding party. He was aware that Robert E. Lee was headed for a major battle in Pennsylvania. Talk around the camp was that Morgan was considering the possibility of linking up with Lee.[11] He would simply cross the state of Ohio and meet a victorious Lee in Pennsylvania. But in his heart, he was anxious to get back to his pregnant wife.[12] As events would unfold, Morgan would come within nine miles of the Pennsylvania border and make a deeper thrust into the North than Lee or any other Confederate army.

On the same day he crossed the Cumberland for the second time, the Battle of Gettysburg was in its second day. By July 4, Lee retreated after suffering devastating losses. Fighting with Lee at Gettysburg was Morgan's other brother-in-law, General A.P. Hill. That same day at ten o'clock in the morning, the South suffered another major defeat when Lt. General John C. Pemberton surrendered Vicksburg and 29,500 starving Confederate soldiers to General Ulysses S. Grant. General Pemberton later explained why, after so many weeks of siege, he had chosen July 4 to surrender. He said that he knew the Northern officers and soldiers would be in a festive mood because of the national holiday and thus he hoped for better treatment.[13] The terms of the Vicksburg surrender were that all the Confederate officers would be permitted to retain their side arms, one horse each, and all their personal property. All the men surrendering had to sign a paper that they agreed not to fight again until they were exchanged.[14]

Riding with General Morgan were four of his five brothers: Calvin (36), Richard (27), Charlton (24) and Thomas (19). John at thirty-eight-years old was the oldest. His youngest brother, Francis Key (18) did not go along on this raid as he had accompanied John's pregnant wife, Mattie, to Augusta, Georgia. He did join the General on Morgan's last raid into Kentucky in 1864. On September 10, 1862, Francis Key enlisted as a private in Co. I, 2nd KY Cav. He was later promoted to quartermaster sergeant.[15] He was named after Francis Scott Key who wrote the U.S. national anthem, "The Star Spangled Banner." Key was inspired to write the poem, "Defense of Fort McHenry," as he watched the bombardment aboard a ship in the Baltimore harbor during the War of 1812. His verse was put to the tune of an English drinking song, "To Anacreon in Heaven." During the Civil War, it was adopted informally as an anthem by the Union Army. The U.S. Army officially endorsed it during World War I. Congress adopted "The Star Spangled Banner" as the national anthem on March 3, 1931.[16]

The Morgan brothers were related to the celebrated composer through their grandmother, Catherine Grosh Hunt who was a first cousin of Francis Scott Key.[17] Also riding with the Morgans was their brother-in-law, Colonel Basil Duke. He was twenty-five years old at the time of the raid, thirteen years younger than the General.

The opponents, who would be involved in this twenty-four-day chase, had fought on the same side during the war with Mexico as Brevet Lt. Col. Braxton Bragg,[18] Brevet Capt. Henry Judah,[19] Lt. Edward Hobson, Lt. John Morgan, Pvt. Calvin Morgan and Pvt. Frank Wolford. They had battled shoulder-to-shoulder and back-to-back at the Battle of Buena Vista defeating Santa Anna's force of 16,000 men.[20]

The man who would command and lead the chase was Brigadier-General Edward Henry Hobson. He served under General Henry M. Judah, commander of the Second division, XXIII Corps stationed in Cincinnati. General James Murrell Shackelford, commander of the 8th KY (Union) Cavalry and the First Brigade, Second division, XXIII Corps. In turn, they all reported to Major-General Ambrose E. Burnside, who, in March 1863, assumed command of all troops in Kentucky as part of the Army of the Ohio.[21]

After riding 130 miles through Tennessee as the hunter, in the next 900 miles Morgan's men would be the hunted prey in an exciting chase beginning just above the Kentucky-Tennessee border. Generals Judah, Shackelford and Hobson were all aware of Morgan's presence south of the

Cumberland River as he moved back and forth along the Tennessee border. The Federals had patrols and pickets keeping an eye on Morgan's movements, even watching his campfires at night from across the river. But during the last week of June, Morgan kept out of sight of the river, and was so profoundly quiet that the Federal commanders, who had been watching him for ten days, concluded he had returned to Bragg's main column near Tullahoma. All vigilance north of the river slackened. Videttes along the bank were recalled and sent to their several commands.[22]

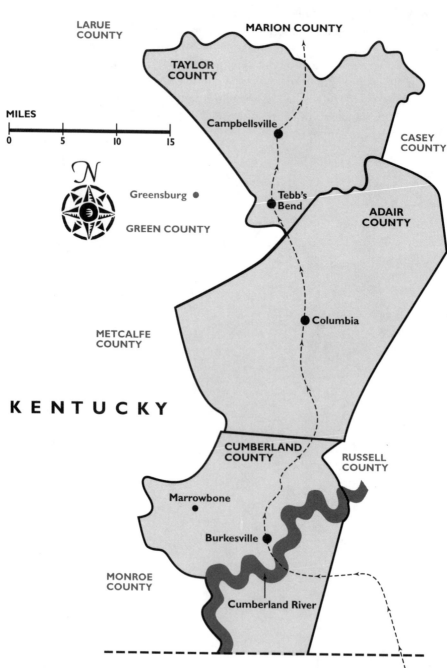

LARUE
COUNTY

MARION COUNTY

TAYLOR
COUNTY

MILES

0   5   10   15

Campbellsville

CASEY
COUNTY

N

Greensburg ●

Tebb's
Bend

ADAIR
COUNTY

GREEN COUNTY

METCALFE
COUNTY

Columbia

KENTUCKY

CUMBERLAND
COUNTY

RUSSELL
COUNTY

Marrowbone

Burkesville

MONROE
COUNTY

Cumberland River

TENNESSEE

CUMBERLAND COUNTY, KY

FOUR

"Naked as Jay-Birds!"

Wednesday, July 1

When Morgan returned to the Cumberland River, he found it very high. It was out of its banks, a quarter of a mile wide.[1] A perilous current and floating driftwood threatened their crossing. He had no large fording craft to accommodate the transfer of 2,500 men and horses. So he was obliged to have some flatboats built to augment the few canoes he had.[2] Under the cover of darkness, he began crossing the raging Cumberland River at two locations. Horses were unsaddled and driven into the swollen stream in groups of twenty or thirty at a time. When they made it across, they were caught, hitched and resaddled. Using two flatboats and a couple canoes, the men crossed. A canoe was loaded with twelve saddles and with two at the oars; the men, inexperienced at rowing, struggled in the surging waters, which lapped perilously within inches of the canoe's edge.[3]

Hundreds of Confederates stripped their clothing off and placed their "uniforms" in the canoes with the rifles. Once they gained the other shore, they dressed themselves and picked up their weapons. There were incidents when several hundred of Morgan's men had just come ashore and were immediately greeted by hostile fire. Not waiting to get dressed, they grabbed their rifles and got off a round.[4] Dropping their rifles, they picked up their pistols and went charging into the Union pickets firing above their raiders' yells. The shaken Federals exclaimed, "They're naked as jay-birds!"[5] Unnerved by the sight and never having confronted such "wild" men, the Union troops turned and fled from the scene. Naked men in battle hadn't been seen since Sparta fought Athens thousands of years ago in the Peloponnesian War (431-404 B.C.).

10:00am, Thursday, July 2

The entire command forded the river. First to cross was Col. Duke leading the First Brigade and the artillery company at Burkesville with his two improvised flatboats and canoes. Col. Adam R. Johnson's 10th KY Cav. led the way for the Second Brigade at Turkey-Neck Bend.[6] Johnson had no

19

craft for crossing. Men and horses plunged into the river and struggled against the current to cross. Col. Johnson reported that in addition to precipitous banks, the enemy were hovering on the river and harassing him as far as they could. Capt. Lorenzo Dow Hockersmith in Johnson's command wryly noted, "We crossed at Turkey Neck Bend under many difficulties. There was a large force of Federals on the opposite side of the river who, from some cause, were very much opposed to our getting over to the Kentucky side. Had it not been for the assistance rendered by Duke, we would have had a warm time before we could have gotten into our own state."[7]

Hobson and Judah, twelve miles away in Marrowbone, Kentucky, had been trusting that Morgan would not cross the swollen river, which Duke had described as a "Millrace."[8] That mistake was a critical error in judgment. Before the Federals could move to Burkesville in force to resist, two Confederate regiments and portions of others were across.

<u>Thursday, July 2</u>

General Shackelford suggested he lead a reconnaissance with his brigade in the direction of Burkesville.[9] General Hobson concurred and was of the opinion that Morgan had not concentrated his forces as yet. The Union advance was given to Lt. Colonel Holloway with a detachment of the 3rd KY Cavalry (USA). Then came Col. Benjamin H. Bristow with the 8th KY Cavalry. They were followed by the 12th KY Infantry, Colonel William A. Hoskins; the 22nd IN Battery, Captain Benjamin F. Denning; Capt. Hammond and Co. K, 65th IN regiment. They had proceeded three miles when word came from General Judah to halt their entire command. Within minutes, Shackelford received orders to march his command back to Marrowbone. Colonel Bristow and Col. Richard T. Jacob had ridden so far ahead that they were already making arrangements to cut off and capture one of Morgan's regiments. Just then, Judah's orders were received to cease their action and return to Marrowbone.[10] This was one of the first of several major blunders General Judah would commit in trying to catch Morgan on this raid.

Colonel Frank Lane Wolford and Union detachments from three regiments, about 300 cavalrymen, skirmished with Quirk's scouts. Captain Thomas Quirk, Co. M, 2nd KY Cav. was the captain of Morgan's scouts. His left arm was shattered by a minie ball and Morgan lost the services of his best scout on this raid.[11] Lt. Kelion Franklin Peddicord, one of Quirk's scouts operating with the 14th KY Cavalry, put it bluntly, "Only one man received a wound. Captain Tom, whose rein arm was broken."[12] But Morgan's men drove the Union cavalry back to Marrowbone, where Federal artillery checked the Confederates' advance. Before the Union force could reorganize itself, Morgan's entire force was halfway to Columbia. Hobson, Judah and Shackelford were getting their first taste of rapidly developing and rapidly changing cavalry warfare, Morgan-style. The chase had begun.

ADAIR COUNTY, KY

<u>Friday, July 3</u>

The first town Morgan's force came to was Columbia.[13] On its out-skirts, they met 150 men of Col. Wolford's 1st KY Cavalry and battalions of the 2nd and 45th OVI (Ohio Volunteer Infantry) under the command of Captain Jesse M. Carter. After a brief fight, the captain fell mortally wounded. Another captain, Brent Fishback of the same regiment, fell back into the town and fought house-to-house. After another hour they withdrew toward Jimtown, leaving Columbia in Confederate hands. In the engagement, Morgan's men captured six prisoners. Three of Wolford's men were wounded and two killed, including Captain Jesse Carter. The raiders suffered two killed and two wounded. Among the Confederate wounded was Captain Jacob T. Cassel, Co. A, 2nd KY, who was shot in the thigh. He was placed in an ambulance wagon and, in that way, continued through the raid.[14]

Lt. Colonel Robert Alston, Morgan's chief of staff commented, "Our men behaved badly at Columbia, breaking open a store and plundering it. I ordered the men to return the goods, and made all the reparations in my power. These outrages are very disgraceful, and are usually perpetrated by men accompanying the army simply for plunder. They are not worth a ____, and are a disgrace to both armies."[15] Many of Morgan's men and officers were native Kentuckians and they felt a kinship toward the residents of the Bluegrass State. Alston's reaction reflected those feelings. But once they were north of the Ohio River, the stores and homes belonged to the "enemy" and criticism of similar plunderous acts was muted or condoned.

By nightfall of the following day, the regiment was seven miles beyond Columbia, with other units of the division strung out far behind. It was three o'clock the morning of July 4 before the rear regiment entered Columbia, bivouacking in the streets. Duke in the meantime had sent Captain Thomas B. Franks, Co. I, 2nd KY Cav., and scouts forward to reconnoiter the Tebb's Bend bridge at Green River. Franks reported back before dawn that the Yankees at the bridge appeared to be expecting an attack. They were busy as beavers, he said. All through the night the scouts heard the ringing of axes and the crash of falling timbers.[16]

TAYLOR COUNTY, KY

FIVE

An Ominous Sign

Morgan's quick breakout from Columbia vaulted his forces a day's ride ahead of pursuing Federals. They camped six miles from the Green River Bridge in Taylor County on present Hwy. 210 just off Hwy. 55 South.

Morgan approached the bridge at Tebb's Bend. It was being defended by two hundred men of the 25th MI (volunteer) Infantry and 8th MI under the command of Colonel Orlando H. Moore.[1]

Colonel Moore had heard of Morgan's advance across the Cumberland River, about forty miles away, the day it occurred. His troops were holding a blockhouse at the bridge over the Green River. He knew he could not defend his fortified position. Morgan's artillery would have been able to shell him from higher ground. For the impending fight, he chose the highest ground available, a mile or so south of the bridge. It was on a bluff in a sharp bend of the river where he would be safe on three sides and could make Morgan fight according to plan on the fourth side. The Confederates would have to approach on a narrow front where their superior numbers would be of little advantage.[2]

The Union soldiers felled trees to form an abatis (an obstacle of trees with sharpened ends aimed at the enemy). Farther in front, they quickly dug a trenched-fortification. Behind and before this was open ground. Col. Moore's plan was that each position, when abandoned by his troops and overrun by the enemy, would leave them defenseless before his fire. The entrenched men were behind special earthworks construction within a horseshoe loop of the river.[3]

3:30am, Saturday, July 4

Morgan was up front before the sun rose, ordering Captain Edward P. Byrne to open with the battery that wounded two Union defenders.[4] After one round was fired from a Parrott (rifled cannon) at six-hundred yards from the barricade, Lieutenant Colonel Joseph T. Tucker was sent forward under a flag of truce with the following hand-written message to the Union commander[5]:

Headquarters Morgan's Division
In the Field, in front of Green River Stockade, July 4, 1863.
*To the Officer commanding Federal Forces at Stockade, near Green
   River Bridge;*
**Sir: In the name of the Confederate States Government, I demand
an immediate and unconditional surrender of the entire force under
your command, together with the Stockade.**
I am, Very Respectfully,   Jno. H. Morgan
                                            Comdg Division of Cav. C.S.A[6]
                                            7 O'clock A.M.

Moore replied, "Present my compliments to General Morgan and say
to him that the Fourth of July is a d__d bad day for a surrender, and I would
rather not." Unable to dislodge Moore's men with artillery, three of Morgan's regiments, the 5th, 7th and 11th KY, made seven frontal assaults and
each was repulsed. Some of the Confederates reached the felled trees, but
became so entangled that none were able to penetrate to the Union position,
although there were many hand-to-hand encounters.[7] While the main battle
was raging, a Confederate force tried to reach Moore's rear. A cavalry charge
was launched on some forty men of the 8th MI under Lt. M.A. Hogan who
had remained near the bridge, but it, too, was turned back. Another unit of
Morgan's men was sent to scale the steep bluff on Moore's right flank, but
the Union colonel blew the bugle and led a reserve company to repel them.[8]
According to Col. Moore, the fighting lasted three and a half hours.[9]

10:30am, Saturday, July 4

Morgan realized that the position could not be taken without losing
more men than he could afford. He sent in a flag of truce—this time asking
permission to remove his wounded.[10] Northern troops helped deliver some
of the wounded Confederates in front of their lines. It had been especially
costly for Morgan's forces. Among the Confederates killed were: Col. David
Walter Chenault (11th KY), Major Thomas Y. Brent, Jr. (5th KY), Captain
Alex H. Tribble (Co. B, 11th KY), Capt. M.D. Logan (Co. I, 7th KY), 1st Lt.
George W. Holloway (Co. B, 5th KY), 1st Lt. Frank A. West (Co. H, 11th KY),
1st Lt. Robert H. Cowan (Co. I, 7th KY), 1st Lt.C.N. Kirtley (Co. K, 7th KY),
2nd Lt. William W. Baldwin (Co. A, 11th KY), 2nd Lt. James Ferguson (Co. A,
5th KY) and 2nd Lt. Thomas J. Current (Co. C, 5th KY). Among the Confederate dead and dying were two brothers, Ausey Dunn Cosby and John Cosby.
A third brother, Oliver, stayed behind to care for his brother Ausey who, in
a day or two, 'died of his wounds.[11] After burying his brother, he caught up
to and rejoined Morgan's forces. All three were privates from Co. B, 11th KY.
In all, thirty-six of Morgan's men were killed and forty-five wounded. One

report said that the Confederate losses were fifty killed and 200 wounded. The Union casualties were six killed and twenty-three wounded.

After Morgan learned of the cost to his forces and the lack of headway made in the attack, he ordered his men to withdraw and he went six miles downstream to another point of the Green River and crossed at a ford where Col. Roy Cluke's 8th KY Cav. had crossed earlier.[12] When the remnants of Chenault's 11th KY withdrew, Joseph W. Bowman, Adjutant was wounded. He, Pvt. John E. Benson, Co. H, 11th KY and others were been left behind to be taken prisoner. The wounded, both Union and Confederate, were treated by Asst. Surgeon J.N. Gregg of the 25th MI Infantry.[13]

Basil Duke, in his book, *History of Morgan's Cavalry,* said that the "seriously wounded and dead were left under the charge of Surgeons and Chaplains, who received every assistance, that he could furnish, from Colonel Moore, who proved himself as humane as he was skillful and gallant."[14] Confederate Col. Robert Alston said of Col. Moore, "He is a gallant man, and the entire arrangement of his defense entitles him to the highest credit for military skill. We would mark such a man in our army for promotion."

General Morgan, with grim appreciation, sent a letter to Col. Moore via a noncombatant saying, "that for his gallant defense of Tebb's Bend, he promoted him to be a Major-General of the Yankee army."[15] After the war, Moore was commissioned a major in the regular army and spent the remainder of his military career on the frontiers fighting Indians.

The night of July 4, while the raiders rested around their camp fires, General Morgan's younger brother, Thomas, sang the song, "Lorena," which had been written by a Zanesville, Ohio, minister, H.D.L. Webster.[16]

> The years creep slowly by, Lorena;
> The snow is on the grass again;
> The sun's low down the sky, Lorena;
> The frost gleams where the flowers have been.
> But the heart throbs on as warmly now
> As when the summer days were nigh;
> Oh! The sun can never dip so low
> Adown affection's cloudless sky.
>
> A hundred months have passed, Lorena,
> Since last I held that hand in mine,
> And felt the pulse beat fast, Lorena,
> Though mine beat faster far than thine.
> A hundred months—'twas flowery May,
> When up the hilly slope we climbed,
> To watch the dying of the day
> And hear the distant church bells chime.

Lt. Thomas Morgan was a talented musician and could play both the fiddle and guitar. He would accompany himself while he entertained the men. Among the songs most favored during the war years by folks North and South were "The Last Rose of Summer" (1813), "Home Sweet Home" (1823), "Annie Laurie" (1835), "Listen To The Mockingbird" (1855), "Dixie" (1860), "The Bonnie Blue Flag" (1836), "Lorena" (1837) and "The Battle Cry of Freedom" (1863).

That same day, the Confederate stronghold at Vicksburg surrendered. Moving along with Morgan's large force were sutlers and others, each of whom had his own reason to join in this adventurous mission. One old gentleman from Sparta, Tennessee, had come north with this Dixie division to get a barrel of salt at Burkesville. Once he had made his purchase, he realized his dangerous situation. He could try to retrace his steps back to Sparta alone and risk fearful dangers. He might even have to abandon his treasure of salt. Or he could stay within the protective cover of the raiders as they moved north and eventually reenter the safety of the South when Morgan's men would return from their raid. Two weeks later, when he was deep into Ohio, constantly attacked by militia forces, he tearfully lamented to one of Morgan's officers, "Captain, I would give my farm in White County, Tennessee, and all the salt in Kentucky, if I had it, to stand once more—safe and sound—on the banks of the Calf-killer creek."[17]

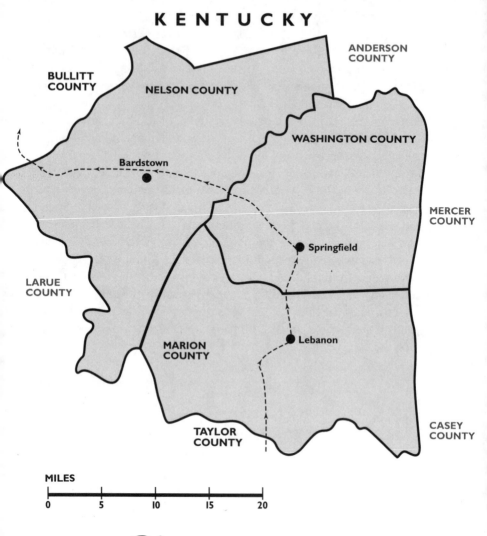

K E N T U C K Y

BULLITT
COUNTY

ANDERSON
COUNTY

NELSON COUNTY

WASHINGTON COUNTY

Bardstown

MERCER
COUNTY

LARUE
COUNTY

Springfield

MARION
COUNTY

Lebanon

TAYLOR
COUNTY

CASEY
COUNTY

MILES

0   5   10   15   20

MARION, WASHINGTON & NELSON COUNTIES, KY

<u>6:30am, Sunday, July 5</u>

About six miles from Bardstown, Lt. Thomas W. Sullivan, 4th U.S. Cavalry, came upon a small contingent of Morgan's advance guard. He was not aware how close he was to Morgan's main body. With his company of just twenty-five men, they chased the small Confederate group through Bardstown. There, they halted because their horses were exhausted. He was informed that the town was surrounded by 300 to 400 of Morgan's cavalry. Realizing his precarious position, Sullivan took possession of a large livery stable and erected a small breastworks of planks and manure within the stable to command the gate. He purchased provisions for his men to last as long as their ammunition would hold out. The lieutenant posted pickets on the corners of the main streets and waited for the inevitable attack. In a few hours, he would get Morgan's response.[18]

<u>9:00am, July 5</u>

In Lebanon, the Confederate raiders met the 20th KY Infantry (Federal), a force of 380 men under the command of Lt. Colonel Charles S. Hanson, occupying the town.[19] The Union colonel's brother was Confederate General Roger W. Hanson who had been an honored guest at the wedding of John to Mattie. The Union regiment were seasoned fighters. They had seen action at Shiloh, Corinth, Perryville and Nelson's Cross Roads. But the fighting they were to experience at Lebanon in the duration of time and severity of fighting would eclipse them all. Lt. Col. Hanson was a native of Lexington, Kentucky, and he knew John Hunt Morgan. The Confederates sent in a flag of truce and demanded that the Union garrison surrender. Hanson sent Morgan his respects but declined the offer. Before Morgan's scouts had circled the town and cut the telegraph wires to military headquarters in Louisville, Hanson had received orders to hold out on the assurance that reinforcements would arrive in a few hours.[20]

The raiders set up their two Parrotts on a hill over looking the Union defenses. They intended to reduce the Union garrison without storming their stronghold. For several hours the four Confederate cannons fired but could not quell the enemy's return fire. In fact, Union sharpshooters advanced on the Confederate artillery, making it difficult for them to be used effectively.

The 8th and 9th MI Cavalry and the 11th MI Battery under the command of Col. James I. David were approaching on the Danville road to reinforce

Lt. Col. Hanson.[21] When scouts reported their approach, Morgan ordered an assault on the Union garrison and, at the same time, he sent Col. Johnson with his brigade to the Danville road to cut off reinforcements. Now after seven hours of fighting, Duke's regiment rushed forward with Morgan's nineteen-year-old brother, First Lt. Thomas H. Morgan (Co. I, 2nd KY) in the lead cheering the men on with his enthusiasm and bright nature. From a window above the railroad depot, a Union soldier sighted on young Morgan and pulled the trigger. Tom was fatally wounded in the chest, the bullet piercing his heart. His last words were, "Brother Cally, they have killed me," and he collapsed into his brother Calvin's arms.[22] Col. Alston observed, "This was a crushing blow to General Morgan, as his affection for his brother exceeded the love of Jonathan to David." After the staggering losses at Tebb's Bend and the shocking death of Thomas Morgan, Lt. Col. James Bennett McCreary commented that "The commencement of this raid is ominous."[23]

SIX

"Twenty-Five Damned Yankees

<u>11:30am, Sunday, July 5</u>

While Morgan's main force was fighting fiercely to the south in Lebanon, an advanced detachment of several hundred Confederates, of Co. C, 2nd KY, descended on Bardstown in three columns from three directions. They were led by Captain Ralph Sheldon. In the first attack, two of Lt. Thomas Sullivan's men were killed. One, Pvt. Bartholomew Burke, Co. H, shouted as he fell mortally wounded. His last words were, "Lieutenant, did I fall like a soldier?" Immediately after this repulse, Captain Sheldon sent in a flag of truce, demanding the Union force's immediate surrender. Sullivan rejected surrender, replying, "I hope to gain the esteem of General Morgan by a gallant defense." After a ten-minute pause, firing resumed and continued all evening. In the dark, Sheldon had his men stretch ropes across the streets to prevent anyone from escaping on horseback in the dark. The Confederates also tried unsuccessfully to set fire to the stable.[1] In this attack, three privates from Co. C, 2nd KY were killed. They were: James Bullitt, Fredrick Edwards and Moses Savage, CSA.

<u>4:00pm, July 5</u>

In Lebanon, Hanson surrendered. Tom's death was not the only one suffered by Morgan's men. In all, nine Confederates were killed and twenty-five wounded. Among the dead were Lt. William Gardner, Co. D, 10th KY; 3rd Sgt. William Jones, Co. A, 2nd KY; Sgt. M.C. Franklin, Co. F, 2nd KY and privates: Logwood, Hawkins and Walter Ferguson, Co. A, 2nd KY. Pvt. R.J. Worsham, Co. A, 2nd KY was one of the wounded. Among the captured was 3rd Lt. John J. Rager, Co. B, 9th TN. Union casualties were six killed and sixteen wounded. The six Union dead were Sergeant Joseph Slaughter, Corporal John House, and privates P.C. Daniels, Jesse Edwards, Sam Ferguson and Eugene McCarty.

Young Tom was buried in the garden of the Reverend T.H. Cleland in Lebanon.[2] After the war, his body would be brought back to Lexington for burial beside his brother, John.

Many of Morgan's men wanted to execute their Union prisoners because they had killed John's brother, Tom. John's brother, Charlton, grabbed Lt. Col. Hanson by his long, flowing beard, shook a fist in his face and shouted, "I'll blow your brains out, you damned rascal."[3] But General Morgan, his eyes filled with tears and grief-stricken, rushed into the captured railroad depot. With drawn pistol, he stood between Hanson's men and his own and declared, "I'll shoot the first one who molests a prisoner." He then turned to Hanson and said, "When you get home, if it is any gratification to you, tell Mother you killed brother Tom."[4] Actually, General Morgan accused Captain H.S. Parrish of shooting his brother.

Among the Union prisoners John Morgan had captured was his former business partner and brother-in-law, Sanders Bruce.[5] Sanders' sister, Becky, was the General's first wife. She had died two years earlier from a chronic illness.

Morgan wasn't the only general who was mad at Hanson. Despite his prolonged and stubborn defense, General Burnside was angry with Hanson. So much so that he had him arrested. But by July 14, Burnside recanted and sent the following telegram:

> General Hartsuff, Lexington, Ky:
> General Robinson, Frankfort, Ky:
> General Boyle, Louisville, Ky:
> **Hobson is close on Morgan's heels, in Clermont County. Morgan will evidently try to cross at or near Maysville. You can release Colonel Hanson from arrest. I am satisfied I made a mistake in arresting him. Please tell him so.**
>   A.E. BURNSIDE, *Major-General.*[6]

In the aftermath of the battle in Lebanon, Kentucky, the Confederates took possession of a large quantity of ammunition, many fine rifles, an abundant supply of medicines, and a field full of ambulances and wagons.[7] General Morgan was able to arm all his men who were without weapons, and furnish ammunition to those who were sorely in need.[8]

Morgan couldn't take his prisoners back to camp in Tennessee. With two Michigan regiments moving toward him, Morgan ordered Alston and a detachment of twenty mounted men to quick-march Hanson and the other prisoners six miles at saber-point to the village of Springfield, where they would be administered the oath of parole.[9] During the march, a merciful rain fell and revived a great number who might have died from exhaustion. At least two Union soldiers died on this forced march. The death of Sgt. Joseph Slaughter, Co. B was described in the *Cincinnati Daily Commercial* (July 24, 1863), "One of our brave boys fell exhausted on the ground, one of whom, 1st Sergeant Joseph Slaughter, of company B, becoming faint and weary, was clubbed by them with a musket until dead! Another, Sam Ferguson, private Co. I, when worn out, got upon a horse. He was ordered in a gruff voice, by one of the villains to get down. He did so and fell in the mud and water of the road. I and another gentleman placed him in a wagon. He died that night, poor fellow."[10] After leaving Springfield, Morgan's main column headed for Bardstown.

4:00am, Monday, July 6

Upon arrival at Bardstown, Captain Sheldon and Co. C, 2nd KY, was detached at Muldraugh's Hill to reconnoiter toward Louisville, and to rejoin the column at Bardstown.[11] But before leaving Bardstown, General Morgan had to deal with Lt. Sullivan's small group entrenched in the stable.

As daylight broke, Captain Sheldon brought in a flag of truce demanding Sullivan's immediate surrender, telling him, "If you refuse, we will blow you to hell with our artillery." Sullivan's answer was, "I am obliged to the General's kind intentions, but it is our duty to trouble him a little longer."[12]

After a few minutes, rapid fire commenced and it continued until one of Sullivan's sentinels on top of the stable reported four pieces of artillery in position about 100 yards from the stable. The message shouted down to Sullivan was that the streets were crowded with Confederate troops, far more than the few hundred they encountered the day before.

Realizing that any further resistance was fruitless, Sullivan took a flag of truce and left the stable. Col. Richard Morgan approached him and asked what he wanted. The Union lieutenant answered that he was now willing to give up and accept the terms of surrender where his men would be treated as prisoners of war. Col. Morgan shouted, "Go back. You have already refused these terms twice. You have no right to demand them now." The Confederate colonel ordered his guard to force Sullivan back into the stable. On his return under a flag of truce, he was fired upon several times. Residents of Bardstown, sympathizers of the Confederates, had been observing the conversation between Col. Morgan and Lt. Sullivan. When the lieutenant, carrying the flag of truce, was fired upon, they cried out, "Shame! Shame!"[13]

Hardly had Sullivan returned to the stable, when a Confederate entered under a flag of truce and demanded unconditional surrender. The lieutenant told the flag bearer that he had laid down his arms. "General Morgan can treat me as a prisoner of war or satisfy his thirst for slaughter. Whatever he chooses." Col. Morgan assured him he would be treated as a prisoner of war with this admonition, "You don't deserve it because of your foolishness and stubborn resistance."

The General grudgingly complimented Sullivan's men by saying, "You twenty-five damned Yankees have cost me twenty-four hours."[14]

Back in Springfield, Morgan's Chief of Staff, Col. Robert Alston, offered his Union prisoners a chance to sign a "Parole of Honor" and be released unharmed. Up until May 1863, when the agreement on the exchange of prisoners broke down, these paroles were common. If a prisoner would swear "not to bear arms against the Confederate States, or to perform any military or garrison duty whatsoever," and sign a document attesting to this oath, he would be released unharmed. In the case of these Union men, they would return home. Then they would receive written notification from the Union government that their paroles were at an end because an exchange had occurred with the Confederacy for men of equal rank. But men on both sides violated their paroles by returning to the war without learning whether they had been exchanged.[15]

Col. Alston had remained behind with a small staff of twenty men to process their Lebanon prisoners and have each sign a parole so they could be released. This detained the Colonel for two hours after Morgan's command had left. Wet and chilly from the aftermath of a heavy downpour, Alston was worn out and his horse was tired and hungry. As night fell, he stopped to feed her at an abandoned farmhouse. Falling asleep, he was aroused by one of his men. They started out to rejoin the command.[16]

When he reached the point on the Bardstown road where he expected the Second Brigade to encamp, he was halted by a party of 9th MI Cavalry under Lt. Ladd. Supposing them to be Morgan's pickets, Alston rode up promptly to correct them for standing in full view of any one approaching. To his mortification, he found himself a prisoner of Federal troops. In his own words, "My God! how I hated it, no one can understand." As Ladd searched his prisoners for weapons, he found Alston's diary, which he subsequently turned over to his superiors. All we know of its contents is a brief passage, "another day of gloom, fatigue and death." It is unclear whether the diary contained information about Morgan's plans and his intent to cross the Ohio River. Alston gave his word of honor that he would take his men to the nearest Federal military post and surrender them on the following day.[17]

On the day following his capture, Alston made contact with Morgan, who sent word that he considered Alston's parole invalid by the new Federal standards, and ordered him and his troops to rejoin the invasion force. Alston released his men but sent word to Morgan that, whatever his legal status under the laws of war, he considered himself bound by his personal pledge to Lt. Ladd. Alston went to Lexington and turned himself in to General Burnside. The Union general also considered Ladd's parole of Alston illegal and found himself in the ludicrous position of having to tell Alston that General Morgan had been right in ordering him to ignore the parole. Burnside was impressed with Alston's sense of honor, but could not send him back to Morgan's invading army. He placed Alston under guard and sent him to the military prison camp at Camp Chase in Columbus, Ohio.[18]

6:00am, Monday, July 6

Leaving Greensburg, Hobson, accompanied by the 9th KY cavalry (USA), hastened their pace for the next twenty miles and reached Campbellsville by daybreak where he linked up with Shackelford. Together, they rode another fifteen miles to Lebanon.

10:00am, July 6

Morgan's division rode out of Bardstown heading west over the Shepherdsville road. They marched steadily all day, passing through Lebanon Junction.

1:30pm, July 6

General Hobson arrived in Lebanon with his command, the 9th and 12th regiments of the Kentucky cavalry. Also General Shackelford's command consisting of the 8th KY Cav. regiment and a battalion of the 3rd KY and one section of the 22nd IN Battery. Soon after his arrival, he was joined by 1st KY Cavalry, 2nd E. TN Mounted Infantry, 2nd and 45th OH Cavalry, 7th OH mounted infantry and Linn's howitzer battery of four mountain howitzers, under the command of Col. Wolford.[19] The 7th OH was known as the "River Regiment" because many of the men came from counties along the Ohio River.[20] Adding to the force was the 14th IL Cavalry led by Col. Horace Capron. General Judah's forces remain farther back, delayed at the flooded Green River which had risen ten feet, preventing him from getting across.[21] Hobson ordered that his slower moving units of infantry and artillery be detached and report to General Judah, who was being delayed at Vaughn's Ferry on the flooded Green River.

SEVEN

Treachery Within the Ranks

Not all of Morgan's men were killed by the enemy. As they approached Lebanon on July 4, they took and held a local citizen under guard for a short time to prevent him from alerting the Union garrison in the town. While he was under the guard of Captain Murphy, the Confederate officer confiscated his watch. When Captain Magenis, the adjutant general of Morgan's division, discovered the theft, he reported it to Morgan. Murphy was ordered arrested.[1]

3:00pm, Monday, July 6

Capt. Murphy learned that Magenis had caused his arrest. He rode alongside, and in full view of General Morgan, drew his pistol and fired severing Magenis' carotid artery, causing a mortal wound. The General cried out and men turned their faces to see what was causing the sudden commotion. As Magenis fell from his horse, with blood gushing out of his mouth, his only remark was, "Let me down easy." In the next moment he was dead. Later, Col. Alston wrote that Captain Magenis must of had a premonition of impending death. "He told me on the morning of his own demise, 'How dreadful to reflect that we were marching on to engage in deadly strife, and how many poor fellows would pass into eternity before the setting of yonder sun.' His admonition was a presage of his own fate before the sun was to set."[2]

The night before crossing the Ohio, General Morgan ordered a court-martial to try the murderer, but Murphy escaped, never to be seen again. Duke said of Magenis, "There was no officer in the entire Confederate army, perhaps, so young as he was, who had evinced more intelligence, aptitude and zeal, than had Captain Magenis. Certainly, there was not among them all a more true-hearted, gallant, honorable gentleman."[3]

4:30pm, July 6

General Burnside apprised of the disposition of Hobson's force and Judah's army, decided that because of Hobson's better position, close on Morgan's trail, Hobson should lead the chase. He sent the following orders to Hobson[4]:

(Telegram)   Cincinnati, Ohio, *July* 6 – 4:30 p.m.

General Hobson: It is reported that a small portion of Morgan's command was at Harrodsburg this morning, but the main body went from Springfield in the direction of Bardstown. You will combine the commands of General Shackelford and Colonel Wolford, and, after ascertaining as near as possible the direction of General Morgan's route, you will endeavor to overtake him or cut him off. Please telegraph at once the composition of your own brigade, and also that of Shackelford and Wolford. You are authorized to subsist your command upon the country, and impress the necessary horses to replace broken-down ones. This should be done in a regular way. Morgan ought to be broken to pieces before he gets out of the State [Kentucky]. Answer at once.

A.E. BURNSIDE,
Major-General.

5:00pm, Monday, July 6

Hobson reported to Burnside that his force now numbered 2,500 men. Within a half hour, Hobson was leading his force toward Bardstown.[5] The order effectively removed Hobson from Judah's authority and granted him the independent action to fulfill Burnside's orders. He also learned that Morgan had lost ten to fifteen officers and a number of men in fights at Marrowbone, Green River Bridge and Lebanon, Kentucky.

12 Mile Island

OLDHAM COUNTY

New Albany

Louisville

Corydon

JEFFERSON COUNTY

SHELBY COUNTY

INDIANA

OHIO RIVER

Mauckport

Morvins Landing

SPENCER COUNTY

Brandenburg

West Point

BULLITT COUNTY

Muldraugh

MEADE COUNTY

Garnettsville

Bardstown Junction

Lebanon Junction

BRECKINRIDGE COUNTY

NELSON COUNTY

Bardstown

HARDIN COUNTY

KENTUCKY

Elizabethtown

MILES

0   5   10   15

LARUE COUNTY

N

GRAYSON COUNTY

HART COUNTY

BULLITT, JEFFERSON, HARDIN & MEADE COUNTIES, KY

EIGHT

A Feint Towards Louisville

Turning north, Morgan's column entered Bardstown Junction along the Louisville & Nashville Railroad line twenty-five miles south of Louisville. Accompanying Morgan on this raid was George A. "Lightning" Ellsworth. He could scale a telegraph pole at any point in the raid and tap into the lines to overhear messages being sent from one Union command to another. In this way, Morgan could be informed immediately of his enemy's plans, where their troop movements were, and what they knew about Morgan's presence. Morgan would use Lightning's skills to send misinformation (false messages) to the enemy reporting Morgan's movements in directions that the General never planned to go. There are several versions of how the Canadian-born telegrapher earned his nickname: One was because he could tap out messages so quickly on his mobile telegraph key. Another was that he once climbed a telegraph pole only to be knocked to the ground when lightning struck, and lived to tell about it.

There, at dusk, Ellsworth entered the Bardstown Junction telegraph office to find the operator wearing a uniform recently issued to Union telegraphers. It included a dark blue blouse, blue trousers with a silver cord on the seam, a natty buff vest, a forage cap with no ornaments or marks of rank. Pointing his pistol to the head of the telegraph operator, James Forker, Ellsworth said, "Hello, sonny. Move one inch except as I tell you, and you'll be buried in that fancy rig."[1] Listening to incoming messages, Ellsworth learned that Morgan was expected to attack Louisville. He also learned about a Union passenger train coming north from Nashville. When the railroad superintendent in Louisville asked, "Has the train passed north yet?" Ellsworth told Forker, "Tell him yes." Forker did so, and in a few minutes later the train was surrounded by gray-clad Confederates south of the trestle, which the raiders had set on fire.

In the exchange of gunfire, one Union soldier was killed. The thirty passengers and the dozen surviving soldiers were made to disembark and line up beside the track. They were relieved of hats, boots, money and jewelry. Money was removed from the express company's safe. The U.S. mail was seized, opened for cash and eventually burned in a series of small fires. A correspondent of the *New York Herald* lost his gold watch to a lieutenant and his pocketknife to a private. Morgan, dressed in a roundabout jacket, gray trousers and cavalry boots, with no insignia of rank, chatted with the women passengers. They persuaded him to allow the train to return south to Elizabethtown.[2] The female passengers praised Morgan and said he was a gentleman.

5:00pm, Tuesday, July 7

Hobson was hard-pressed to find rations for his own men. He halted at Bardstown Junction on the L&N Railroad. Morgan had exhausted the supplies of the people in the areas through which the pursuing Union troops would pass. With thousands of soldiers to feed, Hobson stopped and requested that a train be sent from Louisville with supplies. This scarcity of food would change later when he and his men rode through the friendly and accommodating populations of Indiana and Ohio. But for now, Hobson's hungry forces waited patiently at the railhead junction. This delay would put the Union pursuers twenty-four hours behind Morgan and allow the Confederates sufficient time to successfully cross the Ohio River virtually unopposed.[3] Hobson's ponderous column of men, ammunition and ambulances was three miles long.

From stragglers, Hobson learned that Morgan was headed for the river. Realizing he could not overtake Morgan if the raiders planned to cross the river, communicated with Brigadier-General Jeremiah T. Boyle, commanding the Army of Ohio's District of Kentucky in Louisville, advising him of Morgan's move toward Brandenburg. He requested that a Union gunboat be dispatched to thwart any crossing of the Ohio.[4]

This lightning raid was to carry him through three states, and Morgan's men had to do a lot of "horse-trading." Once a Confederate's horse was exhausted, he would find a fresh one from a nearby farm and exchange steeds. During the course of this twenty-four-day ride through Kentucky, Indiana and Ohio, it has been estimated that Morgan's men used 15,000 horses.[5] If Morgan started with 2,500 men, that would mean that each of his men would have ridden an average of six horses in the journey through Kentucky, Indiana and Ohio. The large pursuing Federal cavalry also needed "fresh" horses, as well. One of Morgan's captains, Thomas Coombs, said, "One man would frequently ride five horses down in one day. Mount a fine, fresh horse in the morning, start off at a dead run, and before ten o'clock (in the morning), he would hardly be able to put one foot before another, then ride him up to a fine stable, change saddle and bridle, turn the tired horse loose in the lot and go ahead again."[6] As the Confederate raiders entered the final lap of their journey through Ohio, most of their original Kentucky thoroughbreds had been abandoned and "traded" for fresh farm horses accustomed to pulling a plow. These agrarian steeds were not conditioned for the torturous, fast-paced chase, which required that the Dixie soldiers change their horses much more frequently. Morgan's men were reluctant to leave behind any healthy horses that their Union pursuers could use to close the gap between them. It was not unusual for a Confederate trooper to ride along, holding the reins of one or more "surplus" horses so as to deny their accessibility to their pursuers. In an effort to discredit Morgan's acquisition of mounts, Union General Jacob Cox wrote this poem[7]:

> John Morgan's foot is on thy shore, Kentucky, O Kentucky!
> His hand is on thy stable door, Kentucky! O Kentucky!
> You'll see your good gray mare no more,
> He'll ride her 'til her back is sore
> And leave her at some stranger's door, Kentucky, O Kentucky!

NINE

To the River

Morgan's forces headed west of Louisville sending 130 men commanded by Captain William J. Davis, Assistant Adjutant General of the First Brigade, to scout the vicinity east of the Falls City.[1] Morgan hoped to give the impression that the city was about to be attacked, and divert attention from the main river crossing at Brandenburg in Meade County, Kentucky. Davis' diversion was to include cutting telegraph wires, burning railroad bridges and creating the impression that his was Morgan's entire force. He was then to lead Co. D of the 2nd KY, and Co. A of Cluke's regiment, to Twelve Mile Island, seize boats and cross the river. Morgan directed Davis to join him in Salem, Indiana.

At Garnettsville, Col. Johnson dispatched Captain Samuel B. Taylor (Co. E) and Captain H. Clay Meriwether (Co. H), both with the 10th KY, to advance on Brandenburg and capture boats to effect their crossing.[2] On their way to Garnettsville, they burnt the trestle of the L&N Railroad between West Point and Muldraugh Hill in order to delay the pursuit of the Union forces.

<u>10:00am, Tuesday, July 7</u>

That morning, the two captains and the 10th KY Cav. arrived in Brandenburg and set about the task of procuring boats to ferry the 2,280 surviving Confederates across the river into Indiana.[3] The town was so far north, it was not garrisoned by any Union troops. Many of the town's citizens were so apathetic or Confederate in sympathy, there was no resistance. The Meade County sheriff, who was a Union sympathizer, took refuge in the Denton home, where the children persuaded him to crawl under a bed to hide.

Another area resident, N.B. Stanfield, was sitting in the office of a hotel when someone shouted, "Here come the boys!" Coming down the main street was Capt. Sam Taylor's company and some of the Meade County boys. Stanfield knew Taylor quite well because Sam had stayed at Stanfield's home while raising his company. He asked Stanfield to go to the wharf with him and hail the first passing boat. Stanfield, wearing a white linen suit, waved a white flag to the *John T. McCombs,* while Taylor's men concealed themselves inside on both sides of the wharf's boat door. When the *McCombs* landed, the Confederates jumped aboard the big Anderson & Louisville packet and took possession.[4] Some of the fifty passengers began laughing as they debarked. There are conflicting eyewitness accounts that the passengers had to pay to get off. Others reported they were not robbed.

The raiders then took the boat out into the river and anchored her. Along came the *Alice Dean,* a side-wheel packet, wheel hub-built, owned by the Dean Company of Cincinnati. It had been recently built for the princely sum of $42,000.[5] It was bound for the Queen City with a mixed cargo from Mound City, Illinois. It operated from Memphis to Cincinnati. As Captain James H. Pepper was piloting his steamboat, the *Alice Dean,* he passed the village of Brandenburg and saw another steamer, idle in mid-stream, seemingly in distress. The Confederates, aboard the *McCombs,* had hoisted these signals, pretending that their boat was aground and required assistance. As soon as the *Alice Dean* pulled alongside, Morgan's men took his mooring line and made the steamers fast. While Captain Pepper was asking what was needed, the dusty, sweat-stained raiders swarmed aboard. There were several Yankees on board, going home on furlough, and they were paroled.

3:00pm, Tuesday, July 7

Morgan's main column entered Garnettsville in Meade County and went into camp.[6] Garnettsville was just east of Otter Creek about two miles south of the Ohio River. At this point, Morgan could have taken one of the many roads that crossed Kentucky in either direction. He could have gone west through the western part of the state and encountered no hostile force. He knew that Hobson was a good fifty miles to his rear. So his plan to cross the Ohio River was not to escape Hobson's pursuit, but rather to intensify the chase, attracting more Union cavalry now that he was about to cross into the North and invade their hometowns. For the next several weeks, Indiana and Ohio would be preoccupied with capturing Morgan, and its citizens would be screaming for arms and military protection.

5:00pm, July 7

The capture of the two boats did not go unnoticed by Federal eyes. Union men in Brandenburg communicated with Lt. Col. William J. Irvin of the Indiana Legion (home guard) who was in Mauckport, a couple of miles downriver, across from Brandenburg. A short time after he received this intelligence, he hailed the *Lady Pike* as it headed up river. The boat turned back to Leavenworth, Indiana, for a cannon and additional assistance. It returned at midnight with a six-pounder and thirty men of the Crawford County artillery company from Leavenworth. Having delivered its cargo, the

Lady Pike withdrew. The artillery company was commanded by Captain G.W. Lyons and Colonel Woodbury. Without limber or caisson, the cannon was lashed to the bed of a farm wagon from which the body had been stripped. In this manner, it was transported through the woods, fields and creeks. En route, the gunners were forced to unload the gun and place it on an old, rotted boat to float it across Buck Creek. It was finally brought to a point on the river opposite Brandenburg at Morvin's Landing, just east of Mauckport.[7]

The little cannon was planted in front of an old abandoned log house, a short distance from the river bank. The Indiana militiamen concealed the cannon with haystacks in a farmer's yard. Quietly, the militia took time to aim the cannon, training the barrel on the *John T. McCombs*. The undertaking was aided by the illumination of the natural gas wells on the Kentucky shore. This task accomplished, Indiana's civilian soldiers waited in nervous anticipation for Morgan's next move.[8]

Some oil wells had been drilled on the river bottom lands at the upper edge of Brandenburg. But no oil having been discovered, the great flow of gas from them had been set on fire, resulting in a constant blaze reaching thirty to fifty feet high. It was this brilliant and wonderful spectacle that illuminated the Confederates' activities and mesmerized the Hoosier contingent.[9]

Midnight, Wednesday, July 8

Morgan marched from Garnettsville with his main force heading for Brandenburg about ten miles away.

9:00am, July 8

The General and his men arrived in Brandenburg. As a kind of celebration to toast their impending invasion of the North, a group of Confederate officers went into E.C. Ashcraft's hotel and rolled out three barrels of whiskey upon the sidewalk. One of the sons of Dixie with an ax burst in the heads of the casks and invited his comrades to have a drink. Soldiers in passing would stop long enough to fill their canteens, and soon 150 gallons of high powered whiskey was well distributed among the men in gray. One of Morgan's men, perhaps having too much to drink, entered a building where Miss Carrie Doyle was teaching music. He climbed upon the piano and began to walk back and forth on its keys.[10]

Not all of Morgan's men were happy at the news that they were about to invade the North. A private, named Patton Troutt, had been born in Sumner County, Tennessee. At the age of fifteen, he had been ordained a deacon in the M.E. Church South. As a deeply religious and patriotic youth, he joined Morgan's division to defend his home in Tennessee. As he moved with Morgan's column north on the Great Raid, they came to the Ohio River at Brandenburg. There he made a critical decision to go no farther. He said, when told that they were about to cross the river into the north, "I have no quarrel with those people. I am perfectly willing to fight for my home land [Tennessee] and my rights, but making war on civilians in the north, I cannot do so." He knew that if he deserted and was apprehended, he would be court-martialed and executed. He took that gamble and returned to his Tennessee home where he was met with hostility from his neighbors. In 1867, he moved to Illinois, and in 1882, he moved his family to Kansas.[11]

Morgan met with Captain Hines at dockside to hear his report of conditions in Indiana, the roads, the towns, and what help or resistance might be expected from the people. Back in May, with Morgan's division lying south along the Cumberland, Hines was sent with some men from the 9th KY Cav. to establish a "convalescent camp" or "dead horse camp" in Clinton County, Kentucky. Here, horses that were unserviceable were fed bluegrass and given attention to bring them back into top form.[12]

Then, becoming bored in his "get well" camp, he received permission from Morgan to take about eighty "picked men" across the Cumberland River on a secret mission into Indiana to contact the "Sons of Liberty" and such organizations as the "Copperheads, Knights of the Golden Circle" and other Southern sympathizers who might aid and abet Morgan's planned incursion into Yankee territory.[13] While Hines was determining what support Morgan might expect in Indiana, the General asked Basil Duke to examine possible fords of the upper Ohio River. Hines later asserted that the very success of Morgan's raid depended upon keeping the expedition "carefully concealed" and relying upon the "surprise and celerity of movement." The information Hines was to gather on his Indiana mission was to ascertain what type of resistance forces Morgan would confront when he entered the Hoosier state and what aid he might expect to receive. Hines' mission was an important part of Morgan's invasion strategy of the Northern states.

Pvt. John Conrad was among five men from Co. K, 9th KY that had temporarily transferred into Hines' scouting unit. Conrad, in his memoirs, quoted Hines as saying, "We are going where there will be a great deal of fighting and a great deal of hard riding. If there are any of you who do not wish to go, who feel that they will dread the long and tiresome march, the weary and sleepless watches – now is the time for them to ride out." Not a man stepped out. "We were all anxious to serve with our captain," wrote Conrad.[14]

Hines and his raiding party crossed the Ohio River near Cannelton, Indiana, on the night of June 17, 1863. Hines passed himself off as a Federal officer and his unit as "Indiana Grays" ...hunting deserters and absentees from the Union Army. Their destination, Hines informed them, was French Lick, the home of a man named Doctor William A. Bowles. Bowles was the leader of the Copperheads in Indiana.[15] Near Paoli, the Confederates were met by a strong force of Home Guards. Hines said they were Indiana Grays. The guards escorted them to Paoli, where the townspeople set a long table in the square to feed the weary "Union" troopers. In the middle of the meal, some troopers rode up and informed the mayor that he had been hood-winked.[16]

Somehow Hines managed to extricate his men and they were able to lose their pursuers. Hines then went to meet with Dr. Bowles about raising an army of Copperheads who would take over the state, assassinating the state and local government officials, seizing the state arsenals and turning on the home guards. The meeting was interrupted when an informer rode up to tell Bowles that a provost marshal's patrol was on its way to arrest "Hines, General Morgan's guerrilla." Hines and his men left Bowles' home and set out for the Ohio River, which they reached on June 19. They captured a small tug near an island and started to cross the horses when a Union force of "regiment strength" arrived, accompanied by an armed steamboat. Hines retreated to the island and fought off the first wave of Federal troops that splashed ashore. But the steamboat, *Izetta,* lobbed shells all around them, forcing them to retreat up the island.[17]

Realizing it was a hopeless situation, Hines gathered his men about him to give them a choice of surrendering or swimming under fire to the Kentucky side. Hines stripped to his drawers, put his money and revolver in his hat and struck out. Twelve men, including John Conrad, chose to swim with him. The Federals tried to run them down with their tug, but the Confederates on the island kept up such a steady fire at the tug's bridge that its skipper was forced to pull back beyond the island. But before the tug had pulled away, Union infantrymen on the decks had killed three of Hines' troopers. One, directly in front of him, sank without a sound. When they reached the Kentucky shore, they turned and waved to their comrades, then vanished in the woods. The Confederates on the island raised a cheer, broke their rifles and marched down to the beach under a white flag to surrender.[18]

At the time of the Hines' raid into Indiana, the governor, Oliver P. Morton, was away in New York City trying to obtain funding for his state's government. Just prior to the raid, the Indiana General Assembly was at a standstill. Republicans had bolted from the legislature in an attempt to prevent the majority Democrats from passing bills that would severely curtail the powers of Governor Morton and hinder his support of the war effort. As a result, no appropriation bills were passed, thus leaving the Republican administration with no funds to run state government. Because of this political stalemate, the governor had gone to New York to solicit funds that he carefully managed to keep the state solvent until the next General Assembly in January 1865.[19]

On July 6, Hines and his men captured a train on the Louisville and Frankfort Railroad carrying a "fortune in gold" to Union General Rosecrans. On board the train was Colonel John H. Harney, editor of the *Louisville Democrat* and a prominent Kentucky Copperhead. When General Burnside received the news of the train raid by Hines, he sent an outraged note to the provost marshal at Lexington demanding that Hines be captured at any cost. Burnside offered $1,000 to the officer who captured Hines and his men.[20]

In Cincinnati, the *Gazette* reported:

"Morgan is in the state [Kentucky]…Colonel Harney, the Copperhead editor of the *Louisville Journal*, met Hines last night, saying, 'I'm delighted to meet you…Morgan is coming.' This is enough. There is panic and it is increasing…"[21]

On July 7, the day before Morgan's arrival at the river, Hines and the dozen survivors of his Indiana raid arrived at Brandenburg and met Captains Samuel B. Taylor and H. Clay Meriwether. Now on July 8, Hines rejoined Morgan at the dock in Brandenburg and informed the General of the conditions he observed in Indiana. He advised him of what support he might expect from local sympathizers and the strength of the defending forces they might encounter. At the end of their conversation, the General informed Hines that because Captain Thomas B. Franks had been wounded at Lebanon, Kentucky, he was to take command of the scouts, the third officer to replace Tom Quirk within a week.[22]

Even though Morgan had captured two sizable boats, it still took many crossings to transfer all his men to the Indiana shore. The first to cross on the *Alice Dean* was the veteran 2nd Kentucky with Hines leading the scouts. They were followed on the *McCombs* by Col. W.W. Ward's 9th TN regiment known as "Ward's Ducks." The men crossed without their horses, and when they landed, they fought as infantry until their horses could be transported.[23] They went inland to secure the shore and make it safe for the boatloads to follow. Morgan watched the troop transfer as an honored guest in the home of Col. Robert Buckner on the hill west of Brandenburg.[24] Buckner was a veteran of the War of 1812.[25] The home is located on an eminence that offers a panoramic view of the Ohio River valley. Morgan and his officers were able to view the river for several miles in both directions, and could thus detect the possible approach of Federal troop transports and gunboats. The slow, steady speed of such vessels would allow the raiders ample time to prepare their defenses.

Today, the river at this point, is much wider[26] and deeper than it was in 1863. These changes were brought about by the series of dams and locks built by the U.S. Army Corps of Engineers. The Ohio River is about 600 meters wide (1,968 feet) at the point where Morgan crossed. The Parrott guns were very accurate at one mile (5,280 feet), two and a half times more than the width of the river. Even the Indiana militia's small howitzer was able to lob shells across the river. Morgan's twelve-pounders had a 1,300-yard range, a six-pounder had a 1,200-yard range.

TEN

Get Across the Ohio and Burn the Boats!

<u>8:00am, Wednesday, July 8</u>

With daylight and the lifting of the river fog, the one hundred Indiana defenders could see the *John T. McCombs* bringing its cargo of Confederate troops toward them. Brazenly, Col. John Timberlake shouted across the river, "Shut down the steam on the *McCombs* and send over the steamer *Alice Dean* or I will blow you to hades in five minutes."[1] Some of Morgan's men on the wharf answered, "Oh hell, old man, come over and take a drink."[2] *There is a Morgan's Raid historical marker at this site.*

Lt. Col. William J. Irvin of the Indiana Legion ordered Captain G.W. Lyons to fire his six-pounder at the approaching vessel with a view to sinking or disabling it, thus preventing the crossing of the raiders. Irvin's command was countermanded by Provost Marshal (Col.) John Timberlake of the 81st IN who claimed precedence in command and ordered that the gun instead shell the Confederate cavalry on the opposite bank.[3] Timberlake was concerned that Morgan had civilian hostages aboard the boat and didn't want to risk innocent lives.[4] The Hoosier artillery was able to fire two unanswered bursts. This unexpected fusillade caught Morgan's troops by surprise. Their first shot pitched into a Confederate group on the river bank, scattering it, and wounding Captain W.H. Wilson, acting quartermaster of the First Brigade.[5] The second struck the texas of the *McCombs,* near the pilot house.

Two Parrott guns under Lt. Elias D. Lawrence of Byrne's Kentucky battery were on the east hill in the courthouse yard. Captain E.P. Byrne had placed the two howitzers in a pasture. They sighted in on the Hoosier artillery with deadly accuracy. The first shot fell short. The second struck the high bank just below the old log cabin. The third went crashing through it. This had the effect of scattering the whole force. At first, the Indiana militiamen tried to carry the piece of artillery off with them, but continued fire from Lawrence's battery induced them to leave it where it rested.[6] The cannon had been loaded for a third shot when its crew deserted it. One of the militiamen, Cortez M. Miller, stood on the wagon carriage, coolly broke a musket cartridge, emptied the powder into the vent of the gun and fired the last shot by touching it off with a lighted cigar. The shot went wide of its mark.[7]

The militia retired to the hoped-for safety of a wooded ridge several hundred yards away from the river. There was a swale or low swamp-like space nearly a quarter of a mile back, in an open field, upon which there was a growth of small timber that served to furnish some protection, at least from view. Many of the fleeing militia took refuge in it, while others continued their rapid and unabated withdrawal. The raiders opened fire on the fleeing crowd and concentrated upon this little wooded space. A Confederate shell landed on a log on which two Indiana men had stopped to rest. It killed both Lt. James H. Currant of the Mauckport Rifles, a resident of Heath Township and forty-six-year-old Georia R. Nantz of nearby Laconia.[8]

Upon gaining the shore, Colonel William Walker Ward and Major Thomas B. Webber at once pressed on toward the ridge. Even without their cannon, the Indiana forces continued to return fire. They withdrew from the exposed shoreline and retreated up Buck Creek in southern Harrison County, skirmishing as they went.[9]

Col. Timberlake's "Hoosier Hawk-eyes" were joined by others led by Col. Lewis Jordan, Sr. (6th Regiment, Indiana Legion) of Corydon and Captain William Farquar (Harrison County Mounted Hoosiers). Altogether there were about 300 volunteer men. At the top of the South Hill, one mile below Corydon, they planned to make a more determined stand, even though they knew they were heavily outnumbered. Three requests went out to New Albany for men and weapons, but despite assurances that help would be sent, none was dispatched.[10]

The small Federal gunboat *Springfield*, which General Hobson had requested, came downriver and tried to interfere. She was boarded up tightly with tiers of heavy oak planking, in which embrasures were cut for guns, of which she carried three bronze twenty-four-pounder howitzers on each side. Her approach had been watched with great interest from the promontory in Buckner's back yard. The boat was commanded by Ensign Joseph Watson. Then, when she was about one mile of the town, her intentions became known. Basil Duke described her appearance upon the scene. "Suddenly checking her way, she tossed her snub nose defiantly like an angry beauty of the coal pits, sidled a little toward the town, and commenced to scold. A bluish-white, funnel-shaped cloud spouted out from her left hand bow and a shot flew at the town, and then changing front forward, she snapped a shell at the men on the other side."[11]

Captain Byrne transferred the two Parrotts to an eminence just upon the river and above the town, and answered her fire. While the gunboat dueled with the Parrotts for about an hour, the troop-ferrying stopped and many of Morgan's forces withdrew, out-of-sight to the woods behind the town. The duel was watched with breathless interest by the whole division on both shores, and General Morgan exhibited an emotion he rarely permitted to be seen.[12] Shells from the *Springfield* rained down on Brandenburg. One went through Judge Percival's kitchen, struck the stable at the old jail and buried itself in a hill. Another struck the Hotel Meade and went through the building to the lower floor. One hit the levee, wounding one of the Confederates and killing three horses. Another shattered a tree in front of a building on the main street. It was estimated that fifty shells fell on Brandenburg, but not a soldier or civilian was killed.[13]

Having exhausted its ammunition, the *Springfield* backed out and steamed from the scene, retreating up the river to New Albany.[14] Morgan's ferrying operations resumed. Watson sent a telegram to Lt. Commander Fitch saying:

U.S.S. Springfield, Off New Albany, *July* 9, 1863.
Sir: I engaged John H. Morgan this morning at Brandenburg. I have been fighting nearly all day. He is crossing over into Indiana. He has 10,000 men and several pieces of heavy artillery. He has his batteries planted at three places commanding the river. We still have boats below town to operate with me. He wants to hold that place until he re-crosses.

JOSEPH WATSON
Acting Ensign, Commanding.

5:00pm, Wednesday, July 8

Almost eight hours after the ferrying began with several interruptions from Federal gunboats, Morgan's troops were evenly distributed on both sides of the river.[15] Duke's brigade in Indiana, Johnson's still in Kentucky. It would take almost another eight hours to complete the transfer of troops from Kentucky into Indiana. The gunboat *Elk,* accompanied by the steamboat, *Grey Eagle* with a detachment of the 71st IN under Colonel Biddle, and a section of artillery from the 23rd IN Battery under 2nd Lt. John W. Ross, came in sight of the Brandenburg crossing. The *Elk* fired its first shots at the *Alice Dean*. It broke through the steamboat's deck. Morgan's Parrotts, which had been left in place, began dueling with the Federal boats and after a few minutes of action, the *Grey Eagle* and the *Elk* withdrew to Louisville. The *Elk*'s captain said that his boat was only bullet-proof, and he feared that Morgan's artillery would sink him.[16]

(Telegram)   Cincinnati, *July* 8, 1863.

General Boyle:
The following has just been received from New Albany:
I have sent one gunboat and a battery this afternoon. At what point
on the river is Hobson? Has he any means of crossing? I can
scarcely believe that Morgan has crossed the river with his whole
force. Hobson should not be deceived.

> **A.M. PENNOCK,**
> **Fleet Captain, and Commanding Station.**
> A.E. BURNSIDE,
> *Major-General.*

(Telegram)   Garnettsville, *July* 8, 1863 – 5 p.m.
(Via Bardstown Junction, 9:10 p.m.*)*

Capt. A.C. Semple, Assistant Adjutant-General:
Captain: We are at this place with cavalry force. John Morgan has
crossed the greater portion of his command into Indiana. Learn
from reliable authority that he has captured 2 packets at Branden-
burg. His object may be to use them in that vicinity, after he gets
through with the people of Indiana. We have pursued with all haste;
have lost no time; and it is evident that he failed in doing as much
damage in Kentucky as he expected. Cannonading at the river. We
will advance in a few minutes.

> E.H. HOBSON,
> *Brigadier-General.*

Commanding Morgan's rear guard was Lt. Col. James McCreary, 11th
KY. About midnight, with the moon illuminating the hills overlooking the
river, a company of Hobson's advance pressed upon McCreary's force. The
Confederates kept up a steady fire, which drove back the Federals. Half of
McCreary's force had descended to the river to be transported. His depleted
rear guard was exposed and he found himself in a critical and dangerous
position. In McCreary's book, *The Journal of My Soldier Life,* he describes
that moment. "By the interposition of Divine Providence, a heavy fog suddenly, and whilst hot skirmishing was going on, enveloped friends and foes,
and the Yankees halted. Under this fog I crossed my command over the
river. As I moved up the hills of Indiana, the enemy moved down the hills of
Kentucky."[17]

One of Morgan's men, Captain Jacob Mitchell Board, of the 9th KY
wrote, "We served as the rear guard. We were in continuing skirmishes with
the enemy until we made our last stand on a steep hill near the Ohio River.
We were run over and captured by superior force." But Captain Board

escaped and made his way back into central Kentucky. The Board family history says that the Captain used a disguise to make his escape. It has never been definitely determined what form that deception took, but some members of his family hint that he disguised himself as a woman.[18]

On its final trip, the *Alice Dean* carried the artillery that had saved the day for the Confederates. Once Morgan's forces had completed the river crossing, he ordered that the boats be burned. Like Hernan Cortez, the Spanish conquistador, who had ordered his boats burned 344 years earlier, Morgan wanted his men to realize that they were going to stay awhile in the North. The *Alice Dean*'s dry timbers were torched and she was set adrift. She burned to her deck and sank beneath the water to settle at the mouth of Buck Creek near the Indiana shore. However, the order to destroy the *McCombs* was countermanded by Col. Duke. Before the war, Duke's family had used the *McCombs* many times for the family's commercial business. Duke was a friend of the boat's commander, Captain Ballard. He spared it and sent it on its way upriver to Louisville so it couldn't be used by the pursuing Union troops.[19]

Some elements of Morgan's 6th KY and 2nd KY were captured in Kentucky before they could cross into Indiana. Those taken to prison in Lexington included: Wm. H. Keller, Geo. C. Gordon, Christopher Chinn, Jr., Wesley Roberts, Wm. R. Allen, John Kane, Jr., Robert Crouch, all of the 2nd KY Cavalry; J.M. Rosch, T.M. Bass and George L. Boswick of the 6th KY Cavalry.

7:00pm, Wednesday, July 8

Hobson received information that Morgan had captured two boats and was crossing into Indiana. He had reached a fork in the road. One led to Rock Haven, three miles away; the other to Brandenburg, twelve miles distant. He chose to go to Rock Haven to communicate with the officers in command and checking to see if the gunboat he requested was available to help him thwart Morgan's crossing. He learned that the boat was twenty miles away, at the mouth of Salt River. The night being dark and his troops fatigued, he did not deem it prudent to attack the enemy. At an early hour the following morning, he moved forward, and arrived at Brandenburg at seven o'clock in the morning.[20]

The Louisville newspaper reported the following:

Louisville, July 8.—A meeting of citizens was held tonight to take measures to provide for the defense of the city. It was addressed by General Boyle, who stated that although there was no immediate danger, it was necessary that measures be taken to organize the citizens for their own defense. The matter was submitted to the City Council, which met at nine o'clock, when the following resolution was passed by the meeting, that all male citizens between the ages of eighteen and forty-five be enrolled into companies for service if required, and that all such who refuse to be enrolled shall be sent North. We have the usual reports the ubiquity of Morgan's forces around us, but they are considered the mere fancies of excited people, as no considerable number of armed rebels are known to be near our city.

Military Study of Brandenburg Crossing

Today, U.S. military officers being trained in the ROTC program at Indiana University- Purdue University at Indianapolis study Morgan's Raid beginning with his crossing at Brandenburg (Kentucky) and concluding at the Battle of Corydon (Indiana). They consider five elements: **OCOKA** – Observation, Cover & Concealment, Obstacles, Key Terrain and Avenues of Approach.

Observation: Once Morgan's men occupied the town of Brandenburg, they posted pickets on the hills above to keep an eye out for any river traffic that may spell danger for their intended river crossings. From the vantage point of Mr. Buckner's home west of the town, they could observe the river in both directions for several miles. Men were posted in the rear to warn of the approach of Hobson's advance units.

Cover & Concealment: The advance companies took possession of the *John T. McCombs* and used it as cover to pretend that it was in distress. This tricked the *Alice Dean* into coming alongside to render aid. Once the two boats were secured to each other, the Confederates were able to capture the latter and take it over. The majority of Morgan's men were concealed in the town to avoid being exposed to enemy fire, militia observation and naval bombardment.

Obstacles: The biggest obstacle was the river. To cross it, they needed boats. Complicating matters was the appearance of the Union gunboat, *Springfield,* and the hostilities with the Indiana Legion militias, which delayed the transfer of men. Throughout the raid, especially in the northern states of Indiana and Ohio, the Confederates had no reliable food supply. They had to live off the land, which meant that they had to procure food from homes in the areas through which they passed. In unfriendly territory, this meant they took food by force, threat, intimidation or simply stole it if the home was vacant. Almost as important as the food supply was the constant need for fresh horses to stay well ahead of the pursuing Union cavalry. These, like the food, were taken by force from farmers and townspeople.

Key Terrain: Around Brandenburg were rolling hills and forested vegetation. The crossing at Brandenburg was selected because of the break in the river hills, making it an easy place to access the river.

Avenues of Approach: Morgan's men primarily moved over roads because they had four pieces of artillery. They came into Brandenburg from the southeast by way of Bardstown Junction and Garnettsville via today's Rt. 448.

SCOTT COUNTY

CLARK COUNTY

New
Philadelphia

Salem

I N D I A N A

Pekin

Carwood

New
Providence

WASHINGTON COUNTY

Palmyra

FLOYD COUNTY

12 Mile Island

CRAWFORD
COUNTY

New
Albany

Louisville

Corydon

K E N T U C K Y

HARRISON
COUNTY

New
Amsterdam

Frake's Mill

MILES

Mauckport

Laconia

Morvin's Landing

J.T. McCombs

Alice Dean

0   5   10   15

OHIO RIVER

N

Brandenburg

INDIANA
CLARK & FLOYD COUNTIES, IN

Eleven

Confederate Thunderbolt Strikes Indiana and Ohio

<u>Wednesday, July 8</u>

Captain William Davis, assistant adjutant-general of the First Brigade, with his men were to create a diversion northeast of Louisville and if possible, cross the river and rejoin Morgan at Salem, Indiana. He seized two boats and succeeded in getting himself and nearly half his men and their horses across before two gunboats, the *Springfield* and *Victory,* appeared on the scene and opened fire. One of Davis' boats was forced ashore on Twelve Mile Island where thirty men were later captured. The remainder of Davis' force, forty-two men under Lt. Josiah B. Gathright, Co. A, 8th KY, left stranded on the Kentucky shore, successfully made it back to Confederate lines in Tennessee.[1] Sixteen of those who made it across to Indiana were captured by Col. Lewis Jordan's 6th Regiment Indiana Legion. Forty-seven others, led by Captain Davis, made the crossing successfully into Indiana. They entered the central part of Clark County, taking by force the best horses they could find from wayside farms. They went through the Muddy Fork Valley north of Carwood, passed through Broomhill and came out onto the New Albany and Salem dirt road by way of the Broomhill Lane. Their first stop was the Milton Hallett farm, where they asked for something to eat. Having nothing cooked, Mrs. Hallett set out a basket of apples and told them to help themselves to the ripe peaches on a tree in her back yard. In short time, all the apples and peaches were gone. The peach tree died soon thereafter.[2]

Mrs. Hallett's brother had taken the family horse to help defend Corydon, so Davis' men found none in the stable. But Morgan's main column must have been more successful in procuring Hallett's horse, because he came home on foot.[3]

Farther along, they had better luck at the William Burns farm. William and his son, Sam, had just finished cultivating a patch of potatoes with "Old Charley," their claybank horse. As the father was unharnessing the animal, one of Morgan's troopers rode up on a horse that was obviously worn out. He removed his saddle from his mount and placed it on Old Charley, remarking as he did so, "Captain, I guess I'll have to trade horses with you. I'm leaving you a mighty fine beast."

He then hurried to catch up with his comrades, but he could hardly get Old Charley to go any faster than a fast walk. That evening, when the Federal troops fired on the Confederates, the rider tried to make Old Charley jump a rail fence. Instead, the horse simply fell down, causing his rider to be captured.[4]

The raiders approached New Providence. A log house occupied by the William Fordyce family stood just west of the William Borden home. Both houses had an unobstructed view down the railroad. They were the first to see the raiders coming. The Fordyces had named one of their sons Lincoln. So when they found out that the newcomers were Confederates, they hid Lincoln in a closet lest Morgan's men should kill him.[5]

Captain Davis stationed guards on all roads leading out of town. Anyone might come in, but nobody was allowed to leave. Jerry McKinley rode his gray-roan stallion into town and hitched him to a sycamore sapling down by the creek. The raiders soon confiscated the beast, but Jerry borrowed another and dashed for home. The Confederate guard ordered him to halt, but somebody yelled, "That man's deaf!" and the soldier did not shoot. George Jackson had come down from the north Knobs with a brand-new rifle of which he was very proud. One of Morgan's men approached him and asked to see his gun. The fellow took it and struck the barrel across the iron rail of the railroad track, bending it so it was useless. Homes were searched and any guns found received the same treatment. After nearly two hours in New Providence, Davis prepared to move on. He had learned that Morgan had already left Salem. He now began to look for someone to guide him northward through Washington County so he could catch up with the main column.[6]

Samuel Blankenbaker had just ridden into town to get some medicine for his sick wife. Davis asked him if he knew the way to New Philadelphia. "I reckon I do," Sam replied. "I was born there." Davis wouldn't listen to his pleas about his sick wife. He made Samuel get up on Jerry Jackson's stallion and lead the way. On the way to Pekin, some of the soldiers stopped at the Packwood home looking for horses. While they were there, they took a blackberry pie. One of the Packwood's sons, Jesse, saw the raiders and counted forty-seven Confederates.

Davis' group went up the Pekin Knob, then turned to the right across the hills and went down into the Lower Blue River Valley about two miles east of Pekin. They were watering their horses in the river when a company of Union cavalry under the command of Captain Hare came in sight of them. Davis saw that the only road of escape led in an easterly direction. He wanted to go north to join Morgan. While he was trying to make up his mind, one of the Confederates, Jerry Jackson, dashed up a dead-end lane and the other raiders followed him. The Federal cavalry fired on them, killing one and wounding four. About nineteen surrendered, and the rest disappeared into the woods and made their escape going north along a country lane bordering the Souder and Martin farms. Davis was among the prisoners. Sam Blankenbaker, riding the borrowed gray-roan, galloped from the scene and didn't stop until he returned home to his sick wife.[7] *There is a historic Morgan's Raid stone monument one mile east of Pekin on Henryville Road.*

Davis was taken back to New Albany that night. The other prisoners were brought back to New Providence and lodged for the night in the schoolhouse on the public square. Jesse Baker was the only member of the home guard who didn't get his rifle bent. He had come into town just as the Confederates were going out. Sam Denny was the only man in town who still had a horse. At first sight of the invaders, he had hidden his horse in a hollow. The remaining nineteen Confederate prisoners were taken to New Albany the next day and confined to jail.[8]

Word had reached Indianapolis that Morgan was crossing the Ohio into Indiana. With their state threatened, thousands of volunteers in the Indiana capital and surrounding areas flocked to Indianapolis to join in the fight against Morgan. On July 8, thirteen regiments were formed that day for the express purpose of repulsing Morgan's raiders. Thus were briefly born the 102nd-114th Indiana. Four days after Morgan had left the state, Tuesday, July 17, all thirteen regiments were mustered out.[9]

One year earlier, a chemist-druggist in Greencastle, Indiana, couldn't wait to get in the fight to keep the country unified. His motto was "The Union Forever!" His name was Eli Lilly and his drugstore was at the southeast corner of Public Square in Greencastle.[10] He had been married only a year and had a son, Josiah, who was but a few months old.[11] His pharmacy became the recruiting station for a light artillery company that he described as "The Lilly Hoosier Battery! The Crack Battery of Indiana!"[12] He began to organize the 18th IN Artillery on July 7, 1862, and by August 24, he had attracted 156 enlistees to serve in his battery.[13] Their army pay was $13 per month. He was elected the company's captain. The company roster included two first lieutenants, two second lieutenants, one first sergeant, one quarter-master sergeant, six sergeants, twelve corporals, two buglers, two black-smiths, two wagon makers, two harness makers, one wagoner and 123 privates. His battery boasted that it had six ten-pounder Parrott guns.[14]

He joined John T. Wilder's brigade, which also included the 17th IN Infantry. Wilder's troops had been armed with the new Spencer repeating rifle, which could shoot fifteen rounds a minute.[15] Wilder had arranged for the financing of these weapons with his hometown bank in Greensburg, Indiana, when the Army brass in Washington refused to purchase them.[16] From his headquarters in Murfreesboro, Tennessee, on March 20, 1863, Wilder ordered nine hundred of the new "Henry's Rifles" from the New Haven Arms Company. But the manufacturer informed Wilder that they could not fulfill such a large order. The Winchester Company, with their fifty-three employees, were only able to produce 200 guns per month. A com-petitor, a salesman for the Spencer Carbine Company, saw his opportunity, stepped in and filled the order.[17]

Wilder's brigade was incorporated into General Rosecrans' force in Tennessee and in the latter part of June, Eli Lilly's company advanced on General Braxton Bragg at Tullahoma. Bragg was anxious for Morgan's raid to begin to take some of the pressure off and allow him to withdraw to Chat-tanooga. Wilder's brigade also saw action at Hoover's Gap and Chicka-mauga. At the entrance of Hoover's Gap in Tennessee, Colonel Wilder found that his brigade was almost nine miles ahead of their division. The 1st KY Cavalry (CSA) was on duty when Wilder's sudden, unexpected advance took them by surprise. Brigadier-General William B. Bate rushed his brigade to the front, and for over an hour they gallantly attacked Wilder's entrenched and outnumbered brigade.[18]

Company E of the 72nd IN Infantry had overrun its position and began to withdraw to their lines. While being fired on by the Confederates, the company came upon three small children trying to find their way out of the woods amid the shower of bullets. When the two sides saw the youngsters, they both stopped firing. Sgt. Wilhite of the 72nd IN Infantry dismounted, helped them over a fence and headed them toward a house that was out of range of the battle. The fighting then resumed and Co. E went about its busi-ness of fighting its way back to the brigade.

The battle continued throughout the day, with charge after charge of Southern men being repulsed by a storm of Yankee bullets from the new repeating rifles. Wilder was ordered to withdraw immediately, but refused and steadfastly maintained that he could hold his position and would take responsibility for the consequences, even under threat of arrest. He was accurate in his assessment, and the last attack of the day was easily repulsed. That evening, Union reinforcements arrived. General George H. Thomas declared that he had not expected to capture the gap for three days, and henceforth Wilder's men would be known as the "Lightning Brigade." This action at Hoover's Gap was the first encounter with repeating rifles and began the expression that traveled around the Confederate army for the remainder of the war: that the "Yankees could load on Sunday and shoot all the rest of the week."[19]

In later action, Eli Lilly joined the 9th IN Cavalry as a major and was captured by Confederates.[20] By the time he was mustered out June 30, 1865,[21] he had attained the rank of colonel. After the war, Eli would become the patriarch of one of Indiana's wealthiest and most civic-minded families. The family business would become Eli Lilly and Company, one of the world's premier pharmaceutical firms,[22] and found America's foremost philanthropic fund, The Lilly Endowment.[23]

7:00am, Thursday, July 9

The Union forces, led by Hobson, arrived at Brandenburg only to see that Morgan had completed his crossing and the *Alice Dean* was burning across the river. The *John T. McCombs* had departed for Louisville. As the river fog lifted, Hobson saw the Confederate rear guard disappearing into the wooded Indiana hills. The Union's chase would now be delayed twenty-four hours.[24]

HARRISON COUNTY, IN

TWELVE

The Battle of Corydon

Once inside the Hoosier state, Morgan's main force passed Mauck-port and headed for Corydon, the state's original capital (1816-1825).[1] *There is a Morgan's Raid historical marker one mile east of Mauckport on S.R. 135. Another is at the Mathew Welsh Bridge near Mauckport.*

While the *Alice Dean* was still burning, some of Morgan's men stopped for breakfast at the home of Jacob Sherman, just outside of Mauckport. When Sherman realized that a boat owned by the Louisville and Evansville Mail Company was due at Brandenburg, he slipped away in search of a horse. He found that the raiders had taken his two steeds, so he mounted his mule and rode upriver opposite Rock Haven, Kentucky. He saw the boat coming and hailed her to stop. He shouted the danger of what might happen if they continued on to Brandenburg. The boat turned about and saved itself from suffering *Alice Dean*'s fate. Years later, a bell was presented to the citizens of Mauckport to recognize this brave deed.[2] The State of Indiana also reimbursed Sherman $450 for the loss of his horses.[3]

As the Confederates advanced, they captured many of the Indiana volunteers. About eight miles north of the river, they took their prisoners to the school house near Phillip "Pete" R. Lopp's mill on Buck Creek and went into camp at Frake's Mill for the night. At this time, it was discovered that Lopp's mill had been set on fire. Lopp, who was among their captives, appealed to Morgan to save his grist and saw mill. But a Confederate courier told the General that they had been fired on from someone in the mill. Morgan refused to save it, and it was destroyed.[4] Later, it was learned that a Mr. Overton had fired on the raiders while being outside of the mill, and had escaped.[5] Years later, the State of Indiana would reimburse Mr. Loop $2,861 for the loss of his mill.[6] Morgan then addressed his home guard prisoners and said if they would go home and promise not to take up arms against him, he would parole them and they would not be disturbed.[7]

The main body of the Indiana Legion under the command of Col. Lewis Jordan had pulled back as far as Rev. Peter Glenn's house, four miles south of Corydon. Here, the Hoosier infantry remained until ten o'clock that night, while one hundred cavalry and mounted citizens were sent on the roads south to scout and watch for the approach of Morgan's men.[8] Several small engagements occurred Wednesday afternoon through Thursday morning.

During the afternoon of July 8, John Dunn, Co. D, 5th KY was killed near Glenn's home which was on Shiloh Road near the intersection with the Mauckport road. Believing that the shots that killed Pvt. Dunn had come from the Peter Glenn home, the Confederates fired into the residence and severely wounded John Glenn, Peter's son, through both thighs. Peter, a noted abolitionist, was also seriously wounded. Curtis Burke, "Hutty" Hutchinson and several other Confederate soldiers received orders to burn the house. They entered the home and saw Catherine Glenn, Peter's wife, who declared that there were no armed men in the house. Paying no attention to her, they took a fire from the stove and commenced igniting the beds and bookcase.[9]

In a few minutes, Peter Glenn and his son, John, came bouncing down the stairs and tried to put out the fire. Hutchinson attempted to stop the fifty-seven-year-old reverend who pitched into him and tried to take his carbine away. In the scuffle, Hutchinson found the old man was stronger than he was. Hutty called to Huston Garvin, "Shoot him! Shoot him!" Garvin then cocked his gun and pressed the muzzle against the older man's side. Peter Glenn instantly released his grip on the gun and said, "I give up." Being weak from his abdominal wound, he staggered out and ran to a shade tree before he collapsed to the ground. The flow of blood could not be stopped and Peter Glenn soon bled to death. By this time, the home and barn were engulfed in flames. John Dunn lay in the shade of another tree. Lizzie, John's wife, and Catherine were ordered to care for the dying raider. They bathed his face but death was inevitable. The Home Guards buried him on the wooded hillside in back of the burnt-out Glenn home.[10]

There are conflicting stories about events that led to Peter Glenn's death. Mrs. Glenn said that her husband did not kill John Dunn and didn't even own a gun. Glenn's grandson, Charley, who was a boy of seven at the time of the raid, said he had been hiding behind a flour barrel when the raiders began shooting at the home. Charley said that his grandfather told him not to be afraid and that he had killed one of the rebels.[11] In Col. Lewis Jordan's report, he said Morgan's forces induced Rev. Glenn to come out of his house under a white flag of truce, whereupon they shot and killed him.[12] The reason for this action was not because of any gunfire coming from his home, but rather because he was supposed to have been well-known to the Confederates for his stand on the abolishment of slavery. In this version, another of Rev. Glenn's grandsons, Reuben, said that the reverend's son,

John, was crossing the road to the barn on the west side when one of the raiders called for him to halt. But before he took another step, he was shot. His mother, sister and youngest brother, William, dragged him into the shade under a tree. They bathed the wound and tried to stop the bleeding. Some of the raiders became tired of waiting for the reverend to show himself, so they hoisted a white truce flag. When he came out of hiding, they killed him. Reverend Glenn is buried on old Rt.135, five miles south of Corydon in the Jordan Cemetery.[13]

(Telegram)   Louisville, *July* 9, 1863.
   Major-General Burnside:
   Morgan has certainly crossed the river with about 3,000 men and five or six pieces of artillery. He was in camp last night 4 miles from Corydon.

                                                    J.T. BOYLE,
                                                    Brigadier-General.

11:30am, Thursday, July 9

In the absence of telephones, runners on horseback were dispatched to various parts of the county to alert farmers and townspeople of Morgan's approach. There were a lot of Paul Reveres on this hot July day. Farmers left their harvest fields, merchants quit their places of business and all hastened to the defensive line just south of Corydon.

The Corydon defenders had built a defensive position and breastworks made of logs, stones and fence rails. Wormwood rails were plentiful, so they were laid and stacked as an impediment to a cavalry charge.[14] *There is a "Battle of Corydon" historical marker at this site on Old S.R.135, south of Corydon.*

Scouts brought word to the defenders one mile below Corydon that Morgan's force was approaching on the Mauckport Road. By now the defense line had swelled to 450 home guards and citizens under the command of Col. Lewis Jordan, assisted by Provost John Timberlake and Maj. Jacob Pfrimmer (6th Legion Cavalry). The defenders formed a battle line about 2,000 feet across with the extreme west wing, resting on Amsterdam (Heidelberg) Road and the opposite end, close to the Laconia Road (S.R. 337),[15] near the brow of the hill south of Ed Aydelott's home.[16] To the east of Mauckport Road (Old S.R. 135) were heavy woods, uneven slopes and underbrush, which made it difficult for a cavalry charge. The drawback to this terrain was that the land's elevation prevented either party from seeing each other before the enemy was almost upon them. Fifteen- year-old W.B. Ryan, who was in Capt. John T. Heth's regiment, described it this way, "Our position was unfortunate, because the brow of the hill obscured our field of vision so that it was impossible to see the enemy until he was upon us."[17]

12:00pm, Thursday, July 9

Scouts brought word to Col. Jordan that the enemy was approaching in strong force along the Mauckport Road. Readying their squirrel guns and old muskets, the raw, untested citizen-soldiers braced themselves. They whispered words of encouragement to one another as they crouched behind their barricades. When the rattling sounds and hoofbeats signaled the approach of Morgan's advance guard, the militia resolutely aimed their weapons, determined to drive the invaders from their land.[18] The main body of the Confederate force came up the Mauckport Road (Old S.R. 135).[19] They traveled past a patchwork quilt of farms with stitch-lines of trees delineating property boundaries. They approached the cross roads of Old S.R. 135 and Heidelberg Road. There the Corydon defenders had placed most of their force in a heavily wooded area reinforced with split rail fences.

Defending Corydon against Morgan's 2,200 alligator soldiers were 450 home guards which comprised the 6th Regiment, Indiana Legion led by Col. Lewis Jordan, Sr. The Legion was comprised of the following home guard units: Ellsworth Rifles (Corydon) commanded by Major Thomas McGrain, Jr., and Capt. John Heth; Harrison Guards (Corydon) commanded by Capt. Abraham M. Stephens; Harrison Mounted Hoosiers (Corydon) commanded by Capt. William Farquar; Scott Guards (New Amsterdam) commanded by Capt. James B. Carnes; Lawson Grey Rifles (Elizabeth) commanded by Capt. Samuel Lawson; and the Spencer Guards (Corydon) commanded by Capt. George W. Lahue.[20]

12:30pm, July 9

A company of Morgan's advance guard made an appearance along the Laconia Road and was repulsed three times by the Spencer Guards under the command of Captain George W. Lahue. The Spencer Guards were picketed about three-quarters of a mile in front and to the east of Col. Jordan's line of defense. In that fight, the Indiana forces suffered another death when Harrison Steepleton was killed. Before that skirmish was completed, Morgan's men made their appearance in full force.[21]

Major Thomas McGrain, Jr., commanding the Ellsworth Rifles on the line near Amsterdam Road, had a full view of the approaching Confederates who filled the road for nearly a mile. The Ellsworth company was splendidly armed with new Henry repeating rifles,[22] which had just been invented three years earlier (1860). The Henry was the first magazine rifle used in quantity by the Union Army. A tubular magazine under the barrel held from twelve to fifteen rim-fire copper cartridges of caliber .44 short. It weighed about nine and three-quarter pounds and had a brass casing.[23] The Confederates had a similar comment about the Henry rifle complaining "that damn Yankee rifle can be loaded on Sunday and fired all week."[24]

The Ellsworth company didn't have the natural ground cover enjoyed by the defenders in the center. Their numbers were exposed by the broad flat farmland through which Amsterdam Road ran. Stands of corn, not yet ripened to their full height, offered minimal cover for the crouching farmer-soldiers. Because of the unhindered visibility, the defenders could see the approaching Confederates a mile away.[25] As soon as the raiders came into range, the Ellsworth Rifles opened fire. All along the western wing, the defenders began firing. The Confederate advance was checked and they began to flank both ends of the defensive lines. Because of their overwhelming numbers, Morgan's men were able to keep up a steady fire in front, while moving large numbers around the flanks. On the left (west), Col. W.W. Ward's 9th TN moved around Maj. T. McGrain's Ellsworth Rifles. On the right (east), Maj. T.B. Webber led the 2nd KY around Capt. G. Lahue's Spencer Guards.[26]

Even though Morgan's men were not clothed in regulation uniforms, their training and experience were far above what the undrilled and undisciplined Harrison County farmers were capable of matching. In their farm clothes and city attire, they crouched behind their barricade of "toothpick" fences.

Col. Richard Morgan's advance guard and the Quirk Scouts charged the breastworks, but the militia men resolutely defended their rail piles. In the exchange, 2nd Lt. Spencer Roane Thorpe, Co. A, 2nd KY was severely wounded in the shoulder and unhorsed. He was serving as Col. Morgan's Acting Adjutant.[27] The barricade was too high for the horses to jump easily. Some of the horses fell headlong, carrying their riders with them in a violent melee. A few of the riders including Lt. Leland Hathaway, an adjutant in Col. Morgan's regiment, displaced the top rail, clearing the hurdle.[28] Lt. Thorpe was one of thirty-three wounded Confederates who were taken to the Corydon Presbyterian Church, which was serving as a field hospital. Left behind for treatment, he was officially captured on July 10 and removed to the General Hospital in New Albany, Indiana. Two of his brothers who were accompanying him on the raid, Captain Patrick Henry Thorpe, adjutant to Col. Duke and Pvt. Andrew Thorpe, Co. E, 14th KY, were unscathed and continued on the raid with General Morgan.[29]

Nathan McKinzie, a citizen, was killed in the exchange of gunfire. The Ellsworth Rifles and a squad of thirty others held the invaders in check for fifteen minutes, compelling them to dismount.[30] For about twenty-five minutes, the Hoosier men held their ragged defensive line. The overwhelming numbers of Confederate cavalrymen was straining the thin line of defenders. Simultaneous flanking movements by the 2nd KY on the right and the 9th TN on the left increased the pressure.[31]

Col. Adam R. Johnson, ordered Lt. Elias D. Lawrence to fire his two Parrotts.[32] The artillery barrage unnerved the militiamen with shells, making an "ugly kind of music" over their heads.[33] Col. Jordan said, "When the enemy opened with three pieces of artillery, with shell and shot, and they appearing in such overwhelming numbers, seeing my forces could no longer successfully contend against such odds, I gave the order to fall back to Corydon."[34] The retreat turned into a rout as the Corydon defenders ran as fast as they could. Isaac Lang, belonging to the Scott Guards, died of heatstroke in the battle.[35] Those who were able to get away were mostly cavalry and mounted citizens. The retreating Corydon defenders raced down the hill, across Big Indian Creek and headed toward town. Those who were in Indiana cavalry companies or mounted infantry had the best chance of escape. Some raced through Corydon's streets and kept going north, leaving the town far behind.

Earlier, Levi G. Saffer, a member of Capt. Samuel Lawson's home guard unit, had approached the toll gate at the eastern side of Corydon, when he was told by W.N. Tracewell to hasten to the ridge south of the town. "There's going to be an engagement there in about twenty minutes," Tracewell urgently warned. On arriving at the defensive line, he was told to hold his position and watch the summit of the rise of land in front and hold his fire until he could see their belts. Levi then describes what happened. "I had not seen a single raider, and did not know for certain that there was one within five miles of us. But suddenly there came a stunning report from a clump of timber in front and a little to our right. Accompanying that report came a screeching noise through the air far over our heads, and nobody yet in sight upon whom we could test our marksmanship.[36]

"The third report sent a shell crashing through the top of a poplar tree causing a large branch to fall near one of our companies. That entire company became panic-stricken and started down the hill toward Corydon. A few minutes later, we were told to take care of ourselves. Quite a lot of us got away, but over a hundred of us ran right into the hands of the raiders. I was one of that unlucky number.

"When we were ordered to lay down our arms, I was standing on the bank of the Little Indian Creek. The water was about two feet deep and very muddy. I just dropped my gun into the creek. I found it there at ten o'clock the next morning, safe and sound. One of my neighbors from near Elizabeth refused to lay down his gun, and started on a dead run toward a nearby corn field. He was built for speed and he made the most of his structural advantages. The raiders wasted considerable ammunition in a fruitless effort to check his speed. At first he was in easy range, but with weeds and growing corn fast on either side of him, he escaped without the smell of powder on his garments. The raiders cheered him lustily; and they laughed and shouted as though they were glad to see him escape.

"Our guns were scarcely out of our hands when two or three villainous looking wretches began exploring our pockets. I was not in a very pleasant humor, and I resented this indignity in terms more personal than any civil code would sanction, and in languages not found in the Bible. My antagonist emphasized his reply to my remarks with a right-hander that put my left eye in mourning for the time being. Inasmuch as he got nothing at all and I got a black eye, I thought it well enough to let it go at that. We were marched down to the court house and drawn up in line to be paroled."[37]

A commissary department for the Corydon defenders had been set up and supervised by David Jordan. Headquarters was the Jordan residence. Bread, cakes, pies, meat and other edibles were gathered together in great quantities and Mr. Jordan expected to issue these rations in true military style. In the midst of performing his complex duties, he heard a shrill commanding voice ring out, "I'll take charge here now and you get some tubs, buckets and pails and go draw some water out of that well." A quick look around and Mr. Jordan realized he was surrounded by Confederate cavalry. There on his doorstep, he was made prisoner and throughout the day, he drew water for Morgan's men.[38]

William Heth, who as the keeper of the toll gate at the east entrance of Corydon, was shot and killed by Morgan's men as they made their way over the Plank road and came in from the east. Jacob Ferree, also a citizen who held the office of county commissioner, was mortally wounded and died shortly thereafter. Other wounded citizens included Caleb Thomas and John Glenn.[39]

After the field was taken by the Confederates, they planted a battery on the hill south of town. Firing two shells into the village, they struck near the center of the town's main street. One exploded but did no damage. Seeing that the contest was hopeless and the continuance of the fight would only result in unnecessary loss of life, Col. Jordan hoisted the white flag and surrendered the town.[40] Three hundred and forty-five men were paroled by General Morgan. At Mauckport and Corydon, Union and citizen losses included Jacob Ferree, Rev. Peter Glenn, William Heth, Isaac Lang, Harrison Steepleton, James Currant, Nathan McKinzie and Georia (Jeremiah) Nantz.[41] Confederate's deaths included Pvt. Greene Bottomer, Pvt. John Dunn, Pvt. Albert Womack and eight unidentified.[42]

1:00pm, Thursday, July 9

Corydon's little Presbyterian church was the first public building Morgan's troops saw as they entered the town from the south. The Confederates entered and turned it into an improvised hospital for their wounded and dying soldiers. Sheets were placed over the dead in the church's fenced yard. The wounded were inside, where some of the younger girls were given the task of fanning and keeping the flies off them.[43]

General Morgan commandeered Jacob W. Kintner's Eagle Hotel as his headquarters. While he was dining there, the innkeeper's daughter, Sallie, brought him the Corydon newspaper, the *Weekly Democrat*. The General read of the South's two military losses: Lee's Gettysburg defeat and Vicksburg's fall. Morgan was visibly crestfallen by the news.[44]

The raiders remained in Corydon until five o'clock in the afternoon, looting the stores and threatening to burn three mills unless a ransom was paid by their owners. One hour was given to raise the money. The three mills owned by Robert Leffler, Harbin M. Applegate and Wright & Brown were compelled to pay $500 each,[45] a figure that had been negotiated down from $1,000 each.[46] You might call it an "introductory rate" since these were the first northern mills to take advantage of this offer. Many of the town's citizens were also robbed of cash. Among them, Willison Hisey had $690 in cash and valuables totaling $786.87 taken from him. Samuel J. Wright's store was robbed of $5,524.11 in merchandise and $4,303.34 in goods were taken from Douglas Denbo & Co.[47] The Denbo family suffered an even greater loss when Mrs. Cynthia Booker Denbo, who was a "large woman," collapsed of exhaustion after the Confederates made her carry water many times up a steep hill. She was also made to drink from every bucket to be sure she didn't put poison in the water.[48] She never recovered and passed away July 16, 1863. She was fifty-six years old and is buried in the little Denbo cemetery about two miles south of Corydon.[49] When the Confederates rode out of town, they left behind eleven of their wounded to be cared for by the Corydon citizens.[50] *There is a Morgan's Raid historical monument in the Corydon Courthouse yard.*

Another Corydon lady died as an aftermath of the raid. Miss Abie Siemmons, who had moved to Corydon with her parents from the State of Maine, was devoted to the Union cause. She stood for hours with many other townspeople in the dust and heat of a July sun and handed water to the weary Union soldiers who entered the town in pursuit of Morgan. The excitement and fatigue of the two days were too much for her. Typhoid fever set in and she died within three weeks.[51]

Sixteen-year-old Attia Porter, a Corydon schoolgirl, wrote a letter to her cousin, Private John C. Andrews, 43rd IN Infantry, Co. C. Following are excerpts from her letter[52]:

Dear Cousin—

We have had rather exciting times in Indiana for the last few weeks, and have had a few of the miseries of the south pictured to us though in a small degree. On the doubly memorable ninth of July, a visit was paid to the citizens of Corydon and vicinity by Morgan and his herd of horse thieves. We heard Tuesday night that they had crossed the river and had disgraced the soil of Indiana with their most unhallowed feet. Our home guards skirmished with the rebs from the river to [Corydon] and on one of the hills overlooking the town had a grand battle. The battle raged violent for thirty minutes, just think of it! And on account of the large number of the rebs, we were forced to retire which our men did in good earnest every one seemed determined to get out of town first but which succeeded remains undecided to this day. After the general skedaddle, Col. Jordan wisely put up the white flag and we were prisoners to a horde of thieves and murderers. Father was fighting with his Henry rifle but they did not get him or his gun. One of our brave boys run three miles from the rebels, and really run himself to death. He stopped at a house and fainted and never came to. I think that was the awfullest day I ever passed in my life. The rebs were pretty hard on the copperheads but they did not take a thing from us. They kidnapped our little negro and kept him three weeks but he got away from them and is now at home safe. I expect you are tired of hearing about Morgan so I will stop. I have not got time to write much more or I will be late for the stage. So goodbye.

Attia

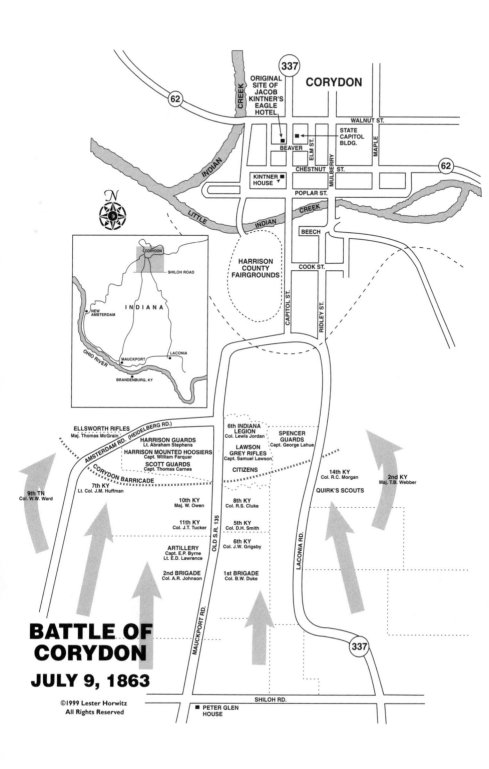

CORYDON

337

ORIGINAL
SITE OF
JACOB
KINTNER'S
EAGLE
HOTEL

WALNUT ST.

STATE
CAPITOL
BLDG.

BEAVER

CHESTNUT ST.

KINTNER
HOUSE

POPLAR ST.

62

BEECH

HARRISON
COUNTY
FAIRGROUNDS

COOK ST.

CREEK

INDIAN

LITTLE

INDIAN

CREEK

N

CORYDON

SHILOH ROAD

INDIANA

NEW
AMSTERDAM

LACONIA

OHIO RIVER

MAUCKPORT

BRANDENBURG, KY.

ELLSWORTH RIFLES
Maj. Thomas McGrain

AMSTERDAM RD. (HEIDELBERG RD.)

6th INDIANA
LEGION
Col. Lewis Jordan

SPENCER
GUARDS
Capt. George Lahue

HARRISON GUARDS
Lt. Abraham Stephens

HARRISON MOUNTED HOOSIERS
Capt. William Farquar

LAWSON
GREY RIFLES
Capt. Samuel Lawson

SCOTT GUARDS
Capt. Thomas Carnes

CITIZENS

CORYDON BARRICADE

14th KY
Col. R.C. Morgan

2nd KY
Maj. T.B. Webber

9th TN
Col. W.W. Ward

7th KY
Lt. Col. J.M. Huffman

QUIRK'S SCOUTS

10th KY
Maj. W. Owen

8th KY
Col. R.S. Cluke

11th KY
Col. J.T. Tucker

5th KY
Col. D.H. Smith

ARTILLERY
Capt. E.P. Byrne
Lt. E.D. Lawrence

6th KY
Col. J.W. Grigsby

2nd BRIGADE
Col. A.R. Johnson

1st BRIGADE
Col. B.W. Duke

OLD S.R. 135

LACONIA RD.

MAUCKPORT RD.

337

BATTLE OF
CORYDON

JULY 9, 1863

SHILOH RD.

PETER GLEN
HOUSE

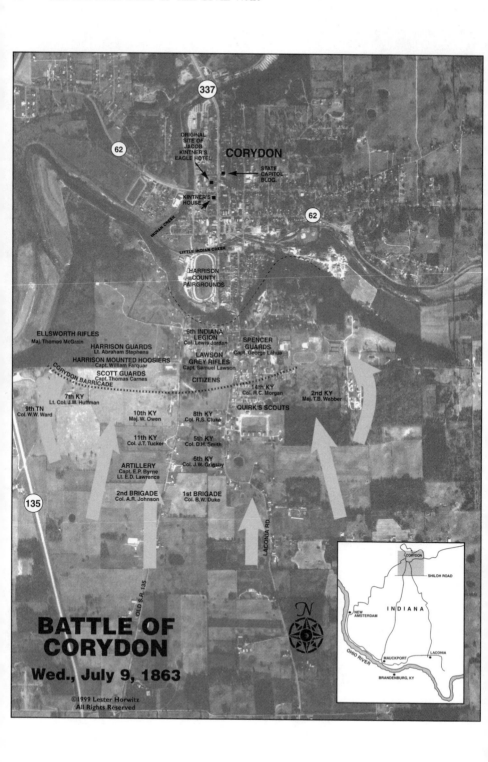

337

62

ORIGINAL
SITE OF
JACOB
KINTNER'S
EAGLE HOTEL

CORYDON

STATE CAPITOL
BLDG.

KINTNER'S
HOUSE

INDIAN CREEK

LITTLE INDIAN CREEK

HARRISON
COUNTY
FAIRGROUNDS

62

ELLSWORTH RIFLES
Maj. Thomas McGrain

6th INDIANA
LEGION
Col. Lewis Jordan

SPENCER
GUARDS
Capt. George Lahue

HARRISON GUARDS
Lt. Abraham Stephens

HARRISON MOUNTED HOOSIERS
Capt. William Farquar

LAWSON
GREY RIFLES
Capt. Samuel Lawson

SCOTT GUARDS
Capt. Thomas Carnes

CORYDON BARRICADE

CITIZENS

14th KY
Col. R.C. Morgan

2nd KY
Maj. T.B. Webber

7th KY
Lt. Col. J.M. Huffman

9th TN
Col. W.W. Ward

10th KY
Maj. W. Owen

8th KY
Col. R.S. Cluke

QUIRK'S SCOUTS

11th KY
Col. J.T. Tucker

5th KY
Col. D.H. Smith

ARTILLERY
Capt. E.P. Byrne
Lt. E.D. Lawrence

6th KY
Col. J.W. Grigsby

135

2nd BRIGADE
Col. A.R. Johnson

1st BRIGADE
Col. B.W. Duke

LACONIA RD.

OLD S.R. 135

N
S

BATTLE OF CORYDON

Wed., July 9, 1863

CORYDON

SHILOH ROAD

INDIANA

NEW
AMSTERDAM

MAUCKPORT

LACONIA

OHIO RIVER

BRANDENBURG, KY

Military Study of Battle of Corydon

The five elements of **OCOKA** (Observation, Cover & Concealment, Obstacles, Key Terrain and Avenues of Approach) are the key points to consider how the terrain will affect the impending battle.

Observation: Military leaders consider the ground that will allow them to observe the enemy throughout their area of operation and consider fields of fire in terms of the characteristics of available weapons. In their reconnaissance, advance Confederate units probed the defenses to determine the location and strength of the Corydon militia. The Confederates approaching on Amsterdam Road could be seen a mile away. The attack was not a surprise because the soldiers on both sides could see each other. The initial contact on the Laconia Road was met with heavy fire from the Spencer Guards, who repulsed the Confederates three times. The raiders approaching on the Mauckport Road were at a disadvantage because of the uneven and the heavily wooded terrain. Their inability to see the Corydon militia made it difficult for the Confederates to determine the size of the defending force. For the militia, the uneven terrain and view-obstructing woods created areas of dead space that were not defensible.

Cover & Concealment: Military leaders look for terrain that will protect them from direct and indirect fire (cover) and ground observation (concealment). On the western flank, the Ellsworth Rifles, firing their new Henrys, forced Morgan's mounted infantry to dismount and seek cover. The only area that offered concealment was the large stand of trees to the east of Mauckport Road. The bulk of the defenders had sought the shade and shadows in the several wooded acres where they could best conceal their presence. The trees and split-rail fences offered cover, which helped protect the militia from bullets.

Obstacles: Military leaders consider the effect of restrictive terrain in their ability to maneuver. Because of the uneven and forested terrain on the Mauckport Road, the raiders had their fields of fire obscured and could be surprised when the defenders opened fire. The high fence rails and heavy forestation also presented obstacles to the mounted cavalry which operate best in open, unfenced fields. In some cases, the Confederate cavalry had to dismount and fight from hill-to-hill, from tree-to-tree. For the Confederates, the 450 determined home guard militiamen and their familiarity with the battle terrain was their biggest obstacle. For the Corydon defenders, the biggest obstacle was the overwhelming size of the attacking force and its superiority in weapons and training.

Key Terrain: This is any locality or area whose seizure or retention affords a marked advantage to either combatant. Leaders consider key terrain in their selection of objectives, support positions and routes in the offense, and on the positioning of their units in the defense. The Corydon militia selected as their best defensive position a high ridge with several acres of wooded terrain. It was one mile south of Corydon between the town and the approaching raiders.

Avenues of Approach: An avenue of approach is a route of an attacking force of a given size leading to its objective or key terrain in its path. In the offense, the leader identifies the avenue of approach that affords the greatest protection and places him at the enemy's most vulnerable spot. In the defense, the leader positions his key weapons along the avenue of approach most likely to be used by the enemy. Morgan's men primarily moved north over three roads that converged on Corydon: the Mauckport Road, the Laconia Road and the New Amsterdam Road.

The four principles of **OFFENSE** used in today's army are **CATS**: Concentration, Audacity, Tempo and Surprise.

Concentration: Morgan's offense divided his forces so each column could concentrate on different defending groups.

Audacity: The Army says it is when you know your unit is not at 100% strength but you persevere because of the importance of the mission and the tenacity of your commander to succeed.

In this battle, Morgan didn't have to be audacious. His sheer overwhelming numbers carried the day. Capt. Hines' earlier reconnaissance into southern Indiana alerted Morgan to the size and strength of the local militias.

Tempo: This is the speed and rate of the operation. Morgan's flanking movements and artillery barrages made it painfully clear to the Corydon defenders that it was an uneven battle. Within thirty minutes, Morgan's men gained the field and the defenders were routed.

Surprise: The Army says to attack the enemy when it is unaware of your presence or from an unexpected direction. There was no surprise when Morgan appeared. The defenders were waiting for him and they knew from which direction he would come. This was one engagement where Ellsworth's deceptive use of the telegraph was of no use. Later skirmishes or the lack of confrontation were aided by Ellsworth's misleading telegraphic memos.

The five key principles of **DEFENSE** are **Preparation, Security, Disruption, Mass & Concentration** and **Flexibility.**

Preparation: The Corydon defenders prepared their positions as best they could in the time allowed. They took advantage of tree cover and built

Brigadier-General John Hunt Morgan, CSA

Colonel Basil Wilson Duke, CSA

General Braxton Bragg, CSA
Commander, Army of Tennessee

Major-General Ambrose Everett Burnside, USA
Commander, Army of the Ohio

Colonel Richard Curd Morgan, 14ᵗʰ KY

Captain Charlton Hunt Morgan, ADC

Captain Calvin Cogswell Morgan, ADC

First Lieutenant Thomas Hunt Morgan, Co. I, 2ⁿᵈ KY

─ Four Morgan brothers who accompanied General Morgan on his Ohio-Indiana Raid ─

Brigadier-General Edward Henry Hobson, USA

Major-General William Starke Rosecrans, USA

Major-General Simon Bolivar Buckner, CSA

Major-General Henry Moses Judah, USA

A4

Colonel Benjamin Henry Grierson, USA
(page 2)

Ordnance Sergeant Henry Lane Stone,
9th KY, CSA
(page 5)

Captain Thomas Henry Hines,
Co. E, 9th KY, CSA
(page 5)

Colonel W.C.P. Breckinridge, 9th KY, CSA
(page 8)

Colonel Orlando H. Moore, 25th MI, USA
(page 22)

Colonel Adam Rankin Johnson, 10th KY, CSA
(page 19)

Orphan Brigade Kinfolk, Louisville, KY

Captain Thomas Quirk, Co. M, 2nd KY, CSA
(page 20)

Captain Ralph Sheldon, Co. C, 2nd KY, CSA
(page 29)

Orphan Brigade Kinfolk, Louisville, KY

1852 Sharps Carbine
Percussion, breech-loading, single fire, 52 cal.
The classic weapon carried by Confederates.

Navy Colt Revolver
6 shots, 36 cal., 2.63 pounds, 13 inches long.
Slightly smaller and lighter than the Army Colt.
A favorite among Morgan's men, many of
whom carried a brace.

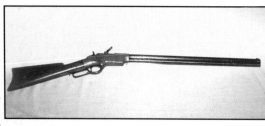

1860 Henry Repeating Rifle
Brass case, 12-shot repeater, 44 cal., 9.75 pounds.
Used by Union troops and Ellsworth Rifles at Corydon.

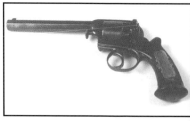

1851 English Revolver
Made by Adams & Deane, makers to HRH Prince Albert.
50 cal., 5 shot, double action. Has ruby-color gemstones
in handle. Presented to Capt. John Morgan in 1854,
a gift from his uncle, Francis Key Hunt.

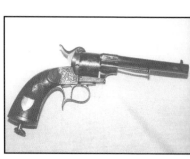

Morgan's Saddle
One of General Morgan's saddles.
From the Behringer-Crawford
Museum, Covington, KY

Lexington Rifles Shako
In 1857, John Morgan organized
a local militia company in
Lexington, KY. Members wore
this handsome black-felt hat
trimmed in leather and gold braid
with brass letters"L R" (Lexington
Rifles) below a brass eagle.
From the Kentucky Military History
Museum, Frankfort, KY

1848 LaFaucheux Presentation Pistol
6 shots, pinfire, ornate carved wooden grip.
Brass shield on handle engraved:
"Col. Wm. W. Ward, 1st KY Cav."

Ransom Paid

Note, dated July 10, 1863, written by General Morgan, alerts other members of his raiding force that the owners of the Allen Manley woolen mill in Salem, Indiana, have paid for "protection from violence by the Confederate troops" under his command.

Colonel Frank Lane Wolford
1st KY Cavalry, USA
(page 20)

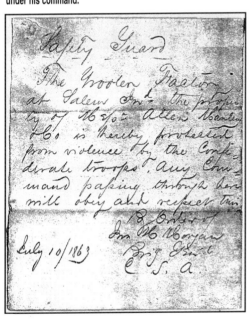

Parole of Honor

As Morgan's men captured Federal troops and citizens, they were given the opportunity to sign a parole and return to their homes. This parole was signed by William Burchfield in Harrison County, Ohio, just three days before General Morgan and his troops were, themselves, captured in Columbiana County, Ohio.

A8

George A. Ellsworth, Morgan's telegrapher
(page 37)

Captain William J. Davis,
First Brigade AAG, CSA
(page 40)

Farmer from Calf-Killer Creek, TN
(page 25)

Brigadier-General Jeremiah Tilford Boyle, USA
(page 38)

Captain Samuel B. Taylor, Co. E, 10ᵗʰ KY, CSA
(page 40)

Colonel Eli Lilly, 18ᵗʰ IN Artillery, USA
(page 57)

Captain H. Clay Meriwether, Co. H, 10ᵗʰ KY, CSA
(page 40)

Private John Conrad, Co. K, 9ᵗʰ KY, CSA
(page 43)

History of Kentucky 1896

Morgan's Raiders ride into Brandenburg, KY
(page 40)

The *Alice Dean*, a side-wheel packet, burned by Morgan after transporting his men across the Ohio River into Indiana.
(page 40)

MORGAN'S RAID
July 8-13, 1863
Despite naval and militia opposition, General John Hunt Morgan, commanding about 2,200 Confederate cavalrymen, began his Indiana Raid by crossing the Ohio at this point, July 8, 1863.
(ERECTED BY THE INDIANA CIVIL WAR CENTENNIAL COMMISSION — 1963)

Colonel Robert Buckner's home, Brandenburg, KY
(page 45)

Battle of Corydon historic marker, Corydon, IN
(page 62)

Georia Nantz tombstone, Corydon, IN
(page 48)

Corydon battlefield. The local defenders hid behind split-rail fences. The Confederates had four cannons.
(page 64)

Corydon monument lists Confederate dead on side facing the south. On the reverse side, facing north, is the list of Corydon defenders who died in battle.
(page 67)

Mary E. Shaffer
She raised Joe Keefey after he was left behind
by one of Morgan's men who was reluctant
to further endanger Joe's young life.
(page 74)

Joe Keefey as a man.
(page 74)

Joe Keefey and the Shaffer family on their farm in Corydon, IN.
(page 74)

Major-General Lewis "Lew" Wallace, USA,
author of *Ben-Hur*.
(page 90)

Oliver P. Morton, Governor of Indiana
(page 76)

Burning a railroad depot,
a favorite target of Morgan's men

GEN. JOHN MORGAN'S
TROOPS GOING EAST
CAMPED HERE SATURDAY
NIGHT JULY 11 1853.

Jefferson Co. Hist. Society.

James C. Rawlings home, Dupont, IN
(page 93)

Morgan's raid marker, St. Rt. 3, Dupont, IN
(page 93)

Colonel J. Warren Grigsby, 6th KY, CSA
(page 97)

Carl & Margaretha Yaeger, New Alsace, IN
(page 100)

Franz Vogelgesang, New Alsace, IN
(page 100)

Henry Yaeger, New Alsace, IN
(page 100)

Compass used by Morgan on Ohio-Indiana raid.
(page 109)

Golden Lamb, formerly the Lebanon House.
where Clement Vallandigham accidentally shot himself
(page 103)

"Morgan Muffler"
One of the silk handkerchiefs made from
a bolt of cloth found in the street after
the raid of Harrison, Ohio.
(page 108)

Reverend B.F. Ferris' one-room schoolhouse,
where Morgan camped the night of July 12, Sunmansville, IN
(page 99)

Colonel Leroy S. Cluke, 8ᵗʰ KY, CSA
(page 122)

Lt. Col. James Bennett McCreary, 11ᵗʰ KY, CSA
After the war, he was elected governor of Kentucky
(page 106)

Clement Laird Vallandigham
Born in Lisbon, Ohio, he opposed the government's
prosecution of the Civil War. He believed that the South
should not be coerced into reentering the Union.
He blamed the war on Lincoln and the Republicans.
Lincoln banished him to the Confederacy. A month later,
he left the South and sought refuge in Canada.
(page 103)

fences. Modern soldiers would dig foxholes, trenches, and if time allowed, dig tunnels and reinforced breastworks. Some of the men in Corydon decided that *discretion was the better part of valor* and, in their judgment, chose to go north and get out of town. The decision to run, rather than resist, was repeated in dozens of Indiana and Ohio towns through which Morgan's men raided. Corydon was one of the few villages in which a significant number of local men stood their ground and fought the invaders.

Security: This goal is to protect your troops within the perimeter or battle line. This can include reconnaissance beyond the defensive line to give early warning. Everyone should know the fields of fire and avenues of approach.

Disruption: The object is for the defense to thwart the assault. To accomplish this, you want to annihilate the offensive reconnaissance. This will prevent them from going back and reporting what they saw to their commanders. Captain Lehu and his Spencer Guards laid down fire on Morgan's advance scouts to prevent their reconnaissance mission. It was designed to kill the will of the enemy to go any farther.

Mass & Concentration: The massing of troops and heavy weapons (cannons) is the main effort to stop the enemy. Major McGrain and his Ellsworth Rifles opened fire with several dozen Henry rifles to stop the Confederates' initial advance.

Flexibility: This is the ability to take the defense and adapt it to the attack from the offense. These could be secondary and alternate defensive positions. In the case of the Corydon defenders, there was no fallback position except to withdraw into the town. To keep Morgan's men from completely encircling them, they fell back to keep the enemy to their front and flanks. Under devastating fire, they broke ranks and ran for their lives.

As the raiders left Corydon, they rode north past the home of David Shaffer, the local veterinarian. His wife, Mary, was standing outside watching the seemingly endless parade of Confederates pass her home. One of Morgan's men stopped his horse and motioned to her to come to the fence. She saw that a young child was sharing the saddle with the soldier. He told her that he had picked up the youngster in Tennessee. But after the long and hazardous ride, he feared for the child's safety, especially now that they were in hostile territory. It was not clear to Mary how the child came to accompany the cavalryman on the raid. But now she was being asked to take the boy for safekeeping, to remove him from harm's way. She empathized with the child's plight because she had three sons close in age. Her agreement that the child deserved better than to continue on the raid was enough for the raider. He quickly swung the young boy from his leather perch, over the fence and set him beside Mrs. Shaffer. Before she could have second thoughts, the soldier rode away to rejoin his comrades.

She brought the boy into her home and questioned him. "What's your name?" Hesitatingly, he answered, "Joe Keefey." "How old are you?" she asked. "Eleven," he replied. Mary looked at his small size and thought he was much younger. After making an unsuccessful effort to locate his parents, the Shaffers raised Joe as one of their children. He married a Corydon girl, Rose Foster, and they had four children: Alvin, Nobel, Hazel and Lola. In 1911, The Keefey family and Floyd, the Shaffer's oldest son, moved to St. Sebastian, ten miles west of Mt. Carmel, Illinois, just across the Indiana border.[54]

(Telegram)   Louisville, *July* 9, 1863.
General Burnside:
Judah is at Litchfield, on the left and south of where he ought to be. He refused to obey my orders because they did not come from General [George L.] Hartsuff. I will send you the dispatches to and from him. Have ordered [Mahlon D.] Manson, with three regiments, to report here at once; I can return him on short notice. Hobson is at Brandenburg, waiting for transportation to cross the river, which has been sent.

J.T. BOYLE,
Brigadier-General.

"Glory to God! Morgan's come!" exclaimed some fervent Copperheads in southern Indiana, as the Confederates halted to water their horses. "We're in sympathy with you, boys," they continued. The raiders answered back, "If you sympathize with us, you d__d cowardly hounds, why don't you fall in and fight with us? The raider continued, "But no, you're d__d careful to stay home and get all the advantages you can of the Yankees, and then\ abuse them whenever you dare. Bring that mare here and let me put my saddle on her." With that, he left his exhausted animal as a memento for the now less than enthusiastic Copperhead.[55]

The size of Morgan's cavalry invasion into Indiana was heralded as a much larger force than it actually was. A newspaper in the Indiana capital reported:

> **INDIANAPOLIS, July 9.**—Morgan's forces consisting of infantry, artillery and cavalry, and numbering between 6,000 and 8,000 crossed into Indiana and captured Corydon. Our forces are falling back. It is supposed the rebels are marching on New Albany and Jeffersonville, where large quantities of supplies are stored. Troops are being organized throughout the State and sent forward as rapidly as possible. Business was entirely suspended here today, and the citizens were forming companies for self defense. One regiment has been raised since last night. It is reported that two citizens were killed at Corydon when the rebels entered the town.[56]

Upriver at Cincinnati, General Burnside received a dispatch from Union Naval Commander Leroy Fitch that Morgan's forces crossing the Ohio River numbered 10,000 men.[57]

5:30pm, Thursday, July 9

Fitch arrived at Brandenburg and sent a telegram to General Burnside in Cincinnati. A portion is as follows:

(Telegram)   U.S.S. Moose
Off Brandenburg, Kentucky *July* 9, 1863.
I arrived here between 5 and 6 P.M. and much to my disappointment and sorrow found the enemy had effected a crossing by means of two steamers captured. On my arrival here I found General Hobson's forces coming into town following General Morgan. I hope with the aid of merchant steamers, he will have his entire force across the river before midnight and after Morgan.
LEROY FITCH
Lieutenant Commander.

Several transports arrived at Brandenburg that evening and Hobson began transferring his men to Indiana. The first of Hobson's troops to cross the river was Col. Wolford's 1ˢᵗ KY Cavalry. They were now almost a day's ride behind. The task was completed by two o'clock in the morning, July 10, and he renewed the chase. The Union forces, including ammunition wagons, ambulance train and troops, made a column three miles in length, a force as large or larger than Morgan's.

Word spread along the route that the Union troops would need food. Indiana women responded with joy and enthusiasm, preparing many good things to eat, especially fried chicken. Hardened troopers were complaining that there was too much food. "The food was fine," said Hobson, but he had heard the women sing "Rally Round the Flag Boys" so many times, he complained, "his clocks ticked it and the crickets on his doorstep sang it."[58]

General Hobson reported, "Never on earth has there been a more enthusiastic reception of troops than we received all through Indiana and Ohio. Hundreds, yes, thousands of people giving up their last morsels of provisions to aid us in overtaking the invaders, while thousands of beautiful young ladies and enthusiastic matrons and children handed us water and bread as we passed their doors. It was one grand cheering procession, urging us forward and enlivening our march. Yet Morgan was able to outmarch us upon fresh horses stolen from the country for five miles on each side of his line of march. We gathered what fresh horses we could. Notwithstanding all our efforts, more than five hundred of our men were left on the line of march without horses in place of their exhausted ones."

When Hobson's men seemed a little disheartened, Colonel Wolford could be seen riding along the whole line cheering them forward by his smile, inspiring enthusiasm and heroic example. Voices could be heard after he passed exclaiming, "We will overtake Morgan yet, because Colonel Wolford said so."[59]

Now that the Confederates had entered Indiana in force and were plundering its southern towns and threatening to attack Indianapolis, the state capital, Governor Oliver P. Morton realized how defenseless and exposed his people and property were. In rapid-fire succession, he sent three telegrams on the same day to General Burnside in Cincinnati, appealing for immediate military aid.

(Telegram)   Indianapolis, *July* 9, 1863.
   General Burnside:
   The information received here indicates that Morgan will march into the interior of Indiana. Are there no troops in Kentucky that can be spared and sent into Indiana?
                                                    O.P. MORTON,

Governor of Indiana.

(Telegram)   Indianapolis, *July* 9, 1863.

General Burnside:
I ask that the Seventy-first Indiana and Twenty-third Indiana Battery, recently sent to Kentucky, be immediately ordered back to this State for its protection – the protection of our towns from burning and pillage. Indiana has repeatedly sent all her troops to protect Kentucky. I now ask the return of some for our own protection.

O.P. MORTON,
Governor of Indiana.

(Telegram)   Indianapolis, *July* 9, 1863.

General Burnside:
Can't you send some cannon to this place from Cincinnati or Columbus, to be placed in batteries immediately? We have nothing here but small-arms. The rebels have occupied Corydon, in Harrison County. I am organizing militia as fast as possible.

O.P. MORTON,
Governor of Indiana.

The Confederate invasion was being met by raw Hoosier volunteers who had supreme confidence in their natural martial abilities. The *Lawrenceburg Democratic Register,* evidently stating from inaccurate preliminary reports that only a part of Morgan's force had entered Indiana, lamented that it was "a pity that the whole command did not cross over, for it is morally certain that not one of those now on this side of the river, or those who follow, will ever return except as prisoners." In Madison, Indiana, the editor of the *Courier* was even more assured of a victory, insisting that the city was "actively prepared for a war fandango. So if the Secesh [secessionists] pay us a visit, our rollicking Legion and Homeguards will teach the plunderers their steps, put them through their paces and finish by initiating them in the salutatory mysteries of the gallopade."[60]

Governor Morton issued a call to "all able bodied white male citizens" from all over the state to organize in companies.[61] Despite the grandiose rhetoric and overwhelming enthusiasm, the Indiana militia lacked the military capabilities to seriously challenge a veteran guerrilla cavalry force. Hasty attempts were made to organize companies around the state. This proved to be a chaotic effort as few men had any military experience and those that did often bickered over who should be in charge. Some areas failed to organize in time because the people still doubted that the raid was in progress until it was too late. More detrimental to the safety of the state, however, was the lack of arms and ammunition. A great number of companies had none at all. In other cases arms were either such obscure makes or so outdated that the proper ammunition was no longer produced. Not only were arms and ammunition not in the hands of the defenders of the state but there were few available to ship them, so while Morton was busy obtaining a shipment of muskets from St. Louis, ammunition was frantically being prepared in Indianapolis.[62]

Thursday, July 9

Col. William P. Sanders, commanding the 5th KY Cavalry (Union), was given orders to march to Eminence on the Lexington and Louisville Railroad in Kentucky. He reached that point about eight o'clock on the morning of July 10. That same day, he continued to march, reaching Westport on the eleventh. At this place, his troops were put on boats and headed up river where he reported to General Manson near Vevay, Indiana. On Manson's instructions, he proceeded to Cincinnati where his command was sent to Avondale and Camp Dennison, arriving there on the thirteenth. On the next day, July 14, he reported to General Hobson and joined his command to continue the chase after Morgan.[63]

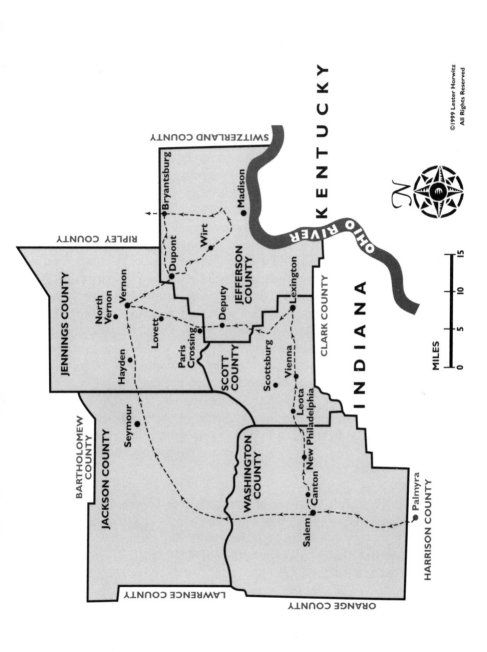

THIRTEEN

The Hoosier Zigzag

Like a broken field runner, Morgan's forces zigzagged through Indiana. The result of a lack of preparation was predictable. By executing simple flanking movements, Morgan was able to easily sweep aside the few forces, such as those at Corydon, that dared to attempt to slow him down. The Confederates made a feint toward Indianapolis and headed north through New Salisbury. George Franz Diedrich and his family were having supper when they heard of Morgan's approach. Interrupting their meal, they fled to the nearby woods, taking their livestock with them. Later, they returned to find that the raiders had eaten the meal that had been placed upon the table. Only a few cans of food remained in the house.[1] At Palmyra, the raiders encountered 350 militia who fled without offering any resistance.[2] Seeing the size of his force, the Palmyra militia decided Morgan had "the right-of-way."

Between Palmyra and Salem, Morgan's men went into camp for the night. One very heavy-set woman was out in her yard near Palmyra giving Morgan's men a tongue-lashing as they rode by. The General halted for a moment to hear what the lady was saying. Then he told one of his troopers, "Give the lady enough cloth to make herself a dress." Then realizing how much material it might take, he added, "Give her the whole bolt. She'll need it."[3]

8:00am, Friday, July 10

Outside Salem, a group of Morgan's men captured a Quaker who strongly objected to being made a prisoner. One of the Confederates asked him,

"Are you strongly opposed to the South?"

"Thee is right, I am."

"Well did you vote for Lincoln?"

"Thee is right. I did vote for Abraham."

"Well what are you?"

"Thee may naturally suppose that I am a Union man. Cannot thee let me go to my home?"

"Yes. Yes. Go and take care of the old woman."[4]

9:00am, Friday, July 10

Major Thomas Webber's 2nd KY was ordered to Salem. First Lieutenant A.S. Welch and a dozen men of Co. L rode ahead, taking the extreme advance. As they neared Salem, they saw the militiamen forming a defensive position. Without hesitation, they charged into them. The militia numbered about one hundred and fifty, but they were badly armed and raw recruits. The defenders were routed and Welch pursued them as they fled toward the town. The Confederates' advance was soon joined by Captain William H. Jones and a detachment of Company M, 2nd KY. Together, they drove the militia pell-mell into the village. Two or three hundred Home Guards were collected into the town square. But when the remainder of the 2nd KY thundered into town, the militiamen fled in haste, scattering their guns in the streets. Salem was taken without a shot being fired.[5]

In the town square, they discovered an old swivel gun that had been used by the townspeople to celebrate Christmas and the 4th of July. Its 18-inch barrel was loaded to the muzzle with nails, slugs and bits of rusty chain, ready to give the raiders a roaring welcome. A young man, deputized to fire the gun, was astounded to see the onrushing cavalry. He dropped the burning coal he was holding by a pair of tongs. Before he could pick up another to light the fuse, the Confederates swarmed over the cannon and captured its frightened gunner.

Basil Duke, seeing what happened, commented, "The shuddering imagination refuses to contemplate the consequences had that swivel been touched off."[6] A short halt was made in Salem to feed the men and horses. General Morgan used the Persise House on the southeast corner of the square as his headquarters during his brief stay.

Forewarned of Morgan's coming, the railmaster of the Louisville, New Albany & Chicago Railroad depot hid all the railroad gold in a crawl space under a house at 203 Poplar Street in Salem. As a diversion, he took an old yellow strongbox, filled it with tools and locked it. When the raiders found it, they broke it open, looking for gold and valuables, but found only tools. So that their visit wasn't a total bust, the raiders took the liberty to burn the railroad depot, a water tank and two wooden railroad bridges. They ransacked stores, mills, bakeries and saddle shops. From Fred Barkey's shop, Barkey Clark & Co., they stole merchandise amounting to $1,580.[7] They looted whiskey from the saloons, and demanded $1,000 ransom from each of Salem's millers.

In exchange for $1,000 ransom, General Morgan issued a note guaranteeing the safety of the Allen, Manley & Co. Woolen Mill.[8] The courthouse and pavement were crowded with home guard prisoners. They were paroled and quickly turned loose. Fresh horses were taken and new wagons were rigged with new harness and fresh horses. These were filled with captured ammunition. The raiders would have gotten more ammunition except for the alertness of a small boy who flagged down an incoming New Albany-Salem train loaded with ammunition. No one paid any attention when the incoming train stopped and backed up at full speed. The engineer was waving toward town and was shouting warnings. The people in Salem were too far away to hear him, but they were not listening because they were too engrossed with the events happening before their eyes. Outside town, up the stubby slope of the playfield, a young boy came running to warn his father, "Pa, Oh, Pa! Come home. The Rebs...the raiders are coming!" His words were drowned out by the rapid firing of guns on the road beyond the woods. At almost the same time came shouts and cries from the town.

Beezon Hayes hid his best horses in a pawpaw thicket, while Mrs. Hayes gathered an apron full of silver spoons and treasures, which she hid away in the raspberry bushes in the upper garden. She also hid her albums and daguerreotypes. The gray-clad troopers passed through the gate into the carriage-house yard. Some headed for the horse barn, while others turned toward the carriage house. As some rode up to the main house, one raider carelessly turned his horse to graze in Mrs. Hayes' flower garden. "Geo'ge," barked the officer in charge, "Take yoah hoss out of the lady's floweh bed." The Confederate officer was considerate and courteous. Mr. Hayes commented, "He seemed to have excellent control of the men and boys under him."

Mr. Hayes offered to feed the men, hoping to fill their bellies and dissuade their minds from burning barns and stealing stock. Mrs. Hayes refused, but the daughters all pitched in to help. They prepared ham, potatoes, bread, pies and other welcomed dishes. After the men ate, they asked to borrow an ax. They wanted to chop brush to help them burn a nearby railroad bridge. To be sure he got his ax back, Mr. Hayes accompanied the group to the bridge. Once there, he was taken prisoner.

"But I can't stay," he protested, "The woman folks are alone at the house. They'll be afraid. And I can't walk to town, because of my rheumatism." The officer in charge questioned him about his loyalty to Lincoln and finally told him he was free to go back to his house. *There is a Morgan's Raid historical marker in Salem in front of the Washington County Courthouse and another on S.R. 135 near Salem.*

A newspaper report read:
INDIANAPOLIS, July 10.— The rebels captured Salem this morning, burned the depot of the Louisville, [North Albany] and Chicago Railroad and took 500 home guards prisoners. No par-

ticulars of the fight received. A prisoner who escaped, reached Seymour this evening, says General Morgan's forces, 7,000 strong with six pieces of artillery, left Salem this afternoon, moving eastward; supposed purpose to strike the Indianapolis and Louisville Railroad at Vienna and Seymour. General Hobson, with forty-five hundred cavalry, was at noon today in close pursuit, being fifteen miles in the rear. When last heard from, the rebels were at Canton. The home guards were retarding the progress of the rebels by felling trees and bushwhacking. Brigadier-General [Henry B.] Carrington has assumed command of the Indiana Militia, and has already assigned a large portion of the companies to report to regiments and brigades. At least fifty thousand will have reported for duty tomorrow morning.

The Louisville, North Albany & Chicago Railroad was reimbursed by the State of Indiana for $13,918.75 in damages.[9]

The Confederate column swept across the landscape of prosperous farms. Captain Coombs, Co. K, 5th KY described the scene. "'Twas a calm still morning. All nature had put on her most attire. The steady breeze from the Sunny South caused the forest through which we threaded our winding pathway to appear a living green. I was in command of a scout, a mile to the left of our advancing column. Ascending a gentle slope to a wide plateau of elevated ground, the eye looked over a beautiful landscape to the west, north and east for miles upon miles. On my right, over fields of waving grain, waiting for the sickle, I could just discern our advance guard in command of Colonel Dick Morgan. My eyes followed him leading his gallant men to within two hundred yards of a large, fine dwelling.

"Suddenly and unexpectedly, a sheet of flame lit up the doors and windows of this palace, and one of Colonel Dick's men fell, to rise no more. The advance was checked, but only for a moment. The yell with which our boys went at them was conclusive evidence of their indomitable courage, as well as their certainty of success. Ten minutes elapsed before I reached the scene of the conflict. Colonel Dick and his men had all left, and only the sounds that broke the solemn stillness was the roaring of the flames as they fast encircled the beautiful mansion, and the heart-rendering cries of the wife and children. The owner lay mortally wounded on a lounge in the garden surrounded by his wife and children, who had thus at one fell blow been bereft of husband, home and father.

"Close to the burning house lay two men that a few minutes before had been our enemies, and close behind them lay, weltering in blood, one of our own men who was always foremost in the fight. I turned from this melancholy spectacle and rode onward ruminating upon the horrors of this unjust war, and thinking of my far distant home."[10]

JACKSON & SCOTT COUNTIES, IN

2:00pm, Friday, July 10

Leaving Salem, Morgan marched rapidly toward Vienna on the Indianapolis and Jeffersonville Railroad tracks. General Hobson's force was twenty-five miles behind. While the Confederates' main column turned east through Canton and New Philadelphia heading for Vienna.[11] Morgan dispatched a group of scouts to proceed north and east to Seymour to burn bridges on the Ohio and Mississippi Railroad for which the railroad was reimbursed by the State of Indiana for $16,476.86 in damages.[12] *There is a historical monument in Scott County in the Morgan Raid Rest Park on S.R. 56.*

The citizens of Salem sent the following telegram to General Burnside in Cincinnati:

> **Rebels are pushing for Lexington, Greensborough or Madison and will try to cross river at or near Warsaw [Kentucky]. They are pushing with great rapidity, and will cut the Jeffersonville Railroad at Vienna tonight... For God's sake, get up the river, seize all flats and steamboats and guard Warsaw Flats. Morgan's whole division is about 7,000 or 8,000; three 24-pounder Parrotts and two 12-pounder howitzers. I would not be surprised at his reaching Ohio by tomorrow morning.**

Heading up the Lexington-Vienna road, raiders stopped at the home of Margaret Bloss Tatlock in Canton. Some of the men sought rest under shade trees, while others came up to the front door and knocked. Margaret was baking bread in the kitchen. Her husband, Willis, was away, fighting in the war. She had been warned that the raiders were in the vicinity, so she had hidden her horses. Answering the door, she was asked about her horses. She told them there weren't any. They smelled the fresh baking bread and asked if they could have some. Margaret informed them that the bread wasn't ready, as yet. They said they would wait out front until it was. When the bread was finished, they took it back to the shade trees and ate. After they had finished, they moved on. An hour later, she decided to go down to the trees where they had been. One of the soldiers had left his sword behind. She picked it up and brought it back to the house. It has been a family heirloom ever since.

At Vienna, the Confederates bivouacked for a brief period. The townspeople were terrified, because Northern newspapers had published wild tales about Morgan's "terrible" men. George Ellsworth, Morgan's ace telegrapher, entered the telegraph office at the railroad depot and attempted to send a bogus telegram to throw off Morgan's pursuers. His message was "Morgan's men were at Salem," but the telegrapher at Jeffersonville recognized from the click of the instrument that something was wrong.[13] Ellsworth gleaned the news from wires being sent from Louisville and Indianapolis and learned that Indiana citizens had been told to cut down trees and blockade all the roads Morgan's men were likely to travel.[14] George Ellsworth's deceptive efforts using the telegraph would materially aid Morgan's raid through Indiana and Ohio by spreading false information about Morgan's location and intended path. The raiders permitted Pete Ringo, the stationmaster, to remove his personal belongings from the railroad depot before they torched it.[15] Without any hindrance, they marched through Vienna. *There is a Morgan's Raid historical marker at Vienna on S.R. 356.*

North of Vienna is Scottsburg. On the outskirts of the town, Stephen H. Woolridge, one of Morgan's men, found that his horse could go no farther. Nearby, he saw a farmer at work in a field. He rode up and "confiscated" a high-headed sorrel, leaving his jaded horse behind. The farmer's wife had come to the field with dinner in a basket. Steve relieved her of her package and its provisions. He could hear the irate granger and his wife cursing him as he rode away. Woolridge and his sorrel were both captured at Buffington Island and Steve was sent to prison at Camp Douglas. After the war, he returned to his home in Mercer County, Kentucky.

But in 1874, Woolridge moved to Kansas and took a section of land in Butler County. About two weeks after he had located on his dirt, he rode over to the nearest farm to be neighborly. At first, he was received hospitably. But after a little while, he noticed that his host and wife kept eyeing him sharply. He became more and more uncomfortable. Finally, the host blurted out, "Well, I'll be a blankety-blank, if you ain't the infernal rebel that took my horse and dinner back in Scottsburg, Indiana, during the war." The farmer's wife chimed in, "I know it's him, Davy; I know it's him!" Seeing that they had the proof on him, Steve admitted the exchange of horses, and being pretty well heeled, he produced a roll of bills and offered to make good. But his neighbors refused to accept the money and said, "I was mad enough to have killed you at the time of the deed. But I have often thought the matter over and have long since come to the conclusion that had I been in your situation, I would have done the same."[16]

11:00pm, Friday, July 10

A detachment of Morgan's men rode into the village of Lexington. Morgan and some of his officers checked into the Meyer's family home across from the courthouse for bed and breakfast. Forewarned, the county's treasurer took the public funds and "mulched" them into his tomato patch at his home.[17] *A Morgan's Raid historical marker is in Lexington on S.R. 356.*

4:00am, Saturday, July 11

A scouting party from the 9th IN Legion, led by Colonel Samuel B. Sering, made a pre-dawn probe into Lexington, unaware that General Morgan was asleep in the Meyer home. Sering stared into the darkness and could make out the forms of men sleeping on the bedrolls in the yards throughout the town. Those guarding Morgan's temporary headquarters raised their guns, preparing to fire. Realizing that they had stumbled into the lion's den, they turned tail and fled, but not before several were captured by the awakened raiders.[18]

JENNINGS & JEFFERSON COUNTIES, IN

8:30am, July 11

Rebecca Robinson of Deputy, Indiana, about 12 miles northeast of Scottsburg, lived less than a half-mile from the road over which Morgan's division passed. She said that beginning in the early morning, they [Confederates] were passing her home almost throughout the day. "The most exciting event was when a bunch of rebels come into the yard, clamoring for something to eat. One insistent fellow attempted to go into the kitchen in spite of a refusal of my stepmother to admit him. She flourished a butcher knife in his face saying, 'I'll let you know I am one of the blue hen chickens from the State of Virginia and if you make any further attempts to enter here, I'll cut your heart out!' Eyeing her intently for an instant, the rebel said, 'I know them Virginians will fight like the devil and I have no doubt you mean what you say.' He went away and left her, for the time being, mistress of the situation."[19]

Another woman living in Deputy was not as calm and in command of her emotions as Rebecca Robinson. She was a relative of Rebecca's who is identified as "Aunt Julia." She lived in a large house well appointed with valuable goods and furnishings. Wishing to salvage something of great worth from the impending visit of the plundering Confederate raiders, in her confusion, she selected a mirror and hastily took it to the garden and buried it. She made no effort to save anything else of more value in her home. The family historian, Middleton Robinson, commented, "After all, what is there about a home which a woman prizes more than a looking glass?"[20]

Robbing stores, stealing food, clothes, weapons and valuables paled when compared to some of the harsher actions Union soldiers demonstrated in Southern towns. Morgan's men rarely harmed a man unless he showed an armed resistance, and women were never abused or threatened. Rachel Tignor of Eagleport in Morgan County, Ohio, was helping to care for a wounded Confederate who had been shot along the Muskingum River. He told her that all the raiders had been ordered to respect the womenfolk on the raid, but to take anything they wanted or otherwise needed.[21] Private residences were spared and families were rarely made to vacate their homes.

Within a hundred feet of the road on which Morgan's men were traveling, a young boy named C.H. Caslin was working in the cornfield of his family farm. His older brother, at home on furlough, was away with the Paris home guard. For hours, he watched the Confederates passing his home. His mother was sick. When he went in the house to see how she was, she asked for a cool drink of spring water. When he went down to the spring, he found a large number of Morgan's men drawing water. An officer approached him and asked if he wanted water. He told him his mother was sick and wanted a drink. The officer ordered his soldiers to stand back and allow the boy to fill his bucket.[22]

If Morgan's men found an empty home, it was because the owners chose to vacate the premises before the Confederates arrived. Many times, when the raiders found a home occupied, they went elsewhere in search of food. Sometimes, after they were served a meal with a modicum of hospitality in a home they had invaded, they offered to "pay" with cash: some with Confederate dollars, but mostly with "greenbacks" stolen from other Northerners. If they did enter an occupied home, they were usually courteous and "gentlemanly." These actions reflected the family training, attitudes and inherent qualities that prevailed in the South. This does not mean that all the Confederate soldiers, nor all of Morgan's men were "Southern Gentlemen." There were a few "bad apples" who accompanied Morgan on his Indiana-Ohio raid. Morgan dealt with them harshly if they didn't follow the guidelines he set forth for the treatment of civilians. Basil Duke later would be called upon to "arrest" renegade Confederate soldiers who defied their generals and the CSA.[23] Neither side was pure and innocent of reprehensible actions. But for the most part, Morgan's men were a chivalrous group of warriors.

The following telegram was sent by another native Ohioan who would become the 20th President of the United States. He dispatched it to the Union general commanding troops in the South. It illustrates the difference between the actions of Morgan's men to Union troops invading the southern states and private property.

(Telegram)   Headquarters Department of the Cumberland,
Tullahoma, Tenn., July 8, 1863.
Maj. Gen. George H. Thomas:
The general commanding [Rosecrans] regrets to learn that straggling soldiers are committing outrages on citizens, by thieving and robbing. Great irregularities have been observed in foraging. In many instances provisions and forage have been taken without giving the proper receipts. Soldiers and foraging parties have been allowed to straggle from their commands and commit outrages. This general commanding directs corps commanders to take vigorous measures to correct this evil.
Very respectfully, your obedient servant,
J.A. GARFIELD,
Brigadier-General and Chief of Staff.[24]

Telegrams were the fastest form of communications in 1863. The telephone wouldn't be invented until 1876[25] and the first radio station wouldn't go on the air until 1920.[26] Morse code using a series of dots (DITs) and dashes (DAHs) was created by Samuel F.B. Morse in 1838.[27] Telegraph operators were trained to read this code and transfer the message into telegram form so it could be read by anyone. The operator had an important responsibility in society. He was the messenger of good news and bad. General Morgan depended on his personal telegrapher, George Ellsworth, throughout the raid for intelligence gathering and for the dissemination of false information about the raiders' movements and intentions. Morgan asked Ellsworth to contact the telegrapher in Madison, Indiana, to determine how large a military force, if any, was guarding the town.

Luther Martin was alone in his telegraph office in Madison, Indiana, when the stillness of the hot July day was broken by the familiar Morse code clicks. Martin, who had been sitting back in his chair with his feet up on his desk, sat straight up. The chatter (didididit dahdahdah didahdah), when deciphered, was asking about the town's defenses and "How many soldiers in Madison?" The eighteen-year-old was young in years but an old hand at the telegraph key. His senses had been trained so keenly that he could identify the sender of the incoming message by the rhythm and tempo of the clicker. Each telegrapher routinely developed his own cadence and tap when sending a message on his "key." In telegraphic jargon, this was known as his "fist."[28]

Luther was instantly suspicious. The sender didn't identify himself. He knew that a telegrapher always identified a transmission by inserting his name and point of origin at the front of the message. For example: "Martin-Madison Ind," or "Turner-Cincinnati Oh." His suspicions increased when his ears told him that the rhythm and tempo was that of a "foreign sender." Forewarned that Morgan might be headed toward Madison, he suspected that it could be a Confederate sender. He knew he didn't have time to confer with the city's military commanders and their small force encamped six miles from town. Unless he could frighten Morgan away from Madison, his town could be captured and subjected to looting, extensive property damage, bodily injury and possibly death of some of its citizens. Circumstances called for a big lie. A whopper! Here is his telegraphic reply to Ellsworth's inquiry.[29]

> **"Martin-Madison Ind—We have three government gunboats at the landing and others coming. Many soldiers are already here from Rising Sun, Lawrenceburg, Aurora and Vevay and others are on the way. The Union commander here has altogether 25,000 men ready to meet any attack made by Morgan."[30]**

The telegrapher at Indianapolis heard Ellsworth's question and Luther Martin's reply. He flashed a warning, somewhat akin to the "Hey Rube!" alarm signal of the circus world, "Rebel on the Line!" There was no rebel on the line for long because when Morgan was advised that he'd been discovered, he had Ellsworth snip the telegraph wire to prevent the alarm from being spread.[31] But Luther's quick thinking saved the town. Morgan dispatched Colonel D. Howard Smith to make a feint against Madison in order to keep the perceived troops massed there from coming out and causing him any trouble.[32]

For the next forty-five years, the citizens of Madison celebrated July 12 as "Luther Martin Day" and honored their local telegrapher with parades and speeches. Even schools and factories were closed. George Washington is remembered for never telling a lie. Luther Martin is fondly remembered for telling a really big one![33]

Morgan's division left Lexington and moved quietly through Deputy and Paris Crossing. By the late afternoon, they arrived in sight of Vernon on the Madison & Indianapolis Railroad. Here, Morgan's scouts sent toward Seymour rejoined the main force,[34] which had skirted south of Hayden (then Hardenburg), tearing up and burning a section of railroad track. Confederates placed the ties on top of burning crossties, causing them to bend and become unusable. Some of the Hayden Home Guards spotted a few raiders destroying railroad property. One of Hayden men, Burbon Winkler, wanted to shoot into the group of raiders. But the others stopped him, saying they were afraid to open fire for fear that the noise would attract a much larger Confederate force, one that they would be incapable of fighting. When the raiders sighted the home guard, they ran away.[35]

<u>6:00pm, Saturday, July 11</u>

In Vernon, Morgan found an enemy of volunteers and militia in great force numbering about 2,000. Unlike other Indiana towns that were easy pickings, the men from Dixie came up against a stubborn group of citizens. About six in the evening, Morgan's force was halted on the road between Dupont and Vernon. The Confederate General sent a small force to the vicinity of Vernon to reconnoiter.[36] They sent in a flag of truce demanding the surrender of the place. Brigadier-General John Love (Union) was due to arrive soon. Colonel Williams took the summons to surrender and replied that he "was abundantly able to hold the place, and if General Morgan got it, he must take it by hard fighting." Morgan expected a surrender, for in a short time he sent a second flag with a similar summons. Colonel Williams refused to receive the second message, but detained the bearer of the truce flag until the arrival of General Love, which occurred soon after. Love at once sent back his answer, "No, I want you to surrender." General Love began making preparations for a fight. He sent a flag of truce to Morgan requesting two hours for women and children to vacate the area before the hostilities began. Morgan's reply was that he would grant thirty minutes and then begin firing his cannons.[37]

General Love told the women and children they had safe passage to leave the town before Morgan's expected artillery attack. The noncombatants were removed to a woods nearby where they would be protected. Love kept his force on alert and expected the fighting to begin at any moment. Minutes dragged by. Hours passed, but no attack developed. Meanwhile, Major-General Lewis "Lew" Wallace had left Indianapolis by train with

1,300 soldiers to reinforce General Love and the 61st MI defending Vernon.[38] Reaching Vernon late at night, Wallace learned that Morgan had skirted the town and had moved on. By three-forty on the following morning (July 12), Love telegraphed Burnside in Cincinnati, "Information I believe reliable leads me to believe he [Morgan] declines a fight and is hastening towards Madison. Information looks as if his command was wearied out and he is anxious about his escape."[39] *There is a Morgan's Raid historical marker at the Jennings County Courthouse in Vernon.*

General Wallace then telegraphed Burnside that Morgan was headed south toward Dupont. He further reported, "Col. Hobson with all his force is after Morgan and is almost at his rear."

About eight miles outside of Vernon, some thirty or forty raiders stopped at the farmhouse of Victor Milhous. Mr. Milhous said that he and his family were treated with respect. Nothing but food was demanded, and payment was tendered by several of Morgan's men. The farmer said that they appeared to have plenty of gold, silver and greenbacks. One of Morgan's men very cordially invited him to visit his home in Dixie "when this cruel war is over." Milhous gave his opinion that the "Rebel's chances for getting home to receive company, were rather slim." The Confederate replied saying, "I suppose you would be pleased to hear that I and all my comrades were killed or captured?" The Hoosier farmer assured him that he was correct in his supposition. "I like your honesty," was the Confederate's reply.[40] Another of Milhous' "guests" expressed great disgust at "Northern sympathizers." He said, "If they sympathize with the South, why don't the d__d cowardly traitors come and fight for us?"

Deciding not to challenge the defenders of Vernon, Morgan rode south to Dupont.

FOURTEEN

Dupont Pays the Price

<u>8:00pm, Saturday, July 11</u>

Once encamped in Dupont, Morgan's advanced companies began destroying the Madison & Indianapolis Railroad. Telegraph lines were cut. The railroad water tank, the depot, warehouse, a train of twelve cars, the Big Creek bridge (south of Dupont) and the Graham Creek bridge (north of town) were all burned.[1] The railroad was reimbursed by the State of Indiana for $15,135.90 in damages.[2] The raiders broke into the town's stores, robbing them of clothing, boots, shoes and cash. They rounded up and captured eighteen old men and a boy named J.F. Lewis. All the prisoners were placed in Frank Mayfield's store. A guard was placed at the front and rear doors. Eventually, one of the guards spied the young boy and said, "What are you doing here?" The boy replied in a quavering voice, "You captured me." The Confederate, realizing the humor of his remark, said, "Go on. See how quick you can get home." The young cub scuttled home as fast as his trembling legs would carry him. The old men were eventually released.[3]

<u>10:30pm, July 11</u>

Morgan's main body arrived. As they rode past the home of Miss Sally Trousdale, a young school teacher, the raiders spotted two American flags fluttering from staffs on her front porch. As they approached the home to tear them down, Sally stepped onto the porch armed with a broom. This fiery, red-headed patriot was not intimidated by the raiders' guns or threats. General Morgan saw the face-off and came to the lady's rescue. He gave orders to have a guard posted to protect her and allowed her flags to remain as they were. Morgan continued to show, by example, how he wanted his men to be respectful of women. Hours later, when the raiders departed the town, the flags were still fluttering in the evening breeze.[4]

From the Frank F. Mayfield pork house in Dupont, the 2,000 Confederates removed 2,000 hickory-cured, canvass-wrapped hams; enough so that every raider could have a ham slung from his saddle.[5] Mayfield's dry goods store, Mayfield & Nichols, was also robbed of merchandise. Years later, Mayfield would by compensated by the State of Indiana: $2,925 for the hams and $2,960 for the stolen dry goods.[6]

<u>3:00am, Sunday, July 12</u>

The General and his staff entered the home of Thomas Stout where they planned to spend the night. Mrs. Stout and her daughters were awakened to fix the General and his staff a breakfast of fried ham and eggs, hot biscuits, canned fruits, buttermilk and coffee. Other housewives around Dupont were preparing breakfast for many of Morgan's men. The General was not finished with the Stout family. With a promise of valuable reward, Mr. Stout was asked to guide the raiders to the Michigan Road. He was forced to ride a horse without a saddle. After twelve miles, they reached the Michigan Road where he was told to dismount and walk back to Dupont. The greenback reward he had been promised was overlooked and he returned home with empty pockets.[8]

<u>6:30am, July 12</u>

At a nearby home, Pirene Vallile was having breakfast with her family. They could hear the raiders riding by their home as they left the town. Occasionally, a few raiders would stop in and ask for food. One picked up a crust of bread and offered to pay for it, but Pirene's mother refused. When one soldier came in and found the table bare, he asked her to bake some bread. She declined saying, "It is Sunday, and I don't cook much on the Sabbath." The soldier replied, "Well if you can't cook, I can." The housewife reluctantly baked the bread as he watched her. As it came out of the oven, another Confederate came in and asked for a piece. She broke off a piece of bread and gave it to him. The soldier who had been patiently waiting for the bread to bake admonished the woman saying, "Don't you give any more of that bread away. It is mine!"[9] Other Confederates stopped in at the modest home of James Rawling. His wife, Margaret, spent the entire day cooking for the raiders, several of whom asked her to cook the hams they had stolen from the Frank Mayfield pork house in Dupont. In appreciation, they offered to pay her for her efforts. When Morgan's men left, Mrs. Rawlings found herself cooking for Hobson's Federal troops who were in pursuit.[10] *Two historical Morgan's Raid markers are on S.R. 7 near Dupont and another two are on the Jefferson Proving Grounds.*

<u>8:00am, July 12</u>

Morgan's rear guard left Dupont. Three of Morgan's men fell behind no more than two hundred yards and were captured. Mr. Stout described Morgan and two of his officers:

Morgan was about six feet tall, and well built. He was wearing his famous linen coat and despite his travel stains was a rather commanding personality. He had a short upper lip, so shrunken that his front teeth were somewhat exposed. His complexion was sandy and his hair quite thin on top. Otherwise, he was not extraordinary.

Colonel Cluke was a couple of inches or so taller than Morgan, was very slender, having a thin sharp face and a very resolute eye. He looked to me to be more dashing and daring than Morgan.

Colonel Basil Duke was more interesting than either of the others. He was a small man but firmly built and muscular. He was by far the most intelligent looking of the officers, his eyes indicating his intelligence at the same time revealing a hardness like flint. His men obeyed him instantly and admitted he could be very severe.

2:00pm, Sunday, July 12

Hobson's cavalry entered the town. From that time until seven o'clock that evening, when the last of the Union soldiers passed, Dupont citizens were wild, almost frantic with joy.[11]

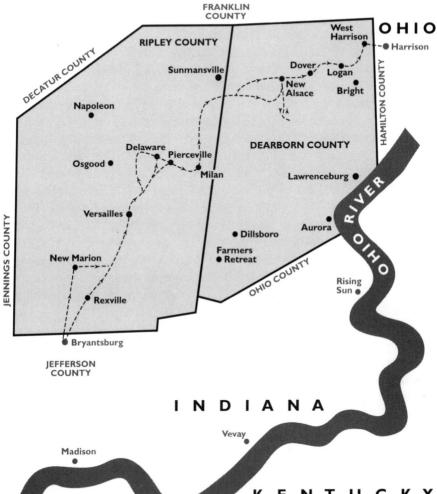

FRANKLIN
COUNTY

OHIO

RIPLEY COUNTY

West
Harrison

● Harrison

DECATUR COUNTY

Sunmansville ●

Dover

Logan ●

New
Alsace ●

Bright ●

HAMILTON COUNTY

Napoleon ●

DEARBORN COUNTY

Delaware ●
Pierceville ●

Osgood ●

Milan ●

Lawrenceburg ●

JENNINGS COUNTY

Versailles ●

Dillsboro ●

Aurora ●

RIVER

New Marion ●

Farmers
Retreat ●

OHIO

OHIO COUNTY

Rexville ●

Rising
Sun ●

● Bryantsburg

JEFFERSON
COUNTY

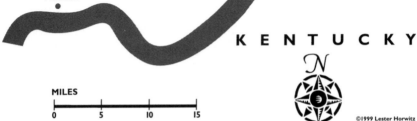

I N D I A N A

Vevay ●

Madison ●

K E N T U C K Y

N

MILES

0   5   10   15

©1999 Lester Horwitz
All Rights Reserved

RIPLEY COUNTY, IN

<u>7:30am, Sunday, July 12</u>

Leaving Dupont, General Morgan took an easterly course to Bryantsburg, turned north and passed through Rexville *(Morgan's Raid plaque on S.R. 421)* and Versailles between one and two o'clock that afternoon *(Morgan's Raid historical marker at Courthouse)*. Col. Richard Morgan entered the county courthouse and demanded the funds from the county safe. He found the treasury was in the charge of deputy B.F. Spenser. Hours earlier, the country treasurer, William Duley, had buried most of the money leaving, some reports say, $5,000 cash to satisfy the raiders' desire for loot. Handing the colonel the cash, Morgan asked, "What are those?" pointing to a number of purses that lay in the safe. "They are purses of money placed there by several widowed ladies for safe-keeping," Spenser answered. Richard Morgan turned to walk away, saying, "Keep them safe. I never robbed a widow yet."[12]

Near the courthouse was the local Masonic lodge. Official Masonic badges ["jewels"] fashioned from silver French francs were too much of a temptation for one of the raiders. He seized the box of coin-silver jewelry and stashed them in his saddlebag. When General Morgan heard of the robbery, he commanded the jewelry be returned and dealt harshly with the perpetrators.[13]

General Morgan was a Mason and instructed his troops not to harm anyone who was a Free Mason. Morgan was a member of the Lexington Kentucky Lodge No. 25. Other prominent Kentuckians who were Masonic members included Henry Clay, Gen. Simon B. Buckner, CSA, Gen. John C. Breckinridge, CSA, Gen. George B. Crittenden, CSA, his Union General brother, Thomas L. Crittenden, USA, Governor Beriah Magoffin and even Union Col. Frank L. Wolford (Morgan's dogged pursuer).[14] This is another instance in which John Morgan's respect for his Masonic brotherhood transcended political, social and military considerations.

Earlier, Col. James H. Cravens, of Osgood,[15] had organized several militia into companies of 100 each to defend Versailles. Each company had a captain. As they were organizing, they heard horsemen approaching the town over the plank road. Mistaking the troop of horsemen for militia reinforcements, they were quickly overwhelmed by Morgan's hard-charging guerrillas.[16] The Confederates relieved them of their weapons and destroyed them. General Morgan addressed his prisoners threatening them with dire consequences should they ever take up arms again against the Confederacy. With that, he paroled them and told them to go home.

At the same time, Hobson was entering Dupont. The Union general stopped only briefly to accept food which the town's citizens had prepared. Then they resumed the chase. Some Federal soldiers were left behind to round up horses left behind by both raiders and Hobson's troops. The horses were then to be auctioned, with the proceeds to go to the State of Indiana. Years later, Indiana would use some of these funds to reimburse farmers who had lost horses to the raiders.

Confederate Col. J. Warren Grigsby was detached with his 6th KY to burn road bridges near Versailles, that included bridges over Laughery Creek and Greasy Run. He dashed into the town where several hundred militia had gathered to devise the best means of defending the place.[17] Grigby's surprise entrance broke up the council meeting. The defenders "donated" a large number of horses to the Confederate cause. Some of these men rode north to Osgood and on to Napoleon where they camped for the night. A squad of sixty Confederates moved on Osgood and burned the bridge on the Ohio and Mississippi Railroad. While Grigsby turn north, Col. Basil Duke passed through Pierceville, burning a bridge there and another near Milan.

Near Pierceville, a Methodist preacher, Rev. Horsley, who was deaf, did not hear the raiders' command to halt. They shot and killed him. As Duke led the main column toward (Old) Milan *(Morgan's Raid boulder marker on S.R. 101)*, General Morgan and a smaller group followed a parallel road in the same direction. Turning north, they stopped south of Sunmansville (Sunman).[18] All along the way, home guards, called "Minute Men," and a lesser number of regulars harassed Morgan's progress. Confederate Captain L.D. Hockersmith observed, "They were everywhere and on every hand and some of them seemed to understand how to shoot and occasionally they did effective work."

To clear the path of felled trees, General Morgan formed a new unit, which he called the "Ax Brigade." When Morgan's men encountered these obstructions, the Confederate axmen had to undo the enemy's work and clear a path for the raider's column. The command "Halt! Axes to the front!" would be heard quite often.[19]

FIFTEEN

Last Day in Indiana

Morgan's quick penetration of Ripley County had begun to alarm farmers in adjacent Dearborn County. Several farming families living south of Dillsboro herded their livestock, gathered their worldly possessions and, together with their women and children, sought refuge away from the main road which led to Lawrenceburg. They headed south to the small village of Opptown well off the beaten track in Caesar Creek Township. Most of these first generation Americans had emigrated to Indiana from Hanover, Germany.[1] In a log-built structure, the St. John Lutheran Church, they gathered to ask for deliverance from the Confederate raiders. Their prayers were answered when the gray regiments turned north instead of east and headed for Sunmansville. After the war was over, the local residents marked this historic event by changing the name of their village from Opptown to Farmers Retreat.[2]

Morgan considered the next two days would present the greatest danger to his entire expedition. Getting around and past Cincinnati without engaging a large Federal force was imperative if he was to maintain a safe distance in front of Hobson's pursuing force. It would take quick wits and some help from Lady Luck. Normally, Morgan would rest his troops at night, blow reveille at three o'clock in the morning, and break camp at sunrise. From Sunmansville, he planned to ride through the night until he was well past Cincinnati. It was a thirty-five-hour ride covering ninety-five miles, ending in Williamsburg, Ohio.[3] The raid's longest continuous ride. Confederate Col. James McCreary said of this achievement, "If there be a man who boasts of a march, let him excel this."[4]

<u>4:00pm, Sunday, July 12</u>

Morgan's advance guard selected a camp site about two miles south of Sunmansville. The area is known as St. Paul, named after the Methodist church and cemetery alongside S.R. 101 where it intersects with the Old Harrison Road.[5] *There is a Morgan's Raid boulder marker near St. Paul's Church on S.R. 101 at Country Road 900N.*

A one-room rural school, in which the Reverend B.F. Ferris taught, was chosen as Morgan's headquarters. That modest structure, years later, was refaced and expanded to a five-room residence. But that night, General Morgan slept on a blanket in front of the teacher's desk. His slumber was often interrupted as his officers came in to report. The Reverend Ferris and several other Sunmansville area men were held prisoner in the one-room schoolhouse.[6]

4:00am, Monday, July 13

General Lew Wallace and several hundred Union militia had arrived in nearby Sunmansville, but were unaware of Morgan's presence two to three miles away.[7] Duke said, "Here twenty-five hundred militia lay loaded into box cars. We halted to rest, and, unconscious of our presence, although we were close upon them, they moved off in the morning toward Cincinnati."[8] Actually, their train went south to the defense of Lawrenceburg, Indiana. Residents in the area who were aware of the closeness of the Union and Confederate forces, feared a major confrontation when the new day dawned. But they would learn, to their relief, that Morgan had headed east for Cincinnati, while their militiamen had gone south to Lawrenceburg.[9]

5:00am, July 13

Morgan left the Sunmansville area, skirted west of Weisburg (seven-thirty in the morning), and headed for Hubbles Corner. There, at the Gutzwiler blacksmith shop, Nicholas Hartman's father was having a young horse shod. Seeing the approach of the Confederates, Hartman jumped on his horse and headed home two miles away. Two of Morgan's men saw him and gave chase. They fired several shots at him, but missed. On his fresh horse, he outrode them. As he turned down the road to his home, the raiders followed the dust cloud stirred up by his horse's hoofs. They stopped at the first home, the Klee's residence, but did not find him. At the second house, which was his, he stopped only long enough to tell his wife not to tell the raiders anything and rode on to hide in the dense woods.

When Morgan's men stopped at the Hartman home, again they failed to find him. This time, they demanded something to eat, and Mrs. Hartman gave them bread, hard cheese and cider. When they finished eating, they rode away and gave up the chase.[10] Morgan's forces passed through Hubbles Corner and headed for New Alsace, where Rev. Ferris and the raider's other prisoners accompanying the Confederates were released to return home.

8:00am, Monday, July 13

In New Alsace, a prosperous village of 600 inhabitants, Morgan's men found three blacksmith shops, two beer breweries, sixteen saloons, two wagonmaker shops, five shoemaking shops, one furniture shop, one casket shop, a tin store, two hotels, six country stores, two flour mills, one saddler shop, four dancing halls, two bakeries and a few other trade shops.[11] The town was on the main route to Cincinnati. Cattlemen and farmers passed through as they drove their herds and took their produce to market. To quench the thirst of these dust-covered travelers, more than a dozen saloons lined the route through this small town. Many of these taverns offered facilities in which cattle could be penned and fed while their owners relaxed over a brew.[12]

Word of Morgan's coming had preceded his arrival. The men, especially the blacksmiths of the village, took their horses several miles north of town and hid them in a wooded area. Elizabeth Vogelgesang was the proprietor of one of the saloons. Her late husband, George, had been the town's first blacksmith.[13]

When Morgan's men arrived in New Alsace, they entered the Vogelgesang tavern and demanded food. Elizabeth let them know that she was a widow, and she played upon their sympathies by walking with a limp. She and her niece, Philomena, fed the men a hearty breakfast. Philomena's parents had died in Kentucky a few years earlier and their children were given to various relatives to "raise" as was the custom. Philomena's mother was Elizabeth's sister. She worked to keep up with the soldiers' appetites. She was grateful that the men were well-mannered and proud of their southern politeness. As an ironic twist after the war, Philomena's brother, who had ridden with Morgan on his Indiana-Ohio raid, went searching for his siblings scattered over several states. When he finally traced Philomena, he discovered that she had served him pancakes when he had passed through New Alsace that morning. During that stressful encounter, they had failed to recognized each other.[14]

Across the street from Vogelgesang's tavern, Eva Margaretha Yaeger was alone in her grocery store. Her only son, Henry, age 20, had been a Union soldier with Co. D, 83rd IN Volunteers. He had been killed at Vicksburg about three months earlier, on April 11, 1863. When word of Henry's death reached the family, her husband, Carl, suffered a heart attack and died May 2, 1863.[15]

Another group of Morgan's men entered widow Yaeger's grocery, but they had no sympathy for the mother of a northern soldier. She, in turn, was grieving and angry with the young raiders because other men in the Confederate army had caused the deaths of her husband and son. The soldiers broke open barrels of molasses, vinegar and whiskey. They gleefully allowed the contents to flood the floor. They ate what food they could grab and vandalized the rest of the store. Finally, one of Morgan's officers appeared in the doorway and ordered them to leave.[16]

Having had a restless night in Sunmansville the night before, Morgan commandeered two taverns near the center of the village and made them his headquarters for a brief time. One was Tony Blettner's, which is Klump's Tavern today. Nearby, in Jacob Gephard's tavern, General Morgan slept four hours in an upstairs room. He had twenty-four men guarding him. Two guards in the room, two at the door, two in the hallway, and the rest on the road to watch for any sign of the pursuing Union army.[17] Today, Gephard's tavern is the residence of Thomas and Kathy Klump.[18]

Leaving New Alsace, they crossed Tanner's Creek and burned the bridge. The raiders pressed on to Dover where some of Morgan's men stopped at James Murtaugh's tavern for refreshments.[19] The Confederate column entered the crossroads village of Logan and headed down the winding North Dearborn road (Old S.R. 46) that descended to the Whitewater River. *There are historical markers of Morgan's Raid on Dearborn Road at Alsace, Dover and Logan. In West Harrison, there is a boulder marker on State Street.*

Three miles from Harrison, Morgan passed through Bright, Indiana. A funeral was in progress. Outside the church, horses were tethered to the hitching post. A man in the funeral party was standing in front of the church as the raiders rode past. He saw the Confederates unhitching the fresh horses and leading them away. He stepped forward and spoke to General Morgan. "Sir, I too am a Southerner. But where I come from, we have respect for the dead." With that, the General called out to his men, "Leave those horses alone." He turned and rode away.[20]

A similar incident occurred on the road between Dover and Logan. A horse-drawn hearse was taking the body of William Glardon's son to the Huber/Briggs Cemetery. Undertakers always took pride in having powerful, showy horses pull their black, shiny hearses. The temptation was too great for Morgan's cavalry. The undertaker's horses were unhitched, harnesses removed and cavalry saddles slung over their backs. The Confederates left behind their jaded steeds to convey the hearse the rest of the way to the cemetery.

To the people of southern Indiana who had not been introduced to the firsthand realities of war, Morgan's system of replenishing his mounts through the impressment of horses from ordinary citizens was seen as an unmitigated act of theft, and Morgan's name was seldom mentioned without colorful adjectives attached to it such as "King of the American Freebooters" or, more commonly, simply "horse thief."[21] At this time out west, the penalty for horse stealing was the hangman's noose. But with respect to the personal safety of the inhabitants of the state, Morgan's men were compassionate compared to the destruction the Union forces inflicted upon the people of the South. In a letter following the raid, one Union soldier admitted to his wife that Morgan's actions were "no werse than we serve the sitayns hears [near Winchester, Tennessee] for we take everything we can get and burn eny thing of thare fences and tare thare houses down and burn them...we take every thing they have we don't leave the first thing for them to live on thare is lots of them now starving for want of soup to eat." Another wrote simply, "You all have now realized some of the horrors of civil war."[22]

Back in Louisville, at Union army headquarters, the military was being beseeched by suffering families of the men who were away in the army. The colonel in command sent a telegram to the mayor of Louisville asking for the city's help.

(Telegram)   Louisville, Ky., *July* 24, 1863.
Hon. William Kaye, Mayor of Louisville:
Sir: As I am overrun with applications from the poor wives and children of soldiers now in the field, serving the government, for assistance to keep them from starving, I deem it my duty to call your attention and that of the city council to the fact. You must consider that the prices of provisions and fuel are much enhanced, while the soldier's pay remains stationary at $13 per month, so that many of these honest, poor people are forced by pinching necessity to ask for charity. I am now issuing Government rations, without orders, at my personal risk, to many families, who would otherwise starve. And certainly a great city like Louisville could, with little effort, raise a fund for the support of the indigent families of soldiers. I see that Northern cities are appropriating hundreds of thousands of dollars to purchase exemptions and support the poor families of their soldiers, and I respectfully request that the council of the city of Louisville consider the matter.
Respectfully,

M. MUNDY,
Colonel, Commanding Post.[23]

Morgan's men crossed the bridge at West Harrison on the Ohio border. Between Dover and Logan, Col. Cluke and the 8th KY riding rear guard looked back and saw a low dust cloud,[24] rising above the treetops. He spurred his horse forward to inform General Morgan that Hobson's cavalry were only a few hours behind them. Some of the German settlers in New Alsace told Hobson that Morgan's men had left their town only two hours before his entry.

Morgan was leaving Indiana and Dearborn County. As they passed through the county, they "shopped" at two of Dearborn's major stores. At W.W. Davidson & Co., they left with $6,200 in merchandise. At Leonard & Simonson's store, the tab was $12,870.[25]

Two miles before Hobson crossed the Great Miami River, two men in a wagon, P.F. Chrisman and his nephew, Matthew Dill, were compelled to stop in the road opposite the residence of Mr. Butts. The large number of Union forces pursuing Morgan choked the road and blocked their journey. Mr. Butts came down to his gate to see the army pass, and give them refreshments and a cheering word as they passed. Mr. Butts noticed that his Butternut neighbors [southern sympathizers] weren't cheering now for Vallandigham, an Ohio Democrat who wanted to make peace with the Confederacy.[26]

Clement L. Vallandigham, born 1820 in New Lisbon, Ohio, was exiled by President Lincoln to the Confederacy for his "treasonous" statements. Southern leaders didn't receive him with open arms, so he fled to Canada for sanctuary. He returned to Ohio in June 1864 and played a major role in framing the National Democratic Party's peace plank that helped bring about the Democrats' defeat in the November presidential election. After the war, he practiced law. In June 1871, he was counsel for a Butler County (Ohio) man who, charged with murder, had obtained a change of venue to Warren County (Ohio). His case hinged on the theory that the victim could have killed himself. In his room at the Golden Lamb (known then as the Lebanon House), he was preparing his final address that he would make to the jury the next day. Demonstrating his theory, he pulled his pistol from his trouser pocket, and in a freak accident, the gun fired a bullet into his abdomen. Mortally wounded, he died the next morning. The defendant, in a new trial, was acquitted.[27]

Some of Hobson's men asked Chrisman if it was true that he was a Vallandigham man. The Butternut replied that he couldn't deny it. With that, the Federals ordered them to unhitch their two horses and attach them to their artillery limber. The Southern sympathizers were made to march on foot until they came to the river. Once they had waded over, they were allowed to return home having suffered for their unpatriotic remarks. Chrisman later remarked that he would have preferred death to the humiliation that they were placed under in the presence of at least fifty of their neighbors. Like the Confederates who had pilfered horses from area farms a few hours earlier, the Union troops offered no receipt to the butternuts for appropriating their two horses.[28] One of the Union soldiers explained their treatment of the Vallandigham men, "We can stand the bullets of Southern Rebels, but we can't bear the insults of Northern traitors."[29]

Many Indiana Home Guards were out looking to engage Morgan's men. A tragedy occurred at Hardintown (Hardinburg), two miles from Lawrenceburg. Col. James Gavin was informed that Morgan had taken Harrison, turned back and was advancing on Lawrenceburg. He took prompt measures to meet the Confederate threat. He sent out his own regiment, the 104th IN Volunteers half a mile beyond Hardintown, where a strong defensive barricade was constructed and a line of battle was formed along the towpath of the canal.

Col. Kline G. Shryock, commanding the 105th IN Volunteers was ordered to take a position half a mile in the rear. About nine o'clock at night, while marching to the assigned position, the 105th came around a short curve in the road. In the darkness, the 104th saw the advance of the 105th and mistook it for Morgan's men, who were actually thirty miles away on the outskirts of Cincinnati. They began shooting, and the 105th returned the fire. Col. Shryock immediately sensed what was happening. Impervious to the fusillade of bullets, he rode along the road, yelling at his men to stop shooting and killing one another. Although he was promptly obeyed, it was too late to prevent a serious catastrophe. Before the firing subsided, six men were killed: Lt. William E. Hart, Sgt. John Gordon and privates Oliver P. Jones, William Faulkner, Ferdinand Hefner and John Porter. Eighteen were wounded.[30] Among those was Pvt. David S. Gooding, who had served as a state senator and circuit court judge before taking up arms. The next day, the *Daily Cincinnati Enquirer* reported, "They had been lively and jubilant during the evening, but the termination was a sad one."[31]

11:00am, Monday, July 13

Just before Morgan reached the Ohio border, his columns crossed the sturdy oak bridge over the Whitewater River. As the last man passed, it was set on fire. Its destruction caused a delay of many hours, forcing the Federal forces to find a navigable ford elsewhere on the river where they could bring their artillery across.[32]

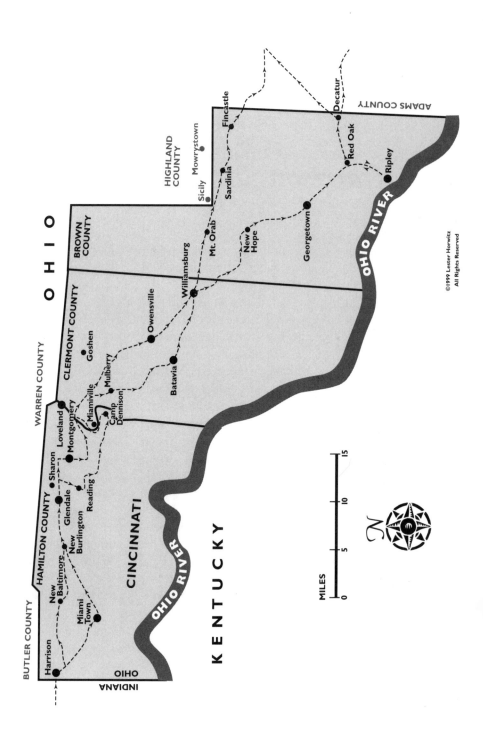

BUTLER COUNTY

HAMILTON COUNTY

WARREN COUNTY

OHIO

CLERMONT COUNTY

BROWN COUNTY

HIGHLAND COUNTY

ADAMS COUNTY

Harrison

Miami Town

New Baltimore

Glendale

New Burlington

Sharon

Reading

Loveland

Montgomery

Miamiville

Mulberry

Camp Dennison

Goshen

Owensville

Batavia

Williamsburg

Mt. Orab

New Hope

Sicily

Sardinia

Mowrystown

Georgetown

Fincastle

Red Oak

Decatur

Ripley

CINCINNATI

OHIO RIVER

OHIO RIVER

KENTUCKY

INDIANA

OHIO

MILES

0 5 10 15

N

OHIO
HAMILTON COUNTY, OH

SIXTEEN

Harrison Shopping Spree

<u>Noon, Monday, July 13</u>

As the Confederate raiders moved eastward into Ohio, panic was their advance guard. Ohioans prepared as best they could for their arrival, but in most instances this consisted of mobilizing the home guards, principally old men and very young men, who were no match for the invaders. Ohio would pay a penalty because its sons had responded so enthusiastically to the government's call for volunteers. When danger threatened their homes and families, the cream of Ohio's fighting men were elsewhere—at Gettysburg, Vicksburg and major military engagements far from Buckeye soil.

Morgan crossed over the Ohio border into Harrison. Of his original force of 2,500 men, he had almost 2,000 remaining. Duke said, "We had not two thousand left."[1] They had either been killed, wounded or captured. Those who had survived, were extremely tired, having been in the saddle for eleven days with very little sleep. As they crossed the state line, Morgan looked back and said, "I'm glad to be leavin' Indiana." He had no idea that Ohio would prove to be much worse than anything he had experienced to date.

During the Civil War, Ohio had more people living in the state (2.5 million) than any other in the nation except for New York (4 million; NYC 900,000) and Pennsylvania (3.3 million). Illinois had 2 million and Virginia had 1.5 million. Morgan had just left Indiana (1.5 million) and Kentucky (1.2 million). Ohio had almost twice as many people as the two states he had just ridden through. He was to be amazed and depressed by the vast number of Ohio men who were of fighting age, not yet in the army.[2]

The people of Harrison had been warned that Morgan was heading their way, but they were not sure when to expect him. The town's merchants had closed and locked their stores and remained home to be with their families in case Morgan rode into their community.

As Morgan entered Harrison, his first impression was very favorable. Of Harrison, Col. James McCreary wrote in his journal, "Today we reach

Harrison, the most beautiful town I have yet seen in the North—a place, seemingly, where love and beauty, peace and prosperity, sanctified by true religion, might hold high carnival. Here we destroyed a magnificent bridge [over the Whitewater River] and saw many beautiful women."[3]

Eight of Morgan's advance pickets rode into town, up Market Street [Harrison Avenue] at a full gallop. They halted Richard Simmonds and his wife, Mary, as they traveled south, half a block from Minors Hotel. The old gentleman was ordered out of his spring wagon and told to unhitch his horse. At first he was speechless. Then recovering from shock, he asked them to allow him and his lady to go. After some further reflection, the Confederate soldiers told him to get in his wagon and go. The old couple drove up the street where they were met by more raiders, who, without ceremony, took their horses, and the old folks were left to trudge home.

The locked stores offered no impediment to Morgan's men. They simply broke down the doors and helped themselves to whatever they wanted. They took food, saddles, bridles, spurs and cash. Harrison merchants who reported losses included Fredrick Rink ($1,500), Charles E. Brunner ($315), Josiah T. Bailey ($18) and Abram S. Clark who ran the post office ($112 in cash, postage and envelopes).[4] Morgan also threatened to burn mills near the town if they didn't pay a $1,000 ransom each.[5] All across Indiana and Ohio, Morgan extracted these payments accumulating large sums of Federal greenbacks. A favorite source for ready cash was the post office. In each town, Morgan's men would go through the mail looking for cash. Maybe that's why today, they advise, "Don't send cash in the mail."

In raiding the Harrison stores, the "shoppers from Dixie" also took unusual merchandise such as ladies' hats, veils and dresses. Some tied bolts of cloth [see the following letter] to their saddles and dragged them like a train behind them. Once they had their fun, they cut them loose. One young raider was observed to have a bird cage with three canaries, which he carried for two days. Another had a chafing dish on the pommel of his saddle until an officer forced him to throw it away. Another slung seven pair of skates around his neck, and chuckled over his acquisition. A Harrison resident observed, "They pillaged like boys robbing an orchard. It seemed to be a mania, senseless and purposeless." With the deprivations they had seen in the South, they used these "shopping" opportunities to stuff their pockets and saddlebags with merchandise they could give their girlfriends or families upon their return.

After resting for three hours in Harrison, feeding themselves and their horses, reading the mail and local newspapers to get news about the war, they rode out into the vast Ohio countryside in mid-afternoon, aware of the potential danger that the big city to their right represented.

In a letter written by Hannah Grubbs, a resident of Harrison, she describes what happened when her great-grandmother Schultz found a discarded bolt of cloth in the street.

> In the War between the North and South, the Rebels came through here, burnt the bridge after they crossed the White Water River at Harrison. Rode into Harrison entered the dry goods stores. Took bolts of yard goods out into the streets caught hold of the loose ends and rode their horses through the streets, unrolling the goods in the streets. My Great Grandmother Schultz gathered up some of this soiled yard good, which turned out to be squares of silk, handkerchiefs all in one long bolt. She hemmed these by hand and gave to her grandchildren, of which one was my own father, Herman Haas, and this is one of those squares or handkerchiefs. They called them "mufflers" then. Morgan's raid passed through Harrison July 13, 1863 at 12:30pm.
>
> Mrs. Hannah (Haas) Grubbs

The silk "Morgan Muffler" handkerchief and the letter have since been passed down to Mrs. Grubbs' great-granddaughter, Anita Mitchell, who resides in Harrison.

At the Trinity Methodist Church, local tradition holds that several of Morgan's men entered the building, even riding their horses up the stairs into the sanctuary. It is said that some lit a fire inside the church to cook their food. When they left, they took two silver chalices and a silver pot. In 1972, a pawn broker in Atlanta called the church in Harrison, Ohio, and said they had three silver items with the church's name engraved on them. So, 109 years after the raid, the items were returned to their rightful owners and occupy a place of historic honor in the United Methodist Church of Harrison.[6]

Hamman Hersh Roudebush, a thirty-two-year-old farmer, lived south of Harrison near the bend of the Whitewater River which, today, is on Kilby Road. Before Morgan's men had entered Harrison, his twenty-two-year-old wife, Emeline, had taken a two-wheeled cart and their best horse and driven over to see her sister Sarah. Her sister and husband, Henry Roudebush, were expecting a child at any moment, and Emeline wanted to be with them. Hamman had been warned of Morgan's arrival, so he secluded his horses in a wooded valley on his farm. Then he realized that his wife might be in danger if she was driving her buggy home. Just as Hamman expected, Emeline left her sister's home after the baby was born. Soon, she was overtaken by Morgan's men. One raider piled his booty and some of his weapons in her buggy and told her to take him to Harrison. There she had to wait while the Confederates looted the stores. Then, with her carriage piled high with stolen merchandise, she was told to drive her buggy and follow the column out of Harrison.

As they came up the hill, Hamman came upon his wife's buggy in the procession. He tried to grab his wife and pull her to safety. One of Morgan's men drew his bayonet and shouted, "How dare you accost this fine lady?"

"I dare, because she is my wife!" Hamman insisted. The jovial Confederates forced him to ride on, but not before he could whisper in Emeline's ear, "Really whip the horse when you pass New Haven Road." For he knew that his prize horse could outrun any mount Morgan had. Needless to say, Emeline had a very exciting ride home. She told her husband, "The ride was worse than the raiders. They were perfect gentlemen."[7]

Before leaving Harrison, the raiders threatened to set fire to three mills and a distillery unless a ransom of $1,000 was paid for each building. The cash was immediately paid and pocketed by Morgan. He also coerced several local Harrison men to accompany him as guides to point out the best roads. He sought out local maps, but the best course of action, which he used throughout the raid, was to force local men to lead his column along the best routes. After they had served their purpose, they would be told to dismount and walk home. Morgan would often ride in the command van with the farmer guides. He bluntly warned each one that the compasses he carried would tell them if they were being led in the wrong direction.[8] Death, he told the frightened farmers, would be the penalty for misdirecting them. These pathfinders were referred to as "guides" or "pilots."

In tracing Morgan's path, his columns followed roads and well-worn pikes. The reason was simple. He had four (some eyewitnesses said six) pieces of artillery: two twelve-pounder howitzers attached to his Second brigade and two three-inch Parrotts attached to the First.[9] Parrotts were a new artillery innovation developed during the conflict. They were much more accurate than howitzers because the interior of their barrels were rifled, grooved to create a spin as the shell traversed the length of the cannon tube. The spin improved the accuracy. So much so, that a door could be targeted and hit a mile away.[10] These artillery pieces were too heavy and cumbersome to drag across plowed farm fields. Thus, Morgan was forced to confine his march over improved roads.

SEVENTEEN

Let's Split!

<u>3:00pm, Monday, July 13</u>

The bugles sounded "Boots & Saddles" and the column moved out of Harrison. Morgan sent a small force toward Hamilton to the north, but this was a diversion. Before reaching Hamilton, they would turn east and head for Loveland. Some of the area residents were captured and then paroled. But before letting them go, Morgan let them overhear that he was planning to attack Hamilton in Butler County. Upon their release, he hoped they would inform Burnside of Morgan's plans. His main body of troops was split. Five hundred were sent southeast to Miamitown. The remaining 1,500 followed him northeast.

<u>4:00pm, July 13</u>

Major Keith, headquartered in Hamilton, reported to General Burnside:

(Telegram)   Hamilton, Ohio, *July* 13, 1863 – 6.30 p.m.

Enemy's advance through New Haven about 4 o'clock. New Haven is 16 miles from here. At that place they divided, part coming this way [Hamilton] and part going farther west. I have about 600 men, but only about 400 armed. Will fight to the last.[1]

KEITH,
Major, Commanding.

Not long after, Major Keith sent another report to Burnside:

(Telegram)   Hamilton, Ohio, *July* 13, 1863.

Another scout is in. Says the enemy have encamped at Shakertown [north of Cincinnati], 15 miles from this place, southwest. There are of the militia 500 men; 170 without arms; 10 of those armed without ammunition. We have of Dayton Guards 138 men. Two companies have just come in from Dayton, and are armed. Want ammunition, Austrian muskets. Governor Morton [Indiana] has just telegraphed that he has sent us one brigade and has 5,000 in pursuit of the rebels.[2]

KEITH,
Major, Commanding.

110

5:00pm, Monday, July 13

The bridge over the Great Miami River at New Baltimore was burned[3] in an effort to delay Hobson's cavalry pursuing him. At the Miamitown bridge, the home guard "tore up" the bridge to prevent the Confederates from crossing the river.[4]

As Morgan's advance scouts left Miamitown, they came in contact with Major Bill Raney commanding twenty-three militiamen. Raney was a Cincinnati detective. He had his men posted behind trees and fences so as to command the road for some distance without being exposed themselves. As Morgan's advance scouts came into sight, twenty-three rifle balls rained upon the raiders. Two Confederates fell dead and three were wounded including Lt. William Kirby, Co. G, 10th KY Cav. Morgan's scouts returned the fire, killing one of Raney's most valuable men, a member of Collins' 11th OH Battalion recruited for Indian service. [5]

The three wounded Confederates were taken prisoner. Lt. Kirby demanded to be treated as a prisoner of war. He said, "I am an officer and a gentleman from Kentucky and am entitled to respect." Raney replied, "I always treat a man as a gentleman until I find him to be otherwise. And I always treat a man as honest until I find him to be a thief." By way of illustrating his principle, Raney thrust his hand into Kirby's shirt bosom and drew out half a dozen pairs of ladies' kid gloves, some ribbon, ladies' silk hose, and some other articles of finery stolen from a store or the wardrobe of a lady of means. As Raney's men were rounding up their prisoners, they encountered what appeared to be an old, feeble man leaning on the arm of a sturdy, sunburned countryman, who, to all appearances, was humanely offering assistance to the old veteran. This sham would have succeeded, had not the good Samaritan looked a trifle too sharp out of the corners of his eyes as they passed the militia men. Raney thought he spied the twinkle of a rogue's eye. He ordered the two men to be taken into custody. Upon examination, the sunburned man proved to be Ike Snow, one of Morgan's most valuable and efficient scouts.[6]

8:30pm, July 13

Morgan's two columns joined up at the Colerain Pike near Bevis. Here they rested until midnight. While encamped, the General asked Col. Johnson if any of his men were familiar with Cincinnati. Johnson responded by saying that two of his troopers had been reared there and that Captain Sam Taylor had lived there for many years. Morgan asked to talk with them. Taylor, Lt. John McLain and Taylor's cousin, joined the officers for a conference and instructions.[7] The three troopers hastily changed into farm clothes acquired in Indiana and rode down Colerain Pike to Cincinnati to learn of Burnside's troop strength and disposition.[8] They were to rejoin the raiders after their reconnaissance. All three were reported to have ridden into Cincinnati and out again without incident. Yet, the following day, the *Daily Cincinnati Enquirer* reported that one of Morgan's men was caught spying in the city.[9] The newspaper identified him as Henry McCauley. After several hours, Capt. Taylor and Lt. McLain returned and told General Morgan that most of the town was in utmost confusion and there was no appearance of any advance against Morgan.

Had Morgan directly attacked Cincinnati and the city surrendered, there would be a long delay in getting boats with which to cross the river. In that time, the net would have been drawn around his force, preventing a safe crossing into Kentucky. Even if he could recross the river, he would have shortened the raid by many days, releasing the Union troops that were pursuing him and abandoning the primary goal that the raid was planned to accomplish.[10] The objective was to keep significant Union troops tied up in pursuing him and divert them from attacking Braxton Bragg's forces as they retreated to Chattanooga.

The Roebling Suspension Bridge, the first permanent span over the Ohio River at Cincinnati, would not open for traffic for another three and a half years [January 1, 1867].[11] The construction of the suspension bridge had begun before the outbreak of the war. In the year or two before the hostilities began, the Kentucky legislature was reluctant to authorize the completion of the bridge. Since the Commonwealth of Kentucky owns the Ohio River, the bridges spanning it are under the control of the Bluegrass State. The legislators who sympathized with the South were concerned that if the bridge was completed, the North would use it to advantage to supply their troops occupying the South. Further, they saw the bridge as an easy avenue for slaves, escaping to the North, to hurdle the giant moat.

Although Morgan may have intended to prolong the raid to the utmost, he planned to maintain a route that was not too far from the Ohio River, so that he might avail himself an opportunity to recross.

EIGHTEEN

Waiting for Morgan

Since entering Ohio, no organized military force stood directly in Morgan's path. General Burnside, commanding thousands of troops stationed in Cincinnati, was waiting for word as to Morgan's whereabouts. David Tod, Ohio's governor, had taken the same action as Governor Morton of Indiana. From Columbus, he called all the militia in the southern half of the state to arms. All able-bodied men from thirty-two counties, about 50,000 men, were ordered to four assembly centers except for those who were in counties bordering the river. They were to stay put and prevent the Confederates from crossing the Ohio River back into Kentucky or West Virginia.[1]

Those nearest Cincinnati were to report to General Burnside. Those next to the east were to report to Lt. Col. George Neff at Camp Dennison. Those in the central block of the southern tier were to report to Camp Chase at Columbus. The balance from southeastern Ohio were to rally at Camp Marietta in the city of the same name. General Burnside feared that Morgan might try to release the Confederate prisoners in Camp Chase, so he sent a telegram to Brig. Gen. John S. Mason in Columbus:

(Telegram) **How many prisoners have you at Camp Chase at the present time?**
At eight o'clock that evening, Gen. Manson answered: **We have about 900.**[2]

News of John Morgan's crossing the Ohio River more than a hundred miles downriver and marching almost unopposed across Indiana caused the citizens of the Queen City to be filled with awful terrors. Uniformed soldiers stationed in the city were hailed as "their preservers" by grateful Cincinnatians. They were elated and proud from the adulation that met them from every side. They were feasted, feted, flattered, petted, pitied and praised. The railroad depot was thronged with ladies and gentlemen, and every soldier became a hero. Lt. William Dustin of the 19th OH battery was especially impressed when one black-eyed, impulsive young woman, standing before him, exclaimed, clenching her little fists, "I have always gloried in being a woman; but today—O, give me a man!" The lieutenant, anxious to gratify her, responded without a smile, "You can have me, miss!"[3]

Everybody wanted to take a soldier to supper. The spirit of hospitality was overpowering. Even the German coffeehouse keepers seemed to have contracted the hospitable epidemic. When soldiers stepped into a saloon to quench their thirst, they were usually greeted with "Drink some peer mit me, poys; ask for everyting you vant, und it don't cost you nothing; der soljer poys can haf all der beer in dis house a'ready!" Needless to say, these invitations were heartily accepted, and beer and pretzels, bologna and cheese disappeared like magic.[4]

Union General Jacob Cox, Commander of the District of Ohio, did his best to prepare the city for defense. He divided Cincinnati into four districts or wards. The first commanded by Brig. Gen. Samuel D. Sturgis with headquarters at the Broadway Hotel. (See Sturgis' following proclamation ordering Cincinnatians to report.) The second under Major Malcolm McDowell was headquartered at the Burnet House on Third Street. The third under Brig. Gen. Jacob Ammen had its offices in the Orphan Asylum. The fourth was commanded by Col. Granville Moody with his command post at the Finley Methodist Episcopal Chapel.[5]

On July 13, Cincinnati's mayor, Len A. Harris, issued a proclamation in the *Daily Cincinnati Enquirer* commanding all businesses to close and all able-bodied men in Cincinnati to report by eight o'clock in the morning to the nearest ward to be organized, trained and be ready to defend the city in the event that Morgan showed.[6]

Following the mayor's proclamation, another was issued by General Sturgis, commanding the First District:

> **The Enrolled Ohio State regular militia of the First District of the City of Cincinnati will parade to-morrow, July 14, 1863, at eight o'clock A.M., in their respective sub-districts. All who fail to comply with the above will be considered as deserters, and treated accordingly.**

Sturgis' commander, Brigadier-General J.D. Cox, wasn't really sure Cincinnati men were going to be needed. But he felt they should at least be organized. This is evident by his order:

> **After the militia have been paraded, and their company organization so completed that they can be rapidly and systematically called into service, details will be made of such companies, etc., as may be needed for immediate use, and the remainder will be allowed to go to their homes, subject to future calls. It is therefore, of advantage to the citizens that the primary organization be completed with the greatest speed.[7]**

The Union's superior number of forces stationed in Cincinnati was neutralized by a Confederate ruse. As they entered Ohio, Ellsworth's messages tapped out a false warning that Morgan was going to attack Hamilton, Ohio, and another column was seen heading directly for Cincinnati. Some captured locals were allowed to overhear Morgan's plan to attack Cincinnati, then released to spread Morgan's "confidential plans."

What did the thousands of regular troops in Hamilton and Cincinnati do? Naturally, they waited for Morgan's imminent attack. Why dispatch troops to the suburban areas if Morgan is heading straight for them? So they waited and waited. Meanwhile, a six-mile-wide window of opportunity lay before Morgan's columns. They could ride unopposed past the confused, heavily armed and potentially dangerous, giant metropolis and reach safety just beyond it. Burnside, at this time, had been receiving wildly exaggerated reports of the size of Morgan's force. He was told that the Confederates had 4,000 troops—twice as many as Morgan possessed.[8]

What Mayor Harris and the Cincinnati military didn't realize was that as the city's manhood was assembling to be "organized" and trained, Morgan was already tearing across the northern suburbs. The mayor was in the dark, Gen. Burnside was just as confused, and the city of Cincinnati was in a panic.

General Burnside was not only worried about Morgan attacking Cincinnati, he was concerned about the draft riots going on in New York, which were front-page stories at that time in Cincinnati.[9] If riots broke out in his town, he would need his troops to quell the rowdies, just as battle-worn veterans, fresh from Gettysburg, had been quickly moved to New York to put down the disturbances there. General Henry W. Halleck, the general-in-chief in Washington, DC, had telegraphed Burnside to leave Cincinnati and move toward East Tennessee to cover the left flank of General Rosecrans and attack General Buckner in Knoxville.[10] While Burnside feared an imminent attack from Morgan, and draft rioting in the streets, he looked with dread and indecision at Halleck's telegram asking him to inform Washington what he planned to do.

Halleck was concerned about Burnside's slow response to his orders. He seemed distracted, in another world. He was right. Burnside had his hands full with the elusive and threatening Morgan.

WAR DEPARTMENT

(Telegram)   Major-General Rosecrans, *Tullahoma, Tenn.:Washington, July* 13, 1863–10:30am

General Burnside has been frequently urged to move forward and cover your left, by entering East Tennessee. I do not know what he is doing. He seems tied fast to Cincinnati.

H.W. HALLECK, *General-in-Chief.*[11]

At this moment, the man, who would have the best opportunity of capturing Morgan, was sitting in Covington, Kentucky, across the river from Cincinnati. He was Major George W. Rue. A week and a half earlier, he was commanding the 9th KY Cav., USA, as part of Shackelford's command in pursuit of Morgan in southern Kentucky. He had become ill and his regiment left him behind at a farm house. Upon recovering, he became anxious to return to his regiment, but they were now somewhere in Indiana chasing Morgan. He put on his uniform and went to the nearest railway station to take a train to army headquarters in Cincinnati. The conductor refused to let him board the train, saying that unless a soldier had a pass from a superior officer, he would not be allowed aboard a train. Rue returned to the house of a friend and exchanged his uniform for civilian clothes. He stepped aboard the next train and was soon reporting to General Burnside.[12]

Burnside told him he had no idea where Rue's regiment was, but if he would agree, he could take over the command of the Covington Barracks, which included four hundred U.S. infantry troops and a thousand horses. There was also a detachment of seventy men from his old regiment, the 9th KY which had been left behind by Shackelford.[13] As Morgan approached Cincinnati, there were indications of a draft riot, or an uprising of sympathizers with the Confederates in some of the worst districts of the city. Fearful of the unrest in the city, General Burnside asked Major Rue to bring his forces across the river, by boat, and camp in a park near the heart of downtown. There were not enough stables to house the thousand horses, so Rue set up a stable near Fountain Square.[14]

The local Cincinnati newspapers, the *Daily Enquirer, Gazette* and *Commercial* issued special editions every few hours featuring dispatches received by Burnside. They kept their tired printers setting type by hand, trying as best they could to keep up with fast-breaking events.[15] Newspaper reporters were stationed in downtown Cincinnati at Burnside's military headquarters in the Burnet House on the north side of Third Street, west of Vine Street. They were permitted to publish reports of Morgan sightings as couriers brought dispatches into the city. That night, there were hourly editions hastily set in type and sold on the streets to anxious, adrenaline-hyped crowds who couldn't sleep for fear of Morgan's threatened appearance.

> **Burnside's Headquarters: 11:30 PM.** A courier arrived having left Cheviot at half past eight PM, with information for the General. Cheviot is only seven miles from the city. He states that about five hundred of Morgan's men had crossed the river at Miamitown, and attacked our pickets, killing or capturing one of them. Morgan's main force, said to be three thousand strong, was then crossing the river. A portion of the Rebel force had been up to New Haven, and another had gone to New Baltimore and partially destroyed both of these places. The light of the burning towns was seen by our men. When the courier left, Morgan was moving up, it was reported, to attack our advance.[16]

Morgan's main column headed northeast to New Burlington. On that hot July night, clouds blanketed the sky, allowing not the faintest celestial light to pierce the solid blackness. In the darkness, the extended line of tired Confederate horsemen had to remain extremely alert, or they could easily lose their way. And many did. Basil Duke said, "It was a terrible and trying march. Strong men fell out of their saddles, and at every halt the officers were compelled to move continually about in their respective companies and pull and haul the men, who would drop asleep in the road. It was the only way to keep them awake. Quite a number crept off into the fields and slept until they were awakened by the enemy."[17] Captain Thomas Coombs of the 5th KY said, "Many is the hour that I have set astride my bay pony fast asleep, trusting solely to his unerring instinct to follow the column and keep at the head of my company."[18]

> **Burnside's Headquarters: 1:00 AM.** A courier just arrived from Colerain, with dispatches. He reports that the enemy, supposed to be two thousand five hundred strong, with six pieces of artillery, crossed the Colerain Pike in the dark at Bevis, going toward New Burlington, or to Cincinnati and Hamilton Pike in direction of Springdale.[19]

As Morgan approached Glendale, through which the Cincinnati, Hamilton & Dayton Railroad (C,H&DRR) ran, he was concerned that a large force of regular troops might have come up from Cincinnati by train and could pin his forces between theirs and Hobson's troops coming up fast in the rear. What Morgan didn't know was that a trainload of soldiers including the 19th OH Battery had left Cincinnati that night destined for Hamilton, Ohio, twenty-five miles to the north. The train crossed Morgan's path on the C,H&DRR line just thirty minutes before he crossed that point. Like two ships that passed in the dark, neither was aware of each others' presence.[20] Morgan expected to be confronted by the concentrated forces of Judah and Burnside. He anticipated great difficulty in eluding or cutting his way through them. He believed that the great effort to capture him would be made as he crossed the C,H&DRR. To deceive the enemy as to the exact point where he would cross the railroad, he sent detachments in various directions to create the impression he was marching to Hamilton and a detachment toward Cincinnati.

> **Burnside's Headquarters: 1:30 AM. A dispatch from Jones' Station states that the enemy are now encamped between Venice and New Baltimore.**

> **Burnside's Headquarters: 2:00 AM. Another dispatch says the enemy are coming in, or a squad of them, from New Baltimore toward Glendale, for the supposed purpose of destroying a bridge over the Cincinnati, Hamilton and Dayton Railroad near Glendale.[21]**

The train load of Union troops arrived in Hamilton at two o'clock in the morning. Their unexpected arrival caused alarm among the citizens, who had been sleepless for two days in expectation of Morgan's momentary arrival. As the cannon were being unloaded, scores of invitations to breakfast were thrust upon every battery member. Every man generally accepted, as far as the capacity of the men would permit. It was a legend among the boys that one of their number accepted and did ample justice to four distinct invitations to breakfast before ten o'clock in the morning.[22]

> **Burnside's Headquarters: 2:15 AM. A dispatch from Hamilton says it believed that the main portion of Morgan's force is moving in that direction going east, while he has sent squads to burn bridges on Cincinnati, Hamilton & Dayton Railroad, and over the Miami River, but he may turn and come down this way on some roads leading through Walnut Hills or Mt. Auburn.[23]**

Except for the train to Hamilton, no other north-bound trains were permitted to depart the Cincinnati depot that night.[24]

This was not the first Confederate invasion of Ohio nor the first time Cincinnati was threatened by Morgan. In early September 1862, Morgan was part of the force led by General Edmund Kirby Smith through Kentucky. To defend Cincinnati, General Lew Wallace had a pontoon bridge erected over the Ohio River over which tens of thousands of "squirrel-hunters" crossed into Northern Kentucky to stop the Confederate threat to the Queen City. At the same time, General Albert Gallatin Jenkins leading 350 Confederate cavalry crossed the Ohio River at Buffington Island and raided the Ohio towns of Portland and Racine in Meigs County. The purpose of their raid was to acquire horses and arms. They took twenty-five horses and shot and killed a "deaf and dumb" man who could not hear their order to halt. They recrossed the river below Racine at Wolf's Bar and once more entered West Virginia.[25]

Back at Cincinnati, Smith and Morgan's forces probed the Union defenses in Northern Kentucky made up of forts placed at strategic points along the ridge of Kentucky hills. Between the forts, a lacework of trenches, manned by Ohio and Kentucky farmers and businessmen, presented the Confederate advance with a formidable and deadly hurdle of firepower. Smith decided to fall back and was never to threaten Cincinnati again. But a year later, Morgan would return by the back door.

NINETEEN

"Veiled" Threat in Glendale

3:00am, Tuesday, July 14

The raiders rode into Glendale in the dead of night and instead of finding it bristling with troops, they found the town sound asleep, unaware of the danger in its midst. Morgan captured the telegraph office in the train station and "Lightning" went to work on the key, dispatching dire warnings of Morgan sightings on the outskirts of Cincinnati.

In the darkness of the early morning hours, the 800-900 residents of Glendale were awakened by the sound of thousands of hoof beats. One resident described looking out his window and seeing gray ghosts riding by. "They looked very strange. Some were wearing women's hats and <u>veils</u>. They came into our homes, raiding our kitchens for food and looking for valuables."

The reason Morgan's men were wearing ladies' hats with veils was to protect their faces and nostrils from the clouds of dust that the horses were stirring up.[1] These suburban pikes were not paved; they were no more than dirt roads. The veils screened out the dust and made breathing easier. Hats kept the netting in place. Not very military, but certainly effective.

Some of the Glendale residents, having been alerted by the noise, attempted to hide their horses. One, who successfully did, was Anthony Harkness who had been Glendale's second mayor. His home, built in 1852, had a smokehouse. In the basement of this small brick building, he hid his prized carriage horses.[2]

Instead of being a dangerous encounter with Union forces, the Confederate riders passed through Glendale without a hostile shot fired. Just beyond, Morgan burned the canal bridge and rode into Sharon [Sharonville]. David Hulse, a resident of Sharon, in his letter of July 19, 1863, described the raiders' visit.

> We were awakened early Tuesday morning to find the enemy in our midst. They were several thousand. They were in our stables, stores and kitchens. They were about four hours passing through.
>
> Three local men, Vanhise, Smyzer and Miller hitched up a wagon, took some bedcord and set off in pursuit of the Rebels. They began collecting horses that the Rebels had discharged.

They were successful in collecting several horses before they got too close to the rear guard pickets, who took them prisoner, took their horses and what money they had with them. They were forced to accompany the Rebels for another twenty miles before they were told to dismount and walk home.

Morgan's men departed Glendale. But hidden in the barn of John R. Wright at 140 Fountain Avenue were two Confederate soldiers. Like many that night who were physically unable to keep up the pace of the exhausting, all-night journey, they had sought rest and sanctuary. They were aided by two young Glendale boys who led them to the Wright's barn. When Mrs. Wright learned what was happening, she felt sorry for the men and fed them until they were able to move on.[3] As Morgan's men rode east away from Glendale, they spread out like many rivulets rather than remaining together as one cohesive force.

Three main reasons that might have contributed to this unusual occurrence: (1) "Lightning" Ellsworth's successful efforts misled Union troops by using the telegraph to send false information of Morgan's location and direction; (2) relief that they were past the danger zone of being attacked by Burnside's troops in Cincinnati and Hamilton; and (3) the darkness of the moonless night made it difficult to maintain visual contact between units.

The two brigades diverged. General Morgan leading the Second Brigade to the southeast, Col. Duke leading the First northeast. Each of these groups split again and again, taking main roads in different directions. As the raiders spread across the East Sycamore area, they were scattered as much as six miles apart. West of Glendale, they had raided about eleven farms over a single ten-mile route. East of Glendale, they raided more than seventy farms in the next ten miles.[4] They spread themselves like a fishing net over the northeastern part of Hamilton County. But instead of fish, they were hauling in fresh horses and depriving the pursuing Union troops from obtaining any for themselves.

Another reason for the unusual divergence of troops was the moonless night. Duke said, "In this night march around Cincinnati, we met with the greatest of difficulty in keeping the column together. General Morgan, who rode at the head of the second brigade, marched in advance. But Cluke's regiment riding at the rear of the First Brigade straggled, halted and delayed. A great gap would thus open between the rear of one brigade and the advance of the other. We who were behind were forced to grope our way as best we could. The night was intensely dark. When the night is calm, the dust kicked up by the passage of a large number of horses will remain suspended in the air for a considerable length of time, and it will also move slowly in the same direction that the horses which have disturbed it have traveled. We could trace it by noticing the direction in which the dust 'settled' or floated. We could also trace the column by the slaver dropped from the horses' mouths."[5] So, in the inky darkness, the First Brigade wandered northward toward Loveland and entered Montgomery Pike about where today it intersects with Interstate 275. They turned south and headed down Montgomery Road into the village of Montgomery and then turned east again going toward the Little Miami River.

On July 13, a spy was caught and imprisoned. A July 14 article in the *Daily Cincinnati Enquirer* reported, "Yesterday morning a well dressed young man, named Henry McCauley, was arrested by a member of the Twelfth Rhode Island regiment, on suspicion of being a spy. He was very inquisitive, inquiring about the number of troops in the city, their equipment, &c, and indeed, as we are informed, his entire conduct was such as to induce his arrest. As soon as papers were found in his possession which confirmed the suspicion that he was one of Morgan's spies. He gave his name as Henry McCauley, and said he was an East Tennessee refugee. He was placed in the Hammond-street Station house."[6]

South of Glendale, near Carthage, John Ivens, a merchant, was alerted that two of Morgan's raiders were in his stable confiscating his horses. This happened on the afternoon of July 14. Ivens seized two revolvers, ran out of his house and confronted the intruders. He arrested them and turned them over to the military stationed in Carthage.

Morgan's main columns, at the time of the Carthage incident, were more than twenty miles away, to the east in Clermont County. These two Morgan stragglers had lost their way during the moonless night of July 13. They weren't the only ones. During that night, Morgan's columns had become strung out over many miles. In the pitch-black night, scattered groups had lost sight of the men in front, and without guides, wandered off in many directions hoping to catch up. Some were too ill to go on. Many were suffering from chronic diarrhea. Most of the men were exhausted from being continuously in the saddle for eleven days with hardly a respite. They were worn down and demoralized with tremendous fatigue. Some slipped out of their saddles to lie down for a few hours of sleep, only to be awakened the next morning by Union soldiers taking them prisoner.[7]

Colonel Leroy [Roy] S. Cluke, commanding Morgan's rear guard rode up to where Colonel Adam "Stovepipe" Johnson was seated in his saddle. Showing signs of exhaustion, he said, "I'd give a thousand dollars for an hour's sleep!" With that, the Texas colonel reached over, grabbed the reins and began leading Cluke's horse. Cluke's huge six-foot frame instantly leaned forward, over the saddle, and he fell into a deep sleep.[8]

TWENTY

While Sherman Slept

<u>3:30am, Tuesday, July 14</u>

Northeast of Carthage is the town of Reading. In that community, some of Morgan's men came upon the Catholic boarding school, Mt. Notre Dame De Namur, "The Mountain." The school, high on a hill overlooking the community, had opened just a few months before the Civil War started. Sister Alphonse was appointed Mistress of Boarders and also taught in some of the higher branches. Sister Mary [Lucy Pine] assisted in the studies and art. Sister Aloysius was the principal music teacher. The school opened with eleven sisters and seven novices. During the war period, the number of boarders grew from thirty to as many as one hundred twelve.[1]

Many of these young women were from the southern states. Their parents had sent them there to be in a place of safety during the war. The teachers had to use a great deal of tact to prevent disputes arising among the pupils, whose sympathies were naturally divided between the North and the South. This was especially difficult because Union Gen. William Tecumseh Sherman's daughter, Maria "Minnie" Ewing Sherman, one of the general's eight children, was a resident of the school. Sherman, a native of Lancaster, Ohio, wrote to his daughter, "We must fight and subdue those in arms against us, but we mean them no harm." He sensed the underlying anger in the school when he advised his daughter, "Do not use the words 'rebels' and 'traitors' when referring to Southerners." For a man who became one of the Confederacy's greatest antagonists, Sherman began the war with a fondness for the South. In 1859, he was first superintendent of Louisiana Military Seminary in Pineville, Louisiana. He had many Southern acquaintances whom he admired.[2]

At the time of Morgan's raid, Sherman had been serving as a corps commander in U.S. Grant's victorious campaign at Vicksburg, Mississippi. A little more than a year later, Sherman would make his savage "March to the Sea," which would bring unprecedented destruction and "total war" to the South. In 1880, fifteen years after the war had ended, the devastator of Georgia addressed a crowd of 5,000 uniformed veterans at the Ohio State Fair in Columbus warning them, "There is many a boy here today who looks on war as all glory. But, boys, it is all hell! You can bear this warning voice to generations yet to come. I look upon war with horror, but if it has to come, I am here."[3]

Morgan's men had no idea that Sherman's daughter was sleeping in the dormitory building as they searched the stables for horses. Like his Confederate counterparts, Sherman felt his daughter would be safe on the "mountain" in this remote Cincinnati suburban community.[4]

The Sisters had been alerted to Morgan's approach, and the Mt. Notre Dame workmen concealed the horses in the lower story of St. Joseph's Building, used as a laundry. They covered its floors with sawdust to prevent the pawing of hoofs from being heard. The Sisters' prayers asked that Morgan's men not hear the horses' neighing. The Confederates searched the stables to no avail, and left, making their way downhill toward the town of Reading to the relief and satisfaction of the boarding school's community.

4:00am, Tuesday, July 14

After passing through Glendale, Morgan's two main columns separated. The northern column, heading toward Loveland, was now being led by Col. Duke. General Morgan accompanied the southern column toward Camp Dennison.

4:30am, July 14

General Morgan stopped at the farm of John Schenck, in an area called East Sycamore. Today, it is known as Deer Park. Mr. Schenck was a pharmacist and operated a drugstore at the southwest corner of Ninth and Main Streets in downtown Cincinnati.[5] On his East Sycamore farm, he raised devon cattle.[6] When he and his wife, Amelia, and eleven children[7] received word of Morgan's coming, the family removed all the furniture in the parlor and piled hay on the floor.[8] Placing his two fine Spanish horses in the room, he had the shutters closed and a cloth hung over the front door. Before the General's party arrived, an advance group approached the house. A member of the family, dressed in a nurse's uniform, advised them that there was a sick child suffering from smallpox confined in the home. Fearing that they might get infected, they left and searched unsuccessfully for horses. The raiders rebuffed some workhorses that the druggist had left in the barn.[9] By the time the General arrived, conditions must have changed because the *Daily Cincinnati Enquirer* reported that Morgan <u>did</u> have breakfast at the Schenck farm. In any case, Schenck's ruse worked because no claim was made to the Ohio Commissioners for any horses taken by the raiders. Mr. Schenck described that Morgan's column took one and a half hours to pass his farm. That's not including Duke's "northern" column.[10]

John Schenck had been active as a sympathetic "conductor" in the Underground Railroad, hiding slaves who had made their way across the Ohio River. The Schencks had smuggled a black family by the name of N. Thompson onto their 175-acre farm and allowed them to use a vacant log cabin and farm the land until the Civil War ended.[11] Two of the Thompson daughters went on to become well-known poets of their day.[12] Despite the Fugitive Slave Act, which was enacted as part of the Compromise of 1850, the Schenck family, like many in the North, ignored it and aided and protected a family of slaves from being recaptured and returned to the South. This clandestine group hid themselves with the family's prize horses when the Confederates rode through and "visited" the property before the sun rose on the morning of July 14, 1863.

TWENTY-ONE

Camp Dennison's 600-Gun Salue

While Morgan was having breakfast, Lt. Col. George W. Neff, of the Union's 2nd KY Infantry[1] and military commander of Camp Dennison (January 15-July 24, 1863),[2] was making preparations to "greet" Morgan. Neff surmised that Morgan wanted the large number of fresh horses and mules that would be found in a military camp. To prevent this from happening, he had most of the horses, mules and as many wagons as they could pull sent to Cincinnati for safekeeping. Fifty wagons were unable to be taken to Cincinnati, so Neff had them pulled to Camp Shady with extra saddles and riding gear. (Shady has been identified as being three miles east; another source reported it six miles "above" Camp Dennison. It has also been described as being fifteen miles from Williamsburg.) The lieutenant colonel hoped that the wagons and gear would remain undetected.

Neff also sent to Cincinnati other camp articles of value which included surgical instruments, medicines, important records and a large amount of money belonging to the soldiers. He dispatched men from the camp to fell trees and construct abatis at the main approaches to impede the Confederates' advance. He ordered Captain William von Doehn and Captain Procter, 18th U.S. Infantry, to throw up some rifle pits on the crossroads and Madisonville Pike. He then took a train as far as Foster's Crossing to examine all roads and bridges, placing pickets and sending out scouts. He also placed pickets and scouts at the bridges at Morrow and Fort Ancient.

General Burnside sent a telegram to Neff asking, "What is the exact amount of your force, armed and unarmed?" Neff replied, "Seven hundred armed; 1,200 unarmed." Then Neff advised Burnside that Morgan's artillery was in position on a hill on the north side and was shelling the camp.[3]

Neff's wife and the wives of other officers had fled the camp earlier and sought refuge in a farmhouse up the Goshen Pike. They had all taken their personal valuables, family silver, jewels and some of the camp's cash and post records for safe-keeping, and planned to stay until the danger passed.[4] One of Duke's patrols, on a search for fresh horses, found Mrs. Neff and other officers' wives huddled in the farmhouse. When she later

126

told her husband about it, she said Morgan's men had taken all their mounts, but "had offered no insult to the ladies, asking them for water, and conversing with them most politely."

6:00am, Tuesday, July 14

General Hobson moved out of Harrison on Morgan's trail. His men were tired, but worst of all was the condition of their jaded horses. Morgan didn't leave much in the way of suitable horses for Hobson's men to pick from. This was so glaringly apparent that the following telegram was sent to General Burnside:

> **General Hobson moved from Harrison on Morgan's trail at 6 o'clock this a.m. Horses are worn out and Morgan will have to be checked from the front or Hobson will not overtake him.**
> J.A. CRAVENS, *Lieutenant and Aide to General Hughes.*[5]

7:00am, July 14

On their way to Camp Dennison, small groups of Morgan's men left the main column, as was their practice, to look for fresh horses in farms nearby. One group startled Tom Boone, a member of an Indian Hill pioneer family and descendant of Daniel Boone. Tom was walking near the intersection of Given and Shawnee Run roads early in the morning. One of the strangers demanded to know, "Friend or foe?" It was known that Hamilton County had many southern sympathizers, Butternuts and Copperheads. Boone quickly replied, "Friend!" He was then asked directions to a certain farm, which he innocently gave. The anxious horsemen rode off, allowing Tom to go on unmolested.[6]

Camp Dennison was the Union's largest military hospital in Ohio during the war. The camp was originally organized at the request of Governor William Dennison who served in that office from January 9, 1860 to January 13, 1862. The camp was named as a well-deserved tribute to Ohio's governor. The site had been selected by George B. McClellan, commander of the Ohio militia and laid out by Capt. William Starke Rosecrans,[7] the man who, when he became a general, would menace General Bragg at Tullahoma, precipitating Morgan's Ohio raid. Rosecrans chose a site on the large, level tract of ground between the Little Miami River and the line of hills to the west, immediately below Miamisville. The tract had many advantages. It was large enough to accommodate up to 15,000 men, with space for drill and parade grounds, and all of it was level. During the four-year war, more than 75,000 men were mustered in at the camp.[8] The Little Miami

Railroad ran through the area, providing good communications with Cincinnati as well as Columbus. The river furnished an ample supply of water, and Cincinnati was near enough for all essential purposes, including a quick march into Kentucky, yet not so near as to create undue disciplinary problems with the men.

A major portion of the 700-acre camp site was owned by Dr. Alfred Buckingham among others. He leased it to the State of Ohio for $12 to $20 per acre. For two years, Dr. Buckingham was in charge of the Seventh Division hospital corps. Beginning April 1861, the camp's first commander was General Jacob Dolson Cox, who would later become governor of Ohio (January 8, 1866-January 13, 1868). Down the middle of the camp ran the Little Miami Railroad. On the west side of the tracks was a row of seventy wooden hospital buildings stretching from one end of the camp to the other. Each hospital barrack measured one hundred twenty feet by twenty-four feet and held 200 beds.[9] Col. Neff had furnished the sick and wounded men with weapons and twenty rounds of ammunition each. He posted them in rifle pits on the hill southwest of the hospital, at points commanding the approaches to the camp.[10]

On both sides of the tracks were the village and sutleries (camp shops) of Camp Dennison. On the east side were the officers and enlisted men's huts measuring twelve feet by eighteen feet, large enough to house a dozen men. Each company had its own street running east and west open to the parade and drill ground. At the other end of each street, facing the hills in the west, was the officers' hut, with a cook shack behind that.

When the camp was established in 1861, it was laid out to accommodate a dozen regiments. Tents also dotted the landscape as recruits in large numbers began to arrive. Originally, it was planned as a central point to receive recruits, arm, clothe and train them. The camp took on a dual purpose when there was an outbreak of measles among the soldiers in the camp. Hospital barracks were built. These medical facilities assumed an even greater importance after the Battle of Shiloh (April 6-7, 1862), the first great bloody battle of the war in which there were more than 12,000 Union casualties. In particular, those wounded who were natives of Ohio were sent by boat and train from Pittsburg Landing to Camp Dennison. Thereafter, the camp's mission was to provide hospitalization for those wounded in battle and serve as a recruiting, training and discharge facility. During the war, 30,000 Northern lads from Kentucky, Indiana and the majority from Ohio received military training to convert them from farmers to soldiers.[11]

Just one week before Morgan's men made their appearance at the camp, the Second Battalion of the 11th OH Cavalry was formed under the command of Lt. Col. Wm. O. Collins. The first battalion had been organized in the spring of 1862, and was assigned to Indian warfare. It had marched 700 miles in twenty-six days to Ft. Laramie, Dakota Territory, and went on severe duty in the western plains and mountains.[12] The second battalion of the 11th would soon be traveling east instead of west in pursuit of Morgan's raiders.[13] The 11th was only one of many Federal units that was being held in reserve at Camp Dennison for the protection of the city of Cincinnati.

Beginning two days before Morgan made his appearance at Camp Dennison, Lt. Col. Neff began making inspection trips of main roads leading to the camp and bridges spanning the Little Miami. Those soldiers who were not hospitalized and convalescents who were almost ready to return to duty were sent by Neff to defend the many bridges spanning the Little Miami River.[14]

7:30am, Tuesday, July 14

Morgan's column came into view of the armed convalescents, many from the Corps of Invalids (43rd Co. of the Second Battalion),[15] who were entrenched in rifle pits on the camp's hilly perimeter. Their number had swelled to six hundred[16] by volunteers, unarmed militiamen who had been arriving during the preceding day and evening. All of them had been armed with rifles and ammunition delivered just in time that morning by train from Cincinnati. Morgan was "welcomed" with a 600-gun salute aimed at him. Morgan decided he would have to pay too dear a price for any horses in the camp.[17] The approaches to the camp were blocked by felled trees that Neff's men had chopped down just a few hours earlier. Morgan answered the "salute" with a few shells from his artillery, but the camp's defenders were well protected in their trenches.

Morgan bypassed Camp Dennison and headed north to cross and destroy the railroad bridge over the Little Miami River leading to Miamisville. But two companies of state militia commanded by Lieutenant Smith of the 21st OH Battery were dug in. Captain Procter of the 18th U.S. Infantry commanding 150 men including some camp convalescents had been following Morgan's rear guard.[18] As the Confederates charged the bridge defenses, they were met by the combined fire from front and back. Morgan was forced to seek cover. For the next hour, both sides banged away at their opponents. In that engagement, Captain Procter lost four men taken prisoner and one convalescent Henry Meyers (Myers), Co. D, 5th OH was killed.[19] Five raiders were taken prisoner, including one of Morgan's lieutenants. Finding that he could not cross at Miamisville, Morgan effected an undisturbed crossing two miles upstream.

In a diary kept by James Given living in Perin Mills (Perintown/Perinville), located five miles southeast of Camp Dennison, halfway between the camp and Batavia, the following entries were made:

Tuesday, July 14, 1863—Hazy & smoky. Tom gone to town. Pat & Maloney began toplow corn & the word came that Morgan was approaching Camp Dennison, when we all left for that point but I came home at night.

Wednesday, July 15, 1863—Foggy but clear morning. Great Morgan excitement at sunrise. General Shackelford Cavalry Brigade began to pass our house & in the course of $2^1/_2$ hours about four thousand passed in search of Morgan forces & about 50 of them took breakfast & fed their horses with us. They took great numbers of the neighbors horses & one from us. The Militia turned out. Pat & Maloney with them & went to Camp Dennison & then to Batavia & got home on Thursday evening. Paid Maloney $2.00 & Pat Devine $3.00.

TWENTY-TWO

Thoroughbreds in Trade

<u>4:00am, Tuesday, July 14</u>

Just before Morgan tangled with Neff's defenses, Duke's column had moved out of Sharon and headed for the village of Montgomery. Residents of the Crist House on Zig Zag Road lowered a bag of jewels into the well by the kitchen door. Another villager put his horse in the parlor and locked the door, telling the raiders that their children were inside with the dread disease, smallpox.[1]

Both Confederate columns were feverishly seeking fresh mounts. Raiding parties spread out over a six-mile area, entered barns and led away clusters of farm horses. Many were pilfered while the farmers slept. Some, who were early risers, had Morgan's men enter their barns while they were feeding their animals. In the face of armed soldiers, the farmers stood back and offered no resistance as their valuable horseflesh disappeared over the horizon.

In several cases, one in particular, the Confederates "traded" their tired horses for those of Montgomery farmer, Nicholas Todd. Todd's losses were much greater than most, which usually represented the theft of one or two horses. When Nicholas and his son, Isaac, went out to their barn, they found the raiders had taken four horses, one buggy and one set of harness.[2] At first, Mr. Todd was angered by his loss. But after those jaded Bluegrass horses regained their strength, he discovered he was the proud owner of two fine Kentucky thoroughbreds. When his son, James, a captain in Co. K of the 138th OVI,[3] returned after the war, he and his brothers began racing the horses as trotters and won many events. They and several Todd generations to follow declined the opportunity to run the farm instead, and operated a successful race horse stable and training track. The Todd trotting stables were located in Swaim Field in the Village of Montgomery. Their race track was behind the present site of Moeller High School. Nicholas Todd was also compensated by the State of Ohio when they recognized his claim and paid him $650 for the horses and buggy the raiders took.[4]

Another, who had a similar twist of fate, was William W. Fletcher, who was married to Lydia Buckingham. Fletcher had a thirty-acre farm just north of Camp Dennison along the banks of the Little Miami River almost

131

across from Miamisville. Like many others, he claimed damages for the loss of two horses to the Morgan's guerrillas. But he soon discovered he had received an exceptional trotting horse in trade. He was more than compensated by the racing cups and cash winnings he brought home thereafter.[5] For him, like Todd, it was a bonus. The state paid him $300 for his claim.[6]

The following letter, dated July 22, was published in the *Cincinnati Commercial* newspaper on July 24, 1863. It is a description of events as seen through the eyes of a Hamilton County resident in East Sycamore (just west of Montgomery). It is a graphic description of what Morgan's men looked like as they rode through the villages in the eastern part of Hamilton County. The words, spelling, grammar and punctuation are as originally written in the language of that day.[7]

You are aware that we have seen them; <u>entertained</u> them (unwillingly) in our houses; that our stables have been plundered; that a part of the harvest remains in the field, without horses, except the jaded, sore-backed, bony, lame ones, which Morgan traded us, to bring it to the barns. On Tuesday, the 14th instant [current month], at early dawn, the inhabitants hereabouts were aroused from slumber by the clattering of hoofs upon the stony pike, and the clanking of stirrups (I suppose, as I didn't see any sabers or the like). On peeping through the window, I recognized them immediately as secesh, from their hard looks, their clothes of many colors and fashions, and their manner of riding.

They did not ride in any kind of order, unless it was disorder. As many as could, rode abreast. Some galloped, some trotted, and others allowed their horses to walk slowly while they slept in the saddles. They were not uniformly dressed. Some wore a whole suit of the well-known blue which designates our [Union] soldiers; others had part of a suit, but most of them were arrayed in citizens' garb. Some were barefoot, some bareheaded, and one, I noticed, wore a huge green veil. Probably he was ashamed of his company, and took this method to conceal his grim visage while in the presence of decent people. Some wore jackets outside of their coats, as though they dressed in a hurry. Perhaps their keen ears had detected the sound of Hobson's cavalry behind. Some had ladies' gaiters, dress-patterns, and the like, protruding from their pockets; and one bootless, hatless, shirtless being held his suspenderless pants in one hand, while he held the bridle with the other, and heeled his horse to a gallop.

Well, I had not continued my rebel-gazing long before one of them dismounted and wanted "yesterday's paper, if you please." I couldn't see it! Very soon the house, yard, barn, and fields were overflowing with "Southern chivalry." They were evidently very tired and sleepy, and, judging from their questions to each other, "How far do you think the blue-jackets are behind?" I should say as much frightened as we were. "How far is it to Cincinnati?" and "Have you yesterday's paper?" were the principal questions asked. In some houses of this vicinity, they turned over beds, peeped into cellars, cupboards, drawers, closets, and even babies' cradles, in search of arms, ammunition, "greenbacks," and sich, while others were not disturbed. They helped themselves very liberally to such eatables as could be found, besides ordering the women to prepare more. Of course, they took horses. They just gobbled up every body's, except—well, perhaps his were lame, blind, or fractious. Generally, they made no distinction between the property of Copperheads and that of "Abolitionists," as they call all unconditional Union men. 'Cause why? They either did not know their friends, or else they considered the Northern Butternuts beneath the respect of Southern rebels, horse-thieves, freebooters, guerrillas, or whatever else they may call themselves.

A young farmer, George McGee by name, residing near Montgomery, made a brilliant dash among them, fired, and slightly killed one, though not altogether! Another farmer, Mr. Landenburg, residing near Sharonville, fired among them, and wounded one of their number. He was captured, but released after having enjoyed a ride of a few miles with the "chivalry." Most persons in this part of the world considered discretion the better part of valor, and held their temper until the last invader had vanished. Like a sudden clap of thunder came Morgan among us, and passed off to the east like a meteor, leaving the natives gazing after him in stupefied horror, rubbing their eyes, and wondering whether it was all the dream of a nightmare, or a reality. Quite a number of men and boys followed in Morgan's train—keeping a safe distance behind, however—hoping to recover their stolen horses.

One old Pennsylvania Dutchman, who resides in this neighborhood, by some means, lost but one of his horses; he mounted the other and hastily pursued the flying secesh. When near

Batavia, he mingled a little too closely with them, as may be proved from the fact that they took the horse he rode, with saddle and bridle. It is told that he gave vent to his enraged feelings by saying to the "Reb" who took his horse: "That is my horse; I wish him good luck; I wish he preak your neck!" "What's that?" thundered secesh. "I wish my horse good luck; I wish he preak your neck!" repeated the candid German. "Reb" rode on. It is said that certain Butternut individuals, whom I might name, shouted for Vallandigham, and Glory to God, Morgan's come!' on the approach of the rebels—all of which I can positively assert to be true. To sum up the whole thing. Morgan's aim was evidently not [to] fight, but horse-stealing.

Another eyewitness account was penned July 14, 1863, into the Butterworth family diary. The Butterworth farm, owned by Quakers and a "stop" on the Underground Railroad for harboring runaway slaves, was located in Warren County just north of Clermont County, close to but not in the direct path of Morgan's raid. You'll note that, to the person making the entry, it was just another day on the farm.

It appears that the rebel John Morgan, with about 3,000 cavalry guerrillas, has made a dash into Indiana and into Ohio & has passed the Little Miami Rail Road & damaged the same this side of Camp Dennison. Wherefore no papers reached Wilmington today. There is great running to and fro, and military preparation—under the call of the Gov. of Ohio. All the organized Militia are rushing from here to Camp Dennison. Ed finished plowing the big field.[8]

Two other brief anecdotal stories occurred in Warren County. The first is about Mary Jane Brandenburg, a small, rosy-cheeked child. Her mother had heard that Morgan might be headed her way. Her husband, Silas, was away in the army fighting in the south. She gathered everything she could carry along with her children and hurried down the road to a rendezvous where she would join others. She had told Mary Jane to take her clothes. As they ran along, the mother noticed that Mary's face was turning scarlet. In sudden alarm, they stopped to rest. The problem was discovered when Mrs. Brandenburg realized that Mary had put on all the clothes she could wear, one over another. The hot July day had done the rest.[9]

In northern Loveland in Warren County, just north of Hamilton County, Sarah Todd Jones, a sharp-tongued Southern sympathizer, spied some of Morgan's men removing her horse from the stable. She rushed out to intercede. She pleaded with the Confederates, "I am a Rebel. All my sympathy is with the South. I'm a Southerner. Please don't take my horse!" The Morgan trooper holding the horse paused to consider his reply. "Well, if it's true that you support our cause," he said as he led the horse away, "then we thank you for your donation." As he rode away, he swept his hat off in a grand gesture. Forever after, if Sarah's tart tongue became unbearable, someone was sure to mention Morgan.[10]

5:30am, Tuesday, July 14

One additional eye-witness account comes to us from a letter handed down through the generations. Written on July 17, 1863 (three days after the raid) and signed by Jerusha June, it was to her sister, Eliza A. McKown. From the names she mentions in her letter, it appears that she lived near the village of Montgomery, a northern suburb of Cincinnati.

> Kind sister, I seat myself to let you know that we are all well at present but there has been rather unfortunate news regarding our horses. On Tuesday morning at about half past five o'clock, I'm looking out of the window. I beheld five of John Morgan's men coming across the meadow. Right towards the house they came and went into the stable where father was feeding (them). They never said a word, but untied the two young horses and took them out, and then told father they were for John Morgan's command, and rode off. They said they would leave Old Charlie. But they had not been gone but a little while until a couple of others came and took Old Charlie and left. And others came and wanted something to eat, and we give them all the bread we had baked. There are about a thousand that came out on the Montgomery Pike by John's and they saw John Morgan and so did father. And the rest of his men came out there by Mr. Hieatt's and they had six pieces of cannon with them.

6:45am, July 14

Duke moved his column along the Little Miami River, heading north toward Loveland. Along the way, he raided homes for fresh mounts. The sun rose in the eastern skies ahead. The black blanket of overcast, which had obliterated the moon and stars, had been blown away. The sky was a pale blue unmarred by clouds. He could see the Little Miami River from a hill overlooking Nathaniel Humphrey's ninety-acre farm. A cool, fresh morning breeze stirred the trees. Duke commented, "The fresh morning air is invigorating. It's having a cheering effect upon my men."[11] Duke's regiments rode down the hill toward the river, stopping at one of Humphrey's barns to help themselves to two horses. Nathaniel, his wife, Elizabeth, and their young daughter, Louella, hid in the root cellar as hundreds of Confederate raiders rode past their home and barns.[12]

TWENTY-THREE

An Unscheduled Train Stop

7:30am, Tuesday, July 14

The raiders forded the Little Miami River at Dungan's Crossing[1] and entered Clermont County. At the top of the embankment, they came upon the Little Miami Railroad. On the tracks, they placed an obstruction, a wedge of cross-ties end on end in a cattle guard.[2] Two years before, Horatio Buckingham had given up his Hamilton County home south of Miamisville when Camp Dennison incorporated his property into their training grounds. He moved north of Miamisville into Clermont County along the railroad line that ran between Loveland and Camp Dennison.[3] Now, hundreds of Confederates were waiting, concealed in a cornfield along the north line of his farm.[4] The raiders had placed a formidable obstruction by filling up a cattle guard with cross-ties, standing end-upward on a curve, so that the engineer could not see it until it was too late to stop the train.[5]

Shortly, a distant whistle alerted them to an approaching train. Aboard its five cars were 150 unarmed recruits heading for Camp Dennison.[6] Among the passengers was a band of musicians from Columbus going to Camp Dennison to join the army.

There were four passenger cars, a baggage-express car, and the locomotive "Kilgore." As the train passed the hidden Confederates, they opened fire. The train's engineer, John T. Redman, increased the speed to forty miles per hour, hoping to outrun the hail of bullets.[7] "The train shot past us like a blazing meteor," wrote Lt. Kelion Peddicord, "and the next thing we saw was a dense cloud of steam about which flew large timbers. Our next sight startled our nerves, for there lay the monster floundering in the field like a fish out of water, with nothing but the tender attached. Her coupling might have broken, for the passenger carriages and express were still on the track, several yards ahead. One hundred and fifty raw recruits were on board, bound for Camp Dennison. They came tumbling and rolling out in every way imaginable."[8]

The train struck the obstruction with great force. The locomotive shot up into the air and overturned killing the fireman, Cornelius Conway, and severely injured the engineer. The passengers were taken prisoner. Morgan paroled them, and together with Conductor W.H. Roberts, the "parolees" marched off to Camp Dennison.[9]

Among the Clermont County claims, The Little Miami, Columbus and Xenia Railroad Co. asked for and was granted $13,700 for the loss of their train. Redman, the injured engineer, made a claim for "Surgeon bills of $90 and Loss of Services resulting from injuries received, in the amount of $1,216," for a total of $1,306. Payment of his claim was refused by the state.[10]

<u>8:00am, Tuesday, July 14</u>

In Loveland, Captain Williamson, who commanded the 116-man Loveland militia, dispatched twenty scouts to reconnoiter along the Little Miami River south of the town.[11] Commanded by Lt. Paxton and Sgt. Ramsey, the Loveland volunteers followed the twisting course of this major tributary that flows all the way to the Ohio River. It also serves as the irregular boundary between Hamilton and Clermont Counties. One of Paxton's relatives, Col. Thomas Paxton, had followed this same river bank, when sixty-eight years earlier, he was the first settler to build a log cabin between the Little Miami and Scioto rivers. He founded the pioneer community called Paxton.[12] Years later, the inhabitants would rename the community Loveland.[13] As Lt. Paxton stared at the sky ahead, he could see wisps of smoke. Could it be a home on fire or a brush fire in the densely forested riverbank? He wondered, "What's burning?"

The scouts picked up their pace and soon came upon the raiders burning the train. They could see that among the baggage car contents, now enveloped in flames, were musical instruments. The Columbus musicians were glad to still be alive and well after the horrible train wreck and only briefly being prisoners of the enemy. They had abandoned their musical instruments, for now it was Confederate booty. They got away with their lives and they would play another day.

Lt. Paxton directed Sergeant Ramsey to take ten men and attack the left flank of the raiding force. Taking cover, he gave orders to begin firing. The sergeant succeeded in shooting one of the raiders in the neck.[14] By Morgan's order, he was carried to Ward's Corner and left to die there.[15] Paxton could see that his small force was greatly outnumbered. He had accomplished his mission, to find the enemy. Quickly, the civilian scouts withdrew and galloped back to Loveland to report the enemy's presence. Captain Williamson asked Loveland residents Henry Hamer and Daniel Lockwood to furnish fresh horses, and he led his militia to harass Morgan's rear guard all the way to Boston, now known as Owensville.[16]

One Loveland militia member was trying to avoid duty. He asked the captain to be excused so he could go home. He said, "I have a necessity to change my breeches." The captain said that once he got home, he was to stay there, "as such a man would demoralize any company."[17]

In Morgan's column, there were several hundred wounded soldiers. Because they were behind enemy lines, the General did not want to abandon his wounded. Unless their wounds were critical, they were placed in wagons and rode with their comrades. Some were left behind with northern families to be cared for and nursed back to health. Like the soldier who died at Ward's Corner, there were many Morgan men who ended their march in a northern grave. It was reported that a Confederate was buried in full military "regalia" in a Miamiville cemetery.

8:30am, Tuesday, July 14

Shortly after Duke's column had crossed the Little Miami River into Clermont County, so did Morgan's column farther to the south. The General followed the river till he met up with Duke. Together, they rode north toward Branch Hill, where they picked up Branch Hill-Guinea Pike and rode southeast. The horsemen easily negotiated the steep path as the road twisted uphill for half a mile from the river valley to the top of the hill. The artillerymen had a more difficult time, as their horses strained to pull the howitzers and Parrotts to the top of the lengthy rise. Just a few hundred feet beyond the crest, the river could no longer be seen, but one could peer across the wide abyss and see the hills of Hamilton County, which they had negotiated earlier that morning. Patches of river fog remained drifting in the air above the Little Miami River Valley.

Morgan came upon Camp Shady, three miles east of Camp Dennison, and the hidden park of seventy-five army wagons. They put a torch to the army cache Col. Neff thought he had safely concealed.[18] It was reported that one of the local men Morgan kidnapped to guide him to Williamsburg was the son of Thomas Paxton and grandson of the first man to settle the area in 1798. At Mt. Repose, Morgan sent a company up the road toward Goshen. The rear guard fought a skirmish with the Tod Scouts, a local militia unit, under the command of Col. Joseph Wheeler.

TWENTY-FOUR

A Romance of Morgan's Rough Riders

<u>10:30am, Tuesday, July 14</u>

One of the men in the company that Morgan dispatched toward Goshen was a Virginia-born trooper named John H. Anderson. On the road that ran from Goshen to Belfast, he and another Confederate stopped at the farm of David Deerwester. Anderson and his traveling partner were hungry and they asked Deerwester's daughter, Catharine, if they could have some food. They followed her into the farmhouse and took seats at the kitchen table. She and her mother did their best, on short notice, to prepare a meal for two weary and hungry, armed and uninvited guests. While they waited for the food, they talked politely to Catharine about her farm and inquired how many horses her family had. Anderson noticed how attractive Catharine was and soon his thoughts were of her, not of food and horses. Catharine noticed the attention, too. John was just over six feet tall. Catharine was about five foot five.

By the time they had finished their meal and rose to leave, Anderson blurted out a promise, "I'll be back after the war and I'm going to marry you!" Checking the list of people who made claims after the raid, Catharine's father, D. Deerwester, was not among them. It would seem that John Anderson changed his mind about taking any horses from Catharine's farm. He probably was anxious not to make a bad impression on his future bride and father-in-law. True to his word, he returned and married Catharine on November 8, 1866. John Ringer, Justice of the Peace, united them as husband and wife. They had six children: four sons (Albert, John, David Daniel and Charles) and two daughters (Sarah and Elizabeth).[1]

This was not an isolated case. There were other Morgan men who returned after the conflict to marry Northern girls they met on the raid. In Dupont, Indiana, Josephine Mayfield had cursed the raiders for stealing thousands of her father's hams. One of the Confederates, nineteen-year-old Harry H. Snook, replied, "You sure are purty, Ma'am when you're in a temper. After we lick you Yanks, I'll come back and marry you."[7] He kept his word. Another romance blossomed when a Confederate prisoner was taken to the jail in Zanesville. He spied an Ohio beauty and tied the knot after the hostilities ceased.

Private Joe Williams, Co. K, 10th KY, was severely wounded in Ohio. He was carried into a home, bleeding badly. At first the ladies of the house protested that their floors and carpets would be ruined. His comrades left hurriedly, saying that Joe's mother was a woman of means and would amply repay them for any care and attention they would give her beloved son. After the war, Joe returned to marry one of the daughters who had nursed him kindly. His gratitude was great, and his affection for her became so strong that he wanted her to become Mrs. Williams.[2]

12:30pm, Tuesday, July 14

Most of Morgan's men headed south down the pike toward Boston (Owensville). The road they were traveling was a great scar, running through rich fields of corn or meadows lush with summer hay. Morgan's cavalrymen were drained of strength. The sky was unmarred by clouds, the merciless sun beat upon the raiders, making them feel, one soldier remembered years later, as if they were being broiled over embers. They were caked with dust and sweat, their faces cracked and bleeding. Many of the homes they passed were empty of men because they had been called to Cincinnati for training to defend the city against an attack from Morgan. The women watched from door stoops, fear on some of their faces, hatred on others. They were not disturbed by the raiders. Many of Morgan's men were too weary to eat, too wretched to leave the road and ride a few feet into a farmyard for food or water.[3]

In a letter from Boston, dated July 29, 1863, fifteen days after the raid, a young lady who signed her letter "Irene" wrote,

> Two rebels rode up to us at the gate and asked, "If we had seen anything of Morgan?" My sister, Anne, told them "No." Then they inquired if they could have some food and feed their horses. One said he would like some coffee but tea was already brewed. In they came and ate very polite.
>
> But they were the hardest looking men I ever saw. They had U.S. belts and guns. One asked for their bill. Anne told him, as payment, to "catch Morgan." He looked pretty grave but said nothing. We pretended we thought they were Union and they let us think so. Later, we heard that Morgan took every horse out of town and along the road where he went and made women bring out bread, pies and cakes for them as they were in too much of a hurry to dismount. They took some local men to pilot them.

<u>1:00pm, Tuesday, July 14</u>

The roads leading to Boston had been twisting and hilly. At places, mature trees arched over the roads, offering shade from the burning sun. At some points in the road, care had to be taken with the artillery carriages and limbers, not to go off the edge of the narrow dirt roads. At some points, the roads dropped off steeply one hundred feet or more. On the other side of Boston, the land was flat and the roads were straight. Fertile farmland and untouched meadows stretched to the horizon. Lines of dense trees defined the borders of one farm from another. Everything was green and in full bloom. It was another hot and humid July afternoon, with no cooling rain in sight. The morning coolness was now only a memory.

Riding along in the rear guard of Morgan's long column, Col. Duke spotted several of his cavalrymen standing beside a home where a table had been placed in the yard. As he rode up, he saw that freshly baked pies covered the table. Duke admitted, "I have always been fond of pies." His men were hesitating, looking but not eating. "What's the problem? Don't the pies taste any good?" Duke inquired. One of the troopers answered, "We haven't tasted them yet. They could be poisoned." "Here, hand me one," Duke commanded. Reaching down from his saddle, a trooper handed one up to him. He took a mouthful, relishing the sweet fruit flavor of the still warm apple pie. Eyeing their commander for two or three minutes and seeing that he was suffering no ill effects, the half-dozen pies found quick-takers and soon only a few crumbs remained of the peace-offering.[4] Food, placed on tables outside of the home, was a tactic used by many housewives hoping to pacify the raiders' hunger and keep them from entering their homes looking for food.

<u>2:30pm, July 14</u>

At a fork in the road where a brick home stood, Morgan sent a company to Batavia, which was southwest, while his main force continued toward Williamsburg. It was a common practice for Morgan to split off a company of men to have them take one road while he took another. Later they would reunite at a distant crossroads. This gave his men a better opportunity to forage for food, fresh horses and booty. And his force could inflict a wider swath of damage and destruction on Northern supply points. As a guerrilla fighter, he didn't always feel the need to have large numbers of men. Under his skilled leadership, a few good men could cause great damage to targets behind enemy lines.[5] On some previous raids, Morgan would disguise himself as a farmer or drover and enter Federal lines to seek accurate information about the enemy.[6] Once, he masqueraded as a Union officer wearing a blue U.S. overcoat over his uniform. Riding alone, he approached a group of Northern soldiers. With bravado, he placed himself in command of the Yankee group and led them into an ambush to be captured.

A contingent of Confederates rode into Batavia and set up pickets at each end of the main street (Rt. 32). The Batavia bus was coming up from Cincinnati with passengers and the mail.[7] During the Civil War, a "bus" was a stagecoach-type wagon drawn by horses. It traveled about six miles an hour, depending on the road. Passengers, thankful they didn't have to ride a horse, paid ten cents a mile. Inside, it seated ten passengers, five deep and two abreast. Additional commuters could sit on the bus' roof with the mail sacks. On top, there was precarious space (no seat belts) for another six riders.

Sitting outside the carriage in the driver's seat and holding the reins was Whig Holloman. He had been warned that the town was in the hands of the Confederates.[8] But Whig felt duty-bound to deliver his passengers and the mail. He drove into town with his four-horse "omnibus" and parked in front of the village tavern.[9] Immediately, the raiders took the mail sacks and began searching for cash. Others took hold of the six horses and began unhitching them. Before he knew it, Whig was out of business. Tears filled his eyes as his horses were led away.[10] Whig wasn't the only Batavian to lose his horses. Claims were made that Morgan's men left town with fifty-seven of the area's horses.[11]

On the outskirts of town, a Batavia farmer by the name of Solomon Mershon went into his barn to find his two horses missing. Suspecting that the Confederates had taken them, he angrily went into town where the Confederates were congregating and began searching for his farm animals. Finding one, he challenged the stalwart man in gray who was riding it. The dispute became quite heated. Other "Johnnies," observing the confrontation, suggested that the rights to the horse could be settled by an honorable, fair fight. A space was cleared among the one hundred amused Confederates. As the word was given, and according to the rules agreed upon, they began to pound each other. The Confederate was forced to quit, whereupon Mershon mounted his steed and rode away to round after round of "rebel yells." Protected by a strong sense of Southern honor and American humor, the horse and Mershon were left unmolested.[12]

Beyond Batavia, the company of Morgan's men entered a plank road, which magnified the sounds of the passing column. Iron shoes clumped rhythmically on the dry wood, trace chains jangled and axles squealed and groaned. Men riding in wagons experienced the washboard effect created from the bouncing ride that no springs could soften.[13]

Just south of Batavia is the small community of Bantam in Tate Township. A Bantam farmer was called up to duty by his home guard regiment. He took his squirrel hunter's rifle, a blanket and two days' cooked rations. Before leaving, he told a neighbor that he had hidden his life savings in a springhouse near the East Fork of the Little Miami River. In the ensuing action, he was killed and his fortune has never been discovered.

In another community near Williamsburg called Clover, Hermon Stone got together with three of his cronies and decided to bushwhack Morgan. The armed quartet set off in a covered wagon. They traveled toward Williamsburg over today's Ohio Rt. 133. As they reached the dip where the road meets today's S.R. 32, one of Morgan's scouts topped the rise and spying the horse-drawn wagon, whipped out his revolver. At the sight of the Colt 44, the Clover contingent hightailed it out of the rear of the wagon, leaving it as bounty for the raiders.[14]

TWENTY-FIVE

Williamsburg, the First Good Rest in Weeks

<u>4:00pm, Tuesday, July 14</u>

Morgan's advance guard rode into Williamsburg, which at that time had about 2,000 inhabitants.[1] Over the next two hours, the remainder of his force converged on Clermont County's largest town. Most rode down today's Rt. 276, a straight shot from Boston (Owensville). The remnants of the company from Goshen continued to raid homes as they passed about three miles east of Boston. Morgan set up his headquarters on the northeast corner of Third and Main streets in the village tavern, Kain House,[2] whose proprietor, John Wesley Kain, had a livery and stable connected to the house. Morgan decided his men could pause and get their first good night's rest in weeks. Basil Duke, in his book, indicated that this overnight rest at Williamsburg was the best they had since leaving Tennessee. He wrote, "Feeling comparatively safe here, General Morgan permitted the division to go into camp and remain during the night."[3] They had ridden ninety-five miles from Sunmansville, Indiana to Williamsburg in thirty-five hours. It ranks as the war's longest, most continuous march made by so large a body of cavalry. Duke said it was "the greatest march that even Morgan had ever made."[4]

In other towns, he had problems with his men breaking into stores that sold liquor. He couldn't afford to let them get drunk and pass out. The enemy was too close behind. Everyone had to stay sober and keep their wits. By setting up his headquarters in the town's tavern, he could keep his eye on the liquor supply. But the General did order 136 meals from Mr. Kain.[5] Morgan preferred sleeping in hotels rather than joining his men in field tents. So that night, he and six of his officers slept in soft beds on the second floor of Kain's hotel adjoining the tavern. Built in 1816, Kain's House & Tavern was torn down in 1907.[6]

<u>7:00pm, July 14</u>

Morgan made sure his men were getting the food they needed and fodder for their horses. Some of his force was camped on the Bethel Road from the bridge to the hill, part in the town and part on the roads to Boston and Batavia. He ordered his men to turn their horses in to the grain fields on the edge of town so they could feed during the night. Then he took a look around Williamsburg. He came to the home of the town's leading citizen, John Lytle,[7] brother of General William Lytle. Before the town was named Williamsburg, it was called Lytlestown.[8]

On the doorsill of Lytle's Main Street homestead, he carved with his saber, "John Morgan, July 14, 1863, 3000 men."[9] He impressed upon Mr. Lytle to advise any Union army soldiers in the area to get out of town. "If they come near us or give us any trouble, we will burn your town down," the General admonished.

When Morgan entered Kentucky on July 2, he had about 2,500 troops. By the time he crossed the Ohio River into Indiana, he had 2,200. When he entered Ohio on July 13 at Harrison, his men numbered just under 2,000. Reaching Williamsburg, he was down to 1,900. But for some unknown reason, he etched "3,000" men into the stone. *Today, that doorstep has been preserved and can be viewed by the public. It is set at curbside, directly across the street from the old high school on Main Street in Williamsburg.*

9:30pm, Tuesday, July 14

General Hobson's forces, on the heels of Morgan's column, encamped at Newberry, fifteen miles from Williamsburg, to feed and rest his troops and animals.[10]

In sharp contrast to the devotion and loyalty Morgan's cavalrymen exhibited to their leader, Capt. George Harris, an officer of Morgan's artillery, turned his back on his commander in Williamsburg. Harris' father was a paymaster in the U.S. Navy and a friend of General Burnside's. Young Harris yearned to be restored to his father and renounce the Confederate service. Before the outbreak of the war, he was attending State University at Nashville. He became a lieutenant of the cadet corps and was ordered to guard state buildings. He and his corps were swept up by the Confederacy and fought for the South at Corinth and Shiloh.

Eventually, his artillery battery commanded by Captain E.P. Byrne had fought at Shiloh, was detached and joined Morgan. He experienced Morgan's exciting raids causing destruction on the Union's wealth and strength. Alone with his own unhappiness, he thought of his father and prayed that fate would allow him to be reunited with his dad and end his participation in the rebellion. Williamsburg gave him that opportunity. He wanted to tell his tale to General Burnside and be permitted to atone his Confederate service.

Being camped overnight so close to Cincinnati, where Burnside had his headquarters, was Harris' best chance to get away and seek the protection of the Union general. George met twenty-year-old Byron Williams on the street and engaged him in conversation. He told him he would leave the Confederate service if he could do it without being caught. Williams secreted Harris in the garret of his father's two-story brick residence at the northwest corner of Gay and Front streets (112 Gay St.). That night, three of Morgan's officers, Captain Dan E. Ray, Chaplain Moore and Captain Henry Hines, all slept in the Williams' bedrooms directly below the attic where Harris was hiding. Before retiring, they had joined the Williams family at the supper table where "Parson" Moore gave a blessing before the meal.[11]

After Morgan's men left town without him, and Hobson's men rode through, a Union officer was sent back to arrest the Confederate soldier who was supposed to be there. Captain William Ulrey, a native of Boston (Ownensville), had reported that such a man was there. Hobson's squad returned to Williamsburg to look for Harris. As the Union soldiers passed Williams and Harris on the street, Williams introduced Harris as an old college chum who was visiting him during vacation.

The second night, Harris hid in the cornfield. The next day, Harris dressed himself in a neat, plain black suit that he had taken out of an Indiana store. Dr. S.S. Walker and Frank A. Warden accompanied him to General Burnside. The General allowed him to take the oath of allegiance to his father's flag. His father sent him abroad because of failing health, hoping it could be restored in the peaceful English countryside. But George died at sea, in sight of land a few months after the Ohio raid. He was buried in a churchyard near London.[12]

3:00am, Wednesday, July 15

Reveille was sounded at three o'clock in the morning, almost simultaneously, in both Morgan's and Hobson's camps. Hobson's forces stirred and rode out, while Morgan prepared to leave Williamsburg. By eight o'clock, Morgan's rear guard had crossed the wooden bridge that spanned the East Fork of the Little Miami and burned it.[13] There was no need to destroy the bridge because the East Fork of the Little Miami, at that time, was virtually dry. As Morgan left town, he impressed into service a guide who led them out the plank road toward Mt. Orab and Sardinia.

Hobson, too, requested guidance from a local who took him first to Batavia, arriving there at nine o'clock. Hobson learned he had been taken the long way, which was five miles out of his way. It further delayed his troops.[14] At this point, he realized that he was being slowed by his artillery and had need to obtain fresh horses, which he found to be a near impossibility. He decided to split his command in two. He assigned Col. August V. Kautz to advance with his brigade composed of the 2nd and 7th OH Cavalry. Behind Kautz came Col. W.P. Sanders who had just reported on the morning of July 14 leading the 8th and 9th MI Cavalry Regiments and one section of the 11th MI Battery.[15] Kautz moved out quickly with 400 men and advanced toward Winchester, arriving there six hours ahead of Hobson's main force.

Hobson's forces, now totaling about 3,000 mounted infantry and artillery, arrived in Williamsburg about one o'clock in the afternoon. They simply rode around the burnt Williamsburg bridge and continued after Morgan. They stopped only long enough to partake of the cooked food that had been provided liberally by the ladies of Williamsburg. A buffet had been set up outside on tables along the main street.[16] Long boards were laid across barrels and boxes, and were laden with a wide variety of foods and beverages. Buckeye belles were to match the Hoosier housewives in preparing generous spreads for the boys in blue.

A member of Hobson's artillery, Samuel Hayford of Indiana, was riding atop a limber wagon. He reached down and accepted a cup of coffee proffered by a Williamsburg miss. After drinking it, he stepped down to return the empty cup. In trying to get on again, he missed his footing and fell under the wheels. In critical condition, he was carried to an office room at Third and Main, where he died that night. He was buried in the village cemetery.[17]

TWENTY-SIX

Mayor Leads Cincinnati Cavalry

Two days earlier, a brave Len A. Harris, mayor of Cincinnati, made an offer to General Burnside which was reported in the early morning issue (July 14) of the *Daily Cincinnati Enquirer:*[1]

CITIZENS: I have said to the General commanding this department that three thousand mounted men could be obtained in this county [Hamilton] to pursue Morgan. He has given me the opportunity to try the experiment. Will you respond to the call? If so, let all who will join in the undertaking and can procure a horse, report at my office this morning with two day's rations. You will be organized and armed at once, and will march today. I will go with you. Experienced officers are ready to lead you. Officers not now in service who have a fancy to take the trip after Morgan, will please report to me at my office, at eight o'clock this morning.

Answering the mayor's call to form *the Cincinnati Cavalry*, 480 "cavalry troops" with 120 horses and one thousand infantry reported for duty. Their commander, "Colonel" Harris, the Mayor, was preparing to give chase when General Henry Judah arrived Tuesday morning by steamboat with a force of cavalry from Louisville. The only problem was that they had left many of their jaded horses behind at the Falls City (Louisville). Judah, in need of 500 fresh mounts, demanded that the *Cincinnati Cavalry* give up theirs to his men. General Burnside accommodated him.[2] About the only order the *Cincinnati Cavalry* Colonel was able to issue was "Dismount, go home and leave your horses behind."

The short-lived effort, though, was graciously recognized by General A. Burnside when he lifted martial law after six o'clock, the evening of Thursday, July 16. The newspaper's issue of that date reported:[3]

He [General Burnside] desires to express his sense of obligation to the Mayor of the city, and the officers and men of the independent battalion, for the energetic zeal manifested by them in organizing and tendering their services of that body of troops. He deeply

> regrets that the necessity of using all the horses and cavalry arms
> and equipment in his hands, for the use of the United States troops
> in motion [led by General Judah], prevented his arming and equip-
> ping the battalion for immediate service. Nothing but the lack of
> horses and equipment would have prevented his accepting their
> very handsome offer.

The *Daily Cincinnati Enquirer* also reported, "About one hundred
Rebel prisoners from Kentucky, and of Morgan's gang in Ohio, were brought
to the city, yesterday, and lodged in the military prisons." Another report on
July 14 stated that "Thirty-three of Morgan's men were captured at different
points yesterday, and brought to this city, and confined in the military prison.
The greater portion were captured at Glendale, the balance at different places
along the country roads. General Morgan's Assistant Adjutant General,
Colonel Alston, was captured at Lebanon [Kentucky], yesterday, and
brought to this city and confined in the military prison on Columbia street."[4]
Colonel R.A. Alston was captured the evening of July 5 on the road from
Lebanon to Bardstown, together with an escort of twenty men by Lt. Ladd
of the 9th MI Cavalry.[5]

General Burnside thanked the 3,490 men who had volunteered for the
Independent Volunteer Companies to defend Cincinnati. He told them to
"continue on duty and report as heretofore to General Matthews, until
relieved and discharged by regular order."

Burnside also recognized and showed his appreciation to Hoosier volunteers in this published dispatch.[6]

> To the volunteer troops of Indiana, who have patriotically and
> promptly marched at the call of their civil authorities, great praise
> is due; and the General commanding [Burnside] returns his thanks
> for their assistance both to them and the Governor of that State
> [Morton], by whose order they were assembled and organized.

As Morgan's vanguard blazed across Cincinnati, the Queen City's populace had been stirred out of their apathy. Fighting spirits erupted and many
clamored to go after the enemy. Men sought to join volunteer militia. A typical newspaper article read[7]:

> BOHEMIAN SCOUTS—Captain J.F. Hruby, who has seen service
> during this war, is raising a volunteer militia company, and invites
> young men who wish to enroll their names in a volunteer company

to call at his headquarters, at the drug store, south-west corner of Fifth and Vine streets. Only a few men wanted to fill the company to the maximum number.

At the same time Morgan was terrifying the Queen City, the Horn & Newcomb Minstrel show was preparing to open at the Smith & Ditson Hall in downtown Cincinnati. The article in the *Daily Cincinnati Enquirer* reported, "They have been anxiously looked for, for some time, and their advent will give relief to the stern excitement which has for days gripped our warlike citizens. Horn & Newcomb have just fulfilled a most profitable and triumphant engagement in St. Louis. The cry will be 'still they come'—not Morgan and his raiders – but the 'unterrified,' to witness their performances, and enjoy a hearty laugh. 'Tis well, some of our citizens have lost flesh in learning the drill in this heated town, and now they may laugh and grow fat again."[8]

Leaving Williamsburg, Morgan's goal was to reach Buffington Island where he hoped to cross into West Virginia and safety. Just three weeks earlier, on June 20, West Virginia had entered the Union, carving itself out of the northwestern counties of Virginia. As far back as August 1861, the citizens living in the western hills of Virginia had passed ordinances to create a new state of Kanawha with its capital at Wheeling.[9]

Back in Indiana, Governor Morton, a Republican, was being attacked by the Democrat's paper, the *Indianapolis Sentinel*. The newspaper criticized the governor for poor judgment in his offer of Indiana troops to help chase Morgan through Ohio, whose people "manifested no sympathy [for] us, instead of sending them [Indiana troops] home to take care of their crops."[10]

In reaction to this criticism, Morton sent a telegram to General Burnside.

(Telegram)   Indianapolis, *July* 15, 1863.
General Burnside:
The Indiana troops now in Ohio are composed almost entirely of farmers and business men, and their presence at home is much needed. I hope you will relieve them from duty as soon as it is consistent with public safety.[11]

> O.P. MORTON,
> *Governor of Indiana.*

Burnside immediately acknowledged Morton's telegram and told him, "I will order transportation for all Indiana troops at an early hour to-morrow morning."[12] The commander of the Army of the Ohio also contacted General

O.B. Willcox in Indianapolis and told him to let the militia of Indiana be allowed to return to their homes as well, in accordance with Governor Morton's wishes. "I am satisfied that their services will no longer be needed in this emergency, and their interests at home need looking after," Burnside concluded.[13] Now that Morgan's men were wholly within Ohio, it was up to the Buckeye volunteers and the pursuing regulars to slow down and capture the Confederate Thunderbolt.

Most of the Indiana militia which had followed Morgan into Ohio and around Cincinnati, gave up its chase and returned to their homes. Some regular Indiana cavalry units committed themselves to remaining with Hobson's force until Morgan was captured The Tod Scouts had returned to the Cincinnati area on Wednesday.[14] By this time, Burnside realized that Cincinnati was out of danger.

About twelve days earlier, General Judah had been trapped at the flooded Green River in Kentucky for thirty-six hours. He had marched to Leitchfield,[15] thinking that Morgan would retreat. Morgan didn't. Judah guessed wrong. He was so far behind Morgan's column, he decided to give up the direct pursuit and return to General Burnside's headquarters in Cincinnati. On the morning of July 9, Judah marched his force, with haste, back to Elizabethtown, where men and horses were loaded on trains and carried to Louisville. There cars were exchanged for steamboats.[16] On the morning of July 14, they arrived at the Cincinnati wharf. His forces consisted of the 111th OH, 5th IN, 11th KY Cavalry, 23rd MI and 107th IL Mounted Infantry, two sections of artillery and four mountain howitzers.

Burnside held General Judah's forces in Cincinnati to help in its defense should Morgan attack. He now dispatched Judah and an entire division, including horses and artillery, by boat with instructions that they should land at any point on the Ohio River that they felt they may contact Morgan on his way to recross the river. Judah's flotilla was made up of his flagship, *The Bostona* and nine others. They included *The Scioto, Undine, Swallow, Saline, Bostona #2, Fisher, Emma #2, Wren* and *Silver Moon.*[17] As the fleet steamed up the Ohio River towards Buffington Island, boats were dispatched from the *Bostona*, the headquarters' steamer, every few hours to get reports of scouts and citizens on the movements and whereabouts of Morgan.

After Morgan had passed around the city and no uprising or riot developed, Major George Rue met with Burnside and gave him his opinion that no troops following Morgan would be able to capture him. He suggested that he be allowed to go by train to get in front of Morgan.[18]

Three days later, Burnside came to the same conclusion and ordered Rue to take his best men and horses, arm them as needed, and proceed by train to Bellaire in Belmont County across the river from Wheeling, West Virginia.[19] Three trains were used. One for the men, one for horses, and one for the three pieces of artillery from the 15th IN Battery under Lieutenant Tarr. They boarded at the Little Miami depot and rode to Columbus which they reached Friday morning, July 17. Major Rue, leading the 9th KY was joined by a detachment of the 8th MI under Lieutenant N.S. Boynton. All together, they totaled 325 cavalry men.

BROWN COUNTY, OH

TWENTY-SEVEN

Colonel Morgan Visits Georgetown

General Morgan left Williamsburg in Clermont County and led his force as it rode into Ohio's Appalachian country. For the next twelve days, he would ride through nineteen of the twenty-nine Appalachian counties in the southern and eastern sections of the state. Beyond Williamsburg, Morgan again split his forces into two columns. His brother, Col. Richard Morgan, led his 14th KY regiment on a southern route, passing through Bethel, Georgetown and on toward the Ohio river town of Ripley.[1]

<u>9:15am, Wednesday, July 15</u>

Col. Richard Morgan's men entered Georgetown following the Georgetown-New Hope Road. There was little opposition because most of the armed men had gone to Ripley after having been told that Morgan would probably try to make a crossing there.

As the Confederates passed the Brown County courthouse, they stopped at the home and shop of Henry Brunner, the town's cobbler. Mr. and Mrs. Brunner had moved into their new residence on Apple Street just three months earlier. It was in the center of a row of similar attached homes. There were two smaller rooms in the rear south wall, which served as living quarters. A hallway divided them from the long room in front, which was the cobbler shop. The bedrooms were upstairs. Coal stoves were used to heat the home. But on this hot July day, the stoves stood idle and the windows were open to catch any breeze.

Many of the Confederate riders stopped and asked Mr. Brunner to repair their boots and shoes. He did so, without quarrel, as long as his supplies lasted. Meanwhile, the raiders asked Mrs. Brunner to feed as many as she could. In appreciation of their hospitality and cobbler services, the Confederates allowed the Brunners to keep their two horses in the barn behind the home. Other area residents were not as fortunate, and lost their horses to the marauding bands. The raiders also missed the bucket of good silverware which the Brunners had lowered into their well, despite the fact that the Confederates had drawn many buckets of water from the same well.[2]

Hiding his valuables was foremost on the mind of the town's only banker, F.J. Phillips. His was a privately owned bank that was uninsured. The King-Phillips Bank had $60,000 in gold coins, which Mr. Phillips placed in bags. He entrusted this princely sum to a servant who had worked for the Phillips family for many years and served as the bank's janitor as well. Mr. Phillips instructed him to take the money to a dense woods, which was located on the east side of the Free Soil Road, close to the premises owned by Mr. Ellis, the county surveyor. There, he was told to bury it.

When the Confederates swept through Georgetown, they picked up a black man claiming he was an escaped slave. He was never seen again in the town. Mr. Phillips and other townspeople did a considerable amount of digging and excavation, searching for the bank's hoard, but to no avail. The money was never found. In the 1870s, there was a depression throughout the United States that caused a financial panic. Large withdrawals were made from all financial institutions, including the King-Phillips Bank. These withdrawals, combined with the $60,000 gold-coin loss, forced the bank to cease business and close its doors. The bank's losses resulted in several suicides of prominent individuals and businessmen of Georgetown.

Five years after the war, a black couple of the same name as the missing elderly black man came to Georgetown. They were seen around the area for several days. When they first walked into the village, they seemed to have no visible means. Yet, when they left, they had sufficient money to buy a team of horses and a surrey, which they paid for with gold coins.[3]

Colonel Richard Morgan's command headed south toward Ripley, crossing Straight Creek, Washburn Run and Redoak Creek. At Ripley, Morgan's men investigated the possibility of recrossing the Ohio River. But scouts reported to Col. Morgan that they observed a heavy concentration of militia around the river town.

(Telegram)   July 14, 1863.

General White, *Catlettsburg:*

Morgan is making for the Ohio River, near Ripley. He may be kept from crossing by the gunboats, and he may go above to cross. General Hobson is but 10 miles in his rear with a large cavalry force. They both camped in Clermont County, Ohio, last night. We hope to catch him.

A.E. BURNSIDE
Major-General.[4]

Dick Morgan could see the gunboats offshore. On board one of the tin-clads was Brigadier-General Mahlon D. Manson. On July 15, Manson reported from Maysville that Morgan's troops had been seen five miles from Ripley at noon. Fifty minutes later, Gen. Manson reported that the Confederates were within a mile of Ripley. The Ohio River was deep at this point. Col. Morgan and his brothers had been assured that these gunboats would not be able to navigate the shallow stretch around Buffington Island. Realizing that a river crossing at this point was hopeless, the Colonel turned his troops northeast. Later, General Manson reported Morgan was seven miles north of West Union at North Liberty.[5]

In the same area, the raiders approached Eckmansville from the southwest. A local physician, Dr. Van Meter, took a shot at the oncoming Confederate cavalry. After firing his weapon, the doctor hid from view. Another resident of the hamlet, William Johnston, happened to be in the same vicinity. The raiders, seeing no one else in the area, determined that Johnston was their aggressor. They summarily fired, killing him on the spot. When they discovered their mistake, they threatened the citizens of Eckmansville, telling them their homes would be burned if they did not identify who had fired among them. The Reverend David McDill, pastor of the Cherry Fork United Presbyterian Church, was accused by the raiders of knowing who the culprit was and where he was hiding. The reverend refused to divulge any information. When Dick Morgan's men realized he was not going to talk despite their threats, McDill was released unharmed the next day.

The inscription on Johnston's tombstone in the Cherry Fork Cemetery reads, "WILLIAM JOHNSTON came to his death by a ball in the head, fired by a rebel guerrilla, in the Village of Eckmansville July 15, 1863. Aged about 60 years."[6]

Heading for West Union, they passed through Taylorsville in Huntington Township. They stopped at James Madison Stafford's blacksmith shop on Pike Street to have him shoe all their horses. Being the only smith in the small town, he was under intense pressure to do the job quickly, so that Colonel Morgan's force could resume their journey. A piece of hot iron chipped off and fell down into Stafford's boot. He complained of the heat, but his plea to stop fell on deaf ears. The raiders' menacing gestures convinced him that a burn was better than a bullet. The raiders must have sensed how closely they were being followed because no sooner had Morgan and his men left, than Union troops followed right on their heels. James Stafford was exhausted and his leg ached. But he was so mad at the Confederates, he welcomed the boys in blue and worked until he had shod all the Union soldiers' horses as well. His rage overcame his pain. The sore that resulted never healed but the wound bothered him until the day he died.[7]

Reaching West Union after dark, Col. Richard Morgan camped for the night. Among Hobson's forces that followed Col. Morgan through West Union was seventeen-year-old Private John A. Cockerill. His father, Col. Joseph Cockerill, 70th OVI, was a native of West Union. Son, John, had enlisted as a drummer in the 24th OVI regimental band. But a War Department order of September 10, 1862, abolishing regimental bands, knocked Pvt. Cockerill out of the war, but only briefly. He reenlisted as a bugler. He was soon to find himself carrying a musket and chasing after Morgan through Adams County, Ohio. As he followed the Confederates through his hometown of West Union, he stopped for a hurried meeting with his mother and sisters.[8]

A letter dated July 15, 1863, from a daughter living in West Union to her mother, is an eyewitness account of the Confederates' movement through the area closely pursued by Union cavalrymen. Her estimates of the size of these forces were greatly exaggerated. Morgan's force, she said, numbered 6,000, while the Union pursuers were 8,000. At that point in the raid, Morgan had 2,000 and Hobson's forces were about 3,000.

Dearest Mother:

The Rebels are upon us, they say! The people have gathered hastily. New rumors come every hour. One lady has fainted on the pavement, up street, a little later and she springs on her horse and dashes away to the country. Here goes a wagon-load of hastily-packed goods, to be hid out of town, for the Rebels want only horses, goods and money. People are hiding money and other valuables. I have put up my sewing "for good" now, the men have taken their guns and gone out to the roads by which the Rebels are expected to enter town to "Bushwhack." There are thousands of Rebels, what can 100 men do against them?

They are nailing the shutters downstairs. We've all put on such clothes as we'd wish to wear away in case they burn the town, and filled satchels with such things as must be saved. Here comes Laura with one of the pictures that hung on the parlor wall; it must be saved, for "we are afraid he might be killed out there." And so it is.

Later evening [15th]: We have been waiting for hours—yet nothing definite is known. Just this, the Rebels are only 7 miles away, therefore, we expect them. We have sent our men some supper. It is almost dark. Someone coming from the place where the enemy is camped, says they intend to camp in West Union tonight. Every woman has her pocket and bosom full of money, jewelry and watches. Some hid their bread in the tall weeds in the garden, also bed-clothes, etc.

Dark! The men have come back from the woods, a wise move on their part.

July 16th. We slept secure last night. The Provost Marshal and Captain O slept out in the woods among the hills, for fear they should be taken prisoners and paroled. The news! The news! Morgan with about 6000 men passed through Russellville (3 or 4 miles from Aunt's) captured our mail boy and hack and tore up our mail out about Winchester somewhere, went on through Jackson and out toward Portsmouth, taking horses, money, whiskey and bed-clothes. But Lo and Behold, only four hours behind comes Burnside with about 8000 cavalrymen, treading upon the very heels of the Rebel Morgan!! There may be a tremendous battle before they get out of Adams County.

Morgan must be caught now—Burnside's Army have followed him from Tennessee and it will be a hard thing for him to escape; a line of gunboats moves along the Ohio, with thousands of soldiers to keep the Rebel horde from crossing the River, and couriers are constantly passing from our Army to them [the gunboats] with orders which way to move.

Evening [16th]: We are feeding 141 [Hobson's] cavalrymen. I have gathered one basketfull of bread and butter and meat—everybody is bringing something. I came toiling in from a cross street with my basket load in one hand and a dish of pickles in the other. Laura is waiting for me with a big pan of bread, butter and pie, and such a nice plate of fried steak. One soldier leans over with his plate, on horseback, asking for a dinner for just four.' I fill his plate with my fingers and away he goes. They feed their horses on the pavement. These men are from Georgetown and Ripley. At last they dash away, a whole street full—to overtake our Army. Just to think! Both these tremendous armies have been within 7 miles of us, and so close together!

Friday morning, 17th. Frank came home at 2 o'clock this morning. He says he never saw such a dirty, ragged set of men as Burnside's—thinks he saw about 4 miles of the Army, and that the whole Army was strung out 15 miles in length. Oh, success go with our soldiers, now that they are so near, may they strike one good blow!

Well, we'll take time to calm down now. I shall go from here next week. Don't know whether to Winchester or Brown Co yet. We are all well. Hoping to hear from you soon. I am,

Yours affectionately, Lena[9]

TWENTY-EIGHT

Beeline for Buffington

General Morgan was convinced that his best chance to cross the Ohio River would be at Buffington Island. There, he was told, the river would be only about two feet deep, too shallow for the Union gunboats. On July 17, the *Daily Cincinnati Enquirer* reported that the Ohio River was only thirty inches deep at Buffington. Even if a boat was able to make it through, it wouldn't be able to maneuver too well. Morgan felt that with his Parrotts, he would put a couple of shells through its hull and sink her. His best route would be a straight line across the State of Ohio to the Buffington bar and escape.

His choice was the northern passage through Mt. Oreb [Orab], White Oak, Sardinia, Fincastle and Winchester, burning every bridge he could to slow Hobson's pursuit. His path, almost due east, followed the Appalachian Highway which, today, closely parallels S.R. 32.

One resident of Sardinia was unaware of Morgan's tactics. Anxious that Morgan not get his cash, he went to the nearby covered bridge over the East Fork, White Oak Creek just west of Sardinia near where Hamer Road meets today's Old S.R. 32. There in the upper rafters he hid his money. In the high, dark shadows, he confidently assured himself that no one would ever see it. The bridge was about 115 feet long. It had been built five years earlier in 1858 by John and Edward Boyle, bridge builders from Fayetteville. When the raiders came through the area, they did little damage—except for the bridge. They burned it.[1] The Confederates would burn a second covered bridge. It was 115 feet long over the North Fork at White Oak Station. The two bridges each cost more than $1,800 to rebuild.[2]

Heading for Sardinia was John Porter, a young lad nine-years-old. His dad, John W. Porter, had sent him with a bag of wheat to a mill near Sardinia. John rode from his family farm in Mowrystown in Highland County, to the Brown County mill just five miles away. After the grain had been milled into flour, he began his return trip through a deep woods. He came to a crossing that required him to remove some rails. As he was clearing his path, he heard the sounds of Morgan's men close by. In his haste to ride away quickly, his sack dropped from the horse's back. Later that night, his father retraced his path in search of the sack of flour and found it. Alerted to the

Confederates' close proximity, he hid his horses in the woods. The raiders did not come to their home, but they could hear them in their camp.[3]

On the Neal farm between Yankeetown and Cloverlick Creek, the family was warned by riders that Morgan's men were headed their way. The Neal family hid their horses in the big woods, while many men who lived in the area crouched in the tall corn that was flourishing along the creek. Bedding and clothing were concealed among the gooseberry bushes quite a distance from the house. The women stayed with their clothing and bedding. Every time they heard hoof beats, they would shudder at the thought "Here they come!" But it always turned out to be some friendly neighbor or another messenger. So it went all night long, but no raiders materialized. Later they learned that Morgan's main column passed to the north of them.[4]

To the north along today's S.R. 32, General Morgan's column was approaching the Adams County line. Less than three miles from the main road was the Fincastle farm of Joshua and Mary Carey. Joshua was away serving in the home guard. His wife, Mary, was at home with her children, Rudolph, Bill, Sallie and Catherine. Her father-in-law, Isaac Carey, who lived on the adjoining farm, rode up to warn her that Morgan's men were heading her way. She had just finished baking bread. She wrapped the loaves in towels and hid them under bolster pillows on the spare bed. Isaac took the horses into the woods to hide them. All the available men in Fincastle assembled in the small village. A contingent of Morgan's men reached the brow of the hill overlooking the town. Below, they could see men milling about in the streets, but it was too far to make an accurate assessment of the force. An elderly black man told the raiders, "They got the militia down there awaitin'." Morgan decided to avoid Fincastle. The Confederates turned around and went back to the crossroads and headed east for Winchester.[5]

The raiders were amazed to see the large number of able-bodied Union men who were not, as yet, in uniform and were available to be called up as reserves. This contrasted with the South, which had drained every adult male to fill its armies; for most Confederates who fell, there were few able-bodied men to take their place. Basil Duke wrote, "We had frequent skirmishes with them daily, and although hundreds were captured, they resumed operations as soon as they were turned loose [paroled]."[6] As 3rd Sgt. Robert T. Bean, Co. I, 8th KY was riding along, one of Morgan's officers rode up to his side and asked Bean, "What do you think of the situation now?"

Bean, feigning ignorance asked, "What do you exactly mean?"

The officer said, "What do you think the chances are for the Confederacy to win?"

Bean replied, "None."

"What are your reasons for such an opinion?" asked the officer.

"Look around at all the well-kept farms, stocked with all kinds of animals for the prosperity of the owners," Bean observed. "We in the South have not used a paintbrush on our houses since the war commenced or made a rail to fence our lands."

The officer agreed with Bean and asking him to keep silent about what they had spoken about, he rode off.[7]

As the Confederate column rode across Ohio, Morgan kept a force in front and one at the rear to fend off and scatter militia groups and armed citizens. The sharp crack of a squirrel gun, shotgun or rifle almost every hour could be heard. This would be immediately followed by a volley from Morgan's scouts or flankers. Squads of citizens and Yankee soldiers would be marched to the rear under guard, where if the Confederates had time, they paroled the offenders and had them swear to go home and behave themselves. Sometimes, a raider was too severely wounded to sit on his horse. He would be left at a farmhouse so his wounds would heal. In some cases, a father, brother or friend, too brave and affectionate to leave the wounded man alone, would remain, even though their concern might mean prison or death.[8]

North of Brown and Adams counties is Highland County. Anticipating the conscription law of March 1863, the leading newspaper of Highland County reported on February 4, 1863, that trouble was brewing with Indians on the far-western border (not California). It was believed that the situation was especially grave in Utah. Earlier, in 1861, William O. Collins, a prominent resident and lawyer of Hillsboro, county seat of Highland County, Ohio, received authority from Washington, DC, to recruit a regiment of cavalry that was later designated the 11th OH. Collins was in his early fifties and had been a former member of the Ohio legislature. He was rather old for military service, but he was given the rank of lieutenant colonel. Captain Lot Smith, a Mormon frontier officer, made the following observation of the Ohioan, "Col. Collins is decidedly against killing Indians indiscriminately and will not take any general measures, save on the defensive, until he can ascertain satisfactorily by whom the depredations have been committed, and then not resort to killing until he is satisfied that peaceable measures have failed."[9]

Southern Ohio in the early months of the Civil War was populated by southern emigrants whose loyalties vacillated between Union and Confederate persuasions. These farmers were especially susceptible to the agricultural depression precipitated by Lincoln's closing of the southern markets in 1861. It was a hotbed of Copperheadism, Negrophobia, and the political machinations of Northerners with Southern sympathies.[10] Young Quaker men in these southern Ohio counties preferred to enlist in a volunteer regiment under the leadership of neighbors and friends rather than be drafted into a brigade that might be commanded by someone who was a stranger to their ways and beliefs.[11] Others who chose to enlist in the Collins battalion were those with southern sympathies who did not want to fight their friends in the Confederacy, but preferred to go west and deal with the Indians.[12]

. A month before Morgan's raid into Ohio, the provost general for Ohio began enforcing the Conscription Act. Four days before Morgan entered Brown and Adams counties to the south, a twenty-four-year-old Quaker, Hervey Johnson, from Leesburgh, ten miles north of Hillsboro, presented himself at the county seat where he joined the Collins battalion. His enlistment bounty amounted to $100, with $25 paid up front and the remainder payable when he mustered out.[13] His battalion had been organized at Camp Dennison on June 26, 1863. Almost immediately, his company joined up with General Hobson's column pursuing Morgan through the southern Ohio counties.[14]

After Collins' battalion participated at the Battle of Buffington Island, the 11th OH Volunteer Cavalry was detached. The Quakers, southern sympathizers and adventurers, were sent west to Salt Lake City, the Nebraska Territory and the Oregon Trail where they would protect settlers, wagon trains, mail routes, the transcontinental telegraph, railroads and stage coaches. Instead of facing Confederate fire, they endured the rugged, icy winters of the plains and tangled with war parties of Sioux, Cheyennes, Shoshoni and horse-stealing Utes.[15]

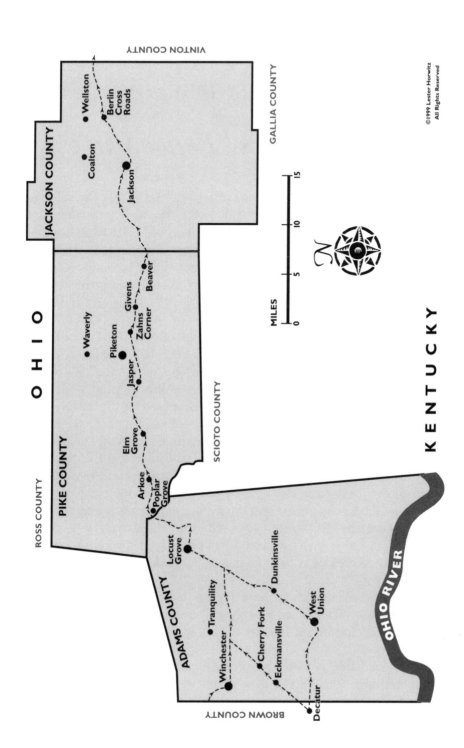

OHIO

ROSS COUNTY

PIKE COUNTY

JACKSON COUNTY

VINTON COUNTY

Wellston
Berlin Cross Roads
Coalton
Jackson

Waverly
Piketon
Givens
Jasper
Zahns Corner
Beaver

Elm Grove

Arkoe
Poplar Grove

SCIOTO COUNTY

Locust Grove

Tranquility

Dunkinsville

ADAMS COUNTY

Winchester
Cherry Fork
Eckmansville
West Union

Decatur

BROWN COUNTY

GALLIA COUNTY

KENTUCKY

OHIO RIVER

MILES

0 5 10 15

N

ADAMS COUNTY, OH

TWENTY-NINE

Winchester's "Fenced In"

Leaving Brown County, a group of raiders went south of Winchester (Scott post office) on the road to Eckmansville. The townspeople of Winchester had been alerted in the early morning hours of July 15 when a farmer rode down the main street calling out, "The Rebels are coming!"[1] The word was that Morgan and his men were killing, looting and burning structures. Little time was had for reading the Bible, but folks prayed as they waited.[2]

<u>8:30am, Wednesday, July 15</u>

When General Morgan entered this village of 600, he made the Burns Hotel (also identified as the White Hotel) his headquarters.[3] He had no desire to tarry long, as he knew that Hobson's Union cavalry was "hot on his heels." He awaited the arrival of the Aberdeen-Hillsboro stage, which was due in mid-afternoon. He wanted the mail on board and the Cincinnati newspapers, which would tell him what effect his raid was having on the North. Rather than wait for the stage to arrive, he sent out a detachment to intercept it. The raiders found the carriage and stopped it on the east side of the creek on the Winchester-North Liberty Road (present-day Ohio Rt. 136 south of Winchester). They forced the driver, Gilbert Paul, off the coach, and the vehicle was driven into town with its booty of mail pouches and newspapers. Also on board was Mrs. Nancy Lockwood, who was returning to Winchester from West Union where she had been visiting her father, Nicholas Burwell. She saved her money from falling into Confederate hands by hiding it in her petticoats.[4]

Morgans' advance scouts went directly to the home guard's building, carried out their muskets and broke every one. They tore down the large American flag, fastened it to a horse's bridle and dragged it through the dusty street.[5]

In Winchester, guards were placed at all intersections, corners and alleys. Residents who were in their homes were told to stay. No one was allowed to leave the village, but people living in the vicinity were permitted to enter. Once they came in, they found themselves "fenced in."[6]

One who found himself trapped was a Union soldier, a Captain Hines. Two Confederate soldiers were guarding him in front of the town's drugstore. He complained of being sick, and asked if he could go in and get some medicine. The request was granted. When he came out, he saw his guards were distracted. Quickly, he stepped in an adjoining door, telling the lady, Mrs. Jerome deBruin, that he was being held prisoner by the Confederates. He begged her to hide him. She took him out the back way to her mother-in-law's home. Mrs. deBruin led him to her cellar, removed some stones, making a hole large enough for him to creep in along the top of the wall, into which he crawled. He lay there all day until the Confederates left town. The raiders raised quite a stir over his escape and made many threats to the townspeople.[7]

Stores were looted. Some raiders paid a visit to the deBruin home seeking keys to Mr. deBruin's store. He was away serving in the army. After a while, they returned the keys, apologizing and promising not to disturb the store again. It is believed that when they saw that the Masonic Lodge Room was over the store and there was evidence of Mr. deBruin being a Mason, the Confederates declined to loot or vandalize his store.[8] A similar occurrence happened in Jacksonville (Dunbarton), about twelve miles east of Winchester. As the raiders approached the Kilpatrick's Inn, they saw the Masonic emblem of compass and square on the inn's sign. Some of Morgan's men entered and spent several hours enjoying their food and resting on the inn's comfortable beds. The Confederates did not molest any of Kilpatrick's property, but that could not be said for the rest of the community.[9]

Out on Winchester's Main Street, six-year-old Ben A. Smith was sitting on a bench with some teenage boys and girls. Ben had been warned by his mother, Mary Ann, "Don't eat nothing from the hands of the enemy. It might be poisoned." When some of Morgan's men came by with a quantity of stolen candy, Ben refused to accept it. He admitted he was "scared to death." One big trooper pulled out a revolver and said, "Now eat." Ben ate and lived.[10]

Morgan's men entered Winchester's government building, seized the mail and opened all envelopes in search of cash. The town's postmaster, Johnny Frow, walked in and said to Morgan. "I am postmaster here and in the name of the U.S. Government, I demand you return the mail."

The General replied, "I am the postmaster today and also the U.S. Government. You get out before I kick you out." Frow found the exit.[11]

Looking through the mail, Morgan discovered the latest newspapers. He scanned them for news about his movements and his pursuers. He rode out to the old cemetery and spoke to his men, explaining their dangerous situation. They agreed to renew their march and took the Grace Run route for

Harshaville, Wheat Ridge, Dunkinsville, Jacksonville and Locust Grove, where they would wait for Col. Richard Morgan and his men to rejoin them. At Locust Grove, the raiders were less than four miles southeast of the Serpent Mound, one of Ohio's ancient architectural mysteries situated along Brush Creek.

East of Peebles, Ohio, flows the Scioto Brush Creek. On Coffey Hollow Road, which runs through the Brush Creek Forest, lived Mary Ann Garmon Murphy. Her husband, Darius, had joined the 109th OVI. His regiment was fighting in Mississippi. It was dead of night and Mrs. Murphy was alone with her children. In the stillness of her remote cabin, she heard a band of horsemen coming up the road. She quickly extinguished the candles and warned the children to be very quiet. She closed and locked the shutters and secured the heavy oak door with a thick board. She could hear them running off her cow and two workhorses. Frustrated at being unable to enter the home, the raiders could be heard cursing and howling. Besides the farm animals, they took as much horse feed as they could carry. They could be heard riding off down the road to Locust Grove. The next day, some of the neighbor men came to check up on them. They told her that the intruders were members of the "infamous Morgan Raiders."[12]

The raiders took over the county's oldest brick building, Wickerham Inn, built before 1805. Peter Noah Wickerham, whose family owned the building, noted in his diary two weeks after the raid, "My grandfather's brick house, an old tenement, was abandoned to the rebels; clusters of them were still sleeping on the floor."[13]

7:30am, Thursday, July 16

On the Peebles-Locust Grove Road known as Zane Trace, Nancy Wickerham Sharpe was home with her two babies, Anna and Charlie. Mr. Sharpe had left early that morning to stack wheat for a neighbor. She had just finished the ironing and the clothes were hung on the rack. Bread was freshly baked for supper and the milking had been completed when some men came galloping up the road shouting a warning that General Morgan and his men were coming. She had hoped that this was a false rumor like others she had heard before. She did not have long to wait. She saw what appeared to be thousands of Confederate raiders coming up the "Big Road."

Her first thought was for her babies. She grabbed them and some blankets, thinking she might have to spend the night with them in the woods. Once outside her home, she saw women and children running to the home of a known Southern sympathizer. She decided to follow. He welcomed them all and offered any protection he could give. He, too, was frightened and didn't know if he could convince the raiders of his "sympathy." He put his refugees into one room and locked the door. He then cooked and made ready all the food he had in the house including hams, shoulder and sides of cured meat.

When the raiders arrived, Mrs. Sharpe managed to look out of a small window. She saw them around a big bonfire burning feathers off chickens, and to her, it appeared as if they were eating them raw. She thought they seemed starved to death. Later, when Morgan's men left without bothering anyone in the house, she returned to her home only to find nothing left to eat. Her fresh milk and baked bread were gone. All her canned fruit and cured meat had disappeared. Her mother had given her a stone jar of canned blackberries. It was found down the road in a fence corner with one of her silver spoons. The jar top had been knocked off clean with a deft stroke. The saber mark was quite visible.[14]

Not only had all the food been taken, but much of their clothing, too. The next day, a neighbor said she saw a raider riding through Locust Grove wearing Mrs. Sharpe's cashmere shawl wrapped around him. The following day, thousands of Union troops came through town in hot pursuit. They halted only long enough to eat where they could find food. They seemed as hungry as Morgan's men, who had eaten or destroyed nearly all the food along the way. Mrs. Sharpe's neighbors, the Platters, fed Hobson's troops cooked hams and sides of meats they had hidden from the Confederates.[15]

When the Union troops left Locust Grove, three of Morgan's men, who were ill, had been left behind. The Platters took them home and kept them until they were well enough to leave. When the Confederates got back to their homes in the South, they wrote and thanked the Platters for their kindness.[16]

One Locust Grove resident was an Irishman of large size and great bodily strength. He had much experience in contracts and jobs on public works in the State of Ohio. He was Edward L. Hughes. He had settled down on a valuable farm near Locust Grove, where he had resided for many years, raising a large and respectable family. Hughes paid little attention to rumors of Morgan's invasion on the grounds that he was a man of high repute and he was known as an opponent of the war. But on the morning of July 16, Morgan's scouts confiscated two very fine horses belonging to him. Hughes appealed to General Morgan to return his horses. But to his sorrow, regardless of how much he opposed the war, Morgan would not return his property. Thereupon, Hughes instantly concluded that if he were to offer to guide Morgan's forces, the General might be induced to return his horses. Hughes led Morgan's forces down Sunfish Valley across the Scioto River, through Piketon and on to Jackson.[17]

At the Jackson courthouse, Hughes became unruly from too much drinking in the local tavern. Morgan dismissed him and left him horseless and at the mercy of the townspeople. When Hobson entered Jackson, Hughes was arrested for treason and sent at once to jail in Hamilton County. There, he was brought before the U.S. Commissioner in Cincinnati where witnesses for the government were heard. The case was continued to allow Hughes to get statements from witnesses who would agree to testify on his behalf. Bail was set and he was ordered to appear in court again on August 27, 1863. He and his attorney boarded the train from Cincinnati to Hillsboro that stopped at Locust Grove.

August 27 came and went, and Hughes did not make his court appearance. He had fled the country and taken up residence in Montreal under Queen Victoria's flag. He had used his valuable property to underwrite his bail. With his disappearance, the bail was forfeited by the U.S. Commissioner and an indictment of treason was made against him. That's how matters stood against Hughes, his family and property until President Lincoln's Amnesty Proclamation in 1863.

On the advice of his attorney, Hughes returned to his Locust Grove home and appeared in U.S. Court, where he took the oath required in the proclamation. The forfeiture of his property was dropped, and he again became a citizen of his community. But the antagonism he sensed from his neighbors caused him to pull up stakes and move out west. Quite a lot of trouble for trying to recover only two horses.[18]

8:00am, Thursday, July 16

Just east of Locust Grove, Mrs. David Boyd was warned of Morgan's approach. She and her children loaded two wagons with everything she considered would be stolen by the raiders. She led her family, two teams of horses and wagons to a wooded hillside overlooking her farm. There, they remained concealed, although they were near enough to have a clear view of their home and anything that might occur there. The only thing they left behind was a mare that Mr. Boyd kept for one reason only. The mare raised exceptionally fine colts. Otherwise, she was a problem. She refused to be haltered or even caught outside the stable. This she entered only voluntarily. But her fine colts earned her a home.

The mare was grazing in the lot near the barn when Morgan's men paid a visit. The Boyd family, on the hill above, watched what happened. Morgan's men looked around and in the house, but found little to interest them. They then discovered the mare. They quickly started the chase, but the mare easily eluded them. Several times, the Confederates tried to encircle the horse, but each time she plunged through the ring of weary horses. In desperation, the raiders gave up and rode away.[19]

THIRTY

"Axes to the Front"

<u>8:15am, Thursday, July 16</u>

Morgan's column, having reunited with his brother Richard's detachment at Locust Grove in Adams County,[1] now entered Pike County at Poplar Grove riding down Chenoweth Fork Road. As they crossed the small bridge over the Chenoweth Fork Creek, the main column stretched for several miles, including not only mounted cavalrymen but also wagons and buggies carrying the sick and wounded. Clouds of dust rose among them reaching to the tops of the surrounding hills.[2]

About two miles southeast of Poplar Grove, the Kendall family saw the local home guard ride by at a gallop. A few minutes later, the raiders arrived. They discovered a barrel of flour and ordered Mrs. Kendall to start baking bread. The girls in the house began filling pans with dough and popping them into the hot oven. The hungry Confederates would rush in, pull the pans from the oven, grab the half-baked bread, burning their hands, rush from the house, leap on their horses at a run, and all the time trying to eat the dough. Some of it was partially baked.[3]

Above the little village of Arkoe, a few of the raiders stopped at the Lewis Beekman property. While some took a drink of water, another took Beekman's horse from the barn. Foraging around the farm, one raider noticed some bee hives. Searching with enthusiasm, he found the cache of honey. When the raiders left, Beekman found himself poorer by one horse and twenty pounds of honey.[4]

Finding food for the thousands of Confederate cavalrymen was a daily quest. Every morning, the captain of each company would appoint a man for each mess to go ahead of the command and scatter out to the farmhouses for miles on each side of the road, and by ten or twelve noon, they would return to their respective companies with sacks full of bread, cheese, butter, preserves, canned peaches, berries, wine cordial, canteens of milk and everything good that the Buckeye and Hoosier pantries yielded.[5]

Farther down the road, today's S.R. 32, a contingent of raiders stopped at the farm of William Henry. The site today is Elm Grove. Mr. Henry had taken the horses and livestock to the woods for safe keeping. But his wife,

Jane Smith Henry, refused to leave her house. At 65, she had lived a full life, including using her home as a station for the Underground Railroad. She was not cowed at the thought of meeting John Hunt Morgan face-to-face. But Morgan was not among the soldiers who came riding through the front yard and flower bed. One young Confederate was ordered to look inside the house to see if it was occupied. He did so without knocking. He was greeted with a well-placed broom handle. The next moment, Mrs. Henry emerged from the front door and ordered the rest of the men to remove their horses from her flower beds.

She had heard, she informed them, that they were Southern gentlemen. She expected to be treated like a lady. If they wished something, they could ask for it. But she would not tolerate any more men riding recklessly through her yard.

The company's captain, taken aback at first, ordered his men to show the lady the respect she desired. He then inquired if Mrs. Henry would cook a meal for the soldiers of his company. She did, inviting them to water their horses at the creek behind the barn. When the meal was finished, Mrs. Henry requested and received a receipt for the services she had rendered. This receipt has remained in the possession of her descendants, even to this date.[6]

The stories of the raiders who stopped at homes along the raid route leave the impression of a group of young men possessed of a considerable sense of humor and a certain gallantry. They left stories that would be retold and laughed about for more than a century.[7]

But the raiders were soon to show an uglier side in Pike County. It demonstrated an undercurrent of hatred that existed in many of the men. Morgan was a man of unquestioned personal courage and fought strongly for what he believed. But now, in the midst of a terribly punishing journey, deep in enemy territory, Morgan simply could not demand the discipline to keep 2,000 men in line. He had tried early in the raid. At Columbia, Kentucky, on July 3, some soldiers had broken into two stores and stolen considerable goods. When apprised, Morgan personally arrested the thieves and punished them. Later, he attempted to punish an officer for stealing a watch from a Kentuckian. But by July 16, tight discipline was lacking and Pike Countians were to suffer for it.[8]

Ohio Governor David Tod and General Ambrose Burnside had both appealed to the citizens of southern Ohio to obstruct Morgan's route in any way they could. The object was to slow down the raiders to give the pursuing Union forces an opportunity to catch up and capture the Confederate force. The best way was to cut down trees, so they blocked the roadways. Had Morgan's force been comprised only of cavalry, this tactic would have little effect. They could have easily ridden around such roadblocks. But the

Confederate column also included four heavy cannons and many wagons for the sick, wounded, stolen merchandise and horseless troopers. Many of his men who had ridden their mounts until they could go no farther, and were unable to find fresh horses, were forced to ride in wagons until new steeds could be found for them. In a telegram dated July 15, Governor Tod received a wire from Burnside's headquarters stating, "I have ordered roads obstructed with trees, and planking of bridges removed in his [Morgan's] front, so as to enable our troops to overtake him." [9]

By July 16, the Confederates began encountering felled trees blocking the roadways. This soon became a routine occurrence. Morgan organized an ax brigade to clear these obstructions. In Col. James McCreary's diary entry for July 17 he wrote, "Today we find our road badly blockaded and 'axes to the front' is now the common command."[10]

Benjamin Chestnut and his son, Isaac, received word about nine o'clock in the morning that Morgan's men were coming down Chenoweth's Fork. They discussed the best place to cut down a tree and decided on a location near the settlement of Tennyson. The road dropped off on the left side and a well-placed tree could stop the column for a time. The two men, along with Benjamin's brother, picked up axes and a saw and rode to the spot. Working hurriedly, they chopped down the tree. The noise of the falling tree attracted the attention of the Morgan scouts who were just around the bend. Spurred on by the sound of falling timber, they rode up and captured the Chestnut men. While one raider gathered up the men's horses, another forced the Chestnuts to cut up the tree they had just fallen. After which the raiders demanded the men's money pouches. Benjamin protested, "Hey, that's plain robbery!" But with guns pointed at them and the unsmiling faces of the rough-looking raiders, he was convinced that further argument was futile and might prove fatal. The three men walked to the top of the hill to wait for Morgan's almost 2,000 troops to pass.[11]

A short distance down the road was a grain mill powered by the flow of Sunfish Creek. The mill was owned by Stewart Alexander, a Pike County commissioner, and served a large number of farmers in the area. The Alexander family, including at least six children,[12] lived a short distance from the mill and had received word of Morgan's approach only a brief time before the raiders came into view. What happened next is best described in a letter written by Lina Silcott Shoemaker, Stewart Alexander's granddaughter.[13]

As I remember my mother told about it. My mother, Lavina, was 9 years old at that time and was a little helper with the chores. So on the morning of the Raid at her home, she with her brother and sister had gone berry picking. Had filled their pails and returned home to the news that Morgan's Raid was close and coming their way. They of course were frightened. So gathered up the Baby Henry and the rest of the children decided to hide in the woods until Morgan's Men passed through. My Grandfather Stewart Alexander at that time was the owner of a mill that ground wheat into flour and corn into meal. And people for miles around came there to get supplies. At that time he had flour and meal stored in barrels a good supply ahead.

So the Rebels arrived. Grandma and Grandpa stood their ground. The men were hungry and they made no secret of it. They cleaned up all supplies Grandpa had in the house and cellar. Then [the raiders] went to the mill. They rolled out barrel after barrel of flour, knocked the end out and let the horses eat and tramp through it until it was all gone. Then they repeated the action with what [corn] meal he had ground. They [Alexanders] had a large jar of honey in the cellar. It contained nothing but spoons when the children arrived back home. They [Morgan's men] asked Grandpa if he had a gun. Having lent it to a neighbor a week before, he did not know the neighbor had returned it. So he answered No. In searching they found it in the closet. One said as you have no gun this is ours then took it. They also took Grandpa's horses and left old poor worn out ones.

They burned the [covered] bridge [a 125-foot wooden structure] across Sunfish [creek]. They were desperate. There had been some trees cut and fallen in the road [over which] they wanted to go. So they took two of Grandpa's sons prisoners to help them cut their way through.

Grandpa at once called on his neighbors for more wheat and corn. And as soon as the Rebels had left, [he] went to grinding. He knew how they had cleaned up things at his home. What they (the rebels) didn't eat, they destroyed. So Grandpa furnished them all [his neighbors] with flour and meal. My mother said, "Never in her entire life had anything tasted better than Grandma's corn cakes that evening." Grandma then went on preparing for the [Union] men coming.

Once more, Morgan divided his command sending a small group over Yankee Hill to Long Fork Road. The larger column continued on the main road in a northeast direction around the hill to Stoney Ridge (via Jasper Road) and on south to Jasper, where both groups merged.[14]

At the beginning of the Civil War, the Ohio militia was in a deplorable state. In January of 1863, a militia reorganization law went into effect. Every able-bodied man between the ages of eighteen and forty-five was to enroll. Its members would only be called out to defend their locales in case of attack. A second group, the Ohio Volunteer Militia, on the other hand, was to be fully armed, trained and ready to move at an hour's notice.[15]

Men enlisted in the Ohio Volunteer Militia for a five-year term and would at the completion of this period be exempt from further military service. This organization was later to become the National Guard. Most of the Pike County volunteer militia had been ordered by Governor Tod to be stationed at Camp Chase near Columbus to protect the state capital. With the cream of Pike County's fighting men hundreds of miles away, it fell to Pike County's "second string," the regular militia, to hold the day and protect the imperiled town. Led by Andrew Kilgore, chairman of the Pike County Military Committee, the remaining men decided that Jasper should be defended.

Gathering up their saws, axes and guns, they moved to a spot north of town where trees could easily be fallen across the road. The barricade would provide cover for the townspeople as they attempted to hold off the raiders. It was a motley crew. Besides Kilgore, there was Samuel Cutler, his assistant; Thomas Rose, the town's doctor; and others.

The Confederates' advance guard discovered the barricade and reported it to Morgan. The men behind the barricades waited nervously. It was nearly one o'clock and the sun was burning. The men steeled themselves for the cavalry charge that they expected at any moment. They could see the dust cloud coming south toward Jasper, but as yet, Morgan's men were not in sight.

John Hunt Morgan was a veteran of such encounters. He knew that the men behind the barricades were most likely untrained and untested under fire. Most defenders would be two to three times as old as the average age of Morgan's young, fleet phalanx. A charge directly into the barricade would undoubtedly overrun the position, but in the process, some of his men would probably be wounded.

To minimize this danger, he had several companies of his Second Brigade dismount and fire a volley at the defenders. No one had warned them that Morgan's men usually fought as mounted infantry, on the ground, not in the saddle. It came as a shock to suddenly, and without warning, have hundreds of rifles open up on their fragile defenses. It did not take long for the defenders to see the hopelessness of the situation, and after firing a few rounds, the men decided to beat a hasty retreat. Several men found themselves prisoners marching at gunpoint back into town.[16]

THIRTY-ONE

McDougal's Fatal Encounter

The town of Jasper was named after Revolutionary war hero, Sgt. William Jasper.[1] It was a bustling canal town of 160 people, and Joseph McDougal was a community leader. At forty-seven years old, he was a schoolmaster, deacon of the Methodist Church and a man of some means. McDougal and his wife, Elizabeth, had five children ranging in age from one to seventeen.[2]

McDougal was among those captured at a barricade on the Jasper Road, and marched back to town. The common procedure was to take the prisoners' guns and make them take an oath not to participate against Morgan again. The prisoners would be paroled and allowed to return to their homes. Morgan detailed this duty to a company commander. In Jasper, the duty fell to Captain James W. Mitchell.[3]

Some of the raiders apparently had made fun of their prisoners as they marched them back to Jasper. Most of the captured townspeople said nothing, but McDougal, a staunch Unionist, answered back. The Southerners immediately concentrated their verbal abuse on McDougal, who continued to get his own points in. He may not have realized nor cared that his remarks were particularly offensive to Captain Mitchell. Money was taken from the prisoners' pockets. When it was found that McDougal only had a dime on him, he was asked if that's all he had. He answered, "Yes, and that is more than I wants you to have."[4]

When the prisoners were lined up to take the oath, Mitchell ordered McDougal taken out of line and led across the canal bridge to the river bank. There he was placed in a canoe. Two of the raiders were told to take aim and fire. One shot struck McDougal below the right eye and the other hit him in the chest, wounding him fatally. The mystery is, what did McDougal say that so provoked and offended the Confederates that they decided to execute him? Certainly, the raiders had heard all kinds of negative things said to them in the previous two weeks, but none had precipitated the shooting of an unarmed civilian. Nor is there any indication that any of the other Jasper civilians were shot.[5] McDougal is buried in the Jasper Methodist Church. On McDougal's tombstone is inscribed:

Joseph McDougal
Was shot by John Morgan's men July 16, 1863
Aged 47 ys. 7 ms. 9 ds.
Blessed are the dead which die in the Lord
From henceforth; yea saith The spirit
That they may rest from their labors
And their works do follow them.[6]

Whatever angered Mitchell must have spread through the entire col-umn. The Confederates' destruction of Jasper was violent and thorough. In addition to ransacking all the shops in town and stealing everything they could carry, they set fire to buildings, barns, stables and mills. The raiders' wrath was turned on the town's shopkeepers and they stole merchandise from Andrew Kilgore ($5,400), Sam Green and Henry Mark ($4,400), William F. Truesdale ($3,300) and Samuel Cutler who made a strange claim that the raiders had stolen fifteen plows valued at $75.[7] Were the raiders planning to do some farming along the way? Charles Miller's lumber mill was destroyed, including his stacked lumber and his mill tools. Miller's canal boat was one of two the raiders burned. The other belonged to Jonathon Gray. It was brand new, still sitting on its stocks. The canal bridge was also torched. Even Joseph McDougal's widow had her horse stolen.[8]

Morgan's men did not ride through Jasper unscathed. All along the nine-hundred mile ride, the raiders were shot at by hastily formed militia groups or farmers. When individual soldiers became separated from Mor-gan's main column, they were vulnerable to attack. Leaving the relative safety of the main force was necessitated by the need to seek food and fresh horses.

One of Morgan's volunteers was Joseph W. Whitfield, a farmer from Madisonville, Kentucky, near Morton's Gap. He joined Morgan's command August 1, 1862, and was mustered into Co. I of the 10th KY Cavalry under the command of Colonel Johnson. Now, almost a year later, he was riding with Morgan through Jasper dead-tired and saddle-sore. He was in a semi-slumbering state, not really aware of what was happening around him. He had a chicken strapped low on his saddle. He had picked it up on the out-skirts of Jasper. He thought the chicken was dead. But when his horse broke into a gallop, the chicken's head bumped against the horse and it let out a squawk. The bird's shriek so startled Joseph that both he and the chicken fell off the horse. The fowl attempted to flee and Joe chased it for several hun-dred feet before grabbing it by the tail. Citizens watching this comical scene, closed in and before he realized it, he was taken prisoner.[9]

Among the claims made by residents of Jasper, Crastilas K. Marquis asked to be reimbursed $5.80 for serving "meals to 29 rebels."[10] Leaving

Jasper, the Confederates crossed the Scioto River, burned the bridge and headed to Piketon. The destruction of the Scioto Canal bridge delayed the pursuing Union cavalry by five or six hours according to Col. August Kautz who was leading Hobson's "flying" brigade. A temporary bridge had to be built, so Kautz didn't reach Jackson until late at night on July 17.[11] Twenty miles to the north, the Chillicothe militia were waiting for Morgan to appear. They were so frightened of an encounter with the raiders that when a cloud of dust appeared on the horizon, they burned a bridge over Paint Creek, which was only a foot deep at the time.[12] It wasn't Morgan. It was some of their own miltia.[13]

3:00pm, Thursday, July 16

The people of Piketon had set up barricades across the road. The smoke and flames of Jasper could be seen easily. Piketon defenders had little inclination to stay and argue. Morgan was soon riding unopposed into the town. It was larger than Jasper with a wider variety of businesses. Except for one store, the wholesale ransacking and burning so common in Jasper did not occur in Piketon. Most of the thefts were for particular purposes such as Dr. Edward Allan (drugs and medicines), William Patterson (buggy, harness and blacksmith tools), Charles Cissna (horse, harness and grain), and Andrew Kellison (shoes and boots valued at $200).[14] When the Confederates stopped at the town's hotel run by Mike Nessler, one of the raiders began to pull up the thrifty old German's cabbages. "Oh, don't do that, Captain," pleaded Mike, knowing full well his visitor was a sergeant. "We need them for winter." The soldier was persuaded with a quarter not to disturb the cabbages under which the innkeeper had buried all his money.

On a hill overlooking Piketon, Henry Brown and his family were living in a farmhouse. When word reached them that Morgan's Raiders were heading their way, they quickly took their most valuable possessions, silver spoons, and stuffed them up the fireplace chimney to hide them. Morgan's men arrived and demanded that hot food be cooked for them. Having little choice, the Browns lit the fireplace, knowing full well the heat might melt the silver. Suddenly, Morgan's men became alarmed, mounted their horses and rode off. The Browns were able to extinguish the fire before any damage was done to the silver. They mounted these flat-handled silver spoons of a colonial design onto a wood rack, which they proudly displayed above the mantel. Visitors to the home were regaled with the story of how the spoons survived the close call.[15] Mr. Brown also placed a claim for a horse that was stolen by the raiders for which he was reimbursed $125.[16] A century later, local thieves broke into the home and made off with the family's historical silver treasure.[17]

THIRTY-TWO

A Bridge Beyond

As they left Piketon, Morgan detailed a company of men to go up the Scioto River just south of Waverly. A bridge had been built there by James Emmitt.[1] He owned a Chillicothe distillery. But most of Emmitt's investments were in Waverly. He constructed the Emmitt House, founded and operated a bank, sawmill, grist mill, furniture factory, lumber yard and a large general store. He organized and helped build the Springfield, Jackson & Pomeroy Railroad and was its first president. At one time, he paid one-third of all the taxes in Waverly and one-tenth of Pike County's taxes. He had promised the people of Pike County, he would build a bridge in return for getting the courthouse moved from Piketon to Waverly.[2] It was located on what is now S.R. 220 East and it was only two years old.[3] Morgan's men went to a nearby farmer's field, collected a batch of straw and soon had the bridge blazing. Only part of the bridge burned. But the cost to repair and replace the bridge was more than the bridge's original cost.[4]

There was a strong suspicion that some Piketon natives could not resist the opportunity to get revenge on Jim Emmitt and informed Morgan's men of the bridge's location. Emmitt, as president of the Scioto Bridge Company, turned in a bill to the Morgan's Raid Claim Commission for $12,000 damage. The Claim Commissioners looked into the matter and discovered that the bridge had cost only $10,000 new. They were not receptive to Emmitt's inflationary plea and allowed him (after depreciation) $8,000.[5]

Morgan's main body headed east over Pike Hill on what is now old S.R. 124. In 1863, this area was settled mainly by people of German descent, many much more comfortable with the German language than English. It must have been interesting to hear the raiders with their southern drawls trying to converse with Pike Countians in their heavily-accented English.[6]

Four miles beyond Piketon, the road split with the north fork going directly east to Givens Station. The south fork turned into Germany Pike. Perhaps because the Germans were pacifists, they had not hidden their horses and livestock. The raiders, who had little regard for pacifists, took all the horses they sighted. From Piketon to Beaver hardly a horse was spared.[7]

6:00pm, Thursday, July 16

In the evening, General Judah reached Portsmouth, in Scioto County, by steamer. Three regiments of cavalry disembarked from twenty-four trans-

177

ports. He began to procure supplies for men and horses. He had some trouble in convincing the loyal people of that town that they ought, in consideration of liberal compensation in cash, to furnish a sufficient train of wagons to carry his extra baggage and ammunition. A little coaxing, emphasized in special cases by resolute-looking fellows with drawn sabers, was successful in getting the transport he needed.[8]

Meanwhile, on the north fork, Bill Givens was determined not to surrender his horse without a fight. He took his gun and hid himself in the stable with his horse. He had a clear view of the door. Bill planned to unload on the first Confederate who entered. He heard the approach of Morgan's men and expected one or two, but from the sound, he could tell there were hundreds. Givens decided to stay quiet. Soon the stable door was swung open and his horse was led outside. Bill was undetected, but to his chagrin, he realized Morgan's men had set the stable on fire. His situation became perilous before the raiders moved on and Givens had a chance to escape.[9]

Just before leaving Pike County, Morgan's advance guard rode through the little town of Beaver at seven o'clock in the evening.[10] The main body began arriving sometime later. Riding as fast as he could, one local man rode through the county to warn people of Morgan's approach. As he rode past the Butcher home in Beaver, Mr. and Mrs. Butcher were sitting on their front porch. They saw a Confederate soldier right behind him. The raider shot through the Pike Countian's shirt-tail as it flopped in the air. But this Civil War version of Paul Revere kept on going and yelling at the top of his lungs, "The Rebels are coming, the Rebels are coming!"[11]

Morgan's men had ridden from Locust Grove to Beaver in the space of twelve hours.[12] There were less than a dozen homes and a few stores in the village, most of them were two-story wooden structures.[13] The raiders stopped at the shops, where they looted bolts of calico and muslin. As they did throughout their ride, they tied the ends of the fabric to their saddles and dragged the bolts through the dusty roads.[14] While Morgan's cannons were parked in front of one of the buildings, a curious boy shoved his head into the barrel only to become stuck. The Confederates had quite a problem extracting his head. Morgan's wagons loaded with the sick and wounded were parked on the corner where Dr. B.L. McCaleb lived. Carl Buehler, a Beaver resident, offered glasses of wine to Morgan's men, saying, "A soldier is a soldier."[15]

Some of Morgan's troops stopped at Spangler's blacksmith shop. They asked the smithy to repair some shoes or replace horseshoes where needed. After supplying their needs, he was surprised when the soldiers wanted to pay him for the new shoes and repairs.[16] One last stop before leaving Beaver was at the home of the James family. Mrs. James had put her bread in the oven when the Confederates arrived. They took all her bread, even though it was only half done. The Confederates ate it immediately, saying they were starved.[17]

9:00pm, Thursday, July 16

Gen. Judah led his sizable force out of Portsmouth over the knobs in a northeasterly direction toward the old Pomeroy stage road.[18] Portland and Buffington Island were thirty miles distant. Portsmouth was under martial law. Five gunboats had arrived to guard the city's riverfront. Even after thousands of General Judah's cavalry force rode off in search of Morgan, regiments of infantry remained to protect the town, a major manufacturing center of war materiel.[19]

One humorous incident occurred as Judah's forces headed east. As they approached the town of Thurman on the border between Jackson and Gallia counties, the townspeople had been alerted that Morgan might be heading their way. Like many towns in the north, they had a flagpole in the center of their village with the American flag proudly displayed. Seeing the large cloud of dust, they mistakenly thought it was Morgan's men coming, so they hurriedly took the flag down to prevent the Confederates from desecrating it. As Judah's men quickly passed Thurman, the citizens realized their error and hurriedly raised the flag again. But, in their haste, the flag was accidentally displayed upside down, which is a distress signal. As Judah looked back at the town and saw what appeared to be a distress signal, he turned his troops and rode back to Thurman. The embarrassed citizens apologized for delaying the Union troops and Judah turned his troops once more to the east and continued toward Pomeroy in Meigs County.[20]

Thursday, July 16

In West Virginia, Colonel Rutherford B. Hayes was standing in a telegraph office to find out what was happening in other theaters of the war. He was present when a wire arrived telling about Morgan's raid into Ohio. As commander of the 23rd OVI, he took a personal interest in this news because his home and family were in Cincinnati. He sent a dispatch to Charleston, West Virginia, asking if there were any steamboats there. When the answer came back that there were two, he directed that they be sent at once up Loup Creek, a tributary of the Kanawha River. Then he galloped back to camp to find Brigadier-General E. Parker Scammon of the 3rd Division, 8th Army Corps. He explained to the General the opportunity before them. He would march the troops to Loup Creek, board the steamers and shortly be on the Ohio River in position to intercept Morgan. After a sharp controversy, Scammon was persuaded to allow Hayes to take the 23rd OVI and the 13th WVA in the effort to stop Morgan. Scammon would shortly follow Hayes with two more regiments.[21]

<u>10:30pm, Thursday, July 16</u>

By this late hour, Morgan's force had passed through Beaver and out of Pike County into Jackson County. Early on the morning of July 17, another cavalry force came riding down Chenoweth Fork. It was a Union brigade commanded by Colonel A.V. Kautz hoping to make contact with Morgan and slow him down until Hobson's main force could catch up.[22]

The Union soldiers were hard-pressed for fresh horses. The raiders were sweeping up all the good horses ahead of them, leaving only the poorer ones for the Union troops. Part of Kautz's group was the 7th Ohio Cavalry recruited from the southern counties through which Morgan was raiding. Seven men were from Pike County. Madison and Harvey Stephenson perhaps bore the hardest feelings about Morgan. Jasper was their home and they needed no other incentive to go after Morgan.[23]

On July 17, Kautz wired Burnside:

I command the advance of General Hobson. Have just arrived at Jasper with 400 men. Gen. Hobson is on the road between Piketon and Locust Grove, about six hours behind, with his main force. I shall move in twenty minutes toward Jackson, where Morgan is now reported to be.[24]

Burnside wired back to Kautz:

There are 2,000 or 3,000 militia waiting for Morgan at Berlin, six miles from Jackson. Judah is somewhere between Gallipolis and Jackson with cavalry.[24]

Hobson wired Burnside:

Militia has failed to intercept the rebels. My progress has been impeded by tired horses, bad roads, and by the destruction of bridges over Scioto River and the canal which parallels the river.[25]

Kautz's brigade began capturing stragglers from Morgan's force as soon as they started down Chenoweth Fork. These stragglers had simply rode themselves into exhaustion. In fact, even after their capture, their behavior was often that of a sleep walker.[26]

Just outside of Jasper, a detail of Co. L of the 2nd OH Volunteer Cavalry came upon a Confederate straggler. But this soldier still had some fight left in him. He fired on the approaching detail, wounding Sergeant William P. Cowan. The raider was captured, but Cowan's wounds were found to be serious. He was taken to Dr. Thomas Rose at Jasper. The doctor, after examining Cowan's wounds, advised that he was too seriously wounded to be moved. Cowan was left at Jasper where he struggled valiantly, but on July 27, 1863, he succumbed to his wounds. He was the second man to die in Pike County as a result of Morgan's Raid.[27]

Arriving in Jackson at night, Kautz's brigade was met with cheers and fried chicken.[28] They were just twelve hours behind Morgan. The Colonel remained with his men in Jackson until three o'clock in the morning, July 18. During that time, he was joined by Colonel Sanders with detachments of the 8th and 9th MI and two pieces of artillery.[29]

<u>Friday, July 17</u>
The 19th OH Battery left Hamilton and took the train to Cincinnati where they arrived in the afternoon and went into camp near the Brighton House. By two o'clock the following morning, they were being shipped by rail to Chillicothe, where they were promptly furnished with a generous dinner by the ladies of the town. From there, they proceeded to Scott's Landing and awaited orders from Col. Benjamin P. Runkle, of the 45th OVI, who was temporarily in command of the regular troops and the militia. One section of the battery was sent to patrol the fordable points on the river between Marietta and Steubenville, while two artillery pieces were sent by boat up the Muskingum River to McConnellsville, under the command of Lt. Wm. Dustin.[30]

This was Dustin's first action in Ohio. Back on April 22, 1861, he had enlisted in the 14th OVI, commanded by Col. J.B. Steedman. As a private, he took part in the battles of Philippi, Laurel Hill and Corrick's Ford in western Virginia. In July 1862, he was mustered out and returned to the employ of the railroad company. Civilian life must have been too dull, because within a few weeks, Dustin joined the 19th OH Battery, organized by Joseph C. Shields. This time he signed up for three years of service. Because of his field experience, Shields chose him as one of his three lieutenants. The other two were Robertson Smith and Charles W. Harris.

The remaining men of the 19th stayed in camp at Scott's Landing, where they were joined by the Pickaway Minute Men and Hocking Valley Rangers. Col. Runkle, knowing the difficulty of feeding such irregular forces as he had under his command, issued an order to the citizens to furnish cooked provisions for the troops. The order brought a generous supply of ham, pie, biscuits, cheese and chickens.[31]

THIRTY-THREE

Newspaper Wars

6:00am, Friday, July 17

Forewarned of Morgan's approach, the citizens of Jackson sought to hide their horses, knowing that the raiders were seizing every available horse. Many in town took their horses to the sheltered hollow, where they were left under the shelves of overhanging rocks. A few residents stood guard over the horses in their equine sanctuary. Later, the townspeople decided that since heaven was a place for being saved, they named the hollow "Horse Heaven."[1]

The advance guard of the Confederate column rode into Jackson. Ed Selfridge, brother of Provost Marshal C.W. Selfridge, saw the raiders gallop down Main Street toward the Isham House. He spurred his horse in an effort to escape. Several raiders pursued him firing at his back. But his horse was swift and he made his escape as he headed for Hamden.[2] Most of the townsfolk offered no resistance. The raiders found a number of people assembled, and all the men were taken prisoner and marched to the fairground.[3] Morgan's main forces arrived in the early morning. Morgan and his staff rode in and stopped in front of the Isham House. The proprietor, John French, had locked the door after the first scouting report, but he and his friend, Elijah Meacham, were still inside. When Morgan demanded admission, French at first hesitated, but soon he concluded that it would be better to open the door. Morgan and his staff registered like regular guests, and soon porters were busy serving them whiskey. One of the staff officers, Colonel Peter Evans, and Meacham had been classmates at Ohio University a few years earlier and recognized one another. As a result, Meacham was released.[4]

Colonel Duke and about fifty men appeared in front of the Valley House on the southwest corner of Portsmouth and Pearl streets. Duke asked the lady on duty, "Is this the best hotel in town?" She answered, "No indeed; this is the poorest; it has no landlord." "Well," he said, "We will take what you have and we want to sit at the table, please, and have all the coffee you can give us." When she brought the coffee, Duke said, "Miss, just put that in a tin cup for me."[5]

William Aleshire was an eyewitness to Morgan's entry into Jackson which had about 1,000 residents. Here is what he wrote:

> Early on the morning of July 17, I was two miles east of Jackson. Fourteen of us were gathered at the home of Nelson Aleshire. We saw a band of Morgan's men galloping over the farm of J.H. Stephenson gathering up his horses. Soon, two of them came riding up the Gallipolis road and stopped at Nelson's house. They ordered us to come down to the road and surrender. We were very ready to do so because we could see more of the band riding up the road. By this time, 25 Rebels had come up and they wanted to know if we were bushwhackers. We answered "No" of course.
>
> Then one of them ordered us to fall into line and he marched us to Jackson, leaving the other Rebels at Nelson Aleshire's. We were marched up to the Isham House and an officer came out and we were all compelled to take an oath not to serve against the Confederacy until exchanged.
>
> When we reached Jackson, it was crowded with Rebels, some lying asleep in the shadow of the houses, others riding about with bolts of muslin and calico over their saddles.
>
> At that time, D.D. Dungan and A. Robbins kept a store below the National Bank. The Rebels broke in at the rear, and began stealing. Mr. Robbins went up to the Isham House and got Morgan to go with him to drive away the men. Mr. Robbins was acquainted with John Morgan, having been captured by him once in Kentucky. I was sitting near the Cavett block talking with William West, when I saw the men running out of Robbins' store like so many scared sheep and West told me that Morgan had driven them out.
>
> West asked me if I would like to see Morgan, and of course I did. We went around to the back door and stepped in and there was Robbins sitting on the counter about 15 feet away and John Morgan standing a little farther leaning against the counter, his musket set on the floor, with its barrel resting in the hollow of his arm.
>
> They were talking, and Robbins said, "War is a very bad thing and we all feel the effects of it." Some remark nettled Morgan and he straightened up and swore viciously at Robbins. We thought he was going to shoot. We were standing there listening and eating sugar out of a barrel, but when Morgan raised his gun, we did not want any more sugar, and left at once. We feared to hear the gun crack, but it did not and we soon saw Robbins and Morgan come out together talking very nicely.
>
> At fifteen minutes of 9 o'clock, July 17th, the order was given to march, and by 9 a.m. the last Rebel was gone. [6]

The raiders burned the Buckeye crib at Berlin and the mill of Rufus Hunsinger & Co., for which Mr. Hunsinger was reimbursed $5,000 by the State of Ohio after the war. Two flour mills in Jackson were spared when their Butternut owners were compelled to pay a ransom of $2,300. Both loyal Union citizens and Confederate sympathizers received the same treatment at the hands of the Confederates. The drugstore of Dr. I.T. Monahan, a notorious Copperhead, was gutted of its contents by Morgan's men and robbed of $500 cash.[7]

Another act of the raiders' vandalism was the destruction of the office of the county's Republican paper, the *Standard,* which was forced to discontinue publication until September 3, 1863. Morgan's men threw all the newspaper's printing equipment out of the second-story window above the First National Bank.[8]

When Union troops commanded by Colonel Carpenter arrived in Jackson a few hours after the raiders' departure, some of them joined a mob, entered and destroyed the rival *Express* office, which was the Democratic organ in the county.[9] The destruction of the *Standard* office created much sympathy for its editor, and his loss turned out to be his gain. Union soldiers rallied to his support and remained loyal subscribers until his death in 1887. The *Express* resumed publication a few weeks before the *Standard,* and the warfare between the two papers continued more bitter than ever before.

Some of Morgan's men entered Jackson's Masonic Lodge rooms and came into the street attired in the robes of the order. General Morgan sharply reprimanded them and ordered that they return the costumes.[10]

Young William Asbury "Berry" Steele, known as the "Drummer Boy of Shiloh," was only fourteen when President Lincoln called for volunteers in the War of the Rebellion. He served as drummer boy with the 1st OH Artillery. When Morgan's men burst into Jackson, Berry was home on furlough. He hid his drum under the bed, went outside and climbed a tall poplar tree to hide. They searched, found the drum and destroyed it. But he escaped their attention.[11]

Another Jackson soldier, who was home at the time, was Mark Sternberger. He was with the 129th OVI stationed at Cumberland Gap, Tennessee. Sergeant Sternberger was on recruiting duty when the news came that the raiders were near. Being in uniform, he discreetly took to the woods, where he spent the night. At daybreak, he went to a farmhouse seeking food and rest. The house was deserted and being quite tired, he lay down and went to sleep. Later, he was awakened by the sound of voices and horses galloping by. Looking out the window, he saw the raiders going toward Berlin on the road in front of the house. He quickly tossed his uniform in the closet and jumped into bed just as two raiders appeared, searching the house. They questioned him and he responded in a very weak voice, "The family has gone but I am too ill to go with them." He heard them report that there was nobody in the house except a sick man. There was no further search of the house and soon the sound of the marchers died away in the distance.[12]

10:00am, Friday, July 17

Colonel Kautz left Piketon with 400 men followed by Colonel Sanders with Michigan cavalry. They were at least twenty-five miles behind Morgan's forces. General Hobson was six hours behind Kautz on the road between Locust Grove and Piketon.[13]

The Ross County militia under Colonel Ben P. Runkle tried to hold the hills commanding the road near Berlin Crossroads, just east of Jackson and south of Wellston. They fought Morgan's men as the raiders traveled east along the Wilkesville-Pomeroy Road. After Morgan had passed, Runkle began to move his men toward Buffington Island. The militia leader reported that his troops had killed the Confederates' guides near Hamden north of Wellston.[14]

(Telegram)   Berlin, July 17, 1863, 2 pm

General Burnside:
The enemy renewed his attack on my front, and in double my numbers, out-flanking me on my right and left. They had several pieces of artillery, part rifled; shelled my position and made demonstrations to surround me. After the militia heard the shells and my men had been driven out of the town, it was as much as I could do to hold my position, and impossible to take the offensive. I would not move the undrilled militia at all. We detained them over three hours, killed four, and this was all I could possibly do. The enemy withdrew on the Wilkesville and Pomeroy road. The 2nd Ohio Cavalry did not arrive. Colonel Gilmore with 1,000 men failed to arrive, leaving but 1,500 men. They burned the furnaces. I await orders.
BEN P. RUNKLE, *Colonel.*[15]

(Telegram)   Cincinnati, July 17, 1863

Colonel Runkle, Berlin:
Send messenger and copy of this dispatch to General Hobson to hurry up and overtake Morgan tonight. If he can get his artillery and 1,500 men up he can whip him I think. You can join Hobson with any mounted forces you have. Morgan ought to be caught.
A.E. BURNSIDE, *Major-General.*

(Telegram)   Hamden, Friday, July 17

General Burnside:
The rebels have made a demonstration against my forces. We have driven them back, killing two. We hold the roads and heights adjacent. The 2nd Ohio Volunteer Cavalry passed through Piketon at 8 o'clock in pursuit.

BEN P. RUNKLE, *Colonel.*

(Telegram)   *Cincinnati, July 17,* 1863
Colonel Runkle, Hamden:
As the enemy have passed you all you can do is telegraph and send messengers by swiftest conveyance to Athens and other points along the Marietta and Cincinnati Railroad and to Pomeroy to get out the militia and obstruct the roads. Do this speedily and thoroughly. A very short delay of Morgan must enable our forces to overtake him. Communicate also with General Hobson and our other commanders and urge them forward. Report where the enemy is from time to time. Have you heard from General Judah?

A.E. BURNSIDE, *Major-General.*

(Telegram)   *Hamden, July* 17, 1863
General Burnside:
I forwarded your dispatches by swift courier to Hobson. I have not heard a word from General Judah. I suppose he turned east below Jackson so as to strike the Gallipolis road. I have sent Colonel Gilbert with his regiment to Athens. Will do all in my power to carry out your instructions.

BEN P. RUNKLE, *Commanding.*

The following day, July 18, Colonel Runkle sent this telegram from Hamden to Ohio's governor, David Tod:

Gov. Tod: I have sent Col. [Joseph] Hill, with my mounted men and best infantry, to Marietta by rail. I follow to Marietta. I hope he will reach the river before Morgan. *A kingdom for drilled men and artillery.* One thousand drilled men can take every man Morgan has.

GUERNSEY
COUNTY

Zanesville

MUSKINGUM COUNTY

Cumberland

Zeno

NOBLE
COUNTY

FAIRFIELD
COUNTY

Ruraldale

Eagleport   Rokeby

PERRY COUNTY

OHIO

New
Lexington

Portersville

Triadelphia

McConnelsville

Chapel Hill

Corning

Buchanan

New Straitsville

MORGAN COUNTY

Logan

HOCKING COUNTY

Murray
City

Nelsonville

ATHENS
COUNTY

Marietta

Starr

WASHINGTON
COUNTY

Creola

Athens

Belpre

Parkers-
burg

Zaleski

Blennerhasset
Island

McArthur

Albany

Coolville

VINTON COUNTY

Hockingport

Hamden

MEIGS COUNTY

Tuppers Plains

Harrisonville

Reedsville

WEST
VIRGINIA

Chester

Long
Bottom

Wilkesville

Salem
Center   Langsville

Bashan

Pomeroy

Rutland

Bald Knobs
Portland

Stiversville

Ewington
Vinton

Middleport

GALLIA
COUNTY

Buffington
Island

Cheshire

Racine

Ravenswood

Porter

OHIO

RIVER

Addison

Gallipolis

JACKSON COUNTY

MILES

0   5   10   15

©1999 Lester Horwitz
All Rights Reserved

N

THIRTY-FOUR

"Our Last Night in the North"

As the raiders left Berlin, they captured Abraham Morris, the town's mail carrier. He had a reputation as a "conductor" on the Underground Railroad through the northern part of the county. He had been helping many runaway slaves escape from Kentucky to freedom. Morris was now forced to lead the Confederates away from Berlin to their next stop in Wilkesville.[1]

3:00pm, Friday, July 17

In Wilkesville, Caroline Carr was assisting her brother, Marshall, the village postmaster, when four of Morgan's men carrying a Confederate flag rode into town. Marshall Carr, alerted to Morgan's coming, took down the American flag and concealed it with some valuables in a field high above the village. He did such a good job, he never found where he had hidden his money. Soon, the town was filled with Morgan's horsemen. General Morgan and Basil Duke came into the post office, took the mail, and left a guard at the door. The mail was taken to the home of Dr. William Cline, where Morgan set up his headquarters.[2] It is said that Dr. Cline's wife, Ruth Virginia Althar, was a first cousin of John Hunt Morgan.

Dr. Cline was one of the richest men in Vinton County, owning 1,400 acres of land and several shops in the town, including the drugstore. Because of his wealth, Dr. Cline was able to provide the Morgan staff with fine meals and sleeping quarters. Unknown to the General was that Dr. Cline was an ardent abolitionist and operated a station on the Underground Railroad.[3] His servants were freed slaves who had found a haven in the North. After the raid, Dr. Cline submitted a claim for the loss of two horses and a buggy. The doctor's home and greenhouse were not molested, but his feed bins were raided and his general store across the street from his home was looted of boots, clothing and dry goods. Ms. Carr's parents' store suffered the same treatment.[4]

At the post office, some of the raiders found newspapers telling of the pursuit. They gathered at the Douglas Tavern in the village to read the news and do some fine cursing. Later that evening, Col. Dick Morgan, John's brother, returned to the post office and wrote a letter to his mother. The following morning, all the mail was returned except for one letter. That letter was found near Hockingport in Athens County, where it had been thrown away by the raiders with other articles after the Battle of Buffington Island.[5] As he went to sleep in the comfort of Dr. Cline's bedroom, General Morgan's prayer was that this would be his last night in the North. Tomorrow, he planned to cross the river at Buffington Island and rejoin Bragg's command in Tennessee.

When General Morgan arose the next morning, he found his black valet and his wallet stuffed with greenbacks were missing. Missing, too, was Abraham Morris, who had taken Morgan's servant with him. The General realized that he had no time to search for either.[6] The pursuing Yankee army was closing the gap and the Buffington Island crossing was less than a day's ride ahead. As the raiders were leaving Wilkesville, they burned the barn of Caroline's uncle, Fred Carr, on today's Rt. 124 near the edge of town. One of the Confederates, who was ill, was left at the home of James Blakely where he was cared for until his death a few days later. At first, Wilkesville citizens thought his body should be buried on the farm of some Copperheads who lived in the vicinity. Instead they buried the dead soldier in the village cemetery. Relatives of the soldier were notified. They wrote expressing their gratitude and later the body was removed to his Southern birthplace.[7]

9:00pm, Friday, July 17

In the nearby town of Athens, 250 of the Athens Volunteer Militia and a squad from Bedford in Meigs County, collected wagons and set off on the road to Wilkesville. Word was that the raiders were encamped there. The small militia force was commanded by Major de Steigner, Major Guthrie and Captain Dana. As they passed John Hibbard's place, Captain A.D. Brown requested quilts to protect his "College bred gentlemen from the night air." Throughout the night, the men tramped along the road. As the gray light of dawn broke in the east, they stopped for breakfast which was provided when a wagon arrived an hour later.[8]

At six o'clock in the morning, the Union force marched toward Harrisonville which they reached by ten. Here they rested and ate again from a table spread by the roadside. Scouts went forward and returned several hours later to report that the raiders were in force at Rutland in Meigs County. While resting, they were fed dinner.[9] Three citizens of Harrisonville reported that they had been forced to feed Morgan's men when they had passed through town earlier. Benjamin F. White said he fed twenty-five raiders. Nicholas Stanart said he had to feed 100 and John Ball 125.[10] In both Rutland and Harrisonville, local men were impressed as guides. In Rutland, they took James Giles. In Harrisonville, Robert Combs was taken. The latter returned home nine days later.

At two o'clock in the afternoon, the Athens volunteers were given orders to "fall in." Once they were on the road, they were told to "bout face." After much confusion, their commanders admitted they were not going to pursue Morgan. The men were told that their maneuvers were meant merely to defend Athens. With that, they were ordered to return home. For the Athens volunteers, the campaign was over.[11]

Meanwhile, Major George Rue's three trains had reached Columbus and because Morgan had burned the Panhandle bridges, the trains were transferred to the B&O. They reached Bellaire in the evening.[12]

Burnside ordered Rue to leave the trains in Bellaire and intercept Morgan as he came into the town. But Morgan did not come. The next morning, Burnside ordered them to reload the trains and go fifty miles up the river to Steubenville and take the first road out into the country and hunt for Morgan. As soon as men and horses were on the trains, Rue ordered them to pull out of Bellaire, leaving instructions for the artillery to follow.[13]

THIRTY-FIVE

The U.S. Navy,
the Union's Secret Weapon

On July 9, when Morgan crossed the Ohio into Indiana, the river's depth at Buffington was just two feet—ideal fording conditions and too shallow for gunboats.[1] But four days later, heavy rains in West Virginia mountains raised the river to almost six feet at Buffington. More importantly for the Union forces, it allowed the tinclads and troop transports to range much farther upriver than usual.[2]

From Cincinnati, the Federal navy escorted the soldier-laden transports of General Henry M. Judah upstream to Portsmouth. As the bluecoats disembarked to chase the Confederates overland, the General asked Lt. Commander Leroy Fitch, of the *USS Moose* to guard the nearby river sector. Fitch deployed a blockade some forty miles in length around Pomeroy. "This might have been considered an extravagant use of boats," Fitch later confided, "but the river was so low and fords so numerous that a less number might not have met with such a favorable result."[3] General E. Parker Scammon stationed at Fayetteville, West Virginia, marched his command to the Kanawha River, boarded boats and went downriver to Gallipolis, where they joined Fitch in patrolling the upper reaches of the Ohio River.[4] Several river steamers had been converted to gunboats by placing cannons aboard manned by the 19th OH Battery.[5]

Despite the rise in the river, it was necessary for Fitch to "warp" his gunboat upstream. Assisted by a tow from the steamer *Imperial,* skippered by Captain T.J. Oakes,[6] and followed by the lighter draft, *Allegheny Belle,* they passed over Letart Falls and other obstructions before reaching Buffington Island, the blockade position to which Fitch had assigned his own flagship. He anchored the *Moose* off Little Sandy Creek on the West Virginia shore and waited.[7]

The Ohio River was an important objective that Morgan knew he needed to cross before he could be safe among a sympathetic population. After skirting Cincinnati, his plan was to cross at the safest point. His scouts, who had reconnoitered the river in June, had told him that Buffington Island would be an ideal crossing point. Not only would it be shallow enough for horses to wade across, it would be too shallow for Union gunboats to approach the area. With only militia forces in front of him, Morgan was confident they would offer but token resistance. Other than using his Parrotts to cover his river crossing, Morgan had no plans to deal with the gunboats. But a twenty-eight-year-old regular naval line officer from Indiana named Leroy Fitch did.

When the river fell in the late spring of 1863, as it did each year about this time, Fitch took the opportunity to visit Cincinnati. There, he personally supervised the outfitting of three new tinclads, the *Victory*, the *Reindeer* and the *Moose*. The latter was his flagship for future missions. As he checked the workmen placing the thin armor and mounting the cannon, he may have taken a moment to reflect on his command steamer. The *USS Moose* was a newly constructed 189-ton sternwheeler steamboat that briefly bore the name *Florence Miller II* before its purchase and commissioning into Union service on May 20, 1863. The vessel was 154 feet, 8 inches long, 32 feet, 2 inches wide at the beam and had a five-foot draught. Once outfitted with armor and six 24-pounder smoothbores, the *Moose* could produce a flank speed of six knots in calm waters.[8]

The first word that Fitch received in Cincinnati about Morgan's activities was the raiders' crossing the Ohio River at Brandenburg, Kentucky. Thinking it was only a small band that had seized the steamers *McCombs* and *Alice Dean,* he wired his immediate superior, Fleet Captain Alexander M. Pennock, of the disturbance and promised that the tinclad *Springfield,* on patrol between Evansville and Louisville, would arrive on the scene in a few hours.[9]

Then returning to the Cincinnati wharf, he boarded the *Moose* and accompanied by the *Victory,* they steamed for Louisville. Arriving there on July 9, the commander was handed a wire sent from New Albany, Indiana, by Acting Ensign Joseph Watson, skipper of the *Springfield* telling of his inability to stop Morgan's crossing at Brandenburg.

Fitch grew fearful that two tinclads, the *Silver Lake* and *Fairplay,* which he had dispatched to help the *Springfield,* might be taken by surprise should they reach Brandenburg. Misled as to the number of raiders, as well as to their objective and speed, he immediately passed orders for the *Moose* and *Victory* to raise steam and push over the Louisville falls to the rescue. A few miles downstream, he sighted the *Springfield*. Hauling close, Fitch communicated with Watson and then directed that all three boats continue at full speed to Brandenburg.

Towards six o'clock in the evening, the mini-fleet arrived off the Kentucky town only to find Morgan had completed his crossing. Unhappy to have missed this chance for battle, the commander signaled his squadron to "round to."[10]

With Morgan's escape, the naval command was saddled with one of the war's most recurrent problems—faulty information. No one knew for sure where the Confederates were at any given time or where they might appear next. Interviews with citizens living along the Kentucky shore were fruitless. Officers of the Federal army either did not know where the raiders were, which was usually the case, or believing they knew, seemed to "think it beneath their dignity to inform or communicate with a naval commander." Frustrated in his personal efforts to obtain intelligence, Fitch was forced to rely on newspaper accounts "for all my information" and the reports in the panic-stricken press were the most inaccurate of all.

Faced with this intelligence gap and aided only indirectly by small daily telegrams from the Cincinnati office of Area Commander Ambrose E. Burnside, whose information-gathering problems were just as difficult, Commander Fitch was forced to make his own estimates. "With the river running around him," the commander decided that his best move would be to post a string of gunboats along the Ohio to guard as many of the accessible crossings and shallow fords as possible. As an added safety measure, he issued a general order forbidding all unarmed steamers to run without convoy.[11]

After scouting Louisville, the Confederate force of Captain Davis chose this time to effect a crossing of the Ohio River. They soon were sighted near Twelve Mile Island above Louisville by the vigilant tinclads. Moving up fast, the *Victory* and *Springfield* began shelling the men crossing. Sixty-three managed to get across. The rest were scattered or captured. Fitch received a wire from Burnside informing them that Morgan was at Vernon heading toward Madison, Indiana. Fitch determined to "keep on Morgan's right [flank]." As they headed upriver toward Cincinnati, Fitch ordered the destruction of every flat, skiff or scow encountered in an effort to deprive the southerners of possible fording craft.[12]

General Burnside had his cavalry forces spread thinly over several states to cover a multitude of duties, not the least of which was the pursuit of Morgan and his men. When General Alexander S. Asboth based in the western Kentucky rivertown of Columbus, requested cavalry troops from Burnside, he received the following response.

(Telegram)   General Asboth, *Columbus, Ky.:* Cincinnati, Ohio, *July* 17, 1863.
All my cavalry are after Morgan in Ohio, east of the Scioto River. I
have to hold the entire line of the Louisville and Nashville Railroad,
the Cumberland River, and Eastern Kentucky, so that I really have
not a man to spare. What kind of force do you need, and how
much? Are there not plenty of gunboats on the river?
A.E. BURNSIDE, Major-General[13]

9:00pm, Friday, July 17

The Federal troops under Hobson arrived in Jackson. They found the
burned remains of the town's railroad depot. The Union general decided to
stop and rest his troops for the night. By three o'clock the following morning, he was on the move again, going east toward Pomeroy.[14]

THIRTY-SIX

Vinton Loses Its Bridge

<u>5:00am, Saturday, July 18</u>

Leaving Wilkesville, Morgan's column headed south and east toward the Ohio River and their anticipated crossing at Buffington Island. They crossed into Gallia County through the small village of Ewington, heading south to the larger town of Vinton. Lydia L. Matthews was attending Turkey Run School. When the townspeople were warned of Morgan's coming, she became frightened because her brothers were all away in the Union Army. Although Lydia had only recently arrived for daily classes, she and the other children were sent home to their parents. Her father was busy hiding their horses and cows far from the house in a deep hollow where they could not be found easily.[1]

Seventeen-year-old Anselm T. Holcomb was standing on Vinton's main street as thousands of Confederate horse soldiers clattered into the village three abreast and in close order. Anselm noted that the soldiers consumed all the patent medicines, especially those with an alcohol flavor. They also helped themselves to all the merchants' tobacco and cigars. A shot rang out, and Anselm was accused of firing the shot at a Confederate officer. Another raider quickly vouched for Holcomb and he was let go. Later, Anselm learned that another youngster had fired the bullet and ran to hide in the closet of the village minister.[2]

After the raiders had crossed the covered bridge over Big Raccoon Creek, they burned it. The bridge would not be replaced for well over one hundred years. Today, a swinging bridge has been built on the abutments of the original span.[3] *There is a Morgan's Raid historical marker at the bridge.* Turning north, the Confederates exited the county through Morgan Center. Next stop was Meigs County and the coveted river crossing near Portland.

<u>6:00am, July 18</u>

Col. Rutherford B. Hayes (later to become the 19th U.S. President) and two Union regiments arrived at the port of Gallipolis. When he heard that Morgan was farther up river, he loaded his men back abroad his two steamboats and made for Pomeroy.[4]

MEIGS COUNTY, OH

THIRTY-SEVEN

Last Lap to Freedom

The militia of Rutland, anticipating a visit from Morgan, had burned the bridge over Leading Creek at McMaster's mills on July 17. They had also felled trees across the road, hoping to delay the Confederates and give Hobson's men an opportunity to catch up.[1]

5:00am, Saturday, July 18

The force from Dixie entered Meigs County through Salem Center.[2] At first, Morgan encountered the felled trees blocking the road. They had been strategically placed so that if his men had gone off on one side, they would have had a steep hill to negotiate. On the other side, there were steep cliffs. So the Confederate column had to stay on the road or it would have been in trouble. Wagons or horses pulling cannons were stopped dead in their tracks where a tree had been dropped in the right place. By strategically picking where they wanted to drop a tree, Ohio citizens were able to make a significant delaying blockade of Morgan's progress.

After crossing Strong Run Creek, Morgan's advance guards came to the Williams' farm, just west of Salem Center. There, they stole one drum and fiddle from John Williams. Perhaps one of the Confederates was planning to start his own musical group on his return to Dixie. Williams was reimbursed $10 by the State of Ohio for the loss of his two musical instruments.[3] On the eastern side of town lived Benjamin Gorby. He had just received letters from his two sons in the Union army. To help their father who had been scratching out a living, they had sent him $30 in their letters to home. The Confederates found the mail and removed the cash. The State replaced every penny pilfered.[4]

Splitting his forces once again, the Confederate General sent half his force north toward Dexter and Harrisonville, while he continued toward Langsville and Rutland.

As he came down the road, Morgan saw the burnt timbers of the bridge that had spanned Leading Creek.[5] Today, it's a small creek, but in 1863, it was a deep and wide body of water with a dam and a mill beside it. Still,

Morgan was undeterred. On the east side of the creek, a small group of people from Langsville took a few shots at him.

Nothing serious. Not enough townspeople and certainly not of the fighting caliber to stand up to thousands of trained soldiers. So Morgan had a few of his men come around the hillside and cross over the dam. He still had the problem of crossing Leading Creek with his wagons and artillery. A few Confederates crossed the creek and captured some of the citizens. The other townsfolk headed for the hills to save their necks. The captured townspeople were forced to build a makeshift bridge to facilitate the crossing of his cannons and huge array of wagons.

Upon entering Langsville, he found the town deserted, except for Mrs. McKnight and her twin, two-week-old daughters who were frightened and seeking sanctuary in their little house with a lean-to back. Unknown to General Morgan, her husband, Captain William McKnight was part of the Union force pursuing him. True to his chivalrous code, the General posted guards around Mrs. McKnight's home so she would not be disturbed or endangered.[6] In fact, he made himself a guest of Mrs. McKnight while he waited for the bridge to be built.[7]

Six hours later, when Captain McKnight entered Langsville as part of the pursuing Union force, he stopped for ten minutes to visit his wife and infant daughters and check how they had fared during the Confederate occupation.[8]

During this interim, a group of raiders split away and headed south of Langsville with hopes of getting around the creek. They came to the J.L. Parkinson farm searching for fresh horses and food. A few of the Confederates, upon entering the Parkinson home, saw some pictures of Union generals on the wall. One soldier advised Mrs. Parkinson to remove the pictures, because, as he put it, "We have some pretty tough customers in our outfit." Mrs. Parkinson took them down, hid them, and went on to fix dinner for the soldiers. Her ten-year-old son, Jimmy, was given the job of holding and caring for the horses while the soldiers ate inside.[9]

As Morgan left town, the men from Langsville were still waiting up the hill on his left. As they started up the grade, the Langsville men allowed all the Confederates to ride by and then shot at the three men riding abreast in the rear of the column. They hit and killed the one in the middle. His companions supported him around a bend in the road and then left him along the roadway. Abner Hubbell at first buried the Confederate in the ravine. Later William Stevens and John Shafer of Langsville put the body in a feed box and buried it in an unmarked grave. The deceased was a young man in his late teens. On his body, they found his name and address. They wrote to his widowed mother in Tennessee. She replied that she wanted him placed in a box so it could be removed at a later date. Hubbell wrote and told her that this had been done, but she was never heard from again.[10]

At the farm of Waldo Strong in Salem Township, the raiders "traded" four broken-down horses for an equal number of fresh ones. Saddles, bridles, bacon, flour and 100 bushels of corn "disappeared" too. Mr. Strong submitted a claim of $650.50. The state compensated him with an even $600. He was one of 381 people in Meigs County to lose farm animals and property to the marauding Confederates. Mr. Strong later stated that the raiders did "treat his family in a most gentlemanly manner."

At the home of a Mr. Durst, Morgan's men threatened to burn the house unless Mrs. Durst told them where they had hidden their horses. She replied, "Burn away, the horses are worth more than the house." The rejected raiders rode away, taking nothing and leaving the home untouched.[11]

8:00am, Saturday, July 18

Morgan's next stop was Rutland, a town founded by New England people who were Revolutionary War veterans coming out to claim land grants. The town was famous in the area prior to the Civil War because of its activities and support of the Underground Railroad. The townspeople had gotten into a legal hassle with the people in Virginia (later West Virginia) across the river. The case went to the Ohio State Supreme Court.[12] Rutland citizens feared that Morgan knew that they had been helping slaves escape. Suddenly, a Southern army showed up on their doorsteps. If Morgan had any knowledge of Rutland's part in the Underground Railroad, he certainly didn't indicate it. He did no real damage, but most of the local people, fearing retribution, were taking no chances and deserted the town.

Now, as Morgan came into Rutland, he felt the press of time. He knew he was getting close to the river. He had been thinking about getting across the Ohio and escaping. He had lost time because of the felled trees, burned bridges and other incidents. Being unfamiliar with the area, he sought out a "pilot." He had his men search the town looking for a man who could guide him. They found the town's blacksmith, Joseph S. Giles, hiding in a fruit cellar. They forced him at gunpoint to get on a horse and accompany them.

A mile beyond Rutland, they passed through Cook's Gap, a low place through the hills. Morgan made a right turn. He was heading toward Middleport. As he rode by a house at an intersection, a man by the name of Halliday Hysell, a Union soldier, home on leave, heard a commotion outside. He stepped out on the porch in his uniform. He may have been intoxicated and began to curse the raiders.[13]

Across the intersection lived seventy-four-year-old Doctor William N. Hudson, a graduate of a medical school in Philadelphia. As the doctor approached his home, he could hear his neighbor denouncing the raiders in very expressive language. He headed across the street to warn his hard-of-hearing neighbor to be quiet. A Confederate trooper hearing the cursing and spotting the doctor running away, shot and killed Hysell and mortally wounded the doctor in the groin, shattering the thigh bone near the joint. He died a week later.[14]

Giles, the smithy captured in Rutland, told Morgan that he could cross the river because Middleport had a ferry. The General turned to his guide and asked, "Okay, now where do I go to get into Middleport?" The answer was, "It's right straight up the road there."[15]

A Union company had arrived in Middleport from Marietta the preceding midnight. They took up positions on Jacobs' Hill and sent out pickets and scouts. One of the scouts was a Middleport resident, George Womeldorff. He went to his home to relieve himself of some money he had on his person. He found his home deserted. Mrs. Womeldorff had taken their children and valuables to Fisher's coal bank, where a number of frightened women and children had taken refuge. Womeldorff was obliged to face the enemy with $200 in his possession.[16]

While reconnoitering, Womeldorff ran into several Confederate advance scouts and was taken prisoner. He was relieved of his $200 bankroll and brought into the raiders' column, where he discovered that Horace Holt of Rutland was a prisoner, too. While Holt was complaining about his stolen horse, Womeldorff saw that the Confederates were distracted and made his escape. He came riding back to his company on Jacobs' Hill, bare-headed and yelling like a Comanche Indian, "Boys, Morgan's coming!"[17]

The Middleport/Pomeroy militia were waiting for Morgan at the top of the hill. The road was narrow and steep on both sides, so the Confederates were riding into a bottleneck. They found it difficult to get through. After trying unsuccessfully a couple of times, Morgan came back and said to Giles, "Okay, where's the next best place to get out of town?" His response was, "Well, Pomeroy is right next door. It also has a ferry. But if Middleport knows you're coming, their ferry will be long gone and so will Pomeroy's." Morgan asked, "Where's the next best place to cross?" Giles thought for a moment and answered, "You can cross the river up at Buffington Island at Portland. There's a shallow place up there."[18] Morgan had been heading for Buffington, but he was ready to cross the river before reaching the island if the opportunity presented itself. So from this point on, Morgan's goal was to reach Portland and Buffington Island. The focus was the river...*Always the River*.

But between him and Portland lay Pomeroy, the county seat of Meigs County. The town of Pomeroy hugs the Ohio River shoreline. Most of the town is only two streets deep because the streets dead end abruptly at the base of overhanging high cliffs. The citizens of Pomeroy were waiting for Morgan's arrival. Charles E. Walker, a lad of fifteen, joined a dozen other boys on the cliff behind the Wildermuth Brewery. They hid among the rocks and trees, where, safe from the fire of gunboats, they could see the battle if there should be one. Anchored along the river shore overlooking Pomeroy, five U.S. Navy gunboats stood ready to open fire should the Confederates try to occupy the town. Morgan's advance scouts first turned down Union Avenue and then entered Thomas Fork Road, where the road over Lincoln Hill crosses the creek. The picket guards stationed on the hill above fired their little cannon and hurried back to town to give the alarm, "They are coming, boys, they are coming."[19]

As Morgan's men rode around the perimeter of Cincinnati, many lost their way
in the moonless night. They lit torches for signs of hoofprints and horse slaver.
(page 117)

Cincinnatians armed themselves for the expected
attack from Morgan's forces. Most adults stayed
awake the night of July 13 to read and hear
reports of Morgan's presence in the suburbs.
(page 114)

Len A. Harris, Mayor of Cincinnati
offered to lead Cincinnati Cavalry in pursuit of Morgan
(page 149)

82

Hamman Hersch Roudebush,
Harrison, Ohio farmer who tried to rescue his wife.
(page 108)

Emaline Avery Simonson Roudebush,
Hamman's wife who was "captured" by Morgan's men.
(page 108)

The Schenck home, Deer Park, Ohio
General Morgan's breakfast stop, July 14, 1863
(page 124)

John Schenck,
Cincinnati pharmacist and prize cattle breeder.
(page 124)

Henry Wager Halleck, General-in-Chief
Union Army, Washington, DC.
General McClellan felt that Halleck was
"the most hopelessly stupid of all men in
high position." Gideon Welles summed it
up by stating that Halleck "originates nothing,
anticipates nothing...takes no responsibility,
plans nothing, suggests nothing, is good for
nothing." In March, 1864, Halleck was
replaced by Ulysses Grant and reassigned
to chief-of-staff.
(page 115)

Lt. Col. George Washington Neff, USA
Camp Dennison commander during Morgan's Raid.
(page 126)

Major-General William Tecumseh Sherman, USA
His daughter, Minnie, was in harm's way.
(page 123)

**Top: Camp Dennison
Military Headquarters**
Waldschmidt House

Middle: Camp Dennison
Railroad ran through middle of camp.
To the left are the hospital barracks.
To the right are parade grounds,
officer huts, headquarters building
and sutleries.
(page 128)

Below: Camp Dennison
Tents to house the enlisted men.
(page 128)

Nicholas Todd home,
Montgomery, OH
(page 131)

Loveland, OH
Log cabin and fresh horses

(page 148)

Officers and Sergeants of Co. B, Cincinnati Zouaves

6

Top: Confederates derail train in Clermont County, OH (page 137)

Middle: Morgan's men waited in ambush around bend for train traveling from Loveland to Camp Dennison.

Below: Colonel Basil Duke offers to test pies while his men watch to see if they are poisoned. (page 142)

Lt. Kelion Franklin Peddicord, 14th KY, CSA (page 137)

**Kain's Tavern,
Williamsburg, OH**
(page 145)

Izella Cadwallader, Williamsburg, OH

Byron Williams home, Williamsburg, OH
Where Captain Harris hid in attic.
(page 147)

Williamsburg Omnibus
Like one Whig Holloman drove to Batavia
(page 143)

Elva Market, Camp Dennison, OH

**Catharine Deerwester
and John Anderson**
shortly after they married
(page 140)

Henry Brunner's home and cobbler shop, Georgetown, OH
(page 154)

Canal boats at Jasper, OH
(page 174)

Above: Train depot at Branch Hill, OH

Bottom: Spangler's blacksmith shop, Beaver, OH
(page 178)

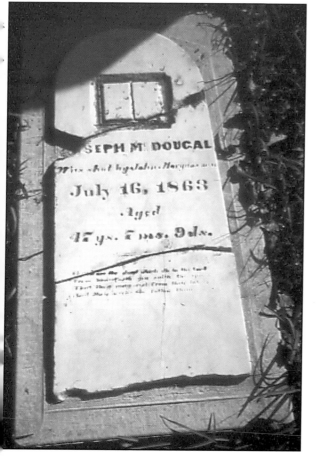

Top left: Joseph McDougal

Top right: Captain James W. Mitchell, Co. G, 11th KY, CSA

Left: McDougal's grave stone in Jasper, OH Methodist Church yard. Vandals had broken stone Into several pieces which have been cemented together.

(page 174)

Colonel Benjamin P. Runkle, 45th OVI, USA
(page 181)

**Colonel Rutherford B. Hayes
23rd OVI, USA**
(page 179)

Gunboats being built at Cincinnati
(page 192)

Above: Home of Dr. William Cline, Wilkesville, OH
(page 188)

Right: Morgan bridge in Vinton, Gallia County, OH replaced bridge burnt by Confederates.
(page 195)

Kim Sheets Schuette, Gallipolis, OH

12

Above: Streets in Pomeroy, OH are one or two blocks deep because town is built against overhanging cliffs.
(page 200)

OHIO
HISTORICAL
MARKER

MORGAN'S RAID ROUTE

General John Hunt Morgan led a force of 2,000 Confederate cavalrymen into Meigs County on July 18, 1863, during a forty-six day raid north of the Ohio River. After a skirmish with the 23rd Ohio Infantry, the Confederates paused to drink and replenish their canteens with cool spring water found here in Rocksprings. Nearby, Isaac Carleton, a Meigs County native, was shot and wounded by a Confederate soldier. After suffering set backs at Chester and Buffington Island, Morgan surrendered eight days later near West Point in Columbiana County. The surrender field was the northernmost point ever reached by Confederate forces during the Civil War.

MEIGS COUNTY HISTORICAL SOCIETY
OHIO TRAVEL AND TOURISM
THE OHIO HISTORICAL SOCIETY

6-53

1997

Captain William McKnight, USA
(page 197)

The "Gauntlet" on Thomas Fork Road through which Morgan's men fought on their way to Chester.
(page 201)

Entrance to Rutland, OH
(page 198)

Top: Bridge at Chester, OH over the Shade River.
(page 202)

Above Left: Home in Chester where General Morgan asked Col. Johnson to join him on the porch.
(page 203)

Above Right: Colonel August V. Kautz, 23rd Army Corps, First Division, Third Brigade, USA
(page 216)

Below: Bashan-Stiversville Road from Chester to Portland.
(page 204)

Major William G. Bullitt, 6th KY, CSA
(page 217)

Lieutenant Leland Hathaway, 14th KY, CSA
(page 207)

Orphan Brigade Kinfolk, Louisville, KY

Lt. Colonel Cicero Coleman, 8th KY, CSA
(page 243)

Colonel D.H. Smith, 5th KY, CSA
(page 212)

Top: Colonel William P. Sanders, 5th KY, USA
(page 78)

Bottom: Lt. Commander Leroy Fitch, US Navy
(page 191)

Major Daniel McCook
Fathered three Union generals and, at age 63, volunteered for Army duty and was mortally wounded at Battle of Buffington Island.
(page 230)

Union gunboats shelling the Confederates on the banks of the Ohio River.
(page 214)

President Abraham Lincoln, USA
(page 252)

President Jefferson Davis, CSA
(page 37?)

Brigadier-General James Murrel Shackelford, 8th KY, USA
(page 20)

Major Thomas Webber, 2nd KY, CSA
(page 25?)

THIRTY-EIGHT

The Pomeroy-Middleport Gauntlet

<u>11:30am, Saturday, July 18</u>

At a fork in the creek, the Confederates came upon a wedding reception for Samantha Smith. Morgan's men "invaded" the wedding party, partaking of the food and refreshments meant for the guests.[1] Then he headed east, trying to get to Portland where he could cross the river. Here he ran into a trap set up by the people of Pomeroy and Middleport. This sizable force was commanded by General Scammon and included Col. Rutherford B. Hayes, with four regiments brought up from West Virginia.[2] They joined the local militia led by Capt. R.B. Wilson and an artillery company under Capt. John Schreiner.[3]

When Scammon arrived at Pomeroy with two regiments, he sent this telegram:[4]

(Telegram)   Pomeroy, *July* 18, 1863.
General BURNSIDE:
I have just arrived here with two regiments infantry, and will have two more to-night. Can you give me any information that would be useful?

E.P. SCAMMON,
Brigadier-General.

The Union plans were to stop Morgan in a natural canyon with very steep hills on both sides and an abundance of rocks and trees. When the Confederates rode into this area, they were riding directly into concentrated gunfire. Because of the hillsides and rocks, Morgan was unable to flank his enemy, who were using the terrain effectively. The men of Middleport, who had forced him off the Middleport hill, were coming down the road behind him. Morgan was frustrated that he had no alternative route to reach the river. He had to run the gauntlet, which forced him into the canyon's narrow space.[5] The same emotion he felt when the federal gunboat sought to thwart his river crossing at Brandenburg, showed itself once more.

201

Scammon's larger group lay in wait at the tops of the hills at the end of the canyon. Included among the men who sighted down their guns at the desperate Confederate troops riding the hellish gauntlet of Thomas Fork Road was Second Lieutenant William McKinley, Jr. (later to become the 25th U.S. President) of the 23rd OVI, Co. D.[6] Morgan was angry because he couldn't get at his adversaries. In Basil Duke's book, he wrote, "In passing near Pomeroy, there was one continual fight, but, now, not with the militia only, for some regular troops made their appearance and took part in the programme. Colonel Grigsby took the lead with the Sixth Kentucky, and dashed through at a gallop, halting when fired on, dismounting his men and dislodging the enemy, and again resuming his rapid march. Major Webber brought up the rear of the division and held back the enemy, who closed eagerly upon our track."[7]

Finally, at the other end of the canyon, Morgan broke through into open flat land. Now, his cavalry had the advantage over the militia caught in the open fields. He charged through them and didn't stop until he came to an area called Rocksprings. There, he rested his men briefly while they replenished their canteens and took care of the wounded. Then they headed toward Chester.[8]

12:00 Noon, Saturday, July 18

Sarah Wells Irwin was taking her baby, Henry, and going to visit her brother, Harrison Wells. She and a neighbor lady were walking to her brother's home. As they started to cross the road to Chester, they discovered it was being used by General Morgan's troops. At that moment, General Morgan happened to come by and he halted his column to allow the two women to cross the road. Sarah's husband, Asbury, was in the Union Army and was part of the cavalry looking for Morgan's column.[9]

About the time Morgan had stopped at Rocksprings, Generals Shackelford and Hobson were leaving Rutland and General Judah had arrived in Pomeroy. The two pursuing Union groups were starting to converge on Morgan's column. Judah followed the River Road through Minersville, Syracuse, Racine[10] and then east across the mid-county road toward Portland. Judah reasoned that if Morgan's intent was to try to cross the Ohio, he was going to follow along the river road, hoping to cut him off. By this time, Morgan was the hunted and getting more desperate, depressed and despairing.

1:00pm, July 18

Morgan's men entered Chester, ten miles from Buffington Island. After his column had crossed the Chester bridge over Shade River, they set it afire.[11] The Chester carding and saw mill, built in the early 1800s, was about fifty feet away. It caught fire from the sparks of the burning bridge. Inside the mill, many Chester area residents had grain and lumber stored, ready for processing. Everything inside was destroyed, along with the building structure. The mill's owner, Benjamin Knight, received $3,500 compensation from the State of Ohio, which gave him the funds to replace the structure.[12] After Morgan's raid, the mill was rebuilt and continued in operation until the 1930s.

In the confusion of the burning mill, Joseph Giles, the Rutland guide, successfully found a hiding place and couldn't be found. Morgan needed an immediate replacement. His men searched the town and couldn't find one. General Morgan declared that he would not march without a guide. While he waited, Morgan sat on the porch of a crossroads store. Nearby was a well where his men were filling their canteens. As Colonel Johnson rode up, General Morgan gave him a bright smile and invited him to stop and rest a spell with him on the gallery. "All our troubles are over," the General said, "the river is only twenty-five miles away. Tomorrow we will be on Southern soil."[13] After delaying for ninety minutes in an unsuccessful search, feeding his men and horses, Morgan relented and struck out for Portland on his own. This halt would prove to be disastrous, as it caused the Confederates to arrive at the river after nightfall.

From Chester, the Confederate troopers struggled over winding dirt roads that rose to precipitous hilltops and then plunged into a verdant overgrowth of lush green hills wearing their full summer garb of green. Rising above the dense vegetation, wisps of dust stirred by the horses rose like low flying clouds, revealing the slow, steady pace of the anxious and tired Dixie soldiers.

On the western side of the boot that forms Meigs County is the Ohio River town of Racine, between Syracuse to the north and Antiquity to the south. It is on the opposite side of Meigs County across from Buffington Island. On Friday, July 17 at eight o'clock in the morning, twenty "Minute Men" reported to Racine's Pleasant View school house, which is three miles north of Racine and six miles due west of Portland. Their officers included Captain Ephriam Aumiller, First Lt. Dan Roush and Second Lt. Sam Davis. The men were not sure where Morgan planned to cross the Ohio River. They felt it would either be Wolf's Crossing or Buffington Island. Waiting, they camped at Pleasant View until Saturday night. Captain Aumiller left the company to reconnoiter and was captured by some of Morgan's men. They were eager to have him pilot them to the river and avoid the Union troops. As they passed through the woods near Bashan, Aumiller jumped from his horse, and although they were firing at him, he succeeded in making his escape through the brush.[14]

Reaching Bashan, a small village and birthplace of the noted writer Ambrose Bierce, Morgan's column encountered a funeral procession. The horse-drawn hearse and small entourage entered the crossroads at the same time the Confederates did. Morgan and his men very respectfully stopped, got off their horses, took off their hats, let the funeral procession go by and then remounted. The sight of fresh horses pulling the hearse was too good to pass up. He went to the head of the funeral procession, stopped the hearse, had the casket taken out and carefully laid on the field. He then had some of his wounded men placed in the hearse, which then joined Morgan's procession.[15] This bedraggled column stretched for several miles and it included an eclectic variety of spring wagons, buggies, coaches, vans and, now, a hearse.

Morgan gave orders for the advance guard to arrest or hold anyone they met or overtook on the road. Colonel Adam Johnson described what happened next. "We had hardly traveled a mile when the advance guard picked up a man, old and gray-bearded, who had been riding toward us. Morgan at once began to question him about crossing the river. He assured us that Long Bottom was about twenty miles down the river, but the ford was much deeper. Morgan concluded to take the right-hand road, and this proved to be a disastrous mistake, as by turning in that direction [to Portland] we were advancing toward the gunboats."[16]

Then turning east again on the Portland Road, they followed the road to Bald Knobs. There, the narrow trail wound southeast to Stiversville. From here, it was only a mile and a half directly east to Portland and the river. Fewer than 1,900[17] dog-tired Confederates descended out of the hills to the flat valley covered with crops of wheat and chest-high corn. The raiders crossed Lauck's Run on the Allen farm, marched across the Commons to Tunis Middleswart's 130-acre farm.[18] It was ten o'clock at night and Morgan's men were now on the banks of the Ohio just north of Portland.[19] Most of the force turned right and followed the Old Portland Road south along the river toward Buffington Island. It was dark, and Morgan had to decide whether to cross the river tonight or wait until morning.

At this point of the river, Morgan found that the promised shallow ford was gone. Because of recent flooding conditions, the river had risen from its easily fordable two feet to an unexpected depth with fast and dangerous currents. Also, he learned that a defensive fortification had been erected overlooking the crossing. Morgan's scouts were unable to tell him how many Union troops were manning the trenches and breastworks. Union Colonel W.R. Putnam had sent Captain D.L. Wood with 200 men, fifty mounted scouts and two pieces of artillery from Marietta.[20] Wood had spread his small company to make it appear he had more men.[21] This fortified point was rumored to have cannon defenses, which, in fact, it did. Without a guide familiar with the local terrain, the darkness masked hidden dangers that would be exposed with the first light of morning. Wood was determined, despite his small force, to deceive the Confederates and stand his ground. To emphasize his resoluteness, he told his men that they were to fight, not run. "If you see me running away, then shoot me. Because if I see you running, I'll shoot you!"[22]

Had Morgan's raid occurred two weeks earlier when it was originally scheduled, the water level at Buffington Island would have been only two feet deep, too shallow for Union gunboats to get close to this crossing point. Morgan could see that any attempt at crossing would need to be delayed until the next morning. Lady Luck was turning away.

Although he appreciated the importance of crossing the river at once, it seemed an impossible task. In the intense darkness, they could not see the ford and they were without guides. He determined that the Union fortifications would need to be cleared before his men could safely make the exposed crossing. He called a hurried council of war with his lieutenants. It was suggested that the heavier wagons be abandoned and a dash made to some point farther upriver, where fords might be passable. It was even pointed out that if two hundred wounded men were left behind with the wagon train and the four guns, the able-bodied men might swim the Ohio as they had swum the Cumberland. Without a moment's hesitation, Morgan vetoed this proposal. He would save all – or run the risk of losing all.[23] Resigned to spending the night on the Portland shoreline, the Confederate wounded were lifted from the motley train of carriages and wagons and laid tenderly upon the softer earth. Before they fell into a deep sleep, they gazed upon the West Virginia shore like the Promised Land illuminated by the light of the moon, soon to be obscured by a blanket of river fog.[24]

As the town of Portland began to fill with weary Confederates, eight-year-old Charlie Price, at the urging of some family members, went to the town's pole where the American flag was flying. His father had given him an auger to bore the pole down and save the flag. They were afraid if he used an ax, the noise would attract the raiders who would burn or destroy the flag. He was told not to bore any holes in the ground with the auger as it would dull the bit. He bored holes in the ground every ten steps but he later admitted, "I would never have thought of it if they hadn't told me not to do it."[25]

<u>4:30pm, Saturday, July 18</u>

Hobson received a dispatch from Col. Kautz who was in Rutland (Meigs County):

> **The rebels tried to force an entrance into Pomeroy, and have been repulsed. Captain Higley, Seventh Ohio Cavalry, left Morgan's rear an hour ago on Chester road, between 7 and 10 miles from here. They are supposed to be marching for Buffington Island, about 25 miles from here, where they will try to ford the river. It is too high, however, and the gunboats are on alert. General Scammon commanded at Pomeroy. No serious damage done. I have stopped to feed and rest, and shall push on to-night. An intelligent lady, at whose house Morgan was this afternoon, thinks they consider their case hopeless unless they can cross at Buffington Island to-night.**
>
> AUGUST V. KAUTZ, *Colonel Second Ohio Cavalry.*
>
> **P.S. – I have no communications with General Judah, but the country people saw him today marching on Pomeroy. He could have been in Morgan's front to-day [this morning] by marching about 25 miles last night. The rebels are bent on crossing to-night, but they cannot do it.[26]**

THIRTY-NINE

The Net Tightens

During the night, the Union forces were converging on Buffington Island from two directions, the west and the south. Colonel Kautz rode through Rutland six hours behind Morgan. Intelligence reports indicated that the Confederates would try to cross at Buffington Island, so he rushed through Pomeroy and on to Chester. Finding no one there, he followed the trail toward Portland.[1] Close behind were the bulk of the forces of Hobson, Shackelford and Wolford. Judah's thousands of fresh Federal cavalry and artillery completed their mid-cross county trip and were approaching along the river road from the south and would arrive at Buffington Island just before sunrise. Hobson's legions of cavalry and mounted infantry were pushing forward in all haste to engage the seemingly trapped Confederates. While all parties were converging, a blanket of river fog enveloped the valley, obscuring any hint of moonlight.[2]

Morgan had ordered his men to start a hasty construction of flatboats to aid the sick and wounded in their anticipated crossing. A few crudely constructed craft were fashioned and dozens of men clambered aboard ready to paddle across the wide, rushing river. A mile and a half upstream, Lieutenant Leland Hathaway found a number of leaky flatboats. In the darkness, he had his patrol set about caulking the seams.[3] Portland resident William Baringer had his ferry confiscated by the Confederates. Morgan ordered Duke to place two regiments as near the earthwork as he thought proper. The artillerists were similarly positioned and assigned the task of providing protective cover once the river crossing began.[4] Nineteen hundred Confederates, laden with the spoils of war, reduced to a few rounds of ammunition each, peered into the Stygian darkness, wondering how close the enemy positions were. Exhausted, most found repose in sleep.[5]

Five to eight thousand Union cavalry filled the hills and clogged the roads, converging on this soon-to-be-bloody Buckeye battlefield. Across the river, directly opposite the mid-point of Buffington Island, Commander Leroy Fitch had anchored his Federal gunboat, the *Moose,* at the mouth of the Little Sandy Creek along the West Virginia shore.[6]

2:00am, Sunday, July 19

Fitch anxiously got underway and moved over Sand Creek Shoals, intending to move close to the southern foot of Buffington Island. But the very dense fog prevented him from getting too far into the chute between the island and the Ohio shore. He settled down to await the morning and better visibility. The *Imperial,* which had towed Fitch's flagship over the Letart Falls, awaited orders to tow the *Moose* farther up the chute.[7] Fitch had positioned his fleet of tinclads at different points along the river where Morgan might try to cross.[8] These included the *Victory, Reindeer, Springfield, Elk* and *Naumkeag.* The unexpected appearance of the U.S. Navy just offshore would surprise and shock Morgan and his men. He had been assured that the river would be too shallow to allow these gunboats to threaten his crossing. Judah advanced blindly in the fog. In his desire to ascertain his enemy's positions, he personally led an advanced scouting party along the river road toward the island.[9]

Buffington Island is located opposite the mouth of Little Sandy Creek, which flows from West Virginia into the Ohio River. On the Ohio side, Dry Run Creek empties into the river at the southern tip of the island. The island is one-quarter mile wide and 1.2 miles long. It consists of 150 acres of land. Originally referred to as Amberson's Island after John Amberson, a late 18th century squatter, it acquired its present name in the early 19th century from first owner Joel Buffington, who farmed the land. It is forty-three miles south of Marietta, Ohio, thirty miles south of Parkersburg, West Virginia and twenty-five miles south of the much larger Blennerhassett Island.[10]

The Ohio shore overlooking Buffington Island is a valley about two miles in length, with the island anchoring the southern end. The valley floor is about 600 feet above sea level. The ridge that surrounds the valley rises to 700 feet and at its highest points are well over 800 feet. The ridges slope down to the valley and come to within 800 yards of the river.[11] The north ridge parallels the river for several hundred yards, then closes toward the bank of the river. There, massive stone cliffs stained by the ages serve as unscalable hurdles walling in the valley.

A road from Pomeroy entered the valley through the southern opening. A second road from Chester dropped into it midway along the ridge perpendicular to the Ohio shoreline. The little town of Portland hugged the Ohio River above the northern tip of Buffington Island. The island is approximately 1,000 feet from the eastern shore of West Virginia and only 200 feet from the Ohio shore. On July 19, 1863, it was even closer because there were no dams or locks, which have since raised the level of the river significantly.[12]

General Morgan chose the northern end of Portland, commandeering the Middleswart home[13] as his headquarters and advising the family to find accommodations elsewhere. Many of his men tore down Middleswart's fence railing and used it to cook and heat their meals that evening. Luckily for Mr. Middleswart, the raiders didn't find the money he had hidden under one of the fence posts.[14] Many of Middleswart's neighbors had uninvited guests over for dinner. Mrs. James Hysell served twenty meals to the raiders before she was permitted to retire. Mrs. William Bell, Middleswart's neighbor to the south, fed thirty raiders.[15] Some of the local men who were impressed into becoming unwilling guides were Clayton Middleswart and Henry Bell. They successfully escaped, and eluded their captors as they were being escorted over the James Anderson farm. While their Confederate guards stopped to let down a fence rail, they fell behind and fled down a gravel bank. Two other Portland residents, Mr. Fitch and Mr. Daugherty, were both taken prisoner by Morgan's men, but the next day when the battle started, they were released.[16]

Susan Bogard and her husband, Abner, were employed in the Williamson's home. She was baking a corn-pone bread. A Confederate rode up and ask if he could have some of the pone to eat. After she handed him a piece, he thanked her and said, "I expect we are going to get it down here. You had better come down after it is over and have a look." After the battle, she did go look and found the soldier, to whom she had given the bread, lying dead on the field.[17]

Half a mile south, closer to the northern tip of the island and the menacing earthworks, Duke hunkered down for the night. Capt. Byrne positioned two howitzers on the Anderson Price farm, overlooking the approaches to the ford at Buffington Island. Lieutenant Lawrence had the two Parrotts pulled up a hill to cover the expected crossing. From this advantage, he could direct fire on any gunboats that threatened safe passage over the bar. The few dozen homes that made up this river town were mostly occupied by women and children. It seems that when the men heard that Morgan was coming, most had business to attend to out of town. Many women and children took refuge in the basement of the Hoback family, one of the few homes in town that had a basement.[18] There, they spent an anxious and fitful night.

2:15am, Sunday, July 19

General Scammon had moved his forces from Pomeroy to Ravenswood in West Virginia, opposite Buffington Island, to capture Morgan's men if any were to make a successful crossing. To the relief of Captain

Wood, Scammon ordered him to evacuate his position guarding the ford. He knew that his militia force was inadequate to stop an onrush of thousands of Confederates. After pushing their artillery down a ravine, they retreated to the river bank where the *Starlight,* the boat that had brought them down from Marietta, lay at anchor. Attached to the steamer was a barge laden with sacks of ground meal. Pushing off, the boat became grounded onto tree stumps partially hidden underwater. Unable to free the craft, they began dumping the sacks of grain overboard to lighten the boat. Despite the commotion, the Confederates were not alerted that the defensive position was being abandoned. Once freed, they crossed safely to Ravenswood on the West Virginia side of the river.[19]

The stage was set on Ohio's only Civil War battlefield. Shortly, the rising sun would begin to burn away the fog, and the sound of crickets and frogs would be drowned out by the thunder of cannon, bursts of gunfire, screams of wounded and dying, shells exploding, desperate yells of trapped men and the chaos of battlefield hysteria. But for now, night and the enveloping fog muffled the movement of thousands of men and gave no hint of the legendary confrontation that would erupt with the dawn.

5:00am, Sunday, July 19

Throughout this summer night, the cool, predawn breezes caused misty clouds to rise from the warm river waters. Dense fog spilled over the Ohio River banks into the valley, obliterating the roads and farmhouses. Both the West Virginia mountains and Ohio hills overlooking Portland rose like spires piercing these earth-bound, opaque clouds.

5:15am, July 19

The tops of the trees overlooking the valley caught the first rays of sun about a quarter after five.[20] For a brief time, the enveloping clouds had a pale rose tint. Below, the Portland corn fields remained in darkness shrouded in a river fog. Hawks rose and began their silent circling, seeking prey. The Confederates had been roused from their fitful sleep and had been quietly preparing for the long-sought river crossing. Breakfast, as sparse as it was, had been consumed. Today, they hoped they would enjoy their next meal on southern soil, served to them by sympathetic Dixie belles.

FORTY

In a Fog

As daylight illuminated the morning scene, Col. J.W. Grigsby led the 6th KY Cavalry and Col. D.H. Smith took the 5th KY Cavalry into the thick fog that shrouded the valley. They moved to attack the hastily fortified earthworks commanding the ford. The fortifications, they found, had been abandoned and the cannon had been spiked and thrown over the bluff. Morgan was informed that the way was clear. Duke directed Col. Smith to take the 5th KY and picket the road to Pomeroy.[1]

Coming from the opposite direction, on the same road, was a scouting party with General Judah included among the advance detachment. The road was as crooked as a ram's horn and had innumerable roads and lanes leading from it at all sorts of appreciable and inappreciable angles. At each of the by-roads, General Judah stationed a sentry with instructions to point the right road as his main column followed farther to the rear. Many of these sentries fell fast asleep while waiting in the darkness. Their horses would walk away in search of something to graze on.[2]

Upon learning of this dereliction of duty, General Judah ordered three men be placed by every intersection, and ordered those who remained awake to take those who fell asleep under guard to headquarters, where they would be punished. While Judah's command had momentarily halted, a staff officer approached, leading a frightened colored man. The black man said that he had just gotten away from Morgan's men. He told the General where the Confederates were and how their forces were disposed. But upon a raking cross-examination, the frightened man stumbled. At once, he was called a liar. Judah thought his tale had been embellished and refused to listen to anything else the man had to say. Staff officers interposed in vain with the plea that the fellow's story was sustained by reasonable probability. But Judah sneeringly silenced them and military discipline forbade them from making any further comments.[3]

Lieutenant Armstrong with a detachment of the 14th IL Cavalry was sent for. Judah directed him to proceed with his company of seventy-five men toward the river. The lieutenant was not ordered to load his pieces, nor given the slightest hint to be prepared for a sudden meeting with the enemy.

211

Behind Armstrong's company rode the General and staff, and behind them was Captain Henshaw with a piece of artillery. After they had descended the hills, they entered a narrow lane bordered on each side by wheatfields, in which the grain was standing in shocks. On each side were high fences that were "horse-high, hog-tight and bull-strong."[4] The fog was so dense, the men could hardly see the men in front who were lost from view in the white gloom.[5] The Union advance group had just crossed Groundhog Creek and were approaching Dry Run near the southern tip of the island.

Just before the sound of gunfire alerted the combatants that a battle had commenced, some Confederate cavalry members of the 9th TN, under the command of Capt. J.D. Kirkpatrick, pushed across the Ohio in a small flat-boat. Later in the day, Artillery Capt. E.P. Byrne, Capt. John Sisson and Cpl. Robert Barksdale Moss of Ward's 9th TN would be among those who suc-cessfully crossed the river at the Buffington bar.[6] In all, some thirty to fifty men got across the Ohio River during the battle.[7] Captain N.M. Lea (Co. F, 2nd KY) and Capt. John A. Cooper (Co. L, 2nd KY) would cross later that day leading most of Companies F and L of the 2nd KY Cavalry.[8]

5:30am, Sunday, July 19

Judah's small group had approached within six hundred yards of the river when a gust of air, hot as the breath of an oven, came down the valley. Some of the fog lifted with the speed of a curtain rising on stage. The sun illuminated the brilliant green scenery. The Federal party was stunned to see a strong skirmish line of gray jackets, on foot, and not more than a hun-dred yards to their left and front in a place called "Buffington fields."[9]

The Confederate force had cautiously advanced, on foot, through the fog about 500 yards when they, too, came upon the unexpected Federal force. On the instant that the two parties discovered each other, the Confed-erates led by Col. Smith reacted first with a rattling volley from a hundred carbines. The Federal company was trapped in the narrow lane. Union carbines carelessly dangling were slow to give answering fire. The first effect was a recoil on the part of Judah's group. After the first shots, the Confederates dropped their carbines and charged the lead men, firing their pistols and yelling like devils. The Union's recoil degenerated into a scrambling, rush-ing, tumbling panic. The lead horses of Henshaw's gun were killed by the first shots. The team to the gun and limber were hopelessly entangled and formed an ugly barricade in the lane blocking the General's staff and escort.[10]

To those who had been persistent in warning Judah that they may be going into a trap, it was a vindication of their judgment and comical, sweet revenge to see the General's discomfort due to the consequences of his own arrogance. General Judah ducked behind his horse's neck to shield himself from the bullets coming his way. He managed to extricate himself and doubled back to seek the safety of his main column. The affair lasted about 20 minutes. By then some of the fog had disappeared, and the opposing lines had a clearer view of each other.[11]

The Confederates took fifty prisoners and wounded six. Among those captured were Capt. R.C. Kise, assistant adjutant general; Captain Rue, aide-de-camp; and Captain Henshaw. Staff officer, Lt. Fred W. Price was mortally wounded and was carried off by Morgan's men, along with Henshaw's piece of artillery.[12] Colonel Smith posted his men at the southern extremity of the valley with the ridge on his right flank. At this point, the ridge angles westward.[13]

Four-year-old J. Hoback awoke early Sunday morning to find the others still sleeping in the stillness of the basement. He quietly went upstairs and outside to see what was happening. He saw a crowd of Confederate soldiers and to him, it was a grand sight. He wandered across the street and down the river bank for quite a distance. All at once, Union guns on the hill behind the town cut loose and the shells began to burst over the river bank. Young Hoback moved with the crowd of stampeding Confederates so he wouldn't be trampled. One big, broad-shouldered Confederate soldier with a sandy mustache picked him up and asked where he lived. Amid the bursting of shells and the general uproar, he carried the child to Hoback's front door. He handed the child a cake and told him to stay inside. With that, the man in gray turned and disappeared into the din.[14]

FORTY-ONE

The Battle at Buffington Island

It is called the Battle of Buffington Island, yet the fighting occurred in, above and below Portland, not on the island itself. Then why didn't they call it the Battle at Portland like the Battle at Corydon? It's because Buffington Island is a landmark in the Ohio River just as is Blennerhassett Island, twenty-five miles farther upstream at Belpre, Ohio, across from Parkersburg, West Virginia. Buffington, jutting out into the river, offered a "bar" or shallow fording point across the Ohio River, which on July 9, 1863, was only two feet deep.[1] Morgan's objective was to reach this island, which would allow his troops to safely cross the treacherous river. Portland just happened to be next to the island. And that's where the conflict took place. The village is about one mile from its northern to its southern tip and about 800 yards wide at its southern extremity.[2] The battlefield area ranged over a three-mile stretch extending above Portland to almost two miles south of the village. Much of the acreage had chest-high corn with ripened plumes, adding a golden glaze over fields of green.

7:00am, Sunday, July 19

Overhearing the sound of gunfire, the officer of the deck, aboard the *Moose* informed Commander Fitch. The *Moose* was at the southern end of the island. Fitch's report detailed what happened next.[3]

I heard musketry on my port bow and a little ahead. Thick as the fog was, I at once got up anchor, and, feeling the way up, managed to get into the chute between the island and mainland. Getting fairly in the chute, the fog lifted, when I saw a portion of Morgan's force coming down the river just on the edge of the bank at full speed, as though they were making a charge. They had with them two pieces of artillery, which I think was their intention to place them at the head of the chute, to prevent my getting through. I at once opened fire on this squad with two bow guns, when they wheeled and took back up the river again.

214

Pushing through as fast as possible, I got above the head of the island and nearly opposite the enemy's left flank, when I again opened fire from the broadside guns.[4]

7:15am, Sunday, July 19

Easing in, the *Moose* picked up Captain John J. Grafton, a member of Judah's staff, who had been briefly captured when Judah had blundered through the fog into Duke's pickets. Grafton made his escape and was able to give Fitch his first good intelligence as to the relative positions of the opposing forces as he last knew them. The naval firepower of solid shot and exploding shells burst among the congested ranks of gray-clad soldiers, wagons, ambulances and artillery caissons. Morgan was taken by surprise at the appearance of the Federal gunboats that his scouts had informed him would not be able to operate in the upper part of the Ohio River.[5]

Commander Fitch was never quite sure where his twenty-four-pounder shells were landing. Both Yankee and Confederate soldiers later agreed on the confusion the shells caused as they roared overhead. Fitch guided the *Moose* up the chute, the narrow body of water between the Ohio shore and Buffington Island. He headed for the northern tip of the island, where he could see concentrations of troops.[6]

7:30am, July 19

Although Fitch remained basically ignorant of the changing bluecoat maneuvers ashore, his fire upon the Confederates was deadly. Col. Basil Duke cursed what he believed was more than one tinclad and "heartily wished that their fierce ardor, the result of a feeling of perfect security, could have been subjected to the test of two or three shots through their hulls."[7] Duke was correct. Naval shells were coming in from more than one boat. When the Confederates had abandoned their two howitzers when fired upon by the *Moose,* Fitch went ashore and had one of the guns placed on the deck of the *Allegheny Belle.*[8] Aiming his cannon aboard the *Belle* and seeking revenge was Nathaniel Pepper, son of Captain James Pepper, former skipper of the ill-fated *Alice Dean.*[9]

7:45am, July 19

General Judah, rejoining his division, ordered the 5th IN Cav. under Colonel Butler to move down the same road from which he had been entrapped. Throwing out a strong line of skirmishers, the dismounted regiment advanced briskly, forming a line as soon as the ground would permit. The 14th IL Cav. followed close in the rear as a reserve. The 11th KY Cav.

made a detour to the right, and swung around to form on Butler's right. At the same moment, Lt. John O'Neil of the 5th IN Cavalry led his company over fences and up the hill where the two Confederate Parrotts had been positioned. They captured the battery and turned it on the retreating Confederates. Col. Grigsby, leading the 6th KY, made a valiant counterattack to retake the Parrotts, but was driven off and joined the Confederate withdrawal. The Union advance cut off a portion of the 5th KY.[10]

Judah's line was now formed and began to flank Smith's regiment. "The shoe was now on the other foot." At Corydon, the Confederates' superiority in numbers of men allowed them to easily outflank the Indiana Legion home guard and quickly overwhelm the Hoosier defenders. Now, with a four to one ratio favoring the Union forces, Morgan's Raiders found themselves being outflanked. Smith gave orders to rally to their horses which was executed silently and in order. As they drew back to Duke's position, they encountered a withering storm of bursting shells, the heaviest concentration of artillery fire they had ever witnessed.[11] In this dash, two of the Confederate's artillery pieces and the one captured from Henshaw were recaptured. Within five minutes, Judah's four pieces were in position and opened fire. The Federal and Confederate lines were fully engaged less than a half mile apart. The Union forces pressed upon the Confederates, crowding them back toward the point where the river road runs over a narrow strip and close to the bluff.[12] The opening round of the battle had been going on for one hour. During this period, Duke rallied two regiments of 500 men and ordered them to dismount and hold the line while he sent several couriers to General Morgan asking for the 2nd Kentucky to be posted on the ridge and reinforce his thinly held line. Colonel Johnson offered Duke a detachment of his own brigade to occupy the ridge on Duke's right. Duke declined, believing the 2nd KY would soon arrive.[13]

Colonel Smith with fewer than 150 men extended his line to the right in an effort to get a few riflemen onto the ridge. Some of the raiders climbed so high they found themselves above the low lying fog. The battlefield was hidden from sight, but they saw the flashes when Judah's guns fired, and could hear the shells screaming up the valley.[14]

8:00am, Sunday, July 19

Coming in on the road from Chester, Colonel Kautz's advance of 200 men[15] came under fire from Johnson's pickets. They were about two miles from Portland. Kautz feared that Morgan was already crossing the Ohio River. He knew that Colonel Sanders was an hour behind with the Union artillery. Rather than wait for the larger force to catch up, he ordered his small band of cavalry to charge into the valley, hoping to disconcert the Confederates and interrupt their crossing.[16] Hearing *Moose*'s bombardment, the Union cavalry charged with renewed courage and an appetite for battle sharpened by the long chase.[17]

Warned of the approach of Kautz's flying column, Colonel Adam Johnson dispatched Captain Bennett and his company to scout the road. He reported back to Johnson that a heavy body of cavalry was advancing. Orders were given to hold the enemy in check.[18]

Kautz's men drove Col. Johnson's rear videttes in from the Chester road. Johnson reacted by deploying his main force to meet Hobson's spearhead. Down the Chester road came some of the Union's finest cavalry units, stones rolling from under the hurrying hoofs, regimental flags waving in the breeze created by the downhill rush.[19] Whitelaw Reid, the newspaper correspondent, saw the battle unfolding and wrote, "As Hobson's guidon [pennant] fluttered out in the little valley by the river bank, every member of that little Rebel band that had defiled a hundred thousand knew the contest was over. They were almost out of ammunition, exhausted, barely 2,000 strong. Against them were Hobson's 3,000 and Judah's still larger force."[20]

Neither Judah nor Hobson were aware of each other's position until the battle was virtually over.[21] The left flank of Duke's line was only 300 yards from the river. It was manned by the 6th KY led by Major William G. Bullitt. Even though the 6th KY was almost surrounded and their ammunition almost exhausted, they held Judah's troops in check, maintaining their position and withdrew as Duke commanded in an orderly fashion.[22] Fighting along with Duke and Smith were Col. R.C. Morgan and Col. W.W. Ward.[23]

Other Federal units, moving in from the west, would soon join in the attack on Duke. In addition to Colonel August V. Kautz with the 2nd OH Cavalry, there would be the 7th, 8th and 9th MI led by Colonel William P. Sanders (5th KY Cavalry) and 7th OH Cavalry led by Colonel Israel Garrard.[24] Kautz with the 2nd OH Cavalry rode north along the base of the ridge and struck the wagon train from the flank. Morgan's men were down to their last five rounds.[25]

The Confederate forces were in a crossfire from three directions: west, south and east (the river). Union cavalry forces were attacking simultaneously from both directions, and the U.S. Navy gunboats were shelling without fear or favor. Southern soldiers groaned and cursed, forgetting it was the Sabbath.[26]

Duke and Johnson engaged the bulk of the Federal forces on the middle and southern ridges overlooking the river. Col. Johnson's line, confronting Hobson, was formed at right angles to Duke. In the unsheltered surface of the valley, everyone was exposed to shellfire.[27]

9:00am, Sunday, July 19

Following in Kautz's footsteps, Col. Sanders' command arrived with an artillery battery. The 9th MI, led by Capt. W.B. Smith, dismounted and deployed as skirmishers in front of Duke. They filed to the left and formed a line along the edge of the deep green, tightly packed cornfield and were ordered to commence firing as soon as their battery opened its barrage. Capt. Smith sent one of his staff officers to reconnoiter from the top of a hill near the cornfield and select a position for their battery.[28] They found a clearing about 120 feet above the valley floor, overlooking Portland, with Buffington Island off to the right.

9:20am, July 19

Within twenty minutes, the orders were executed, a section of the 11th MI Battery had climbed the steep hill and commenced firing. They could hear Judah's artillery on their right and the heavier Dalhgren guns being fired by the *Moose*. Following the 9th MI Cavalry onto the field was the 9th KY (USA), led by Colonel Richard T. Jacob, moving to the right. Lt. Col. Adams with the 1st KY Cav. (USA) headed to the left. The 3rd OH and 8th MI charged the center, forming along the cornfield fence and began to fire without waiting for the signal gun. After twenty minutes, the Confederates were driven from the cornfield. Lt. Col. Grover S. Wormer ordered the 8th MI Cav. to remount and make a charge against the Confederates. For two miles, the Michigan battalions poured volley after volley from their Spencer carbines into the retreating gray ranks.[29] Isolated skirmishes had been ranging from Ground Hog Creek in the south to the Middleswart Cemetery upriver.

General Hobson, Col. Sanders and their staff, standing on a hill overlooking the conflict, found themselves exposed to exploding naval shells. A shot or two caused a hasty transfer of Hobson's headquarters into a ravine for protection.[30] Over all the field a thin blue haze of smoke was slowly spreading. In the maelstrom of soldiers and horses, the men became hopelessly entangled with other regiments and separated from their sergeants and officers. Bugles screamed quick urgent calls at cross-purposes. The Confederate forces formed to the "rear of the line" three times and kept the pursuing Union cavalry at bay. But as they approached the end of the valley and saw that there were but two avenues of escape, the men broke ranks and rushed for them. The Federal cavalry came up and dashed pell-mell into the crowd of fugitives.[31]

This hasty and desperate move was exactly what Commander Fitch had been seeking. On the enemy's left flank at a point less than two miles above the island, the *Moose* opened on the protective Confederate cannons.[32] Basil Duke described the scene.

> The dreaded missiles passed overhead and their hiss increased the panic. A shell struck the road throwing up a cloud of dust. Troopers began unloading their booty of the raid. Shoes, parasols, skates, bird cages were scattered to the wind. Long bolts of muslin and calico spun out in banners of brilliant colors, streaming in the morning sunlight. The wounded and terror-stricken occupants of the ambulance wagons urged the scared horses into headlong flight. Often they became locked together and were hurled over as if by an earthquake. Occasionally a solid shot or unexploded shell would strike one, and dash it into splinters. The remaining section of Confederate artillery tumbled into a ravine as if the guns had been as light as feathers. The gunboats raked the road with grapeshot. In a moment the panic was complete and the disaster irretrievable.

Unable to retreat back up the ravine, the Confederates broke into a rout. Some threw down their arms and clawed their way up the bank, heading for the woods. The Federal troops charged into the woods after them. Major Edgerly went to the right, Major Mix to the left. Soon they began bringing in captured raiders. They pressed on over rocks and hills until they captured 573 prisoners with their horses and equipment.[33]

FORTY-TWO

Morgan Escapes,
Duke Captured

Shielded by Duke's gallant rear guard effort, Morgan's men speedily descended a steep ravine[1] toward the river. They were moving in perfect order from the field. Some, striving to make their way out of the valley at the north end, ran afoul of howitzers attached to the second brigade, causing guns and wagons to roll headlong into the steep ravine.[2] General Morgan was leading his men up the river bank. General Hobson had been informed by Portland citizens that there was no road up the river and that the hills were impassable. Despite these obstacles, more than 1,000[3] men were being led safely out of the valley of death. As the main Confederate body moved north, there were skirmishes here and there. They rode over the Anderson property, just north of Middleswart's farm. There the young Anderson son saw a raider throw a sack behind a log. Upon investigation, he found it to contain money. Other raiders abandoned greenbacks as they fled the battle scene. Another stash was found in a teacup by the side of the road. Some of Morgan's men buried money or hid some in hollow trees, perhaps hoping to recover it at some later date.

Cut off from the General's successful retreat, his brother, Col. Richard C. Morgan, hastily backtracked with remnants of his regiment along the road to Stiversville and Bashan. They had arrived at a point near Bashan Church when General Shackelford's force engaged Colonel Morgan's group. A spirited fight ensued. Shackelford's official report describes what happened.

I at once reversed my column, and, on arriving near Bashan Church, found the enemy in force. He occupied a dense woods, an old field, and the mouth of a lane through which the road ran. Our lines were formed promptly; the 9th Kentucky Cavalry, Colonel Jacob, on the extreme right; the 12th Kentucky Cavalry, Colonel Crittenden, on the extreme left; the First, Third and Eighth Kentucky Cavalry in the center; the 45th Ohio held in reserve. After fighting an hour, the First, Third and Eighth Kentucky Cavalry were ordered to charge. With drawn sabers gleaming in the bright sunlight, and a yell that filled the foe with terror, they rushed upon him, and he fled at their approach.[4]

Colonel Jacob noticed that his men were shooting with great precision, as he saw Confederates falling rapidly. He feared that his men were thinking of their dead comrades at Marrowbone who had been shot down after surrendering. Believing that the situation might get beyond his control, Col. Jacob galloped between the two lines at imminent risk of his life and called upon the Confederate forces to throw down their arms and surrender or he could not save them. They did and he gave a peremptory order to his men to cease firing, which they obeyed.[5]

Back at the river, Captain Byrne rode his horse into the Ohio River and successfully made a dash for freedom.[6] He was followed by members of various regiments who stripped themselves of clothing and tossed away their weapons. They ran through the swift waters rippling over the sand shallows of the Buffington Bar and plunged into the angry and powerful currents of the flooded Ohio River. Seeing some of Morgan's column crossing the ford, the *Moose* and the *Allegheny Belle* shifted fire to the men in the water. Fewer than thirty men made the crossing successfully.[7] Broad-brimmed hats could be seen floating among the debris from flooded homes upriver. One who successfully swam across the river to safety was Capt. Thomas Bronston Collins, Co. F, 11th KY Cav. Farther upstream, fifty men of the 9th TN, led by Captains J.D. Kirkpatrick and John Sisson, managed to launch one of the repaired flatboats and crossed before the Federal forces discovered them.[8]

Waiting on the West Virginia side for any Confederates who might successfully cross the swollen river were elements of Col. Hayes' regiments who reported that they gathered more than 200 prisoners, who they promptly took down river to Gallipolis.[9]

The scene in the rear of the Confederate lines was utter confusion. Stragglers were circling about the valley in a delirium of fright, clinging instinctively, in all their terror, to their horses and booty. Two Portland men taken prisoner for use as guides, Fitch and Daughtery, escaped over the riverbank in the confusion, when the gunboats opened fire on the Confederates massed along the shore.[10]

10:15am, Sunday, July 19

Col. Johnson successfully withdrew and followed Morgan's path to safety. But Col. Duke, Col. Smith, Capt. Thorpe (who had acted as adjutant general of the first brigade since the detachment of Captain Davis below Louisville), Capt. Campbell and forty other officers and men were cut off by the charge of the pursuing 7th and 9th MI. Duke's group sought refuge in a wide, deep ravine on the left of the road by which they had been seeking to escape. The whole country was thickly covered with shrub brush and trees.[11] Duke's band was about two miles north of Portland, but not more than a few hundred yards from the Ohio River. At the bottom of the ravine, a creek flowed toward the river.

11:00am, Sunday, July 19

After forty or fifty minutes, Duke began to hope that he would not be discovered, and that under cover of the night, his group might safely leave their covert area, cross the river and avoid capture. But one of Major Mix's soldiers followed the tracks that the Confederates' horses had made in descending into the ravine. He came to the edge of it and looked down. When Duke realized he had been sighted, he led his party out of the ravine, intending, if there were only a few Union stragglers, to cut through and get away. But upon reaching higher ground, he was confronted by a detachment of cavalry numbering about eighty men in the immediate vicinity. Convinced that resistance and escape were impossible, he signaled his willingness to surrender.[12]

Sergeant Charles F. Doke of the 9th MI Cavalry accepted his surrender and led them out of the hills. Captain Theodore F. Allen and Lieutenant McColgen, of the 7th OH Cavalry, led a platoon to give them safe escort. Allen was surprised to learn that one of his prisoners was Col. Basil Duke. Captain Allen later commented, "Basil Duke bore himself with dignity, and I would not have known that I had him if one of the other prisoners had not accidentally disclosed his identity." After escorting the Confederate group into the Federal lines, Capt. Allen found that, during his absence, Colonel Garrard had continued the pursuit of General Morgan through the gorge. Before leaving, he left behind a detachment of the 7th Ohio Cavalry with orders to remain and guard the prisoners on the river bank until further orders were received from him.[13]

As the guards and prisoners sat near the river bank in the oppressive heat of the late morning, first one man then another asked permission to go to the water's edge to wash his face. Soon, one-half of the men, both Union and Confederate, were washing their hands and faces and digging the dust out of their eyes, ears and nostrils. As Allen later reported:

> This proved to be such a halfway sort of business and so unsatisfactory that the men asked to go in swimming. Recognizing the merit of the request, I gave permission for one-half the

guards to go in swimming together and the other half to stand by and take their turns. The men stripped off and soon both sides, "Yankees" and "Johnnies" were splashing in water together, enjoying the most necessary bath they ever had in their lives. The first detachment having completed their scrubbing, the second detachment took their turn.

While men were bathing, one of the Confederates turned to me and pointing to the naked soldiers in the water, said, "It is difficult to tell t'other from which," meaning that he found it difficult in telling "Yankee" from "Johnnie" when they were stripped naked. I debated in my mind whether there was any danger of "getting the babies mixed" but a glance at the men in dusty blue on the shore with their Spencer carbines re-assured me, and I permitted the boys to gambol in the water to their hearts' content.[14]

After the bath, the guards shared the fried chicken in their haversacks with the prisoners. They were spread out on the grass under the shade of trees in regular picnic fashion, resting and waiting for orders. One of Duke's officers came forward and presented Captain Allen with a small Confederate flag about the size of two hands. Allen accepted the flag and asked the officer his name. "Captain Hines," he replied.[15]

Two Union colonels, William P. Sanders and Grover S. Wormer, were walking among the prisoners. Wormer noticed that Sanders was acquainted with a good many of Morgan's men, addressing them as "Jim, John, Joe, Frank," and so on. He asked if anyone had seen Richard Guthridge (one of Morgan's men) and was told he was up the line. Soon they found him at the bank of the river, washing himself. Col. Sanders said to him, "Hello, Richard. What are you doing here?"

"I suppose you know."

"Have you had a hard time?"

"Oh no."

"When did you hear from home?"

"Not very lately. We have been too busy to read letters."

"Dick, have you got any money?"

"No."

With that, Col. Sanders gave him the last four dollars he had. As he walked away, Wormer asked Sanders, "Who was that man?" Col. Sanders answered, "He is a brother of the young lady to whom I am engaged."[16]

While Hobson's, Scammon's and Judah's troops had been held at bay for several hours, Morgan made a desperate dash north through a narrow defile and escaped with more than 1,000 men.[17] Using a Portland prisoner, David F. Pearson, as a guide, the General led his men through a ravine and to safety beyond the gunboats' range.

1:00pm, Sunday, July 19

Colonel Kautz was directed to report to Shackelford to intercept Morgan.[18] Meanwhile, General Judah sent a telegram to Burnside saying that General Hobson had joined him and that they were now operating together, with Judah in overall command.[19]

2:00pm, July 19

Judah reported to Burnside that the prisoner total brought in by Hobson had reached 575.[20]

2:30pm, July 19

Half an hour later, Judah reported that Col. Wolford has brought in another 275 prisoners.[21]

Among the 700 captured included Duke and two of Morgan's brothers (Richard and Charlton), Col. Ward, Lt. Col. Huffman, Maj. Bullock, Maj. Bullitt and thirty officers. Union Col. J.E. McGowan, who was on General Judah's staff, said of the defeated Confederates, "No men could have behaved better than they did in their circumstances."[22]

FORTY-THREE

Mopping Up

The Buffington Island-Portland battlefield was strewn with one of the most unique collections of vehicles ever assembled for the transport of military supplies and baggage. It contained every sort of four-wheeled conveyance: lumbering omnibuses, a monstrous two-story peddler's wagon, a dozen or more hackney coaches used as ambulances, a number of barouches, top buggies, open buggies, express wagons, spring wagons and farm wagons. Oh yes, a hearse, too. Their loads resembled little of a military nature. Spread over the ground and in the wagons were bolts of calico, drugs, groceries, confectionery, boots and men's, ladies' and children's shoes.[1]

Lying hidden among the scattered goods was a broken gold watch that had belonged to twenty-year-old Pvt. Peter Dozier, Co. B, 11th KY Cav. When he realized he was about to be captured, he smashed it against a tree to prevent the gold watch he had inherited from his father from falling into Yankee hands. He dug down and hid it near the base of the tree so it couldn't be seen. Many years later, Peter's children would give him a gold watch to "take the place" of the battered one he left on the Buffington Island battlefield.[2] After the war was over, Marin Price returned to his Portland, Ohio, home and had a vivid dream in which a gold watch was buried under a hickory tree in front of Tunis Middleswart's home. He went to the place and began digging. Marin soon uncovered a gold watch, which he kept for many years and showed it around to anyone who would listen.[3] Was it Dozier's watch?

Lester Fitch, just fifteen-years-old at that time, said, "Everything you would want was strung through the woods from Dewitt's Run to Portland."[4] General Hobson, viewing the merchandise, food and clothing strewn over the battlefield, offered the Portland residents an opportunity to pick up and keep anything they wished.[5]

But all the booty taken from Indiana and Ohio homes was not abandoned on this field. The thousand Southern soldiers who had escaped with General Morgan had still retained some of the trinkets and valuables taken during this hard-driving expedition. Most of the personal property would never be recovered. An exception would be the engraved silver chalice and cups pilfered from a Harrison (Ohio) church. More than 100 years later, they would be returned by a pawn shop in Atlanta, Georgia.[6]

The Battle of Buffington Island had begun at five-thirty that morning[7] when Col. Smith's Confederates blundered into General Judah and his advance guard.

Noon, Sunday, July 19

General Hobson reported that Col. Basil Duke and his command were brought to him, and soon thereafter, they were joined by Colonels Smith, Huffman and R.C. Morgan. Seven hundred prisoners were encircled by Spencer-armed Union guards.[8] Some of the boats that had brought General Judah's forces from Cincinnati to Portsmouth would now transport the prisoners back to Cincinnati.

Scarcely had the field around Portland been cleared of the enemy and proper orders sent to the different brigade commanders, when a column of cavalry was discovered coming up the river to Hobson's right.[9] An orderly from some other command came dashing up to General Hobson and stated that General Judah's command had been engaged with the enemy that morning, that the column Hobson saw was Judah's force, and the general desired to have it identified.[10]

This was the first Hobson had heard directly from General Judah since leaving Marrowbone near the Kentucky-Tennessee border, eight hundred miles to the rear. As soon as Judah learned it was Hobson's command, he came upon the field and assumed command of all forces, including Hobson's. General Hobson protested against it. In his official report, he stated:

> I told him it was true that he was my superior officer, and could do so, but that I had been placed in command at Lebanon, Kentucky, by special order from General Burnside, and, from the disposition of my forces, it was impossible to give him my plans, and the matter should be referred for adjustment to department headquarters; that, fortunately for the country, but a small portion of my command was here; that most of it was following Morgan, under orders from me, Thus I became separated from my command, which has gone in pursuit of the fleeing rebels, I with my staff, being detained awaiting orders from General Judah.[11]

General Burnside was informed of this controversy, and responded to the effect that Hobson had been in pursuit for many days, and had done a good job, and he must not be balked. He went on to warn Judah that if he did so, he would incur a heavy responsibility, which would bring its retribution. In his telegram to Judah, Burnside thanked General Hobson and said the nation thanked him, too. Burnside also ordered Judah to allow Hobson to retain a separate command of his own after so long a chase.[12]

This settled the matter so far as General Judah was concerned, but by the time it was received, Hobson's brigade, in obedience to his orders on the morning of the nineteenth, were many miles away, in hot pursuit of Morgan and the scattered fragments of his command.[13] Hobson realized that he had been delayed so long by Judah, that he would not be able to catch up to his forces now being led by General Shackelford with Col. Wolford as second-in-command.

Having been reprimanded by General Burnside, an angered Judah told Hobson to take charge of the prisoners while he took a boat to Pomeroy where he would spend the next few days venting his frustration. To save face, he sent a telegram to General Burnside saying that he was going to Pomeroy with some artillery, and the pursuit of Morgan would continue.[14] Finally, three days after the Buffington battle, Judah abandoned any further pretext that he was conducting the chase and sent a telegram to Burnside saying that he was leaving Pomeroy "to bring down another batch of prisoners" to Cincinnati.[15]

While Hobson had been "detained" by Judah, Shackelford and Wolford were in close pursuit and did not attempt to communicate with Judah. Even though they were hot on his trail and would surround and do battle with General Morgan in the week ahead, the man who would have the best opportunity to capture Morgan, Major George Rue, was resting impatiently in Cincinnati getting reports by telegraph.[16]

At nine o'clock in Pleasant View, the Sunday morning stillness was broken by the sounds of gunboats firing their cannons. The "Minute Men" broke camp and headed for Bald Knobs, where they met Hobson's men who had just captured a company of Morgan's men. Two brothers, Daniel and Washington Holter, were part of the Pleasant View militia contingent. Washington captured one of the raider's horses and took it back to his farm in Racine. When Holter removed the saddle, he found its back was raw from being under saddle so long. One Confederate had told him he had kept one horse under saddle for eighteen days.[17]

A Confederate company of eighty men, which had earlier captured Captain Aumiller, hid in the woods until Sunday evening. After dark, they headed for the sandbar at Wolf's riffle less than a mile south of Bowman's Run. Several other local inhabitants had been captured and were being used as guides. They included Charles Guise, Fred Bergshicker and Harry Wolf. Heading north of Racine, the Confederate group stopped at Washington's barn and took out the horse he had brought home that morning. When they saw its condition, they left it alone.[18]

The Middleport home guards, who had been dismissed from their Jacobs' Hill positions the day before, heard that Morgan had been defeated at Buffington Island. Twenty militia members headed south. At Bowman's Run, a creek that empties into the Ohio River between Syracuse and Racine, they came upon eighty Confederates attempting to cross the river.

"Halt, who comes?" they challenged.

"A company of Morgan's men," was the firm reply. "How many of you are there?" the Morgan stragglers asked.

Exaggerating their numbers, a Middleport picket answered, "There are 5,000 men right around you." With that, the Confederate company gave themselves up and were led into the Middleport militia camp.[19] The Middleport volunteers had captured seventy-six privates, two lieutenants, one surgeon, all their arms, equipment and a goodly amount of stolen goods.[20] The prisoners were taken to the dormitory of the Cheshire Academy. An observer in Cheshire described the raiders as "more like a motley array of Falstaff's ragamuffins than chivalry gleaming in purple and gold."[21] A large number of Middleport residents, out of curiosity to see a real live raider, went to Cheshire to look at them. One remarked that they were "a fine looking set of men, but dirty and sassy." Mrs. A.E. Dumble said, "They seemed in good spirits. Some were enjoying their first wash since leaving home. Others were playing cards in the broiling sun while others were singing Rebel songs, 'Dixie,' 'Red, White and Red,' and 'Maryland, My Maryland.' They were fine singers. Our boys gave them in return, 'Red, White and Blue,' and 'We'll Rally Round The Flag, Boys.'"[22]

The next day, the home guards marched eighty-two prisoners down to Gallipolis where they were quartered in the Frost House, a hotel on the corner of Grape Street and Third Avenue, until they were transferred to military prisons.[23]

FORTY-FOUR

Capture and Surrender: A Partial Victory

One Confederate officer was glad the long ride was over. He was Capt. Andrew Jackson Bruner, Co. C, 11th KY Cav. Because of a leg injury, he had covered 600 miles of this raid riding sidesaddle carrying his crutches.[1]

In addition to the 700 captured, Dr. D.K. Scriven (or Scriver), of the Ohio militia, reported fifty-seven Confederates killed[2] and sixty-three wounded on the Buffington Island battlefield. Doctor Scriven reported burying seven Confederates and local citizens said they buried "47 rebels."[3] Some of the Confederate dead who were identified were: Lt. R.G. Marriner, Co. C, 2nd KY; 1st Sgt. James T. Scott, Co. I, 8th KY; 2nd Corp. Edward O. McKenzie, Co. B, 8th KY; F.M. Brown (Co. F), J.A. Beckham (Co. C), Samuel Dearborn (Co. C), G.W. Hensley (Co. E), C.H. Yeagle (Co. B), all privates in the 8th KY. Another fatality was Pvt. Augustus Castillo, Co. K, 11th KY.

Among the wounded and captured were: Col. Basil W. Duke; Col. Richard C. Morgan, Capt. Charlton H. Morgan; Col. Joseph T. Tucker, 11th KY; Capt. J.T. Cassell, Co. A, 2nd KY; Henry Lane Stone, Ord. Sgt, 9th KY; 2nd Sgt. J.A. Edgar, Co. A, 2nd KY; 3rd Sgt. H.S. Bethard, Co. A, 2nd KY; 2nd Corp. V.F. Sullivan, Co. A, 9th KY; 3rd Corp. I.L. Hudson, Co. A, 9th KY; Pvt. George Swango, Co. D, 5th KY; Pvt. J. Swango, Co. D, 5th KY; Pvt. Thomas Edward Dailey, Co. C, 7th KY; Pvt. James E. McMurray, Co. I, 7th KY; Pvt. William Henry Tucker, Co. C, 8th KY; Pvt. William H. Hunter, Co. K, 8th KY; Pvt. William E. McCormick, Co. K, 8th KY; Pvt. John Conrad, Co. K, 9th KY; Pvt. Peter Dozier, Co. B, 11th KY; Pvt. James Cosby, Co. B, 11th KY, Pvt. Aaron Robert Lynn, Co. F, 10th KY and all of the following from Co. C, 10th KY: Pvt. Charles Ausenbaugh, Pvt. Butler Ausenbaugh, 3rd Sgt. Robert L. Baker, Pvt. Alfred N. Beckner, Pvt. William Claxton, Pvt. William R. Dillingham, Pvt. Charles Eison, Pvt. J.W. Hamby, Capt. John Hampton Hamby, Pvt. James C. Hopper, 3rd Corp. Nathan B. Howell, 1st Corp. David H. Howton, Pvt. Nathan J. Hunter, Pvt. Isaiah Jackson, Pvt. Winfield Scott Lamb, Pvt. Thomas Sidney Lewis, Pvt. William Murray Nichols, Pvt. Francis A. Pasteur, Pvt. Hubbard L. Scott, Pvt. George R. Scott, 2nd Lt. Benjamin White and Pvt. David White.

The following prisoners were from Co. A, 9th TN: Captain Micajah Griffith; 2nd Sgt. Richard Strother; 3rd Sgt. John Soper; 4th Sgt. James H. Coleman; 1st Cpl. Clay Raymor; 4th Cpl. Patrick E. Youree; Pvt. John S. Askew; Pvt. H.H. Coleman; Pvt. James Dill; and Pvt. Dewitt C. King. Prisoners from Co. E, 9th TN were: 2nd Lt. David Anderson Carr; 1st Sgt. John Wesley Branham; 4th Cpl. Charles H. Slayton; Pvt. Granville Cline; Pvt. William Eli Durham; Pvt. William C. Harrison; Pvt. William T. Key; Pvt. Daniel Methews; Pvt. G.W. Maynard; Pvt. George O'Hair; Pvt. Robert J.L. Purseley; Pvt. William B. Reed; Pvt. John A. Reese; and Pvt. Elisha T. White. From Co. D, 9th TN was Pvt. William Anderson Barrett. The Union forces captured all of Morgan's artillery and the wagon train of spoils.[4]

Also among those killed in this engagement was Union Major Daniel McCook of the famous "Fighting McCooks." When the Confederacy seceded, Daniel McCook enlisted at age sixty-three and died in battle at age sixty-five. Daniel was born 1798 in Canonsburg, Pennsylvania. In 1826, he moved his family to New Lisbon, Ohio, and later to Carrollton, Ohio. At the beginning of the war, he was in Washington, D.C., and although sixty-three years old, he at once volunteered his services to President Lincoln. Each of his eight sons also responded to the call for troops. Except for one, all became commissioned officers. These included one major-general, two brigadier-generals, one colonel and one surgeon.[5] Only one, 17-year-old Charles M. McCook, who was killed in the first battle of Bull Run, declined a commission, preferring to serve as a private volunteer.[6] Before the war, Daniel had a law practice with Edwin Stanton, later Lincoln's Secretary of War. In the U.S. Army, he served as a paymaster. Despite his advanced age, he joined the chase after Morgan, because he was seeking revenge for the death of his son, General Robert L. McCook of the 35th OH.[7] He had been told that his son had been killed by a Captain Frank B. Gurley, a member of Morgan's guerrilla group in Tennessee on August 4, 1862.[8]

Major Daniel McCook, the father, insisted on joining a vidette in front of Lt. Armstrong's company when Judah's advance scouts made its initial probe in the thick fog at five-thirty that morning. He was advised not to go, and other officers pointed out to him that he did not know what Gurley looked like, and that no one in Armstrong's command had any personal knowledge of him. He joined the vidette, giving a mock salute and dashed out of sight into the fog, his fine sorrel charger seeming to partake of the spirit of his master. The little party he was with almost rode into the Confederate skirmish line before either saw the other. He, Lieutenant Price and one soldier were killed at the first fire. Major McCook's body was pierced by three balls. His horse, watch and Henry rifle fell into Confederate hands.[9]

Mortally wounded, he was first taken to the Anderson Price home and then to the river, where he was placed on a boat heading for Cincinnati. But by the time it docked at Portsmouth, his life had ebbed away.[10] A monument to Daniel now stands just south of Portland, near the spot where he fell by the side of the road. He is buried in Spring Grove Cemetery in Cincinnati.[11]

Captain Gurley was captured and taken to Nashville where he was tried by a military commission for the murder of General Robert McCook, Major McCook's son. He admitted the killing by his men but he said he had done it while he was a regularly commissioned officer of the Confederate government. The court that tried him decided that the killing was a legitimate act of war. The decision was confirmed by President Lincoln. As an ordinary prisoner of war, Gurley was later exchanged with others[12] and returned home a hero.

McCook was one of three Union officers killed on the raid. The other two were Captain Jesse Carter (at Columbia, Kentucky) and Lt. Fred W. Price, killed alongside McCook at Buffington Island. In addition to the three officers, eighteen Union enlisted men suffered mortal wounds.[13] Many of the Union and Confederate wounded were taken to the Williamson home, which served as a temporary hospital during the Buffington battle.

BATTLE OF BUFFINGTON ISLAND

SUN., JULY 19, 1863

9th MI CAV. Capt. W.B. Smith
8th MI CAV.
7th MI CAV.
5th KY CAV. (USA) Col. W.P. Sanders
9th KY CAV. Col. R.T. Jacob

2nd OH CAV. Col. A.V. Kautz
1st KY CAV. Col. F.L. Wolford
7th OH CAV. Col. I. Garrard
8th KY CAV. Lt. Col. Holloway
12th KY CAV. Col. W. Hoskins
2nd E. TN Mtd. Inf. Col. J.P.T. Carter

11th MI BATTERY
GENERAL E.H. HOBSON
GENERAL J.M. SHACKELFORD

GEN. MORGAN'S Withdrawal

10th KY CAV. Maj. W. Owen
11th KY CAV. Lt. Col. J. Tucker
2nd KY CAV. Maj. T.B. Webber
8th KY CAV. Lt. Col. J.M. Huffman
14th KY CAV. Col. R.C. Morgan

GENERAL MORGAN'S Overnight headquarters

MIDDLESWART

1st BRIGADE Col. B.W. Duke

BELL

PORTLAND

2nd BRIGADE Col. A.R. Johnson

9th TN CAV. Col. W.W. Ward

ARTILLERY BATTERY Capt. E.P. Byrne

6th KY CAV. Col. J.W. Grigsby

5th KY CAV. (CSA) Col. D.H. Smith (withdrew to this position after initial encounter with Gen. Judah)

Capt. J. Grafton boards Moose

PRICE

Abandoned Earthworks

MOOSE

WILLIAMSON (BOGARD)
James Williamson residence temporary field hospital

BUFFINGTON ISLAND

OHIO RIVER

5th KY CAV. (CSA) (5:30AM)

11th KY CAV. Lt. Col. W. Riley

GENERAL H.M. JUDAH

11th OH CAV. Col. J. Bond
23rd MI CAV. Col. M. Chapin
5th IN CAV. Col. Butler Lt. J. O'Neil
14th IL CAV. Col. H. Capron
107th IL CAV. Col. J. Kelly
IL Battery Capt. E. Henshaw

ALLEGHENY BELLE

WEST VIRGINIA

Inset map

Chester
Long Bottom
Pomeroy
Bashan
Minersville
Syracuse
Racine
Letart Falls
Portland
Buffington Island
Great Bend

MEIGS COUNTY

OHIO RIVER

OHIO

WEST VIRGINIA

Gen. Morgan's and Gen. Hobson's Route ●●●●
Gen. Judah's Route ▬ ▬ ▬

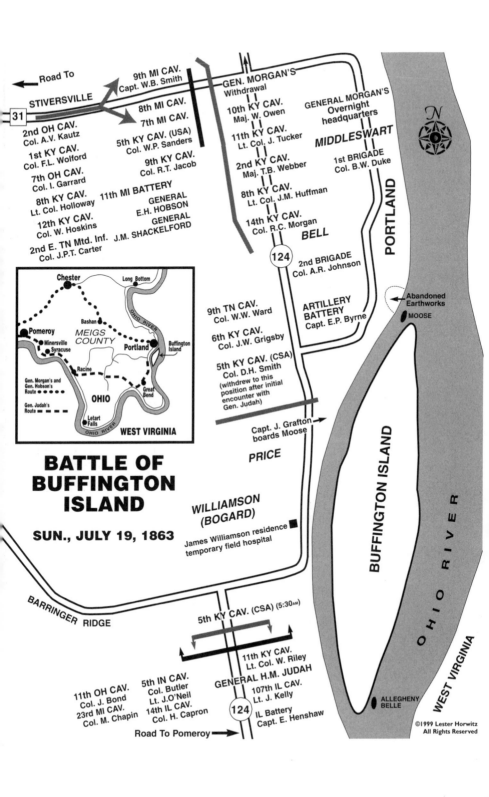

Road To STIVERSVILLE

31

9th MI CAV.
Capt. W.B. Smith

8th MI CAV.
7th MI CAV.

GEN. MORGAN'S
Withdrawal

10th KY CAV.
Maj. W. Owen

GENERAL MORGAN'S
Overnight
headquarters

MIDDLESWART

2nd OH CAV.
Col. A.V. Kautz

1st KY CAV.
Col. F.L. Wolford

7th OH CAV.
Col. I. Garrard

8th KY CAV.
Lt. Col. Holloway

12th KY CAV.
Col. W. Hoskins

2nd E. TN Mtd. Inf.
Col. J.P.T. Carter

5th KY CAV. (USA)
Col. W.P. Sanders

9th KY CAV.
Col. R.T. Jacob

11th MI BATTERY

GENERAL
E.H. HOBSON

GENERAL
J.M. SHACKELFORD

11th KY CAV.
Lt. Col. J. Tucker

2nd KY CAV.
Maj. T.B. Webber

8th KY CAV.
Lt. Col. J.M. Huffman

14th KY CAV.
Col. R.C. Morgan

1st BRIGADE
Col. B.W. Duke

BELL

124

2nd BRIGADE
Col. A.R. Johnson

9th TN CAV.
Col. W.W. Ward

6th KY CAV.
Col. J.W. Grigsby

5th KY CAV. (CSA)
Col. D.H. Smith
(withdrew to this
position after initial
encounter with
Gen. Judah)

ARTILLERY
BATTERY
Capt. E.P. Byrne

Abandoned
Earthworks

MOOSE

Capt. J. Grafton
boards Moose

PRICE

PORTLAND

BUFFINGTON ISLAND

WEST VIRGINIA

Inset map:

Chester

Long Bottom

OHIO RIVER

Pomeroy

Bashan

MEIGS COUNTY

Minersville

Syracuse

Racine

OHIO

Letart Falls

Portland

Buffington Island

Great Bend

OHIO RIVER

WEST VIRGINIA

Gen. Morgan's and
Gen. Hobson's
Route

Gen. Judah's
Route

BATTLE OF BUFFINGTON ISLAND

SUN., JULY 19, 1863

WILLIAMSON
(BOGARD)

James Williamson residence
temporary field hospital

BARRINGER RIDGE

5th KY CAV. (CSA) (5:30 AM)

11th OH CAV.
Col. J. Bond

23rd MI CAV.
Col. M. Chapin

5th IN CAV.
Col. Butler
Lt. J.O'Neil

14th IL CAV.
Col. H. Capron

11th KY CAV.
Lt. Col. W. Riley

GENERAL H.M. JUDAH

107th IL CAV.
Lt. J. Kelly

IL Battery
Capt. E. Henshaw

124

Road To Pomeroy

ALLEGHENY
BELLE

OHIO RIVER

WEST VIRGINIA

Military Study of Battle of Buffington Island

Using the same five elements used in our review of the Corydon battle, we apply them to the battle at Buffington Island: **OCOKA** – Observation, Cover & Concealment, Obstacles, Key Terrain, and Avenues of Approach.

Observation: The Union forces felt certain that Morgan's forces had not been able to cross the swollen Ohio River. Heavy fog in the valley obscured any trace of Confederate campfires. General Judah personally conducted an early morning probe to ascertain the location of the Confederate troops. The Confederate commander could not see his enemy because of the fog cover, nor could he see the one hundred or more Union troops believed to be manning an earthworks commanding the intended crossing point at Buffington Island. The Confederate commander also sent pickets along the road opposite the southern end of Buffington Island to warn of the Union approach.

Cover & Concealment: The Confederates positioned their cannons to cover their planned crossing. They believed that the river was too shallow for gunboats to maneuver. If that was the case, a few well-placed shells from their Parrotts would sink the boats if they did appear. As long as the fog persisted, the Confederates' planned early-morning crossing would go uncontested.

Obstacles: For the Confederates, the deep, raging river was the greatest hurdle. Added to this were several gunboats that rained shot and shell over the heads of frantic men and horses. Finally, there was the overwhelming number of Union troops descending the hills above the valley, sealing off avenues of escape.

Key Terrain: A two-mile valley of farmland framed by the Ohio River on the east and surrounded on all other sides by heavily forested hills. To the north, there were no roads, only steep ravines and unscalable rock outcrops that hugged the shoreline.

Avenues of Approach: Judah's troops came in from the south along the river road. Hobson's forces followed Morgan's route taken the night before, coming east from Chester down to Portland.

OFFENSE: The four principles of offense used in today's army are **CATS:** Concentration, Audacity, Tempo and Surprise.

Concentration: The Union's offense was composed of two battle groups. One led by Hobson, the other by Judah. Each Union General had a force of between 3,000 and 4,000 men. Hobson concentrated his artillery on the hills above, while his cavalry fanned out left and right after entering the valley from Chester. Judah advanced on a broad front from the south catching the Confederate forces between his regiments, Hobson's men and the gunboats on the river.

Audacity: The Confederates knew that they were not at 100% strength but they persevered because they had their backs to the river and their commanders were determined to allow General Morgan to escape with as many men as possible. In this battle, the Union forces didn't have to be audacious. Their sheer overwhelming numbers eventually prevailed.

Tempo: This is the speed and rate of the operation. Beginning with the unexpected contact between Col. Smith's 5th KY and Gen. Judah's advance scouts at five-thirty in the morning along the Pomeroy road south of Portland until Col. Basil Duke and his party were flushed out of a ravine north of Portland just before noon, the fighting was continuous and without letup. The battle picked up in intensity as more Union units and Navy gunboats arrived on the scene. The lines of opposing forces were fluid. There were times when the Confederate forces would stand and fight then withdraw to another defensible line. At other times, it was a running battle, with chases and skirmishes as pockets of Confederates found themselves surrounded and depleted of ammunition.

Surprise: The Army advocates to attack the enemy when he is unaware of your presence or from an unexpected direction. There were several surprises in store for the Confederates starting with the encounter with Judah on the Pomeroy Road surprising the 5th KY. The next surprise was the appearance of the Navy gunboats belching their deadly Dahlgren cannonade. The Confederates were expecting Hobson's legions to come down the Chester road but not in such great number.

DEFENSE: The five key principles of defense are **Preparation, Security, Disruption, Mass & Concentration** and **Flexibility.**

Preparation: The Union soldiers from Marietta prepared an earthworks position which dominated the Buffington Island ford. This stopped the Confederates from crossing the Ohio River as soon as they arrived in Portland. General Morgan planned to storm this position in the early morning, only to find it had been abandoned during the night.

Security: Its goal is to protect your troops within the perimeter or battleline. This can include reconnaissance beyond the defensive line to give early warning. Everyone should know the fields of fire and avenues of approach. Col. Duke sent the 5th and 6th KY to picket the Pomeroy road. Col. Adam Johnson had his 11th KY picket the Chester Road, the only other road leading into the Portland valley area.

Disruption: The object is for the defense to thwart the assault. To accomplish this, you want to annihilate the offensive reconnaissance. This will prevent them from going back and reporting what they saw to their commanders. There was little opportunity for the Confederates to nullify the Union reconnaissance. The Union forces knew where Morgan's men were, trapped in the small valley overlooking Buffington Island.

Mass & Concentration: The massing of troops and heavy weapons (cannons) is the main effort to stop the enemy. These tactics were used with great success by the Union cavalry, infantry, artillery and gunboats. Despite the uneven ratio of four Union soldiers to one Confederate, General Morgan was able to extricate the majority of his force to fight another day.

Flexibility: This is the ability to take the defense and adapt it to the attack from the offense. These could be secondary and alternate defensive positions. With the Union attack coming from the south, east and west of Portland, General Morgan sought an escape route north through what appeared to be impassable terrain. While he was so engaged, Col. Duke and Col. Johnson fought a delaying action, which permitted General Morgan to lead more than 1,000 men out of the Union trap.

FORTY-FIVE

"Go On. Save Yourself!"

The men who escaped with Morgan rode to another crossing fourteen miles upstream[1] to Reedsville at a point opposite Belleville, West Virginia. Along the way, Morgan took Joseph Randolph as hostage.[2] Randolph, a ferryman, was building a new house at the time and was in the woods cutting timber when captured. He was forced to act as a guide to the ford at Reedsville. They followed today's Meigs County Road Number 9, an old Indian trail.[3] As they passed the home of Sarah Hetzer, some of the men asked her to fix them a meal. She did, and they ate it in her front yard.[4] Once they reached the ford, Randolph was released.

The crossing began, led by Colonel Adam R. Johnson. The colonel recalled, "I determined to cross at all hazards. Forming the men who were with me in column of fours, I appealed to them to keep their ranks and make a show at least of an organized force. There was hardly a company in the whole division that was not represented in this body of men. I assured them I would lead them across the river."[5] Three hundred and sixty managed to cross to safety into West Virginia.[6] General Morgan himself was nearly across the river when Leroy Fitch commanding the *Moose* reappeared and began firing upon those crossing. Shells exploded among the swimmers, killing several and frightening the horses.[7] Seeing that the bulk of his command was still stranded on the Ohio side, he had to decide whether to complete his crossing of the river and join the 360 who had made it safely into West Virginia or return and lead the 700 who were still stranded in Ohio.[8]

George Ellsworth was beside Morgan as he started to return to the Ohio side. Ellsworth offered to go back with him. "No, Lightning," Morgan said, "go save yourself if you can."[9] This is a testament to Morgan's leadership. He could have made it to safety, but he chose to fulfill his responsibility as their leader, accepting its dangers and consequences. Once again, he demonstrated that he placed their safety above his. That one act, that singular decision, demonstrated clearly why his men held him in such high esteem. He was as devoted to them as they were to him.

As he was returning to the Ohio shore, the General saw one of his black servants called "Box" entering the water on a big farmhorse. John called out to him to return to Ohio. But Box replied, "Marse John, if they catches you, they may parole you. But if this boy is catched in a free state, he ain't going to get away while the war lasts."[10] Despite the shells and the swift current, Box made his way safely across into West Virginia. If Box had stayed in Ohio, he could have sought freedom through the Underground Railroad, which would have helped him escape to Canada. But his ties to his family in Lexington, even though they were in slavery, had a greater emotional pull.

Swimming for the West Virginia shore, Colonel Johnson was alongside Lieutenant Meade Woodson, Co. A, 10th KY. Woodson was riding an immense Norman horse, common to Ohio farms. Halfway across, the lieutenant's horse turned on its side and floated against Johnson's mare. Woodson was unable to swim and the great weight of the Norman horse began to sink Johnson's steed. The Colonel jumped from his horse into the river and caught hold of the cantle of his saddle. He urged and coaxed her until she actually dragged the heavy weight to the other side. Johnson's whole attention was on saving Woodson, and he had not observed what was happening behind him. As they reached the shore, he directed Woodson to take the horses to the woods, and ordered all those who had been following to go to the same point.[11] Many of Johnson's own regiment, the 10th KY, were among those that made it to safety, including Willis Washington Johnson, no relation to the colonel. Col. J. Warren Grigsby (6th KY) made it across. Two bothers, 2nd Lt. Edward H. Crump and Sgt. John C. Crump, both of Co.F, 2nd KY, also survived the crossing.

As Col. Johnson had pointed out, he was leading men from virtually every regiment including Ward's 9th TN. Among the Tennesseans escaping across the river from Co. A were: Calvin Hardin (company bugler); Pvt. S. Albert Christman; Pvt. J.H. Hardin; Pvt. John W. Hugle; Pvt. J.F. Jackson; and Pvt. D.A. Mitchell. Those from Co. E were: 4th Sgt. James Wesley Rippy; Daniel H. Alory (company bugler); Pvt. Richard Banks Bransford; Pvt. William Thomas Duffer; and Pvt. John M. Rippy.

Capt. S.P. Cunningham, assistant adjutant general of Morgan's Division, described his harrowing crossing.

> In dashed the Colonel followed by Lieutenant Woodson, Captain Paine of Texas, young Rogers of Texas [one of four "Private Rogers" from the Lone Star state on the raid], Captain McClain, A.C.S. 2nd Brigade, and myself. My poor mare, being too weak to carry me turned over and commenced going down; encumbered by clothes, saber and pistols. I made but poor progress in the turbid stream, but recollections of home, of a

bright maiden in the sunny South, the pressing need of soldiers, and an inherent love of life, actuated me to continue swimming. Behind me I heard the piercing call of young Rogers for help; on my right Captain Helm was appealing to me for aid; and in the rear my friend, Captain McClain, was sinking. I hear something behind me snorting! I feel it passing! Thank God, I am saved! A riderless horse dashes by. I grasp his tail. Onward he bears me, and the shore is reached! Colonel Johnson on reaching the shore seizes upon a ten inch piece of board, jumps into a leaky skiff and starts back to aid the drowning. He reaches Captain Helm, but Captain McClain and young Rogers are gone.[12]

Looking across the river, Col. Johnson sadly saw a number of hats floating on the surface. He knew that each hat represented a brave comrade who had found a watery grave. Johnson described how he felt.

Words are inadequate to express my desolation, and even wild thoughts of suicide flashed through my brain. Just then one of the hats was lifted out of the water, and a faint voice came to me, saying, "Oh, Colonel, can you do anything for me?" I recognized Captain Neil Helm, one of my truest friends and most faithful followers, one who had been with me on the plains of Texas and had never failed me when surrounded by the savage Comanches. I determined to rescue him or die. Seeing an old skiff on the bar, I rushed to it and shaking it from its sandy bed, I skimmed it over the ground as if it were a feather, and pushing it with a mighty force into the river, I sprang in and jerking out one of the seats with superhuman effort, paddled to him just as he was about to sink. He had barely strength left to grasp and hold on to the stern of the boat.[13]

By this time the gunboats were on us, and the soldiers gathered on the bow looked down on us with guns in hand. Helm, believing they were going to shoot, pleaded with me to jump into the river, but knowing the skiff would soon sink, I paddled with all my might toward shore. The skiff sank before we reached the bank, and I jumped into the water to assist Helm and found it shallow enough to wade. Seizing him I dragged him on the sandbar. All this time there was not a shot fired at us and not a single shell was thrown on that side [West Virginia shore] of the river. This was an act of humanity I am glad to record. We were still in short range, and Helm, believing they would shoot, begged me to leave him. When I refused, he jumped to his feet and declared he would walk, and I supporting him, we reached the woods where the men were now gathered. Believing they would soon have a force in pursuit of us, I moved the men as rapidly as possible across the mountains, and traveling by unfrequented roads, we reached Green Briar country, [West] Virginia. When we first came in sight of fields of harvested wheat and green waving corn, I am sure each one of us felt as much pleasure as did Moses of old when he first viewed the Promised Land.[14]

Not all of those reaching West Virginia fled immediately inland. Near the Wells farm, on the upper side of Lee Creek two miles above Belleville, West Virginia, sixteen-year-old Foster Wells met some of the Confederate troopers and offered to guide them to safety. Before departing, one Butternut squad prepared an ambush for the steamers. As the unsuspecting gunboats passed, the raiders fired two volleys of musketry at a range of less than twenty yards. Amazingly, only two Yankee sailors were hurt. Accepting the challenge, the *Moose* replied with her starboard battery, killing nine of the bushwhackers. With their guns elevated to fire over the riverbanks, the two Federal tinclads began a general bombardment of the area, concentrating on the roads leading inland.[15]

Many of the Union shells passed over the Wells homestead, with some cutting limbs from the tops of surrounding shade trees. Before the last naval shell exploded, the Confederate survivors had been directed to the Elizabeth Pike and the hills leading to the Little Kanawha Valley.[16] Among those who had safely made it across to the West Virginia shore was the fourth Cosby brother, Oliver. Four of the brothers in Co. B, 11th KY, Ausey, John, Oliver and James, had started the raid with Morgan. At Tebb's Bend at the Green River Bridge, two had been killed, Ausey and John. At the Buffington Island battle, James was captured. Now Oliver was part of the "lucky" 360 who had escaped from Ohio and were on their way back south. But Friday, July 24, he was captured in West Virginia and spent the rest of the war in prison at Rock Island, Illinois.[17]

One more crossing was attempted about two miles north of Reedsville, across from the mouth of Lee Creek. Again, a few raiders made it across before the *Moose* made its final appearance, ending any further attempt to cross. Morgan was discouraged to find the Union tinclads had the ability to maneuver in such shallow waters. Finding the water upstream too difficult and too many shoals to warp, the boats rounded to and returned to Buffington Island.[18] Fitch realized that with the river water level falling, it was imperative that he get below Buffington that evening or his craft could be grounded. Later, the body of Pvt. William Withers, Co. E, 9th KY, who drowned trying to cross the river at Reedsville,[19] was claimed by relatives and returned to Kentucky for burial.

One of Morgan's men who was captured when trying to escape north of Buffington was George Nolan of Shelby County, Kentucky. In a diary written by Julia Cutler, a resident of the Marietta area, she describes him. "I was resting in my room. I heard a bustle in the road in front of my house. Going to the window, I saw quite a crowd gathered round a buggy and two or three cavalry scouts. I heard a pleasant voice say, 'Yes, I'm a live rebel.' He was a pleasant faced, young looking man, a Kentuckian and son, he said, of a Union man. He appeared to be well educated and ought to know better than to be a rebel and a robber. He had been with Morgan through Tennessee, Kentucky, Indiana and Ohio. His feet were swollen, so that he could wear but one of his gaiters, from constant riding. He ate dinner under guard and was sent to Camp Marietta."[20]

With the Battle of Buffington Island decided in the Union's favor, the Yankees could not agree who was responsible for the victory. General Judah laid great stress upon the overwhelming force he mustered to throw against the weary raiders. General Hobson thought his relentless pursuit was primarily responsible for Morgan's discomfiture. Militia commanders proudly pointed to the work their volunteers had done in barricading roads and slowing down the enemy column. Nobody gave the rampaging Ohio River the credit it deserved, although the Union Navy could never have operated across the shallow bars and fords if the waterway had not been unseasonably high.[21]

The skipper of the *Imperial* had no doubts, "I think the credit belongs to the gunboats. They were at all the fording places and kept him [Morgan] from crossing, checking him until the troops could arrive and complete the work."

Colonel G.S. Wormer of the Michigan cavalry said that the Federals' better equipment made the difference. "Our arms, the Spencer rifle, proved as before, a terror to the Rebels. They thought us stronger than we were, since each man could pour seven shots into them so rapidly."

Lieutenant Commander Leroy Fitch was so elated with the results, he dispatched a telegram to Gideon Welles, the Union Secretary of the Navy. It was not a particularly modest message. "After chasing Morgan nearly 500 miles, at last met him on the river at this point. Engaged and drove him back, capturing two of his pieces of artillery. He abandoned the rest to General Judah. The enemy broke in confusion from the bank and left his wagon train, many horses and small arms in my possession. Several were killed, twenty-five or thirty wounded and twenty horses captured. Have but two men wounded slightly. Our shell and schrapnel created great confusion in the Rebel ranks, killing and wounding many."

A few hours after the battle was over, Captain Wood and the Marietta volunteers, who had built the earthworks which had stopped Morgan from attempting a crossing on the night before the battle and then fled leaving the ford unguarded, walked into the Federal camp. They were ordered to stand watch over the captured Confederates who had pulled up shocks of wheat and thrown themselves down on these rough pallets and fallen asleep.[22]

General Judah did have words of praise for the local militia. He said, "Under Captains Smith and Hoston, the Meigs County Home Guards persistently annoyed the enemy for a distance of from eight to ten miles by desultory fire which harassed him [Morgan] much and materially interfered with his procurement of supplies."

FORTY-SIX

The Chase to Cheshire

Morning of Monday, July 20

General Shackelford received a report that the "enemy" was moving in the direction of Eight Mile Island near Cheshire. In the haste to get away from the gunboats shelling Morgan's men on the Ohio shore, a group led by Lt. Col. Cicero Coleman, became separated from General Morgan's main force which was moving northeast to Tuppers Plains. Coleman's group doubled back to the southwest toward Rutland. Shackelford's forces chased them for fifty-seven miles.[1]

2:30pm, July 20

In Cheshire, just south of Rutland, all was quiet until a man rode into town hollering at the top of his voice, "The Rebs are coming back and they'll be here in ten minutes!" The news was a shock to the Cheshire militia.[2] They thought that all of Morgan's men had been captured at Buffington Island. Franklin Smith, one of the Cheshire militia, was standing near the Guthrie Hotel. He decided to give himself a furlough. He ran and hid himself in a nearby wheatfield. Smith remained there until he saw the Union troops drive the Confederates out of Cheshire.[3]

The detachment of Morgan's men riding toward Cheshire included Lt. Col. Cicero Coleman, 8th KY; Maj. William G. Bullitt, 6th KY; Lt. Col. James B. McCreary, 11th KY; Capt. Robert D. Logan, Co. I, 7th KY; Capt. L.D. Hockersmith, Co. C, 10th KY; Capt. T.H. Shanks, Co. B, 6th KY; Capt. Thomas M. Coombs, Co. K, 5th KY; AQM E.T. Rochester, 6th KY; Adjutant J. W. Alcorn, 6th KY; 1st Lt. John D. Bryan, Co. A, 6th KY; 1st Lt. W.P. Crow, Co. B, 6th KY; 1st Lt. George C. Nash, Co. K, 6th KY; 2nd Lt. John S. Hughes, Co. A, 6th KY; 2nd Lt. David M. Prewitt, Co. A, 6th KY; 2nd Lt. Charles H. Powell, Co. K, 6th KY; 2nd Lt. Michael Jewett, Co. K, 6th KY; Surgeon D. Drake Carter, 6th KY; Sgt. Major James W. Schooling, 6th KY; and Pvt. William Lafayette Clayton, Co. K, 10th KY. Like Col. Johnson's group crossing at Reedsville, Coleman's group included more than a dozen Tennesseans. From Co. A, 9th TN were: Pvt. Robert Hardin; Pvt. J.W. Hickerson; and Pvt. Benjamin Settle. From Co. B were: Cpl. William P. Hatch; Pvt. Thomas R. Furgesson; Pvt. Robert J. Harris; Pvt. William Anderson Lovel; and Pvt. James N. Morris. From Co. D were: Cpl. William Haywood Ross; Pvt. John H. Fergason; Pvt. James Riley Gammon; Pvt. Francis H. Grant; Pvt. Hugh B. Kyle; Pvt. Lemuel Montgomery; and Pvt. George W. Whitescarver. From Co. E were: 1st Lt. Littleberry B. Moncrief; Pvt. Alfred Center; and Pvt. William Alfred Rippy. Others included 2nd Lt. John N. Crossway, Co. C; Pvt. J.B. Cocke, Co. C; 1st Lt. John D. Stalker, Co. F; and Pvt. James A. Harris, Co. F.

3:00pm, Monday, July 20

This splinter group of Confederates hoped Eight Mile Island would provide a good ford. Before entering Cheshire, two local men were captured and made to act as guides. One was an old man named Galbreth, the other a young man named Swishes. The latter was riding a fine horse, which they took from him and gave him one of their lesser horses to ride bare back. Galbreth took some of the Confederates to the head of Eight Mile Island while Swishes accompanied a group to the foot. The beach was lined with mounted men ready to cross the Ohio River. A few succeeded in crossing before they saw a boat coming up the river. Mistaking it for a gunboat, the raiders retraced their steps back toward Cheshire.[4]

Watching the action from the northeast window of her home was Alvira Gates. She had been forewarned that Morgan's men might be returning to Cheshire following the Buffington Island battle. She wrapped her family's gold watches, silver spoons and other trinkets and threw them down an ash-hole in the side of the dining room fireplace. She hid her money in the clothing of her infant. She saw a cloud of dust ascending in a continuous line as the raiders followed along the banks of Kyger Creek. In back of the village, they let down a fence and crossed over into Gates' Lane. Some came into her yard, dismounted and asked where all the "Yanks" had gone. They asked for something to eat. Alvira went inside and gave them some bread, which they took greedily. Others were hurriedly washing at the well. When they came up to the house, they asked for pies. She went into the pantry and brought out two. She began to slice them, but they told her to stop. Instead, they removed the pies from the pans, tied them up in their handkerchiefs and hastened away.[5]

The Confederates' rear guard included Capt. Thomas Coombs leading a detachment of the 5th KY and Capt. Robert Logan with elements of the 6th KY.[6] They warned that Col. Wolford's Union cavalry was in close pursuit.[7] The advance of the 45th OH was led by Lt.Colonel Ross.[8]

<u>4:00pm, Monday, July 20</u>

At the foot of Coal Hill, they crossed a narrow bridge over Little Kyger Creek, rode 300 yards, dismounted, hitched their horses in the woods and waited for the Union force to cross the bridge. When Wolford's advance guard crossed the span, the Confederates opened fire. The startled Union troops stopped in the confusion of gunfire, while Col. Coleman's group ran to remount their horses and rode to the top of a high bluff four miles behind Cheshire, only to find themselves surrounded. With their last rounds of ammunition expended, surrender was inevitable.[9] General Shackelford reported that the skirmish had lasted an hour. It involved Federal troops led by Colonel Adams with the 1st KY Cav. and Captain Ward of the 3rd KY Cav. making a flanking movement and taking possession of the only road on which the Confederates could retreat.[10]

A flag of truce was sent up the hill to Lieutenant-Colonel Coleman, who asked for time to consider the terms of surrender. The Confederate commander came down and asked for a personal interview with Shackelford. Coleman requested an hour, but the Union general granted him forty minutes.[11] Terms of surrender were agreed to about sunset.[12] The Federal troops thought that they had captured the remnants of Morgan's forces, including John Hunt himself. When the Confederate prisoners were all accounted for, Morgan was not among them. Shackelford concluded that General Morgan had given him the slip during the forty minutes in which the surrender terms were being negotiated.[13] But like the old shell game, Morgan wasn't there. With almost 800 men, he was keeping a low profile twenty miles north in the isolated hills between Meigs and Athens counties.[14] Without realizing it, Shackelford's presence at Cheshire, just below Athens County, put him in a good position to resume the chase, when Morgan's presence was discovered. On July 22, Morgan's men were spotted due north, near McArthur and Zaleski.[15]

Coleman and company were taken to Cheshire and arrived about dark on July 20. There they joined the others taken as prisoners at Buffington. Capt. Hockersmith later commented that "Wolford and his men treated us with kindness and consideration."[16]

As Coleman's group had been heading for Cheshire, a half dozen men from Co. C, 9th TN split themselves from the larger group just south of Rutland and headed west towards Ewington where they were captured. They were: Pvt. Elmore Harris Green; Pvt. John Barnett Kizer; Pvt. John F. Patton; Pvt. James Payton; Pvt. Daniel H. Smith; Pvt. John Henry Alexander Turnage; and Pvt. William Turnage.

The Confederate prisoners captured at Coal Hill, Bowman's Run, Ewington and Buffington Island were imprisoned in the three-story Cheshire Academy Dormitory. The structure was new, having been built in 1862.[17] Officers of the command, including Col. Coleman, Lt. Col. Tucker, Lt. Col. McCreary, Captains Logan and Coombs, received a parole of honor, quartered at the hotel and were given liberty of the town of Cheshire.[18]

Among the Union men who had the responsibility of guarding and accompanying the captured Confederate officers was a squad of Cincinnati militia who had arrived on July 20. They turned out to be a first-rate set of men for the duty, all being ex-soldiers who had been discharged on account of wounds or sickness.[19]

FORTY-SEVEN

Steamboatin' to Prison

<u>Monday, July 20</u>

Under the guard of the 12th OH Infantry, the Confederate prisoners were escorted to the river, where they were put aboard steamboats the *Starlight, Henry Logan, Imperial, Tariscon* and *Ingomar*.[1] In a telegram sent nine o'clock on the morning of July 20, General Judah reported that the Confederates on the two boats consisted of "704 prisoners including 48 commissioned officers."[2] In a telegram sent two days later, he increased the total to 711 stating that there were "663 enlisted and 48 officers." The same day, he sent a second telegram to General Burnside increasing the total prisoners on the *Starlight* and *Ingomar* to 790.[3]

<u>Wednesday, July 23</u>

The Confederate prisoners at Cheshire, officers and men, were taken to Cincinnati on the steamers *Golden Era, Navigator, Marmora, St. Louis, J.H. Done, Ida May* and *Odd Fellow*.[4] They arrived the next day but remained aboard the steamers while they were anchored out on the river during the night. The following morning, they left the boats and were marched to the Ninth Street Prison, where they were reunited with Colonels Duke, Smith, Morgan and a great number of field and line officers.[5]

In his telegram of July 22 from Pomeroy to General Burnside, Judah listed the following number of Confederate prisoners sent by various boats to Cincinnati:

On the *Starlight* and *Ingomar*	790
Sent separately by Hobson	96
To be shipped from Pomeroy	227
To be shipped from Cheshire	1,100
Shipped by General Scammon	160
Number who crossed the Ohio River	100
Total	2,473

General Judah said that Colonel Duke had told him that Morgan had 2,800 men ready to cross at Portland (Buffington Island), "and I believe him." Duke had added almost a 1,000 "phantom" soldiers to the tale he told

247

Judah. In Capt. Hockersmith's book, *Morgan's Escape,* he indicated that there was less than a company that escaped to Cheshire, so the 1,100 quoted by Judah was greatly exaggerated. In his book, *History of Morgan's Cavalry,* Duke said they left Indiana and entered Ohio with less than 2,000 men. Working with that figure, here are estimated Confederate numbers that are probably closer to the accurate figures:

Men who escaped Buffington Battle with Gen. Morgan 1,050
Men captured at Buffington Island/Portland 700
Men captured at Pomeroy and Cheshire combined 150
Men captured by General Scammon... 25
Men lost in Ohio before Buffington battle....................................... 70
Total number of Confederates who entered Ohio............................ 1,995

The prisoners found their guards to be courteous and understanding. Because they were regular soldiers, the Ohioans knew how the fortunes of war can turn a fighting man into a prisoner within minutes, and they showed respect for men who had been under strain for so long. Along the riverbanks, civilians were not so understanding. The raiders could hear insults and threats shouted from every town's wharf boat. During the night, some of the Confederate prisoners, because of overcrowding, had to sleep on the decks. A few slipped over the side and swam for the West Virginia or Kentucky shore and freedom.[6]

One of those who was captured at Buffington on July 19 was Private Thomas W. Jackson, Co. A, 6th KY. Like most privates and noncoms, he would be sent to Camp Morton in Indiana and then to Camp Douglas in Illinois. Others would be imprisoned at Camp Chase near Columbus or Johnson's Island in Lake Erie. But a separate, nonmilitary confinement awaited the Confederate officers. Private Jackson was unable to escape off the boat. Angry that he could not continue the fight against Lincoln's legions, he made plans, once he was free, to join Emperor Maximilian of Mexico and continue his personal battle against the Union. Like most Southerners, he was fighting for a cause, which for him, did not cease with surrender. Soldiers' pay was incidental to his determination. On his company's muster roll card in 1863, prior to accompanying Morgan on his Indiana-Ohio raid, Jackson answered when asked, "When were you last paid?" His written answer was, "Never paid."[7]

The next day, the boats docked at the foot of Broadway Street in Cincinnati. There was a crowd on the wharf. One of the unidentified Confederate prisoners was nattily dressed in a neat-fitting suit of black broadcloth, with silk tie and patent leather boots to match. Under his hat was a thick growth of black, slightly curly hair. He wore a full beard, which was long, black and very curly. His face had a rather thin aquiline nose, firm mouth, kept resolutely closed, and a pair of keen black eyes. He was well aware of his rather sharp appearance and handsome good looks. He took advantage of the commotion among the mob on shore to step down the gang plank while some of the Union officers were mounting their horses. At the foot of the plank, he addressed the officer in charge of the guards who stood with ranks open to receive the prisoners. He identified himself as an officer of the boat.[8]

Naturally, he was believed. Slipping through the ranks on his right, he mingled with the crowd and made his way around the railway offices on the corner of Front and Broadway. He entered the first barber shop he came to and had his hair trimmed close, his beard cut down to an inch in length, and shaved into a "Burnside," a fashionable cut among the "nobs" at that time. His next stop was a clothing store where he purchased a wide-brimmed straw hat and long linen duster. He even ordered a silk tie to be delivered to the Spencer Hotel. He checked into the hotel, completed his disguise and drank and chatted with the Federal officers until evening when he took the mail boat to Louisville. From the relative safety of the Falls City, he wrote and mailed a letter of thanks to Capt. D.W.H. Day and others of General Judah's staff. He said that he regretted that he had to leave in such unceremonious style. He added that he must be excused because he could not wait for them to make the "grand round" of Louisville with him; but, really, his engagements called him South.[9]

With the exclusion of the few who got away, several hundred including seventy Confederate officers were marched under a strong guard from where they had landed at the foot of Main Street[10] up to the city prison on Ninth Street. One resident living on East Fifth Street near Pike, rushed to his door to see a body of 200 unarmed men dressed in gray, with about a third of their number in blue on each side with muskets in hand. The whole mass was on a run in the middle of the street hurrying to the depot of the Little Miami Railroad.[11]

The value of the Union Navy's river squadron in repulsing Morgan's attempted crossings is hard to overestimate. With little knowledge of the Confederates' disposition, Lt. Commander Fitch had organized and used his limited fleet in a most successful manner. Navy Secretary Gideon Welles was so pleased that he sent the commander an official commendation on July 27. Three days later, both Generals Ambrose Burnside and Jacob Cox wrote to Admiral Porter with praise for the Navy's role. Fitch, Morgan's most determined naval opponent, died at his Indiana home in 1875 at the age of forty. *The Moose* was sold on October 9, 1865. Redocumented at the *Little Rock,* she plied the rivers until fire destroyed her at Clarendon, Arkansas on December 23, 1867.[12]

After Morgan slipped away at Buffington Island, General Shackelford asked for volunteers to stay in the saddle continuously without eating or sleeping until Morgan was captured. Everyone stepped forward, but only 500 sound horses could be found, so with that many, plus several hundred mounted Ohio and Pennsylvania militia who joined along the way, he resumed the chase. His forces included Colonel Horace Capron and 157 men of the 14th IL, Colonel Wolford with detachments of the 1st KY, 2nd TN, 45th and 2nd OH. Colonel Jacobs remained behind with his command to guard the prisoners.[13]

Following Buffington Island and Cheshire, Morgan now had less than one-third of his original force. Still capable of maneuver, his goal was to lead his remaining men to safety across the Ohio River while eluding his pursuers.

Morgan took his remnant force north. Having lost all his cannons, wagons of wounded and spoils of war at Buffington Island, he was no longer limited to travel over passable roads. He was able to escape his pursuers by scaling hills over goat-like trails and slipping around roadblocks, dodging traps and moving faster than resistance could be organized.

Up in Hockingport (Athens County), the townspeople could hear the Sabbath morning stillness shattered with the sound of cannonading. Distinctly, and in rapid succession, fourteen discharges were heard. Then all was still. Everyone was put on alert. They could see smoke down the river. Two citizens, E.H. Stone and John Lytle, jumped into a skiff and started in the direction of Buffington Island. As the duo approached Belleville, they spotted a large party of Morgan's men approach the river and plunge in. A space of fifty yards along the river bank was filled with men and horses. The *Moose* steamed into view and fired a couple of shells among them, killing and drowning many. Continuing up river, the crews of the gunboats could see dozens of raiders coming down Parker's Hill, about a mile below Hockingport. A round or two from *Moose's* naval guns dispersed the crowd back into the safety of the hills.[14] The men returned to give Morgan a negative report, so he turned west and encamped the night of July 19 between Tuppers Plains and Coolville.

Several of Morgan's men needed medical attention. The local physician, Dr. Edward Tiffany of Tuppers Plains, gave medical care. In fact, after the Confederates moved on, the few wounded remained with Dr. Tiffany to convalesce for up to six weeks before they were turned over to the Union military.

There in the dark on the night following the Buffington Island battle, General Morgan reviewed his options and knew that he needed to reorganize the seven to eight hundred men he was leading. His mission was clear: Try to avoid the thousands of Union troops and militia who were tracking him and find an escape route over the Ohio River that was too shallow for the gunboats. He had lost all but one of his colonels. Only Cluke remained. He named Major Thomas B. Webber, the fiery leader of the 2nd KY, as acting colonel of the First Brigade,[15] combining two hundred men of his 2nd KY regiment with about the same number surviving from other regiments of Duke's brigade.[16] Webber should have been in a hospital, not in the saddle. For days he had suffered from dysentery so debilitating his aides had to help him get on his horse. He refused to follow a surgeon's suggestion that he drop out and surrender. It was small wonder the raiders called him the "Iron Man."[17]

Col. Roy S. Cluke, of the 8th KY, replaced Adam Johnson as commander of the Second brigade.[18] As darkness fell over the Ohio hills, he set his men to building large campfires. At the General's signal, they were all lighted at once. A few minutes later, under cover of darkness, the newly reorganized companies mounted up, formed in columns of twos and stealthily rode away. The old campfire trick was successful. Union patrols sighted the winking lights from afar, and all through the night Federal cavalry units were moving into position to surround what they believed was John Morgan's last camp of the raid.[19]

When morning came, the raiders were far to the west, doubling back away from the river. For the next two days they followed obscure trails through isolated hill country, avoiding all towns. Their whereabouts during this time were such a mystery to Union pursuers that even General Burnside reached the conclusion that Morgan and most of his men had escaped to West Virginia.[20] In a telegram, Burnside would tell Washington, DC, that Morgan had deserted the Confederate remnants still trapped in Ohio.

Morgan's "disappearance" worried Burnside. He was not really sure where the chief Confederate raider was. He had other pressures on him beside locating and capturing Morgan. He was concerned that draft riots in other cities might spread to Cincinnati. Some Army officers on Burnside's staff had no faith in his ability to lead and thought that he was often irrational and indecisive. He seemed to be afraid to commit troops to attacking General Bragg's Army of the Tennessee. The following telegram was sent in secret cipher code from Burnside's headquarters to President Lincoln.[21]

PRIVATE   Cincinnati, Ohio, *July* 20, 1863.
     (Received, in cipher, 7:40pm)
     His Excellency ABRAHAM LINCOLN,
                    President of the United States:
**I advise you to relieve Maj. Gen. A.E. Burnside from command of
the Department of the Ohio immediately by telegraph. He has been
plausibly pursuing a policy hostile and adverse to your wishes and
instructions and those of the Secretary of War and General-in-
Chief. Send some thoroughly brave man to take his place. I cordially recommend [Joseph] Hooker, who is a brave man, and will be
very popular. We are on the eve of important events, which require
you to pursue the course I suggest. We are threatened with mobs
and riots and bloodshed throughout the entire Western country.
Orders 38 has kindled the fires of hatred and contention, and Burnside is foolishly and unwisely excited, and, if continued in command,
will disgrace himself, you, and the country, as he did at Fredericks-
burg.Please acknowledge the receipt of this dispatch. I am
absolutely right. [Stephen] Douglas was my preceptor.**
                         J.M. CUTTS,
     Captain Eleventh Infantry, Judge-Advocate Dept. of the Ohio.

Monday, July 20

The next morning, the raiders came upon a funeral procession for
Lydia Cowdry, who had died Saturday in Coolville. Morgan wanted the
fresh horses pulling the hearse. But the funeral party pleaded to allow them
to take the body to the cemetery for burial and then they would return and
the Confederates could have the horses. But the promise wasn't kept, so
they took hostages for guides. These included Bill Hull, John A. Johnson,
Myron Barker, Benjamin McAfee, Joe Carsey, George Withey and Tim
Gray. They didn't take them far before they were released.[22]

Morgan's weary group continued their westward journey across the
top of Meigs County. They captured five horses at Tuppers Plains, then
seven at Alfred. They pushed on to Burlingham when they appropriated
nineteen horses before turning north and entering Athens County. In all,
they had confiscated 266 horses in Meigs County. The largest group, fifty-
eight, came from the Harrisonville area, while fifty-five were taken from
Rutland.[23] The vast majority of these pilfered horses had been seized before
the Buffington battle.

FORTY-EIGHT

Riding the Athens-Meigs County Line

Several hundred Union soldiers had been stationed in the town of Athens to help defend it against the approaching Morgan threat. The ladies of Athens County demonstrated their patriotism by providing the following provisions each day. An article in the *Athens Messenger* reported[1]:

During the week of the Morgan raid, provisions were furnished for the soldiers in Athens as follows:

Friday, July 17—Dinner on the College Green for 65, supper for 300.
Saturday, July 18—Breakfast for 200; lunch and coffee at the depot, at three o'clock for upwards of 300; supper for 80
Sunday, July 19—Breakfast for 90; dinner for 100; supper for 110.
Monday, July 20—Breakfast at 5 o'clock a.m. for 150; at 6 a.m. for 90; dinner at 12 p.m. for 100; at 1 p.m. for 90; supper at 5 p.m. for 90; at 6 p.m. for 68.
Tuesday, July 21—Breakfast for 90.
Wednesday, July 22—Breakfast at 4:40 a.m. for 112.
Friday, July 24—Lunch at the depot for 300.

The numbers of soldiers being fed, as noted above, did not include many others who were temporarily quartered in private homes and hotels, which were reported to be filled to overflowing. The Athens War Committee had asked surrounding communities to donate food. Among the many contributions received, Nelsonville, in the northern part of Athens County, provided four wagon-loads.[2]

Nine miles northeast of Athens is the small two-block town of Amesville.[3] There, the home guard was led by Captain John Patterson and First Lieutenant Charles Henry. Long before word of Morgan's coming was heard in the hills and hollows, the home guard had been drilling on horseback every Saturday afternoon. At the conclusion of each drill, they would have a horse race. When word came that some of Morgan's men were seen at Long Bottom (Meigs County), Orville Potter, a resident of Athens and a member of the home guard, enthusiastically suggested, "Let's go over and see them!"

The others in the group didn't seem inclined to join him. "Well, I'm going!" said Orville as he turned his fine, dapple gray mare eastward. Sitting astride his bay horse, "Prince," Charles Henry warned, "If you ride that mare over there [Long Bottom], you'll come back afoot." Potter went. The raiders took the mare and that's the last he saw of her.[4]

Soon word came to Amesville that Morgan was heading their way. As Athens prepared to defend itself, so, too, did the families in the rural area of Amesville. Charles Henry had inherited a large portion of his father's 240-acre property. Charles, in turn, had given away acreage and farms to his sons as they married. As each son tied the knot, he was given a farm with a house on it. When a daughter entered into matrimony, she was given a feather bed and a cow. That was the custom in the area. The land was being parceled out quickly because Charles had ten children by his first wife and nine by his second.[5]

The current Mrs. Henry with her three sons and one daughter gathered up their feather beds and other valuables. They tied the bed ticking with rope to their two black mares and took off for the wooded hills. As the horses climbed the slope, the bed material began shifting and appeared ready to fall off, so the older sons stuck their caps between the ropes and the horses' hides to hold them in place. Upon reaching their thicketed hideaway, they bedded down for the night. But Amesville was not on Morgan's itinerary. Many years later, the youngest son, Carlos, remarked, "Morgan didn't visit us at all."[6]

To avoid the city of Athens, the Confederates stayed close to the Meigs County border. Traveling west, they turned south again toward Ewington in Gallia County.

FORTY-NINE

Give Us Your Guns and Go Home

<u>Monday, July 20</u>

By order of Col. Peter Kinney of the Ohio militia stationed at Camp Portsmouth,[1] Lt. Col. Sontag, with a detachment of 500 men from the First Scioto militia, proceeded by train heading north to Jackson. Morgan was reported prowling about in the Jackson and Gallia County hills. At Keystone Station, ten miles south of Jackson, Sontag split his force into two. He ordered Major Slain (Slane) to debark the train with 200 men, while he continued onto Jackson. Slain was given orders to march east to Ewington. At Jackson, Sontag took the Berlin Road planning to meet at Ewington. Sontag's men had no rations and they had to wait for dinner at Jackson. The Lt. Colonel also had to procure wagons to haul blankets, extra clothing, footsore and sick soldiers.

(Telegram)   Col. George W. McCook,   *July* 20, 1863.
Chairman of Jefferson County Military Committee
Have a force in readiness to proceed down river to meet raiders under Morgan.

W.T.H. BROOKS, *Major-General.*

<u>3:00pm, July 20</u>

After a long delay, they left Jackson. They expected to form a junction with Major Slain after a twenty-mile march. Sontag's militia volunteers were untrained and unaccustomed to long, forced marches. Many whose feet were already worn to blisters could hardly be persuaded to go from Berlin to Latrobe Furnace, which was more than seven miles from Jackson. When they reached Latrobe, it was quite dark, and the men could go no farther. Sontag estimated that Slain was six miles down the road. Lt. Colonel Sontag sent couriers to communicate with the Major Slain.[2] That night, it rained.[3]

255

Tuesday, July 21

The following morning, they resumed their march, went two miles to another furnace, where they heard that Morgan's men had been seen. As the Lt. Colonel's group moved along the road to Ewington, more couriers were sent forward to make contact with Slain.

Sontag's advance scouts were captured by Morgan within a few miles of Ewington. Sontag was surprised and found himself surrounded by Confederates. Under a flag of truce, the militia officers concurred that prudence and humanity demanded a surrender. So they did. Sontag also revealed to Morgan where Slain's force might be found. That detachment was also surprised and captured without resistance.[4] Morgan paroled the officers and men. Down to their last two rounds, the Confederates now took possession of Sontag's 395 French rifled muskets with 15,000 rounds of ammunition. At this point, General Morgan requested of his men, "All who have horses unable to travel will ride to the front." Fifty-four rode forward. He briefly addressed them: "I am going to turn you over to Colonel Sontag. He will treat you as prisoners of war." With this parting message, he turned and led the rest of his force away. Colonel Sontag proved to be a gentleman and a soldier. He permitted the Confederates to turn their horses over to either the local citizens or the U.S. government. They were marched to Portsmouth, Ohio, where they were placed on a packet and sent to Cincinnati.[5] Upon hearing of Sontag's debacle, Col. Kinney preferred charges against both Sontag and Slain and forwarded it to Adjutant-General Hill.[6]

A telegram sent by the president of Chillicothe's military committee to Governor Tod said:

> **I have reliable information that Morgan and five hundred of his men dined three hours ago at Iron Valley Furnace, six miles south of Hamden. I am also informed they are now moving towards McArthur. We cannot get dispatches to Zaleski, Athens and Marietta; we suppose wires are cut.**
>
> N.L. WILSON, *Pres't.*

The Confederates entered the county from Gallia County coming from Ewington. They crossed the Marietta & Cincinnati Railroad, followed today's Rt. 160 northwest to Vinton Station, two miles east of McArthur and three and one half miles southwest of Zaleski. They followed present Routes 9, 6 and 7, which run north into Madison Township to the site of a charcoal-burning iron furnace called Vinton Furnace, which is located on the Elk Fork of Raccoon Creek.[7] On their way to Vinton Furnace, they raided the place of Anthony L. Beard near Reed's Mill. They took two horses, saddles, bridle and Mr. Beard's pistol. On the other side of the furnace property, they took four horses from James Freeman. The manager of the furnace was Isaac Brown. Morgan's men noticed that Brown had a fine horse. Before Brown gave up his horse, he asked Morgan, "Give me a receipt so I can collect it off the government." Morgan was glad to oblige and handed him a voucher.[8]

1:00am, Wednesday, July 22

Following Rt. 93 north, the Confederates went into camp at Andrew Wolf Karn's farm on the Logan Road, some four miles north of Creola. The pursuing Union troops rose early that morning and went northwest on Madison Township Road 7 and Elk Township Road 18 to Old Rt. 50 between McArthur and Prattsville. As they approached Vinton Station, which was on the B&O line, they passed the homestead of a farmer named Dowd.[9]

Old man Dowd had two sons in the Union Army and a twelve-year-old son still at home. When he had heard that Morgan was coming, he sent his son to hide their horses in the woods. Dowd and his son were working in the field when they got word that Union troops were coming and that they were taking all the horses that Morgan had missed. Dowd unhitched his team, placed his young son on one and told him to take them to the woods and hide them as before. Before the boy reached the woods, a Union patrol, spying the lad, rode up and yelled for the boy to come back. The youngster kicked his horse and kept going. The Union troopers raised their guns and began firing at young Dowd. Turning to the NCO in charge of the patrol, old man Dowd began to raise hell. The Union cavalryman protested, "We need remounts. Morgan has taken most of the horses in the country." Dowd responded angrily, "I have two sons serving in the Union Army and now Union troops are trying to shoot my other son."[10]

6:00am, July 22

Morgan rose and continued in the same direction for a few miles, turned east along today's Rt. 56 when he was within one mile of New Plymouth. He entered Hocking County heading for Starr.

FIFTY

Starr's and Stripes

<u>8:00am, Wednesday, July 22</u>

At thirty-five years of age, Lavina Eggleston was postmistress at Starr. She was a direct descendent of Josiah Bartlett, one of the signers of the Declaration of Independence. Her great uncle was Benjamin Eggleston, a congressman from Cincinnati during Lincoln's presidency and very much involved in the Underground Railroad. Eggleston Avenue, in Cincinnati, is named for him.[1]

A horseman came to warn Lavina that Morgan's Raiders were headed her way. She took down the U.S. flag for fear that the raiders would desecrate or destroy it. Her husband and some other men took horses from the area and hid them in a hollow. When Morgan arrived, he found no horses and no flag, but he did go through the mail. Before leaving the tiny town, they "freed" twelve horses from their owners, the largest cache of mounts in Hocking County. Morgan's men rode away heading for Nelsonville in Athens County.[2]

Another telegram from the military committee in Chillicothe informed Governor Tod:[3]

(Telegram)
Information just received by horse telegraph, that Morgan was within two miles of Logan this four (4) P.M.
D.A. Schutte, *Secy. Ross Co. Mil. Com.*

On July 30, well after Morgan left Hocking County, several dry goods stores ran the following ads in the *Hocking County Sentinel*.[4]

(Ad #1)
We have been living the last two weeks upon the excitement of war, and now inorder to get down to the attractions of peace, go to the store of Rochester & Sons, and examine their nice Dress goods, tall piles of calicoes, muslins etc., at low prices and thank your stars that Morgan's thieves did not come this way and confiscate them!

9:00am, Wednesday, July 22

The Confederates crossed the Hocking River at Nelsonville. The small town was unprepared for the mid-morning arrival of Morgan and his raiders. An article in the *Hocking County Sentinel*, a day or two earlier, stated that "Morgan had been defeated and only a few stragglers were still loose. No doubt is entertained of the total destruction of Morgan's force. Our citizens need have no further apprehensions of seeing Morgan in this neighborhood."[5]

The Confederates were exhausted. Camping on the commons west of Nelsonville, they remained in town for two hours. The raiders helped themselves to all the food the housewives had cooked for dinner that day. The citizens could do nothing as they watched Morgan's men set fire to the old Factory Bridge over the Hocking Canal and burned or damaged ten canal boats: *Forest Rose, Swan, Hibernia, Ontario, Fame, Eureka, Quebec, Valley, Comstock* and *Virginia*. The fire spread to the Lorenzo Dow Poston coal works. One boat was ignored. Its owner, Charles Stuart, was able to convince Morgan that his boat, *The Custer,* was really a house boat instead of a coal boat. The General also spared the Steenrod flour mill from destruction when hearing the tearful pleas of Mrs. Steenrod.[6]

The militia who could have been mustered to defend Nelsonville had previously been dispatched to Athens upon hearing reports that it was Morgan's next destination. After seizing thirty-six horses,[7] raiding the town's four stores and taking all the supplies they could carry, the Confederates moved out about twelve-thirty in the afternoon and continued on to Buchtel and Murray City.

General Shackelford with a little more than 400 Union cavalry entered Nelsonville about six hours after Morgan had departed.[8]

A few days after Morgan rode out of Nelsonville, the *Hocking County Sentinel* reported:

Morgan burned some 10 of 12 canal boats for which act of devilishness, if for noother, Morgan and his band ought to suffer death by slow torture.

<u>Wednesday, July 22</u>

During the day, at least twenty of Morgan's men, mostly members of Co. F, 2nd KY, were captured. Taken prisoner were: Major T.B. Webber; First Lt. W.T. Dunlap; 5th Sgt. Wm. D. Cloud; First Cpl. C.L. Brackin; Pvt. C.W. Appling; Pvt. H.C. Barton; Pvt. Wm. Berry; Pvt. John Betty; Pvt. Thomas Brown; Pvt. Robert Daniel; Pvt. Jno. P. Fennell; Pvt. Thomas Hawkins; Pvt. John Hope; Pvt. Ben Jones; Pvt. Joseph Long; Pvt. John Mathews; Pvt. Columbus Moore; Pvt. W.W. Meglone; Pvt. J.S. Towles and Pvt. T.L. Yancey.[9]

<u>12:30pm, July 22</u>

(Telegram)   Headquarters Twelve Miles from Logan,
Eleven and a Half Miles from Plymouth.

General Burnside: The enemy passed this point this morning at 7 o'clock, led by Morgan himself, with a force variously estimated from 400 to 2,000; I think he has about 600 men. From the absolute want of horses, we are forced to pursue him with a little [over] 400 men. I think he is trying to cross the Muskingum River and reach the Ohio at a point above navigation for gunboats. Our horses are terribly jaded; yet we will pursue the enemy to the utmost capacity of men and horses.
Very respectfully,

J.M. SHACKELFORD,
Brigadier-General, Commanding Brigade.

General Judah was "out-of-the-loop" when he sent a telegram on this date to General Burnside saying, "I believe Morgan crossed [into West Virginia] himself on Sunday night. The Confederate force remaining in Ohio does not exceed 300 and is under the command of [Col.] R.S. Cluke."

General Burnside, wanted to pass along this tidbit to his General-in-Chief in Washington, DC. In a telegram, he inflated the numbers. He even intimates that General Morgan has deserted his men.

(Telegram)   Maj. General H.W. Halleck   *Cincinnati, Ohio, July* 22, 1863.

It is now thought that Morgan has deserted his men, leaving his force under command of Col. [R.S.] Cluke. We have all his other colonels, including Duke, who has been the managing man of all Morgan's raids; 2,321 prisoners thus far captured. The number of (Morgan's men) killed and wounded by gunboats and our own force will not fall short of 150. Morgan's force when he entered Indiana did not vary far from 3,000 men, so that his band is com-

pletely destroyed, and the circumstances under which he left his command have ruined his reputation as a leader.

A.E. BURNSIDE,
Major-General.

An hour or so later, Burnside received an eyewitness report that Morgan was indeed still in Ohio, and with a larger force than reported earlier. He then sent a telegram to General Judah who was still languishing in Pomeroy. He said, "Received report from Nelsonville [12:20pm] stating that Morgan passed through with a much larger force than mentioned in your last dispatch." Judah had claimed that Morgan's men in Ohio now numbered less than 300, while the actual number was more than double.

FIFTY-ONE

Heading for the Muskingum

<u>3:00pm, Wednesday, July 22</u>

Morgan entered the county along the road to New Straitsville. He then turned east through Whipstown (today known as Hemlock)[1], where they rested in a wheatfield. In the Whipstown area, the raiders took five horses.[2] Following the road, they approached the West Fork of Sunday Creek. A young woman spotting the dust cloud stirred up by hundreds of horses, began yelling, "Morgan is coming! Morgan is coming!" She was pointing toward Whipstown. Two farmhands who worked for Benjamin Sanders shouldered pitchforks as rifles and started marching up the road to see what all the commotion was about. At the first rise in the hill, they almost looked down into the mouths of Morgan's horses. They turned around and came back— not marching, but running in terror! At the barnyard, they swiftly unhitched a team and each jumped aboard a steed, harness and all. Off they dashed toward Buckingham, where they turned up a hollow, thus saving two horses and sets of harnesses and, of course, themselves.

Morgan's men arrived at the Sanders' farm and stated what they wanted. They took three horses including the family favorite "Old Rach" (short for Rachel) and one mule. They watered their horses at the water trough in the corner of the yard and came inside the house and took all the prepared food. Morgan's men, Mrs. Susannah Sanders said, "Comported themselves as true Southern Gentlemen. They offered no threats, nor threatening gestures. Morgan had those men strictly under his command."

One of Morgan's young troopers came to the side door and knocked. When Mrs. Sanders appeared, he removed his saddle from his mount in order to show her the saddle sores on the horse's back, caused by not having a saddle blanket or a poor excuse for one. "Would you have Ma'am," he said, "a piece of rug or something that would do me for a saddle blanket?"

Susannah disappeared to return shortly with one of her best quilts, which she gave the young cavalryman. She had, at that moment, three sons of her own off fighting for the Union, somewhere in the South. She thought, "Wouldn't it be nice if some kind-hearted mother way down there would do one of my boys a good turn when he stood in need of it." Her sons, William, Camm and Spencer were cavalrymen, too.

Mr. Sanders was not at home when Morgan paid a visit and took away the family horses. He wasn't ready to say goodbye to them. He mounted one of the horses that had been saved and set off the following morning to follow the raiders' trail. After he had ridden forty to fifty miles, he heard shooting up ahead, volleys of it. He stopped and waited until the shooting became sporadic. As he moved ahead, he could see a man who seemed to be commanding blue-coated men. He identified himself and told of Morgan taking three of his horses. The Union commander allowed him to pick out his own horses. Imagine his pleasure when he found "Old Rach." He tied his horses together in a chain-like "remuda" and headed back for his homestead in Perry County. He had been gone almost a week. Unfortunately, one of his horses died soon after he returned, a victim of hard riding.[3]

4:00pm, Wednesday, July 22

In Buchanan (later renamed Millertown),[4] the raiders stopped at Joseph Rodgers' home where, according to Rogers, he "fed 50 rebels." As many as fourteen horses were taken from the farmers in the Buchanan area.[5] Millertown is between Drakes and Corning.

5:00pm, July 22

At Hartleyville, a few miles south of Buchanan, the raiders came upon Dr. William H. Holden making house calls. They relieved him of his horse but permitted him to retain his saddlebags containing his instruments and medicines. Carrying the bag over his arm, he continued making the rest of his calls. Down the road, a farmer was hauling a wagonload of hay. His team was halted, the harness stripped from the horses and he was left sitting on the load, a much astonished individual. Stopping at a home for something to eat, some of Morgan's men came upon a group of women engaged in a "wool picking party." By the time Confederates departed, there was little food left for the partygoers.[6]

They passed through Corning and took a little-used road to Chapel Hill. The small hamlet of rude log cabins was originally named Thompsonville after the town's founder, George Thompson. But with the establishment of a post office, it had to change its name because a similar name already existed in the state. Thompson, as the town's first postmaster, renamed the village "Chapel Hill."[7]

Seven-year-old Kitty Crider was living on Sunday Creek, near Chapel Hill. She could hear a rattling noise as Morgan's men traveled on the ridge road above her. Her mother thought the noise was made by galvanized tin someone was taking home to make a new molasses pan. Her father met up with them and was told to "halt!" He dismounted, threw the rein over a post and walked away. In the company of others, he followed behind the raiders, hoping his horse would break away. He never recovered his valuable riding horse, saddle or bridle.[8]

"Widow Wiley," who lived in the same vicinity, welcomed Morgan's men into her home. She made them pancakes until her supply of flour and other food was exhausted. She was offended when someone asked if she had looked in the stable for her horse. She said these men were "gentlemen and would not steal a horse." But her stable was empty when she looked. Eventually, after Morgan was captured, some horses were given back to the owners who could identify them. The "Widow Wiley" walked a long distance to the place where the horses were held. She whistled to her horse, it came to her and she fed it sugar. She was permitted to take her horse home.[9]

From Athens, Ohio, Governor Tod was informed by telegram[10]:

> **Morgan passed Chapel Hill, twenty two miles north of this [Athens], on Zanesville road, at ten o'clock last night, aiming to cross Muskingum at Eagleport, seven miles above McConnelsville."**
> M.M. GREEN, *Chrm. Mil. Com.*

Another telegram from Green in Athens, on July 22, told the Governor:[11]

> **Message from Gen. Shackelford, at Nelsonville, 6 P.M., asks that Morgan may be checked in front, stating that he cannot be caught unless impeded in front, as he has taken all fresh horses. Morgan's forces, at 6 P.M., fed on section 3, Washington township, Hocking county."**

Earlier that afternoon, Governor Tod telegraphed to Zanesville that Morgan was at McArthur in Vinton County and his object was "to strike the Ohio River above the reaches of our gunboats, and he may visit your place."[12] The Governor requested that 100 scouts be sent to Perry and Morgan counties. The governor's message was received by T.J. Maginnis, chairman of the military committee at Zanesville. Maginnis had the courthouse bell rung and read the notice to the assembled crowd. The *Zanesville Courier* printed notices and they were soon posted.[13]

A committee was appointed to secure horses. "Pale faces and trembling tongues were not uncommon," said the *Courier*.[14] The governor's dispatch had produced much excitement in McConnelsville and along the river above. As Morgan was heading for the Muskingum River, it became evident that his objective was either McConnelsville or Eagleport. Only these two towns had fordable passes over the river. Morgan was trying to avoid the larger towns that would have better defenses. At Eagleport, Morgan expected the ford to be unguarded.

3:00pm, Wednesday, July 22

A company of 150 Zanesville men galloped away to patrol the Muskingum River and the Maysville Pike.[15] That same afternoon, Colonel Joseph Hill, who had left Marietta on the steamer *Jonas Powell* with 500 men and two brass field pieces, sent a message that he was at Nelsonville and was steaming toward McConnelsville.[16] It appeared that Col. Hill was not too anxious to confront Morgan. Hill was notified that Morgan would cross the river at Eagleport, yet he chose to land his 500 troops at Stockport, ten miles below McConnelsville. Three times during the night, he was urged to head Morgan off or let some of his officers go after the raiders. He refused. By nine o'clock on the morning of July 23, when Morgan was crossing the river at Eagleport, Hill passed McConnelsville. By ten-thirty, he landed two miles south of Eagleport and allowed Capt. Marsh to lead a company up the river road to Eagleport where he learned that Morgan had passed that point two hours earlier. Col. Hill unloaded his two field pieces and had them fire token rounds, even though Morgan's men were nowhere in sight.[17]

5:00pm, July 22

A regiment of the 86th OH arrived by train in Zanesville under the command of Col. Lemert from Columbus. Lemert took two mounted companies to Deavertown for picket duty. The others remained in Zanesville under the command of Lt. Col. R.W. McFarland.[18]

At dusk, Morgan left Perry County at Portersville. As the raiders came through town, the parents of Anna Newlon feared the Confederates would enter their home. They hid little Anna and her sister by placing them in a trundle bed which they pushed under a larger bed. Morgan's men had another seven miles of riding ahead before they would stop for camp. They didn't bother to pause for meals but they did take six horses in the Portersville area. A total of forty horses were taken in the two Perry County townships of Monroe and Bearfield, through which the raiders rode.[19] Anna remained still for what seemed hours. She could hear the clicking of swords as troopers passed her home. For years afterward, Portersville mothers frightened their children into obedience by simply saying, "Morgan will get you!"[20]

The raiders rode past the farm of Thomas Pettet on the border between Perry and Morgan counties. Thomas and his wife, Jane Barron Pettet, and their five children, Thomas, Samuel, George, Ann and Harriet, took in oil drillers as boarders for the noon meal. Grandmother Julia Roger and Aunt Fleeta helped the family prepare the dinner by rising early and baking fourteen pies daily. On that particular day, Grandmother Roger had just placed the fresh-baked pies on the sill of the open kitchen window to cool. As the raiders rode through, they spotted the pies. They were so distracted by the delicious bakeries, they never bothered to look for the family's horses.[21]

General Morgan entered Morgan County at Deerfield Township near today's S.R. 37. He skirted northwest of Triadelphia.

9:00pm, Wednesday, July 22

Col. Z.M. Chandler, who was later to teach business courses in the Zanesville High School, led ten Ohio militia scouts into Morgan's picket line. Taking the Zanesville scouts prisoners, the raiders exchanged horses with the militia and relieved them of their watches and greenbacks.[22] The raiders continued riding through five Nelson farms (P.J., Jas., P.S., W. and J.W.) stopping to rest at the two-story log cabin on John Weaver's farm at the headwaters of Island Run. His group of 600 ragged troopers gathered about the Weaver's farm buildings and house. Morgan dismounted and, with a cramped gait of one who had spent too much time in the saddle, walked over to the front door where Weaver and his family stood.[23]

Fear and astonishment were written on their faces. "We are putting a guard around your house," Morgan said. "You and your family will not be molested, but you must not come out until we are gone. You might get hurt." He entered the house and walked to the bedroom where he pulled the straw tick from the bed and dropped it on the floor. He threw himself upon it and at once fell asleep.[24] His men camped for the night in the surrounding orchard. Groups of raiders took Weaver's fence railings and built fires over which they cooked the food products they had found on Ohio farms, homes and stores.[25]

Mr. Weaver's wife, Nan, had a baby only a few weeks old, but she stayed up much of the night making griddle cakes and biscuits for some of Morgan's men. In the barn, the men found many bushels of freshly threshed wheat. It is said that they fed very little of it to their animals for fear that their horses might get colic or cramps when they rode them hard the next day. Yet, Mr. Weaver made a claim for reimbursement for the following items taken by the raiders: one horse with saddle and bridle, 100 bushels of wheat, four tons of hay, clothing and one barrel of salt. Although many other Ohio citizens asked to be compensated for "feeding meals to rebels," Mr. Weaver made no such claim.[26]

FIFTY-TWO

The Eagleport Crossing

<u>Midnight, Thursday, July 23</u>

Thomas L. Gray of Deavertown set out with several companions to look for Morgan. They included Reeves McAdoo and James Foraker. Gray and his friends were lightly armed, carrying two old guns. They were soon joined by Jacob Knapp who was armed with an ax. Later, they were joined by Peter Mast and George Swytzer. Stopping in the dark at Joe Helmick's place, the six adventurers heard that half a dozen raiders had, some hours before, secured food and gone in the direction of Eagleport. At first, the group decided to cut down trees to cut off the enemy's retreat. As Knapp started in with his ax, it was decided that the noise would warn the raiders of their presence.[1]

Just below John Bankes' house, the road forks, and as they approached this point, they heard horsemen coming up the creek. The clank of sabers told them that they were soldiers. It was about an hour after midnight and it was very dark. Halting in the road and remaining quiet, the Deavertown gang waited for the approach of the enemy. When the riders were only a few feet away, Mr. Gray, in a voice with as much authority as he could muster, shouted, "Halt, dismount and give up your arms." Not knowing how many Union men surrounded them, the raiders surrendered. Not a shot had been fired. The Confederate captives included a Captain Williams and four men. When they saw young Jacob Knapp with his ax upraised, one of the raiders put his spurs to his horse and galloped away into the darkness. The prisoners were marched to Helmick's mill, where they were held until morning. During the night, one of the raiders escaped. The others were turned over to the authorities in Zanesville.[2]

<u>2:00am, July 23</u>

Lt. Col. R.W. McFarland left Zanesville heading south on the steamer *Dime* with 500 men, four companies of the 86th OH, intending to keep Morgan from crossing the Muskingum River.[3]

Early that morning, Morgan rode into the southeast corner of York Township. He took John Weaver with him to show him the way. After a few miles, General Morgan told Weaver he knew where he was so "you may go back home. Walk slowly and when my last man passes you, do not turn around and don't run."[4] Morgan followed the Island Run gorge to where it wound toward the Muskingum River south of Eagleport. On the outskirts of Eagleport, one of the town's more timid citizens, a Mr. Forgrave, took refuge in a nearby pig pen. A Confederate trooper saw him enter, and following him into the pen, discovered him crouched behind a matronly looking sow that was in the process of feeding a number of newborn offspring. "Halloa!" shouted the Confederate soldier. "How did you git here? Did y'all come in the same litter?" With all the adversity the raiders had endured, their good humor still remained. "Come on out of there you d__m fool," said the young raider, rapping the plank covering the sty with the muzzle of his carbine. "Come out of there before some of our foragers shoot you for a pig."[5]

Another Eagleport-area citizen was watching the raiders ride two abreast down the Island Run from the bluffs above. Twelve-year-old "Lon" Woodward had walked from his farm to Alonzo Jones' place which stood on a hill overlooking the run. The two Jones boys had declined Lon's offer to join him for a look-see. "The rebels might shoot at us." So he trudged on alone to the brow of a hill near the line of Jim Boal's farm. Here he found his father's roan mare, "Julia," tied to a tree. From behind a beech tree, his father, John F. Woodward of Lemon Hill, was shooting at the Confederates with his squirrel rifle. After firing three shots, the raiders sighted Woodward's location and returned fire. Twenty rounds slammed around the beech tree and flushed Woodward out. He ran for his horse and headed for safety. Young Lon ran along with the 600 raiders, but they were some 300 feet below in the gorge. He watched the action unfold from his perch in the bluffs among the trees. He thought, why go down when the whole play was set before him as a scene upon a stage.[6]

8:00am, Thursday, July 23

Morgan's advance guard rode toward Eagleport. Lon saw Delphine Devol run for the river just a block away from his Main Street store. Mr. Devol sold general merchandise including dry goods and groceries. Many times, Lon had carried eggs and butter from his family farm to sell to Mr. Devol. Now Devol could be seen jumping into a skiff and he began to row across the Muskingum River toward Rokeby. One of Morgan's lieutenants shouted to the fleeing Eagleport merchant, "Come back here, d__n you!" On the hill above, Lon could hear Mr. Devol's reply, "You go to h__l!" and he rowed to the eastern shore and safety.

Another Eagleport merchant, William Price, heard the shooting and realized that Morgan's men had entered the town. He quickly filled a pocketbook with the contents from his cash drawer. He fled out the store and into a field. Some of the raiders called to him to return or they would shoot. As he turned to walk back through a field of timothy, he dropped the wallet into the tall hay. After the Confederates left town, Price recovered his money.[7]

All along the Rokeby front, across the river from Eagleport, squirrel rifles were popping. Shotgun roars reverberated off the cliffs overlooking the river. A bullet fired by a Mr. Finley from Theobold Weber's home across the river struck one of Morgan's troopers, Tommy McGee, mortally wounding him. With the aid of men riding beside him, Tommy was tied to his saddle. He managed to stay on his horse until he crossed the river and was some distance beyond.[8]

But most of the guns being fired by area citizens did not have the range to do much damage. At the command of the Confederate lieutenant, twenty or more of Morgan's men drew their horses parallel with the river. Resting their carbines across their saddles, they commenced to return the fire toward the Weber and McElhiney houses.[9] As Theobold Weber's wife leaned over to make a bed in the front room, a bullet crashed through the bedroom window. Had she remained standing, she would have been killed with a minie ball in the head.[10] With their lives now in danger, the Webers and their daughter, Lib, fled for safety into the hills behind their home.[11]

While they were away, the raiders were determined to burn the home because they knew rifle fire had come from the direction of the home. But they were stopped by two elderly Rokeby men who vouched for the fact that no one to whom the home belonged fired any shots. Later, when they returned, they found their home stripped of food, quilts, blankets, sheets and pillows and a yard full of spent bullets.[12]

Theobold Weber's daughter, Lib, wrote to her sister two days after the raid (Saturday, July 25), describing Morgan's raid. Her sister was away teaching school.

Dear Sister, I will now try and write you a few lines to let you know that old Morgan has not got us yet, but he came pretty close near taking us Thursday.

The first we knew that Morgan was near here was last Wednesday evening, two men came riding down the road fast. One of them had stopped here before. They said a dispatch came to Zanesville and Marietta, and they thought they would come to McConnelsville, so that is where they went. Twenty more came down and they followed where the first ones went.

Well, there were men riding here all night. The next morning about 4 o'clock, there was about twenty men stopped and wanted breakfast and their horses fed. They said they had taken five of Morgan's men near Helmick's Mill.

Someone said, "Morgan is coming down Island Run." I did not believe it until I saw them all start back again toward the ferry and the Captain hollering for every man to get his gun. I was out milking. Then some men started for McConnelsville as fast as their horses could carry them. I never felt a bit afraid until I heard them firing guns near the mouth of Island Run.

Pretty soon we could see them [Morgan's men] coming up Andersons, all on horses, with their arms glittering.

Ann Jones had just come with butter. We ran in the house. There were so many folks off on Dutch Hill. They had been up all night scouting. Some of them were here. They told us to go in the house while they would shoot. But we begged them not to shoot, for we knew that such few men as they could not do anything with so many. But they stood in our door and fired at them. In an instant, the bullets were flying back here. There were four or five that went through the house. They had made us all go in the back yard. You never saw people so scared in all your life. We thought it was not safe to stay here, so we started for the woods.

They could not see us on the other side of the river, for our corn in the lot. A bullet came within a half foot of Mrs. Brown's head. We got on Winchell's hill. I mean on the left side of the Run as you go up. We could hear them shooting all the time but could not go to the edge of the hill to see them. The road was full [of raiders] from Delph Devol's down as far as you could see. They made Mr. Winchell ferry them over. Stood over him with guns until they all got across.

There were about 700 of them. They started up the road. Didn't go farther than Frew's, when they saw the boat landing at Bells with [Union] forces. So they started back as hard as they could get. They took across the hill out toward Barrs. While our infantry, that the boat brought down, took up the hill by Bell's. Then we came home.

We had left all the doors open. When we came in you never saw such a looking house in your life. Everything was upside down. The woman's trunk was bursted open and all her things scattered over the floor. All the stockings out of the closet on the floor. Not a bite to eat in the house. They had taken all our best meat, flour, quilts, two comforts, all of Pap's and Dave's pants, my kid gloves and purse, and eight or ten dollars in money. They went to the bar room and the whiskey they did not drink, they let it all run away. I mean everything that was in the bar room, whiskey, wine and cigars, all were gone.

We went out yesterday where they had the fight. I saw one dead Rebel. They had buried one the day before. There was fifteen killed altogether. I guess they took the rest and buried them. There was only one of our men killed, and he does not live around here [see Harry Kelly, below.] They have got a wounded Rebel over in Devol's warehouse. They think he will get well again. He was shot through the shoulder. That wounded Rebel at Devol's is so sassy.

I got a letter from George yesterday. They were on a branch of the Little Hocking when he wrote. I also got one from him Wednesday. I did not answer either. We heard you were coming home today. I must stop. Lib.[13]

Harry (also identified as Henry) Kelly, of Logan in Morgan County, had lost three horses to the raiders a few days before. Harry was the assistant manager of the Logan Furnace, having left his job at the Zanesville Blast Furnace several months earlier. He said good-bye to his wife and five little children and left to pursue Morgan and retrieve his horses. From time to time, he would take shots at Morgan's rear guard. At last, Harry stood on the hill overlooking Eagleport where he could see the Confederates below waiting to cross the river.[14]

On another hill where Lon Woodward stood, he was joined by a Private Walker of Deavertown. Walker was home on furlough and had come over in the wake of Morgan. He brought along his musket and forty rounds of U.S.A. ball in his leather cartouche. He saw the scramble on the opposite shore. Changing the cap on his weapon, he took aim and fired at the Confederates downriver. His second shot brought an angry outcry from the raiders, who thought Walker was one of them. "You d__m fool, don't you know you're shooting at your own men?" Then directing his bullets across the river at a raider on a white horse, he shouted, "You darn fool, don't I know who I'm shooting at?"[15]

With his telescope, Morgan scanned the hills above Eagleport, thinking Walker's shot had come from the hill where Kelly stood. As he ranged his glass along the escarpment of the bluff, Kelly came into range, just 250 yards away. The Logan man had been warned by a companion, Alex Stinchcomb of Deavertown,[16] to stay behind a tree. Morgan commanded, "There's that darn Yank that's been popping at us; get rid of him."[17] Standing on Mr. Devol's store steps, three sharpshooters lifted their carbines and fired. Kelly fell, shot through and through by three balls from the Raiders' guns. Kelly's body was brought to Devol's store, wrapped in muslin and placed in a crude coffin.[18] The next afternoon, the body of Harry Kelly went back to Logan in an express wagon driven by Mr. Woodward of Lemon Hill.[19] The *Zanesville City Times* reported in its July 30 edition, "He [Kelly] has left a wife and five children in a rather helpless condition."[20]

The citizens' firing at Rokeby slowed and at last stopped. The hamlet's defenders had taken cover in the cornfields that lay behind the village. Hiram Winchell, who lived at Unity Farm and operated the flatboat-ferry at Eagleport, was hiding behind a store near his boat. The Confederates called him out and ordered him to his boat. Men and horses were loaded and moved across the waterway. As the first boatload crossed, a raider took one look at Hi Winchell's hat and said, "Partner, that's a darn good hat you're wearing. Let's trade." He took the hat from the ferryman's head and placed it on his own, jamming the old one he was wearing over Winchell's brow.[21]

As the Confederate riders disembarked, some turned north and some south toward the McElhiney's farm a quarter of a mile away. Several hundred Bloom and Bristol Township citizens had come to Muskingum to see Morgan's Raiders. They stopped on the eastern shore above the McElhiney place. A squad of a dozen raiders came out of the hollow and surprised the spectators. Everyone ran. They tumbled over fences and ran for the corn or wherever they could get out of sight. Horses were captured before their owners could unloose them. Others were halted and made to come back to give up their steeds.[22]

Morgan's arrival in Eagleport and Rokeby Lock in Bloom Township was vividly recalled in 1938 by ninety-one-year-old Elizabeth McElhiney who was sixteen at the time of the raid.

"Riding their horses along the riverbank [of the Muskingum River] on the Eagleport side [south of the town] directly opposite the McElhiney house, Morgan's men were in plain view of a body of some 500 civilians gathered to defend their property. I was standing beside the man who fired the first pistol shot at the rebels. He was a Mr. Bowers, a miller from Zanesville." The temerity of the civilians brought a reply of minié bullets from the opposite shore and the crowd was rapidly dispelled.[23]

By fording the river, then at low stage, and by using of the ferry, the raiders crossed to Rokeby. After the rain of bullets upon the house, Richard McElhiney ordered his family to leave the home. "We went up the hill," continued Miss McElhiney, "and saw them sack the house. I took all my jewelry and so did my sister. Father had about $2000 in a small wooden box. He buried it in the potato patch behind the house and it was two weeks before he found it again. We had some pancakes left from breakfast, a cake in the cellar and a five-gallon jar of fresh buttermilk. When we returned to the house, the cake and pancakes were gone and so was the buttermilk, but the glass tumblers which they had used to drink the milk, were set inside the jar with never a crack in them. My father lost every shirt he had in the house." When asked whether she had been frightened, she replied, "I wasn't a bit frightened, they weren't going to kill us."[24]

Richard McElhiney did make a $167 claim for payment from the State of Ohio for the following items taken by the raiders: one horse, saddle, clothing, jewelry, watch, gun and $17 cash.[25]

Morgan's group needed more than Winchell's ferry to get them over the river. They had no time to waste what with Shackelford's men in close pursuit. They had heard that there was a ford at Eagleport. Unknown to the raiders, the ford was about one hundred yards below the dam and, at low-water mark, as it then was, does not exceed one hundred feet in width, with a depth for a limited space of not more than four feet. Fifty yards above the ford, the river is seven hundred feet wide, varying in depth from ten to forty feet.[26]

Captain Virgil W. Pendleton, Co. D, 8th KY, rode up to a group of men sitting on the porch of the Devol store. "Do any of you men know the ford?" he asked. Johnny Fouts replied, "I do." Pendleton jerked an order over his shoulder. "Bring a horse!" Pendleton asked, "Does it swim you?" Fouts replied, "No, only in the boat channel. About a hundred feet. I swam cattle there the other day." A private appeared leading a horse. "Get on that horse and show me the ford," said Pendleton. Fouts crossed. When he had reached the eastern bank, the captain shouted, "Now come back." Fouts recrossed and rejoined the raiders on the Eagleport side. Pendleton said, "Now we will cross together," and turning to the raiders behind him he commanded, "Attention! Close up! By twos, march!" and he and Fouts plunged their horses into the Eagleport ford.[27] *There is a monument on Ohio Rt. 60 just south of Rokeby Lock across the road from the W.L. McElhiney property now known as the Morgan's Raid farm. Morgan County Schools now use the Morgan Raider name for their school band and athletic teams.*

FIFTY-THREE

Zanesville Responds

Earlier that morning, in Zanesville, 1,000 rifles and forty rounds of ammunition apiece arrived from Columbus. Mounted men, now well armed, dashed out of the city at a furious rate, heading south. About 1,000 Zanesville men volunteered for service. Four-horse teams were hitched to all of the city's omnibuses to transport troops. Farmers' wagons were pressed into service. An African-American company was organized for duty. When the guns were distributed and there were not enough rifles for everyone, the unarmed men began to make coffee in a big boiler and provided it to soldiers at the courthouse and at the train depot. The suspense was relieved by a number of women who stood on the balconies of the Stacey House hotel and sang patriotic songs. Other ladies furnished the Zanesville militia with food and provisions. About eleven o'clock in the morning, business was suspended and, during this great excitement, a small red wagon came rattling up Fourth Street with four Confederates who had been captured. A Zanesville girl would later marry one of them.[1] At eleven-forty-five, mounted couriers galloped to the Zanesville courthouse with the news that Morgan had crossed the river at Eagleport.[2]

As Morgan's men were leaving the Rokeby hamlet, a Confederate scout saw the smoke of the steamer *Dime* with Lt. Col. McFarland and hundreds of militia aboard. From the distance, the Confederate scout took it to be a gunboat.[3] The boat landed two miles above the Rokeby Lock near Sarah Bell's home. The home guard infantry commenced their march south in pursuit of Morgan's column. They met at Barr's Ridge.[4] Shots were exchanged between the two forces and the raiders gave way, riding through the corn and wheatfields and through the McElhiney hollow. The whole of Morgan's command rode at a gallop and passed out of sight in the gorge.[5]

9:30am, Thursday, July 23

Tommy McGee dropped from his horse. He had been tied to his saddle and brought that far. He was dead. His body was found by Charles Patterson and Dave Bailey.[6] There was a pillow,[7] stolen from David Power,[8] placed under McGee's head. They hastily laid the body under a shelving rock near by, cast some leaves over it and left. The following day, McElhiney's neigh-

274

bors, Jas. Shilling, J.M. Betz, Joseph M. Biggs and Mr. Bailey,[9] took McGee's remains and buried him beside a little stream one and a half miles from the river in "Dead Man's Hollow." They placed a flat rock about six inches by twelve inches, found nearby to act as a crude tombstone and on it scratched a date. There was no name, for they had no idea of the dead Confederate's identity. In 1890, a rumor circulated that relatives of the dead Confederate had searched for treasure alleged to have been buried in the hollow. Jim McElhiney, Richard's brother, decided to satisfy the curiosity of people looking for the grave. McElhiney said he made up the name "Tommy McGee" and scratched it on the flat sandstone. In 1913, a Mr. Hambleton, on a visit to Zanesville, said that he had come through Morgan County long before as a member of Morgan's troops. He visited the grave of his comrade, whose real name, he declared, was Frederick (or John) Rolfe, not Tommy McGee.[10]

To determine which version was true, Elmer Gerlach, in 1989, did genealogical research and proved that the dead Confederate's name was Thomas Milton McGee. At the request of Brian McKee, commander, Sons of Confederate Veterans, Parkersburg, Steve Tatman and Jim Miller jointly donated a new grave marker, which was placed on the farm of Cecil Moore. In 1991, the marker was dedicated. It reads: "McGee, Thomas Milton, Pvt., Co. H, 2nd Kentucky Cav., CSA, KIA July 23, 1863."[11]

For an hour, young Lon Woodward and a group that joined him on the bluff scanned the opposite shore for fresh developments. But Morgan's men were not planning an encore at Eagleport. Instead, a fresh medley of hoof beats and the rattle of sabers were followed by the advance guard of Shackelford's cavalry as they came down Island Run at a gallop. Lon, realizing the danger had past, raced down the hill and ran alongside a pair of blue-coated troopers. "Careful sonny," said one of the unshaven riders, "my horse might step on them feet."[12]

After the danger was ended, people began to realize how much the county had been terrified by a few hundred retreating and exhausted Confederates, and they saw the amusing side of the raid. One man sent a parody to the *Courier*.[13]

**Muskingum's children still turn pale,
When Morgan's name inspires the tale,
And Zanesville matrons long shall tame
The froward [disobedient] child with that dread name.**

On July 20, Lt. Wm. Dustin of the 19th OH Battery took his two pieces aboard the little steamer *Mayflower*, accompanied by 400 "squirrel-hunters," under the command of Col. Hill, with orders to proceed up the Muskingum River. The following morning, when within two miles of McConnelsville, a mounted courier rode up to the river bank and hailed the steamer. He informed Col. Hill that Morgan had just crossed the river two miles above, with the intention of destroying McConnelsville. With the wildest excitement, horses, men and guns tumbled ashore in the quickest manner possible. At "double-quick," they galloped toward the imperiled town.[14]

As they approached McConnelsville, great confusion and consternation were prevailing. The citizens were running aimlessly about in distress, some carrying wearing apparel, and others valuables. The column dashed into town, the riders lashing their horses and the dust rising in clouds from their feet. The rattle of the cannons over the stones, the jingling of sabers, the treble teams drawing the big guns were all novel sights to the people. Some citizens weren't sure whether these were friends or foe. One old lady standing on the pavement seemed to be in a frenzy while her daughter was trying to calm her. As the lead cannon dashed into sight, the old lady screamed, "They'll kill us all; they are going to kill us!" The daughter hastily recognized the blue uniforms, and with joy in her voice, shouted to her agitated parent, "It's our men, mother; they're our soldiers!" The old lady threw up her hands and exclaimed with an intensity of fervor, "Glory to God! Our artillery's coming!"[15]

Lt. William Dustin marched about seven miles up the river toward Eagleport. Hardly a corporal's guard of squirrel-hunters had been able to keep up with his cannons. At this juncture, he discovered the advance guard of Morgan's column about 1,200 yards distant advancing on the road toward him. He promptly ordered the pieces unlimbered, and fired. The first shot made a terrific noise, that was echoed back from wood and hill, and went tearing through a barn standing on the roadside a few yards from the passing Confederate troops. It was so unexpected that it threw the raiders' advance into confusion and forced them to reverse the order of march. In all, forty-five rounds of shot and shell were fired, with no response from the raiders. The artillery group returned to McConnelsville, where they were greeted by prepared food sent out by the grateful people of the town to refresh their "gallant defenders." The citizens of McConnelsville, through their ladies, presented a beautiful little silk battle-flag to the battery as a mark of their regard.[16]

FIFTY-FOUR

The Sign of the Freemason

<u>10:00 am, Thursday, July 23</u>

At Barr's Ridge, the opposing forces met.[1] They were in the woods and fields along the McConnelsville Road. On the road ahead waited Captain Marsh with two pieces of artillery. Cannon fire turned Morgan from the road. To avoid Lt. Colonel R.W. McFarland's force in his rear and the cannon fire in front, the Confederates turned right and rode into McElhiney's hollow.[2] The pursuit continued until two o'clock.[3] Once more, Morgan had eluded his pursuers. His tired cavalrymen rode through Ruraldale in Blue Rock Township, and on through Museville, Zeno and High Hill in Meigs Township before crossing into Guernsey County.[4]

Between Zeno and Cumberland lived Theodore March Frazee, a grocer and harness maker. About three o'clock in the afternoon, Dr. John McCall, a Cumberland doctor, came riding from Zeno past Frazee's home with the alarming news of Morgan's coming.[5] He shouted to them as he sped by. Mr. Frazee hid his good horses, leaving "Old Barney" in the barn. Theodore went back and took a seat on his front porch and waited. When Morgan's men arrived, they started jumping off their horses and racing toward the house, grocery and harness shop. Suddenly, General Morgan shouted, "Halt! The first man who enters that house without orders will be shot! And pay for anything you take in the store." The men, accompanying the General, did not loot the house or shop. Mrs. Frazee later observed that she had seen Freemasonry signs given between the General and her husband.[6]

The Frazee family had a Southern girl working for them and she was told to prepare the best dinner she could for Morgan's men. They were served as long as the food supply lasted.[7] Other Confederates, who came later, took two saddles, bridles, halters, cigars and ten bushels of corn. Frazee made no claim for meals served.[8] But James Culbertson of Cumberland asked $5.00 for serving "forty meals to rebels."[9]

Mary Eleanor Frazee kept a diary for most of her life. Her entry on July 23, 1863, is titled "Morgan's Raiders."

At Theodore Frazee's at Cumberland. Some of his men at Levi's Frazee's. The men had taken all the horses but "Old Barney." Gone to Duncan Falls. Mother and we children took Barney to sheep barn so they would not get him.[10]

Fulton Caldwell, from the town of Caldwell (named after his father, Samuel) in Noble County, was on the road south of Cumberland. He was taking his watch to a jeweler for repair. He was in the company of six other men who lived in the area. They rode along deep in conversation. To their surprise, they were suddenly confronted by several armed men who turned out to be Morgan's advance guard. Fulton, in his diary, wrote that he and the others were "captured by Morgan on July 23." They were all relieved of their mounts as well as Mr. Caldwell's watch.[11]

(Telegram)   *Cambridge, July 23, 1863*

Gov. David Tod: Scouts just in report Morgan came to Cumberland at three o'clock, and left after dark in the direction of Senecaville, about seven or eight hundred strong.

                                        C.J. ALBRIGHT[12]

OHIO

WEST VIRGINIA

CARROLL COUNTY

Dungannon
Lisbon
Gavers
West Point
Millport
COLUMBIANA COUNTY
Norristown
East Liverpool
Mechanicstown
Salineville
Wellsville
Carrollton
Monroeville
JEFFERSON COUNTY
Bergholz
Circle Green
Amsterdam
East Springfield
Toronto
Richmond
Shanghai
Wintersville
Steubenville
HARRISON COUNTY
Mingo Jct.
New Alexandria
Smithfield
Cadiz
Georgetown
Dillonvale
Moorefield
Harrisville
Mt. Pleasant
GUERNSEY COUNTY
New Athens
BELMONT COUNTY
Smyrna
Londonderry
Antrim
Wheeling
Old Washington
St. Clairsville
Cambridge
Bellaire
Lore City
Pleasant City
Senecaville
Cumberland

OHIO RIVER

MILES
0   5   10   15

N

©1999 Lester Horwitz
All Rights Reserved

GUERNSEY COUNTY, OH

FIFTY-FIVE

The Bonnie Blink Ride of Mary McClelland

<u>3:00pm, Thursday, July 23</u>

The Confederate force of about 600 men rode into Guernsey County[1] arriving at Cumberland about midday. They remained there until after dark eating supper, stealing horses and plundering stores. Morgan and his staff were self-invited guests at the Globe House, which was kept by Dr. Stone. The General made this 1840's landmark his headquarters. Guards were posted around the home. In the rear, Morgan's men noticed that the back doors opened into the second floor, because the ground sloped up in the rear.[2] Morgan and his weary staff stretched out on the soft beds in the spacious home's many bedrooms but not before they sampled the doctor's ample pantry. In the rear stable was the physician's horse. Dr. Stone asked that they leave his horse because he had a critically ill patient whom he needed to visit. He offered $75 in place of the horse, and the cash was accepted. After the officers left at ten o'clock at night, another squad of raiders came by and took his horse, despite his pleas.[3] The doctor lost both his cash and equine transportation. The doctor was not alone in the loss of his steed. More than 100 horses were taken from the Cumberland area. Fifteen of them were taken from the McClelland families.[4]

At the same time that Morgan was entering Guernsey County, Dr. James McCall was spreading the news of Morgan's coming. He shouted as he rode north from Zeno. Riding past the home of James McClelland, he gave the alarm. All the McClelland men were in the fields at work some distance from the house. Mrs. James McClelland and her daughter-in-law, Mrs. Alexander McClelland, with her small daughter, Alta, and stepdaughter, Mary, were in the house. Only one horse remained at the homestead. "Bonnie Blink," a three-year-old filly yet unbroken was grazing in the pasture. Mary, with some effort, succeeded in bridling it, jumped on its back with neither saddle nor blanket, and started to race to the men in the field to warn them. She was as spirited as the filly and hung on when the latter cleared the top of the fence rails. Mary had started sidewise, the only proper way for

280

women in that day. But now she threw one leg over the back of the charging horse and rode astride, clutching its mane.[5]

Before she reached her menfolk in the fields, she saw the glint of Morgan's guns facing her. The sun shining on the metal stocks made them seem like a phalanx of spears. She rode through the men, ignoring their commands to halt. Digging her heels into the sides of the filly, she urged it to even greater speeds. When she reached her men in the hayfield, she was so exhausted that they had to lift her from her colt, which they then hid in a thicket some distance from the road. Later in the day, Morgan and some of his men took possession of the McClelland home. There, in the parlor, the General took his army blanket, spread it on the floor and tried to get some sleep. Before he could drift off, he was warned that the Union forces were coming near. In his haste, he rushed out of the home, leaving his blanket behind. The McClelland family have prized it as a trophy of war ever since.[6]

Forcing a local man to accompany him as a guide, Morgan left Cumberland, following the road leading northeast from the town. Riding into the night, Morgan's column reached Pt. Pleasant where they released their Cumberland hostage. In his place, they forced Harrison Secrest, owner of the Elk Hotel in Pt. Pleasant, to guide them to Campbell's Station (Lore City). Between Pt. Pleasant and Hartford (Buffalo) was a covered bridge across Seneca Creek. Locals had removed some floor planks to make it difficult for the raiders to use the bridge, so Morgan's men swam their horses across and the General ordered the bridge burned.[7]

Early in the morning, a group of Confederate stragglers went past a home southwest of Pt. Pleasant on the road north of Cumberland. Trailing behind Morgan's main force, they stopped, dismounted and proceeded to search the stable for fresh horses. Inside they found a dark bay horse, the family's prize steed. While they were taking the horse from the stable, a rider was seen coming up the road. He was slouched over in his saddle and gave no heed to the command of the Confederates that he stop. Believing him to be a Union soldier, they fired and he fell to the ground. On closer examination, they saw that he was John Happs, one of their own men. Like the rest of Morgan's soldiers, he was nearly exhausted and had fallen asleep in the saddle. The men from Dixie could not leave him there in the road to die, neither could they take him with them. They carried him into the home of William LaFollette and demanded that he go for a doctor immediately. LaFollette rode to Pt. Pleasant to search for Dr. Teeter. He found the town still greatly excited from Morgan's recent visit. Dr. Teeter's horse had been stolen, so there was a delay until another horse could be found and the two returned to the badly wounded Confederate.[8]

The doctor probed for the bullet and found it. He said the condition of the wounded man was critical, but that he would recover if proper care was given. Mr. and Mrs. LaFollette were much distressed and were loyal Union people. Nobody else offered to care for him, so they felt it was their Christian duty to do all they could for him. During his convalescence, he wrote some letters to his family. After four months of care, he was able to travel and was taken away by Union officers.[9]

On the main street in Senecaville lived a husband and wife who were deeply interested in the Union cause. Her two brothers had gone to war and when her husband announced that he, too, felt it to be his duty to enlist, she patriotically gave her consent. She promised her husband that she would support herself during his absence by keeping a millinery shop in her home.

Before leaving for his military destination, the husband purchased a pistol, which he loaded and presented to her, jokingly remarking that she should shoot the first rebel who came into the house. She placed the weapon in the drawer of a bureau in the room, and vowed that she would do just what her husband suggested.[10]

3:00am, Friday, July 24

The Confederate advance guard rode through Senecaville. Warned of Morgan's coming, many of the citizens had left town. Those who remained locked their doors fearing that the town would be plundered and buildings burned as, it was rumored, had been done elsewhere.[11]

The milliner heard the hoof beats through an open window and peered out through the blinds. The long line of tired soldiers paid no attention to her or her home until one Confederate, who was riding near the rear of the main body, dismounted in front of her home. She recognized him as Morgan himself, as she had heard him described—a well-built man, about six-feet tall, fresh complexion, sandy hair and beard with a mild face, physically large and powerful. On his breast, he wore a large silver star.[12] He stood facing her window, only a few feet away. Then the promise flashed through her mind, the vow she had made the day her husband left for the war.

She stepped to the bureau, lifted the loaded pistol from the drawer, returned to the window and deliberately aimed it at Morgan's breast. When she was about to pull the trigger, a thought came to her that caused her to lower the weapon. She thought of the anguish that she would experience if some woman of the South would shoot her husband. She was troubled to think that Mrs. Morgan would grieve, and why should she be the cause of such suffering? She returned the pistol to the bureau drawer, just as the Confederate chief came to the door.

He politely inquired about the roads leading from Campbell's Station. After she had engaged in conversation with him for a few minutes, the milliner became composed and told him what she had intended to do. With bowed head, Morgan listened to her story in silence. With an expression on his face that indicated deep emotion, he looked at her steadily for a few minutes and then said, "Do you know why you did not shoot? At that very moment Mrs. Morgan, at our home in Tennessee, was down on her knees praying for my safety. I am sure that she was; several times in the past have I been near death as I was a few minutes ago, and on my return home afterwards I would learn that Mrs. Morgan was on her knees praying for me at the very moment."

With those words, he thanked the woman and bid her a courteous farewell. He mounted his horse and started for Campbell's Station.[13] They arrived there early Friday morning, where Harrison Secrest was released to walk back to his hotel in Point Pleasant.[14]

8:00am, Friday, July 24

Campbell's Station suffered more damage by the raiders than any other place in the county. The bridge over Leatherwood Creek was burned; the home of John Fordyce and his warehouse were burned, but not before the Confederates removed $4,000 cash from the Adams Express Company's safe, of which $2,000 belonged to Thomas Frame. Three freight cars loaded with tobacco that were standing on the railroad sidetrack were also torched.[15] Telegraph wires were cut to prevent information of Morgan's movements from reaching the outside world. The burning of Mr. Fordyce's home was an unusual target for destruction. The Confederates had usually limited their arson victims to commercial mills, transportation resources, bridges and structures that they considered as aiding in the enemy's war effort. The burning of Fordyce's residence, it is believed, was in revenge for a personal grudge against John Fordyce. His son, Lt. S.W. Fordyce had left Guernsey County two years earlier with Union cavalry. He had led a number of destructive raids in Kentucky and Tennessee. Some of Morgan's men had knowledge of the relationship and had been heard to remark, "We are only following Fordyce's plan."[16]

Thomas Regan, section foreman of the Central Ohio (Baltimore & Ohio) Railroad, dispatched his son through the woods to flag down a westbound passenger train that was carrying $50,000. The elder Regan ran the other direction along the railroad tracks until he found a handcar, which he used to reach Cambridge with the news of Morgan's approach.[17]

By now the sun had risen and in an hour Morgan's men were on the outskirts of Old Washington. Citizens of this town could see columns of smoke coming from Campbell's Station. They were sure Morgan would burn their town too.[18]

FIFTY-SIX

"The Most Exciting Day in the History of (Old) Washington"

<u>8:30am, Friday, July 24</u>

Entering Washington, Morgan's column of 670 passed the Colonial Inn.[1] Across the street, a family had hidden their one-year-old daughter, Catherine, in a barrel in the basement.[2] Morgan posted pickets on all roads into town, and permitted his men to rest while housewives prepared meals for them.

The U.S. mail coach had arrived a few minutes earlier and, the driver hearing Morgan's arrival, took off at full whip eastward in the hope he could escape. The raiders gave chase and, after an exciting race, captured the government outfit, ripped open the mail and scattered the contents in the street.

By eight-thirty in the morning,[3] many of the men were camped in the square, but the General and his staff entered the American House,[4] a two-story hotel at the southeast intersection of two roads (present-day Rt. 285/Old National Road and Morgan's Way). Of the proprietor, James Smith,[5] the General demanded dinner for his staff. The lower level of the hotel had a walkout to the back. The basement level was cooler on this hot July day. It was here that Morgan and his staff took their meal unaware that mailbags were hidden in an adjacent room.[6] After filling their bellies, they took over all the bedrooms in the establishment to get some much-needed rest.

Elizabeth McMullin was sixteen-years-old when Morgan came to town. In 1933, at the age of eighty-six, she gave an eyewitness account of what happened that day.[7]

> We lived at the west end of town. Father had gone to war, and mother, my brother, two sisters and I were left at home. On Thursday, July 23, we heard that Morgan might come our way. Captain John Laughlin, who lived south of town, was home on furlough. He was a telegraph operator and, in order to learn of Morgan's movements, he kept close to the instruments all day. The people were advised by him to get ready, as it was his opinion, from what he could gather from the wires, that the rebels would take the road running through our town.

All had confidence in Captain [James B.] Laughlin and they acted on his advice. Valuables were concealed and horses were hidden back in the woods far from roads. The Guernsey County Bank was in Washington then. Mr. Lawrence, Mr. McCurdy and some others took all the money out of the safe and carried it to Wheeling for safekeeping. It was a busy day for everybody and that night nobody slept, excepting the children.

The next morning we could see smoke in the south. It was reported that Campbell's Station had been set on fire. We expected Washington to be burned, too. Nearly all the men had gone to the war. Captain Laughlin changed his army uniform to citizens' clothes and with some boys armed with guns went south to investigate. They soon returned with the report that Morgan was coming. We were all frightened. Captain Laughlin advised us to keep cool and offer no resistance. Nearly all the town gathered at the corner where the Campbell's Station-Winchester road crossed the pike [at the Colonial Inn].

Riding two abreast the rebels came up the road. Rev. Ferguson, our Presbyterian minister, stepped out in front and waved a white handkerchief. The rebels did not pass through as hoped, but dismounted and gathered along the street. They entered homes and ordered dinners to be prepared for them immediately. Morgan and his staff of fourteen men went to the American Hotel kept by James Smith. Rebel guards were placed around the town, two miles on all sides. Anybody could come in, but nobody was permitted to go out.

Just before Morgan arrived Charlie Simms came into town with the mail which he was carrying from Cambridge to Wheeling. The sack was thrown out of the bus and hidden. Charlie drove on but was captured and his horses taken. Believing that the mail was concealed at the postoffice the Confederates went there, took the sacks that had been made up to be sent out and rifled them. They seemed to be looking for letters that might enlighten them as to the movements of the Union army, rather than for valuables.

Morgan and his staff ordered dinner at the hotel and [the] Smiths called in some of us older girls to help prepare it. I waited on the table. Morgan seemed very tired and worried and talked but little during the meal. After eating they all went upstairs and lay on the beds. In the meantime, his soldiers, having eaten their dinners and fed their horses, were lying along the street from one end of the town to the other. They were in Washington two to three hours.

Captain Laughlin kept in communication with General Shackelford who, with his cavalry, mounted infantry and Ohio militia, was following Morgan. Suddenly a gun was fired by one of the rebel guards as a signal that Shackelford was near. Morgan and his staff immediately rushed down the stairs and out into the street. The soldiers ran to their horses, mounted them and headed for the Winchester road. All was confusion.

Looking to the south we saw Shackelford's army gathering on Cemetery hill. We wondered what would happen and we soon learned. They began firing at the Confederates who, in turn, shot back. Women were screaming and children crying. The shooting increased. Above the noise of battle we could hear voices coming from the Federal lines, ordering women and children to run to cellars. I ran into the one that was nearest, where twenty or thirty women and other persons soon gathered.

The firing continued. They were shooting across the town. The Union men were firing from the south; the Confederates from the north. We could hear bullets whizzing over our heads and the crash of broken windows. It was terrible, as we did not know what would happen to us who were in the direct line of fire.

The shooting ceased and we ventured out. Morgan's men had gone towards Winchester and Shackelford's soldiers were sweeping across town. They seemed to be coming from every-where, which was a great relief to all of us. Two rebels lay dead in the street and others were so badly hurt they had to be killed.

Some of the Confederates were cut off from Morgan's main army and taken prisoners. They were placed in the old academy building and guarded until next morning, when they were marched to Cambridge and locked in the jail. They were after-wards taken to Columbus.

Some of us girls went into the room that had been occupied by Morgan at the hotel and on the bureau I found a picture of a young man. One of the Confederates who was among the pris-oners held at the academy said his name was William Cloud, Morgan's physician. I have the picture yet, a reminder of the most exciting day in the history of Washington.

Leading the Union advance was Captain Ward of the 3rd KY Cavalry and a detachment of the 1st KY under Adjutant Carpenter.[8] They drove in the Confederate pickets and as the raiders streamed out of the homes and hotel racing north out of the town, three Dixie cavalrymen lay in the street dead or dying.[9] Several were wounded and eight were captured.[10]

Today, the three men in gray lay buried in a cemetery overlooking Old Washington. The gravestone was erected by the citizens of Old Washington. The inscription says, "Here was laid to rest by the citizens of Washington under public authority, the bodies of three Confederate cavalrymen killed during the battle of Washington July 24, 1863, when a force in command of General John H. Morgan was overtaken and defeated by Federal cavalrymen in command of General James M. Shackelford." On Memorial Day, each year, the "Union" citizens of Washington decorate the granite monument with three gravesite Confederate flags.[11]

Morgan was not exactly "defeated." He hastened on to Winchester (Winterset) and Antrim pursued by General Shackelford's force of more than 1,000 men. While Morgan was resting in Washington, the people in Cambridge, to the west, feared Morgan would come their way.[12]

8:00am, Friday, July 24

A detachment of citizen volunteers moved eastward along the National Road toward Washington, and if Morgan, perchance, should turn to the west, they would drive him back and save Cambridge. The band of patriots was not a large one, but its members displayed considerable courage, boasted of their military prowess, and assured the people that they would protect Cambridge from the raiders.[13]

As the citizens marched toward Washington, they were joined by others living along the National Road. Nothing of importance happened until they reached the Oliver farm at the west foot of Hyde's Hill. Here they met two boys who confirmed that the raiders occupied Washington in force. The Cambridge defenders stopped and a consultation was held. Two mounted scouts were dispatched to advance cautiously toward the enemy's line, gather all information possible, and report to the main body. In the meantime, the volunteers stationed themselves along the road for a distance of a quarter of a mile.

While Morgan was in Old Washington, he placed pickets two and three miles out of the town, on all sides. Several were quartered at a brick house on the Hyde farm. Unaware of this, the two Cambridge scouts approached the top of the hill. Seeing the danger ahead, they quickly turned and, pursued by two of the raiders, rode at a terrific pace toward Cambridge. As they passed their comrades scattered along the road, they shouted that Morgan was coming and that the entire rebel force was in pursuit. At the same time, the two Confederates chasing them came into view.[14]

The terrified army of volunteers immediately dispersed. Wagons were turned around. The drivers did not wait for men to get in. Without their loads, they started toward Cambridge as fast as the horses would take them. Some threw away their guns and fled to the hills and woods. Others took refuge in a house that was near. When the two rebel pursuers reached the scene of demoralization, the volunteer army had disappeared. They entered the house, captured six of the men who had hidden there, and marched them back toward Morgan. As they approached Washington, heavy firing of guns could be heard. Realizing what the firing meant, the two raiders released their prisoners and sought safety for themselves. Thus ended the infamous "Battle of Hyde's Hill." When the members of the volunteer army returned to Cambridge, they were joked about for a good deal afterward. However, they accepted the jests graciously, maintaining that they had shown more patriotism than those who had not ventured out at all.[15]

10:30am, Friday, July 24

In Antrim, eight-year-old S.C. Knouff was living on a farm with his grandmother, mother, brothers and sisters. He heard the Madison College bell ringing fast and loud. At first he thought it might be a fire. But when he went to the top of the hill and looked down into the town, he could see men hurrying with horses in every direction. Just then, Jim Padgitt came to the top of the hill leading two dappled grays toward the hollow where he planned to hide them. Knouff wrote:

> When we reached town, we found everyone frightened. Rev. Knox, the Presbyterian preacher, rode up the street telling people to hide their horses. We stood on the street and in a short time, the Confederates began riding into town. There must have been about 600 of them. They seemed fatigued and did not pay much attention to us. Perhaps they were too anxious to get away from Shackelford who was coming close behind.
>
> Some of them stopped at Tom Gill's store and began looting it. Nobody resisted, of course, and they carried away many things. They took a fine pair of boots that my father had made and left at the store to be sold, before he entered the army. We never saw the boots again.

Morgan was not at the head of his army, but farther back towards the rear. The danger was behind, not in front, and he probably chose a position where he would be able to command in case of emergency. As we watched the Confederates go by, the word was passed along the street that Morgan himself was coming. In my eagerness to see him, I pushed out in front of the crowd. He was riding in a buggy with a darkey driver. When he came opposite me, Morgan asked the darkey to stop the horses. He called me to come to the buggy. "Son," he said, "get me a drink of water." I deemed it policy to obey. I quickly brought him a tin cupful from a well under the house. After he had drunk the water, he returned the cup to me, saying, "Son, I would give you a coin, but I have no money." I felt important, as I was the only person in Antrim whom Morgan seemed to notice.

The people felt relieved when the last of the raiders had passed through town. Presently Shackelford's men began to arrive. They didn't seem to be in much hurry, as they stopped for their suppers. The Antrim women were glad to feed them. It was a great evening, one I shall never forget. [16]

An observer described Morgan's men as they rode past their home. "The men were very tired and very dirty. The horses were mostly jaded Ohio farm horses that could hardly be persuaded to gallop at all. As to their uniforms, Southern soldiers were notoriously ill-clad at that stage of the war. Morgan's men had been riding for more than three weeks with no chance at all to procure clean clothes or even to wash what they had on. Were they all riding horses? No, not always. Some were riding buggies, spring wagons, carriages, a sulkey and a stage coach." [17]

Leaving Antrim, Morgan passed through Londonderry, exiting Guernsey County in a little more than twenty-four hours after entering it. He had traveled the county diagonally about a distance of thirty-five miles.

As Shackelford's men entered Antrim, the skies opened and a downpour drenched the dusty gray uniforms, revealing spots of Union blue. Several troopers were invited into Anna Moss' home, where they were fed. Mr. Moss noticed that some looked pale and exhausted. He went to his store and returned with several bottles of "Gueysott's Sarsaparilla" which he gave to them. [18]

Also in pursuit of Morgan was a detachment of troops led by Col. Cyrus Sarchet. Their night's ride from Winchester to Moorefield told upon pursued and pursuers. The men were drenched to the skin, saddles and blankets wet and heavy, road muddy and slippery, horses jaded and hungry. Many mounts fell by the wayside and their riders were forced to plod along on foot, carrying their saddle and bridle until another horse could be captured. Sarchet's group moved slowly through Antrim and Londonderry, where they came to a halt. The colonel was suffering severe pain in his stomach and bowels. He roused an old friend, Dr. John McCall, living in Londonderry. The physician prepared a medicine to relieve his pain and sent him on his way, rejoicing. Before they reached Stillwater Creek, they could see flashes of light that told him Morgan had burned the bridge after crossing it. Part of Sarchet's command with a battery of two guns made a detour up the creek to another bridge where they crossed.[19]

Those Blue Jackets who forded the river, at the point where the bridge had been burned, crossed by twos, struggling in the mud and water up to the saddle skirts. Once they reached the other side, they turned to those following and yelled "Over!" Then it was up the steep and slippery bank where they reached the road. Those who had successfully forded the river stopped to wait for the detachment that had crossed over the bridge farther up the creek. Once the command was reunited, they laid down to rest on the roadside. Here they camped and took their first sleep since leaving Cambridge. In the morning, the sky was clear and the chase was resumed.[20]

HARRISON COUNTY, OH

FIFTY-SEVEN

Lincoln's Concern About Morgan

On Thursday, July 23, little Ida Hamilton recorded in her diary the excitement that happened that day in Cadiz. "Father and I were out in the country this morning. As we came home, we heard them ringing the bell in town and beating the drum. We thought they surely had good news, but on coming in we heard that General Morgan was only fifty miles from here, and coming in this direction. They were ringing the bell to bring people together to form themselves into companies to protect our homes."[1]

The bell Ida heard was in the tower of the courthouse, and it was in the courtroom of that little brick building that the townsmen met to decide what should be done to defend the county seat. It was determined to establish a military committee for the defense of the county, to telegraph Governor Tod for arms and ammunition, and to send out scouts to locate Morgan and discover his course. The plea for 500 rifles and forty rounds of ammunition for each was dispatched at once to the governor, and the scouts were outfitted and sent into the night in the direction of Cambridge and Morristown. As the meeting adjourned, Cadiz took on an unaccustomed nighttime glow. Every house was lighted because only the children would sleep that night, and the streets were lit by big, flaring torches that were kept on hand for election-night celebrations.[2]

In the Cadiz telegraph office, the sounder began to clatter. It was a telegram from Governor Tod informing the county's military committee that the requested arms and ammunition would be forwarded that day. But would they come in time?

Urgently, the call went out to the distant townships for more men and arms. If Morgan could not be repelled with the lightweight squirrel guns, perhaps they could be overwhelmed by sheer numbers, or so reasoned the military committee. But where was Morgan? The scouts sent out the previous night were not back. Cadiz was not only ill-prepared to meet the raiders, it was also uninformed as to Morgan's whereabouts.[3]

291

Cadiz wasn't the only one in the dark. President Lincoln in Washington sent the following[4]:

(Telegram)   Washington, D.C., *July 24, 1863.*
    Major-General Burnside, *Cincinnati, Ohio*
    What, if anything, further do you hear from John Morgan?
                                                            A. LINCOLN

The next day, Burnside responded.[5]

(Telegram)   Cincinnati, Ohio, *July 25, 1863 – 8:00am.*
    His Excellency, Abraham Lincoln, *President of the United States:*
    Morgan was 4 miles from Cadiz at 6 o'clock, moving toward the river, with our people pursuing him closely and skirmishing with him. This information is from General [W.T.H.] Brooks, who is at Steubenville. I requested him to use the two bodies of cavalry which I sent from here, by railroad, to Bellaire and Cadiz Junction, and I hope he will capture him. They have both been ordered to close in on Morgan by rail.
                                        A.E. BURNSIDE, *Major-General.*

July 24 was not going to be a day that Burnside would remember with particular relish. His first indication of this was a request from General Rosecrans asking when he could expect to get his cavalry back to help him scout General Bragg's maneuvering.[6]

"Your dispatch received," answered Old Mutton Chops. "I am sorry to say we have not yet got hold of John Morgan. He is still out with some 500 of his men, but our cavalry are after him in hot chase. I am confidently expecting to hear of his capture; the whole force is broken up and annihilated. The prisoners are now coming in, both men and officers."

Barely had this excuse been sent when another, more insistent, query came from General Halleck in Washington.[7]

(Telegram)   WAR DEPARTMENT
    Washington, July 24, 1863 – Noon
    Major-General Burnside, *Cincinnati, Ohio:*
    You have not yet replied to my dispatch in regard to your movements toward East Tennessee. You will immediately report the position and numbers of your troops organized for that object. There must be no further delay in this movement. It must be pushed forward immediately.
                                        H.W. HALLECK,
                                        General-in-Chief.[8]

Burnside thought Halleck was crowding him a bit too hard.[9] After all, couldn't he understand that Morgan was still on the loose in Ohio, destroying property, threatening its citizens who were turning to Burnside for help and protection? Burnside must have felt that he could not begin another major endeavor, an attack on Maj. Gen. Simon B. Buckner in eastern Tennessee, until the "Morgan problem" was resolved. To deflect any criticism, he shot back a reply.

(Telegram)   Cincinnati, Ohio, *July* 24, 1863 – 3 p.m.
Major General H.W. Halleck,
General-in-Chief:
Your dispatch received. All of my available cavalry have been after Morgan. There are six thousand troops ready to start...but a large number of mounted troops are necessary to guard our trains and keep communications open when we get to East Tennessee. A very great impediment to this movement has been the removal and destruction of Morgan's forces. I hope to finish him up to-day or to-morrow. Where is the Ninth Corps? Grant promised it to me after Vicksburg.

A.E. BURNSIDE.
Major-General.[10]

Halleck had not won his nickname of "Old Brains" without a reason. Instead of answering Burnside's petulant question about the Ninth Corps, he showed the telegram to Lincoln. The President wrote out a reply in his own handwriting—a reply that seemed tactful and understanding, but in which Burnside could not help reading a hidden reprimand:

"Let me explain. In General Grant's first dispatch after the fall of Vicksburg he said, among other things, he would send the Ninth Corps to you. Thinking it would be pleasant to you, I asked the Secretary of War to telegraph you the news. For some reason never mentioned to us by General Grant, they have not been sent, though we have seen outside intimations that they took part in an expedition against Jackson. General Grant is a very copious worker and fighter, but a very meager writer or telegrapher. No doubt he changed his purpose in regard to the Ninth Corps for some sufficient reason, but has forgotten to notify us of it."[11]

Days before Halleck pressured Burnside to forget Morgan and go after General Buckner commanding the Confederate forces in East Tennessee, Buckner was trying to make a belated effort to help his friend, John Morgan. He ordered Colonel John S. Scott to push from East Tennessee into Kentucky to see if he could draw off any units pursuing Morgan in Ohio. Scott's brigade was composed of the 1st LA, 2nd TN, 5th TN and 10th Confederate

Cavalry regiments; the 5th NC Battalion of mounted infantry, the Brown Horse Artillery with four guns and Robinson's Louisiana Artillery.[12]

It was a last-ditch move, and what good it might have done was nullified by a slow start. Finally, Scott led his force through Big Creek Gap, driving a detachment of the 44th OH Mounted Infantry before it toward Loudon. There was a brisk fight there, and at Mount Vernon and Big Hill. This took many days, and by the time Scott defeated the Northern troops at Richmond, it was too late to help Morgan. He was too far away, and Burnside had no intention of diverting any of his forces to meet a new threat deep in Kentucky. Scott finally retreated under mounting pressure from local troops, and Morgan was abandoned to his fate.[13]

Noon, Friday, July 24

At the same time Halleck sent his telegram to Burnside to start his attack on Buckner, the Confederates' advance guard entered Harrison County, riding through Smyrna.[14] They stopped briefly to raid several stores and appropriate five fresh horses. Merchandise taken from David B. Armstrong's dry goods store totaled $302. The raiders also took twenty-two bridles, five girths, six halters, saddler's hardware and $45 from the cash register of Bartlett Davidson's harness shop.[15] Passing quickly through the town, they descended to the valley of the Big Stillwater at Collinsport (Piedmont). In order to delay their pursuers, they burned the covered bridge over the Stillwater west of town and another over Bogg's Fork east of the village.[16] Harrison County was later reimbursed $600 for the loss of these bridges.[17]

Morgan's men followed the old Cambridge road and advanced upon Moorefield. Dr. S.B. McGavran, of Cadiz, noted the events just prior to Morgan's arrival in the village. "The air was full of rumors of the great destruction of property along the line of march, and the alarm for the safety of family and property became intense. The feeling of insecurity increased when M.J. Brown and John Robinson, of Cadiz, driving a spirited team rushed through the town, furiously driving Jehu-like, announcing that the rebels were coming this way, and would be with us in a short time."[18]

Dr. McGavran noted, "We discovered that the rebels were burning the bridge over Big Stillwater and a few minutes later another smoke looming up about one-half mile east, indicated that the other bridge over Little Stillwater [Boggs Fork] was also being consumed."[19]

2:35pm, Friday, July 24

The Confederates rode into Moorefield and sought food and a catnap. They also did some "shopping" at George L. Wharton's store, carrying off $330 in merchandise.[20] Despite prior warning, the Confederates confiscated twelve fresh horses in Moorefield.[21] Morgan entered the parlor room on the first floor of the Mills Hotel. While the General slept, his body guard, with their revolvers lying upon the chairs at their sides, or on the bed where Morgan was sleeping, occupied the time reading the news, with which they seemed to be well provided.[22] His men filled the yards and sought rest wherever it was available. They did not disturb nor forcibly enter any house where the family had stayed home. They were hungry and freely solicited every house for provisions.[23] At the home of Thomas S. McGee, meals were served to forty raiders.[24] A like number sat down to eat at Samuel West's home.[25] One resident commented, "They exhibited abnormal appetites for pound cake and preserves."[26] One of the homes that was entered belonged to the Rev. Thomas R. Crawford.

When the raiders entered the town, the Reverend had looked out his window and saw that some of the village men were being captured and placed in front of their ranks to act as guides. He described his reaction:

> As having no desire to be conscripted on so short a notice and so unceremoniously, without even an opportunity to hire a substitute, I concluded the best policy would be to desert my house and home for the time being. I greatly regretted leaving my manuscripts and library to the care and disposal of such a motley crowd of roughs.
>
> An aged man, my next door neighbor, whom they did not harm, informed me on my return home that the raiders occupied all my premises, threw open all the doors of our dwelling, and certain of them found one of my last manuscript sermons. He called to his associates, with an oath attached, "A preacher lives here, for I have found one of his sermons upstairs in his study and I am going to preach it." At the same time cautioning his hearers to keep good order. Then at the top of his voice he read a short time, until his rather restless auditory began to stamp with their feet, clap their hands, and many of them shouted, "Amen! Amen!" which ended their mock worship.[27]

The Reverend had joked about not having time "to hire a substitute." During the Civil War, civilian men could pay another man to take their place when they were drafted into the army. This led to some men demanding large sums to act as a substitute. To stop the price from going beyond what most men could afford, the Secretary of War fixed the range of what a substitute could be paid. In the July 25, 1863 issue of the *Steubenville Daily Herald*, an article reported, "The Secretary has fixed the sum from one dollar to three hundred dollars to check speculation and keep down the price of substitutes."

After a three-hour rest, General Morgan rose from his bed and walked to the front door of the hotel. Stepping out upon the pavement, he cast his eye down the street, then turned and walked leisurely up the street unattended.[28] Soon, a shot fired by a picket, warned Morgan of Shackelford's advancing troops who had been delayed by the destruction of the bridges. Four hours had elapsed since entering the village. He gave the order to mount, and the march eastward continued, exiting Moorefield as quickly as they had arrived.[29] *There is a historic monument of Morgan's Raid along Rt. 22 at Moorefield.*

3:00pm, Friday, July 24

When it became apparent that Morgan might head toward Steubenville (Jefferson County), the old courthouse bell brought the citizens together. A militia company was formed with Capt. Frank Prentiss, Walden, Burgess and Boals in charge. That evening, Major-General W.T.H. Brooks arrived with three regiments including the 44th PA militia and established his headquarters in the old C&P passenger station at the foot of South Street with Joseph C. Doyle as temporary train dispatcher.[30]

General Shackelford had been delayed by the burned-out bridges and his full force did not arrive in Moorefield until after dark. Like the Confederates who had preceded them, the Union soldiers needed to be fed, and the local women continued cooking and serving food up to midnight. Most of the Federal force pushed on, but a portion of the men remained overnight.[31]

The raiders took Julius Schreiber from his Moorefield home and used him as a guide as far as the Rankin church. There, Joseph Kirkpatrick was taken and kept prisoner until they were beyond Stumptown. Two miles east, they aroused Joseph Dickerson from his bed and made him guide them to Georgetown.[32] At the intersection of today's S.R. 22 and 519, they turned southeast, taking the road to New Athens. The Confederates, on reaching Stumptown, turned left toward Cadiz, on the Flushing Ridge Road, bypassing New Athens. Then taking a trail through the woods, they came out on present Route 9 (New Athens-Cadiz Road). At the foot of the hill, they took the valley road toward Georgetown. About a mile farther down the road, they stopped for the night in the Tom Worley sugar grove and on W.W. Dickerson's farm.[33]

Shackelford gave up the direct pursuit at Stumptown, where Morgan had turned northward. The Union general chose, instead, to lead his men into New Athens, where he found the village in turmoil.[34] The night on their first day in Harrison County ended with Morgan's men sleeping about two miles north of Shackelford's force of 1,200 in New Athens. Farther to the north, in Cadiz, the county militia prepared to meet the raiders at dawn. The rifles and ammunition promised by Governor Tod arrived about six o'clock Friday evening. Cadiz's military committee had asked each township to send fifty men under their own appointed captain. By eight o'clock, between 700 and 800 armed and equipped citizen soldiers had reported for duty. By ten o'clock, the number had grown to 1,000. They were bivouacked at the Cadiz Fairgrounds.[35] Under the command of Judge S.W. Bostwick, they departed from Cadiz at two o'clock in the morning and marched south toward Georgetown. He positioned his little army southwest of Georgetown and placed it in battle array at the crest of a hill overlooking the valley road.[36]

After several hours of rest, Morgan's men rose at three o'clock and continued on the valley road to Georgetown, turning right before entering the town and going up the hill. The Confederate general sent scouts forward. After riding a short distance northeast, the scouts were astounded to discover the Harrison County militia drawn up in battle lines before them. They hurriedly wheeled and raced back to report the situation to Morgan.[37]

Meanwhile, General (Judge) Bostwick had sent a scout to find General Shackelford's column thought to be in New Athens. The scout reported, "I skedaddled for New Athens. I went into town and it was full of soldiers, and the girls were handing them out pie, bread and butter. I rode up and the girls handed me some pie. I got acquainted with those girls afterwards. I took two or three pieces of pie, then I asked an officer where General Shackelford was. He said he had gone on ahead towards Harrisville."[38]

Not since the bloody skirmish at Old Washington on July 23 was Morgan so threatened. He had two choices: fight or flight. He preferred not to do battle, knowing that Shackelford's more capable forces were near. He could not chance being delayed, but flight would be successful only if he moved fast enough to get in front of Shackelford on the ridge road to Harrisville. Quickly, but in good order, Morgan turned south onto a road that led to the crest of the Harrisville ridge.[39]

The militiamen, three-quarters of a mile away, could see the Confederate movement. They were impatient to fire, despite the long range, but General Bostwick was not. He hadn't marched these inexperienced young men all the way from Cadiz to get them shot up by a hard-bitten troop of professional soldiers. Although the militia held its fire, Shackelford did not.

From his position at Hammond's Cross Roads overlooking Short Creek, the Union general could see Morgan hurrying his men up the road to the Harrisville ridge. Knowing that he could not move fast enough to intercept the raiders, Shackelford ordered his artillery to open fire. The hills of southeastern Harrison County echoed for the first and only time to the thunder of Civil War gunfire. The shelling resulted in the wounding of two Confederates and the shattering of a number of trees along Morgan's route. Despite the shelling, Morgan escaped. His band reached the crest of the ridge ahead of Shackelford and swung left in the direction of Harrisville.

They followed the New Athens-Harrisville Road returning to today's S.R. 519. As Shackelford watched his Confederate quarry disappear behind the ridge, he lamented, "My men are just played out—men and horses both. Morgan's in front of us and gets all the good horses, and we have to take the leavings. We have to rest." They took a two-hour respite.

The Harrison County militia was well fed and rested, but they were without horses. General Bostwick regrouped his men and sent them on a quick march toward Harrisville along present U.S. Rt. 250.[40]

(Telegram)   Newark, *July 24, 1863*

Gov. Tod: The troops under the command of Maj. Way, are just leaving the depot, on the Steubenville road, with orders from me to push on lively to the line of Harrison county, and then proceed cautiously and with great vigilance to Cadiz Junction, and there await instructions from Gen. Burnside. Shall I remain at the telegraph office to-night?

GEO. B. WRIGHT, *Q.M.G. Ohio*[41]

4:00am, Saturday, July 25

Morgan's men entered Harrisville, rounding up nine horses including one from Dr. John Morgan and also took the physician's hat.[42] They helped themselves to food that had been prepared for the pursuing Union soldiers and said "good-bye" to Harrison County.[43] *There is a Morgan's Raid historical monument at Route 250 and Dillonvale Road.*

(Telegram)   Major-General Brooks: Wheeling, *July 25, 1863.*

Morgan is reported to have passed Harrisville about 4 o'clock this morning. It is said he captured some 10 of Sharley's scouts. He will try crossing between here and Steubenville.

W. C. THORPE, *Captain Thirteenth U.S. Infantry, Commanding.*[44]

FIFTY-EIGHT

"I'll Be Damned if I Will Ever Surrender to a Farmer!"

Waiting for Morgan in Steubenville was Col. George W. McCook, chairman of the Jefferson County Military Committee. Just the day before, he had learned that his uncle, Major Daniel McCook, had been killed by Morgan's men at Buffington Island. McCook had a score to settle with Morgan.[1]

7:00am, Saturday, July 25

Entering the county opposite the cemetery gates at the eastern edge of Harrisville, Morgan's force of 600 men followed a rough-hewn road down Long Run through the hamlet of Ramsey. They followed it to Long Run Station of the W.L.& E.R.R. Morgan followed the meanderings of Short Creek. At White Bridge, he forded the creek and headed for Dillonvale.[2] *There is a Morgan's Raid historical monument on Rt. 150 in front of a Presbyterian church in Dillonvale.* Now they were just six miles from the Ohio River at Warrenton ford. But they learned that there was a trainload of Union troops at Portland (Rayland), which was less than a mile west of Warrenton and eighteen miles south of Steubenville. They turned northward up Dry Fork Road just west of Bradley and came toward Smithfield.[3] *There is another historical monument where County Highway 8 intersects with Rt. 150.*

9:00am, July 25

The Smithfield home guard, having heard that Morgan might be coming their way, armed themselves, got on their farmhorses and marched south, led by Captain William Collins who had boasted of his military skill and bravery.[4] These dozen volunteers trotted briskly down Main Street and out of the village. They took the road to toward Mt. Pleasant, where rumors had it, the notorious General John Hunt Morgan and some 480 of his men, were raiding. These brave horsemen had ridden but a mile along the winding road when, suddenly, around a turn, they came face-to-face with the head of a long column of Confederate raiders.[5]

The encounter was abrupt and disastrous. Before they could turn and flee, the Smithfield men were engulfed. Their arms were wrenched from them and thrown into a field.[6] Most of the fifteen horses taken in Smithfield were yielded by its "Home Guard."[7] *There is a Morgan's Raid historical monument on Rt. 151 to the right of the Jefferson County fairgrounds, north of the town.*

Captain Collins was forced to ride a mule at the head of the column. He was told that when Morgan's men entered Smithfield, he should falsely announce that "These are Hobson's men, loyal Union soldiers."[8] On the way, the raiders encountered George D. Cook and William Cope. Once Cook and Cope were among Morgan's column, they were told to get off their horses. Cook did, but Cope refused. The "Union" soldiers drew guns and ordered him to dismount, which he did in a hurry. One of Morgan's staff officers asked Cook who he thought they were. George Cook replied, "I think it's General Morgan and his forces." The Confederate officers dropped behind Cook and said, "That young man knows too much. I think we will take him with us."[9]

The column came to a halt as they entered the main street of Smithfield. Collins called out, "These are Hobson's men. Give them plenty to eat, they need it, and treat them well." With that, the citizens brought out everything they had and laid it before the hungry, half-starved raiders. In the commotion, the people did not discover the mistake until it was too late to hold back their bounty.[10] As the Confederates ate their fill, some of the captured Smithfield Home Guard members slipped away from their captors who were too busy eating and looking for fresh horses. The raiders may have taken their eyes off their captive "pilots" but they did notice a four-horse-drawn stage coach in town. On closer examination, they found it filled with passengers ready to head up the road to New Alexandria. The driver attempted to pull away and escape the Confederates swarming into town. Raiders blocked all avenues of escape. As the driver and passengers looked on, the Confederates unhitched the team, threw the harness to the ground, mounted the horses and rode away.[11]

In the afternoon, Shackelford's men really did appear, tired and hungry. They found little left to eat in Smithfield, but they gathered what horses they could find that had been overlooked by Morgan and pressed on in pursuit.[12]

When Morgan resumed his march beyond Smithfield along Rt. 151, he retained some of the captives, including George Cook, and headed for New Alexandria, which was just three miles from the Ohio River. Before reaching that town, they halted, and the prisoners were ordered to go forward to be paroled. George Cook raised his hand to be sworn when an orderly rode up and ordered him back into Morgan's ranks, saying that General Morgan had so instructed him.[13]

When the line began to move forward again, Cook discovered that he was one of only two prisoners in the column. The other was a Doctor Finley. General Morgan joined the prisoners and said to Cook, "That's a fine mare you are riding." Cook replied, "She ought to be, as she is Morgan stock." The General also commented to his prisoners, "I am surprised at the great number of men here in the North that are not in the Army. Almost everyone down South, that's old enough, is in the Southern Army." Years later, George Cook would comment, "While I was badly frightened when first taken prisoner, I very soon overcame that. This was largely due to General Morgan riding and talking to me so much of the time. I never met a more affable man, and although he showed he was extremely worried, he did not cease for a moment to be the gentleman that he was."

Dr. Finley asked Morgan if he had any idea of getting away. The General replied, "No. I intend to surrender at the first opportunity. It seems like every fence corner turns into a man, and I don't have much hope of ever escaping." The doctor then proposed, "Well, General, you had better surrender to me." General Morgan gave a disdainful look at the doctor and said, "Well, I may surrender to a soldier, but I will be damned if I will ever surrender to a farmer!"[14]

Crossing McIntyre Creek, they destroyed the PC&StL Railroad bridge by fire, entered New Alexandria and began to plunder James Graham's store of boots, shoes, clothing, dry goods, notions and groceries. When General Morgan was apprised of the fact, he ordered his men to desist from further plunder and requested that Mr. Graham lock up his store to prevent any more losses.[15] Graham placed a claim after the raid of $524.75. The state reimbursed him $287.00[16] (wholesale). C.A. Wallace, a merchant in the same town, was more fortunate. When his store was plundered, he made a claim of $418.96. The state paid him $418.00.[17]

(Telegram)   Major Way, *Mingo:*   Steubenville, *July* 25, 1863.

Send up as much cavalry as you can to Alexandria Station, up the Cross Creek Valley. Morgan is thought to be approaching that point.

            W.T.H. BROOKS, *Major-General.*[18]

At the Panhandle Railroad station below Alexandria, they burned the depot and the "Howe" truss railroad bridge. The Steubenville and Indiana Railroad Company received a $3,000 claim paid by the state.[19] The other bridge burned by the raiders was the covered bridge over Yellow Creek, for which the county received a compensation of $2,000.[20] Robert McIntire of New Alexandria received no compensation for the eight-seven gallons of whiskey the raiders took.[21] Young George Cook, an unwilling witness to the raiders' actions, pleaded with the General, "If you don't let me go home soon, I will not be in time to go to Sunday School." Morgan replied, "If you get to Sunday School in two weeks from now, you will be most fortunate." Shortly after that exchange, the General returned and said, "We will take a halt in a short time. You then can return home."[22] *There is a Morgan's Raid historical monument on Rt. 151 at New Alexandria.*

(Telegram)   General Shackelford: Steubenville, *July* 25, 1863.
You can assume command of the forces under Major Way [9th MI Cav.] and Major Rue [9th KY Cav.], and obey any orders given by General Brooks. Don't give up the chase, but push Morgan to the lakes, if necessary. Way is following him, and Rue has gone up the railroad to cut him off from the river.
                              A.E. BURNSIDE, *Major-General.*[23]

As they turned up the road leading to Steubenville, a short distance below Wintersville, the Confederate column stopped at the farmhouse of John Hannah. The General and some of his men entered it to find it empty. Mrs. Hannah and her daughter had fled into the fields to hide. As George Cook approached the house, he saw some raiders leading Mrs. Hannah and her daughter out of the field. When they were brought in, General Morgan assured them that they would come to no harm. He asked Mrs. Hannah to fix him a meal. He then retired to the bedroom for a short nap while the meal was prepared. Mrs. Hannah showed Morgan's servants where to find milk, butter, meats and other eatables, with which they prepared dinner for Morgan and his staff. When it was ready, he was awakened to partake of the meal, which he ate heartily.[24]

When he finished eating, he thanked Mrs. Hannah and offered to pay for the meal. She thanked him and asked that he not take any of her clothes. The General replied in a most courteous manner, "Madam, I have no use for the clothes." As Morgan left the house, he saw George Cook sitting on the high porch steps. Cook asked if he could leave the column and return home. Morgan asked if he had been paroled. "No," George replied.[25]

"Well then raise your hand and swear that you will not reveal what direction we are going or the number of men in my troop…" Morgan began, but he was interrupted as one of his scouts came up and said that Shackelford's men were within a short distance. The General decided that a prompt departure was more important than concluding the parole. George, Mrs. Hannah and daughter sat on the top porch step and watched the company riding away in the direction of Wintersville.[26]

George Cook began walking back toward Smithfield when he saw an abandoned horse in a field eating wheat. Since everyone seemed to be stealing horses that day, he commandeered the horse for himself. After riding a mile or two, he stopped to take an inventory. Tied to the saddle was a bolt of calico, a man's shawl, a woman's shawl and a pair of fine French calf boots. He surmised that it had belonged to one of Morgan's men who had probably fallen asleep and the horse had wandered away. As he was riding, he saw men coming down the hill. His first thought was that they were more of Morgan's men, but soon an officer overtook him and said they were Shackelford's men. He rode with the Union soldier to where Shackelford was and told of his encounter with Morgan. He believed Morgan would go west from Wintersville toward Richmond.

Leaving the Union pursuers behind, he continued his ride back to Smithfield. At the top of a hill, he met a young soldier boy who did not seem to be more than sixteen-years-old. He was riding a broken-down horse and he was crying. He said he was with the 14th IL Cav. and owing to his horse's poor condition he could not catch up to his regiment. George offered to switch horses, retaining the saddle, bridle and other things he had found tied to it.[27]

(Telegram)   Governor [A.L.] Boreman, *Wheeling, W.Va.:*
            Steubenville, *July* 25, 1863.
I shall remain here for the present. Parts of three regiments are on their way from Pittsburgh. They will be stopped between here and Wheeling, until something is known.
                                        W.T.H. BROOKS, *Major-General.*[28]

Of the 2,000 troops coming from Pennsylvania, Colonel James R. Porter's regiment was the first to arrive and was moved to Warrenton, fourteen miles below Steubenville. His presence there may have caused Morgan to turn north at Short Creek to Smithfield. Colonel Bemis' regiment came next and was stationed at LaGrange (now Brilliant). Colonel Gallagher's regiment was first posted at Mingo and then at Rush Run, midway between Warrenton and Brilliant. He had 800 infantry, 350 cavalry and a battery. Thus the fords were guarded and a train, with a full head of steam, stood ready to move the forces from one point to another as needed.[29]

2:00pm, Saturday, July 25

Colonel James Collier was placed in command of the Steubenville militia, 500 strong, by General Brooks and started their march out the old plank road in the direction of Wintersville. The force would have been larger had there been more weapons available. They did take a six-pounder cannon as their one piece of artillery.[30]

4:00pm, July 25

Militia scouts returned to headquarters in Steubenville to report that Morgan's men had moved across Thomas Maxwell's farm at the crossroads just west of Wintersville. They were seen on the Richmond road. A detachment of 100 Confederates left the main body and diverged toward Wintersville.[31] In the Wintersville area, Morgan's men would steal half a dozen horses.[32] *A Morgan's Raid historical monument is at Fernwood Road and Main Street (Rt. 22).*

5:00pm, July 25

About a mile south of the village, Morgan's men encountered scouts of the Steubenville militia led by Captain Prentiss. His company had reached the Dry Fork Road with Morgan's force just ahead of them. The Confederates' rear guard had been deployed in the adjoining field, and as the militia advanced, it fired a volley. One bullet struck one of the Steubenville militiamen, sixteen-year-old Henry L. Parks, in the abdomen. Two days later, he died of his wound.[33] During the subsequent firing, Miss Margaret Dougherty (also identified as Lizzie Duvall) was accidentally wounded by a stray bullet. It passed through her lung while she stood in the window of Thomas Maxwell's house (also identified as the Maxwell Hotel & Tavern) at the fork in the road. Fortunately for the young lady, whatever her name, it was not a fatal wound, as she healed and recovered.[34] After the brief exchange of gunfire, the militia scouts retreated to rejoin their main force on the road to Richmond. Not far behind them were 400 men of the 9th MI Cavalry under Major Way. These men of Shackelford's force overtook the Confederates at Two Ridges Presbyterian Church, eight miles west of Steubenville.[35] *A Morgan's Raid historical monument is on the west side of Rt. 43 near the Two Ridges church parsonage.*

Thirteen-year-old Ross Coe was standing on the porch of his green frame home across the street from the church. Ross, with his mother, Mrs. Benjamin Coe, his aunt, six sisters and brothers, were watching about fifty Confederates come into their yard and surround the house and barn. One of the raiders politely asked Mrs. Coe for water and something to eat. She gave them all the bread and butter she had in the house. Then they warned the women to either get into the house and shut the door, or go over the hill and into the woods because "there's going to be some shooting."[36]

Mrs. Coe and her children decided to seek refuge in the woods at an entrance to a coal bank. From that vantage point, young Ross could see the 9th MI Cavalry and the Steubenville militia advancing up the hill toward the farmhouse. When the militiamen were within 100 yards of the barn, they fired their cannon loaded with scrap iron. In the skirmish that followed, two of Major Way's men were wounded. One died, Martin Kane (also identified as Kean, Keene and Keane), and is buried at the "Two Ridges" church. The other Michigan trooper was wounded in the thigh. He was Pvt. James Nelson Carney. The Confederate, also wounded, was W.G. Page.[37] The two wounded were carried to the Coe house, where they were attended by Dr. Markle. They stayed under Mrs. Coe's care until they both recovered from their wounds.[38]

Young Coe described Morgan's men: "They were dressed on all manner of style, dress coats and ragged pants, stove pipe hats and no shoes, others had good citizens suits. They had all kinds of horses and saddles with riding fat farm horses which looked like they were not far from home. One of the rebs rode a horse and carriage with silver fittings. Another rode one of my father's horses."[39]

The raiders had barely left town before Colonel Collier's main body of Steubenville militia moved in from the east, formed a line on a hill dominating the town and wheeled into place an old six-pounder, loaded with scrap iron. At this critical moment, the van of Frank Wolford's cavalry trotted in from the southwest. The dust raised by Morgan's horses hung over the village. Collier mistook the Union troops for Southerners. His gunner opened fire and assorted bits of hardware smacked against buildings in the center of town. One large piece of iron entered the taproom of Maxwell's Tavern, which only a few minutes earlier had been filled with women and children. Wolford's cavalry dismounted, pulled their carbines from gunboots and prepared to fight for their lives. General Shackelford rode up to take command and at once saw that his men were exchanging fire with Ohio militia. He sent a courier forward under a white flag to Colonel Collier who was standing beside the cannon.[40]

"What are you fools shooting at?" asked the regular officer. Abashed, Collier explained he thought he was engaging the enemy. His scouts then reported that Morgan's force was several miles away, making good their escape on the Richmond road.[41]

(Telegram)   Governor Boreman, *Wheeling, W.Va.:*
               Steubenville, *July 25*, 1863.

**Morgan appears to be going north. His advance at Wintersville, 4
miles west. Major Way is close after him with his cavalry. His
artillery is just discharging from cars. If troops can be sent from
Cleveland to Alliance, they might be useful. All my troops are moving up the river.**

                                        W.T.H. BROOKS, *Major-General.*[42]

On the morning of July 25, the two regiments, one led by Major Way,
the other by Major Rue, arrived by train in the Steubenville area. The men
and horses were fresh from having crossed Ohio by train. Way led the 9th MI
Cavalry following Morgan to Richmond.[43]

Between Steubenville and Richmond was Benjamin Shelley's farm.
The farmer and his wife had been warned that Morgan was headed their
way. Shelley hid his good horses in the woods. As a ruse, he made no
attempt to hide a team of old horses that he kept in the barn. While they
waited, Mrs. Shelley continued to bake bread on her outdoor oven. Shortly,
Morgan's men made their appearance. When asked where his horses were,
Shelley pointed to the barn. A trooper entered and a moment later stormed
out saying, "You're a damn liar. You can't work a farm with those kind of
horses." For solace, the Confederates walked over to the oven and extracted
all the bread leaving with hot loaves in their hands.[44]

(Telegram)   General Brooks: Bellaire, *July 25*, 1863.

**What of Morgan? Can I be of service? I have been following the
Central Ohio Railroad since 7 this morning, ready to head off Morgan. Have 400 of the Eighty-sixth Ohio Volunteers and 600 militia.**

                                        R.W. McFARLAND, *Colonel Eighty-sixth Ohio.*[45]

<u>6:00pm, Saturday, July 25</u>

Morgan passed through Richmond taking another half dozen horses.
Some of his men stopped at a home where the woman of the house
upbraided them for stealing horses and other property. "Madam," they
replied, "we have burned better towns than this. Now, just bring on the
chicken."[46] *There is a Morgan's Raid historical monument at the intersection
of Rts. 43 and 152 in Richmond.*

They continued west for four miles to East Springfield where they
"traded" for nine more mounts. In this town, they raided Dr. Thomas R.
Simpson's home where clothing, three watches, $31 cash and the doctor's
surgical instruments "disappeared" along with his horse.[47] When General

Morgan started to take two horses from "Bill" Huskroff, the East Springfield farmer said, "I would rather give you $360 than lose those horses."

"All right," said Morgan, "show us your money." Huskroff produced the cash.

"The money and the horses both look good to me," said Morgan, as he pocketed the cash and took the horses. Huskroff was "stung."[48]

In the village square, the Confederates cut down a "liberty pole" and handed the colors to a disconsolate young woman who had been protesting their actions.[49] One of the town's practical jokers, John K. Miller (also identified as Mills), thought he would have a little fun at Morgan's expense. He asked to see General Morgan and upon their meeting, he assured him of his sympathy for the South. Then he began to volunteer all kinds of information, which he thought would confuse and mislead the Confederate leader. The General listened quietly and then inquired, "Are you acquainted with this country?" The loquacious Mr. Miller replied, "Yes sir, I know every foot of it." "Then mount that horse. You are just the man I want," came the General's firm command. That was a turn of events that Mr. Miller did not expect. But a glance at the rebel chief's stern face convinced him Morgan wasn't about to listen to any excuses. So Miller adopted a cheerful demeanor, mounted the steed, and took his place in line.[50] *There is a Morgan's Raid historical monument at East Springfield at the intersection of Rt. 43 and C.R. 60 (Circle Green Road).*

FIFTY-NINE

Escape or Capture Tomorrow

R. Mitchell Crabs was a member of Co. K, 2nd OVI home on a furlough. He was visiting with two young ladies, Maggie and Jennie McCullough. He had accompanied them to an afternoon singing rehearsal, which was in progress at the Methodist Church in East Springfield. John Kerr was conducting the group. Outside, the members' horses were tied to the hitching rail. Charles B. O'Connell (also identified as C.E. O'Donnell) opened the front door and loudly announced, "Morgan is coming up the Steubenville road and will be here in about half-an-hour." Immediately the audience dispersed to find and hide their horses.[1] Maggie McCullough ran from the church to her father's general store, where she removed a pocketbook of money from the safe. She started northward from the town where she secreted it among the leaves along a fence. Her sister, Jennie, was safely escorted to her home by Mitchell Crabs. He noted, "By this time, the village was full of 'patriots to the Southern Confederacy' and the citizens were full of fear and confusion. Men and women were alike paralyzed with fear that the village would be burned, and all the horrors of war fully realized."[2] Despite this warning, Morgan's men spied nine horses at the rail which they "acquired." One protested. Miss Celia Davidson, a maiden lady of uncertain years, resisted and prevented the raiders from taking her horse. They had unhitched the horse from her buggy and were trying to take the harness off, when she took hold of the bridle and pleaded so hard that they wilted and left her with her horse.[3]

Minutes before the raiders entered the village, Edgar Graham came riding down the street and said, "The latest word was that Morgan's men were at Wintersville and coming this way." Stewart (also identified as Stuart) McClave, a resident of Nebo, and his companions, William Seaton and John Myers, all laughed at Graham. Their laughter turned to confusion when they saw fifteen men riding down the street. The intruders yelled to them to halt, which they did. Among the Confederate group, they recognized John K. Miller, a resident of East Springfield, talking to the "Rebs" and wondering why he seemed to be familiar to them. Not until later did they find out he was a prisoner and was not able to come and stand with the crowd on the sidewalk.[4]

Then, Capt. Ralph Sheldon, Co. C, 2nd KY, called McClave to step forward, "The second man...step out!" He asked what they wanted of him and the answer was that he would be a guide for the next twenty miles. He was ordered to get on his horse and join their group. "There's no use talking. There's a horse. Get on it and come with me," were the orders, and he obeyed.[5]

Veering north and west, Morgan's men rode through Amsterdam and Circle Green. Four miles farther, they approached just west of Nebo (now Bergholz).[6] *There is a Morgan's Raid historical monument at Bergholz where Rt. 164 spans the creek.*

Captain Sheldon and a Texas Ranger flanked McClave as they rode. Soon they came in sight of the McClave farm. Captain Sheldon asked, "Is this were you live?" Stewart answered, "Yes." Spotting women standing in front of the house, Sheldon said, "Do these women belong to you?" Again McClave answered him that they did. Sheldon told him to ride ahead and tell his family to go back in the house and he would see that they were not harmed. Then quite a number of raiders entered the house and soon ate all the bread and butter they could find.[7]

McClave asked his cousin to bring him a heavier coat than the one he had on. His mother turned to Stewart and asked, "Where are you going?" He responded that he had to accompany these men as a guide. His mother began to cry and plead with Captain Sheldon. "I'll never see my son again!" she wailed. Several of Morgan's men gathered around her and tried to comfort her and told her not to worry. "We'll send him back tomorrow safe and sound, and we'll give him a horse to ride back," they reassured her.[8]

Major George Rue with his trainloads of fresh men and horses were ordered by Major General Brooks to move from Bellaire to Steubenville. Once there, he learned that Morgan had avoided Steubenville and was going northwest heading toward Salineville.[9]

7:00pm, Saturday, July 25

Rue continued as far as Shanghai station (now Empire), where he waited to see if Morgan was going to cross at Shanghai. Once he was convinced that the Confederates were heading north, he ordered his men to mount up and he followed the public road (today's Rt. 213), reaching Knoxville at midnight. There he encamped seven miles north of Wintersville.[10] By following a parallel road east of the one Morgan was taking, Rue was trying to keep his troops between Morgan and the Ohio River should the Confederate general attempt a dash for the river.

On the Elkhorn branch of Yellow Creek, the Confederates camped for the night on Herdman Taylor's farm. Here, Morgan made his usual "arrangements" to dine and sleep for a few hours in Herdman's home.[11] The Steubenville militia marched up to a hilltop and camped within sight of Morgan's pickets.

Mrs. Sara Allen was about to retire for the night when someone knocked at the door. When she opened it, two men said they were "hunting Morgan's raid." They asked for something to eat. Thinking they were Union men, she started to grant their request. On her way to the springhouse, she was told to "halt." Looking around, she discovered the yard was filled with horses and men. When she explained that she was going to the springhouse to bring food for the men, she was allowed to proceed. Mrs. Allen had baked and churned that day, and her loaves of bread and butter must have been very satisfying to the hungry men. Observing that she kept bees, they asked for honey. She brought out a four-gallon crock. The men ate half, taking care not to waste what was left. In all, they consumed fourteen loaves of bread, two pounds of butter and drank ten gallons of milk.[12]

While Mrs. Allen was dispensing hospitality, she must have trembled, because one of them asked, "Are you afraid?"

"Yes, I won't deny it. I am afraid," she answered.

"Well, you need not be," he answered, "we never harm anyone who treats us as you have. When anyone gets contrary, we do sometimes do things we ought not, but we won't molest anyone who treats us right. Besides," he added, "this is nothing to what we have to submit to in the South. Your northern soldiers not only rob us, but they burn our houses and turn our wives and children out, homeless."[13]

Morgan's advance guard, with Stewart McClave as one of their prisoners, stayed the night at the D.G. Allen home while his rear guard stayed at the farm of Thomas McConaughey.[14] This would be Morgan's last night camp.

McClave, John K. Miller, Mr. McIntosh and Mr. Shepherd were placed in a log cabin on the Allen property. Around the cabin, ten Confederates placed themselves as guards. Shepherd waited until all the raiders were fast asleep, and then he turned to McClave and asked, "What are you going to do? Skip out or stay with them?" Stewart quietly replied, "I'll stay until they discharge me." Shepherd said that he had a notion to slip away and break for home, but he finally gave up on that idea.[15]

12:00am, Sunday, July 26

General Shackelford came into Major Rue's camp, north of Wintersville on Resinger Hill near a small mining settlement known as Eastern.[16] Rue was camping two miles away. The General's scouts had alerted him of

Rue's presence. Shackelford wanted to know what kind of force Rue had. The Major told him that he was acting under the orders of General Burnside. Shackelford invited him to join him in the chase the next day. Rue consented on the condition that he be allowed to ride in front and head Morgan off, while Major Way, with the 9th MI Cavalry would attack from the rear. At first Shackelford was reluctant, but he finally consented.[17] Like Rue's fresh men and horses, Major Way's regiment had arrived by rail at Bellaire[18] and then advanced to Mingo Station south of Steubenville.[19]

3:00am, Sunday, July 26

At the Taylor, Allen and McConaughey farms, the signal was given to awake. The Confederates rapped on the fences and doors giving the division's recognition signal, "Lady Washington, Lady Washington." One of Morgan's men had fallen asleep in Allen's sheep stable. He had been overlooked and continued his uninterrupted portrayal of Rip Van Winkle. Long after the sun had risen, he was found.[20]

The General arose and asked Mr. Taylor's sister, Maria, to make chicken for his breakfast. She hastened to prepare the General's meal. But before the chicken could be cooked, Morgan was told that the Union cavalry was closing in. Instead, he took a quick cup of coffee and said to Maria, "We have never been run so hard before."[21] Morgan quickly exited the home taking Taylor, shoeless and hatless, with him for two miles before releasing him. As the men from Dixie passed over the Yellow Creek Bridge near Taylor's property, it is said that a farmer demanded $5 for the passage over his bridge.[22] It is doubtful that raiders "paid" any attention to his request, but the Confederates' rear guard burned the wooden covered bridge to delay Major Way's men and the militia who were thirty minutes to an hour behind them.

When the Union cavalry approached the burned bridge, they found the creek was low. So without any delay, they rode around the smoking timbers and exposed stone abutments, continuing their pursuit. The new bridge, which replaced the old span, was dubbed "Morgan Burnt Bridge."[23]

As some of Morgan's men passed Ed Crister, the miller, living in an old log house, they stopped to feed their horses on the grain by the mill. Seeing Crister, they offered him a drink. Thinking that the whiskey might contain poison, he said, "No, thank you. I'm a temperance man." His neighbors, later commented, "Ed Crister would have gone ten miles for a drink of good whiskey."[24]

About one mile south of present S.R. 39, near Monroeville, David White's family was especially anxious about Morgan's advance. Mr. White had been part of the Underground Railroad network to help slaves escape to

Canada. They took their horses and precious belongings and hid in a ravine north of the house. After Morgan passed, they returned home to find that one of the young Confederate soldiers had been buried on their property. Years later, the boy's father came looking for his son's burial place, removed the body and took it home.[25]

On the border between Jefferson County and Columbiana County, the raiders approached Monroeville, two miles southwest of Salineville. Ezekel and Mary Maple lived on a farm near Monroeville. Ezekel was away when Mary was informed that Morgan was headed that way. She took what little money they had and ran into the field to hide it. Shortly, the Confederates arrived and asked Mary to cook for them. The men said they meant no harm to her or her children. When they departed, they took all the remaining food they could find and took away the livestock. On Ezekel's return, Mary told him the raiders took everything. Together, they went into the field to retrieve the money, but it could not be found.[26]

Monroeville consisted of Pat Kerr's blacksmith shop, Bob Potts' store and about a dozen houses. A sharp slap with a Confederate saber convinced Pat Kerr he should kindle his forge and replace some horseshoes. Bob Potts obligingly opened his store, and the raiders carried out nearly everything of value. Every home was converted into an emergency restaurant to feed the hungry Confederates. They took Jimmy Twiss along to guide them over the back roads.[27]

At the first opportune time, Mitchell Crabs stealthily walked out of East Springfield to the place where he had hidden his horse, "Frank." Escaping north to Salineville, he arrived about ten o'clock at night.[28] He informed the residents of Morgan's coming. Here's how Crabs tells it:

> The men organized a force at once and elected me captain, colonel or general. I do not know which but I have the brevet ever since, and were going to capture Morgan right there, "Be jabbers" Salineville is a mining town. I received the brevet with much satisfaction, of course, but advised that unless I could succeed in obtaining armed forces from General Brooks, their attempts would prove futile, and might result in loss of life and homes, and it would be better to let them pass through quietly.
>
> Arriving at the telegraph office at the railroad station, Frank Rogers, the agent, informed me that he would have to get the privilege to use the wires from the general superintendent to call General Brooks [fifteen miles away in Wellsville]. This obtained, my first dispatch read: "I have just arrived from East Springfield,

Jefferson County, Ohio. Saw Morgan's men, about 600. Send troops to Salineville at once."

I received an answer as follows: "Who vouches for this statement? I have news that they are at Knoxville, Ohio." On receiving this, Mr. Rogers and H.C. Robbins, mayor, promptly telegraphed, vouching for the truth of the statement. In a short time, I received a telegram as follows: "I have sent you 700 infantry under command of Colonel Gallagher."[29]

(Telegram)   Major-General Brooks: Salineville, *July* 25, 1863.

My regiment arrived here at 6 o'clock this morning, and the rebels are outside of the town about 2 miles, on the Monroeville road. I have the regiment placed to receive them when they arrive; have mounted scouts to follow if they should retreat, so I can inform you.

THOMAS F. GALLAGHER,
Colonel, Fifty-fourth Pennsylvania Infantry.[30]

Just west and south of Monroeville (formerly Croxton), Elizabeth McIntosh, from her second-floor bedroom window, decided to count the Confederates riding by including those who came to her farmhouse. When she finished, she had counted 475.[31]

She later described the incident.

They were the dirtiest lot of fellows I ever looked at. If their clothes had ever been gray uniforms, one would never have suspected it. Nearly all wore slouch hats. The ones that came down to the home acted very gentlemanly. They said they were hungry. They demanded bread, cold meats, pies, butter, pickles, jams and spreads of any kind. They went to the springhouse and took all the milk. Some of the rebels with their hands full of things to eat went out to the barn to search for horses. There were none there. They chased the family driving mare all over the big field in front of the barn, but could not catch her. The alarm was given, that the "Yanks" were coming, the rebels ran out the gate, and rode away towards Monroeville. Morgan rode by our place in a carriage drawn by two white horses. He stopped at the gate just long enough to allow some of his men to hand him some of the things to eat, which they had taken from our house.

Shackelford's troops arrived at our house thirty minutes later. It was hard to tell Shackelford's men from Morgan's. The uniforms looked as though they might have once been blue. When the Union soldiers arrived, we hunted up the griddles and commenced to bake pancakes. I baked pancakes all day, and was so busy, I did not get out into the fields as others did to see what was going on. Our home was turned into a hospital that forenoon. Wounded rebels and wounded Union soldiers were brought and laid on our front and back porches. All they seemed to care for was sleep. We treated them all alike.

The rebels behaved better than some of the Union troops, especially those who came around a few days after the surrender gathering up plunder. In some instances, these Union troops made old men take the oath of allegiance and frightened them into paying tribute, after accusing them of giving comfort and aid to the enemy. It was later learned that some of these fellows were only Union soldiers home on furlough, and took this means of punishing so-called "Copper-heads."[32]

8:00am, Sunday, July 26

Sixteen-year-old James Cooper Boice had just been discharged from Co. I, 98th OVI. He had enlisted at fifteen, but because of a medical disability, he was once again a civilian.[33] His older brother, William Allison Boice, was a first sergeant in the same unit and would be killed at Bentonville, North Carolina two years later. James had been helping Robert McMillen carry the mail from Steubenville to New Lisbon via Monroeville while his health was improving. Suddenly, Confederates poured into the small town from the east. Several residents ran for the woods. In a short time, the Confederates were knocking on the doors of every home. Those that had been abandoned, they entered looking for food and other valuables.

Young Boice watched the action from McMillen's doorstep. Several of Morgan's men rode up and asked for something to eat. One soldier requested one thing, another asked for something else. Boice called out the requests to Mrs. McMillen. If she had it, she would say so and brought it to young James, who gave it to the soldier. This kept up until Mrs. McMillen's supply of food was exhausted.

One of the Confederate officers approached Boice and asked if he had heard from Hammondsville (just three miles from the Ohio River) that morning. "Yes sir," he answered, "A man had rode up from there and had gone back a short time ago."

The raider asked, "Are there any soldiers there?"

Boice replied, "Yes sir. About six thousand."

The Morgan officer then asked if he had heard anything from Salineville that morning. "Yes sir. A man [Robert McMillen also identified as Miller][34] was just there and gone back."

"Were there any soldiers in Salineville?"

Boice responded, "No, as they expect Morgan to go by Hammondsville."

Morgan's officer shouted the news and the Confederate column started for Salineville, two miles to the north. Boice waited until the raiders rear guard was a quarter mile away, and then he began to follow them. James Boice wanted to see what kind of reception the "Johnnies" would get. He knew that there was a large contingent of Union soldiers in Salineville (Col. Gallagher's regiment, soon to be joined by Rue's 9th KY), but he had no idea if there were any in Hammondsville. In Boice's own words, "I was afraid there might not be enough at Hammondsville to give them a decent reception. I was thoughtful for their welfare."[35]

Boice was joined by Samuel Twiss, and soon others joined the line following Morgan's trail. About a half mile north of Monroeville, Boice saw Union cavalry, under the command of Major Way, coming through Monroeville. He and the others waited for the soldiers to catch up and then they ran alongside the blue-coated column. By now, Morgan's advance scouts had gotten close enough to Salineville to realize that there was a significant Union force in front of them. They turned and headed back toward Hammondsville, a town to the southeast, but after a quarter of a mile, Way's men who had been chasing them from Monroeville opened fire.

9:00am, Sunday, July 26

In the exchange of gunfire, one of the Union soldiers was wounded. Boice now describes what happened:

> The Johnies ran west across the fields, and our men ran after them. I stayed with the wounded and got some help. Carried the injured soldier to Mr. James Criss' house, which was only a short distance.
>
> Then I started through the corn field as fast as I could to find if any more had been wounded or killed. I soon found a wounded Johnie. I spoke to him and told him I would soon be back with help to care for him. I met Mr. McClelland and told him where the Johnie was. He went there and remained until I got others to help. When I returned, a little Bugler of our Army took me for a Johnie and pulled his gun on me. He could hardly be convinced that I was not a Rebel. Mr. McClelland told him who

I was. We carried the wounded Johnie to the Burson home. We looked around but could not find any others who were wounded. By then the soldiers had got so far away that I did not follow them any farther.[36] *There is a Morgan's Raid historical monument in Monroeville at the intersection of Rts. 55 and 164.*

Major Rue with his fresh horses and men rode out of camp at the break of day and headed for Hammondsville trying to get ahead of Morgan. Gen. Shackelford and Maj. Way continued on the road to Salineville.[37] Shackelford's forces were composed of the 2nd E. TN Mounted Infantry, the 1st KY Cavalry, the 86th OH Mounted Infantry, the 9th MI Cav. and the 14th IL Cav.[38] Accompanying them were the Steubenville militia. Rue reached the edge of Salineville shortly after nine that morning and just missed the skirmish with Morgan.

While Rue was in Salineville, forty Confederate prisoners were brought into town. This group of Morgan's men had been acting as his rear guard and had sacrificed themselves to allow Morgan to escape west toward Mechanicstown. Major Rue, a native of the Bluegrass State, recognized a number of them personally. "They were rebels from my home county in Kentucky. Some I had known from boyhood," he commented.[39]

SIXTY

Last Shots Fired in Anger

<u>Saturday, July 25</u>

The alarm bell rang in the Carrollton Town Hall. A crowd gathered in the hall to learn what was happening and report for whatever duty awaited them. A meeting was called to order by appointing Judge Ambler as chairman. Captain Coppock was appointed chief of command and he set about to organize a militia force with arms and ammunition. Scouts were sent out every road and ordered to report back every two hours to J. Twing Brooks.[1]

<u>7:30am, Sunday, July 26</u>

Morgan's men continued north toward Salineville. Morgan's right was being flanked by Shackelford's force and the Steubenville militia led by Col. Collier.[2] Morgan's scouts, who had been sent ahead to reconnoiter, had gone to the top of the Salineville hill. One or two of the scouts had gotten as far as the "old mill" where the road turns up the hill from Main Street toward Monroeville.[3] They returned and reported that Salineville was full of Union infantry and that a detachment of Federal cavalry was approaching from Hammondsville. Sensing that he was cut off both in front and rear, Morgan instructed his rear guard, mostly the remnants of Cluke's command, to turn and hold the enemy in check while he turned west.[4]

Leading the first charge at Monroeville was Capt. H.M. Rice, Co. H, 9th MI[5] under the command of Major Way. Union troops commenced firing their carbines at the fleeing Confederates. As these weapons would kill at a quarter mile, quite a number were wounded between Monroeville in Jefferson County and the Burson farm in Carroll County.[6] In this rout, it was reported that eight men were killed.[7] In the confusion of battle, Jimmy Twiss escaped unseen by his captors and returned to his home in Monroeville.[8]

317

(Telegram)   Major-General Brooks: Salineville, *July* 26, 1863.
Morgan's forces have divided and taken different roads. Captain [H.M.] Rice, of my command, has just come in with 55 more prisoners. I want some of the captured horses for my command.
                                                                    W.B. WAY.[9]

To outrun Shackelford's cavalry, General Morgan abandoned his carriage drawn by two white horses, and mounted his thoroughbred sorrel, "Glencoe."[10] When his "empty" carriage was searched later by Union troops, they found the General's rations, which consisted of a loaf of bread, two hard-boiled eggs, and a bottle of whiskey. With Lt. Col. George Washington Owen (10th KY), Morgan led his men to Cyrus Moore's farm and the West Grove Cemetery. To avoid being struck by shells being fired by a Union battery, he led his men down a steep ravine. Shackelford's forces declined to follow this rocky, treacherous path.[11]

<u>7:45am, Sunday, July 26</u>
Watching this action from a nearby hill was fifteen-year-old Amos Moore. Standing at the fence at a point that overlooks the Monroeville Cemetery, Amos tells what he saw.

To the right, you can see the Monroeville cemetery and behind that the town. Winding along the ridge a mile away is the Salineville road. I leaned on the fence and looked in amazement at what was happening on the road. Guns were firing rapidly, not in volleys, but continuously at close intervals. I could see two bodies of moving men, one on the Burson farm, and one moving out of Monroeville. I could see the smoke and hear the shots. I could tell from the action of the smoke that the two lines were firing at each other. The line [Cluke's command] on the Burson's hill was not moving while the men who were shooting from the troops coming out of Monroeville were rapidly advancing. Soon I saw men tearing down the fence over on the Burson farm.
Next I saw a man on a sorrel horse [Morgan], followed by several hundred more ride down the steep hill. Some of the horses stumbled and fell, but not many. They came across the valley and were headed right for the spot where I was standing. Just then I noticed what looked like a cannon being brought into the Monroeville Cemetery, and soon a number of shots were fired from Cemetery Hill. The guns could not be depressed enough

and the shots went high over the heads of Morgan's men, who in the meantime had ridden lower down under the hill, out of reach of the battery. Presently I saw them coming up the road through the ravine which led up to the fence where I was standing. I started back for the house, but went in through the orchard just above the barn. Morgan's men overtook me and they were scattered all through the orchard but the main body followed the road down by the barn and the house. They told me I had better run out of the orchard, and into the house, or I would be killed. I did not realize the danger I was in, but soon I heard bullets whistle through the air, coming towards McIntosh's hill, this side of the cemetery.

Morgan's men were in a great hurry; none of them stopped at the barn or house to molest anything but went hurriedly down our lane. They reached the Mechanicstown road and were almost to the West Grove Cemetery, before the Union troops came in sight, along the road leading from Monroeville, and connecting with the Bergholz road near the McIntosh residence. The Union troops rode rapidly down the hill toward the [West Grove] cemetery and opened fire on the fleeing Confederates passing the cemetery. I watched the running fight until Morgan's men all disappeared. I supposed this all occurred within a half an hour. Thirty minutes later, I heard distant firing towards the Boring and Sharp farms.[12]

Here, three of Morgan's men were wounded, two of them mortally. In addition to those killed, there were some wounded and many taken prisoner. Three of wounded Confederates were picked up by Union soldiers and taken to the porch of John Moore. They were given all the attention possible, with frequent drinks of water to quench their thirst and moisten their parched lips, by members of the Moore household. Two of them died where they lay on the porch before the sun went down. The third wounded raider was Frank Bixby who was paroled and rested at the Moore's for six weeks before leaving. The two dead Confederates are buried in the West Grove Cemetery. One is identified as John Miller. The other is identified only as "Unknown, A Mere Boy."[13] The cemetery is tucked in the corner of Brush Creek Township in Jefferson County. But if you take a few steps to the west from the cemetery, you are in Carroll County. A few steps north puts you in Columbiana County. *There is a Morgan's Raid historical monument three miles south of Salineville on Rt. 39.*

It is believed that the two marked graves are not the only burial sites in the area. Two others are thought to be buried together on the Sharp farm. It has also been reported that one Michigan cavalryman died when his horse reared after tangling with a pig. He was pitched and thrown against a fence post.[14]

10:00am, Sunday, July 26

The first batch of Confederate prisoners was brought into Salineville. They had been captured in and around Monroeville. Nine or ten were wounded in the group. They were taken into the warehouse of Pumphry and Irwin, which had been turned into a temporary hospital and made as comfortable as possible. They were given medical attention and provided with food. The other prisoners camped behind the store. One of the raiders was so badly hurt, he was taken to the hotel across the street, kept by the Widow Farmer. Rebecca Irwin's mother, Margaret Coburn, also assisted in taking care of the wounded raider. She took him dainties she had prepared because she felt "It was her duty as a Christian to be kind to the wounded." She said, "He was a nice man and a gentleman."[15]

The final shots of this 1,000 mile raid were fired on the Sharp's farm in Carroll County. Miss Sara A. Sharp was standing outside her home when six of Morgan's men drew up in front of her gate. One said, "You had better go into the house Miss, it's dangerous to be out to-day." Their faces were cut and bleeding and they looked as though they had been riding hard. Sara didn't recognize who they were nor was she frightened. She asked them how they had gotten hurt. They answered that they had been cut by the brush coming through the woods. After they rode away, she ran down the road to her brother-in-law's home to see if he had seen the soldiers. Coming back, she heard shooting farther up the road and soon six riderless horses came galloping down the hill. What she heard was Co. C, 2nd KY under Capt. Ralph Sheldon fighting the final skirmish. In this deadly burst of gunfire, Lieutenant Fiske of the 7th MI Cavalry was severely wounded. He was brought to Ethelbert Sharp's farmhome and placed on the porch, were the bullet was removed. The lieutenant's wife, living in Coldwater, Michigan, was notified and she came to the Sharp farm where she helped to nurse her husband back to health.[16]

(Telegram)   Adjutant-General, *Washington, D.C.:*
Wellsville, Ohio, *July* 26, 1863.
Major Way, Ninth Michigan, reports from Salineville:
I engaged Morgan about 8 o'clock this morning, about 1¹/₂ miles from this town, and, after a severe fight, routed them, killing 20 or 30, wounding about 50, taking 200 prisoners, 150 horses, and 150 stands of small-arms. Have delivered the prisoners and horses to Colonel Gallagher, Fifty-fourth Pennsylvania Infantry.
W.T.H. BROOKS, *Major-General.*[17]

It was here, where Jefferson, Columbiana and Carroll counties meet, that Morgan's forces were split. It was not of his choice, but because of Shackelford's close pursuit, the Confederates were obliged to split into two groups in their haste to get away. Morgan's men had crossed into Fox Township of Carroll County. Cluke's Second Brigade bypassed Union troops by going north on Nickel Road and skirting Riley's Church. They followed Riley Run Creek and picked up Apollo Road to Aurora Road where they paused. Morgan, with the First Brigade, took Ocean Road and turned left at Salineville Road (now S.R. 39). His intuitiveness divined that the other body of his command would travel west from Riley's Church. He reasoned that by taking the first crossroad to the right, Oasis, he would reunite his forces, which is what happened when he entered Apollo.[18]

Once more, Morgan had escaped with several hundred men. The chase continued. The pursuit was getting hotter and the temperature was ninety-five degrees in the shade.[19] Before leaving Fox Township, Morgan stopped at the farm of Mrs. Keziah Morgan Allison. During their conversation, she said she thought she was his cousin. Her sister was Jane Morgan, both being cousins to John. She was not friendly toward the Southern cause, because the son of her sister, Jane, was William Campbell of Salineville, who was with James P. Andrews on the famous raid in Georgia in which the locomotive, "The General," was stolen. Campbell had been condemned to hanging with Andrews when captured by the Confederates. When William Campbell, a large man, was hung, the rope broke and he fell to the ground. When he regained his senses, they compelled him to mount the gallows again and with a stronger rope, the sentence was carried out. Despite this sad episode, Mrs. Allison liked John Morgan as a person. She gave him a badly needed clean shirt and allowed his seriously wounded men to stay at her house while he and the others rode away. The wounded raiders were taken into custody a few hours later by Federal soldiers.[20]

As Morgan left the Allison farm, he moved north toward Riley's Church. There he was met by a Union force and forced to retreat back down

Avon Road. He turned right onto Ocean Road, left onto Salineville and then past the Burson, Boring and Sharp farms. There Capt. Sheldon fought a rear guard action, the last skirmish of the raid. Turning right on Oasis, they came to Apollo Road, which they followed north to Norristown. Left behind was a black horse handler who had been serving the Confederates throughout the raid. His name was Sam and he was about sixteen-years-old. After the skirmish, the Marshall brothers, who lived in the area, went to the spring and found Sam with several horses. The black youth lived with the Marshall family for two years before moving to Detroit.[21]

The Confederates had passed only three miles from Carrollton, where recently deceased Major Daniel McCook had built a home where his four youngest sons were born. One week earlier, he had been mortally wounded at Buffington Island.[22]

Cluke's brigade was the first to arrive on the road overlooking Norristown. There was no sight of Morgan and the First Brigade. There were no Union pursuers. No pressure. They stopped to rest and decide what to do. Should they surrender to the first Union force to confront them? Where was Morgan? Should they go it alone and head east for the river? Where were they? They waited for a sign. While they waited, they looked for fresh horses and something to eat. Time passed and soon Morgan came over the hill and joined them. They would go on, wherever the General led them. Before they could continue, they needed a guide.[23]

<u>10:30am, Sunday, July 26</u>

John H. Carey, of Norristown, who was seventeen-years-old at the time, was walking to the Catholic church with his two sisters. Unaware that Morgan's men were in the vicinity, young Carey was surprised when the Confederates rode up and pressed him into service as a "guide." His two sisters, Elizabeth and Maria, began to cry, expecting never to see him again. Carey took them over the Hanoverton road where they soon overtook Captain William Swaney who also was on his way to church. Swaney was "recruited" as a second guide. As they went past farms, they took fresh horses to stay ahead of Major Way's MI cavalry. Then just west of Millport, they turned east along Merlin Road and entered Columbiana County just above Fink Road.[24]

SIXTY-ONE

"Who the Hell is Captain Burbick?"

Morgan followed Merlin Road out of Carroll County[1] along the "Great road from New Lisbon to Carrollton,"[2] which ran between the Campbell and Mathews farms. The Carrollton road ran through Phillip Haessly's farm[3] as he entered Franklin Township in Columbiana County.

<u>11:00am, Sunday, July 26</u>

The raiders left the road to the right and cut through the fields through Ellie Orr's farm.[4] Morgan's scouts spotted the crowd assembled at the Bethesda Church and mistook the people for Shackelford's troops. For safety, Morgan kept a wooded hill between his troops and the church-going crowd. The Confederates crossed the Cleveland & Pittsburgh Railroad tracks after they passed south of the Bethesda Presbyterian Church. There, they released Carey to return to his sisters because they could see that Capt. Swaney was more familiar with the roads in that area. Alarmed by the report of troops ahead, Morgan caused his column to swing right to the John Cooney farm, and came out on the road leading from Millport to the Bethesda Church. At the church, no one had the slightest idea that Morgan was coming their way, because there was no telegraph office in the area.[5] But once the hundreds of citizens saw the large group of horsemen, they recognized the Confederate peril in the distance and sought to get away. One tried to ride away with the hitching post, forgetting in his haste to untie his horse. The minister's brief sermon was, "Flee from the wrath to come. Go! And wait not on the order of your going."[6]

At this point, Morgan was confronted by a natural barrier. It was a mill-race that was too deep to cross. He threatened to shoot his guides unless they quickly found a way to cross the stream. He was suspicious of being led into a trap and warned his "pilots" with stories that he had shot and killed many guides since he entered Ohio. They followed the railroad tracks down

323

an embankment to a little wooden bridge, which they used to get across the water hurdle.[7] They crossed Elias Willard and John Willard's adjoining farms and continued up the road to Daniel S. McAllister's farm,[8] where they pressed McAllister into service as a guide after taking his horse. Mrs. Cecilia McAllister, when she heard Morgan was coming, declared that she would "broomstick the dirty devil." But when they did show up, she was so frightened, she leaned against the wall and gasped out, "Help yourself."[9] The McAllister farm is where Morgan's 350-400 men had reached the northernmost point of any Confederate force—excepting the St. Alban's raiders—during the war.[10]

At the hill overlooking Dungannon, they saw the Catholic church on the highest point of the little village. Someone had evidently given an alarm, because people could be seen pouring out of windows and doors, tumbling over one another, priest and sermon swallowed up in the quest of self-preservation.[11]

(Telegram)   Captain Oliver, *Alliance:*   Wellsville, Ohio, *July 26, 1863.*
Send word to New Lisbon, as soon as possible, for every man to turn out to meet Morgan's forces coming in from Salineville and Steubenville roads.
W.T.H. BROOKS, *Major-General.*[12]

In New Lisbon, the county seat, the covered bridge at the west end of town had been mined and was ready to be blown up at a moment's notice should the Confederates approach the town.[13] There, three companies of home guard[14] had been hastily formed by men from Center and Madison Townships. Two companies of mounted militia were led by Captain William Hostetter and Captain James Burbick. The infantry company and its vintage artillery was led by Captain James M. Curry, a probate judge. They were not long in waiting to hear news of Morgan's presence. The Sabbath morning quiet had been broken by sounds of cannon roar in the distance coming from Salineville in the south and points west. The militia left New Lisbon and went south on today's S.R. 164 to the Hanover and West Point roads, to intercept and stop Morgan's advance. The infantry under Curry was posted on a hill of Nancy Morgan's farm to the north of the road (present S.R. 518) with the old brass cannon loaded to the muzzle with pieces of nail rod. With their colors flying in the wind, they were ready to mow down Morgan and his men on sight. Impatient for Morgan to come to him, Captain Wm. Hostetter, Jr. advanced his company down S.R. 164 toward Salineville and missed Morgan altogether.[15]

The citizens of Columbiana County knew Morgan was headed their way, but they weren't sure which roads he would take. Eight miles northeast of New Lisbon lived John and Mary Hisey on a 160-acre farm near New Waterford. They were bound and determined that Morgan's men would not get their hands on their life savings. The Hiseys placed their $500 cash hoard into a small, black, steel box and buried it in the pigpen. John smoothed over the freshly dug earth and vowed, "Not going to let that rebel steal all our money!"[16]

Men in Morgan's front ranks stopped at farmhouses and exchanged their jaded horses for fresh ones found in barns or pasture fields. Then, they would drop back into line at the rear. Leaving Franklin Township, they entered Wayne Township. Passing down a ravine that led southeast to Jackson school house, they entered the broad, beautiful valley of the West Fork of Little Beaver Creek, they were going directly east on S.R. 518. On a map, the route looks like a straight line. But, in reality, it is a curving road that winds to the left and then twists to the right, up short hills, and down the other side. It parallels the meandering Beaver Creek, which can be seen, at certain points, flowing on the south side of the road.[17]

The Confederate column rode past the West Beaver Church and James Donaldson's farm. "Captain" Donaldson was away, but they found and led away one horse that he had forgotten to hide. The captain had been busy organizing the Wayne Township Home Guard at the recruiting center and drill grounds at Gavers, just four farms away. But before Morgan's men reached Gavers, Captain Donaldson's home guard had trooped off to Walnut Ridge on the old Salineville-Lisbon Road to await Morgan's approach which they thought would come by way of Salineville from the south. In the Donaldson contingent was Samuel Ewing, treasurer of Wayne Township.[18]

Earlier that morning, Samuel and his eldest son, Frank, had hidden their horses. Sam had also buried a bag of gold belonging to the township. He had dug a hole in the earthen floor of his basement. Watching him was his five-year-old son, Johnny. After he had tamped down and leveled the floor, he turned to his child and said, "Johnny, you must not tell the soldiers about the gold." And as an incentive to obey, Sam ask his wife, Elizabeth, to dress Johnny in his birthday present, a brand-new children's soldiers suit. It was a solid suit of Union blue, brass buttons, cap and all. Johnny grinned and said, "I won't tell."

Just before entering Gavers, the raiders passed the New Lebanon United Presbyterian Church and John Fleming's farm. Unbeknownst to the Confederates, Fleming's was an Underground Railroad station. During daylight hours, runaway slaves were hidden in the root cellar of the barn. When night came, they would be conveyed to the next hideout until they reached Canada and freedom. Had Morgan known what the barn represented, it might have been burned.[19]

Waiting for Morgan's forces at Gavers, Burbick's and Curry's companies had felled several trees across Rt. 518 to block the Confederates' path.[20] Two main roads intersect at Gavers. Rt. 518 runs east and west, while Rt. 164 entered Rt. 518 at the east end of Gavers. From here it took a short jog west paralleling Rt. 518, passing through Gavers before it once again turned south.[21]

Across the road from the home guards' position was the McDonald farm. As the farm was at the intersection of Rts. 518 and 164, the locals referred to it as "McDonald's corner." Next door was Samuel Ewing's place.[22]

Learning that Morgan was in their immediate vicinity, two scouts, Sterling and Cullers, were sent to ascertain his whereabouts. They soon returned and reported the enemy was crossing the north fork of Little Beaver Creek, about a mile back. The militiamen became excited.[23]

Three scouts volunteered to ride forward. Among them were Lieutenant Charles D. Maus and Jess Daily. Watching this beehive of activity was Elizabeth Ewing. She saw and recognized Jess riding William Myers' horse. She strained to see which course the riders would take at McDonald's corner. Would they continue west on Rt. 518 or turn south on S.R. 164 as her husband's home guard group had done earlier that morning? She saw that they continued west. They soon encountered a slight hill, and from there, the road veered right in a semicircle and then left again, following an old Indian path. Coming to the top of a second and higher hill, which overlooked the John Fleming farm, the three scouts found themselves facing the advance guard of Morgan's forces.[24]

Lt. Maus was immediately captured, but Daily, who was mounted on Myers' speedy stallion, and the third scout wheeled their horses about and escaped by a spirited dash back to their company waiting at Gavers.[25] Because the home guard scouts were riding fresh horses, they quickly outdistanced the pursuing raiders, who were shooting from their jaded horses as they tried to catch up. Fence posts on the side of the road exploded as bullets tore into them narrowly missing the Lisbon militiamen obscured by dust clouds and distance. Jess Daily jumped the high barricade of a felled tree that the Lisbon militia had placed across the road. He shouted, "Morgan is coming! Morgan is coming!" Turning to the farm residents watching him from their porches, he warned, "Git in your house and bar your door. They are killin' everyone!"[26] He continued his wild ride all the way back to Lisbon, where he returned the horse to its owner, William Myers, only to have it die from excessive heat and exhaustion.[27]

Faced with impending disaster, Captain Burbick deemed his handful of militia inadequate to cope with Morgan. He ordered them to fall back upon their artillery stationed on the hill. When they arrived, they found only a few men there, among them, Cornelius Curry, Frank Rogers, Jerome Nelson and William Dorwart. The rest, having heard Jess Daily's frantic warning, had fled for their lives. They had spiked their cannon, ripped up their ammunition and took off for the woods. By now, Burbick's force had dwindled to less than a dozen men. One of those who remained, William Dorwart, grabbed the flag staff and said, "By Judas, this is the American flag, and I will die by it!"[28]

<u>11:30am, Sunday, July 26</u>

Elizabeth, Samuel Ewing's wife, had heard Jess Daily's dire warning shouted as he sped past her home. She closed and bolted the door and waited anxiously for the arrival of the gray hordes. Young Johnny Ewing had taken refuge under the kitchen table with his two little sisters, Ida and Nancy. Shortly, Elizabeth could see her yard filling up with Confederate cavalry. A tall man alighted from his horse, came up the path, crossed the porch and rapped on the door. Realizing that there was nothing to be gained by keeping the door barred, she opened it.

The Confederate officer she faced was General Morgan. He said, "Begging your pardon, ma'am. Do you have milk and water in the spring house across the road?" The tall farm woman answered, "Yes sir."

"Well," Morgan said, "if you will share the milk and water with my men, I pledge you the honor of a Kentucky gentleman that no harm shall come to you or yours."

"Certainly," Elizabeth replied, "excuse me, please, while I get my new buckets."

The General stepped into the home and saw little Johnny and his two young sisters under the table. Johnny tightened his lips to be sure that he didn't blurt out where the gold had been hidden. Nancy Morgan, Elizabeth's seventy-seven-year-old mother, who had a home on the north side of S.R. 518, was gently rocking a cradle containing Jim, a husky three-month-old. One of the daughters began to whimper and turning to the grandmother, General Morgan said, "Soothe the child, madam, I assure you of her mother's safe return." Nancy Morgan answered, "From one Morgan to another, I hope you will keep your word." Bowing, the General replied, "Good, then your name is the same as mine. I will keep my promise."

When Elizabeth returned, she was accompanied to the springhouse by one of Morgan's officers saying, "Clear a path for the lady." She carried milk and water to the men until all were satisfied. Helping her serve bread and buttermilk to the jaded troopers was Margaret Hetzel who worked on the

Ewing farm.[29] Then escorting Elizabeth back to her house, General Morgan bowed politely, thanked her for her services, mounted his horse and went to John McDonald's farm next door.[30] He, his officers and their prisoner, Lt. Maus, sat on the McDonald porch while the farmer's daughter, Alice, brought water to him and his men to quench their thirst on this hot July day.[31] From the shade of the McDonald's porch, they could see the intersection of the two main thoroughfares. One went east toward the Ohio River. The other turned left and went north to Lisbon, the home of Clement Vallandigham,[32] the "Copperhead" congressman who caused as much pain to President Lincoln as Morgan did. The General had to decide which road to take. But first he ordered his men to take their axes and remove the tree barrier placed across today's Rt. 518.

12:30pm, Sunday, July 26

Then, he turned to Charles Maus and told him to go under a flag of truce to his commander and tell him, "I do not want bloodshed. If they will allow me, I will pass peaceably to the Ohio River and will not destroy any private property or take anything." Under escort of two officers, Maus, with a white flag, set out to find his militia. They rode only a short way before he could see the remaining militia moving away as they approached. Finally, Maus spotted Captain Curry behind a tree and called to him. Curry wanted to know what the white flag meant. Maus told him to come down and find out, assuring him that he would not be hurt. As the captain came closer, Maus said that General Morgan wanted to talk to him. Just then Burbick came out into the open and agreed to accompany Curry to the McDonald farm, across the road, with Maus to see the General.[33]

Morgan asked Captain Curry upon what terms he would let them through. Curry asked what terms he wanted. Morgan proposed that he be allowed to pass unmolested to the Ohio River and out of the state. In return, he promised that his men would respect both persons and property while in the state. Captain Curry agreed to the terms, hoping to spare New Lisbon from the plundering and destruction that was associated with Morgan's visits. The General then asked the Lisbon captain to accompany him through the country for awhile. Curry declined, saying that he had no horse. Morgan said to Curry, "Captain, let one of your officers go with me a piece. He can fall out of our ranks whenever he pleases."[34]

Morgan turned to his captive, Charles Maus, and asked if he knew the names of any of Curry's officers. Maus said, "There is Captain Burbick on horseback." The General then said to Maus, "Ask him if he would go with me a piece?" Burbick said he was ready to leave at Morgan's pleasure. Curry

Private Oliver W. Cosby, Co. B, 11th KY, CSA
Captured in West Virginia.
(page 240)

Mike McMurray, Houston, TX

Private James E. McMurray, Co. I, 7th KY, CSA
Captured at Buffington Island, OH.
(page 229)

Private William L. Clayton, Co. K, 10th KY, CSA
Captured at Cheshire, OH.
(page 243)

Dale Johnson, Barberton, OH

THOMAS MILTON
McGEE
PVT. CO. H
2ND. KY. CAV. C.S.A.
K.I.A. JULY 23, 1863

Grave of Tommy McGee, Co. H, 2nd KY, CSA
Killed at Eagleport, OH.
(page 275)

C2

John Weaver's farm In Morgan County, OH
(page 266)

Portland home served as temporary field hospital during Battle of Buffington Island.
(page 231)

Ravine north of Portland where Col. Duke and his party hid before being captured.
(page 222)

View of West Virginia hills as seen from the Ohio shore in Portland, OH.
(page 221)

**Morgan's men ride into Old Washington,
Guernsey County, OH**
(page 284)

**Front of American Hotel,
Old Washington, OH**
(page 284)

**Rear of American Hotel,
Old Washington, OH**
(page 284)

**Richard McElhiney's home,
Rokeby, Morgan County, OH**
(page 272)

**Grave of three Confederates
in Old Washington, OH**
(page 287)

James Cooper Boice, Monroeville, OH
(page 314)

**Farm overlooking West Grove Cemetery
where Confederates died**
(page 319)

**Confederate graves in
West Grove Cemetery.**
(page 319)

Ohio farm horses

**Gulley where Sam, the
"horse holder," was discovered hiding.**
(page 322)

C

**West Beaver Church,
Columbiana County, OH**
(page 325)

**Bethesda Church,
Columbiana County, OH**
(page 323)

Farm along West Beaver road.
(page 325)

**The hills, twists and turns
in the West Beaver road
(S.R. 518) on the way to
West Point, OH**
(page 325)

Road to West Point, OH,
Columbiana County

Barn on Crubaugh farm
near West Point, OH
(page 331)

View of S.R. 518 looking
west from surrender site.
Morgan's troops filled this
road for one mile back.
(page 332)

View of S.R. 518 looking
East from surrender site.
Major Rue's force blocked
the road at the crest of the hill.
(page 332)

Surrender monument on S.R. 518, Columbiana County, OH
(page 335)

Major George Rue and his wife flank the surrender monument at its dedication, August 11, 1910.
(page 332)

Johnny Ewing, 5 yrs. Old
(page 325)

Hisey cash box buried in pig pen.
(page 325)

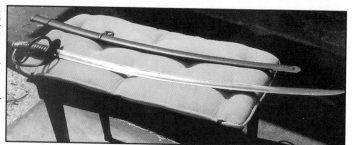

Above: General Morgan's saber and scabbard given to Thomas W. Whitacre, proprietor of the Whitacre House, where Morgan was held until he could be sent by train to Cincinnati.
(page 340)

Below: Market Street in Steubenville, OH during the Civil War.
(page 338)

David Tod, Ohio's governor
(page 113)

Nathaniel Merion, Warden of Ohio Penitentiary
(page 346)

General Ulysses S. Grant
(page 15)

General Robert E. Lee
(page 15)

Ohio Penitentiary with partial remains of 25-foot high wall.
(page 357)

University of Kentucky Library, Lexington, KY

Above: Morgan's men in prison wore high-top leather boots and broad-brimmed hats.

Below left: More of Morgan's men in prison.

Below right: Captain Lorenzo Dow Hockersmith,
Co. C, 10th KY, CSA
(page 356)

Scott E. Sallee, Bowling Green, KY

Escape over Ohio Penitentiary walls. This artist's conception is inaccurate because on the night of the escape, it was raining and the guards sought shelter inside. Both they and their guard dogs were not to be seen when Morgan's group ran across the prison yard and scaled the two perimeter walls.
(page 357)

WINTER ARRANGEMENT.

LITTLE MIAMI AND

COLUMBUS AND XENIA

RAILROADS,

For Cincinnati, Dayton, Richmond, Indianapolis & Chicago.

Without change of Cars to DAYTON and RICHMOND, and only one change of Cars to ST. LOUIS, INDIANAPOLIS & CHICAGO.

On and after Monday, Nov. 16, 1863,

Trains will run as follows:

FOUR TRAINS DAILY FROM COLUMBUS.

(Sundays excepted.)

FIRST TRAIN.

CINCINNATI AND DAYTON NIGHT EXPRESS leaves at 1:25 a. m., stopping at London, Xenia, Dayton, Middletown and Hamilton, arriving at Cincinnati at 7:25 a. m.

Newspaper ad General Morgan read when he planned his escape.
He noted that the train left the Columbus depot bound for Cincinnati at 1:25 am.
(page 358)

Reward Poster
Dated Nov. 28, 1863. Sheldon's first-name initial is missing and Tom Hines' last name is not spelled correctly. Ohioans complained that the reward should have been much higher than $1,000.
(page 362)

$1,000!

REWARD.

Head Quarters U. S. Forces,

Columbus, O., Nov. 28, 1863.

GEN. JOHN H. MORGAN

Captains J. C. Bennett, L. B. Taylor, L. D. Hockersmith, Sheldon T. H. Haines, and G. S. Magee,

Escaped from the Ohio Penitentiary on the night of the 27th instant.

A Reward of $1,000!

Will be paid for the apprehension and arrest of John Morgan, and a suitable reward for the apprehension and arrest of the others.

WM. WALLACE,
Colonel 15th O. V. I. Commanding.

Above: Captain Thomas Hines distracts the attention of a Union patrol in Tennessee so General Morgan, hidden in bushes, can make his escape.
(page 364)

Below: After the Union patrol realizes Hines is a Confederate escapee, he attempts to talk his way out of being hung from a tree. He asks the Federal major what he would have done had he been in Hines' place. "If you were the General's aide, wouldn't you have tried to divert attention away so he could escape?"

John Wesley Hunt
John Hunt Morgan's maternal grandfather
(page 390)

Calvin Cogswell Morgan
John H. Morgan's father
(page 389)

Rebecca G. Bruce
John H. Morgan's first wife
(page 389)

Henrietta Hunt Morgan
John H. Morgan's mother
(page 389)

Above: Birthplace of John H. Morgan, Huntsville, AL (page 389)

Below: Final resting place in Lexington,KY Cemetery (page 374)

Far right: Both the North & South sang about Morgan. (page 366)

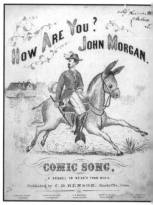

Group of Confederate prisoners in Ft. Delaware (1864) included (left to right):
Back row: Lt. H.H. Brogden, Lt. L.H. Smith, Lt. J.J. Andrews, Col. Cicero Coleman,
Col. Richard C. Morgan, Capt. Charlton H. Morgan, Col. Basil W. Duke, Lt. J.H. Tomlinson.
Seated: Col. Joseph T. Tucker, Capt. Hart Gibson, Lt. J.J. Andrews, J.W.K. Handy,
M. Jeff Thompson, Col. W.W. Ward. Seated on floor: B.l. Key, orderly.

Edward Hibarger, Montgomery, OH

Many years after the war, Morgan's Men Association gather for a meeting. Its first president,
Basil Duke with a white goatee beard, sits in second row behind man in light suit, left of center.

General Morgan with his second wife,
Martha "Mattie" Morgan.
(page 389)

Johnnie Morgan, the General
and Mattie's only child.
(page 390)

"Morgan's Wedding" original painting by John Paul Strain ©

From left to right: Major-General Benjamin F. Cheatham, Alice (Mattie's sister), Mattie's mother (sitting), Charles Ready
(Mattie's father), Mattie, General John H. Morgan, Col. Basil Duke (General's brother-in-law), Lt. General Leonidas Polk
(in Episcopal bishop's robe), Lt. General William J. Hardee, Mrs. Breckinridge, Maj. General John C. Breckinridge and
General Roger W. Hanson. Other groomsmen in the wedding party (not shown) were Horace Ready (Mattie's brother),
Col. George St. Leger Grenfell and General Braxton Bragg.
(page 389)

stood there as Morgan's command passed him, then he went up to rejoin the Lisbon men who had gathered on the hill. He was asked what had become of Burbick. He answered, "He went with the rebels." One of the home guards made a facetious remark, "The rebels have got a new recruit."[35]

As Burbick and Maus joined the Confederate column, they asked Morgan how far he would take them. "Not far," was the reply. The General asked Burbick for the nearest road to Achor. He said it was by way of Elkton. Two miles beyond Gavers, Morgan asked Burbick if he would accept the surrender of his sick and wounded soldiers.[36]

"We have been traveling for forty days, and had a fight every day, and we will surrender to you arms, equipment and horses if you let us go home," the General said.

Burbick answered, I agree. [37]

As they continued to ride toward West Point, Morgan saw a cloud of dust rising along a road parallel to their route. It was Major Rue and detachments of the 9th, 11th, and 12th KY (USA). After having left Salineville, he learned from scouts and telegraph operators that Morgan had crossed the Cleveland & Pittsburgh Railroad near Millport and that the Confederate column was leisurely moving down the West Beaver road, which ran along the north side of the creek for some ten or twelve miles from Salineville.[38] Isaac Williams had been acting as Rue's guide. But when Rue got to the high ground, near the Bethel church, he met Dr. David Marquis of West Point on horseback riding a good horse. Because of the coating of dust on their uniforms, the doctor, at first, thought these were Morgan's men. The major, holding a gun on him, identified his troop as Union men and asked if he was acquainted with the roads leading to West Beaver Creek. He said he was, and stated that he was a physician, lived in West Point, and had practiced medicine all along the West Beaver Valley for a number of years.

Rue said, "You're just the fellow I am looking for. Show us the shortest roads and we'll be sure to find Morgan before noon." After sizing up Rue and his men, the doctor replied, "Come on!"

As they rode, Rue spotted a cloud of dust on the horizon ahead. "Is the West Beaver Creek over there where there's a cloud of dust?" Rue asked the doctor. Dr. Marquis confirmed that it was, and he explained that it goes down the north side of the creek for several miles and then the road turns from the creek and leads to the Ohio River.

Major Rue watched the cloud of dust, which was about a mile distant. It seemed to be moving faster than when he first spotted it. The doctor pointed out that the road they were on would cross the creek and intercept the road about two miles away. Realizing that he had a greater distance to ride than Morgan did to reach the crossroads, Rue ordered his command into a brisk trot.[39]

Morgan had been watching the dust cloud pick up speed and he realized that his jaded horses and dog-tired men would not be able to outrun what appeared to be a large hostile force that was gaining rapidly. He also saw another cloud of dust rising on his other flank. It was Captain Ward with the 1st KY (Wolford's "Wild Riders") on his left and Rue's 11th KY on his right. At this point of the pursuit, it was Kentuckians chasing Kentuckians through Ohio.

Concluding that his capture was imminent, Morgan began to weigh his options. He wanted the best possible terms. He surmised that a lone Ohio militiaman riding by his side, as his virtual prisoner, would be more agreeable to surrender terms than a large regiment of armed militia. Leaving Burbick at the front of the column, Morgan fell back to confer with his other officers and tell them of his decision. He then rode forward and said to Burbick, "Would you accept the surrender of my entire force?"

The Lisbon volunteer asked, "On what grounds do you want to surrender?"

Morgan replied, "My men and officers are to be paroled and allowed to go home. We will give up our guns and equipment except for our side arms."

Burbick hesitated, "I really don't know. I don't understand the nature of a surrender. I am not a regular officer."

Morgan, with an impatient tone, demanded, "Look, I have the right to surrender to anyone I want. Now, will you accept my surrender? I want an answer right off! Yes or no?"

The befuddled Burbick acquiesced, "Yes, I accept."[40]

With that, Morgan took Burbick's riding stick and attached his white pocket handkerchief to it. Morgan then told him to get on his horse, "Glencoe," and ride to the rear quickly because "Your men will soon be upon us. Tell General Shackelford not to molest us as we ride to the river because we have surrendered." Together with one of Morgan's officers, Burbick began to move to the rear of the long Confederate column.[41]

SIXTY-TWO

"General Morgan Demands Your Surrender!"

Rue, despite his fresher horses, saw that Morgan might reach the cross-roads ahead of him. He wanted to get there first and meet the Confederates face-to-face. He asked the doctor if there was a shortcut to the crossroads. The physician suggested that by riding down the creek, they would come to a farm road, not very good, but over which horses could travel nicely.[1]

Rue's troopers increased their gait to a gallop for almost two miles until they found the farm road leading from the creek up through some farm fields. Ahead, they saw a young teenager, George P. Ikirt, sitting motionless on a horse. The lead Union soldier called out, "Do you live nearby?" George answered, "Yes I do." "What's the nearest way out to the West Beaver road to West Point?" the dusty soldier asked. "Turn up the second gulch. It's only a bridle path, but it goes to the main road," the teenager shouted as he pointed.[2] Rue's column rode past the startled teenager and up the hill into David Crubaugh's farm. Crubaugh's young son and daughter were walking from the barn to their house when one of the Union officers reined up and asked the little girl, "Are there any rebels in that barn?" Both children answered, "No!" Satisfied that there were no Confederates in hiding, the blue column rode on to the main pike. It was a fast ride made possible because of good horses. Reaching the main road, they wheeled to the left and rode to the crest of the hill.[3]

Riding a dark-colored horse, raising his field glasses to his eyes and stretching his six-foot three-inch frame,[4] Major Rue exclaimed, "Yonder he comes, boys. We've got him now."[5] The front of Morgan's column had just ridden over the crest of a hill less than a quarter mile away. Under the direction of Major Graham, the Union command of 300 men completed their hasty formation of two columns deep across the road in front of the Crubaugh farm. Out of curiosity, George Ikirt had followed Rue's command and took up a position in the second row of soldiers, even though he didn't have a gun.[6] Union soldiers went to the homes on both sides of the road to warn neighboring residents, the Crawfords, the Burbicks, and the Crubaughs that there was going to be a fight and they would be caught between two lines of battle. They were advised to leave. But several of the farming residents decided to stay in their homes come what may.[7]

Opposing forces were now straddling the Wayne and Madison Townships' line. Morgan, at the front, was on the road between Henry Crawford and David Burbick's farms (no known relation to Capt. Burbick of New Lisbon) in Wayne Township. Several hundred yards away, Rue's forces blocked their path in Madison Township at the Crubaugh lane with one flank anchored at some timberland and the left of the line below the road into an orchard.[8] The Federal troops could look behind, down the hill, and see the West Beaver United Presbyterian Church.[9] Morgan's advance had crested a steep hill and spotted the men blocking the road ahead. The Confederates halted and drew back, leaving a few men to watch the movement of their adversaries.[10]

2:00pm, Sunday, July 26

Morgan, resting on the green grass under on old tree, realized that Burbick was way past the John Hepner farm, too far in the rear for Rue to see the white flag. Raising his body upright, he shouted a "holloo!" and ordered another truce flag to be given to Charles Maus, their prisoner.[11] Major Theophilus Steele and two privates accompanied him toward Rue's lines.[12] Upon sighting the advancing group under a flag of truce, several Union soldiers galloped forward. The Federals asked, "What does this mean?"[13]

One of the Confederates answered, "General Morgan demands your surrender."[14] At this point, Morgan thought he was dealing with another group of Ohio militia, expecting Shackelford's forces to be at his rear.

At once, Major Rue recognized this as a typical Morgan bluff. The Union major, anxious to let Morgan know that he was dealing with Union cavalry, not militia, sent back word that Morgan "must surrender or fight Major George W. Rue of the Ninth Kentucky Cavalry."[15]

Morgan knew that his men closest to Rue's line were low on ammunition. Believing that Shackelford would attack him from the rear, he had transferred much of the remaining ammunition to his forces toward the rear of his column.[16] Morgan then, for a second time, sent Major Steele with a flag of truce to inform Rue that he had already surrendered to Captain Burbick.[17]

"Who the hell is Captain Burbick?" Rue inquired. When told by Major Steele that Burbick was a captain of a militia company from a nearby town, Rue sent word back to Morgan stating that he recognized no other surrender, other than one to himself. "Inform Morgan that he must surrender to me or we will open fire and be damned quick about it!"[18]

In a few minutes the Confederates returned with the announcement that Morgan was willing to surrender to Rue. Then Major Rue with an escort rode over into Morgan's camp. Morgan's men were lying on both sides of the road nearly every one of them was asleep. They had fallen exhausted off their horses and were trying to rest in the shade of trees. There was a cluster of men close to General Morgan anxious to hear what was going to be discussed. But most of the Confederates were scattered along both sides of the road for almost a mile to the rear toward Gavers.[19] The weather was oppressively hot. That Sunday in July was the warmest day of the season with the thermometer, at noon, indicating ninety-five in the shade.[20]

Rue observed, "It was a hot July day and they were the tiredest lot of fellows I ever saw in my life. I rode quite a little distance through his men before I reached Morgan. When I met him he was on a fine Kentucky, thoroughbred sorrel mare." He got off his horse and the men went under the shade of an old oak tree to talk.[21]

The two bearded Kentuckians greeted each other. George Rue's white teeth were framed by a heavy black beard as he spoke, "General Morgan, I'm glad to see you."[22] The General returned the smile when he recognized Rue, a fellow Kentuckian who had grown up just thirty miles from Morgan's home. "You have beat me this time,"[23] the General conceded "If I had to be caught, I'm glad it was by another Kentuckian."[24] They had soldiered together in the War with Mexico. Morgan informed the Union officer that he had already given his parole to Captain James Burbick. The terms of surrender were then discussed at the roadside just a bit more than two miles (2.3) west of West Point, Ohio.[25] After Rue listened to Morgan's explanation of the terms he had reached with Captain Burbick, he said, "Matters must remain as they are until General Shackelford arrives."[26] Then as a conciliatory gesture, Morgan offered him his sorrel mare, "Glencoe," for a trophy. Rue could sense that Morgan was very loath to part with his horse. The Major later commented, "He gave the mare to me, supposing probably that I would take her back to Kentucky where he might some day have the chance to steal her back."[27]

General Morgan also presented trophies to Maus and Burbick. To Lt. Maus, he gave his Colt revolver, holster and riding bridle, saying, "I admire bravery. Keep this as a remembrance of the giver." To Burbick, he offered another horse, saying, "Take this beautiful white mare which I 'appropriated' from a circus in Indiana." Later, Burbick would surrender the horse to General Shackelford.[28]

Shackelford was about three miles back, where he and Wolford had stopped to have dinner at Joshua Patterson's farm. Rue sent word for the

General to join him. He and Col. Wolford rode together to the scene of the surrender.[29]

2:30pm, Sunday, July 26

As Wolford slid off his horse, still limping from the wound that Morgan's men gave him at Lebanon, Tennessee, "Old Meat-Axe," his face breaking into a grin, advanced and shook hands with Morgan.[30]

"I'm glad to see you on this occasion," he said to Morgan.

"You and the Colonel have met before?" asked Shackelford.

"Not as friends," replied Morgan.[31]

Earlier, Major Rue had questioned Burbick about the surrender terms. The New Lisbon captain repeated them. Rue asked Burbick, "What was the size of your force when Morgan surrendered?" He answered, "I had no force. I was only a guide."[32] Later, Rue relayed, to Shackelford, Morgan's claim to have surrendered to Captain Burbick and wanted the terms of the surrender honored. After thirty days and nights of hard riding in pursuit of Morgan, Shackelford lost his temper. He began to bestow some caustic epithets upon the Confederate chieftain for attempting to con him into such terms with such a flimsy story. Col. Frank Wolford, who had been Morgan's prisoner in previous encounters, tried to control the General's temper. "It is wrong to speak harshly to one whose hands are figuratively confined,"[33] Wolford interrupted, "Morgan's terms should be honored."[34]

When Shackelford stated, "No way will I accept those terms," Morgan angrily responded, "Then put us back on the battlefield and let us fight it out."[35] Shackelford answered adamantly, "Your demand will not be considered for a moment. You have surrendered, and the terms were unconditional. You are our prisoners."[36]

With that, the Confederates were instructed to stack their weapons on the lawn in front of David Burbick's log cabin and, if they wished, they could fill their canteens at the Burbick's springhouse.[37] Some Union soldiers took the stacked weapons and carried them across the road to the Crawford cherry orchard and began to discharge them. Tree branches began to snap and fall to the ground. Tree trunks became the targets for hundreds of bullets.[38] Henry Crawford, who lived with his father, Joseph, across from the Burbick farm, later remarked, "It is a mistake to say that Morgan had no ammunition with which to fight longer. If you could have seen our cherry trees, you would have been convinced that he had plenty of loaded guns."[39] Farmers in the area, hearing the sounds of gunfire, wrongly surmised that Morgan's men were engaged in another skirmish.[40]

The surrender had been concluded. Five hours after the Salineville encounter, facing overwhelming odds, Morgan had surrendered in Columbiana County with more than 330 men remaining. Eager to take credit for finally capturing the elusive Morgan, Major George W. Rue sent a telegram to General Burnside, who in turn, forwarded it the next day to Ohio's governor.

(Telegram)   Governor Tod:
Cincinnati, *July* 27, 1863
General Burnside: Salineville, 26th.
I captured John [H.] Morgan today at 2:00 P.M., taking 336 prisoners, 400 horses and arms. Morgan presented me his fine sorrel mare.
G.W. Rue, *Major Ninth Kentucky Cavalry.*[41]

When General Shackelford learned that Rue had already sent a telegram announcing the capture of Morgan, he dispatched another to General Burnside's headquarters in Cincinnati to be sure he received credit. After having chased Morgan through three states, keeping up the pressure for more than 900 miles, he felt he deserved the credit as much as anyone for Morgan's capture.

(Telegram)   Headquarters U.S. Forces
In the Field, three miles south of New Lisbon, via Salineville -
3.20 p.m. *July* 26, 1863.
Col. Lewis Richmond, A.A.G.:
Cincinnati, Ohio
By the blessing of the Almighty God, I have succeeded in capturing Gen. John H. Morgan, Col. Cluke, and the balance of the command, amounting to about 400 prisoners.
J.M. SHACKELFORD
Brigadier-General Commanding.[42]

Basil Duke, in his book, placed the number of Confederate prisoners at 364.[43] Velma Griffin, a Carroll County historian, placed the number surrendered at 384.[44]

Among those who were captured or surrendered in Columbiana County on July 26, 1863, were: General John Hunt Morgan; Colonel Leroy S. Cluke; Major Theophilus Steele, 7th KY; Major Horace A. Higley, Acting ADC; Capt. Thomas B. Boyd ACS; Capt. E. Foster Cheatham AQM; Capt. Hart Gibson AAG; Capt. Calvin C. Morgan; Capt. Thomas S. Morgan; Maj.

W.G. Owen; Capt. Washington C. Shane ADC; Capt. John M. Triggs; Capt. E.D. Warder ADC; Capt. D. Rufus Williams, Inspector General; Lt. J.H. Croxton AAG, Co. E, 8th KY; 1st Lt. J.E. Keller; 2nd Lt. Daniel Cooper; 2nd Lt. R.B. Mitchell, Co. D, 6th KY; 3rd Sgt. Robert T. Bean, Co. I, 8th KY; Pvt. H.T. Seppington; Pvt. J.F. Carter, Co. F, 2nd KY; Pvt. John D. Duval, Co. E, 8th KY; Pvt. Robert D. Grimes, Co. B, 2nd KY; Pvt. David Kent, Co. F, 2nd KY; Pvt. John B. Peters, Co. F, 9th KY; Pvt. William R. Peters, Co. F, 9th KY; Pvt. William Smith, Co. F, 9th KY; Pvt. Bennett H. Young, Co. B, 8th KY; Surgeon J.S. Bemiss; Asst. Surgeon W.B. Anderson; James F. Crouch, AA Inspector General; J.F. Herndon, AQM; James W. Harberry, Orderly; Joseph Derby, Orderly; W.H. Grisard, Orderly; S.B. Ryan, Courier.

Among the Tennesseans captured with the 9th TN were: 1st Sgt. Isaac J. Ragan, Co. A; Pvt. David A. Bridges, Co. A; Pvt. William S. Carter, Co. A; Pvt. Reuben Douglas, Co. B; 3rd Sgt. Thomas T. Grizzard, Co. C; Pvt. Joseph A. Cambell, Co. C; Pvt. James W. Edwards, Co. C; Pvt. James W. Moore, Co. C; Pvt. G.H. Burgess, Co. E; Pvt. David L. Mitchell, Co. E; Pvt. John Waller Overton, Co. E; Pvt. Thomas R. Williford, Co. E; 3rd Lt. Rufus Cornwell, Co. F; Sgt. James M. Allard, Co. F; Pvt. Thomas Haney, Co. F; Pvt. Grant Rice, Co. F; and Pvt. James P. Barnes, Co. I.

General Shackelford seized Morgan's horse, "Glencoe," which had been a gift from Keene Richards, a Bluegrass breeder,[45] and gave it as a gift to General Winfield Scott.[46] General Scott had landed at Vera Cruz In March 1847 and marched to Mexico City during the Mexican-American War,[47] where John Morgan served as a lieutenant and saw action at the battle of Buena Vista.[48]

Less than a week earlier, northern newspapers were reporting the Union victory at Buffington Island. In a letter written to his wife from Corinth, Mississippi, Pvt. James S. Prather, Co. E, 66th IN Infantry said, "I was glad to hear that Morgan and his band was nearly all captured. I saw in yesterday's paper that our men had taken 2,500 of Morgan's men and about 3,000 horses. It also stated that they had captured Morgan himself but it is not believed here." Prather's letter was dated July 25, 1863, just one day before Morgan's actual capture.[49] Prather's instincts had been right when he sensed that Morgan had given his captors the slip at Buffington Island. But now the rumors and reports were true. The month-long raid that had panicked the mid-west was finally over.

Why was it possible for Morgan's horse, Glencoe," to carry him throughout the twenty-four-day raid, while all the other soldiers and officers had to replace their mounts several times during the chase? The answer is that Morgan spent a great deal of his time in his "command van" while en route. It could be a wagon or a buggy. The vehicle and the horses that pulled it were often changed as the raid progressed. Glencoe was tethered to the vehicle and Morgan only mounted his steed when he needed to ride to the front or rear of his column. There were occasions when he had to abandon his "command van," mount Glencoe and speed away. One such occasion happened in Jefferson County between Monroeville and Salineville. He left his coach, mounted Glencoe and rode down the precipitous ravine into Carroll County. Without having to continually carry a rider nor go on fast scouting missions, Glencoe was in relatively good condition after 1,000 miles.

After the Buffington Island engagement, Morgan had managed to elude all Union efforts to capture him for another six days. He taxed his energy and those of his men. For almost a week, he had outmaneuvered General Shackelford and his superior forces and equipment. The raid was over for the weary Confederates. They were alive, and that was one blessing no man overlooked, even with prison camp a few days away. Some hoped for exchange, others for escape; but every one of Morgan's "terrible men" looked forward eagerly to one thing—a chance to rest and sleep. The chase was done. The mission was accomplished.

With the loss of fewer than 2,000 men, Morgan kept a large portion of the Middle West off balance for weeks. It had also rekindled a hope in southern hearts, and instilled fear in the minds of hundreds of thousands in the three states through which the raid was carried out. Seldom in warfare have so few men ridden so far and so fast within enemy lines. And never in any war had 2,500 men fought their way against such odds, damaging but a few private homes and without intentionally harming a single woman or child. It may well have been chivalry's last appearance in a major war.

Basil Duke gave this appraisal of the raid. "The objects of the raid were accomplished. General Bragg's retreat was unmolested by any flanking forces of the enemy, and I think that military men, who will review all the facts, will pronounce that this expedition delayed for weeks the fall of East Tennessee and prevented the timely reinforcement of Rosecrans by troops that otherwise would have participated in the battle of Chickamauga [a Confederate victory]."[50]

With the capture of General Morgan and his remaining men a "done deal," General Burnside could now turn attention to his main objective: to support Rosecrans offensive against Bragg in Chattanooga and lead his army against Buckner in Knoxville. With a cleared agenda and without further delay, he sent the following telegram to the general-in-chief in Washington, DC:

H.W. Halleck, *General-in-Chief*
HEADQUARTERS: Cincinnati, Ohio, *July* 26, 1863
I can now look after the other work you desire done.
A.E. BURNSIDE, *Major-General.*[51]

Bragg was safe, if only for a little while. Later, Gen. Rosecrans would maneuver Bragg out of Chattanooga, his strategic southern stronghold. Then reinforced by Gen. James Longstreet's corps from the Army of Northern Virginia, Bragg would turn, attack and defeat Rosecrans, ending his Union adversary's military career at Chickamauga. Rosecrans would be replaced as commander of the Army of the Cumberland by Major General George H. Thomas, while U.S. Grant assumed command of the newly constituted Military Division of the Mississippi. Then in the fourth week of November, Grant's "army group" routed Bragg's Confederates at the battle of Chattanooga.[52] On April 9, 1865, Gen. Lee surrendered to Grant at Appomattox Courthouse.[53]

4:00pm, Sunday, July 26

Toward evening, the Steubenville militia arrived and helped to take charge of the Confederate prisoners. They would march them down to the Salineville station, which would take about an hour. From there, a train would take them to Wellsville, where the officers would be off-loaded and the remaining prisoners would continue on to Steubenville. The prisoners in coaches and the militia in flat cars would arrive at Steubenville and march up Adams and Markets streets under guard to the Steubenville & Indiana Railroad train, which would take them to Camp Chase in Columbus or other northern prisons. Many of the pursuing Union companies stopped at Steubenville on their way home, where they were the recipients of cordial hospitality by the town's citizens. Market Street was filled with uniformed men of the 2nd TN Mounted Infantry, 1st KY Cavalry, 14th IL Cav., and 8th and 9th MI Cav.[54]

Among many of the Union cavalrymen temporarily encamped in Steubenville was Lieutenant N.S. Boynton, Co. F, 8th Michigan Cavalry. He was awaiting transportation to Cincinnati. Boynton had been part of Major Rue's force that finally captured Morgan. There was nothing too good for the boys of the command that had captured the noted Confederate raider. One old exuberant fellow, with a bright good-looking girl by his side, a daughter as it proved, hunted all around the camp until he found Lt. Boynton and was introduced. "By gosh, Leftenant," said the old fellow, "you are a hull team and yoke of oxen thrown in, Gol durned, if you don't deserve suthing. Say, hain't got nuthing but this gal ter give you. Darn my socks, take her.

She'll make you a bang up good wife, so she will. I would kind o' like to see her yoked up to one of the boys with shulder straps on. Dog on it, you can have 'er, she's peaches."

Lieutenant Boynton blushed, and the girl looked shy. Finally the lieutenant said, "My dear, good fellow, am sorry I can't accept your offer. I have a wife and baby at home in Michigan, and by the way, my wife is a Buckeye girl, too; very much obliged, but I can't accept." "Great guns," exclaimed the old guy, "you don't say, Leftenant. Why, dog on it, you don't appear as you were hitched. Well, I'll be gol durned if I don't give her to some other shulder stropper who helped pull in old Morgan," and away went the old man with daughter in tow.[55]

Back at the surrender site, Shackelford placed Colonel Frank Lane Wolford, the commander of the 1st KY Cavalry (USA), in charge of the prisoners. The column of mounted men, blue and gray together, were on the road marching toward Salineville where they would go by train to Wellsville. John Hunt Morgan rode at the head of the column, with Shackelford on his right. If he was dejected, he gave no sign of it. A few miles along the route, the column crossed a small stream on a timber bridge, Morgan turned in his saddle, out of habit, and softly spoke to Colonels Capron and Wolford riding behind him. He said, with a smile on his face, "Adjutant, see that that bridge is burned."[56]

SIXTY-THREE

Be My Guest

The special train bearing Morgan arrived at the river town of Wellsville early Sunday evening. The General was first taken to the office of J.N. McCullough, in the Bean House, better known as the "railway eating house." McCullough was superintendent of the Cleveland & Pittsburgh Railroad and General Brooks had been invited to establish his headquarters there, the day before, so as to be near the telegraph operators.[1]

Later in the evening, Morgan and his officers were taken to the Whitacre House, located on the corner of Water and Market (Riverside and Fourth). The hotel fronted on the park between Front Street and the railroad.[2] It was owned and operated by Thomas W. Whitacre.[3] Morgan's hotel room had a fine view of the Ohio River and the West Virginia hills on the other side.[4] He could also see the railroad tracks running along the river about two blocks from the hotel. It would be over these tracks that he and his men would be carried to Cincinnati and to prison. Morgan and his officers were given the double parlors on the first floor, the best in the house.[5] The hotel was crowded to capacity, with many of the officers having to share rooms. Colonel Wolford entered room sixty-four, where Morgan had a room to himself. He was looking out of the window, observing the circle of armed Union troops surrounding the hotel. Shortly before midnight, an outer ring would be added, doubling the number of guards stationed every few feet around the Whitacre House.[6]

This was the first opportunity, since the capture, for Morgan and Wolford to be alone. Wolford had been one of the 6,000 Union men and hundreds of Federal officers Morgan had taken prisoner in his many raids. Wolford had been Morgan's prisoner in Tennessee the year before. Now Morgan was his prisoner in Ohio. They had also both served in the Mexican-American War— Morgan as a lieutenant, Wolford as a private. Frank Wolford respected Morgan's military capabilities and he was glad to see that his old adversary seemed to be in good spirits despite his capture.

Wolford respectfully addressed Morgan, "General, while you and your officers are my prisoners here in the hotel, you are my guests. If you wish to have anything to eat, the hotel is serving chicken and dumplings tonight. You'll be served in your rooms. Anything you want, and that includes the bar, the cigar stand and other accessories, is at your service and my expense. Just don't try to leave the hotel." [7]

Morgan was greatly pleased by Wolford's generosity and his appeal to Morgan's honor. He was also cognizant of Wolford's request that Morgan's terms of surrender be honored. He said, "Colonel Wolford, I appreciate your invitation and the consideration you have shown to me and my men. With your permission, I would like to remove my spurs and present them to you as a token of my appreciation." With that, he removed his silver spurs and gave them to Wolford.[8] Virtually everything else of value had either been taken or given away: his horses, bridle, saber and pistols. Because his spurs were still attached to his boots, he had them to offer. It was customary in those days for guests to put their boots outside the door to their rooms, and were supposed to be shined without extra charge. Whitacre's son, Harve, said, "I don't think I ever saw so many boots to be shined as we found early the next morning. I am sure there must have been sixty pairs."[9]

They were taken down to the washroom and cleaned by the porters and by ten-year-old Harve Whitacre. Young Whitacre continued, "I personally reserved for myself the privilege of shining General Morgan's boots. I do not remember whether I was given a tip or not. Tips were few and far between, and were seldom larger that five cents in scrip, silver money had entirely disappeared, and war time fractional currency had taken its place." Later, when it was noticed that Morgan's boots were missing its spurs, it was wrongly suspected that one of the temporary porters had taken them as a trophy.[10]

Besides giving Wolford his spurs, Morgan had earlier presented Thomas Whitacre, the hotel's proprietor, with his saber, scabbard and belt.[11] Those historic artifacts are part of the historical collection in the Wellsville River Museum, a gift from Mrs. Frances Whitacre Morton, whose grandfather received them from General Morgan.[12]

During the evening, there were a number of attempts by people to see General Morgan in person. Even though the hotel was crowded, General Morgan remained in his room with Union soldiers stationed in the hallway as guards. One of those who were eager for an interview with the General was an ex-mayor of Wellsville. He had the reputation of being a good dresser. On this occasion, he donned a spotless white linen suit, with a snowy white shirt front, gold shirt buttons, well-starched standing collar, black silk tie, and a long solid gold watch chain around his neck. He was unable to get a pass from General Brooks. The hallway guards were obstinate and refused to recognize the gentlemen's request to be allowed into the General's room. Having exhausted his efforts with those in authority, he turned to his friend, Thomas Whitacre. "Tom, I must see Morgan. Can you get me in? I want to meet him."

Morgan had just sent a request to the hotel office for a pitcher of ice water. Turning to the ex-mayor, he said, "Sam, how would you like to be a bellboy for a little while?"

"Give me the pitcher of ice water," was his reply and his honor started through the hallway with a pitcher of water in one hand and his well-brushed, shining, high black silk hat in the other. When he approached the guard, he said, "I am connected with this hotel, and I am conveying a pitcher of ice water to General Morgan at his request."

He succeeded in gaining admittance to Morgan's presence. The Confederate chief looked up, and after inspecting the intruder from head to foot, said, "Who are you? Why am I thus honored?"

The reply was, "I am the bellboy. I have brought you a pitcher of ice water. I am the ex...."

Morgan interrupted the speaker at this point and said, "Well sir. This hotel employs the damnedest best dressed bellboys of any hotel I ever stopped at. I thank you for the pitcher of water." The ex-mayor and Morgan both enjoyed the humor of the situation.[13]

As mentioned before, General Morgan also appreciated Wolford's effort to have Shackelford accept the terms of his surrender to Burbick. He was not pleased with Shackelford's outright dismissal of his deal with the Lisbon captain. He had hoped that they would have allowed him to be paroled or exchanged. But Shackelford's disdain for any agreement Morgan had with Burbick, made Morgan mad—angry enough that he made a complaint to Shackelford's superior, Major-General Burnside and Ohio's Governor Tod.[14]

At the request of Governor Tod, L.W. Potter, an attorney in New Lisbon, was appointed to take statements from Burbick and Maus to ascertain what exactly occurred. Potter then forwarded affidavits to the governor in Columbus and General Burnside in Cincinnati.[15] Even the sheriff of Columbiana County offered his opinion.

(Telegram)   Governor Tod: Salineville, *July* 28, 1863.

James Burbick was not acting as captain of any number of men on Sunday, but was there as any other citizen. He volunteered to pilot Morgan without any force.

JESSE DUKE, *Sheriff.* WM. HOSTETTER.[16]

That same day, another was sent to both General Burnside and Governor Tod.

(Telegram)   Salineville, *July* 28, 1863.

I forwarded by special messenger statement of Burbick and Maus that can be relied on. Burbick was not captain of any militia or volunteer force, but acting, on Sunday, as captain of 15 or 20 mounted Home Guards at time of surrender. Major Rue was there, and also General Shackelford. Burbick was acting as pilot for Morgan; his object to keep him from New Lisbon. Maus was a prisoner, and these two were the only Union men with Morgan. The surrender took place 4 miles from Gavers, and when surrounded by Union forces. Wait before acting for special messenger.

L.W. POTTER, *Esq.*[17]

Governor Tod sought an opinion from the Secretary of War, Edwin M. Stanton.

(Telegram)   Hon. E.M. Stanton: Columbus, Ohio, *July* 28, 1863.

I visit General Burnside to-night to settle the question that Morgan raises as to his surrender. From what I can learn of the matter, it is all gammon [to mislead by deceptive talk] on Morgan's part. Allow me to call your attention to a proclamation I send you by mail.

DAVID TOD, *Governor of Ohio.*[18]

Despite General Morgan's protestations, Tod and Burnside concluded that Morgan's "surrender" to Burbick was null and void. As for asking Governor Tod to intervene on his behalf, Tod responded, "I can claim no control over you."[19] His unconditional surrender to Rue and Shackelford would stand and serve as the basis for his capture and imprisonment.

PRISON & ESCAPE

SIXTY-FOUR

Welcome to the Pen

From Wellsville, Morgan and his men were placed on a train to Cincinnati, escorted by General Shackelford. A humorous incident occurred on the trip to Cincinnati. An elderly Irish woman was going up and down the train selling eggs. She kept asking, "Where's Morgan? Just point him out to me." Finally one of the Union troopers pointed, in jest, to General Shackelford and quietly said, "He's Morgan." She turned and walked quickly to where Shackelford was sitting and spit into the General's face.

General Shackelford commented on the train trip. "Never before or since have I witnessed such scenes of excitement as we found at every station, town and city on the road from Wellsville to Cincinnati. The crowds were simply immense and every place we stopped, the men, women and children went into the cars to see the great raider." [1]

Before arriving in Cincinnati, the train also made a stop at the Columbus depot. The Columbus newspaper *Ohio State Journal* described Morgan's reception as he disembarked the train:

> The noted raider, John Morgan, received a very handsome reception yesterday afternoon at the depot—at least so far as numbers are concerned. The desire to see one who had given the citizens of Ohio as much trouble as this Rebel has could hardly have been greater than to see President Lincoln. The hero came on a special train, accompanied by General Shackelford and staff, and several other Union officers. The excitement ran high, and a rush was made for the train. The crowd in front feasted their eyes and made way for others eager to see him. The Governor, General [John S.] Mason, and portions of their staffs were introduced to Morgan and shook hands with him, after which they paid their respects to General Shackelford."[2]

The train arrived in the Queen City on July 28 where the Confederate prisoners remained until August 1. In the *Cincinnati Commercial* newspaper on Tuesday, July 28, a reporter wrote the following eyewitness account of General Morgan's arrival in the city:[3]

Arrival of Gen. John Morgan and Colonel Cluke and Staffs, at Cincinnati.
The anxiously-looked-for party arrived last night shortly after 10 o'clock, over the Little Miami Railroad, guarded by troops under Gen. Shackelford, the captor of Morgan. It consisted of Morgan and Cluke, with their staffs and orderlies amounting in all to thirty-one persons. On disembarking from the train, they were taken in charge by a detachment of the 111th Ohio.

A large crowd was assembled at the depot, and as the prisoners moved, immense numbers were constantly added to it. When they marched down Ninth Street not less than 5,000 persons surrounded the famous guerrilla and his aides. Many of these lookers-on seemed excited, and cried, "Hang the cut throats," "bully for the horse thieves." Several spectators were flourishing pistols, but the guard quickly drove them away.

The field-band of the 111th discoursed "Yankee Doodle" on the march, which the prisoners endured with complete *sang froid* [coolness, calmness]. Morgan, on the way, interrogated the Captain commanding the guard, concerning the whereabouts of his brother; his question on that point being answered, he turned and said, "Pass up that whiskey." The whiskey was passed forward in a canteen, which the General proffered to the Captain, who politely refused. The General then took a long pull.

They were ensconced in the City Prison shortly before eleven o'clock. Before locking them up they were deprived of a large number of pistols which they stated they had been permitted to retain by the terms of surrender. There was a bushel of pistols, all loaded, stowed away in the office of the City Prison last night, all of them revolvers, many of the officers carrying a brace [two pistols].

Morgan is fully six feet high, and of prepossessing, though not imposing presence. He was attired in a linen coat, black pants, white shirt and light felt hat. No decorations were visible. He has rather a mild face, there being certainly nothing to indicate the possession of unusual intellectual qualities.

> Col. Cluke in very tall, rising probably, two inches over six feet. He
> was attired much after the manner of his chief. He is slender, has
> sandy hair, and looks like a man of invincible determination. His
> countenance is not devoid of certain savage lines, which correspond
> well with his barbarities as a leader.
>
> The whole is a counterpart of the squads we have heretofore seen of
> the same command. The same motely dress and the same decorous
> behavior (no great merit in this last trait) distinguishes them.

On entering the Cincinnati prison, General Morgan asked Colonel Braley, commander of the 111th OVI, what had become of his brothers, Richard
and Charlton. After being told that they had been sent to Johnson's Island, a
look of distress passed over the General's face. "Pass up that whiskey," he
demanded. A canteen of whiskey was handed to him, and he took a deep
drink. Thus fortified, he was ready to spend the night in the city jail.[4]

In fact, the Confederate officers, who had been captured at Buffington
and Cheshire, had left their Cincinnati prison on July 27 and boarded a train
bound for Sandusky. The following day they arrived at Johnson's Island,
where they remained for four days before being taken to the Ohio Penitentiary in Columbus.[5]

General Burnside issued strict orders that the prisoners were to receive
no visitors or messages. So when the General's mother took a train from
Lexington to see her sons in Cincinnati, she was turned away.[6] The General-
in-Chief of the Union Armies, Henry Wager Halleck, had been humiliated
many times by Morgan's exploits.[7] The Halleck decision to confine Morgan
and his officers in the Ohio Penitentiary was supposedly based on the belief
that a Union officer, Colonel Abel D. Streight, had been imprisoned with
common criminals in Richmond. Halleck wanted to retaliate in kind. Now
that Morgan was a Union prisoner, Halleck was determined that he be
securely held with no hope for pardon, exchange or escape. He asked Ohio
Governor David Tod if there was room for Morgan and his officers in the
Ohio State Penitentiary in Columbus. After the governor checked with Warden Nathaniel Merion, the reply was in the affirmative. So the order was
given to move Morgan from Cincinnati to Columbus.[8]

Morning of Thursday, July 30

The Confederates were transferred to the Little Miami Railroad and
taken to Columbus,[9] where Morgan, his surviving brothers and many of his
officers were to be confined to the Ohio Penitentiary with the overflow of
noncommissioned men going to other prisons. The penitentiary walls of

solid stone surrounded fifteen acres on the east bank of the Scioto River.[10] A heavy iron gate faced Spring Street. Built in 1815 on the exact spot of the original stockade prison,[11] it was expanded in 1861 with the addition of the 200-foot-long East Hall to relieve the overcrowding already experienced before the onset of the Civil War. During the war, the prison population increased to 2,000.[12]

3:00pm, Thursday, July 30

Rather than going into the Columbus depot, the train stopped at the State Avenue crossing, about 100 yards from the penitentiary's entrance.[13] The Confederates were marched from the train between a human corridor of soldiers, under the command of Lieutenant Irwin,[14] blocking a crowd of curious onlookers. The crowd saw a thirty-eight-year-old man, standing six feet tall. Twenty-four days in the saddle, riding and fighting, had not robbed him of his dignity.

Morgan and his men entered the massive stone and concrete building, and into the Front Hall. The Hall was an area about 700 square feet with mats and carpets on the floor. This part of the prison was quite plush and well decorated. General Mason read off the names of the prisoners, one by one, and then turned them over to the custody of the warden, Nathaniel Merion. The list of prisoners received included one general, one colonel, three majors, seven captains, four lieutenants, and thirteen privates. The prisoners were thoroughly searched and everything was taken from them. The items taken, including money, were put in a package with the prisoner's name on it, then placed in one of the two prison safes. The amount of money was recorded on a ledger, in which the clerk would post whenever the prisoner drew upon the account to make purchases.[15]

After this, the Confederates were conducted to the prison proper. This scene was in sharp contrast to the Front Hall. No carpeting, no rocking chairs, no fancy clocks. Instead, they found a smelly, damp and chilly atmosphere. They were forced to immerse themselves in two big hogsheads filled with hot water and disinfectants. Two black convicts scrubbed them with horse brushes. The same water was used over and over again, but General Morgan was the first to get a bath.[16] Then they were moved to a barbers' room, where the Southern gentlemen lost most of their hair and beards. As Duke described it, "The officiating artists were ordered to give each man's hair 'a decent cut.' We found that according to the penitentiary code, the decent way of wearing the hair was to cut it all off.

"Colonel Smith had a magnificent beard sweeping down to his waist, patriarchal in all save color—it gave him a leonine aspect that might have awed even a barber. He was placed in a chair, and in less time, perhaps, than Absalom staid on his mule after his hair brought him to grief, he was reduced to ordinary humanity. He felt it keenly. I ventured to compliment him on features which I had never seen till then, and he answered, with asperity [irritability], that it was 'no jesting matter.'"[17] The Confederates took the removal of their facial hair as a great affront to their dignity and they bitterly complained to the prison authorities.[18]

From the barbers, they were taken to the East Hall, an eleven-foot-wide corridor of flagstone. A high brick wall was on their right with many barred windows, four levels high. Five tiers of cells were on the left. Metal stairs at either end led to the upper ranges where wooden balconies, three feet wide, provided access to the cells along each range. General Morgan was placed in Cell #35, Range 2, the last cell on that range.

In her diary, Miss Emma Holmes of Charleston wrote this entry on Friday, July 31, 1863, "Alas [John] Morgan, our brave, dashing, brilliant, partisan chief, has been captured, after, by the Yankees' own confession, his most brilliant and destructive raid into the very heart of Indiana and Ohio, how his proud spirit will chafe within his prison walls, as the base foe have decided that his officers and himself will be kept in close confinement until the Tories and negroes who were captured by [Nathan Bedford] Forrest in their raid in Georgia are exchanged."

(Telegram)   General Burnside: Columbus, Ohio, *August 2*, 1863.
Morgan and his officers were turned over to the warden of the penitentiary. Their hair was trimmed and beards shaved for cleanliness. They were not put into prison clothes. They are in separate cells, and allowed two hours in the morning and two in the afternoon for exercise and conversation, and are entirely separated from the convicts.

JNO. S. MASON, *Brigadier-General.*[19]

A week after the surrender, General Shackelford was upset that Major Rue was still getting the credit for capturing Morgan. To rewrite the events as they happened, he sent the following:

(Telegram)   Hdqrs. First Brig., Second Div., Twenty-Third A.C.
Madisonville, August 3, 1863.

Col. Lewis Richmond:

I see that Major Rue still claims the capture of Morgan, under General Burnside. Rue reported to me Saturday night, was acting directly under my orders, a part of the First and Third Kentucky Cavalry being in front with him. Morgan never surrendered to Rue; [when he] came up with him, he sent back to the head of column for re-enforcements. Rue refused to take any action until I got up. In behalf of my command, who followed Morgan thirty days and nights, I appeal to the general to set the matter right.

M. SHACKELFORD.[20]

SIXTY-FIVE

A Letter to Mattie

While in prison, Morgan corresponded with his wife, Mattie. Morgan's own words show his love and respect for his wife, and his religious faith. Here is one of his letters written on August 10, 1863. The letter was sent under a flag of truce, via City Point, care of H. Hazen, Esq., Knoxville, Tennessee. Forwarded care of Col. Charles Ready (Mattie's father), Atlanta, Georgia.

On yesterday, we had a nice box of delicacies sent from home [prepared by his mother], it contained everything nice, from an elegant pound cake to a fine baked ham. And you can imagine "My Dear Wife" how much we enjoyed it. Col. Breckinridge's wife went to mother's and assisted in getting them up. So you see "My Precious One" we are getting along bravely. Get a great number of letters from our Friends in Ky., but would sacrifice every pleasure and comfort to get one single line from "My Lovely Mattie." It would be a treasure. Yesterday, Sunday, passed the greater portion of the day in our rooms. The convicts are not at work upon that day and all are in their cells. We have to keep quiet as they are liable to become unmanageable if they hear any unusual noise. We pass the day reading, the greater portion of the officers reading their Bible—when with you "My Sweet One" it was by far the pleasantest day of the week and I used to look forward to its coming with great pleasure, and was perfectly happy, when I accompanied you to church. But hope "My Darling" the time may soon come to when we may enjoy the same pleasure again. What do you do "My Love" to pass the time, I know not as pleasantly as last winter. Those were my <u>happiest</u> days. Then I was <u>perfectly</u> happy.

It is now eight at night. I occupy one hour each night in reading my prayer book, which you, "Dear One" was so very kind and considerate as to present me with and it has been a great source of pleasure to me. In reading the Psalms, I often try and see if I can pick out the passage you had marked in your Prayer Book and in a number of cases, I know that I am correct.

Good night "My Precious One." May God bless and protect my Darling Mattie. Yours affectionately, Jno. H. Morgan, Brigd-Gnl.[1]

General Morgan wrote to Mattie on an average of two to three times a week, but all letters did not get through. They were limited to one page and had to pass through the prison censorship. Also, incoming mail was similarly scrutinized and censored.[2]

One of the ways Morgan's men, who were imprisoned in the Ohio Penitentiary, helped pass their time in confinement was by signing autograph books. Each Confederate prisoner had his own book, which was circulated among his fellow cellmates. Each man signed one page, sometimes, but not always, including the name of his hometown (or birthplace), identifying the military unit he served in and the cell number he occupied in the penitentiary.[3]

Almost to a man, their writings reflected skilled calligraphy. There was clarity and legibility to each signature. No graffiti, no blasphemy, no doctor's prescription scrawl. Their restrained comments and spare prose reflected a pride and honor to have served under General Morgan. Even though they signed many books, the men did not always sign their names the same way nor embellish the page in the same manner. For example, Basil Duke, in one book, added a Latin phrase at the bottom of the page. But in other autograph books that phrase did not appear. In most books, he wrote, "Basil W. Duke. St. Louis, Mo. 2d Range—Cell No 27, Ohio Penitentiary. Col. Comd'g 1st Brigade, Morgan's Division." But in one book, he added, *"Haesit in latere lethalis arundo, et dulce moriens reminiscitur Argos."*

Duke, married to Morgan's sister, Henrietta ["Tommie"] had studied at Georgetown College and Centre College. He probably studied law under one of the Transylvania [Lexington] professors without enrolling and was admitted to the bar in St. Louis.[4] He was well versed in classical Latin. He had quoted from memory two incomplete verses from Vergil's *Aeneid*, a Latin epic poem recounting the adventures of Aeneas after the fall of Troy. Duke put them together to read, "The fatal dart stuck in his side, and he, dying, remembers sweet Argos." The first half of the line, *Haesit in latere lethalis arundo*, comes from the *Aeneid* 4.73, and is usually found in modern texts as *haeret lateri letalis harundo* (the fatal dart sticks in her side). It describes a wounded doe that escapes the hunter, who does not know that he has hit her, but the doe dies later. Duke substituted the past tense *haesit* for the present tense *haeret*, and the prepositional phrase *in latere* for the less usual but more poetic dative (Latin grammatical case) *lateri*. His spellings of *letalis* and *harundo* are variants less favored by Latinists today. Only a person who knew Latin could make those substitutions, even inadvertently.[5]

The second half of the line from the *Aeneid* 10.782, reads *et dulcis moriens reminiscitur Argos* (and dying, he remembers sweet Argos). Argos was an ancient city-state in southeast Greece, a rival to Athens, Sparta and Corinth. In this part of *Aeneid*, King Mezentius tries to kill Aeneas, but his spear bounces off Aeneas' shield and fatally wounds a Greek ally, Antores. "He is laid low by a wound meant for another, and he gazes at the sky, and dying, remembers sweet Argos."[6]

This brief Latin quote gives an insight into Duke's emotions. That moment was a vulnerable and introspective time of his life. My interpretation is that the dart was the pursuit of the Union forces trying to catch Morgan. But at Buffington Island, the fatal dart bounced off Morgan as he escaped and struck Duke who was captured. As Duke wrote these words, he was confined to prison (which he compared to dying), and was remembering his sweet home in Dixie (Argos). Actually his home was near Georgetown in Scott County, Kentucky, where it still stands.

<u>Saturday, August 1</u>

Fifty-three other officers (thirty-seven from Johnson's Island), including Col. Basil Duke, joined Morgan in the penitentiary.[7] They had been previously imprisoned elsewhere. Capt. L.D. Hockersmith said that three officers were in the prison hospital, among them was Major Steele,[8] who had south to negotiate the terms of surrender with Major Rue. Four other captured officers not assigned penitentiary cells were Captain John M. Triggs, 1st Lt. J.E. Keller, 2nd Lt. Daniel Cooper and Lt. R.B. Mitchell.[9] Major Thomas Webber was not included in the General's group when they arrived by train in Cincinnati nor is his cell number assignment recorded. But it was reported that he spent some time in solitary confinement in the penitentiary because of opinions expressed in his letters as to what should be done to "captured negro soldiers and their officers."[10]

Another of Morgan's officers, who had been taken prisoner during the raid and was excluded from serving his time in the Ohio Penitentiary, was Lt. Col. Robert A. Alston. Because he had voluntarily given himself up when captured at Springfield in Kentucky, General Burnside noted that he had not participated in the Indiana-Ohio raid. He allowed Alston to remain at Camp Chase in Columbus and Burnside was already recommending that Alston be paroled pending exchange with a Federal officer of equal rank.[11]

Upon his transfer from Johnson's Island to the Ohio Penitentiary, Duke stood waiting to be assigned to a cell, a man in one of the upper cells, whom he thought was a convict, spoke to him. He turned to a companion and quietly commented about how friendly the inmates were on such short acquaintance. The "convict," shaven and with a close-cropped haircut, broke into laughter. Only then did Duke recognize his brother-in-law, General Morgan. Charlton, standing next to Duke, exclaimed, "Great God!" For the moment, he could say no more.[12]

Now there were sixty-eight Confederate officers[13] quartered at one end of the prison, away from the regular convict population.[14] All were imprisoned on two levels (ranges).[15] Morgan's men were not required to wear the prison stripes that the convicts had to wear.[16] Each prisoner was placed in his own cell measuring three feet six inches wide, seven feet deep and seven feet high. The walls were brick, the floors concrete and there was a four-inch-diameter hole on the back wall of every cell to allow ventilation. The cell doors had heavy iron grating with bars an inch wide and half an inch thick in a lattice pattern with two-inch-square spaces between them. Each cell was equipped with a bedstead hung on the wall by small iron hinges. During the day, the bed could be lowered to give the prisoner some living space in the cell. Bed ticking, a three-legged stool, a bed prop board (one inch by three inches by thirty-six inches), a sanitary bucket and a gas-burner completed the amenities offered.[17]

Living conditions in the Ohio Penitentiary were far better than in the military prison camps of either army. As P.O.W. camps filled up after the breakdown of exchange, prisoners on both sides suffered from bad water, inadequate sanitation and disease. In southern prisons, food was less abundant and housing usually deficient; the two largest facilities, Andersonville and Belle Isle, provided no shelter from the elements. In the penitentiary, the water was pure, sanitation was up to standard, and the food was so ample that the men gained weight. Dick Morgan was being sarcastic, but the truth came through when he wrote: "At first we thought our fate, a hard one, being sent to a Penitentiary in retaliation for the treatment of Col. Streight's men, but experience has taught us to highly appreciate the institution for abundance of *grub*, cleanliness, fine water, and many other privileges which are granted us, for which we are greatly indebted to the hospitable Warden of this institution."[18]

Warden Merion demanded that the military prisoners follow the same strict rules he enforced on the convict population.[19] Failure to follow them often found the offenders placed in the dungeon in the lower levels of the prison. They were small, damp cubicles sealed on the inside with sheet iron in which prisoners were forced to stand with no facilities except a vermin-infested slop bucket. Lt. Col. McCreary spent five days there and referred to it as "a hell on earth." Others who were sentenced to the dungeon were Capt. Calvin Morgan, Col. Basil Duke, Major Thomas Webber, Major H.A. Higley and Captain E.F. Cheatham. Captain Morgan said that he was covered with green mold when he emerged.[20]

When General Morgan protested the conditions to Governor Tod, he visited the east wing section of the prison and expressed surprise concerning the treatment. He stated that the shaving of heads and beards had been an assumption of authority by prison officials and not by any military order. Tod apologized for "an outrageous and disgraceful act." After his visit, there appeared to be a general relaxation of the rules. The prisoners were granted more freedom of movement, permitted to exercise for longer periods, and given permission to make outside purchases. They were also permitted to receive money and packages from their families.[21]

When word got around in Kentucky that the prison was accepting gifts, the warden's office was deluged with packages from home. For a few days, the Confederate prisoners were surfeited with good things, and then the trap fell. Inspection of the mountain of packages became so time-consuming that the military authorities laid down a new rule: no more edibles or clothing would be received without special permission. Merion took advantage of the ruling to confiscate the provisions, and rather than going to waste, he served them at his own table.[22]

Toward the end of August, General Morgan's mother sent an express package to Warden Merion. It contained clothing and two bottles of cordial. Warden Merion delivered the clothes, but because liquor was prohibited, it was appropriated to the use of those who were sick in the hospital. The Morgan brothers wrote to their mother thanking her, but their letter made clear that she could not visit. Nevertheless, on September 6, she appeared and demanded to see her boys. Merion refused, but promised to distribute the six hams, seven cakes, and other items she had brought.[23]

In his diary, Charlton noted, "My Mother and Mrs. Hoch Gibson arrived here today. They were not permitted to talk to us but were marched out in the hall where Mother and Mrs. Gibson were permitted as an especial favor to peer through the grating at us."[24] Through the prison grapevine, the Morgan brothers had heard she was there. The tall Morgan men stood on tiptoe, watching eagerly through their cell grating to catch a precious glimpse of her.[25] His anger against Warden Merion boiling over, Charlton added, "If a single man of us here ever survives the war, Merion will be held to strict responsibility for his unkindness to us. One who can forget these wrongs has none of the instincts of a man."[26]

An article in the *Steubenville Herald* carried the following story:[27]

Horse-Thieves About— The *Wheeling Intelligencer* of yesterday says that on Saturday night somebody stole six or seven horses from the farm of Mr. Jacob Woods, who resides about four miles from the city, on Bethany Pike. Mr. Somebody is evidently following the bad example of John Morgan—he should consider John's fate, head shaved and an inmate of the Ohio Penitentiary, and be admonished.

SIXTY-SIX

Breakout from "Castle Merion"

There is some controversy as to who discovered the air chamber running beneath the floor of Range 1. Both Captain T.H. Hines[1] and Captain L.D. Hockersmith[2] claimed they were the first to notice that the floors were dry and free of mold compared to the damp walls.[3] Hockersmith said that because he had been a brick mason before the war, his experience in that trade made him suspect that there might be an air chamber beneath the floor.[4] Hines said that he had been reading Victor Hugo's 1862 novel, *Les Miserables,* and was inspired by Jean Valjean's underground escapades. After a cursory inspection, chipping away at a peep hole, suspicions were confirmed. Further investigation revealed that the passageway was large enough to crawl through and that it led to the courtyard. To hide the small hole in his cell, Hines placed a large bag over it.

Work began on November 4. Hines reported that the tunneling was completed on November 20.[5] Hockersmith said the completion date was November 27.[6] Starting with dinner knives, they began chipping away at the six-inch-thick concrete floor. The ground in the air chamber below was hard, so a better digging tool was needed. Jake Bennett spied a rusty garden spade in the prison yard and pretended to trip over it. He secreted it into his greatcoat and smuggled it into the tunnel. Concrete beneath the other six cells was chipped away, leaving only a thin veneer to poke through at the last minute. To avoid breaking through the remaining fragile crust of concrete and to avoid having it discovered, everyone on the ground level tier requested a large wooden board, saying that the concrete was cold during the chilly November nights. A flat board fifteen inches wide and five feet long was provided to each inmate on Range 1.[7]

General Morgan offered to give anyone $50 or $100 to exchange cells with him so he could be next to No. 20, Hines' cell, the night of the escape.[8] His brother, Colonel Richard, offered to let him have cell No. 21 and the General accepted.[9] From the rear, the two Morgan brothers look very much alike in build, size and hair color.[10]

John's strong yearning to escape was driven by his desire to see his wife, Mattie, who was pregnant with their first child, due in late November.[11] His wife had been corresponding with the Federal authorities hoping to have them exchange her husband for a Union officer of equal rank, Brig. Gen. Neal Dow who was a prisoner of the Confederacy.[12] On the day of Morgan's escape, she learned that Union authorities had no interest in releasing General Morgan, whom they considered too dangerous and too important. Upon hearing this news, Mattie began to sob uncontrollably. Her friends called in a doctor who announced, " Her grief has started her labor." That same day, General Morgan learned that the military commander at the prison was being transferred the next day. Knowing this change would probably mean an inspection of their quarters by his successor, Morgan said there could be no delay. He spread the word: "Tonight!"[13]

Friday night, November 27, 1863, it had been arranged that after the midnight visit from the guard, Captain Taylor would descend into the air chamber and give the signal underneath the floor of each cell.[14] "Fortunately," Col. Duke thought, "the only man vile enough to have betrayed the plan was absent in the hospital." Sixty-odd men lay awake, silent and excited—with hearts beating louder and blood rushing faster than the approach of battle had ever occasioned. A few minutes elapsed and then at the signal, the seven sprang from their beds. They hastily stuffed flannel shirts with material prepared beforehand, and made bundles to place in their beds to represent them. Then stamping on the floor, the thin crust of concrete gave way and they crawled into the air-chamber below. Following Captain Taylor who held a candle, they passed one by one along the tunnel until they reached its terminus. With a straight-edge razor, Hockersmith took about twenty minutes to cut away the sod and emerged into the open air and inner yard.[15] He was followed by Taylor and then the others.

Because it was raining, the guard dogs had been brought inside. This allowed the escapees to cross the moonless open yard without detection. Two walls had to be scaled before they were free. The inner wall, twelve feet from the outer wall, was twenty feet high—the outer one, twenty-five feet. It took Taylor three attempts to hook the bent poker before it secured itself onto the outer wall.[16] The rope had been braided from bedsheets by Calvin Morgan.[17] Scaling the wall in the darkness, Morgan reached the top where his hand felt a peculiar cord. His shrewd guess was right. It led to an alarm bell. While two men held opposite ends, he delicately cut it.[18] Using the braided rope, they lowered themselves to the ground. Just then, the General realized that he had left his carpetsack on the other side of the wall, inside the prison. Hockersmith and Taylor both volunteered to go back and retrieve it for him. After everyone was once again safely outside the wall, they tried to dislodge the rope, but the hook held firm. They abandoned the dangling rope and ran for safety.[19] Before parting, Morgan and his men shook hands and whispered words of encouragement to each other.[20]

Besides the General, there was Jacob C. Bennett, Samuel B. Taylor (a nephew of President Zachary Taylor), Lorenzo D. Hockersmith, Ralph Sheldon, Thomas Henry Hines and Gustavus S. Magee. Magee would be killed in battle the following year in Tennessee. Except for the loner, Magee, who was headed for his home in West Virginia, the men paired off. Taylor joined Sheldon to travel to Louisville[21] where they would be recaptured on December 2, six miles from the Falls City and returned to the penitentiary. Hockersmith joined Bennett heading for Covington, Kentucky. In ill health, Bennett parted company with Hockersmith near Ashbysburg on the Green River. Hockersmith successfully rejoined the Confederate army. Hines joined Morgan.[22] The two latter pairs walked to the railroad station, a fifteen- to twenty-minute stroll, and bought tickets for the night express to Cincinnati. Fearing that he would be recognized, the General wore a pair of green spectacles, which he borrowed from one of the other prisoners.[23] Hockersmith said that the General had given him $7 for a ticket.[24] Prior to the escape, Morgan's men had bribed a guard with $15 to give them a copy of the Columbus newspaper. In it, they found the train schedule for the Little Miami, Columbus and Xenia Railroad.[25] The schedule showed that it would depart Columbus at one-twenty-five in the morning, stopping at London, Xenia, Dayton, Middletown and Hamilton, arriving at Cincinnati at seven-twenty-five.

Conductor W.H. Eckert was making up the express when two men approached him shortly after one o'clock in the morning. They wore slouch hats. He took them for drovers. One asked, "When will the Cincinnati train leave?"

"It is due to leave at one-twenty-five," Eckert replied, "but...other trains from which we make up have not arrived."

"Are you going to wait for them?"

"I am not. I shall leave just as soon as I can get my train ready."

Eckert, remembering later, thought the men seemed relieved that he would not delay the departure. They followed him down the station platform, asking numerous questions about the time the train was due in Cincinnati and what connections they could make for Louisville. Eckert noticed that one of them carried a fine gold watch. The next day, he was sure that man was Morgan.[26]

Despite Eckert's intentions, the train left Columbus ten minutes late.[27] When the train pulled out of the station, it was not crowded, but Morgan and Hines had agreed not to sit together.[28] The General chose to sit next to a

Union officer with whom he struck up a conversation.[29] Morgan was afraid that the conductor might ask for a pass, but if he appeared to be an acquaintance of the Union officer, he would not be questioned.[30] But in actuality, the conductor's only concern was that he had paid for a ticket.[31] Hines sat behind them. Hockersmith and Bennett sat near the front, pretending to sleep.[32] All were close enough to overhear Morgan's conversation with his Yankee friend. In a few minutes the train pulled out. By then, the Federal officer and the tall stranger in business clothes were quite friendly, sharing sips of peach brandy from a flask which the "Blue Coat Officer" had offered to Morgan.[33] As the train rumbled past the dark prison, the Union officer glanced at the General and then looked out the window and said, "You know, they have Morgan safe and secure in there!" Morgan wryly responded, "Let's hope that Morgan is always as safe as he is right now!"[34] Hockersmith smiled and then looked out the window as the train passed near the prison walls. He could make out the rope swinging in the breeze.[35]

Not too long thereafter, Morgan excused himself to speak to a couple of acquaintances a few seats up in the coach. In a manner totally natural and at ease, he shook hands with Hockersmith and Bennett, asked about their families, wished them a safe journey, and returned to his seat.[36] Somewhere around Xenia, the train was stopped. These were tense moments for the escapees, who thought their breakout might have been detected and the train had been stopped to conduct a search. They also feared that news of their escape had been telegraphed to railroad stations connecting to the Columbus depot. The four escapees followed the conductor into the telegraph office. Annoyingly, they clung to him, chatting, asking questions and seeing that he received no word of their escape. At Dayton, there was an obstruction on the tracks, which the alert engineer had seen. The "drovers" came forward to find out what was causing this second delay. They helped the train crew remove the obstruction from the tracks.[37]

Soon the train was rolling again and no one had boarded to search for the escapees. Before reaching Cincinnati, the Union officer got off and Morgan settled down for some sleep. Hines, Hockersmith and Bennett relaxed for the first time since they had boarded the train.[38] As they were passing through suburban areas approaching the Cincinnati depot, Morgan and Hines agreed to jump off in case troops were waiting for them in the station. Hockersmith and Bennett said they wanted to remain on board.[39] It was a cool, rainy morning. The time was about eight o'clock in the morning. Originally, the train was due at Cincinnati at twenty-five minutes past seven. But because of the Xenia and Dayton delays, the train would arrive in Cincinnati after eight o'clock.[40] About one-half mile from the depot, Morgan and Hines pulled the emergency cord, but the engineer seemed to ignore the signal. So the pair went out onto the train platform and manually applied the brakes, slowing the cars so they could jump off.[41] As they leapt off, some Union soldiers were nearby and one accosted the tall fellow in the business suit. "What in the hell do you mean by jumping off the cars here?" he demanded. Morgan answered in kind, "What in the Devil is the use of my going into town when I live out here? And besides, what business is it of yours?" He was allowed to go on his way.[42]

The railroad depot was in the western side of the city less than one mile from the river's edge. Morgan and Hines walked toward the river, avoiding busy streets and finally reached the shore across from Newport, Kentucky. Here they found a young, enterprising lad who was ferrying passengers across the Ohio River.[43] At that time, there was no bridge spanning the Ohio. The Roebling Suspension Bridge would not be built and open to the public until January 1, 1867, about three years later.[44] They ask the young man how much to take them across. He replied, "Fifty cents a passenger." Morgan gave him a dollar as he and Hines stepped in. They sat down and waited for the boy to start rowing. The lad sat motionless. "What are you waiting for?" asked Hines. The young "captain" said, "I have room for two more passengers." With that, Morgan produced another dollar and told the youth to start rowing.[45]

As they were crossing the river, the General asked, "Where does Mrs. Ludlow live?"

"Just a short distance from here," replied the youth.

"Will you show me her house?"

"Yes, sir!"

The swift current carried the small skiff downstream so it landed near the Ludlow home. The young captain pointed it out. Ludlow's servant answered the doorbell. The General wrote upon the visiting card, "General Morgan and Captain Hines, escaped." Mrs. Ludlow came to the door and warmly greeted them. Without a moment's hesitation, she ordered horses saddled for Morgan, Hines and her son who would accompany and guide them to safety.[46] She handed Morgan $60 in gold, all she had in her home. "Now go General and ride for your life," Mrs. Ludlow said as she bade him farewell.

Their next stop was at the home of Dr. William Robinson Thomas in Fort Mitchell. Mrs. Thomas cleaned and dressed Morgan's hand, which he had injured in climbing the prison wall, and laundered Hines' trousers, which had gotten muddy in the jump from the train. While the pants dried, she served them lunch. Her two daughters never forgot how Morgan smiled when they asked for a lock of his hair and how afterward he said they were a great improvement over the prison barber. Mrs. Thomas furnished them with fresh horses and had her twelve-year-old son, Will, guide them to their next stop,[47] which was at the home of Henry Corwin near Union, Kentucky. Here, on Saturday, November 28, they spent the night. Corwin's young son, W.P., noticed that the General was not wearing a coat, and that his black trousers were too thin to keep him warm. So, he gave him a pair of blue jeans, which Morgan pulled over his own. On Sunday, they were supplied with fresh steeds and young Corwin served as their guide.[48]

As the General traveled through Kentucky, care, concern and cash were offered by sympathetic men and women. Many brave women who tried to force their money on him were mortified when he refused. Men and horses were at his command as he headed south to rendezvous with his beloved Mattie. One of the horses he received as a gift upon his escape from prison was "Sir Oliver," the steed he was to ride for the remainder of his military career.

Morgan's most famous horse, "Black Bess," was presented to the General by Warren Viley[49] of Woodford County, Kentucky. His legendary mare was lost near Lebanon, Tennessee, when Col. Frank Wolford's 1st KY Union Cavalry and General Ebenezer Dumont's 800 members of the 17th Brigade of the Army of the Ohio charged into the town. Lebanon's streets were filled with 2,000 bluecoats. One hundred fifty of Morgan's cavalry were captured. Morgan, who was staying in a hotel, was caught by this surprise move. He quickly mounted Black Bess and with some of his men rode out on the Rome and Carthage Pike, pursued by Dumont's cavalry. For fifteen miles, Black Bess outdistanced the pursuers carrying Morgan to safety, once again. Arriving at the ferry on the Cumberland River, there was room in the craft for the men but not their horses. Black Bess was left standing at the water's edge on May 5, 1862. He would never see her again.

6:30am, Saturday, November 28

The morning after Morgan's escape, one penitentiary guard noticed the rope dangling from the wall. He sounded the alarm and guards went to see if the Confederate prisoners were still in their cells.[50] Those who had escaped had bunched up pillows, blankets and materials to make it appear as if someone was sleeping in their bunk. For a few minutes, the ruse worked. But when the cells were entered, the dummies were uncovered. Warden Merion was not too concerned about the prisoners' escape, "I don't give a damn if they all got away as long as we still have General Morgan." Running to the upper level to check Cell #35, Range 2, where the General was kept, a guard peered into the cell to see a figure reclining on the bunk with his face toward the wall. The guard called out, "General, are you all right?"[51] The General's brother, Richard, responded to the inquiry by lifting one leg slightly in the air as if he were too tired to talk. Later, one of the guards approached the warden and said that it would have been possible for someone to switch cells with the General. Merion told him to check it out. Col. Dick Morgan was then discovered in the General's cell.

In the air chamber used by the escapees, a note was found signed by T. Henry Hines, Capt. CSA. The address at the top of the note said, "Castle Merion, Cell No. 20. November 27, 1863. *La patience est amere, mais son friut est doux*. The French phrase translates, "Patience is bitter, but its fruit is sweet."[52]

The day after the escape, Col. Wm. Wallace, commander of the 15th OVI, issued a $1,000 reward for "the apprehension and arrest of John Morgan and a suitable reward for the apprehension and arrest of the others."[53] There was a hue and cry from Ohio citizenry that the reward was not large enough, considering the damage Morgan could do if he were allowed to remain on the loose. Remember that Morgan demanded a $1,000 ransom from each mill owner to keep his men from burning down their building. So, Secretary of War Edwin M. Stanton added $5,000 from the Federal treasury and armed the Lake Erie shore patrol if Morgan tried to escape to Canada.[54]

Back in the penitentiary cellblock on November 28, Second Lt. Thomas W. Bullitt (Co. C, 2nd KY) wrote in his diary: "Great God. Be gracious and merciful to us now. Thou has favored us. Darkness. Rain. Oh guide the steps of a beloved commander. May he be great in action and in thought. May he gleam—a bright flaming star in the clouded sky of our country. Save him from the enemies who hunt his track."[55]

After Morgan's escape, the prison authorities posted a sign above Cell #21, which read, "Cell from which Gen. John H. Morgan ESCAPED Nov. 27, 1863." For the next hundred years, Morgan's empty cell became a tourist attraction.[56]

The old penitentiary walls were torn down in 1994. The demolition company, R.S.V. Inc., under the supervision of Robert Stephen Vukelic, sold chunks of "The Great Wall of the Ohio Penitentiary" to anyone interested in owning a piece of the rock. Accompanying the stone fragment was an "Authenticity Paper" and an eight-page brochure relating the history of the pen and bios of "some interesting prisoners of the 1800s." Prominent among these stories is one that is headlined, "Morgan's Raid." The story below it says:

The most famous prisoner at the Ohio Pens history was that of General John Hunt Morgan, General, Confederate States of America. General Morgan and his raiders came up through Kentucky and then raided through southern Indiana and southern Ohio to eventually be captured in Salineville, Ohio, just short of the Pennsylvania line. Morgan and 30 of his command entered the Ohio Penitentiary on July 30, 1863.

The Ohio Pen was becoming famous for holding such a famous general who found his way well to north. But this fame would escalate soon after the discovery of the general's soon to [be] famous escape over the great walls of the Ohio Penitentiary on November 27, 1863 with 6 of his men.[57]

Throughout the South, people gave three cheers at the news of the escape. In Louisville, Coral Owens Hume was beside herself: "Hurrah, Hurrah, Hurrah! I feel like I want to be somewhere, that I can scream as loud as I can. I think I will get into the cellar and then no Yankee can hear me. Yes, Hurrah, Hurrah, Hurrah! For John Morgan and six of his men have escaped from prison."[58]

Morgan and Hines finally reached the Cumberland River, about nine miles downstream from Burkesville, where the Great Raid had started on July 2. They swam their horses across the stream and were soon in Tennessee. So far, they had managed to dodge the Federal scouts which General Boyle,[59] in Louisville, had sent looking for the escaped pair. Many times, when they heard hoof-beats and the whinny of horses, they rode off the road and hid in the woods or underbrush. On one occasion, they stopped at a cabin in the wilderness, and prepared to dismount, when a woman rushed out of the door, and waved them away. They quickly rode back into the woods, unsure of her actions. While they debated their next move, she appeared again and invited them to return to her cabin. She explained that a Federal cavalry patrol had just stopped at her home for water and had informed her that they were looking for General Morgan and Captain Hines.[60]

After a refreshing meal, they rode on into Middle Tennessee, where the people were mostly pro-Southern and where General Morgan was well known. While riding through a small village, one woman almost gave the General away. Upon seeing him, she exclaimed, "Oh, I know who that is!" But instantly aware of her indiscretion, she said no more and walked away. After a couple of days, Morgan and Hines were riding down a mountainside looking for the road to Athens, Tennessee. While the General hid in the shadow of trees, Hines went to a farmhouse to confirm the location of the road. As he returned to where Morgan was hiding, Hines saw a Federal patrol approaching. With quick presence of mind, he rode up to the patrol and shouted, "Hurry up Major or the rebels will escape! Morgan's gone down the road!"[61]

The magic name was enough to make the patrol of home guards follow Hines away from Morgan's hiding place. After a mile or two, they came to a muddy section of the road. It had been raining that day. The Major noticed that there were no hoof prints in the mud. "No one's come this way! Who are you? You're probably a damn rebel!"[62]

Hines answered quietly, "That's true sir. I'm your prisoner." One of the enraged patrol riders threw a noose around Hines' neck, begging the Major to allow him to hang the Confederate. Hines brushed the noose away and asked the Major if he could pose a question. The Major nodded his assent. Hines asked, "Suppose that was General Morgan, as you insist, and I have led you astray. Put yourself in my shoes. If you were a member of his command, wouldn't you have done just what I did?" The officer stared at Hines and pondered the question. Finally, he said, "Boys, he is right. Let him alone." With that, they took Hines as their prisoner and brought him to their camp opposite Loudon on the Tennessee River. He was placed in a log cabin, which already held five other Confederate prisoners.[63]

As the other prisoners gathered around, Hines began telling funny stories. The sentry posted at the door became intrigued with the entertaining tales. Hines chuckled and slapped his leg as if the joke's ending was almost too hilarious to repeat. When he wiped his eyes, he mumbled something. The guard leaned down to catch the words and, instead, caught Hines' knee in the pit of his stomach. Before he could recover, the Confederates were out of the door and scattered into the night, with Hines melting into the darkness. The startled home guards stumbled from their cabins and began shooting wildly. The shots went wide of their mark and the Confederate captain made good his escape.[64] Later, he would be reunited with Morgan in Richmond, Virginia.

SIXTY-SEVEN

A Hero's Welcome

After several close calls, hiding out and traveling for almost a month, Morgan arrived in Columbia, South Carolina, on December 24. He wired his wife, Mattie, in Danville, Virginia, "Just arrived. Will make no stop until I reach you." From the letters he had received from her while he was in prison, he learned that she was in Danville. He arrived there at six o'clock in the morning, Christmas Day. Despite his desire to spend the day alone with his wife, the town celebrated with a military parade in his honor at three o'clock in the afternoon. Mattie had to share her husband with the people because he was their hero. Mayor Thomas P. Atkinson hailed him as the recognized representative of southern chivalry and declared, "Your Yankee oppressors greatly erred in supposing that you were shorn of your strength when they deprived you of your hair; unlike Samson, your power lies not in the covering which God has given your head, but in the vigor which he has imparted in your right arm."[1]

It was in Danville that John first learned of the death of his daughter born the day he escaped from prison. From Christmas to New Year's, John and Mattie stayed in Danville to allow her to recover from her illness so they could travel.[2] He had been made aware that Colonel Adam Johnson had assembled remnants of Morgan's command at Decatur, Georgia.[3] General Buckner had recommended that the more than 300 men who had escaped at Reedsville should be the nucleus for organizing a new cavalry regiment with Johnson as its commander.[4] The Confederate War Department cooperated by instructing all army officers to transfer, and release any Morgan men who had enlisted in their command after the raid.[5] Hundreds more flocked to Johnson's headquarters, enough to make two battalions.[6]

But Morgan's first thoughts were not of taking over Johnson's command, rather he was more concerned about his men still suffering in the Ohio Penitentiary. He planned to go to the Confederate capital in Richmond to see if he could arrange to have his officers transferred to a military prison and then eventually exchanged.[7] He arrived in Richmond during a driving snowstorm at noon, Thursday, January 7, 1864, accompanied by Mattie.

Despite the storm, he was met by thousands of southern men and hundreds of personal friends. The *Daily Richmond Enquirer* ran a front-page story, January 9, about the "grand demonstration of the people in honor of the General." The article said, "to those assembled, the snow storm was unregarded, and the bitter cold became as pleasant as the 'sweet South wind.'"[8]

On January 8, the Richmond populace had celebrated the anniversary of Andrew Jackson's victory in the battle of New Orleans. The newspaper said, "On yesterday the people did not love Jackson less, but Morgan more." A formal reception was held at the Ballard House, where a suite of rooms was given to the General and his staff. All the streets leading to the hotel were densely packed with a mass of people, including the hotel lobby. The article continued, "The modest and gallant Morgan was seen standing in the midst of battle-worn and scarred veterans. The hero of a hundred fights, and, as our readers know, also the hero lately of one of the most remarkable escapes, from the hands of a vandal foe, recorded in modern history." [9]

Morgan's raid into the North and his subsequent escape from the Ohio Penitentiary had a positive effect on southern morale at a time when the South had little to celebrate. In early July 1863, when Morgan began his raid into the North, the South suffered two major defeats. Vicksburg fell and Robert E. Lee's force retreated from Gettysburg. The people of Richmond were singing Morgan's praises. An Italian composer, C.L. Peticolas, was caught up in the adulation and wrote the "Genl. Morgan's Grand March." It was "dedicated to the Officers and Privates of his command." It was "entered according to Act of Congress in the year 1864 by George Dunn in the Clerk's Office of the District Court of the Confederate States of America for the Eastern district of Virginia."[10] This was not the first song dedicated to John (Jack) H. Morgan. When he was but a captain, a song was published titled, "Three Cheers Jack Morgan! A Camp Song."[11]

Morgan had learned that the Union government considered him a special enemy who was to be denied the rights of a prisoner of war if he was captured again. The experience had been so traumatic for John that, after escaping, he resolved never be taken prisoner again. Northern officials were outraged at the breakout, while Southerners hailed it as proof that Morgan could always outwit the Yankees. Through the excitement, and romance of the escape, Morgan became a greater hero than ever.[12]

The Confederacy wasn't alone in writing songs about John Hunt Morgan. In Union-held Nashville, a comic song, "How Are You? John Morgan," was published by C.D. Benson. The sheet music cover says that it is a sequel to "Here's Your Mule."[13] In 1863, in Cleveland, Ohio, another less-reverent song was published, "How Are You, Telegraph?" The lyrics are:

John Morgan paid us a visit, you know;
All booted and spurr'd was he;
With a jolly good gang, four thousand or so,
And cannon numbering three.
He made it his boast, he could gallop straight thro'
What a roystering blade was he!
Buckeyes and Hoosiers, with all of his crew,
Till he heard the bugles of Lee.

Compare the Confederate pride to then Colonel Jimmy Doolittle's April 1942 raid in World War II. While Doolittle's thirty seconds over Tokyo and other Japanese cities did little damage to the Japanese war machine, it gave a great lift to U.S. morale early in the war. In WWII, the Japanese were winning all the battles in the first seven months of the conflict. There was pessimism and sorrow with each allied defeat. Doolittle's daring raid of sixteen B-25 bombers on April 18, showed that the Japanese were not invincible. Like Morgan, Colonel Doolittle was out of action for about four months after the raid because he had to land in China. His bombers' range was too limited to allow him to return to his American aircraft carrier in the western Pacific. He did return to active duty in September 1942, organizing the 12th Air Force.[14]

In the Civil War, the Confederacy had their share of victories in the first 25 months of the war. But as the tide turned in the Union's favor, doom and gloom began to engulf the South. Morgan's raid showed that the North was vulnerable and that the South could still inflict the horror of war on the Yankees' home front. While the raid ended in defeat, it gave encouragement and made folk heroes of Morgan and his men.

On January 1, 1864, John Hunt Morgan issued a proclamation calling for the men of his command to reassemble in Decatur, Georgia. Seeking 1,000 recruits, he received more than 14,000 responses from men in every branch of the service.[15] The fortunes of the Confederacy being in decline, he was unable to provide 800 of these recruits with horses. On his raid into Kentucky in June, the 800 had to walk until a raid at Lexington brought in enough thoroughbreds for every man. This was the first time Morgan's cavalry had to move on foot.[16]

SIXTY-EIGHT

End of the Glory Road

General Morgan raided into Kentucky again in June 1864, but some of his men now began pillaging nonmilitary establishments in eastern Kentucky, robbing the Farmer's Bank of Kentucky in Mt. Sterling.[1] Unwilling, perhaps unable, to restore discipline and now suffering heavier losses than before in a June 12 debacle at Cynthiana, he began to be thought of as less value to the Confederacy.[2] General Bragg, angry at Morgan for crossing the Ohio River, had resigned as commander of the Army of Tennessee on Nov. 29, 1863, being replaced by Gen. Joseph E. Johnston.[3] Jefferson Davis then made Bragg a military advisor.[4] In that position, he helped initiate an investigation to get Morgan relieved of his command, based partly on the Mt. Sterling bank robbery. Some of Morgan's own officers went over the General's head and contacted James A. Seddon, the Confederate Secretary of War, requesting that General Morgan and some of his officers and men be investigated concerning the Mt. Sterling bank robbery. Seddon suspended Morgan as commander of the Department of Southwestern Virginia, a post he had been given after his escape from Ohio.[5] Scouts brought warnings of a Union column moving toward Bulls Gap on the department's defense line to the southwest. Brigadier-General John C. Echols was named to replace Morgan and was due to arrive in Abington, Virginia, to take over command. But Morgan immediately ordered the troops to march into East Tennessee.[6]

Just hours before Morgan was to lead his troops to Tennessee, Basil Duke arrived in Abington. He had been unexpectedly exchanged at Charleston, South Carolina. Duke was shocked by Morgan's appearance. "When I met him for the first time since he had made his escape, he was greatly changed. His face wore a weary, care-worn expression, and his manner was totally destitute of its former ardor and enthusiasm. He spoke bitterly, but with no impatience, of the clamor against him, and seemed saddest about the condition of his command."[7]

A court of inquiry to investigate Morgan's actions at Mt. Sterling was due to convene August 30. But a day or two earlier, Morgan marched out of Abington hoping to engage and defeat the Union force at Bulls Gap. Such a victory, Morgan felt, would once more make him a hero and make it difficult, if not impossible, for his detractors to prosecute him. He rendezvoused

368

with his troops at Johnson City, thirty-five miles northeast of Greeneville, and marched down the valley with 1,600 men and two pieces of artillery. A few miles southwest of Johnson City, at Jonesboro, he telegraphed Mattie on Friday, September 2: "Arrived here at one o'clock. Command has been moved forward." He left Jonesboro that afternoon and rode all night.[8]

His force was composed of Col. Henry Giltner's 4th KY Cavalry, Col. William Bradford's regiment from John C. Vaughn's old Tennessee brigade, and Col. Howard Smith's battalions.[9] Capt. James E. Cantrill, in command of the 2nd battalion, had been forced out of Greene County by Gillem's Union force. He took the advance because he was familiar with the roads. On Saturday morning, several miles from Greeneville, Morgan sent a courier to Cantrill, directing him to halt. The message was that the General and his staff would lead the column. The thought of General Morgan riding the point through hills harboring bushwhackers astounded Cantrill. He sent a lieutenant to warn the General that they had been fired on in this area a few days before. Morgan thanked Cantrill for the information but said he did not apprehend any danger. Morgan had been in Greeneville on several occasions and felt at home in this part of Tennessee. When he rode through the column to the advance position, a cheer went up. It would be the last ovation Morgan's men would give their beloved chief.[10]

In a cold and overcast sky, at four o'clock in the afternoon, Saturday, September 3, 1864, Morgan rode into Greeneville, Tennessee, with 1,600 men. Robert Mason and James D. McGaughey were sitting and chatting on the wooden piazza (porches) of the Mason hotel. They looked up and saw a column of Confederate cavalry halt in front of them. General Morgan could be seen at the head of the column riding his large sorrel horse, "Sir Oliver."[11] Bob Mason thought it best to disappear, so he got up and went into his father's hotel. McGaughey concluded that it would be prudent to vanish as well. Without attracting attention, he meandered down Depot Street and up Irish, retreating into the sanctuary of his father's home at the southwest corner of Irish and Summer streets. Later, he could see a long column of Confederate cavalry continue down the Knoxville road and another body of men going over the long hill on the west side of town along the Rogersville road. As night fell, a light rain increased into a violent storm with frequent bursts of thunder and lightning.[12]

By then, General Morgan had set up headquarters in the home of the late Dr. Alexander Williams. His hostess was the doctor's widow, Mrs. Catherine Williams, mother-in-law of Lucy Williams. Catherine was a distant relative of Morgan's wife, Mattie. The house and grounds occupied the block bounded by Main, Church, Irish and Depot streets. Greeneville had a large number of residents who favored preserving the Union. Perhaps the best known of this persuasion was Greeneville resident Andrew Johnson, who would succeed Lincoln after the April 14, 1865 assassination to become the Seventeenth President of the United States.[13]

There are several versions of how Union forces discovered that General Morgan was sleeping in Greeneville. The first is from a young boy. The second and third involve women.

Version #1: When a Morgan scout, James M. Fry, seized twelve-year-old James Leahy's horse and a bag of meal, Leahy was angered at this treatment. While Fry and his comrades ate supper, the boy led his mare through a cornfield and got away. Young Leahy had been befriended earlier by Union soldiers in the area. He determined to let his Yankee friends know that Morgan's men had occupied Greeneville. He rode to nearby Bulls Gap to the Federal camp to alert the Union troops. At eighty-thirty in the evening, the lad was brought by the picket guard to the quarters of Col. John K. Miller, commanding the 13th TN Cavalry. He told the Union colonel that he lived in Greeneville and had been sent to the mill to have some corn ground. He was returning with the bag of meal when some of Morgan's men seized his meal. At the first opportune chance, he left them and had come directly to the Union camp. His story was simple and straightforward. He could not be moved or changed from what he said. Col. Miller then took the boy at once to Brigadier-General Alvan C. Gillem's headquarters where the lad was again closely questioned. Once Gillem, a native of Middle Tennessee and a West Point graduate, was convinced of the boy's story, Miller sought approval to advance and attack Morgan without delay.[14]

That same evening, Lucy Williams' father, Jacob Rumbough, came to the Williams' mansion to warn Morgan that he should not sleep in the home away from his command who were bivouacked some distance away in a field.[15] It was the same warning that Catherine Williams had given the General.[16] General Morgan did not believe that Federal troops were close enough to present a danger to him or his men. He was not aware that they were in Bulls Gap. Morgan, as a Southern aristocrat, preferred a feather bed to an army cot or the ground. He enjoyed dining in the company of aristocratic women in a comfortable dining room with tablecloth and napkins.[17] Because they were available, he opted to enjoy these advantages of command while most of his men slept on the outskirts of town. General Morgan's penchant for comfort was an invitation to death.

At midnight, in a driving rain, two Union columns set out from Bulls Gap. The first group was led by Lt. Col. William H. Ingerton who had been put in charge of Col. Miller's own regiment, the 13th TN cavalry (USA).

They headed for Greeneville with 500 men. A second body of 600 men followed an hour later led by Gen. Gillem.[18]

As Ingerton neared Greeneville, a farmer was seen running from his house and making for the woods. He was ordered to stop or he would be shot. He threw up his hands and on finding himself among Federal soldiers declared that he was a Union man running from what he supposed to be a rebel conscripting squad. From him, they obtained information that Morgan had his headquarters at Mrs. Williams' house. Further on, a cabin was reached. The female occupant, a black, told that she came from Greeneville about dark, and General Morgan was stopping at Mrs. Williams'. This confirmed the information already gained.[19]

Ingerton's Union cavalry had slipped around the flank of Col. W.E. Bradford, the commander of one of Morgan's three detachments camped in the field. Capt. Christopher C. Wilcox, under Ingerton's orders to "Bring Morgan out dead or alive," took two companies at daybreak on Sunday, September 4, 1864, and slipped into town. Wilcox's people charged into town in columns of four. Near the Williams house they divided. Twenty-five men went up Main Street, another squad up Irish Street behind the house and a third toward the Williams stables on Depot Street. Wilcox's men yelled and fired at the drowsing picket guards, who were caught by surprise. Most of the Confederate troops were camped outside of the town. As Wilcox and Co. G surrounded the house, Captain Samuel E. Northington and his Co. E seized the Williams stables.[20]

Morgan was awakened by the shouts and gunfire. He looked out the window and saw Union troops heading for the Williams home. He pulled on his socks, jumped into bedroom slippers, hastily dressed in pants and a shirt and threw his pistols over his shoulders. With two of his men, he ran down the stairs past Mrs. Williams. Major William D. Williams yelled to Morgan,[21] "For God's sake, General, get out of here, the town is full of Yankees!"

"Where are they?" Morgan asked urgently.

"Everywhere," said Mrs. Williams.

"The Yankees will never take me prisoner again," Morgan remarked as he darted for the back door. Then he paused, gave his hostess a military salute, and said with a smile,

"Goodbye Mrs. Williams, I am all right now."[22]

Tossing aside his gun belt and holsters, he grasped a Colt revolver in each hand and dashed with two others through the door into a garden where they tried to hide themselves among the bushes and vines. For a short while, Morgan and some of his officers sought refuge beneath Saint James Episcopal Church, located off the property's southern corner. It was a small framed building perched atop three-foot-high brick pillars. But as Union soldiers broke into the church's front door, Morgan moved back into the Williams' garden to hide among the gooseberry bushes and vines.[23]

Seeing a soldier wearing a brown jeans jacket ride up to the white picket fence surrounding the garden, Morgan and his men assumed he was a Confederate coming to their rescue. They stepped out, but were surprised when he demanded their surrender.[24]

At that moment Captain Wilcox and several others rode up. The two men with Morgan, Confederate Captain James T. Rogers and staff clerk, L. Claude Johnson, threw up their hands and walked toward Wilcox. Morgan turned to escape. Earlier, they had tried to persuade Morgan to give up, but he had said, "The Yankees will never take me prisoner again." He did not want to be separated from his wife, whom he knew to be pregnant again with another child. In a letter to Mattie, written April 1863, he said, "Darling I love you more than life."[25]

The soldier in the brown jacket was Pvt. Andrew J. Campbell of Co. G, 13th TN (Union) Cavalry. He ordered Morgan to halt, but instead of obeying, the General broke into a run. Morgan had two pistols and was reported to have attempted to fire them at Campbell.[26] After repeating the order twice to stop and surrender, the private raised his gun, aimed and shot. Campbell later said he had no idea who the person was that he had shot.[27] Neither did Wilcox. Morgan exclaimed, "O God!" and fell forward into the vines. The bullet had entered his back, just to the inside of the left shoulder blade, and passed through his heart and out through his left breast. By the time the Union soldiers reached him, he had ceased to breathe and the blood was gushing from the heart. He had on a pair of blue Federal cavalry pants and a dotted muslin shirt, no coat or vest, and was without a hat.[28] Nobody knew who had been killed.

Captain Wilcox came up and directed that one of the captured Confederate officers be brought up in order to identify the body. Captain Henry B. Clay (a grandson of Henry Clay), dropped to his knees beside Morgan, crying, "You have just killed the best man in the Confederacy." Wilcox demanded, "Who is it?" Clay answered sadly, "It is General Morgan."[29]

"My orders were to take him out, dead or alive. And as he is dead, I have no other way to take him," said Capt. Wilcox.[30] The General's body was placed on Private Campbell's horse, taken through the town, and toward Gillem's lines. When Pvt. Campbell brought Morgan's body to Gillem, he was congratulated but received a reprimand for the treatment of the General's body. Gillem had the body laid on a saddle blanket under a tree until the skirmishing ceased. It was then placed on an artillery caisson and escorted to the Williams' house and laid on Lucy's bed. She, together with several of Williams servants and the assistance of two captured Confederate officers, Major C. Albert Withers and Captain Rogers, helped to clean the body and dressed it in a clean shirt, uniform and ceremonial sword.[31]

Version #2: This version of how General Morgan was discovered in Greeneville was revealed in the diary of Sarah Elizabeth Thompson in the archival collection of the Duke University Library. In 1854, Sarah married Sylvanius H. Thompson and had two daughters, Lilly and Harriet. Sylvanius later became a private in the 1st TN Cavalry (USA). He was primarily a recruiter for the Union army. Sarah worked alongside her husband, assembling and organizing Union sympathizers in the predominant Confederate area around Greeneville. In early 1864, Sylvanius was ambushed and killed by a Confederate soldier as he returned from a courier mission to Union troops in Kentucky. Spurred by her husband's death, Sarah continued her work for the Union, delivering dispatches and ascertaining information for Union officers.[32]

Not only was Sarah angry about her husband's death, she also had a personal grudge against General Morgan and his men. On an earlier visit to Greeneville, Morgan and his officers had stayed at the Williams' home across the street from Sarah's home. On one occasion, the General and some of his men paid an uninvited visit to Sarah after her husband's death. They knew of her loyalty to the Union and that she was a widow. While they sat in her kitchen helping themselves to her food, Morgan had said, "You would make some Rebel a good wife, if you were as good a Rebel as a damn Union woman."[33]

When Morgan returned that fateful weekend in September, she saw his arrival at the Williams home through her window. That evening, Sarah managed to slip away in the darkness of the heavy rainstorm. She was a good rider, having often served as a courier for Union dispatches. She rode to Bulls Gap and alerted the Union forces to Morgan's whereabouts.

She returned to Greeneville with the Federal soldiers and reentered her home and watched the events unfold. From her window, she saw Morgan hiding among the vines. She shouted to the Union soldiers, "There he is! There he is!" as she pointed to the small group of Confederates hiding in the Williams' garden. It is said that she hailed Andrew Campbell and declared, "Sir, if you tear the fence down, I assure you, you will find Morgan."[34]

After Morgan was killed and his men captured, the Federal troops spirited Sarah and her children away from Greeneville for fear of retribution and housed them temporarily in Ohio for safety. Later, she would move to Washington, DC, where she was given a job with the post office. That was followed by a government pension. After her death, she was buried in Arlington Cemetery with full military honors, one of the few women to be accorded this exalted distinction. It is believed that this final act was in recognition of her service to the Union for helping to end General Morgan's military career.[35]

Version #3: This version attributes the betrayal of Morgan's whereabouts to Lucy Williams, daughter-in-law of Catherine Williams, owner of the mansion where Morgan was sleeping. Lucy was married to Joseph A. Williams,[36] a Union officer, and had quarreled with Morgan on the General's earlier visit to Greeneville over the arrest of a paroled Union soldier whom Morgan suspected of being a spy.[37] She denied betraying Morgan, but was hounded out of town, driving her into exile in faraway Texas.[38] The Williams family was representative of many in the South where brother fought brother. While Joseph Williams espoused the Union cause, his two brothers, William Dickson Williams and Thomas Lanier Williams, were in the Confederate army. In fact, Major W.D. Williams was on Morgan's staff.[39] The following dispatch carried the sorrowful message to Morgan's wife:[40]

Headquarters Brigade near Rheatown, Tenn.
September 4, 1864

Mrs. General Morgan, Abingdon, Va:

With deep sorrow I have to announce the sad intelligence of your husband's death. He fell by the hands of the enemy, at Greeneville, this morning. His remains are being brought under flag of truce. We all mourn with you this great affliction.

Most respectfully,

H.L. Giltner
Colonel Commanding Brigade.

Later, Mattie confided in a letter to a relative, "My poor husband gambled on life and he lost."[41] John Hunt Morgan was buried first in an aboveground vault at Sinking Springs Cemetery in Abingdon, Virginia, then removed by train to Richmond, Virginia, where he was given a state funeral. In the Confederate House of Representatives, his body was draped with a Confederate flag. He was temporarily placed in a vault in Hollywood Cemetery in Richmond.[42]

In April 1868, Morgan's body was brought from Virginia to Lexington, Kentucky, for burial in the Morgan family plot in the Lexington Cemetery on West Main Street. Also buried in the same cemetery is Henry Clay and Adolph Rupp.[43] A Louisville citizen published a poem lauding Morgan and forecasting his immortality:[44]

Although no marble column rise,
    Above the hero's bed,
To mark the spot where Morgan lies,
    Among the honored dead;
Although no sculptured stone shall tell,
    The stranger passing by
The mournful story how he fell,
    His name will never die;
For glory with a jealous care,
    Shall guard the hero resting there.

After Morgan's death, Basil Duke took command of Morgan's brigade, now reduced to 273 men armed with scarcely fifty serviceable guns. The variety of calibers made it almost impossible to keep a supply of ammunition.[45] On September 15, Duke was made a Brigadier-General.[46] His command swelled in number and he led them in actions at Jonesboro, Greeneville, Carter's Station, Saltville and Wytheville. In the middle of October, Duke took two hundred men to Floyd and Franklin counties, where deserters from various Confederate Virginia armies had congregated and organized what they called the "new State." They had elected a provisional Governor and Lieutenant Governor. This group was causing terrible outrages to the citizens of Virginia. Duke broke up the gang and some two hundred surrendered.[47]

During this period when Duke was their leader, Morgan's men sang this song to the tune of "Blue Bonnets Are Over the Border."

Kentucky's banner spreads
Its folds above our heads;
We are already famous in story.
Mount and make ready then,
Brave Duke and all his men;
Fight for our homes and Kentucky's old glory.

Chorus –
March! March! Brave Duke and all his men!
Haste, brave boys, now quickly march forward in order!
March! March! Ye men of old Kentucky!
The horrid blue coats are over the border.

Morgan's men have great fame,
There is much in a name;
Ours must shine today as it ever has shone!
As it shines o'er our dead,
Who for freedom have bled;
The foe for their deaths have now got to atone.

When the Confederacy's capital, Richmond, fell, Jefferson Davis refused to give up, even after the surrenders of General Lee's and Johnston's armies. He was determined to keep the struggle alive.[48] Duke's force of 600 men, one of five brigades totaling 4,166 cavalrymen,[49] met Davis at Charlotte and accompanied him on his flight from the capital as part of the President's military escort.[50] As they were passing through South Carolina, the first state to secede from the Union, an old lady scolded some of Duke's troopers for pilfering forage from her barn. She called them "A gang of thieving, rascally Kentuckians, afraid to go home, while our boys are surrendering decently." One of the men replied, "Madam, South Carolina had a good deal to say about getting up this war, but we Kentuckians have contracted to close it out."[51] On May 4, near the Dionysius Chenault plantation in Georgia, just across the Savannah River from Vienna, SC, Morgan's men were paid with a portion of the gold brought from Richmond. Each man got from $26 to $32.[52] Federal troops were not paid much more than these loyal Confederate troopers. For example, Corporal Clement K.H. Cochran, who chased General Morgan across Ohio as part of General Hobson's Union force in Co. M, 8th KY Cavalry, received $55.21 when he was mustered out at Lebanon, Kentucky, on September 17, 1863. He had furnished his own horse, saddle and bridle.

On May 8 at Woodland, Georgia, Secretary of War John C. Breckinridge, under whom Duke had served, advised the remaining Morgan men to return to their hometowns. "I will not have one of these young men to encounter one hazard more for my sake."[53] With that order, the last fighting organization of "Morgan's men" was disbanded. President Davis continued his escape until his capture May 10, 1865, at Irwinville, Georgia.[54]

It was Basil Duke, the last leader of Morgan's men, who most eloquently expressed the unspoken emotions of his men as they drifted home to Kentucky, Tennessee and as far away as Texas, "There was no humiliation for these men. They had done their part and served faithfully, until there was no longer a cause and a country to serve. They knew not what their fate would be, and indulged in no speculation regarding it. They had been taught fortitude by the past, and, without useless repining and unmanly fear, they faced the future."[55]

Epliogue:
Morgan's Legacy and Legend

The effects of Morgan's raid were summarized by Col. J.E. McGowan on General Judah's staff:

> He [Morgan] destroyed no supplies; hardly touched, let alone injured, our lines of communication; captured nothing of any moment to him or anybody, save some forage, food, a miscellaneous collection of merchandise, and a comical wagon train. But he delayed the invasion of East Tennessee three months. He thus broke the plan of co-operation, and delayed Rosecrans at Murfreesboro, giving Bragg time to get back the men he had loaned Johnston. Rosecrans was so late in pressing his enemy into decisive action that the enemy had time to obtain reinforcements from Lee [Gen. Longstreet] and Chattanooga. Had Morgan been readily beaten back from Kentucky in a crippled condition, Burnside would have met Rosecrans at Chattanooga by the 20th of July; the battle at Chickamauga would not have been fought; and the war might have ended sooner.

In his book, *History of Morgan's Cavalry,* Col. Basil W. Duke wrote, "The objects of the raid were accomplished. General Bragg's retreat was unmolested by any flanking forces of the enemy, and I think that military men, who will review all the facts, will pronounce that this expedition delayed for weeks the fall of East Tennessee, and prevented the timely reinforcement of Rosecrans by troops that would otherwise have participated in the battle of Chickamauga."

Ohio and Indiana can well be grateful to John Hunt Morgan. He left behind some of the best thoroughbred stock, jaded though they were. Had it not been for the audacity of that colorful Confederate cavalry commander, the Hoosier and Buckeye states would have no Civil War battlefields to commemorate (Corydon and Buffington Island), Columbiana County (Ohio) would not have the honor of being the high-water mark of the Confederacy's penetration into the North, the Ohio Penitentiary in Columbus would have been denied one of its great mysteries and tourist attractions, and countless present-day Ohioans and Hoosiers would have been deprived of the opportunity to boast of ancestral beds occupied by Morgan. In my research, I found more people who claimed he ate in their home, held their children, and slept in their beds in the two and a half weeks he was in Indiana and Ohio than all the homes George Washington was supposed to have slept in during the entire American Revolution. More than 6,570 Ohioans and Hoosiers went on record as having Morgan pay them a house call.

Appendix

Battles & Skirmishes of the Kentucky, Indiana & Ohio Raid (July 1863)

Military actions fought by General John Hunt Morgan's Confederate cavalry division and the Union forces that opposed him were:

<u>KENTUCKY</u>
1863

July 2: **Cumberland River**—Skirmish with 3rd, 8th and 9th KY Cavalry; 12th KY Infantry; 65th IN Battery.

Columbia (Adair Co.)— 1st KY Cavalry; 2nd and 45th OVI. Confederates captured town.

July 4: **Green River Bridge** (Taylor Co.)— 25th MI Infantry under Col. Orlando Moore successfully defended bridge. Many Confederate officers and men killed and wounded.

July 5: **Lebanon** (Marion Co.)— For seven hours the 12th KY, outnumbered seven to one, held off Morgan's attack. Before the Union defenders under Lt. Col. Charles Hanson surrendered, the General's young brother, Tom, was killed.

July 6: **Bardstown** (Nelson Co.)— After holding out overnight, a detachment of 4th U.S. Cavalry surrendered to Morgan.

July 7: **Bardstown Junction** (Bullitt Co.)— Morgan captured train.

July 8: **Brandenburg** (Meade Co.)—Mauckport Rifles, Crawford County Artillery and Indiana Legion have brief artillery duel with Morgan's Parrotts and withdrew to defensive positions south of Corydon. The Federal gunboat *Springfield* made an unsuccessful attempt to halt crossing of Morgan's men from Kentucky into Indiana.

Twelve Mile Island (Jefferson Co.)— Gunboats *Springfield* and *Victory* have better luck stopping many of Captain Davis' diversionary group from successfully crossing into Indiana.

INDIANA

July 9:   **Corydon** (Harrison Co.)—6th Regiment, Indiana Legion: Ellsworth Rifles; Harrison Guards; Scott Guards; Lawson Grey Rifles; Spencer Guards; Harrison Mounted Hoosiers and Citizens. 450 home guards faced 2,200 Confederates.

Palmyra (Washington Co.)—350 militia fled as Morgan approached.

July 10:   **Salem** (Washington Co.)—Home guard surrendered town without a fight.

July 11:   **Vernon** (Jennings Co.)—61st MI Infantry under General Love refused to surrender. Morgan bluffs with a threat of attack while skirting the town to go on to Dupont.

July 12:   **Versailles** (Ripley Co.)—Several hundred militia surprised by the 6th KY.

Osgood (Ripley Co.)—Local militia captured and paroled by Morgan.

Hardintown (Dearborn Co.)—104th and 105th IN Volunteers mistook each other for Morgan's men in the dark and fired at each other. Six men were killed and seventeen wounded before they realized their mistake.

OHIO

July 14:   **Camp Dennison** (Hamilton Co.)—More than 600 convalescents commanded by Lt. Col. George Washington Neff. No fatalities. Camp successfully defended.

Miamisville Bridge on the Little Miami River (Hamilton Co.)— Skirmish with convalescents commanded by Capt. Procter (18th U.S. Regular Infantry) and Ohio militia commanded by Lt. Smith (21st OH Battery) who successfully defended bridge and repulsed Morgan. One convalescent, Henry Meyer, killed.

Train Derailment, Little Miami Railroad (Clermont Co.)—Train destroyed. Two fatalities: Cornelius Conway, train fireman and one raider mortally wounded in skirmish with Loveland scouts commanded by Lt. Paxton and Capt. Williamson.

Near **Goshen** (Clermont Co.)—Tod Scouts attack Morgan's rear guard.

July 17:   **Berlin Crossroads** (Jackson Co.)—Ohio militia under Col. Ben P. Runkle.

Centerville (Gallia Co.)—Skirmish with 9th MI Cavalry.

Near **Hamden** (Vinton Co.)—Skirmish with Ohio militia.

July 18:   **Langsville** (Meigs Co.)—Skirmish with citizens who burned their own bridge.

Near **Pomeroy** (Meigs Co.)—Skirmish with 23rd OVI; 13th WVA, Middleport-Pomeroy-Marietta militia; 3rd Division, 8th Army Corps commanded by General E. Parker Scammon.

July 19:   **Battle at Buffington Island/Portland** (Meigs Co.) —

Hobson's force: 1st, 5th, 8th, 9th and 12th KY cavalry; 2nd and 7th OH Cavalry; 7th, 8th and 9th MI Cavalry; 11th MI Battery and 2nd Tennessee (Federal) Mounted Infantry.

Judah's force: 11th OH Cavalry; 5th IN Cavalry; 11th KY Cavalry; 23rd MI Infantry; 14th IL Cavalry; 107th IL Mounted Infantry, Henshaw's (Illinois) Independent Light Artillery; Ohio militia and two Federal gunboats. In this battle, the Confederates faced four to one odds in the Union's favor.

July 20:   **Hockingport** (Athens Co.)—Skirmish with 23rd OVI.

Coal Hill near Cheshire (Gallia Co.)—Skirmish with 45th OVI.

Cheshire (Gallia Co.)—Skirmish with 1st KY Cavalry; 65th IN infantry.

Ewington (Gallia Co.)—Morgan captured First Scioto Militia, under Lt. Col. Sontag, without a shot fired.

July 22:   **Eagleport** (Morgan Co.) and **Rokeby** (Muskingum Co.)—Skirmish with 86th OVI; 19th OH Battery.

July 23:   **Cumberland** (Muskingum Co.)—Skirmish with 86th OVI under Lt. Col. R.W. McFarland.

July 24:   **Old Washington** (Guernsey Co.)— Skirmish with 1st, 3rd, 8th, 9th and 12th KY Cavalry; 45th OVI; 14th IL Cav. under the command of General Shackelford. Ohio militia under Capt. James Laughlin.

   Harrisville, east of New Athens (Harrison Co.) – Confronted by Ohio militia under General Bostwick and fired upon by Shackelford's artillery.

July 25:   **Smithfield** (Jefferson Co.)—Home Guard captured when surprised by Morgan.

   Near **Steubenville** (Jefferson Co.)—Skirmish with 44th PA militia.

   Wintersville (Jefferson Co.)—Skirmish with Steubenville militia under Captain Prentiss.

   Two Ridges (Jefferson Co.)—Skirmish with Shackelford's forces: 1st KY Cavalry, 9th MI Cavlry, 11th MI Battery, 86th OH Mounted Infantry, 14th IL Cavalry and 2nd TN Mounted Infantry.

   East Springfield (Jefferson Co.)—Skirmish with citizens.

July 26:   **Monroeville** (Jefferson Co.)—Skirmish with 9th MI Cavalry under Major W.B. Way.

   Salineville (Columbiana Co.)—Skirmishes with 9th MI Cavalry; 54th PA Infantry under Col. Thomas F. Gallagher; 1st KY Cavalry, 86th OH Mounted Infantry, 9th and 14th IL Cav. under Shackelford; Steubenville militia under Col. James Collier.

   Near **Mechanicstown** (Carroll Co.)—Skirmishes with forces led by General Shackelford.

   Gavers (Columbiana Co.)—Lisbon militia encountered Morgan who promised not to destroy property or harm anyone else in Ohio if they accompanied him to the river and allowed his men to leave the state peacefully. After a few miles, Morgan "surrendered" on his own terms to Capt. James Burbick of the Lisbon Militia.

July 26:   Near **West Point** south of New Lisbon (Columbiana Co.)—Confrontation with elements of the 1st, 9th, 11th and 12th KY; 8th MI Cavalry; 15th IN Independent Battery of Light Artillery. Final and unconditional surrender first to Major George W. Rue, then to General James M. Shackelford.

Ohio & Indiana Raid Claims

As the raiders had traversed Ohio stealing horses, burning mills, breaking into homes and taking personal property, the people of the Buckeye State started complaining that the state was not giving them adequate protection. The fact was that most of Ohio's able-bodied men were down south, at Vicksburg or a dozen other Dixie battlefields fighting under Grant, Rosecrans and other Union commanders. The state was left exposed, with only young boys, old men or a few men home on furlough to protect its citizens. Governor Tod sympathized with the hue and cry that was directed to his office in Columbus. Members of the Ohio militia and their military committee members began asking, "Who's going to pay us for fighting Morgan?" As early as July 18, a week before the raid was over, Governor Tod began asking people to report their damages and militia services to him for possible compensation.

To the military committees of Ohio counties invaded by Morgan, the governor sent telegrams:

> **Gentlemen: It is important to the State, as well as to the individual sufferers, that I be advised at as early a day as practical, of the extent of the injuries committed by Morgan and those under his command in their raid through the State.**

Once word got out of the governor's concern, the number of claims grew substantially. Governor Tod realized that this was going to be a monumental task, so he appointed a commission to handle the flood of claims that were being made. Only Ohio and Indiana offered compensation "for property taken, destroyed or injured by the Rebel forces, during the Morgan Raid in 1863." Kentucky, being a "border state" and whose citizenry reflected strong sympathies for both sides, never addressed the issue of damages caused by Morgan's many raids into that state. Ohio and Indiana also offered to include similar losses sustained from Union forces pursuing Morgan.

In an act of the Ohio Legislature, passed March 30, 1864, a board of commissioners was appointed to examine and pass upon claims for damages to property during the Morgan raid of 1863. Messrs. Albert McVeigh, George W. Barker and Henry S. Babbitt were appointed the commissioners and revisited the route of the raid. At various points along the route, they conducted public meetings to hear claims from the local citizens. They classified them into "Damages done by (1) the Rebels, (2) by United States troops and (3) by State Militia," respectively.

In all, there were 4,375 claims made by Ohioans in twenty-five counties totaling $576,225 (an average of $131.71 per claim); $428,168 in damages by Confederate troops; $148,057 by Union troops. The State of Ohio paid their state militia $212,319.

Three years after Ohio took action to compensate its citizens, Indiana began to study similar legislation. The Indiana Senate, House of Representatives and the governor approved the legislation in March 1867. The governor appointed John I. Morrison, Smith Vawter and John McCrea. Gen. Thomas M. Brown served as their attorney. On April 4, 1867, the three-man Hoosier commission had its first meeting. In *Report of Morgan Raid Commissioners to the Governor, December 31, 1867,* it is noted that a total of $413,599 (an average of $187.91 per claim) covering 2,201 claims was allowed by the commission. Claims came from nine Indiana counties.

Morgan's Men Reunite

The first reunion of Morgan's men was held April 17, 1868, at the Phoenix Hotel on the evening of his reburial in Lexington. The men pledged fidelity and affection for each other for as long as they lived and resolved "that the memory of our illustrious and beloved leader shall ever be as indelibly stamped upon the tablets of our hearts as his name is written on the undying page of History." Morgan's men met annually through 1883.

An association of the descendants of the men who rode with Gen. John Hunt Morgan, CSA, was formed. Gen. Basil W. Duke served as president of the Morgan's Men Association from its formation until his death in 1916. Others who have served as leaders were Kentucky Governor James B. McCreary, Kentucky Lt. Governor James E. Cantrill, Dr. John A. Lewis of Georgetown College, Col. D. Howard Smith and Kentucky state auditor, M.C. Saufley. Col. W.C.P. Breckenridge, responding to a standing ovation, asked the audience to remember him "simply as one of Morgan's Men."

Morgan's Daughter Appears at Reunion

The most memorable of all was the camp (reunion) in Lexington in 1883 on the twentieth anniversary of the Great Raid. For three days (July 24-26) 300 delegates met in Woodland Park. They had a band, and from the state arsenal they requisitioned two cannon to fire salutes at sunrise and sunset. On Friday, July 24, at 2:00pm, a crowd of more than 1,200 veterans and friends attended a grand ceremony and heard speeches by Duke, William

Preston, and former Governor James B. McCreary. The center of attention, however, was Morgan's only child, eighteen-year-old daughter, Johnnie.

A reporter wrote, "She is a very beautiful girl, sprightly and accomplished." Morgan's men gave her a gold watch and at the public ceremony, when McCreary asked if she had anything to say, she whispered, "Governor, just tell them I love them, and how glad I am to see them." He asked her if she would enjoy shaking hands with the men, and with tears in her eyes, she exclaimed, "Indeed I would."

Morgan's Men Association Continues Today

Today, the association has several hundred members including direct descendants, associate members and honorary members. It is historical and benevolent, a nonpolitical and nonsectarian organization. Inscribed at the base of the statue of Morgan astride a horse, on Courthouse Square in downtown Lexington, is "Gen. John Hunt Morgan and His Men." The two are inseparable.

The Morgan's Men Association has two types of membership. Regular Membership is open to all members of the family of Luther Morgan, the grandfather of Gen. John Hunt Morgan, and to all descendants, both direct and collateral, of those who served honorably in the Confederate Army in the command of Gen. Morgan. Associate Membership is extended to all persons who are interested in maintaining Gen. Morgan's honored place in our nation's history. A special invitation is made to the descendants of the Union soldiers who fought against Morgan's men. Just as the Union opponents were proud of their adversary role, so too are their descendants.

Those who are interested in more information about the Morgan's Men Association or wish to receive a membership application, may write Samuel R. Flora, 1691 Kilkenny Dr., Lexington, KY 40505. (606)299-7679; Fax (606)299-7000.

Battle of Corydon Battlefield
(Harrison County, Indiana)

One mile south of Corydon, Indiana, this five-acre park is at the heart of the battle line on a ridge overlooking the village. Memorial markers, log cabin, Civil War cannon and split rail fences are at the site where 450 home guard citizens attempted to defend their town against 2,200 Confederate cavalry on the morning of July 9, 1863. The park, registered in the National

Register of Historic Places, is open to the public year round (8 am until dark). Admission is free. The battle site park was dedicated in 1977 and is located on the east side of old State Road 135 just south of the Harrison County Fairgrounds.

Each year, students in the R.O.T.C. program at Indiana University are brought to the Corydon battle site by army instructors in the University's Military Science Department. They study the offensive and defensive tactics employed by the opposing forces at the battle scene. Students begin their observations in Brandenburg, Kentucky. They discuss the crossing of the Ohio River into Indiana and follow the path taken by Morgan's raiders until the capture of Corydon itself. The military overview of both the Corydon and Buffington Island battles included in this book are based upon material studied by the students in training at Indiana University.

For additional information about the battle site, contact The Harrison County Parks and Recreation Department, 124 South Mulberry St., Corydon, IN 47112 Phone (812) 738-8236; or the Harrison County Chamber of Commerce, 310 N. Elm St., Corydon, IN 47112. Phone toll free: 1-888-738-2137.

Buffington Island Battlefield (Meigs County, Ohio)

The battlefield site is situated several hundred feet from the island on the valley floor in the Portland, Ohio, vicinity. It is believed that the battlefield covered an area of three to four square miles. A study prepared for the U.S. Congress and the Secretary of the Interior by the Department of the Interior's Civil War Sites Advisory Commission ranked the Battle of Buffington Island in the top 2.6% of all Civil War armed conflicts. It urged the State of Ohio and local governments, organizations, and individuals to work together to preserve and appropriately develop it.

Yet only a four-acre parcel is protected as a state memorial, operated by the Ohio Historical Society and listed in the National Register of Historic Places. The vast majority of the battlefield remains unmarked and unprotected. Unlike the manicured fields of Gettysburg studded with numerous plaques, markers and monuments, the Buffington Island battle site remains pristine rural farmland, and is virtually unchanged in appearance from 1863. There are no walkways crowded with tourists. No regular guided tours. No easy access to view the island where Morgan had planned his long awaited crossing.

There are only two markers. One of Ohio glacier boulders is set in the four-acre outdoor park. The other is nearby on the road where a Confederate bullet felled Major Daniel McCook, patriarch of the fighting McCook family. McCook is buried in Cincinnati. Recently, an aerial flyover using thermal imaging equipment located fifty-five bodies. Most of them were in two mass graves. Four bodies were found beside the home that had been used as a temporary hospital.

For additional information, contact the Meigs County Historical Society, P.O. Box 145, Pomeroy, OH 45769. Phone (614) 992-3810; or the Ohio Historical Society, 1982 Velma Ave., Columbus, OH 43211-2497. Phone (614) 297-2300.

Ohio & Indiana Civilians Killed During Morgan's Raid

In addition to the Union and Confederate soldiers killed, here are some of the citizens from Indiana and Ohio who were killed by Morgan's men or contributed to their deaths during the raid:

1. Nathan McKinzie at Mauckport, Harrison County, IN
2. James Currant at Brandenburg Crossing, Harrison County, IN
3. Rev. Peter Glenn, Lutheran minister, Corydon, Harrison County, IN
4. William Heath, tollgate keeper, Corydon, Harrison County, IN
5. Jacob Ferree, County Commissioner, Corydon, Harrison County, IN
6. Georia (Jeremiah) Nantz, Corydon, Harrison County, IN
7. Harrison Steepleton, Corydon, Harrison County, IN
8. Isaac Lang, Corydon, Harrison County, IN
9. Mrs. Cynthia B. Denbo, Corydon, Harrison County, IN died of heat exhaustion carrying water for raiders.
10. Miss Abie Siemmons, Corydon, Harrison County, IN died of typhoid contracted after an exhausting two days of carrying water for both Confederate and Union troops.
11. James Wright, fifteen-years-old, while trying to hide family horse.
12. John Wible, Washington County, IN
13. William Vance, Washington County, IN
14. Rev. Horsley, Methodist preacher in Pierceville, Ripley County, IN shot because he was deaf and didn't hear the command to halt.
15. John Sawdon, Dearborn County, IN
16. James McDougal, a teacher in Jasper, Pike County, OH
17. Harry Kelly, assistant manager of the Logan Furnace in Morgan County, OH
18. Dr. William N. Hudson, a physician south of Rutland in Meigs County, OH

19. Halliday Hysell, a elderly citizen in Meigs County, OH
20. Cornelius Conway, a fireman aboard the Little Miami Railroad near Loveland in Clermont County, OH
21. Harvey "Doc" Burris near Jackson in Jackson County, OH
22. Henry Meyer (Myer) at the Miamisville bridge in Hamilton County, OH
23. William Johnston an elderly citizen of Eckmansville, OH, who was mistaken for someone else who had taken a shot at the Confederates.

American Presidents Participate in Chase

Morgan's Raid appears on several presidential resumes. It is not common knowledge that the following future U.S. presidents, all born in Ohio, engaged in or helped defend against the raid.

Rutherford B. Hayes, 19th U.S. President (1877-1881). Born in Delaware, Ohio, 1822, died 1893. He entered the army on June 7, 1861. On October 15, 1862, he was appointed colonel of the 23rd OVI. While on duty in southwestern Virginia (shortly to become West Virginia), he was dispatched to Ohio in command of two regiments and a section of artillery for the purpose of finding and stopping the Confederate raiders. Hayes' forces were part of the Union command that engaged Morgan's men at Pomeroy and Buffington Island.

William McKinley, Jr., 25th U.S. President (1897-1901). Born in Niles, Ohio 1843, died 1901.
At age eighteen, he enlisted as a private in the 23rd OVI on June 11, 1861. On September 24, 1862, he was commissioned a Second Lieutenant, Co. D. At the time of the raid, his brigade was stationed in West Virginia under Col. Rutherford Hayes. He saw action at Buffington Island and Pomeroy fighting against Morgan.

Benjamin Harrison, 23rd U.S. President (1889-1893). Born in North Bend, Ohio, 1833, died 1901. He joined the 70th IN Infantry Regiment of Volunteers. Indiana Governor Morton commissioned him a colonel. His unit was brigaded with the 79th OH under Brigadier-General William Thomas Ward in Kentucky. Ward's command was given the responsibility of chasing Morgan's raiders. Harrison did spend time chasing Morgan around Kentucky in the September-October, 1862 period. But he was not involved in the Indiana-Ohio Raid chase.

James A. Garfield, 20th U.S. President (1881). Born in Orange, Ohio, 1831, died 1881.

In June 1863, General William S. Rosecrans asked for the written opinion of seventeen of his subordinate generals on the advisability of an immediate advance on General Braxton Bragg's Army of Tennessee at Tullahoma. Garfield was one of the generals in Rosecrans' command and served as his chief of staff. All the generals wrote opinions opposing the advance except for Garfield. His arguments were so convincing that Rosecrans began plans to engage Bragg. This movement threatened Bragg's withdrawal from Tullahoma to Chattanooga, which triggered events that helped precipitate Morgan's diversionary raid.

The Morgan Family

John Hunt Morgan was born Wednesday, June 1, 1825, at 310 South Green Street in Huntsville, Alabama. His mother: Henrietta (1805-1891). His father: Calvin (1802-1854). His parents had six sons and six daughters (two daughters, Katherine and Ann, died in the cholera epidemic of 1833). Mary died at age ten months. Elenor died at age four months. John Hunt was the oldest (1825-1864); Calvin Cogswell (1827-1882); Catherine Grosh (1834-1920); Richard Curd (1836-1919); Charlton Hunt (1839-1912); Henrietta Hunt (1840-1909); Thomas Hunt (1844-1863); Francis Key (1845-1878).

John was married twice. First wife: Rebecca Gratz Bruce of Lexington (1830-1861) was eighteen-years-old when she was married November 21, 1848 to John, twenty-three. In September 1853, she had a stillborn son. As an aftereffect of her pregnancy, Rebecca developed a blood clot in her leg. Doctors of that time were unable to properly diagnose her ailment. Today's modern medicine would have recognized the problem and successfully treated it. But in antebellum days, physicians said she had "milk leg." This condition was caused by a blood clot, which affected her blood circulation, and her leg turned white. John did everything he could to alleviate her suffering including taking her to Hot Springs, Arkansas, for extensive bathing in the hot mineral springs. The soreness persisted and her condition grew worse. After eight years of suffering, she died an invalid and childless at age thirty-one. John would be a widower for two years before he met and married his second wife, Mattie.

Martha "Mattie" Ready of Murfreesboro, Tennessee (1840-1887), was twenty-two when she married John who was then thirty-seven. They had two daughters. The first was born November 27, 1863, and lived only one day. Their second, Johnnie, was born April 7, 1865, following John's death. Mattie died at age forty-six, twenty-three years after John Morgan's death.

His sister, Henrietta, married Basil Wilson Duke on June 18, 1861 when he was twenty-three. John's other sister, Catherine, was married three times. First to Calvin Morgan McClung, who died February 19, 1857. Second marriage was to General Ambrose P. Hill who fought with Lee at Gettysburg and was killed April 2, 1865. Her third marriage was to Dr. Alex Forsyth, who died September 10, 1875. Catherine survived all three husbands living until September 12, 1912.

His grandfather, John Wesley Hunt, was a founder of Lexington and one of the wealthiest men west of the Allegheny Mountains. It is said that he was Lexington's first millionaire. He had significant investments in merchandising, manufacturing, banking and government securities.

John's father, Calvin, was a very handsome man. Portraits of both John's mother and father hang in the Hunt-Morgan House in downtown Lexington. Calvin won Hunt's permission to marry seventeen-year-old Henrietta on September 24, 1823. Calvin's twin brother, Alexander, visited Lexington and married America Higgins on September 25, 1823. Calvin and Henrietta returned to Huntsville to live. But in 1831, Calvin, having lost his Alabama home in order to pay his taxes, accepted his father-in-law's offer to move to Lexington and manage one of the Hunt farms in Fayette County, Kentucky. Their family moved into a two-story farmhouse on Tates Creek Road. John Morgan was six years old when they relocated to Kentucky. In 1854 when John was twenty-nine, his father died at age fifty-two.

At age seventeen, John enrolled at Transylvania College, Lexington, Kentucky, in 1842 and joined the Adelphi Society, a literary fraternity. In June of 1844, he had a duel with a fraternity brother. Neither was seriously hurt. Following this incident on July 4, 1844, the college's Board of Trustees expelled John from the school. Years later, he referred to himself as a Transylvania alumnus and he gave a large gift of money to the college. He never resumed his studies, but he was not forgotten.

John Morgan stood arrow-straight at six feet tall, weighed 185 pounds. He had curly sandy hair and gray eyes. Early in the Civil War, Carrie Pyncheon of Huntsville wrote in her diary, "Before the town was occupied by the Yankees, I spent an evening with Captain Jack [John] Morgan, our second Marion. He was so mild and gentle in his manners that I would not have taken him for a soldier but for his boots and spurs, so unwarrior-like did he seem."

Sundays had a special meaning to John Hunt Morgan. John married Martha "Mattie" Ready on Sunday, December 14, 1862, in Murfreesboro, Tennessee. Morgan had purposefully delayed the wedding to a Sunday. He said, "Everything important [for better or worse] happens to me on Sunday." How prophetic were his words. He was sworn into the Confederate Army on Sunday, October 27, 1861. The battle that convinced him that he should dispense with the traditional cavalry charge with sabers and operate as mounted infantry instead, was at the Battle of Shiloh fought Sunday, April 6, 1862. His brilliant victory at Hartsville occurred on Sunday, December 7, 1862. His brother, Tom, was killed near the beginning of the Ohio-Indiana raid in Lebanon, Kentucky on Sunday, July 5, 1863. The pursuing Union armies would finally catch up and capture half his remaining force at Buffington Island on Sunday, July 19, 1863. He would be captured at the end of the Ohio-Indiana raid on Sunday, July 26, 1863; and he would be killed in Greeneville, Tennessee, on Sunday, September 4, 1864.

John Hunt Morgan's only child, Johnnie, at age 23 died shortly after she was married leaving no direct descendants. But John's brothers and sisters did. Prominent among the members of the following generation was the son of John's brother, Charlton and his wife, Ellen. Their oldest son was Thomas Hunt Morgan (1866-1945). In 1933, he was awarded the Nobel Prize for his discoveries concerning the role played by the chromosome in heredity. In 1966, the University of Kentucky dedicated its new biology building to Morgan naming it the T.H. Morgan School of Biological Sciences.

Acknowledgments

Special appreciation to Dr. James A. Ramage for his wisdom, guidance and encouragement. A salute of thanks to Edwin C. Bearss for his help in assuring the military and historical accuracy of this manuscript.

The author gratefully acknowledges the following people and organizations, who contributed stories, photographs, documents, sources, their talents, services and assistance, which helped to make this a most comprehensive account of the *Longest Raid of the Civil War.*

ALABAMA
Steve Hettinger, Huntsville
John Motley, Geneva
Ward Sykes Allen, Auburn
Rick Storey, Huntsville

ARIZONA
Norman Berberich, Glendale
Harry Johnson, Jr., Tucson

CALIFORNIA
Neil Allen Bristow, San Diego
William M. Pursell, Hollister
Eileen J. Schenck, Downey
Clarence R. Sterling, Ojai
Maner L. Thorpe, PH.D., Santa Barbara

COLORADO
David R. Swearingen, Colorado Springs

CONNECTICUT
Carolyn Schenck Rose, West Hartford

FLORIDA
Charles F. Cole, Sarasota
Lynn Normile, Indiatlantic
F. John Schoenwetter, Port Orange
Perry G. Snell, Sarasota
Duke Nordlinger Stern, St. Petersburg

GEORGIA
Michael E. Whitfield, Rocky Face

IDAHO
Ben R. Boice, M.D., Idaho Falls

ILLINOIS
Geneva Ankenbrand, Mt. Carmel
Eugene Berberich, Mt. Carmel
Joseph F. Peter, Mt. Carmel

INDIANA
Aurora Public Library District, Aurora
Leo G. Benton, Corydon
Oscar Best, Elizabeth
Martha Bowers, Salem
Bob Breese, Elkhart
James H. Britton, Lawrenceburg
Nina L. Faith, Mauckport
Julia R. Fitzgerald, Pekin
Roger W. Gleitz, Leavenworth
Fredrick Griffin, Corydon
Hayden Historical Museum, Hayden
Michael Heilers, Lebanon
Helen Houchins, Indianapolis
Wilma Howell, Salem
Indiana Commission on Public
    Records, Indianapolis
Indiana Historical Society, Indianapolis
Indiana State Archives, Indianapolis
Indiana State Land Office, Indianapolis
Indiana University, Military Science
    Dept., Indianapolis
Jackson County Historical Society,
    Seymour
Maxine Klump, Guilford

(Indiana continued)
Lt. Col. Donald V. McGuire, Indianapolis
Carolyn McManaman, Lawrenceburg
William H. Prather, Indianapolis
Charles O. Roeger, Seymour
Roger D. Ruddick, Hayden
Salem Leader, Salem
Edward L. Sebring, Vincennes
Charles W. Shaffer, Corydon
John Sickles, Merriville
Richard Skidmore, Hanover
Marjorie Ann Martin Souder, Pekin
Dave Taylor, Lexington
Clarence E. Timberlake, New Albany
Steven E. Towne, Indianapolis
Vincennes Sun-Commercial, Vincennes
Washington County Historical Society,
   Salem
Harley W. Wiseman, Corydon
Jean A. Wiseman, Corydon

IOWA
Ella F. Hartmann, Davenport
Edna L. Jones, Washington

KENTUCKY
Rudy Ayoroa, Danville
Richard M. Bean, Lexington
Larry D. Benson, Cynthiana
Sharon Bidwell, Louisville
James Birchfield, Lexington
Franklin D. Brewer, Southgate
Lisa R. Carter, Lexington
John B. Conrad, Lexington
Sherman T. Dozier, Versailles
The Filson Club Historical Society,
   Louisville
Samuel R. Flora, Lexington
Thomas W. Fugate, Frankfort
Mary Mitchell Gravely, Harrodsburg
Ken Hamilton, Lexington
Joe Hardesty, Louisville
Porter Harned, Louisville
Jack Harrison, Bardstown
Alexander T. Hunt Museum, Hunt-
   Morgan House, Lexington
Gypsie Lee Cosby Jones, Richmond

Kentucky Military History Museum,
   Frankfort
Mary Jean Kinsman, Louisville
Louisville Courier Journal, Louisville
Louisville Public Library, Louisville
Stephen Douglas Lynn, Lexington
Wood C. Meade, Ft. Thomas
Miriam Metz, Louisville
Burton Milward, Lexington
Morgan's Men Association, Lexington
Northern Kentucky University,
   Highland Heights
Orphan Brigade Kinfolk, Louisville
Dr. James A. Ramage, Cold Springs
Bill Rogers, Jr., Frankfort
Freddie J. Rogers, Winchester
Scott E. Sallee, Bowling Green
Dr. Mark J. Schuler, Newport
Betty Gorin-Smith, Campbellsville
W. Hunt Smock, Murray
Edison H. Thomas, Louisville
University of Kentucky, Margaret I.
   King Library, Lexington
James R. Watts, Brandenburg
Jane White, Ft. Mitchell

LOUISIANA
John D. Jackson, M.D., Jefferson

MARYLAND
United States Naval Institute, Annapolis
Gary K. Zimmerman, Bowie

MISSISSIPPI
Hugh H. Rather, Jr., Holly Springs

MISSOURI
Clyde Boice, M.D., Fulton
William Catron, St. Charles

OHIO
Eric Anderson, Jackson
Sue Appleberry, Fairfield
Gary J. Arnold, Columbus
June Ashley, Racine
Keith Ashley, Pomeroy
Robert M. Ball, Caldwell

(Ohio continued)
Batavia Public Library, Batavia
Blaine Beekman, Waverly
Jan Beller, Loveland
Ethel Blackburn, Pleasantville
Charles Blakeslee, Pomeroy
Dallas Bogan, Franklin
Doris Murphy Boggs, Hillsboro
Darlene S.T. Bowling, Waverly
Chris Bradburn, Cincinnati
David A. Brewer, Portland
Timothy R. Brookes, East Liverpool
Marshall Burtt, Loveland
Dorothy L. Bussemer, Zanesville
Izella Cadwallader, Williamsburg
Nan J. Card, Fremont
Denver Carey, West Chester
Carroll County Historical Society,
    Carrollton
Chandlersville Courier, Chandlersville
The Cincinnati Enquirer, Cincinnati
Cincinnati Historical Society, Cincinnati
Cincinnati Public Library, Cincinnati
Mary G. Clark, Wellsville
Oscar Coe, Columbus
Mary L. Cook Public Library,
    Waynesville
Zelma Cornelius, Cleves
Mrs. Marion Cozza, East Palestine
Richard Crawford, Amelia
Daily Jeffersonian, Cambridge
Sandy Day, Steubenville
Delhi Historical Society, Cincinnati
Elmer H. Detwiler, Columbiana
East Liverpool Museum of Ceramics,
    East Liverpool
Kevin Lee Eblen, Copley
Elinor Edmundson, Lewisburg
James W. Ewing, Lisbon
John Ewing, Lisbon
Jackie Fisher, Somerset
Marabel Frecker, Pomeroy
John & Marilyn Fultz, Middleport
Gallia County Engineer's Office,
    Gallipolis
Gallia County Genealogical Society,
    Gallipolis

Gallia County Recorder Office,
    Gallipolis
Bob Garrison, Lebanon
Mike Gerlach, Middleport
Jim Given, Columbus
David Gloeckner, Racine
Richard E. Goodwin, Cambridge
Bill Graver, Cincinnati
Greater Loveland Historical Society,
    Loveland
Eleanor W. Grooms, Sardinia
Guernsey County District Public
    Library, Cambridge
Robert Hale, Cincinnati
Lucille Scott Hamilton, Piketon
William Hanlin, East Springfield
Walt Harrell, Cleves
Harrison County Historical Society,
    Cadiz
Harrison Recreation Commission,
    Harrison
Ruth A. Hart, McConnelsville
Dallas Haydon, Oak Hill
James S. Henry, Waverly
Edwin Grant Hibarger, Montgomery
Gary Lee Hicks, Cincinnati
Jewyl Hina, Lisbon
Leighton L. Hine, Westerville
Tom J. Holden, Columbus
Esther Holland, Loveland
Meryl F. Houdasheldt, Radcliff
Jim Irvin, Cincinnati
Richard C. Isphording, Cincinnati
Jefferson County Historical Assn,
    Steubenville
Dale Johnson, Barberton
Karin Johnson, Pomeroy
Mary L. Johnston, Wellston
Joanne Joy, McArthur
William Justis, Portland
John Kaplet, Old Washington
Steven Kelley, Seaman
Phil Ketchum, Salem
Jack Kindell, Cincinnati
Gloria Kloes, Pomeroy
Judy Klosterman, Loveland
Tutt Lambert, Loveland

(Ohio continued)

Michael Lennon, Cincinnati
Dwight Lewis, Bloomingdale
Marilyn Liles, Lucasville
Joseph Liming, Mount Orab
Jessica A. Little, Cincinnati
Mamie C. Lloyd, Oak Hill
Lucille MacKnight, Cincinnati
Sally Maier, Zanesville
Elva Maphet, Camp Dennison
Cindy Maryo, Miamiville
Dane McCarthy, Millfield
Virginia McCauley, Wellsville
Stanley W. McClure, Harrison
Robert L. McDonnell, Loveland
Nancy McGary, Harrison
Meigs County Commissioners Office,
    Pomeroy
Meigs County Library, Pomeroy
Meigs County Tourism Board, Pomeroy
Lavella Metzler, Columbus
Milford Public Library, Milford
Orloff Miller, Cincinnati
Anita Mitchell, Harrison
Ron Moore, McConnelsville
William J. Moore, D.D.S.,
    Cuyahoga Falls
Russell & Sandy Morris,
    Cuyahoga Falls
Charles A. Murray, Gallipolis
Muskingum College, New Concord
Muskingum County Library System,
    Zanesville
Louella Nagel, Portsmouth
Catherine Naylor, Georgetown
Jon P. Neill, Cincinnati
Michael Neilson, Cambridge
Louis & Nancy Neumann, Maineville
The News Watchman, Waverly
Nobel County Historical Society,
    Caldwell
Albert M. Nutgrass, Loveland
Ohio Civil War Museum,
    Camp Dennison
Ohio Historic Preservation Office,
    Columbus
Ohio Historical Society, Columbus

Ohio Valley District Public Library,
    Peebles
Ohio Valley Visitors Center, Gallipolis
Frank Oligee, West Chester
Sister Louanna Orth SNDdeN, Reading
Greg Parks, Cambridge
Michael L. Penrod, Zanesville
Perry County District Library,
    New Lexington
Melody Eggleston Pesta, Irondale
Marvin S. Phillips, Barnesville
Pike County Chamber of Commerce,
    Waverly
Molly V. Plymale, Gallipolis
Pomeroy Daily Sentinel, Pomeroy
Dr. Lorle Porter, New Concord
Ruth Powers, Pomeroy
Betty L. Pride, Hammersville
Lester Propes, Cincinnati
Puskarich Public Library, Cadiz
George E. Rankin, Carrollton
James A. Reaney, East Liverpool
Jo Ann Richardson, Loveland
Beale and Gail Robinson, North Canton
Jack Roudebush, Cambridge
Rutherford B. Hayes Presidential
    Center, Fremont
Anthony J. Sargenti, Amesville
Floy Jean Scatterday, Jacobsburg
Schiappa Memorial Library,
    Steubenville
Kim Sheets Schuette, Gallipolis
Lenore Sechler, Kensington
Dale E. Shaffer, Salem
Becky Sheperd, Cadiz
James S. Simmonds, Westwood
Helen Skinner, Carrollton
Ray Skinner, Athens
Rich Smethurst, Loveland
Betty Ann Smiddy, West Chester
Thomas D. Snyder, Cambridge
Jacklyn J. Spaun, Long Bottom
Margaret Cotton Spiry, Cincinnati
Lt. Col. Alfred J. Spiry, Sr., Cincinnati
Lora Staats, Mogadore
Jane L. Steibig, Loveland
John Steinle, Loveland

(Ohio continued)
Janet S. Stohlman, Ripley
Suzanne Merion Strachan, Chagrin Falls
William Stubbs, Sardinia
Linda M. Swartzel, Waynesville
Connie Tarter, Milford
Richard J. Taylor, Chandlersville
Mrs. Homer Todd, E. Palestine
Kim J. Torgler, Orrville
Richard E. Troup, McConnelsville
Kathryn Undercoffer, Loveland
University of Cincinnati–
    Classics Library, Cincinnati
Thomas L. Vince, Hudson
The Village Historical Society, Harrison
Vinton County Courier, McArthur
Vinton County Historical Society,
    Hamden
Robert Volz, Cambridge
Charles B. Wallace, Cadiz
Debbie Martin Wallin, Fairfield
Charles L. Ward, Williamsburg
Helen Ward, Deer Park
Wayne Warne, Cambridge
Warren County Historical Society,
    Lebanon
Bob Weaver, Gallipolis
Kermit W. Weaver, Malta
Kristin Weiss, New Lexington
Wellsville Historical Society, Wellsville
John G. Whipple, Berea
William A. White, Sardinia
Aileen M. Whitt, New Richmond
Mrs. Robert C. Willson, Jasper
George Wilson, Columbus
Ida Wilson, West Union
Robert Wirkner, Carrollton
Gene & Ann Woelfel, Harrison
Emmett Wright, McConnelsville

PENNSYLVANIA
Lt. Col. Martin W. Andresen (Ret),
    Boiling Springs
Carole Boice Jones DePaul, Pittsburgh
Glen Speirs, State College
U.S. Military History Institute,
    Carlisle Barracks, Carlisle

SOUTH CAROLINA
James C. Ewing, Ridgeville

TENNESSEE
Stephen D. Cox, Nashville
East Tennessee Roots, Oak Ridge
Paula Gammell, Oak Ridge
Greene County Genealogical Society,
    Greeneville
Tim Heath, Lebanon
Shirley Farris Jones, Murfreesboro
Lynn Llewellyn, Knoxville
Jan Maddux, Greeneville
Major Kevin G. Mason (Ret), Knoxville
The Tennessee State Museum, Nashville

TEXAS
Richard J. Blumberg, Spring
Confederate Research Center, Hillsboro
Peggy Barnes Fox , Hillsboro
Michael A. McMurray, Houston
John Paul Strain, Ft. Worth
Todd Thompson, Southlake

VIRGINIA
Edwin C. Bearss, Alexandria
Blue and Gray Educational Society,
    Danville
Martha M. Boltz, Vienna
Anne B. McLeod, Richmond
Cecil Richardson, Jr., Tazewell
Len Riedel, Danville

WASHINGTON
Lt. Robert J. Abbott, Tacoma

WASHINGTON, DC
The Library of Congress
Naval Historical Center

WEST VIRGINIA
Jeffrey W. Danner, Parkersburg
West Virginia Division of Culture and
    History, Charleston

Cover illustration: Rudy Ayoroa, Danville, KY.
Book cover design: Kim Fieler, Cincinnati, OH.
Maps by Linda Sullivan, Cincinnati, OH.
Photo page layouts by Kim Fieler and Linda Sullivan.
Index by Barbara E. Cohen, Indianapolis, IN.
Typesetting by *d*Best, Inc., Cincinnati, OH with special thanks to
Terry Durrette, Jeff Durrette and Kevin Sullivan of *d*Best.
Marketing assistance by Timothy Pennington, Newtown, OH.
Administrative assistance by Angela Bauer, Cincinnati, OH.

Notes

Preface
1. Diary of Capt. Thomas Munroe Coombs, Co. K, 5th KY. Entry of July 2, 1863.
2. Civil War Society, *Guide to Civil War Armies* (1998).This document indicated that there were nine artillerymen assigned per gun.
3. *Report of the Ohio Commissioners of Morgan's Raid Claims* (December 15, 1864), p. 114.
4. James A. Ramage, *Rebel Raider* (1986), p. 256.
5. Ibid.
6. *Population Centers of the United States* (undated article).
7. Thirey and Mitchel, *Encyclopedic Directory* (1902).
8. Basil W. Duke, *History of Morgan's Cavalry* (1867), pp. 409-410.
9. Ibid., p. 440.
10. Rev. F. Senour, *Morgan and His Captors* (1865), p. 106; Ramage, *Rebel Raider*, p. 251. Morgan dressed as a businessman in his escape from the Ohio Penitentiary.
11. Ramage, *Rebel Raider*, p. 202.
12. *Lexington Herald* (October 19, 1911).
13. Morgan's Men Association.
14. Ramage, *Rebel Raider*, p. 251.
15. Ibid., p. 19.
16. Lowell H. Harrison, *The Civil War in Kentucky* (1975), p. 55.
17. Cecil Fletcher Holland, *Morgan and his Raiders* (1943), p. 219; Roller, *Indiana Magazine of History*, p. 13.
18. Lew Lord, *U.S. News & World Report* (August 15, 1988), p. 52.
19. Albert Hemingway, *America's Civil War*, Vol. 2, No. 2 (November, 1989), p. 12. The name *"Alligator Horses"* is from a song composed by Samuel Woodsworth for Kentuckians who fought at the Battle of New Orleans in 1815.
20. *Merit Students Encyclopedia* (1991), Vol. 8.
21. U.S. Civil War Center—Statistical Summary: America's Major Wars, Internet.

1. Why The Raid?

1. *U.S. Army Field Manual 100-5*, pp. 7-8.
2. Duke, *History*, pp. 410-411.
3. "Lightning and Rain in Middle Tennessee: The Campaign of June-July 1863," *Tennessee Historical Quarterly*, Vol. LII, No. 2, Fall 1993, pp. 158-169.
4. *Official Records of the Union and Confederate Armies*, Vol. XXIII, *Part II-Correspondence,* Chap. XXXV, p. 383.
5. Duke, *History*, p. 409.
6. Undated article, *A Beachhead on the East Bank,* pp. 87-96.
7. Duke, *History*, p. 409.
8. Stephen Starr, *Colonel Grenfell's Wars* (1971), p. 44.

9. Ibid., p. 87.
10. *OR, Part II-Correspondence,* p. 854.
11. Duke, *History,* p. 389.
12. Dee Alexander Brown, *Morgan's Raiders* (1959), p. 173.
13. *Adjutant General's Report,* Ninth Regiment Cavalry, p. 3.
14. *OR, Part II-Correspondence,* p. 944.
15. Duke, *History,* p. 411.
16. John E. McGowan, *Annals of the War* (1879), p. 763.

Notes to Pages 6-12

2. Getting Ready For Battle

1. Holland, *Raiders,* p. 8.
2. Brown, *Raiders,* p. 97; David L. Taylor, *With Bowie Knives & Pistols* (1993), pp. 49-50; *OR, Part I-Reports,* p. 750.
3. Brian Steel Wills, Clinch Valley College, at BGES Morgan Raid Symposium (June 13, 1998).
4. Signature page from autograph book circulated in Ohio Penitentiary.
5. Albert Dillahunty, *Shiloh National Military Park, Tennessee,* p. 9.
6. Duke, *History,* p. 411.
7. Starr, *Grenfell's War,* p. 49.
8. *Webster's American Military Biographies* (1978), p. 202.
9. *Kentucky Adjutant General's Report,* 7th Regiment, pp. 686-688.
10. *State of Tennessee Adjutant General's Report,* 9th Regiment, pp. 527-553.
11. Starr, *Grenfell's War,* p. 49.
12. *OR, Part II-Correspondence,* p. 944.
13. William E. Metzler, *Morgan and His Dixie Cavaliers* (1976), p. 48.
14. Ramage, *Rebel Raider,* pp. 202-203.
15. Barbara Kalfs, *Chillicothe Gazette* (April 22, 1972), p. 3.
16. Steven Woodward, Texas Christian University, at BGES Morgan Raid Symposium (June 13, 1998).
17. Ibid.
18. *Life Magazine* (January 6, 1961).
19. Duke, *History,* p. 176.
20. As explained by Thomas W. Fugate, Curator, Kentucky Military History Museum.
21. Holland, *Raiders,* p. 162.
22. Family history of Pvt. John Conrad, Co. K, 9th KY, p. 194.

KENTUCKY

Notes to Pages 13-18

3. Crossing The Cumberland Twice

1. Ramage, *Rebel Raider,* p. 159.
2. *OR, Part II-Correspondence,* p. 867.

3. Ibid., p. 869.
4. Hemingway, *America's Civil War* (November 1989), p. 56.
5. Duke, *History*, p. 411.
6. Ibid., p. 412.
7. *OR, Part I-Reports,* p. 818.
8. Duke, *History*, p. 414.
9. Ibid.
10. Ibid.
11. Ibid., p. 411.
12. James A. Ramage in personal notes (December 15, 1997), p. 5.
13. Robert S. Henry, *Story of the Confederacy* (1931), p. 263.
14. Henry Steele Commager, *The Blue and The Gray* (1950), p. 671.
15. *Morgan's Division Regiment Rosters,* pp. 582-583.
16. Francis Scott Key, *The Star Spangled Banner*, Internet.
17. James A. Ramage, *The Hunts and Morgans, A Study of a Prominent Kentucky Family* (1972), Abstract of Dissertation.
18. *Webster's American Military Bios*, pp. 39-40.
19. Ezra J. Warner, *Generals in Blue* (1964): Judah (p. 255); Hobson (p. 231).
20. Ramage, *Rebel Raider*, p. 26.
21. Warner, *Generals*, pp. 57-58.
22. Col. J.E. McGowan, *Morgan's Indiana and Ohio Raid* (1879), p. 750.

Notes to Pages 19-21   **(Cumberland & Adair Counties)**

4.   "Naked As Jay Birds!"

1. Duke, *History*, p. 414; Holland, *Raiders*, p. 226.
2. Holland, *Raiders*, p. 226.
3. Henry Lane Stone, *Narrative of Personal Experiences* (April 8, 1919), p. 10.
4. Brown, *Raiders*, p. 180.
5. Hemingway, *America's Civil War* (November, 1989), p. 56.
6. Adam R. Johnson, *Partisan Rangers of the Confederate States Army* (1904), p. 144.
7. Capt. L. D. Hockersmith, *Morgan's Escape* (1903), p. 12.
8. Duke, *History*, p. 414.
9. *OR, Part I-Reports,* p. 639.
10. Ibid.
11. Hemingway, *America's Civil War* (November 2, 1989), p. 56.
12. Brown, *Raiders*, p. 180.
13. Metzler, *Cavaliers*, p. 48.
14. Duke, *History*, p. 419.
15. Commager, *Blue & Gray*, Journal of Lt. Col. Alston, p. 679.
16. Duke, *History*, p. 419.

Notes to Pages 22-28   (Taylor County)

5. An Ominous Sign

1. *OR, Part I-Reports*, Col. Moore's Report, pp. 645-646.
2. Louis Hebel and Owen Phillips, *Courier Journal Magazine* (July 3, 1960), p. 22.
3. Ibid.
4. Duke, *History*, p. 421.
5. Holland, *Raiders*, p. 227.
6. *OR, Part I-Reports,* Moore's Report, p. 646.
7. Hebel and Phillips, *Courier Journal*, p. 23.
8. Ibid.
9. *OR, Part I-Reports,* Moore's Report, p. 646.
10. Metzler, *Cavaliers*, p. 49.
11. Letter from Sherman T. Dozier (November 11, 1996).
12. Duke, *History*, p. 423.
13. *OR, Part I-Reports,* Moore's Report, p. 646.
14. Duke, *History*, p. 423.
15. *Annals of the Nineteenth Ohio Battery*, p. 205.
16. Norris F. Schneider, *Zanesville Times Recorder* (July 28, 1963); Francis Trevelyan Miller, *Poetry and Eloquence from the Blue and the Gray* (1957), p. 350.
17. Holland, *Raiders*, p. 227; Duke, *History*, p. 418.
18. *OR, Part I-Reports*, Lt. T.W. Sullivan's Report, pp. 652-653.
19. *OR, Part I-Reports*, Lt. Col. C.S. Hanson's Report, pp. 647-651.
20. Brown, *Raiders*, p. 183.
21. Basil W. Duke, *The Century Magazine*, Vol. XLI, No. 1 (November 1890), p. 408.
22. Brown, *Raiders*, p. 184.
23. Samuel Carter III, *The Last Cavaliers* (1979), p. 178.

Notes to Pages 29-33   (Marion, Washington & Nelson Counties)

6. "Twenty Five Damned Yankees"

1. *OR, Part I-Reports*, Lt. T.W. Sullivan's Report, pp. 652-653.
2. Holland, *Raiders*, p. 230.
3. Ramage, *Rebel Raider*, p. 164.
4. Metzler, *Cavaliers*, p. 49.
5. Howard Swiggett, *The Rebel Raider* (1934), p. 131.
6. *OR, Part I-Reports*, p. 746.
7. Duke, *History*, p. 427.
8. Senour, *Morgan and His Captors*, p. 113.
9. Duke, *History*, p. 427.
10. *OR, Part I-Reports*, p. 649; *Cincinnati Daily Commercial* (July 24, 1863).
11. *OR, Part I-Reports*, p. 652.
12. Ibid.
13. Ibid., pp. 652-653.
14. Ibid., p. 653.

15. James A. Ramage in personal notes (December 15, 1997), p. 6.
16. John R. Seawright, The Sorrows of the Alstons. Part 18, *Flagpole Magazine,* The Internet.
17. Ibid.
18. Ibid.
19. *OR, Part I-Reports*, p. 658.
20. B. Kevin Bennett, BGES Morgan's Raid Symposium (June 13, 1998).
21. *OR, Part I-Reports,* Telegram July 6, 1863—4pm from Gen. Hobson to Gen. Hartsuff.

Notes to Page 34-36

7.   Treachery Within The Ranks

1. Duke, *History*, pp. 423-424.
2. Commager, *Blue & Gray*, Alston, p. 680.
3. Duke *History*, p. 424.
4. *OR, Part I-Reports*, p. 658.
5. Ibid.

Notes to Pages 37-39   (Bullitt, Jefferson, Hardin & Meade Counties)

8.   A Feint Towards Louisville

1. Brown, *Raiders,* pp. 185-186.
2. Ramage, *Rebel Raider*, p. 166.
3. *OR, Part I-Reports*, p. 659.
4. Ibid.
5. Stone, *Experiences*, p. 12.
6. Thomas M. Coombs letter to his wife Lou (August 14, 1863).
7. Holland, *Raiders,* p. 121; Harrison, *Civil War in Kentucky*, p. 39.

Notes to Pages 40-46

9.   To The River

1. Duke, *History,* p. 428; Brown, *Raiders*, p. 186.
2. Johnson, *Partisan Rangers*, p. 144.
3. Duke, *History*, p. 430.
4. Brandenburg Methodist Church, *The Brandenburg Story* (1963), p. 18.
5. Ramage, *Rebel Raider*, p. 168.
6. Metzler, *Cavaliers,* p. 50; Duke, *History*, p. 428. Basil Duke identified Garnettsville as being in Hardin County. Joe Hardesty with the Louisville Public Library said, according to a Kentucky map published in the late 1800s, it was in Meade County. Hardesty said that the town is no longer in existence, but it had been located about 2.5 miles southeast of Otter Creek Park along today's Route 1638.
7. Taylor, *Bowie Knives*, p. 36.
8. Ibid.

9. W. Fred Conway, *Corydon - The Forgotten Battle Of The Civil War* (1991), p. 51.
10. *Brandenburg Story*, p. 18.
11. Letter from Tim Heath, Lebanon, TN (August 24, 1996).
12. Duke, *History,* p. 430; Metzler, *Cavaliers*, p. 51.
13. Duke, *History*, p. 431.
14. Conrad family history, p. 194.
15. James D. Horan, *Confederate Agent* (1954), p. 25.
16. Ibid., pp. 25-26.
17. Ibid., p. 27.
18. Ibid.
19. Roller, *Indiana Magazine of History*, pp. 3, 6.
20. Horan, *Agent*, p. 28.
21. Ibid.
22. Duke, *History*, p. 431.
23. Ibid., p. 432.
24. Metzler, *Cavaliers*, p. 51.
25. Taylor, *Bowie Knives*, p. 37.
26. Duke, *Century Magazine* (November, 1890), p. 409. In this article, Duke said that the Ohio River at Brandenburg was about 2,500 feet wide ("eight hundred or a thousand yards wide").

Notes to Pages 47-52

10. Get Across and Burn The Boats!

1. Mark Ford, *The Brandenburg Story* (July 13, 1963), p. 19.
2. Taylor, *Bowie Knives*, p. 38.
3. *Corydon Weekly Democrat* (July 14, 1863), p. 1.
4. Corp. W.B. Ryan's account, *Corydon Republican* (July 15, 1909).
5. Metzler, *Cavaliers*, p. 52.
6. Taylor, *Bowie Knives*, p. 39.
7. Ryan, *Republican* (July 15, 1909).
8. Conway, *Corydon, The Forgotten Battle*, p. 55.
9. Taylor, *Bowie Knives,* p. 40; Duke, *History*, p. 432.
10. *Corydon Weekly Democrat* (July 14, 1863), p. 1.
11. Ramage, *Rebel Raider*, p. 168; Conway, *Corydon*, p. 57; Duke, *History*, pp. 432-433.
12. Ford, *Brandenburg Story,* p. 23.
13. Duke, *History*, p. 433.
14. Ibid., p. 434.
15. Taylor, *Bowie Knives*, p. 43.
16. Arville L. Funk, *Morgan Raid in Indiana and Ohio* (1971), p. 5.
17. Commager, *Blue & Gray*, McCreary, p. 682.
18. Jon P. Neill, *Phillip Board - Bluegrass Pioneer* (1992).
19. Taylor, *Bowie Knives*, p. 44; Edison H. Thomas, *John Hunt Morgan and His Raiders* (1975), p. 78.
20. *OR, Part I-Reports*, Hobson's Report, p. 659.

INDIANA

Notes to Pages 55-59   (Clark & Floyd Counties)

11. Confederate Thunderbolt Strikes Indiana and Ohio

1. Brown, *Raiders*, p. 254.
2. John Linza Gibson, *Early Wood Township* (1964), Chapter VII, p. 32.
3. Ibid.
4. Ibid., p. 33.
5. Ibid., p. 34.
6. Ibid., pp. 34-35.
7. Ibid., pp. 35-36.
8. Ibid., p. 36.
9. Funk, *Hoosiers in the Civil War* (1967), p. 169.
10. Ibid., p. 107.
11. David J. Bodenhamer and Robert G. Barrows, *Encyclopedia of Indianapolis* (1994), p. 911.
12. Funk, *Hoosiers*, p. 169.
13. W.H.H. Terrell, *Indiana in the War of the Rebellion* (1869), Vol. I, p. 566.
14. Funk, *Hoosiers*, p. 169.
15. John W. Rowell, *Yankee Artillerymen*, p. 65.
16. "The Steadiest Body of Men I Ever Saw: John T. Wilder and the Lightning Brigade," *Blue & Gray Magazine* (October 1992), pp. 32-36.
17. William B. Edwards, *Civil War Guns* (1962), p. 161.
18. *Blue & Gray Magazine* (October 1992), pp. 32-36.
19. Ibid.
20. Bodenhamer & Barrows, *Encyclopedia*, p. 911.
21. Terrell, *Indiana in the War,* p. 566.
22. Bodenhamer & Barrows, *Encyclopedia,* p. 566.
23. *Daily Cincinnati Enquirer* (February 17, 1998), p. A2.
24. *OR, Part I-Reports*, Hobson's Report, p. 659.

Notes to Pages 60-78   (Harrison County)

12. The Battle of Corydon

1. Taylor, *Bowie Knives*, p. 52.
2. *S&D Reflector* (June 1976), p. 13; Notes from Helen Ballard Crayden, Harrison County, IN.
3. *Report of Morgan Raid (Indiana) Commissioners* (December 31, 1869), p. 31.
4. S.M. Stockslager, *Corydon Democrat* (August 1, 1923).
5. Samuel Pfrimmer, *Corydon Democrat* (March 30, 1927).
6. *Indiana Commissioners Report*, p. 38.
7. Pfrimmer, *Democrat* (March 30, 1927).
8. Simeon K. Wolfe, Editor, *Corydon Weekly Democrat* (July 14, 1863), p. 1.
9. Taylor, *Bowie Knives*, p. 47.
10. Ibid., pp. 47-48.

11. Rev. Wilford and Mrs. Butt, *History of Mt. Solomon Lutheran Church* (1969).
12. Funk, *Hoosiers in the Civil War*, Col. Lewis Jordan's Report, p. 26; Wilford and Butt, *Mt. Solomon Lutheran Church*.
13. Reuben Glenn's notes furnished by Jean A. Wiseman.
14. Taylor, *Bowie Knives*, p. 48.
15. Wolfe, *Corydon Democrat* (July 14, 1863), p. 1.
16. Ryan, *Corydon Republican* (July 15, 1909).
17. Ibid.
18. Taylor, *Bowie Knives*, p. 49.
19. Wolfe, *Corydon Democrat* (July 14, 1863), p. 1.
20. W.H.H. Terrell, *Adjutant General Report,* Vol. III, 1861-1865, pp. 563-567.
21. Wolfe, *Corydon Democrat* (July 14, 1863), p. 1.
22. Ibid.
23. Francis A. Lord, *Civil War Collector's Encyclopedia* (1963), p. 251.
24. Edwards, *Civil War Guns*, p. 158.
25. Wolfe, *Corydon Democrat* (July 14, 1863), p. 1.
26. Johnson, *Partisan Rangers*, p. 145.
27. Duke, *History,* p. 435; M.L. Thorpe, *The Thorpe Brothers of Kentucky of the CSA.*
28. Taylor, *Bowie Knives*, p. 51.
29. Thorpe, *Thorpe Brothers of Kentucky.*
30. Funk, *Indiana Magazine of History* (June 1959), p. 12.
31. Johnson, *Partisan Rangers*, p. 145.
32. Ibid.
33. Wolfe, *Corydon Democrat* (July 14, 1863), p. 1.
34. Funk, *Hoosiers in the Civil War*, Col. Lewis Jordan's Report, p. 25.
35. Ibid., p. 26.
36. Levi G. Saffer, *Corydon Republican* (July 15, 1909).
37. Ibid.
38. Conway, *Corydon, The Forgotten Battle*, p. 76.
39. Funk, *Hoosiers*, Col. Lewis Jordan's Report, p. 26.
40. Taylor, *Bowie Knives*, p. 52.
41. Ibid., p. 55.
42. Names inscribed on the "South" side of memorial stone at Battle of Corydon site.
43. Funk, *Morgan Raid in Indiana and Ohio*, p. 61.
44. Historical flyer prepared by Leo Benton, Corydon historian.
45. Conway, *Corydon, The Forgotten Battle*, pp. 81-83; Taylor, *Bowie Knives*, p. 55.
46. *Report of Morgan Raid (Indiana) Commissioners,* p. 32.
47. Taylor, *Bowie Knives*, p. 53.
48. *Report of Morgan Raid (Indiana) Commissioners.*
49. Mrs. Thomas Keller, Cynthia Denbo's granddaughter in a letter to the editor (July 11, 1947). Note: Rev. Peter Glenn was the mentor of her husband's ancestor, Rev. Jacob Keller.
50. Letter from Roger W. Gleitz, Leavenworth, IN, a descendant of Cynthia Denbo.
51. Taylor, *Bowie Knives*, p. 55.
52. Funk, *Morgan Raid Through Harrison County* (1977); Notes furnished by Fredrick P. Griffin, Corydon historian.
53. Funk, *Morgan Raid in Indiana and Ohio*, pp. 21-22.

54. Letters and conversations with descendants of Mary Shaffer and Joe Keefey: Charles W. Shaffer (Corydon, IN); Geneva Ankenbrand (Mt. Carmel, IL); Norman Berberich (Glendale, AZ); Eugene Berberich (Mt. Carmel, IL); and Joseph Peter (Mt. Carmel, IL).
55. *Annals of the Nineteenth Ohio Battery*, p. 208.
56. *Daily Cincinnati Enquirer* (July 10, 1863).
57. *Daily Cincinnati Enquirer* (July 11, 1863).
58. Theodore F. Allen, Capt. 7th OH Cav., *The Magazine of History* (April 1910), p. 215.
59. Undated newspaper article (circa 1863).
60. Roller, *Indiana Magazine of History*, p. 10.
61. Ibid.
62. Ibid., p. 12.
63. *OR, Part I-Reports*, Sander's Report, pp. 663-664.

Notes to Pages 80-91   **(Washington, Jackson, Scott, Jennings & Jefferson Cos.)**

13. The Hoosier Zigzag

1. Letter from Nina L. Faith (March 5, 1998).
2. Metzler, *Cavaliers*, p. 54.
3. Marjorie Ann Martin Souder, *Outdoor Indiana*, Vol. 40, No. 6 (July-August 1975), p. 34.
4. Lorine Letcher Butler, *John Morgan and His Men* (1960), p. 222.
5. Duke, *History*, p. 435.
6. Ibid., p. 436.
7. *Report of Morgan Raid (Indiana) Commissioners,* p. 43.
8. Taylor, *Bowie Knives*, pp. 62, 63.
9. *Report of Morgan Raid (Indiana) Commissioners,* p. 48.
10. Thomas M. Coombs letter to his wife Lou (August 14, 1863).
11. Taylor, *Bowie Knives*, p. 65.
12. *Report of Morgan Raid (Indiana) Commissioners,* p. 65.
13. E.A. Gladden, Scottsburg, *The WPA Life Histories Collection* (Oct. 10, 1940).
14. Duke, *History*, p. 437.
15. Gladden, *The WPA Life Histories Collection* (Oct. 10, 1940).
16. Stephen H. Woolridge, *Harrodsburg Herald* (1909).
17. Taylor, *Bowie Knives*, p. 68.
18. Terrell, *Indiana in War*, p. 235; Duke, *History*, p. 437.
19. Middleton Robinson, Deputy, *The WPA Life Histories Collection* (February 1938).
20. Ibid.
21. Gerald M. Buckley, *Sunday Times Recorder* (July 24, 1988).
22. Middleton Robinson, Deputy, *The WPA Life Histories Collection* (February 1938).
23. Duke, *History*, p. 549.
24. *OR, Part II-Correspondence,* p. 521.
25. *Alexander Graham Bell,* The Internet.
26. Paul Schubert, *The Electronic Word: The Rise of Radio* (1928).
27. Timo Kaiser, *Encyclopedia* by The Software Toolworks (1991).
28. Letter from Charles F. Cole, Sarasota, FL, great-grandson of Luther Martin (March 30, 1998).

29. Ibid.
30. *Madison Courier* (August 3, 1983).
31. Charles F. Cole letter.
32. Holland, *Raiders,* p. 240; Duke, *History,* pp. 437-438.
33. Charles F. Cole letter.
34. Duke, *History*, p. 438.
35. Letter, dated July 9, 1863, furnished by Roger Ruddick, Hayden, IN, documents events that were happening in "Hardenburg." Resident began writing four-page letter on July 9, but it is not known when it was completed. Morgan's raid came to the town on July 11.
36. Senour, *Morgan and His Captors,* p. 140.
37. Terrell, *Indiana in War,* pp. 236-237.
38. Ibid., pp. 237-238.
39. *OR, Part I-Reports,* p. 733.
40. *Cincinnati Daily Commercial* (July 24, 1863).

Notes to Pages 92-97   **(Jefferson & Ripley Counties)**

14. Dupont Pays The Price

1. Taylor, *Bowie Knives,* p. 84.
2. *Report of Morgan Raid (Indiana) Commissioners,* p. 58.
3. Dr. J.F. Lewis, *The WPA Life Histories Collection* (Oct. 10, 1940).
4. Metzler, *Cavaliers,* p. 57.
5. Terrell, *Indiana in War,* p. 238.
6. *Report of Morgan Raid (Indiana) Commissioners,* p. 61.
7. Taylor, *Bowie Knives*, p. 85.
8. Senour, *Morgan and His Captors,* pp.141-142.
9. A.A. Pender, *The WPA Life Histories Collection* (1938).
10. Lora Schmidt Cahill, *Thunderbolt* (1995), p. 17.
11. Taylor, *Bowie Knives,* p. 95.
12. Minnie Wycloff, Batesville, IN, *The WPA Life Histories Collection* (1938).
13. Taylor, *Bowie Knives*, pp. 97-98.
14. Charles S. Guthrie, *Kentucky Freemasonry: The Grand Lodge and Men Who Made It* (1981).
15. Terrell, *Indiana in War,* p. 239.
16. Thomas, *Morgan and His Raiders,* p. 81.
17. Duke, *History,* p. 439.
18. Ibid.
19. Ramage, *Rebel Raider,* p. 174.

Notes to Pages 98-104   **(Dearborn County)**

15. Last Day In Indiana

1. Telford & Louise Walker, *Our County,* Part 2, Farmer's Retreat.
2. *Aurora Journal Press* (June 3, 1986), p.7-B.

3. Taylor, *Bowie Knives*, p. 104; Keller, *Raid*, 134; Edward G. Longacre, *Mounted Raids of the Civil War* (1975), p. 196.
4. Commager, *Blue and Gray*, p. 683.
5. Bernard McCann, *Lawrenceburg Register* (July 11, 1963), p. 11.
6. Nicholas Hartman, *Lawrenceburg Register* (August 28, 1947).
7. Terrell, *Indiana in War*, p. 242.
8. Duke, *History*, p. 439.
9. Metzler, *Cavaliers*, p. 58.
10. Hartman, *Lawrenceburg Register* (August 28, 1947).
11. *History of New Alsace, Indiana*, p. 153.
12. Letter from Maxine Klump, Guilford, IN (March 19, 1996).
13. Ibid.
14. Ibid.
15. Ibid.
16. Ibid.
17. *History of New Alsace, Indiana*, p. 153.
18. Klump letter (March 19, 1996).
19. *Dearborn County, A Pictorial History* (1994), Vol. 1.
20. Interview with Lillian Mears, Harrison, OH.
21. Roller, *Indiana Magazine of History*, p. 13.
22. Ibid., p. 14.
23. *OR, Part II-Correspondence*, pp. 553-554.
24. Longacre, *Mounted Raids*, p. 195.
25. *Report of Morgan Raid (Indiana) Commissioners*, p. 84.
26. *Cincinnati Daily Commercial* (July 23, 1863).
27. Clement L. Vallandigham in History of Golden Lamb, *Internet*.
28. *Cincinnati Daily Commercial* (July 23, 1863).
29. *Cincinnati Daily Commercial* (July 16, 1863).
30. *Lawrenceburg Register* (July 15, 1971), p. 14; Terrell, *Indiana in War*, p. 246.
31. *Daily Cincinnati Enquirer* (July 16, 1863).
32. Commager, *Blue and Gray*, p. 682.

OHIO

Notes to Pages 106-109   (Hamilton County)

16. Harrison Shopping Spree

1. Duke, *History*, p. 442.
2. Thirey and Mitchel, *Encyclopedic Directory* (1902).
3. Commager, *Blue and Gray*, p. 682.
4. *Report of Morgan Raid (Ohio) Commissioners*, pp. 106, 108, 122.
5. Ramage, *Rebel Raider*, p. 172.
6. Interview with Anita Mitchell, Harrison, OH.
7. Letter from Paul Bennett, Harrison, OH.
8. Allan Keller, *Morgan's Raid* (1962), p. 129.
9. Ramage, *Rebel Raider*, p. 160.
10. Described by Thomas Fugate, Kentucky Military History Museum.

Notes to Pages 110-112

17. Let's Split!

1. *OR, Part I-Reports,* p. 741.
2. Ibid., p. 742.
3. Brown, *Raiders,* p. 207.
4. *Daily Cincinnati Enquirer* (July 14, 1863).
5. *Cadiz Republican* (July 29, 1863).
6. Ibid.
7. Johnson, *Partisan Rangers,* pp. 145-146.
8. Keller, *Raid,* p. 119.
9. *Daily Cincinnati Enquirer* (July 14, 1863).
10. Duke, *History,* pp. 442-443.
11. Rev. Charles Frederic Goss, *The Queen City,* Book I (1912), p. 220.

Notes to Pages 113-119

18. Waiting For Morgan

1. *OR, Part I-Reports,* Governor's Proclamation (July 12, 1863), pp. 737-738.
2. Ibid., p. 744.
3. *Annals of the Nineteenth Ohio Battery Volunteer Artillery,* p. 181.
4. Ibid.
5. *Daily Cincinnati Enquirer* (July 14, 1863).
6. Ibid.
7. Ibid.
8. *OR, Part I-Reports,* p. 740.
9. *Daily Cincinnati Enquirer* (July 15, 1863); Keller, *Morgan's Raid,* p. 120.
10. *OR, Part II-Correspondence,* p. 531.
11. Ibid.
12. Keller, *Raid,* p. 122; Maj. George Rue, *Ohio Historical Quarterly,* Vol. XX (1911), pp. 369-370.
13. Keller, *Raid,* p. 123.
14. Rue, *Quarterly,* p. 370.
15. Keller, *Raid,* p. 122.
16. Henry Howe, *Historical Collections of Ohio,* Vol. I (1900), p. 455.
17. Duke, *History,* p. 444.
18. Thomas M. Coombs letter to his wife, Lou (August 14, 1863).
19. Howe, *Historical Collections* (1898),Vol. I, p. 455.
20. *Nineteenth Ohio Battery Annals,* pp. 181-182.
21. Howe, *Historical Collections,* Vol. I, p. 455.
22. *Nineteenth Ohio Battery Annals,* p. 182.
23. Howe, *Historical Collections,* Vol. I, p. 455.
24. *Daily Cincinnati Enquirer* (July 15, 1863).
25. *Ohio Handbook of the Civil War* (1961), pp. 11-12.

Notes to Pages 120-122

19. "Veiled" Threat in Glendale

1. Keller, *Raid*, p. 131.
2. *Glendale Heritage*, p. 48.
3. Ibid., p. 44.
4. *Report of Morgan Raid (Ohio) Commissioners,* pp. 106-129.
5. Duke, *History*, p. 443.
6. *Daily Cincinnati Enquirer* (July 14, 1863).
7. Duke, *History*, p. 444.
8. Johnson, *Partisan Rangers,* p. 146.

Notes to Pages 123-125

20. While Sherman Slept

1. Sister M. P. Butler, *The American Foundation of Notre Dame De Namur* (1928), pp. 79-80; Denise White, *History of the School* (undated).
2. John Fleischman, Reluctant Warrior, *Ohio Magazine* (August 1983), p. 39.
3. Ibid., p. 37.
4. Butler, *Notre Dame De Namur*, p. 80.
5. Druggist labels from the collection of Helen Ward; *Sycamore Messenger (*February 3, 1977), p. 1.
6. Letter written by Ida Schenck Dittes, Memphis, TN (undated).
7. Dittes letter; *Sycamore Messenger* (February 3, 1977), p. 1.
8. Dittes letter.
9. Ibid.
10. *Daily Cincinnati Enquirer* (July 15, 1863).
11. Dittes letter.
12. Conversation with Eileen Schenck.

Notes to Pages 126-130

21. Camp Dennison's 600 Gun Salute

1. *OR, Part I-Reports*, p. 670.
2. Mary Rahn Sloan, *History of Camp Dennison* (1956), p. 29.
3. *OR, Part I-Reports*, p. 749.
4. Keller, *Raid*, p.132.
5. *OR, Part I-Reports*, p. 747.
6. Eleanor Gholson Taft, *Hither and Yon on Indian Hill* (1962), p. 32.
7. Sloan, *History of Camp Dennison,* p. 30.
8. Walt Schaefer, *Daily Cincinnati Enquirer* (August 4, 1998), p. B3.
9. Sloan, *History of Camp Dennison,* p. 29.
10. *Cincinnati Daily Commercial* (July 24, 1863).
11. Sloan, *History of Camp Dennison,* p. 30.

12. William E. Unrau, *Tending the Talking Wire*, p. 10.
13. Alvin M. Josephy, Jr., *The Civil War in the American West*, p. 250;
14. Al Martellotti, *Highland County Magazine* (1985), p. 31.
15. Byron Stinson, *Civil War Times* (May 1971), p. 25; *OR, Part I-Reports*, p. 671.
16. *Cincinnati Daily Commercial* (July 24, 1863).
17. *Civil War Times* (May 1971), pp. 20-27.
18. *OR, Part I-Reports*, p. 671.
19. *Daily Cincinnati Enquirer* (July 15, 1863); Henry & Kate Ford, *History of Hamilton County Ohio* (1881), p. 92.

Notes to Pages 130-136

22. Thoroughbreds In Trade

1. *Northeast Suburban Life* (August 2, 1995), p. 1.
2. *Report of Morgan Raid (Ohio) Commissioners*, pp. 126-127. Letter written by Jerusha June, Montgomery, OH (July 17, 1863).
3. Letter written by Capt. James Todd, Montgomery, OH (July 6, 1864) from Lucille MacKnight, Cincinnati, OH (January 7, 1998).
4. *Report of Morgan Raid (Ohio) Commissioners*, pp. 126-127.
5. Sloan, *History of Camp Dennison*, pp. 32-33.
6. *Report of Morgan Raid (Ohio) Commissioners*, pp. 112-113.
7. *Cincinnati Daily Commercial* (July 24, 1863).
8. *Butterworth Diary* (July, 1863).
9. Dallas Bogan, *Family History*.
10. Ibid.
11. Duke, *History*, p. 444.
12. Home of the author.

Notes to Pages 137-139   (Clermont County)

23. An Unscheduled Train Stop

1. *OR, Part I-Reports*, p. 671.
2. *Daily Cincinnati Enquirer* (July 15, 1863).
3. Clermont County Engineer's map (1870).
4. Clyde W. Park, *Morgan The Unpredictable* (1959), p. 24.
5. *Daily Cincinnati Enquirer* (July 15, 1863).
6. Ibid.
7. Ibid.
8. Carter, *Last Cavaliers*, pp. 181-182; Brown, *Raiders*, p. 209.
9. *Daily Cincinnati Enquirer* (July 15, 1863).
10. *Report of Morgan Raid (Ohio) Commissioners*, pp. 70-71, 122-123.
11. *Loveland, Passages Through Time* (1992), p. 20.
12. *Loveland...from its beginning* (1976), p. 7.
13. Ibid., p. 13.
14. *Daily Cincinnati Enquirer* (July 15, 1863).

15. *Cincinnati Daily Commercial* (July 16, 1863).
16. Ibid.
17. Ibid.
18. Keller, *Raid*, p. 132; Metzler, *Cavaliers,* p. 60.

Notes to Pages 140-144

24. A Romance of Morgan's Rough Riders

1. Conversation with Elva Maphet, granddaughter of John and Catharine Anderson.
2. G.R. Burdsal, *WPA Life Histories Collection* (October 10, 1940); Taylor, *Bowie Knives,* p. 85; Johnson, *Partisan Rangers*, pp. 385-386.
3. Keller, *Raid*, p. 133.
4. Duke, *Century Magazine*, Vol. XLI, pp. 409-410.
5. Thomas, *Morgan and His Raiders*, p. 22.
6. Holland, *Raiders*, pp. 9-10.
7. James B. Swing, *Historical Souvenirs of Clermont County, Ohio* (1916), p. 38.
8. Ibid.
9. Park, *Unpredictable*, p. 27.
10. Swing, *Souvenirs*, p. 38.
11. *Report of Morgan Raid (Ohio) Commissioners,* pp. 60-81.
12. *History of Clermont and Brown Counties*, Chapter XX, p. 431.
13. Keller, *Morgan's Raid* (1962), p. 133.
14. Tom Fortney, *Cincinnati Post* (January 21, 1972), p. 4.

Notes to Pages 145-148

25. Williamsburg, The First Good Rest In Weeks

1. Howe, *Historical Collections*, Vol. I (1900), p. 408.
2. *Historical Souvenirs of Clermont County*, p. 34; *Olde Williamsburgh* (1996), p. 28.
3. Duke, *History*, p. 444.
4. Ibid.
5. *Report of Morgan Raid (Ohio) Commissioners,* pp. 68-69.
6. *History of Clermont and Brown Counties*, Chapter XX, p. 433.
7. *Historical Souvenirs of Clermont County*, p. 35; Richard Crawford, *Thunder in the Valley* (1985), p. 23.
8. Howe, *Historical Collections*, Vol. I, p. 416.
9. Crawford, *Thunder*, p. 22.
10. *OR, Part I-Reports*, p. 659.
11. Bryron Williams, *History of Clermont & Brown Counties, Ohio* (1913), pp. 431-432; Crawford, *Thunder*, p. 41.
12. The story of Captain Harris deserting General Morgan was a rare occurrence. There were a few other Confederates who chose to desert on this raid, but for other reasons. Another young raider had parents living in Williamsburg on Main Street. They had, a few months earlier, moved from Kentucky. He stayed on with them, but soon after, they all left town.

13. *Historical Souvenirs of Clermont County*, p. 34.
14. *OR, Part I-Reports*, p. 659.
15. Ibid., p. 660.
16. *Clermont and Brown Counties*, p. 433.
17. Crawford, *Thunder*, pp. 31-32.

Notes to Pages 149-153

26. Mayor Leads Cincinnati Cavalry

1. *Daily Cincinnati Enquirer* (July 15, 1863).
2. *OR, Part I-Reports*, p. 656; *Daily Cincinnati Enquirer* (July 16, 1863).
3. *Daily Cincinnati Enquirer* (July 16, 1863).
4. Ibid. (July 15, 1863).
5. Seawright, Sorrows of the Alstons. Part 19, *Flagpole Magazine,* The Internet.
6. *Daily Cincinnati Enquirer* (July 16, 1863).
7. Ibid.
8. Ibid.
9. Patricia L. Faust, *Historical Times Encyclopedia of the Civil War* (1986), pp. 816-817.
10. Indianapolis *Daily State Sentinel* (July 14, 1863).
11. *OR, Part I-Reports*, p. 754.
12. Ibid.
13. Ibid., p. 755.
14. *Daily Cincinnati Enquirer* (July 17, 1863).
15. *OR, Part I-Reports*, p. 656.
16. Ibid.
17. Keller, *Raid*, p. 135.
18. *Ohio Historical Society Quarterly*, Vol. XX (1911), pp. 370-371.
19. Ibid., p. 371.

Notes to Pages 154-158   **(Brown County)**

27. Colonel Morgan Visits Georgetown

1. Thomas, *Morgan and His Raiders,* p. 82; Brown, *Raiders*, p. 210.
2. Letter from Catherine Naylor, Georgetown, OH describing story as told to her by Mr. Brunner's son-in-law, Frank Roth (February 23, 1996).
3. John H. Houston, *News Democrat* (March 17, 1944).
4. *OR, Part I-Reports*, p. 751.
5. Ibid., p. 753.
6. *The People's Defender* (undated).
7. Letter from Paula Gammell, Oak Ridge, TN, whose gr-gr-grandfather was James M. Stafford (June 3, 1997).
8. Homer W. King, *Biography of John A. Cockerill* (1965), p. 18.
9. *Civil War Illustrated Times* (November, 1984), p. 39.

Notes to Pages 159-163

28. Beeline For Buffington

1. Story told by Lynn Gardner, Georgetown, Ohio.
2. *Report of Morgan Raid (Ohio) Commissioners,* pp. 46-47; Ian Cunningham, *News Democrat* (April 24, 1997).
3. Letter from Eleanor Grooms, Sardinia, OH, granddaughter of John Porter (April 8, 1996).
4. Lee Liming, *Neal/Liming Family History,* pp. 21-22.
5. Letter from Denver Carey, West Chester, OH, about his great grandparents, Joshua and Mary Carey (March 9, 1996).
6. Duke, *History,* p. 445.
7. Letter from Richard M. Bean, Lexington, KY, grandson of Robert T. Bean (September 21, 1997).
8. Thomas M. Coombs letter to his wife, Lou (August 14, 1863).
9. Josephy, *American West,* p. 247.
10. Unrau, *Talking Wire,* p. 8.
11. Ibid., p. 9.
12. Josephy, *American West,* p. 250.
13. Unrau, *Talking Wire,* p. 13.
14. Josephy, *American West,* p. 250.
15. 11th Ohio Cavalry History, *Internet*; Josephy, *American West,* p. 250.

Notes to Pages 164-168   (Adams County)

29. Winchester's "Fenced In"

1. Ben Smith, *News Democrat* (September 26, 1946).
2. Stephen Kelley, *People's Defender* (January 24, 1996).
3. Smith, *Democrat* (September 26, 1946); Kelley, *Defender* (February 14, 1996).
4. Kelley, *Defender* (February 14, 1996).
5. Smith, *Democrat* (September 26, 1946).
6. Kelley, *Defender* (January 24, 1996).
7. Ibid. (February 7, 1996).
8. Sherman Beam, *Defender* (1963).
9. James S. Frame, *Defender* (1963).
10. Smith, *Democrat* (September 26, 1946).
11. Ibid.
12. Letter from Doris Murphy Boggs, Hillsboro, OH about her grandparents (March 26, 1996).
13. Kelley, *Defender* (undated).
14. Doris Wickerham interview with Nancy Wickerham Sharpe (1931).
15. Ibid.
16. Ibid.
17. Sherman Beam, *Defender* (1963).
18. Ibid.
19. Stanley Herdman, *Defender* (March 15, 1973).

Notes to Pages 169-173   **(Pike County)**

30. "Axes To The Front"

1. Thomas, *Raiders*, p. 82.
2. Blaine Beekman, *Call Of Conscience, Call Of Duty* (1975), p. 28.
3. Herdman, *Defender* (March 15, 1973).
4. Beekman, *Call Of Duty*, p. 28.
5. Thomas M. Coombs letter to his wife, Lou (August 14, 1863).
6. Beekman, *Call Of Duty*, p. 29.
7. Ibid., p. 30.
8. Ibid., pp. 30-31.
9. Governor Tod's papers relating to the Morgan Raid, No. 40—Telegram (July 15, 1863).
10. Commager, *Blue and Gray*, p. 683.
11. Beekman, *Call Of Duty*, p. 32.
12. Ibid.
13. Letter written by Ethel Blackburn, Pleasantville, OH, great granddaughter of Stewart Alexander (October 8, 1995).
14. Letter written by Lina Silcott Shoemaker, granddaughter of Stewart Alexander.
15. Beekman, *Call Of Duty*, p. 33.
16. Ibid., pp. 33-34.

Notes to Pages 174-176

31. McDougal's Fatal Encounter

1. Jim Henry, Pike's Past, *Waverly News Watchman* (May 19, 1977).
2. Beekman, *Call Of Duty*, pp. 35-36.
3. Ibid., 35; Robert Ervin, *Jackson Journal-Herald* (September 30, 1987), p. 10.
4. J. Henry, *News Watchman* (December 27, 1984).
5. Beekman, *Call of Duty*, p. 36.
6. Kalfs, *Gazette* (April 22, 1972), p. 3.
7. *Report of Morgan Raid (Ohio) Commissioners,* pp. 232-233.
8. Beekman, *Call of Duty*, pp. 36-38.
9. Letter written by Michael E. Whitfield, Rocky Face, GA, gr-gr-grandson of Joseph W. Whitfield (May 27, 1996).
10. *Report of Morgan Raid (Ohio) Commissioners,* pp. 236-237.
11. *OR, Part I-Reports,* p. 662.
12. Sarah Higgins, *Gazette* (March 8, 1997), Lifestyle/C.
13. Whitelaw Reid, *Ohio In The War* (1868), Vol. I, Chapter XII, p. 144.
14. Beekman, *Call of Duty*, p. 38.
15. Edward L. Sebring, *Vincennes Sun-Commercial* (February 20, 1998), p. A4.
16. *Report of Morgan Raid (Ohio) Commissioners,* pp. 230-231.
17. Sebring, *Vincennes Sun-Commercial* (February 20, 1998), p. A4.

Notes to Pages 177-181

32. A Bridge Beyond

1. Beekman, *Call of Duty*, p. 38.
2. *Biographies of State Senators*, James Emmitt, Seventh District, pg. 119.
3. Beekman, *Call of Duty*, p. 38.
4. J. Henry, *News Watchman* (January 10, 1985), p. 8.
5. Beekman, *Call of Duty*, p. 39.
6. Ibid.
7. Ibid.
8. J.E. McGowan, *Morgan's Indiana and Ohio Raid* (1879), p. 755.
9. Beekman, *Call of Duty*, p. 40.
10. Ibid., p. 41.
11. Geneva Keppler, *History of Beaver in Pike County* (May 27, 1965), p. 38.
12. Beekman, *Call of Duty*, p. 41.
13. Keppler, *History of Beaver*, p. 19.
14. Ibid., p. 37.
15. Ibid., pp. 37-38.
16. J. Henry, *News Watchman* (September 26, 1995), p. 4.
17. Keppler, *History of Beaver*, p. 39.
18. McGowan, *Morgan's Raid*, p. 756.
19. Mike Deaterla, *Portsmouth Daily Times* (July 30, 1988).
20. Letter from Mamie C. Lloyd (March 13, 1996).
21. T. Harry Williams, *Hayes of the Twenty-Third* (1965), pp. 153-154.
22. Beekman, *Call of Duty*, p. 42.
23. Ibid., p. 43.
24. *OR, Part I-Reports*, p. 764.
25. Ibid., p. 765.
26. Beekman, *Call of Duty*, p. 43.
27. Ibid.
28. Ibid.
29. *OR, Part I-Reports*, p. 662.
30. *Annals of the Nineteenth Ohio Battery*, pp. 186-187.
31. Ibid., pp. 187-188.

Notes to Pages 182-186   (Jackson County)

33. Newspaper Wars

1. Everette E. Parker, *Jackson Times* (undated).
2. *Jackson Standard-Journal* (January 18, 1899).
3. Ervin, *Jackson Journal-Herald* (circa 1988).
4. Ibid.
5. Ibid.
6. Jack Rhea, *Jackson-Vinton Journal-Herald* (December 10, 1995), p. 15.
7. Rhea, *Journal-Herald*, (1995); Ervin, *Journal-Herald* (circa 1988).
8. Metzler, *Cavaliers*, p. 61.
9. *Early Jackson*, p. 26.
10. Ibid.

11. Ibid., pp. 26-27.
12. Ibid., p. 27.
13. *OR, Part I-Reports*, pp. 764-765.
14. Ibid., p. 772.
15. Ibid., p. 767.

Notes to Pages 188-190   **(Vinton County)**

34. "Our Last Night In The North"

1. *Jackson Standard-Journal* (January 18, 1899).
2. Charles H. Harris, *The Harris History* (1957), pp. 257-258.
3. Ibid., p. 254.
4. *Report of Morgan Raid (Ohio) Commissioners,* pp. 246-247.
5. Harris, *Harris History*, p. 258.
6. *Jackson Standard-Journal* (January 18, 1899); Harris, *Harris History*, p. 258.
7. Harris, *Harris History*, p. 258.
8. *The Athens Messenger* (July 23, 1863).
9. Ibid.
10. *Report of Morgan Raid (Ohio) Commissioners,* pp. 176-177; 204-205; 208-209.
11. *Athens Messenger* (July 23, 1863).
12. Rue, *Ohio Historical Quarterly,* Vol. XX, p. 371.
13. Ibid.

Notes to Pages 191-194

35. The U.S. Navy, The Union's Secret Weapon

1. *Daily Cincinnati Enquirer*, July 17, 1863.
2. Myron J. Smith, *Gunboats at Buffington, West Virginia History*, Vol. XLIV, No. 2, p. 105.
3. Ibid., pp. 105-106.
4. *Diary of Rutherford B. Hayes* (1922), Vol. II, p. 420.
5. *Annals of the Nineteenth Ohio Battery*, p. 187.
6. Keller, *Raid*, p. 182.
7. Smith, *Gunboats at Buffington,* p. 106.
8. Ibid., p. 98.
9. Ibid., p. 100.
10. Ibid., pp. 101-102.
11. Ibid., p. 102.
12. Ibid., p. 104.
13. *OR, Part II-Correspondence*, p. 541.
14. *OR, Part I-Reports,* p. 660.

Notes to Page 195   **(Gallia County)**

36. Vinton Loses Its Bridge

1. Charles A. Murray, Estivaun Matthews & Pauline Rife; *Gallia County One-Room Schools* (1993), p 101.
2. Ervin, *Journal-Herald* (January 8, 1988), p. 10.
3. Gallia County *Welcome* Brochure.
4. Williams, *Hayes of the Twenty-Third*, p. 156.

Notes to Pages 196-200   **(Meigs County)**

37. Last Lap To Freedom

1.   Hardesty, *Historical Encyclopedia* (1883), p. 276.
2.   Hiram B. Smith, *Stock Book of the Newcastle Coal & Salt Co.*, p. 1.
3.   *Report of Morgan Raid (Ohio) Commissioners,* pp. 210-211.
4.   Ibid., pp. 186-187.
5.   Margaret Rigg, *Pomeroy Daily Sentinel* (undated).
6.   Thomas W. Lewis, *Southeastern Ohio and the Muskingum Valley*, Vol. II, p. 586.
7.   Rigg, *Pomeroy Daily Sentinel* (undated).
8.   Ibid.
9.   Ibid.
10. Ibid., Roy Cross, *Athens Messenger* (undated).
11. Smith, *Stock Book*, p. 1.
12. Information related on a Meigs County historical tour (1996) by Mike Gerlach, Meigs County history teacher.
13. Ibid.
14. Hardesty, *Historical Encyclopedia*, p. 276; Lewis, *Southeastern Ohio*, p. 586.
15. Gerlach tour; Lewis, *Southeastern Ohio*, p. 586.
16. A.E. Dumble, *Tribune-Telegraph* (June 5, 1895), p. 5.
17. Ibid.
18. Gerlach tour.
19. Charles E. Walker, Meigs County (Pomeroy) newspaper (1933).

Notes to Pages 201-206

38. The Pomeroy-Middleport Gauntlet

1. Meigs County Pioneer & Historical Society, *125ᵗʰ Anniversary Celebration of Buffington Island Battle* (July 30, 1988), p. 3.
2. Williams, *Hayes of the Twenty-Third*, p. 156.
3. Edgar Ervin, *Pioneer History of Meigs County* (1949), pp. 203-204.
4. *OR, Part I-Reports,* p. 773.
5. Gerlach tour.
6. *Official Roster of Ohio Soldiers* (1883), Vol. III, p. 72.
7. Duke, *History*, pp. 445-446.
8. Gerlach tour; Ed Bearss, BGES bus tour of Buffington battlefield (June 12, 1998).

9. *Meigs County History* (1980).
10. *OR, Part I-Reports*, p. 656.
11. Beulah Jones, *Pomeroy Sentinel* (undated); Hardesty, *Historical Encyclopedia*, p. 276.
12. *Report of Morgan Raid (Ohio) Commissioners,* pp. 192-193.
13. Johnson, *Partisan Rangers*, p. 147.
14. Washington Holter, unidentified Meigs County newspaper (February 15, 1913).
15. Keller, *Raid*, p. 162.
16. Johnson, *Partisan Rangers*, p. 147.
17. Duke, *History*, p. 450.
18. Gerlach tour.
19. Thomas M. Coombs letter to his wife Lou (August 14, 1863).
20. *OR, Part I-Reports,* p. 766.
21. Keller, *Raid*, p. 165.
22. Bennett, BGES Morgan's Raid Symposium (June 13, 1998).
23. Keller, *Raid*, p. 164.
24. Ibid., p. 166.
25. Gayle Price, *The Daily Sentinel* (July 19, 1995), p. 8.
26. *OR, Part I-Reports,* p. 660.

Notes to Pages 207-210

39. The Net Tightens

1. *OR, Part I-Reports,* p. 662.
2. Ibid., p. 656.
3. Brown, *Raiders*, p. 213.
4. Duke, *History,* p. 448.
5. Diary of Capt. Thomas Munroe Coombs, Co. K, 5th KY. Entry of July 19, 1863.
6. Smith, *Gunboats at Buffington*, p. 106.
7. Ibid.
8. Ibid.
9. *OR, Part I-Reports,* pp. 656-657.
10. Smith, *Gunboats at Buffington*, p. 105.
11. Topographical map furnished by the Ohio Department of Natural Resources.
12. Gerlach tour.
13. Price, *Daily Sentinel* (July 19, 1995), p. 8; Gerlach tour.
14. Charlene Hoeflich, *Daily Sentinel* (July 26, 1988), p. 6.
15. *Report of Morgan Raid (Ohio) Commissioners,* pp. 176-177, 196-197.
16. Hoeflich, *Daily Sentinel* (July 27, 1988).
17. Price, *Sentinel* (July 19, 1995), p. 8.
18. J. Hoback, *The Pomeroy Leader* (September 29, 1900), p. 8.
19. Ed Bearss, BGES bus tour of Buffington battlefield (June 12, 1998).
20. Cincinnati Public Library, Technology Dept.; Columbus Weather Bureau.

Notes to Pages 211-213

40. In A Fog

1. Duke, *History*, p. 448.
2. Col. J.E. McGowan, *Morgan's Indiana and Ohio Raid* (1879), pp. 757-758.
3. Ibid., pp. 758-759.
4. Carlos D. Henry, Reminiscences recorded at Amesville, Ohio (May 1, 1963).
5. McGowan, *Morgan's Indiana and Ohio Raid,* p. 759.
6. Metzler, *Cavaliers*, p. 63; Duke, *History*, p. 453.
7. Ibid.
8. Ibid.; Brown, *Raiders*, p. 246.
9. McGowan, *Indiana and Ohio Raid*, pp. 759-760.
10. Ibid., p. 760.
11. Ibid.
12. *OR, Part I-Reports,* pp. 775-776; McGowan, *Indiana and Ohio Raid*, pp. 759-760.
13. Duke, *History*, p. 449.
14. Hoback, *The Pomeroy Leader* (September 29, 1900).

Notes to Pages 214-219

41. The Battle at Buffington Island

1. Ramage, *Rebel Raider*, p. 177.
2. Metzler, *Cavaliers*, p. 62; Duke, *History*, p. 449.
3. Smith, *Gunboats at Buffington*, p. 106.
4. *OR, Fitch's Report.*
5. Smith, *Gunboats at Buffington*, p. 107.
6. Ibid.
7. Duke, *History*, pp. 450-451, 460.
8. In every historical reference, almost without exception, the *Allegheny Belle* is mentioned as being present and participating in the Battle of Buffington Island on Sunday, July 19, 1863. The exceptions are contradictory statements in *Gunboats at Buffington* by Myron J. Smith Jr. published in *West Virginia History,* Winter, 1983, Vol. XLIV, Number Two. On page 106, he states, "…only the *Moose* (was present) to handle Morgan's attempted crossing at Buffington." Smith continues on page 108, "Early Monday morning (July 20), the *Allegheny Belle*, a packet outfitted at Burnside's order and placed under naval authority, joined the *Moose*." On the same page, he describes the *Allegheny Belle* as joining the *Moose* in stopping Colonel Adam R. Johnson's crossing at Belleville which occurred the same day as the Battle of Buffington Island, Sunday, July 19. The text reads, "Although some drowned in the rush of men and the river's swift current, about three hundred men reached the safety of the West Virginia bank before the *Moose* and *Allegheny Belle* were seen rushing up the channel."
9. Keller, *Raid*, p. 174.
10. McGowan, *Indiana and Ohio Raid*, pp. 760-761; Duke, *History*, p. 450.
11. Thomas M. Coombs letter to his wife Lou (August 14, 1863).
12. McGowan, *Indiana and Ohio Raid*, p. 761.
13. Duke, *History*, p. 450.

14. Keller, *Morgan's Raid*, p. 172.
15. Weaver, *Sketches*, p. 302.
16. *OR, Part I-Reports,* p. 662.
17. Ramage, *Rebel Raider*, p. 178.
18. Johnson, *Partisan Rangers*, p. 147.
19. Keller, *Morgan's Raid*, p. 172.
20. Reid, *Ohio In The War*, p. 146.
21. Captain H.C. Weaver, *Sketches of War History* (1896), Vol. IV, p. 305.
22. Duke, *History*, p. 452.
23. *OR, Part I-Reports*, p. 660.
24. Ibid., pp. 662-663.
25. Keller, *Morgan's Raid*, pp. 172-173.
26. Ibid., p. 173.
27. Duke, *History*, p. 451.
28. Col. Grover S. Wormer, *The Morgan Raid* (1898), p. 205.
29. Ibid.
30. Weaver, *Sketches*, p. 304.
31. Duke, *History*, p. 452.
32. Smith, *Gunboats at Buffington*, p. 107.
33. Wormer, *Morgan Raid*, pp. 205-206.

Notes to Pages 220-224

42. Morgan Escapes, Duke Captured

1. Ramage, *Rebel Raider*, p. 178.
2. Brown, *Raiders*, p. 216.
3. Hathaway and Gillespie, *Ohio Historical Society Timeline* (October-November 1985), p.48.
4. *OR, Part I-Reports,* p. 641.
5. Weaver, *Sketches*, p. 308.
6. Keller, *Morgan's Raid*, p. 178.
7. Brown, *Raiders*, p. 215.
8. Metzler, *Cavaliers*, p. 63; Brown, *Raiders*, p. 215.
9. Williams, *Hayes of the Twenty-third*, p. 157.
10. Hoeflich, *Daily Sentinel* (July 27, 1988).
11. Wormer, *Morgan Raid*, p. 207.
12. Ibid., pp. 207-208.
13. Theodore F. Allen, Capt. 7th OH Cav., *Sketches of War History* (1903), pp. 238-239.
14. Ibid., pp. 239-240.
15. Ibid., p. 240.
16. Wormer, *Morgan Raid*, p. 206.
17. Hemingway, *America's Civil War* (November 1989), p. 59; Brown, *Raiders*, p. 218.
18. *OR, Part I-Reports*, p. 663.
19. Ibid., pp. 776-777.
20. Ibid.
21. Ibid.
22. McGowan, *Morgan's Raid*, p. 761.

Notes to Pages 225-228

43. Mopping Up

1. McGowan, *Morgan's Raid*, p. 761.
2. Letter from Sherman T. Dozier, Versailles, KY, great grandson of Peter Dozier (November 11, 1996).
3. Interview with Gayle Price during BGES Bus Tour to Buffington Island Battle site (June 12, 1998).
4. Price, *Daily Sentinel* (July 19, 1995).
5. Weaver, *Sketches of War History*, p. 305.
6. Interview with Anita Mitchell, Harrison, OH.
7. *OR, Part I-Reports,* p. 656; Smith, *Gunboats at Buffington*, p. 106.
8. *OR, Part I-Reports,* p. 666.
9. Ibid., p. 661.
10. Weaver, *Sketches*, p. 305.
11. Ibid., pp. 305-306.
12. *OR, Part I-Reports,* p. 777; Weaver, *Sketches*, p. 306.
13. Weaver, *Sketches*, p. 306.
14. *OR, Part I-Reports,* pp. 780, 787.
15. Ibid., pp. 788-789.
16. Maj. George Rue, *Ohio Historical Quarterly,* Vol. XX (1911), p. 371.
17. Washington Holter, *Pomeroy Leader* (February 15, 1913).
18. Ibid.
19. Meigs County newspaper (1933).
20. Mrs. A.E. Dumble, *The Tribune-Telegraph* (June 5, 1895).
21. James Sands, *Pomeroy Sunday Times-Sentinel* (July 9, 1995), p. B4.
22. Dumble, *The Tribune-Telegraph* (June 5, 1895).
23. Meigs County newspaper (1933).

Notes to Pages 229-236

44. Capture and Surrender. A Partial Victory

1. *Morgan's Division Regiment Rosters*, pp. 82-83.
2. Weaver, *Sketches*, p. 308; *OR, Part I-Reports*, p. 661.
3. *OR, Part I-Reports,* p. 780.
4. Ibid., p. 657.
5. Howe, *Historical Collections* (1898), Vol. I, p. 366.
6. Ibid.
7. Camilla Warrick, *Cincinnati Post* (September 15, 1995), p. 4B; Owen Findsen, *Cincinnati, Enquirer* (June 15, 1997), p. E12.
8. Whitelaw Reid, *Ohio in the War* (1868); McGowan, *Annals of the War*, p. 767; Owen Findsen, *Enquirer* (June 15, 1997), p. E12.
9. McGowan, *Annals of the War*, p. 767.
10. Governor Tod's papers relating to the Morgan Raid, No. 88—Telegram (July 22, 1863); Keller, *Raid*, p. 170.

11. *Queen City Heritage*, Vol. 53 (Spring/Summer 1995), p. 75; Owen Findsen, *Enquirer* (June 15, 1997), p. E12.
12. McGowan, *Annals of the War*, p. 767.
13. *OR, Part I-Reports,* p. 637.

Notes to Pages 237-242

45. "Go On. Save Yourself!"

1. Butler, *Morgan and His Men*, p. 237.
2. Price, *Sentinel*, (July 19, 1995), p. 8.
3. Ibid.
4. John Switzer, *Columbus Dispatch* (April 8, 1992).
5. Johnson, *Partisan Rangers*, p. 148.
6. *Richmond Enquirer* (July 31, 1863); Dee Alexander Brown set the number at 330, *Raiders*, p. 246.
7. Smith, *Gunboats at Buffington*, p. 108.
8. Keller, *Raid*, p. 187.
9. Ramage, *Rebel Raider*, p. 178.
10. Duke, *History*, pp. 453-454.
11. Johnson, *Partisan Rangers*, pp. 148-149.
12. Butler, *Morgan and His Men*, p. 238.
13. Johnson, *Partisan Rangers*, p. 149.
14. Ibid., pp. 149-150.
15. Smith, *Gunboats at Buffington*, p. 109.
16. Ibid.
17. Letters from Sherman T. Dozier, Versailles, KY (November 11, 1996 and September 21, 1997); *Morgan's Division Regiment Rosters*, pp. 78-79.
18. Smith, *Gunboats at Buffington*, p. 109.
19. *Morgan's Division Regiment Rosters*, pp. 20-21.
20. *Julia Cutler and Morgan's Raid* (1960), p. 29.
21. Keller, *Raid*, p. 182.
22. Ibid., pp. 182-183.

Notes to Pages 243-246   (Gallia County)

46. The Chase To Cheshire

1. *OR, Part I-Reports,* pp. 641-642.
2. Sands, *Pomeroy Sunday Times Sentinel* (July 9, 1995), p. B4.
3. Ibid.
4. Letter written by Alvira E. Nye Gates (1828-1915).
5. Ibid.
6. Capt. T.M. Coombs' diary entry (July 20, 1863).
7. Hockersmith, *Morgan's Escape*, p. 18.
8. *OR, Part I-Reports,* pp. 641-642.
9. Hockersmith, *Morgan's Escape*, p. 19.
10. *OR, Part I-Reports,* p. 642.

11. Ibid.
12. Capt. T.M. Coombs' diary entry (July 20, 1863).
13. *OR, Part I-Reports,* p. 642.
14. Lew Ogan, *History of Vinton County* (1954), p. 210.
15. Ibid., p. 230.
16. Hockersmith, *Morgan's Escape,* p. 19.
17. Sands, *Pomeroy Sunday Times-Sentinel* (July 9, 1995), p. B4.
18. Capt. T.M. Coombs' diary entry (July 20, 1863).
19. McGowan, *Annals of the War,* p. 765.

Notes to Pages 247-252   (Meigs County)

47. Steamboatin' To Prison

1. Howe, *Historical Collections of Ohio* (1900), Vol. I, p. 777; Metzler, *Cavaliers,* p. 67.
2. *OR, Part I-Reports,* p. 781.
3. Ibid., pp. 787, 788.
4. Metzler, *Cavaliers,* p. 67; Capt. T.M. Coombs' diary entry (July 23, 1863).
5. Capt. T.M. Coombs' diary entry (July 25, 1863).
6. Duke, *History,* p. 463.
7. Letter from John D. Jackson, MD, Jefferson, LA (December 11, 1996).
8. McGowan, *Annals of the War,* pp. 767-768.
9. Ibid.
10. Goss, *The Queen City,* Book I (1912), p. 340.
11. Howe, *Historical Collections* (1898),Vol. I, p. 777.
12. Smith, *Gunboats at Buffington,* pp. 109-110.
13. *OR, Part I-Reports,* p. 642.
14. *The Athens Messenger* (August 6, 1863).
15. Duke, *History,* p. 454.
16. Brown, *Raiders,* p. 219.
17. Keller, *Raid,* p. 189.
18. Duke, *History,* p. 454.
19. Keller, *Raid,* pp. 189-190.
20. Brown, *Raiders,* p. 220.
21. *OR, Part II-Correspondence,* p. 545 .
22. Letter written "after supper" by Fanny Cooley, living in the Coolville, OH area, to her husband, Leonard, away in the army (July 20, 1863).
23. *Report of Morgan Raid (Ohio) Commissioners,* pp. 176-213.

Notes to Pages 253-254   (Athens County)

48. Riding The Athens-Meigs County Line

1. *The Athens Messenger* (August 6, 1863).
2. Ibid.
3. Jim Albert, *Athens* Magazine (Winter 1988), p. 26.
4. C. Henry, Reminiscences recorded at Amesville, Ohio (May 1, 1963).
5. Ibid.
6. Ibid.

Notes to Pages 255-257   (Gallia & Vinton Counties)

49. Give Us Your Guns and Go Home

1. *OR, Part I-Reports,* p. 672.
2. Ervin, *Journal-Herald* (February 10, 1988), p. 6.
3. Letter written by Fanny Cooley (July 21, 1863).
4. Ervin, *Journal-Herald* (February 10, 1988), p. 6; *OR, Part I-Reports,* p. 673.
5. Johnson, *Partisan Rangers,* p. 391.
6. *OR, Part I-Reports,* p. 673.
7. Letter from Oscar Coe, Columbus, OH (October 5, 1995).
8. Lew Ogan, *History of Vinton County,* p. 218; *Report of Morgan Raid (Ohio) Commissioners,* pp. 246-249.
9. Letter from Oscar Coe (September 19, 1995).
10. Ibid.

Notes to Pages 258-261   (Hocking & Athens Counties)

50. Starr's & Stripes

1. Letters from Melody Eggleston Pesta, Irondale, OH (September 20, 1995 and November 28, 1995).
2. Pesta letter (September 20, 1995).
3. Governor Tod's papers relating to the Morgan Raid, No. 85—Telegram (July 22, 1863).
4. Hocking Sentinel (July 30, 1863).
5. Sheila Blue, *Athens* Magazine (Winter 1988), p. 24.
6. *Report of Morgan Raid (Ohio) Commissioners,* pp. 38-43; Blue, *Athens* Magazine (Winter 1988), p. 24.
7. *Report of Morgan Raid (Ohio) Commissioners,* pp. 38-43.
8. Murra Fowler, *Perry County Tribune* (June 6, 1979), p. 9.
9. *Morgan's Division Regiment Rosters,* pp. 566-571.

Notes to Pages 262-266   (Perry & Morgan Counties)

51. Heading For The Muskingum

1. *Ohio Postal History Journal* (December 1997), p. 7.
2. *Report of Morgan Raid (Ohio) Commissioners,* pp. 226-229.
3. Sanders Lunning, *Community Life Quarterly,* Vol. 10, No. 4, (Winter 1997-98), pp. 15, 29.
4. *Ohio Postal History Journal* (December 1997), p. 6.
5. *Report of Morgan Raid (Ohio) Commissioners,* pp. 226-229.
6. *History of Perry County* (1980).
7. Rev. Msgr. H.E. Mattingly, *Catholic Record Society Bulletin,* Vol. III, No. 1 (January 1977), p. 2.
8. *Herald* (August 6, 1959).
9. Ibid.

10. Governor Tod's papers relating to the Morgan Raid, No. 99—Telegram (July 23, 1863).
11. Ibid., No. 100—Telegram (July 22, 1863).
12. Charles Robertson, M.D., *History of Morgan County, Ohio* (1886), p. 228.
13. Norris F. Schneider, *Zanesville Times Signal* (January 10, 1945).
14. Ibid.
15. Ibid.
16. Robertson, *History of Morgan County*, p. 229.
17. Ibid.
18. Schneider, *Zanesville Times Signal* (January 10, 1945).
19. *Report of Morgan Raid (Ohio) Commissioners*, pp. 226-229.
20. *Perry County History* (1980), p. 24.
21. Letter from Mrs. Harold Scatterday, Jacobsburg, OH (March 16, 1996). Her great grandfather was Thomas Pettet.
22. Schneider, *Zanesville Times Signal* (July 21, 1963).
23. Eck Humphries, *How General J.H. Morgan Invaded Morgan County* (1988), p. 23.
24. Ibid.
25. Ibid., p. 24.
26. Letter from Kermit W. Weaver, Malta, OH (September 26, 1995). John Weaver was his grandfather's brother.

Notes to Pages 267-273

52. The Eagleport Crossing

1. Robertson, *History of Morgan County*, p. 232.
2. Ibid.
3. Robertson, *History of Morgan County*, p. 233; Schneider, *Zanesville Times Signal* (January 10, 1945).
4. Weaver letter (September 26, 1995).
5. Schneider, *Zanesville Times Recorder* (July 21, 1963); Humphries, *How Morgan Invaded*, p. 26.
6. Humphries, *How Morgan Invaded*, pp. 24-25.
7. Keller, *Raid*, p. 198.
8. Humphries, *How Morgan Invaded*, p. 25.
9. Schneider, *Zanesville Times Recorder* (July 21, 1963).
10. Ibid.
11. Elizabeth McElhiney, *Morgan County Herald* (July 12, 1995), p. 4.
12. Schneider, *Zanesville Times Recorder* (July 21, 1963).
13. Letter written by Lib Weber, Rokeby, OH (July 25, 1863).
14. Humphries, *How Morgan Invaded*, p. 27.
15. Ibid., pp. 26-27.
16. Rick Taylor, *Chandlerville Courier*, Vol. 4, No. 15 (July 29, 1993), p. 2.
17. Ibid., p. 27.
18. Robertson, *History of Morgan County*, p. 231.
19. Humphries, *How Morgan Invaded*, p. 27.
20. Schneider, *Zanesville Times Recorder* (July 21, 1963).
21. Humphries, *How Morgan Invaded*, pp. 25-26.

22. Ibid., p. 26.
23. McElhiney, *Morgan County Herald* (July 12, 1995), p. 4.
24. Ibid.
25. *Report of Morgan Raid (Ohio) Commissioners,* pp. 214-215.
26. Robertson, *History of Morgan County*, p. 229.
27. Humphries, *How Morgan Invaded*, pp. 26-27.

Notes to Pages 274-276   (Muskingum County)

53. Zanesville Responds

1. Norris F. Schneider, *Y Bridge City: Story of Zanesville and Muskingum Co.* (1979), p. 217.
2. Schneider, *Zanesville Times Signal* (January 10, 1945).
3. Humphries, *How Morgan Invaded*, pp. 27-28.
4. Taylor, *Chandlerville Courier* (July 29, 1993), p. 3.
5. Humphries, *How Morgan Invaded*, p. 28.
6. *Ohio Historical Quarterly*, Vol. XVIII (1911), p. 99.
7. Robertson, *History of Morgan County*, p. 231. In Robertson's text, he says the pillow came "from a house near the ford." Another historical source says that the pillow belonged to Hi Winchell. But among the items listed for losses and damages sustained from the raiders, Winchell did not mention a pillow. The loss of a pillow was claimed by David Power.
8. *Report of Morgan Raid (Ohio) Commissioners,* pp. 216-217.
9. *Ohio Historical Quarterly*, Vol. XVIII (1911), p. 99.
10. Brian McKee, *Morgan County Herald* (May 1, 1991), p. 4.
11. Ibid.
12. Humphries, *How Morgan Invaded*, p. 28.
13. Schneider, *Y Bridge City*, p. 217.
14. *Annals of the Nineteenth Ohio Battery*, p. 192.
15. Ibid., pp. 192-193.
16. Ibid., pp. 194-197.

Notes to Pages 277-279

54. The Sign of the Freemason

1. Taylor, *Chandlerville Courier* (July 29, 1993), p. 3.
2. Schneider, *Zanesville Times Recorder* (July 21, 1963); Taylor, *Chandlerville Courier* (July 29, 1993), p. 3.
3. Taylor, *Chandlerville Courier* (July 29, 1993), p. 6.
4. Schneider, *Y Bridge City*, p. 217.
5. Taylor, *Chandlerville Courier* (July 29, 1993), p. 6.
6. May Stranathan, *History of Early Cumberland* (1943), p. 23; Taylor, *Chandlerville Courier* (July 29, 1993), p. 6.
7. May Stranathan, *History of Early Cumberland* (1943), p. 23.
8. *Report of Morgan Raid (Ohio) Commissioners,* pp. 218-219.

9. Ibid.
10. Copy of diary entry furnished by Jackie Fisher, Somerset, Ohio.
11. Copy of diary entry furnished by Robert M. Ball, Caldwell, Ohio.
12. Governor Tod's papers relating to the Morgan Raid, No. 112—Telegram (July 23, 1863).

Notes to Pages 280-283 (Guernsey County)

55. The Bonnie Blink Ride of Mary McClelland

1. William G. Wolfe, *Stories of Guernsey County, Ohio* (1943), p. 315.
2. Globe House in Spencer Township (undated), p. 993.
3. Stranathan, *History of Early Cumberland*, pp. 23-24.
4. *Report of Morgan Raid (Ohio) Commissioners*, pp. 94-105; Wolfe, *Stories of Guernsey County*, p. 313. Lewis, *Southeastern Ohio and the Muskingum Valley*, p. 367.
5. Stranathan, *History of Early Cumberland*, p. 22; Col. Cyrus P.B. Sarchet, *History of Guernsey* (1911) Chapter VII, p. 99; Wolfe, *Stories of Guernsey County*, p. 330.
6. Stranathan, *History of Early Cumberland*, pp. 22-23. Wolfe, *Stories of Guernsey County*, pp. 330-331.
7. Wolfe, *Stories of Guernsey County*, p. 304.
8. Ibid., pp. 315-316.
9. Wolfe, *Stories of Guernsey County*, pp. 331-332.
10. Ervin, *Jackson Journal-Herald* (1987); Keller, *Raid*, pp. 207-208.
11. Wolfe, *Stories of Guernsey County*, p. 332.
12. This *milliner's story has been published in several historical sources. Yet there are some details of the tale which cast doubt about its veracity. First is the fact that Morgan was supposed to have approached and entered the home alone. In almost every other recorded instance, the General was accompanied by an entourage of guards who checked out the home before Morgan entered. They usually remained in the room with him or stood guard at the door if he took a rest. The other incongruity was the "star on his breast." In all other descriptions of General Morgan on this raid, he is described as wearing no uniform or insignia of rank. Nowhere else on this 1,000-mile journey has anyone mentioned that there was a star on his breast. Because of these inconsistencies, either the story was a fabrication, or it was someone other than General Morgan who entered the milliner's home. But it is a good story and the only event that has come down to us about Morgan's raid through Senecaville.*
12. Ibid., pp. 332-333.
13. Ibid., p. 304.
14. Sarchet, *History of Guernsey*, p. 100; Wolfe, *Stories of Guernsey County*, pp. 305-306.
15. Wolfe, *Stories of Guernsey County*, p. 306.
16. Ibid.
17. Ibid.
18. Ibid.

Notes to Pages 284-290

56. "The Most Exciting Day in the History of (Old) Washington"

1. Wolfe, *Stories of Guernsey County*, p. 306.
2. Undated newspaper article.
3. *OR, Part I-Reports,* telegram from Gov. Tod to Gen. Burnside, p. 798.
4. Wolfe, *Stories of Guernsey County*, p. 306.
5. Old Washington Historical Walking Tour Brochure.
6. Rose McAfee, *The Jeffersonian Weekender* (July 14, 1973), p. 1.
7. Wolfe, *Stories of Guernsey County*, pp. 318-321.
8. *OR, Part I-Reports,* Shackelford's report, p. 642.
9. Wolfe, *Stories of Guernsey County*, p. 321.
10. *Morgan's Division Regiment Rosters.*
11. Greg Parks, *The Daily Jeffersonian* (July 1996); photo by Michael Neilson.
12. Keller, *Raid*, p. 209.
13. Wolfe, *Stories of Guernsey County*, p. 322.
14. Ibid., p. 323.
15. Ibid., pp. 323-324.
16. Ibid., pp. 324-325.
17. Cambridge newspaper article (undated).
18. Wolfe, *Stories of Guernsey County*, p. 326.
19. Sarchet, *History of Guernsey*, pp. 106-107.
20. Ibid., p. 107.

Notes to Pages 291-298   (Harrison County)

57. Lincoln's Concern About Morgan

1. Charles B. Wallace, Mary R. Ford, Marguerite A. Milliken, John A. Moore, *The Harrisonian*, Number 1 (1988), p. 3.
2. Ibid.
3. Ibid.
4. *OR, Part I-Reports*, p. 799.
5. Ibid., p. 800.
6. Keller, *Raid*, p. 204.
7. Ibid.
8. *OR, Part II-Correspondence*, telegram from Halleck to Burnside, p. 553.
9. Keller, *Raid*, p. 204.
10. *OR, Part II-Correspondence*, telegram from Burnside to Halleck, p. 553.
11. Keller, *Raid*, pp. 204-205.
12. Ibid., p. 205.
13. Ibid., p. 206.
14. *Cadiz Republican* (July 23, 1953).
15. *Report of Morgan Raid (Ohio) Commissioners*, pp. 130-131.
16. Wallace, *The Harrisonian*, p. 3.
17. *Report of Morgan Raid (Ohio) Commissioners*, pp. 132-133.
18. Wallace, *The Harrisonian*, p. 3.

19. Eckley & Perry, *History of Carroll and Harrison Counties*, Vol. I (1921), p. 302.
20. *Report of Morgan Raid (Ohio) Commissioners*, pp. 136-137.
21. Ibid., pp. 130-137.
22. Wallace, *The Harrisonian*, p. 5.
23. Eckley & Perry, *History of Harrison County*, p. 302.
24. *Report of Morgan Raid (Ohio) Commissioners*, pp. 134-135.
25. Ibid., pp. 136-137.
26. Eckley & Perry, *History of Harrison County*, p. 303.
27. Wallace, *The Harrisonian*, p. 4.
28. Ibid., p. 5.
29. *Cadiz Republican* (July 23, 1953).
30. Caldwell, *History of Steubenville and Jefferson County, Ohio*, p. 190.
31. Eckley & Perry, *History of Harrison County*, p. 303.
32. *Cadiz Republican* (July 23, 1953).
33. Wallace, *The Harrisonian*, pp. 5-6.
34. Ibid., p. 6.
35. Ibid., pp. 6-7.
36. Ibid., p. 7.
37. Ibid., p. 8.
38. Ibid., p. 7.
39. Ibid., p. 8.
40. Ibid.
41. Governor Tod's papers relating to the Morgan Raid, No. 124—Telegram (July 24, 1863).
42. *Report of Morgan Raid (Ohio) Commissioners*, pp. 134-135.
43. Wallace, *The Harrisonian*, p. 8.
44. *OR, Part I-Reports*, p. 803.

Notes to Pages 299-307   (Jefferson County)

58. "I'll Be Damned If I Will Ever Surrender To A Farmer!"

1. Malcolm J. Brady, *Steubenville Herald Star* (July 26, 1963).
2. Eileen Cozart, *Steubenville Herald Star* (July 31, 1988).
3. Joseph Doyle, *Frederick Wm. Von Steuben & The American Revolution* (1913), p. 382.
4. Joseph Doyle, *History of Belmont & Jefferson Counties* (1976), p. 460.
5. Ibid.
6. Brady, *Steubenville Herald Star* (July 26, 1963).
7. *Report of Morgan Raid (Ohio) Commissioners*, pp. 168-175.
8. Brady, *Steubenville Herald Star* (July 26, 1963).
9. George D. Cook, *Steubenville Gazette* (July 24, 1913).
10. Caldwell, *History of Steubenville and Jefferson County, Ohio*, p. 190.
11. C. Henry, Reminiscences recorded at Amesville, Ohio (May 1, 1963).
12. Doyle, *History of Jefferson County* (1976), p. 460.
13. George D. Cook, *Steubenville Gazette* (July 24, 1913).
14. Ibid.

15. Doyle, *History of Jefferson County* (1976), p. 460.
16. *Report of Morgan Raid (Ohio) Commissioners*, pp. 168-169.
17. Ibid., pp. 174-175.
18. *OR, Part I-Reports*, p. 803.
19. *Report of Morgan Raid (Ohio) Commissioners*, pp. 172-173.
20. Ibid., pp. 170-171.
21. Ibid., pp. 172-173.
22. Cook, *Steubenville Gazette* (July 24, 1913).
23. *OR, Part I-Reports*, p. 800.
24. Doyle, *History of Jefferson County* (1976), p. 460.
25. Cook, *Steubenville Gazette* (July 24, 1913).
26. Ibid.
27. Ibid.
28. *OR, Part I-Reports*, p. 801.
29. Caldwell, *History of Steubenville and Jefferson County, Ohio*, p. 190.
30. Ibid., pp. 190-191.
31. Brady, *Steubenville Herald Star* (July 26, 1963).
32. *Report of Morgan Raid (Ohio) Commissioners*, pp. 168-175.
33. Doyle, *History of Jefferson County* (1976), pp. 460-461; Caldwell, *History of Steubenville and Jefferson County, Ohio*, p. 191; Brady, *Steubenville Herald Star* (July 26, 1963).
34. Doyle, *History of Jefferson County* (1976), p. 461; Caldwell, *History of Steubenville and Jefferson County, Ohio*, p. 191; Brady, *Steubenville Herald Star* (July 26, 1963).
35. Ibid.
36. Brady, *Steubenville Herald Star* (July 26, 1963).
37. Caldwell, *History of Steubenville and Jefferson County, Ohio*, p. 191.
38. Brady, *Steubenville Herald Star* (July 26, 1963).
39. Ibid.
40. Keller, *Raid*, p. 215.
41. Ibid.
42. *OR, Part I-Reports*, p. 801.
43. *Steubenville Weekly Herald* (July 29, 1863).
44. Letter from Jim Irvin, Cincinnati, OH (October 2, 1995). Benjamin Shelley was his gr-gr-great grandfather.
45. *OR, Part I-Reports*, p. 802.
46. Brady, *Steubenville Herald Star* (July 26, 1963).
47. *Report of Morgan Raid (Ohio) Commissioners*, pp. 172-173.
48. *Report of Morgan Raid (Ohio) Commissioners*, pp. 170-171; Jere H. Simms, *Last Night and Last Day of John Morgan's Raid* (1913), p. 7.
49. Brady, *Steubenville Herald Star* (July 26, 1963).
50. Doyle, *History of Jefferson County* (1976), p. 461.

Notes to Pages 308-316

59. Escape Or Capture Tomorrow

1. Simms, *Last Night and Last Day*, p. 8; *Steubenville Herald* (March 5, 1897).
2. *Steubenville Herald* (March 5, 1897).

3. *History of Christ United Methodist Church Bulletin* (undated).
4. Simms, *Last Night and Last Day*, p. 10.
5. Brady, *Steubenville Herald Star* (July 26, 1963).
6. Velma Griffin, *Steubenville Herald-Star* (July 25, 1988).
7. Simms, *Last Night and Last Day*, p. 11.
8. Ibid.
9. *OR, Part I-Reports*, p. 802.
10. Robert Wilson Schilling, *The Yellow Creek Stories* (1942), p. 146.
11. Brady, *Steubenville Herald Star* (July 26, 1963).
12. Simms, *Last Night and Last Day*, p. 4; Keller, *Raid*, p. 217.
13. Ibid.
14. R. Max Gard, *Morgan's Raid Into Ohio* (1963), p. 41.
15. Simms, *Last Night and Last Day*, p. 11.
16. Mary Peebles, *Carrollton Freepress Standard* (circa 1955).
17. Rue, *Ohio Historical Quarterly*, Vol. XX, pp. 371-372.
18. *OR, Part I-Reports*, p. 800.
19. Ibid., p. 803.
20. Simms, *Last Night and Last Day*, p. 4.
21. Ibid., p. 5.
22. Brady, *Steubenville Herald Star* (July 26, 1963).
23. Simms, *Last Night and Last Day*, p. 6.
24. Ibid.
25. Letter from James A. Reaney, East Liverpool, OH (June 5, 1996). David White was Mrs. Reaney's grandfather.
26. Letter from Mrs. Marion Cozza, East Palestine, OH (March 10, 1996). Ezekel and Mary Maple were her great-grandparents.
27. Simms, *Last Night and Last Day*, pp. 15-16.
28. *Steubenville Herald* (March 5, 1897); Simms, *Last Night and Last Day*, p. 8.
29. Caldwell, *History of Steubenville and Jefferson County, Ohio,* p. 194.
30. *OR, Part I-Reports*, p. 803.
31. Simms, *Last Night and Last Day*, p. 15.
32. Ibid.
33. Letter written by James Cooper Boice describing the incident at Monroeville; Wm. Marion Miller, *Ohio State Historical Quarterly*, pp. 169-170.
34. Miller, *Ohio State Historical Quarterly*, p. 170.
35. Boice letter.
36. Ibid.
37. Rue, *Ohio Historical Quarterly*, Vol. XX, p. 372.
38. Doyle, *The American Revolution* (1913), p. 382.
39. Rue, *Ohio Historical Quarterly*, Vol. XX, pp. 372-373.

Notes to Pages 317-322   **(Carroll County)**

60. Last Shots Fired In Anger

1. *Salem Republican* (July 29, 1863).
2. *Steubenville Weekly Herald* (July 27, 1863).
3. Simms, *Last Night and Last Day,* p. 36.

4.   Ibid., p. 16.
5.   *Steubenville Weekly Herald* (July 27, 1863).
6.   Simms, *Last Night and Last Day*, p. 16.
7.   *Steubenville Weekly Herald* (July 27, 1863).
8.   Simms, *Last Night and Last Day*, p. 16.
9.   *OR, Part I-Reports*, p. 804.
10. Hemingway, *American Civil War* (November 1989), p. 56.
11. Simms, *Last Night and Last Day*, p. 16.
12. Ibid., p. 18.
13. Ibid., p. 17.
14. Letter from Robert Wirkner of Carroll County (February 26, 1998).
15. Simms, *Last Night and Last Day*, p. 37.
16. Simms, *Last Night and Last Day*, p. 19; Wirkner letter.
17. *OR, Part I-Reports*, p. 805.
18. Wirkner letter.
19. *Steubenville Weekly Herald* (July 27, 1863).
20. Schilling, *The Yellow Creek Stories*, pp. 144-145; Gard, *Morgan's Raid*, p. 44.
21. Wirkner letter.
22. Carroll County Historical Society, *Home of The Fighting McCooks* (undated).
23. Wirkner letter.
24. Simms, *Last Night and Last Day*, pp. 19-20.

Notes to Pages 323-330   (Columbiana County)

61. "Who The Hell Is Captain Burbick?"

1.   Wirkner letter.
2.   Letter, documents and maps from Glen Speirs whose parents own the farm Morgan crossed in Franklin Township in Columbiana County (February 26, 1998).
3.   *1870 Atlas of Columbiana County*; *1860 Atlas of Columbiana County*, p. 19; Simms, *Last Night and Last Day*, p. 20.
4.   *1860 Atlas of Columbiana County*, p. 19; Simms, *Last Night and Last Day*, p. 20.
5.   Simms, *Last Night and Last Day*, p. 20.
6.   Ibid., p. 21.
7.   Ibid., p. 20.
8.   *1870 Atlas of Columbiana County*.
9.   Simms, *Last Night and Last Day*, p. 21.
10. *1870 Atlas of Columbiana County*.
11. Simms, *Last Night and Last Day*, p. 21.
12. *OR, Part I-Reports*, p. 804.
13. Roy B. Ewing, *Columbiana Journal* (1963).
14. R. Max Gard, *The End of the Morgan Raid* (July, 1963), p. 9.
15. Simms, *Last Night and Last Day*, p. 22.
16. Letter from Elmer H. Detwiler of Columbiana, OH (March 9, 1996). John & Mary Hisey were his great grandparents.
17. Personally observed by the author; 1849 Wayne Township map.
18. Ewing, *Columbiana Journal* (1963).

19. Ibid.
20. Simms, *Last Night and Last Day*, p. 25.
21. Personally observed by the author.
22. Ewing, *Columbiana Journal* (1963).
23. Simms, *Last Night and Last Day*, p. 22.
24. Ewing, *Columbiana Journal* (1963).
25. Simms, *Last Night and Last Day*, p. 25.
26. Ewing, *Columbiana Journal* (1963).
27. Ibid.
28. Simms, *Last Night and Last Day*, p. 22.
29. Ewing, *Columbiana Journal* (1963).
30. Simms, *Last Night and Last Day*, p. 26.
31. Ibid., p. 22.
32. Ibid., p. 25.
33. Clara McGee, *Buckeye State,* Lisbon Diary (undated).
34. *OR, Part I-Reports*, Curry's Report, pp. 812-813.
35. Ibid., p. 810.
36. Ibid.
37. Rue, *Ohio Historical Quarterly,* Vol. XX, p. 373.
38. Ibid.
39. *OR, Part I-Reports*, Burbick's Report, p. 810.
40. Ibid.
41. Rue, *Ohio Historical Quarterly,* Vol. XX, p. 374.

Notes to Pages 331-339

62. "General Morgan Demands Your Surrender!"

1. Rue, *Ohio Historical Quarterly,* Vol. XX, p. 374.
2. Simms, *Last Night and Last Day*, p. 32.
3. Rue, *Ohio Historical Quarterly,* Vol. XX, p. 374.
4. Brown, *Raiders*, p. 224.
5. Simms, *Last Night and Last Day*, p. 26.
6. Ibid., p. 32.
7. Simms, *Last Night and Last Day*, p. 26.
8. Ibid., p. 27.
9. As observed by the author.
10. Rue, *Ohio Historical Quarterly,* Vol. XX, p. 374.
11. *OR, Part I-Reports*, Maus' Report, p. 812.
12. Butler, *Morgan and His Men*, p. 242.
13. Simms, *Last Night and Last Day*, p. 26.
14. Rue, *Ohio Historical Quarterly,* Vol. XX, p. 374.
15. Ibid.
16. Waight, *East Liverpool Review* (April 18, 1958); Robert C. Cheeks, *America's Civil War* (May 1998), p. 48.
17. Rue, *Ohio Historical Quarterly,* Vol. XX, p. 376; Doyle, *History of Jefferson Co.*, p. 460.

18. Simms, *Last Night and Last Day*, p. 28.
19. Rue, *Ohio Historical Quarterly,* Vol. XX, p. 376.
20. *Steubenville Weekly Herald* (July 27, 1983).
21. Rue, *Ohio Historical Quarterly,* Vol. XX, p. 376.
22. Simms, *Last Night and Last Day*, p. 35.
23. Doyle, *History of Jefferson County* (1976), p. 461.
24. Ibid.
25. As measured by the author's automotive mileage counter.
26. Waight, *East Liverpool Review* (April 21, 1958).
27. Rue, *Ohio Historical Quarterly,* Vol. XX, p. 376.
28. Simms, *Last Night and Last Day*, pp. 23, 26.
29. Metzler, *Cavaliers*, p. 65; Simms, *Last Night and Last Day*, p. 23; Keller, *Raid*, p. 228.
30. Dr. Hambleton Tapp, *Incidents in the Life of Frank Wolford* (1936), p. 14; Metzler, *Cavaliers*, p. 65.
31. Metzler, *Cavaliers*, p. 65.
32. *OR, Part I-Reports*, Burbick's Report, p. 810.
33. Keller, *Raid*, p. 228.
34. Metzler, *Cavaliers*, p. 66; Duke, *History*, p. 458.
35. Brown, *Raiders*, p. 226.
36. *OR, Part I-Reports*, Shackelford's Report, p. 644; Waight, *East Liverpool Review* (April 21, 1958).
37. Simms, *Last Night and Last Day*, p. 27.
38. Ibid., p. 28.
39. Waight, *East Liverpool Review* (April 21, 1958); Simms, *Last Night and Last Day*, p. 26.
40. Ibid., p. 29.
41. *OR, Part I-Reports*, p. 808.
42. Ibid., p. 636.
43. Duke, *The Century* (1891), Vol. XLI, p. 416.
44. Velma Griffin, *Ohioana Quarterly* (Summer 1972), Vol. XV, No. 2, p. 69.
45. Thomas, *Morgan and His Raiders*, p. 54.
46. Brown, *Raiders*, p. 225.
47. *Webster's American Military Biographies* (1978), p. 372.
48. Ramage, *Rebel Raider*, pp. 24-25.
49. Letter from William H. Prather, Indianapolis, IN.
50. Duke, *History*, p. 460.
51. Ramage, *Rebel Raider*, p. 179.
52. Edwin C. Bearss.
53. *Webster's American Military Biographies*, p. 150.
54. Caldwell, *History of Steubenville and Jefferson County, Ohio,* pp. 194-195.
55. Wormer, *Morgan Raid*, pp. 213-214.
56. Keller, *Raid*, p. 231.

Notes to Pages 340-343

63. Be My Guest

1. Wellsville Historical Society, *Wellsville Echoes* (1949), Vol. One, p. 16.
2. Simms, *Last Night and Last Day*, p. 37.
3. *Wellsville Patriot* (July 28, 1863), Vol. XVIII, No. 35.
4. Waight, *East Liverpool Review* (April 21, 1958).
5. Ibid.
6. Simms, *Last Night and Last Day*, p. 38.
7. Tapp, *Incidents in the Life of Frank Wolford*, p. 14.
8. Ibid.
9. Simms, *Last Night and Last Day*, p. 38.
10. Ibid.
11. Wellsville Historical Society, *Wellsville Echoes* (1949), p. 18.
12. *Youngstown Vindicator* (May 28, 1950), Rotogravure Section.
13. Simms, *Last Night and Last Day*, p. 38.
14. Governor Tod's papers relating to the Morgan Raid, No. 155—Telegram (Aug. 1, 1863).
15. *OR, Part I-Reports*, pp. 813-814.
16. Ibid., p. 809.
17. Ibid.
18. Ibid.
19. Governor Tod's papers relating to the Morgan Raid, No. 155—Telegram (Aug. 1, 1863).

PRISON & ESCAPE

Notes to Pages 344-349

64. Welcome To The Pen

1. Waight, *East Liverpool Review* (April 21, 1958).
2. *Ohio Handbook of the Civil War* (1961), p. 8.
3. *Cincinnati Daily Commercial* (July 28, 1863).
4. Metzler, *Cavaliers*, p. 68; Holland, *Raiders*, pp. 251-252.
5. *Cincinnati Gazette* (July 29, 1863).
6. Ramage, *Rebel Raider*, p. 184.
7. *Papers Relating To Confinement Of Gen. Morgan* (July 27, 1863), p. 246; Ervin, *Jackson-Herald* (circa 1988); Keller, *Raid*, p. 274; Ramage, *Rebel Raider*, p. 183.
8. Keller, *Raid*, p. 274; Metzler, *Cavaliers*, p. 68; Holland, *Raiders*, p. 252.
9. Metzler, *Cavaliers*, p. 68; Ramage, *Rebel Raider*, p. 184.
10. Dr. Orloff Miller and Rita Walsh, *Ohio Penitentiary Archaeological and Architectural Document Search* (March 14, 1996), p. 6.
11. Dan J. Morgan, *Early History of the Ohio Penitentiary* (1893), p. 2.
12. Miller & Walsh, *Penitentiary Document Search*, p. 8.
13. Dave Roth, *Blue & Gray Magazine* (October 1994), p. 17.

14. Metzler, *Cavaliers*, p. 68; Holland, *Raiders*, p. 69.
15. Roth, *Blue & Gray* (October 1994), pp. 17-18.
16. Metzler, *Cavaliers*, p. 69.
17. Duke, *History*, p. 469.
18. Horan, *Agent*, p. 39.
19. *OR, Part I-Reports*, p. 815.
20. Ibid.

Notes to Pages 350-355

65. A Letter To Mattie

1. Holland, *Raiders*, pp. 260-261; Williamson papers.
2. Holland, *Raiders*, p. 260.
3. Copies of several autograph books in possession of author.
4. Comment from James A. Ramage.
5. Letter from Michael Lennon, University of Cincinnati Classics Library (July 18, 1995).
6. Ibid.
7. Duke, *History*, p. 469; Ramage, *Rebel Raider*, p. 186; Thomas, *Morgan and Raiders*, p. 86.
8. Hockersmith, *Morgan's Escape*, p. 34;.
9. *Steubenville Daily Herald* (July 30, 1863); Hockersmith, *Morgan's Escape*, pp. 32-33.
10. Duke, *History*, pp. 476-477.
11. Seawright, Sorrows of the Alstons. Part 19, *Flagpole Magazine,* The Internet.
12. Keller, *Raid*, p. 276; Metzler, *Cavaliers*, p. 69; Holland, *Raiders*, pp. 254-255.
13. Duke, *History*, p. 469; Capt. T.H. Hines was quoted as saying there were 70 Confederate officers ("Morgan and sixty-nine of his officers") Horan, *Confederate Agent*, p. 39.
14. *OR, Part I-Reports*, p. 815; Duke, *History*, pp. 470-471.
15. Horan, *Confederate Agent*, p. 39; Duke, *History*, p. 471.
16. *OR, Part I-Reports*, p. 815.
17. Duke, *History*, p. 470, 473; Horan, *Confederate Agent*, p. 39; Hockersmith, *Morgan's Escape*, p. 32; Ramage, *Rebel Raider*, pp. 186-187.
18. Ramage, *Rebel Raider*, pp. 186-187.
19. Holland, *Raiders*, pp. 255-256.
20. Brown, *Raiders*, p. 239; Duke, *History*, p. 474; Keller, *Raid*, p. 276.
21. Metzler, *Cavaliers*, p. 69; Keller, *Raid*, pp. 277-278.
22. Duke, *History*, p. 472; Keller, *Raid*, pp. 276-278; Ramage, *Rebel Raider*, p. 187.
23. Ramage, *Rebel Raider*, p. 187.
24. Holland, *Raiders*, p. 262.
25. Ramage, *Rebel Raider*, p. 187.
26. Holland, *Raiders*, p. 258.
27. *Steubenville Weekly Herald* (July 27, 1863).

Notes to Pages 356-364

66. Breakout From "Castle Merion!"

1. Horan, *Confederate Agent*, pp. 42-51.
2. Hockersmith, *Morgan's Escape*, pp. 27-30.
3. Horan, *Confederate Agent*, p. 42.
4. Hockersmith, *Morgan's Escape*, p. 37.
5. Horan, *Confederate Agent*, pp. 42-51.
6. Hockersmith, *Morgan's Escape*, p. 44.
7. Ramage, *Rebel Raider*, p. 192; Hockersmith, *Morgan's Escape*, p. 44; Johnson, *Partisan Rangers*, p. 365.
8. Horan, *Confederate Agent*, p. 51.
9. Ibid.
10. Holland, *Raiders*, p. 278.
11. Ramage, *Rebel Raider*, pp. 189, 191.
12. Ibid., p. 189.
13. W. Fred Conway, *The Most Incredible Prison Escape of the Civil War* (1991), pp. 60-61.
14. Metzler, *Cavaliers*, p. 74.
15. Duke, *History*, p. 486; Hockersmith, *Morgan's Escape*, p. 47.
16. Horan, *Confederate Agent*, p. 54.
17. Brown, *Raiders*, p. 241; Metzler, *Cavaliers*, p. 74.
18. Ibid., p. 243.
19. Duke, *History*, p. 487.
20. Metzler, *Cavaliers*, p. 75.
21. Ibid., p. 77.
22. Hockersmith, *Morgan's Escape*, p. 48; Metzler, *Cavaliers*, p. 75.
23. Howe, *Historical Collections* (1902),Vol. I, p. 777; Ramage, *Rebel Raider*, p. 195.
24. Hockersmith, *Morgan's Escape*, p. 47.
25. Metzler, *Cavaliers*, p. 74.
26. Holland, *Raiders*, pp. 279-280.
27. Ibid., p. 280.
28. Conway, *Incredible Prison Escape*, p. 67.
29. Duke, *History*, p. 488.
30. Ibid.
31. Metzler, *Cavaliers*, p. 75.
32. Hockersmith, *Morgan's Escape*, p. 47.
33. Horan, *Confederate Agent*, p. 55.
34. Holland, *Raiders*, p. 280.
35. Hockersmith, *Morgan's Escape*, p. 47.
36. Ramage, *Rebel Raider*, p. 195.
37. Holland, *Raiders*, p. 280.
38. Horan, *Confederate Agent*, pp. 55-56.
39. Ibid., p. 56.
40. Brown, *Raiders*, p. 243.
41. Metzler, *Cavaliers*, p. 75.

42. Duke, *History*, p. 488.
43. Ramage, *Rebel Raider*, p. 195.
44. Goss, *The Queen City*, Volume I (1912), p. 220.
45. Howe, *Historical Collections* (1902),Vol. I, p. 778; Holland, *Raiders*, p. 281.
46. Philip Van Doren Stern, *Secret Missions of the Civil War* (1959), p. 165.
47. Ramage, *Rebel Raider*, pp. 195-196.
48. Metzler, *Cavaliers*, p. 77.
49. Brown, *Raiders*, p. 63.
50. Ramage, *Rebel Raider*, p. 194.
51. Horan, *Confederate Agent*, p. 62.
52. Ibid., p. 53.
53. Taylor, *Bowie Knives*, p. 108; Horan, *Confederate Agent*, p. 56.
54. Ramage, *Rebel Raider*, p. 195; Holland, *Raiders*, p. 289.
55. Ibid., p. 194.
56. Photo in *Blue & Gray Magazine* (October 1994), p. 61.
57. Brochure and flyer furnished by R.S.V. Inc, Steubenville, OH with purchase of piece of "The Great Wall of the Ohio Penitentiary."
58. Ramage, *Rebel Raider*, p. 197.
59. Holland, *Raiders*, p. 290.
60. Metzler, *Cavaliers*, p. 78.
61. Horan, *Confederate Agent*, p. 57; Metzler, *Cavaliers*, p. 78.
62. Horan, *Confederate Agent*, p. 57.
63. Metzler, *Cavaliers*, p. 78; Horan, *Confederate Agent*, pp. 57-58.
64. Horan, *Confederate Agent*, p. 58.

FIGHT TO THE FINISH

Notes to Pages 365-367

67. A Hero's Welcome

1. Ramage, *Rebel Raider*, p. 197.
2. Metzler, *Cavaliers*, p. 82.
3. Holland, *Raiders*, pp. 298-299; Ramage, *Rebel Raider*, p. 201; Metzler, *Cavaliers*, p. 82.
4. Ibid., pp. 268-269.
5. Brown, *Raiders*, p. 247.
6. Metzler, *Cavaliers*, p. 81.
7. Holland, *Raiders*, p. 295; Ramage, *Rebel Raider*, p. 199.
8. *Daily Richmond Enquirer* (January 9, 1863).
9. Ibid.
10. C.L. Peticolas, cover of sheet music, *Genl. Morgan's Grand March* (1864).
11. Cover of sheet music on display in Alexander Morgan Museum in Hunt-Morgan House, Lexington, KY.
12. Ramage, *Rebel Raider*, pp. 197-198.
13. Sheet music artifact #:87.107, Tennessee State Museum.
14. *Webster's American Biographies*, pp. 105-106.

15. Ramage, *Rebel Raider*, pp. 201-202.
16. Ibid., p. 213.

Notes to Pages 368-376

68. End of the Glory Road

1. Ramage, *Rebel Raider*, p. 218; Metzler, *Cavaliers*, p. 91; Brown, *Raiders*, pp. 259-260.
2. Metzler, *Cavaliers*, p. 95; Ramage, *Rebel Raider*, p. 226.
3. *Webster American Military Biographies*, p. 204.
4. Faust, *Historical Times Encyclopedia of the Civil War*, p. 75.
5. Ramage, *Rebel Raider*, pp. 230-231; Brown, *Raiders*, pp. 264-265.
6. Brown, *Raiders*, p. 267.
7. Duke, *History*, p. 532.
8. Ramage, *Rebel Raider*, p. 231.
9. Brown, Raiders, p. 267.
10. Ramage, *Rebel Raider*, p. 231.
11. Ibid., p. 233.
12. Richard H. Doughty, *Greeneville: One Hundred Year Portrait* (1975), p. 235.
13. Brown, *Raiders*, p. 268; Ramage, *Rebel Raider*, p. 231; William J. Stier, *Civil War Times* (December 1996), p. 83.
14. Doughty, *Greeneville*, pp. 230-231.
15. Ramage, *Rebel Raider*, p. 232.
16. Roy Morris, Jr., *America's Civil War* (May 1996), Vol. 9, No. 2, p. 6.
17. Ramage, *Rebel Raider*, p. 232.
18. Ibid., p. 234.
19. Doughty, *Greeneville*, p. 232; Ramage, *Rebel Raider*, p. 235.
20. Ibid.
21. Stier, *Civil War Times* (December 1996), p. 84.
22. Ibid.
23. Brown, *Raiders*, p. 270; Stier, *Civil War Times* (December 1996), pp. 84-85.
24. Stier, *Civil War Times* (December 1996), p. 86.
25. Ramage, *Rebel Raider*, p. 237; Brown, *Raiders*, p. 270.
26. Doughty, *Greeneville*, p. 233; Metzler, *Cavaliers*, p. 104.
27. Ramage, *Rebel Raider*, pp. 237-238; Dr. Ramage said that he had found a newspaper article in the Morgan biographical file in the Kentucky Historical Society Library in Frankfort, KY. In the undated clipping, reprinted in the *Philadelphia Weekly Times*, Private Campbell told the reporter that he had no idea it was General Morgan when he shot him.
28. Doughty, *Greeneville*, p. 234; Ramage, *Rebel Raider*, p. 238.
29. Ibid.
30. Ramage, *Rebel Raider*, p. 238.
31. Ibid., p. 238-239.
32. A.A. Hoehling, *Women Who Spied* (1967), pp. 31-32.
33. Doughty, *Greeneville*, p. 239; Hoehling, *Women Who Spied*, pp. 32-33.

34. Hoehling, *Women Who Spied*, p. 38.
35. Ibid., pp. 40-44.
36. Doughty, *Greeneville*, p. 238.
37. Metzler, *Cavaliers*, p. 101.
38. Doughty, *Greeneville*, p. 238.
39. Ramage, *Rebel Raider*, p. 231.
40. Ibid., p. 245.
41. From conversation with James A. Ramage.
41. Stier, *Civil War Times* (December 1996), p. 92.
42. Duke, *History*, p. 549; Brown, *Raiders*, p. 296.
43. Brown, *Raiders*, p. 297; Duke, *History*, p. 541.
44. Duke, *History*, pp. 549-550.
45. Metzler, *Cavaliers*, p. 110.
46. Brown, *Raiders*, p. 312; Duke, *History*, p. 570.
47. Duke, *History,* p. 572.
48. Ibid., pp. 574-575.
49. Ibid., p. 576.
50. Ibid., p. 577.
51. Brown, *Raiders,* p. 315.
52. Duke, *History*, p. 578.
53. Ramage, *Rebel Raider*, pp. 249-250.
54. Jim Tipton, *Find-A-Grave by Cemetery: Lexington Cemetery*, Internet.
55. Ramage, *Rebel Raider*, p. 254.

Index

Note: Page numbers in **boldface** refer to illustrations and captions. Military units are alphabetized as spelled out. John Hunt Morgan is abbreviated as "JHM" in subheadings when reference is to the man (elsewhere, reference is made to "Morgan's raid"). "?" indicates an unknown first name.

Abatis, 22, 126
Achor (OH), 329
Adair County (KY), 21
Adams, Col. Silas, 245
Adams, Lt. Col. ?, 218
Adams County (OH), 156–157, 160, 164–168, 169
Albright, C.J., 278
Alcorn, Adj. J.W., 243
Aleshire, Nelson, 183
Aleshire, William, 183
Alexander, Henry, 172
Alexander, Lavina, 171–172
Alexander, Stewart, 171–172
Alexandria (TN), 13
Alfred (OH), 252
Alice Dean (packet), 41, 45, 47, 49, 51, 53, 59, 60, 192, **A10**
Allard, Sgt. James M., 336
Allegheny Belle (boat), 191, 215, 221
Allen, D.G., 310, 311
Allen, Dr. Edward, 176
Allen, Manley and Co. Woolen Mill (Salem, IN), 81
Allen, Sara, 310
Allen, Capt. Theodore F., 222–223
Allen, Wm. R., 51
Allen family, 204
Alliance (OH), 305
"alligator soldiers," xx
Allison, Mrs. Keziah Morgan, 321
Alory, Daniel H., 238
Aloysius, Sr., 123
Alphonse, Sr., 123
Alston, Lt. Col. Robert A., 21, 24, 28, 32–33, 150, 352
Amberson, John, 208
Ambler, Judge ? (of Carrollton, OH), 317
American Hotel, 284, **C3**
Amesville (OH), 253–254
Ammen, Brig. Gen. Jacob, 114
ammunition: capture of, 30, 82, 256; shortage of, 77–78, 110, 207, 217, 245, 332, 375
Amnesty Proclamation (1863), 168
Amsterdam (OH), 309
Anderson, Albert, 140
Anderson, Catharine Deerwester, 140, **B7**
Anderson, Charles, 140
Anderson, David Daniel, 140
Anderson, Elizabeth, 140
Anderson, James, 209, 220
Anderson, John, 140, **B7**

Anderson, John H., 140
Anderson, Sarah, 140
Anderson, Dr. W.B., 336
Andersonville prison, 353
Andrews, James P., 321
Andrews, Pvt. John C., 68
"Annie Laurie" (song), 25
Antiquity (OH), 203
Antrim (OH), 287, 288, 290
Aplegate, Harbin M., 67
Apollo (OH), 321, 322
Appling, Pvt. C.W., 260
Appomattox (VA) Courthouse, 338
Arkoe (OH), 169
armaments. *See* weapons
Armstrong, Lt. ?, 211
Armstrong, David B., 294
Army of Tennessee (CSA), 1
Army of the Ohio (USA): at battle of Buffington Island, xvii; command of, 16; pursuit of JHM by, 20–21, 361; surveillence of JHM by, 16–17
artillery (Kentucky Battery): at Buffington Island, 207, 209, 215, 216, 218, 219; composition of, 8; in Indiana, 47; in Kentucky, 19; size of, xi; transportation of, 109, 142, 171, 196
Asboth, Gen. Alexander S., 193–194
Ashcraft, E.C., 42
Askew, Pvt. John S., 230
Athens (OH), 186, 189, 253, 256, 264
Athens County (OH), 250, 252, 253–254, 259–261
Athens Messenger, 253
Athens Volunteer Militia, 189, 190
Atkinson, Thomas P., 365
audacity: at Buffington Island, 235; at Corydon battlefield, 72
Audenbaugh, Pvt. Butler, 229
Aumiller, Capt. Ephriam, 203, 227
Ausenbaugh, Pvt. Charles, 229
autograph books, 351
avenues of approach: at Brandenburg crossing, 53; at Buffington Island, 234; at Corydon battlefield, 63, 72
Avondale (OH), 78
"Ax Brigade," 97, 171
Aydelott, Ed, 62

Babbitt, Henry S., 383
Bailey, Dave, 274, 275
Bailey, Josiah T., 107
Baker, Jesse, 57
Baker, 3rd Sgt. Robert L., 229

Bald Knobs (OH), 204, 227
Baldwin, 2nd Lt. William W., 23
Ball, John, 189
Ballard, Capt. ?, 51
Baltimore and Ohio (B&O, Central Ohio) Railroad, 190, 283, 306
bank robbing, 368
Bankes, John, 267
Bantam (OH), 144
Bardstown (KY), 27, 29, 31, 379
Bardstown Junction (KY), 37, 379
Baringer, William, 207
Barker, george W., 383
Barker, Myron, 252
Barkey, Fred, 81
Barkey Clark and Co. (Salem, IN), 81
Barnes, Pvt. James P., 336
Barr family, 270
Barrett, Pvt. William Anderson, 230
Barr's Ridge (OH), 274, 277
Bartlett, Josiah, 258
Barton, Pvt. H.C., 260
Bashan (OH), 203–204
Bashan Church (OH), 220
Bass, T.M., 51
Batavia (OH), 134, 142, 143, 147–148
Bate, Brig. Gen. William B., 58
"Battle Cry of Freedom, The" (song), 25
Bean, 3rd Sgt. Robert T., 160–161, 336
Beard, Anthony L., 257
Beauregard, Gen. P.G.T., 3, 6
Beaver (OH), 177, 178–179, **B8**
Beckham, J.A., 229
Beckner, Pvt. Alfred N., 229
Bedford (OH), 189
Beekman, Lewis, 169
Bell, Henry, 209
Bell, Sarah, 274
Bell, Mrs. William, 209
Bell family, 270
Bellaire (OH), 153, 190, 311
Belle Isle prison, 353
Belleville (OH), 250
Belmont County (OH), 153
Bemis, Col. ?, 303
Bemiss, Dr. J.S., 336
Bennett, Capt. Jake (Jacob C.), 217, 356, 358, 359
Benson, C.D., "How Are You? John Morgan" (song), 366
Benson, Pvt. John E., 24
Bergholz (formerly Nebo, OH), 309
Bergshicker, Fred, 227
Berlin (OH), 180, 184, 188, 255
Berlin Crossroads (OH), 185, 381

Berry, Pvt. Wm., 260
Bethard, 3rd Sgt. H.S., 229
Bethel (OH), 154
Bethesda Church, 323, **C5**
Betty, Pvt. John, 260
Betz, J.M., 275
Bevis (OH), 111, 117
Biddle, Col. ?, 49
Big Hill (KY), 294
Biggs, Joseph M., 275
Bixby, Frank, 319
Blakely, James, 189
Blankenbaker, Samuel, 56, 57
Blettner, Tony, 101
"Blue Bonnets Are Over the Border"
    (song), 375–376
Boal, Jim, 268
Boals, Capt. ?, 296
Board, Capt. Jacob Mitchell, 50–51
Bogard, Abner, 209
Bogard, Susan, 209
Bohemian Scouts, 150–151
Boice, James Cooper, 314–315, **C4**
Boice, 1st Sgt. William Allison, 314
"Bonnie Blue Flag, The" (song), 25
Boone, Tom, 127
Borden, WIlliam, 56
Boreman, A.L., 303, 305–306
Boring family, 319, 322
Bostona (steamer), 152
Bostona #2 (boat), 152
Bostwick, Judge S.W., 297–298
Boswick, George L., 51
Bottomer, Pvt. Greene, 67
Bowers, Mr. ? (miller from Zanesville,
    OH), 272
Bowles, Dr. William A., 44
Bowman, Joseph W., 24
Box (black servant), 237–238
Boyd, Mrs. David, 168
Boyd, Capt. Thomas B., 335
Boyle, Edward, 159
Boyle, Brig. Gen. Jeremiah T., 38, 50,
    51, 62, 74, 363, **A8**
Boyle, John, 159
Boynton, Lt. N.S., 153, 338–339
Brackin, 1st Cpl. C.L., 260
Bradford, Col. William E., 369, 371
Bragg, Gen. Braxton, xv; in Mexican
    War, 16; Morgan's raids in support
    of, 1, 2–3, 4, 8, 112, 337–338,
    377; relieved from command, 368;
    Union attacks on, 58, 292, **A1**
Braley, Col. ?, 346
Brandenburg, Mary Jane, 134
Brandenburg, Silas, 134
Brandenburg (KY): arrival of Mor-
    gan's raiders at, 42, 45; arrival of
    Union forces at, 51–52, 59, 74, 75;
    crossing of Ohio River at, 38, 40,
    45–46, 48–49, 50–51, 192, 379;
    military study of crossing at, 53;
    procuring boats at, 40–42, 51
Branham, 1st Sgt. John Wesley, 230
Bransford, Pvt. Richard Banks, 238

Breckinridge, John C., 96, 376
Breckinridge, Col. W.C.P., 4, 8, 384,
    A4
breech-loading rifles, 10
Brent, Maj. Thomas Y., Jr., 23
Bridges, Pvt. David A., 336
Bright (IN), 101
Brilliant (formerly LaGrange, OH),
    303
Bristow, Col. Benjamin H., 20
Brooks, J. Twing, 317
Brooks, Maj. Gen. W.T.H., 255, 292,
    296, 298, 301, 303, 306, 312–313,
    318, 321, 324, 340
Broomhill (IN), 55
Brown, Mrs. ? (of Eagleport, OH), 270
Brown, Capt. A.D., 189
Brown, Pvt. F.M., 229
Brown, Henry, 176
Brown, Isaac, 257
Brown, M.J., 294
Brown, Pvt. Thomas, 260
Brown, Gen. Thomas M., 384
Brown County (OH), 154–162
Brown Horse Artillery, 294
Bruce, Sanders, 30
Brunner, Capt. Andrew Jackson, 229
Brunner, Charles E., 107
Brunner, Mr. and Mrs. Henry, 154,
    home, **B8**
Bryan, 1st Lt. John D., 243
Bryantsburg (IN), 96
Buchtel (OH), 259
Buckingham, Dr. Alfred, 128
Buckingham, Horatio, 137
Buckingham (OH), 262
Buckner, Col. Robert, 45–46, 53, **A10**
Buckner, Gen. Simon Bolivar, 1, 3, 14,
    96, 115, 293, 337, 365, **A3**
Buehler, Carl, 178
Buena Vista, battle of, 16
Buffington, Joel, 208
Buffington fields, 212
Buffington ford: scouting of, 5,
    191–192; terrain at, 208, 214, 234
Buffington Island, battle of (July 19):
    battlefield park, 386–387; conver-
    gence at, 151, 159, 179, 185, 189,
    191, 194, 199–200, 204–205,
    207–213; description of, xvii, 6,
    214–231, 232, 233, 336, 381;
    escape from, 220–221, 223–224,
    236, 237–242; military study of,
    234–236
Bullitt, Pvt. James, 29
Bullitt, 2nd Lt. Thomas W., 362
Bullitt, Maj. William G., 217, 224,
    243, **B14**
Bullitt County (KY), 37–39
Bullock, Maj. Robert S., 224
Bulls Gap, 368, 370, 373
Burbick, David, 332, 334
Burbick, Capt. James, 324, 326–330,
    332–334, 342–343
Burbick family, 331

Burgess, Capt. ?, 296
Burgess, Pvt. G.H., 336
Burke, Pvt. Batholomew, 29
Burke, Curtis, 61
Burkesville (KY), 19, 363
Burlingham (OH), 252
Burns, Sam, 56
Burns, William, 56
Burnside, Gen. Ambrose E., 1, 16,
    34–35; allegiance pledged to, 147;
    arrest of Hanson by, 30; capture of
    Hines ordered by, 45; and JHM's
    surrender, 335, 348–349; naval
    support to, 193, 249; obstruction
    of Morgan's raid ordered by, 170,
    171; offensive by, 337–338; oppo-
    sition to, 251–252; and parole of
    prisoners, 32–33; protection of
    Indiana by, 76–77, 84, 91,
    151–152; protection of Ohio by,
    110, 113, 115–116, 118, 126,
    149–150, 152–153, 155, 180,
    185–186, 190, 193–194, 201, 224,
    226–227, 251, 260–261, 292–294,
    302, 311, **A1**
Burris, Harvey ("Doc"), 388
Burson family, 316, 317, 318, 322
Burwell, Nicholas, 164
Butcher, Mr. and Mrs. ?, 178
Butler, Col. ?, 215
Butler County (OH), 110
Butternuts. *See* Copperheads
Butterworth, Ed, 134
Butterworth family, 134
Butts, Mr. ?, 103
Byrne, Capt. Edward P., 8, 22, 47, 48,
    147, 209, 212, 221

Cadiz (OH), 291–292, 296, 297
Caldwell, Fulton, 278
Cambell, Pvt. Joseph A., 336
Cambridge (OH), 283, 286, 287–288
Camp Chase (Columbus, OH), 33,
    113, 173, 248, 338, 352
Camp Dennison, 78, 113, 124,
    126–130, 137, 380, **B4**
Camp Douglas (IL), 85, 248
Camp Marietta, 113, 241
Camp Morton (IN), 248
Camp Portsmouth (OH), 255
Camp Shady, 126, 139
Campbell, Capt. ?, 221
Campbell, Pvt. Andrew J., 371, 373
Campbell, William, 321
Campbell family, 321
Campbell's Station (Lore City, OH),
    281, 282, 283, 285
Campbellsville (KY), 33
cannon: deployed at Morvin's Landing
    (IN), 41–42. *See also specific
    types of cannon*
Canton (IN), 83, 84
Cantrill, Capt. James E., 369, 384
Capron, Col. Horace, 33, 250, 339
carbines, 6

Carey, Bilf, 160
Carey, Catherine, 160
Carey, Elizabeth, 322
Carey, Isaac, 160
Carey, John H., 322, 323
Carey, Joshua, 160
Carey, Maria, 322
Carey, Mary, 160
Carey, Rudolph, 160
Carey, Sallie, 160
Carnes, Capt. James B., 63
Carney, Pvt. James Nelson, 305
Carpenter, Adj. ?, 287
Carpenter, Col. ?, 184
Carr, Caroline, 188
Carr, 2nd Lt. David Anderson, 230
Carr, Fred, 189
Carr, Marshall, 188
Carrington, Brig. Gen. Henry B., 83
Carroll County (OH), 317–322, 323, 337
Carrollton (OH), 317, 322
Carsey, Joe, 252
Carter, D. Drake, 243
Carter, Capt. Jesse M., 21, 231
Carter, Pvt. J.F., 336
Carter, Pvt. William S., 336
Carthage (OH), 122
Carthage (TN), 13–14
Carwood (IN), 55
Caslin, C.H., 87
Cassell, Capt. Jacob T., 21, 229
Castillo, Pvt. Augustus, 229
casualties. See wounded soldiers
Center, Pvt. Alfred, 244
Centerville (OH), 381
Chandler, Col. Z.M., 266
Chapel Hill (formerly Thompsonville, OH), 263–264
Chattanooga (TN), 1, 8, 15, 58, 112, 337, 338, 377
Cheatham, Capt. E. Foster, 335, 354
Chenault, Col. David Walter, 23
Cheshire (OH), 228, 243–246, 381
Chester (OH), 202–203, 207, bridge, B13
Chestnut, Banjamin, 171
Chestnut, Isaac, 171
Cheviot (OH), 117
Chickamauga (GA), battle at, 58, 337, 338, 377
Chillicothe (OH), 176, 181
Chinn, Christopher, Jr., 51
chivalry, Southern: evidence of, 87–88, 92, 96, 100, 101, 109, 127, 143, 170, 197, 262, 327–328; ironic mention of, 133
Chrisman, P.F., 103
Christman, Pvt. S. Albert, 238
Cincinnati, Hamilton and Dayton Railroad (C, H&DRR), 117

Cincinnati (OH): arrival of Union forces in, 152, 181; crossing Ohio River at, 112, 360; description of, xiii–xiv; fear of attack in, 113–115, 149–151; path of Morgan's raid around, xiii, 98; preparations for defense of, 114; prisoners in, 226, 247–249, 256, 344–346; threat of draft riots in, 116; Union army in, 78
Cincinnati Cavalry, 149
Cincinnati Daily Commercial, 30, 116–117, 132–134, 344–346
Cincinnati Gazette, 45, 116–117
Cincinnati Zouaves, B5
Circle Green (OH), 309
Cissna, Charles, 176
civilians: death of, 387–388; treatment of, 87–88, 92, 101, 108–109, 310
Clark, Abram S., 107
Clark County (IN), 55–56
Claxton, Pvt. William, 229
Clay, Henry, 96
Clay, Capt. Henry B., 372
Clayton, Pvt. William Lafayette, 243, C1
Cleland, Rev. T.H., 29
Clermont County (OH), 30, 122, 137–153, 155
Cleveland and Pittsburgh Railroad, 323, 329, 340
Cline, Pvt. Granville, 230
Cline, Ruth Virginia Althar, 188
Cline, Dr. William, 188, home, B11
Clinton County (KY), 43
Cloud, Dr. William, 286
Cloud, 5th Sgt. Wm. D., 260
Clover (OH), 144
Cluke, Col. Leroy S. ("Roy"), 8, 24, 94, 102, 121, 122, 251, 260, 317, 318, 335, 345, 346, A16
Coburn, Margaret, 320
Cochran, Cpl. Clement K.H., 376
Cocke, Pvt. J.B., 244
Cockerill, Pvt. John A., 157
Cockerill, Col. Joseph, 157
Coe, Mrs. Benjamin, 304–305
Coe, Ross, 304–305
Coleman, Lt. Col. Cicero, 243, 245, 246, B14
Coleman, Pvt. H.H., 230
Coleman, 4th Sgt. James H., 230
Colerain (OH), 117
Collier, Col. James, 304, 305, 317
Collins, Capt. Thomas Bronston, 221
Collins, Capt. William, 299, 300
Collins, Lt. Col. William O., 111, 129, 161
Collinsport (Piedmont, OH), 294
Colt revolvers, 10, 144, 371, A6
Columbia (KY), 21, 22, 170, 379
Columbia (SC), 365
Columbiana County (OH), 312, 322–343

Columbus (OH): arrival of Union forces in, 153, 190; fear of attack in, 113; prisoners held at, 286; provisions from, 274
Combs, Robert, 190
compensation: paid in Indiana, 60, 83, 84, 92, 97, 384; paid in Ohio, xi, xii, 131, 132, 138, 175–176, 177, 184, 188, 196, 198, 203, 266, 273, 277, 294, 301–302, 383–384
Compromise of 1850, 125
concentration: at Buffington Island, 234–235; at Corydon battlefield, 72
Confederate army: size of, 1; uniform of, 10. See also Army of Tennessee
Confederate States of America: morale in, 366, 367; Northern sympathizers of, xx–xxi, 43, 74–75, 91, 103–104, 127, 161–162, 166–167, 184
Conrad, Pvt. John, 43, 44, 229, A9
Conscription Act of 1863, 161, 162
Conway, Cornelius, 137, 388
Cook, George D., 300–301, 302–303
Cook's Gap (OH), 198
Coolville (OH), 250
Coombs, Capt. Thomas M., 38, 83, 117, 243, 244, 246
Cooney, John, 323
Cooper, 2nd Lt. Daniel, 336, 352
Cooper, Capt. John A., 212
Cope, William, 300
Copperheads, 43, 44, 74–75, 127, 133, 184, 314
Coppock, Capt. ? (of Carrollton, OH), 317
Corning (OH), 263
Cornwell, 3rd Lt. Rufus, 336
Corrick's Ford (VA), 181
Cortez, Hernan, 51
Corwin, Henry, 361
Corwin, W.P., 361
Corydon (IN), battle near (July 9): battlefield park, 385–386; description of, xvii–xviii, 62–68, 69, 70, 216, 380; field hospital at, 64, 67; military study of, 71–73; preparations for, 48, 55, 60–62, 72–73, A11
Corydon Weekly Democrat, 67
Cosby, Pvt. Ausey Dunn, 23, 240
Cosby, Pvt. James, 229, 240
Cosby, Pvt. John, 23, 240
Cosby, Pvt. Oliver, 23, 240, C1
courts-martial, 34, 43
cover and concealment: at Brandenburg crossing, 53; at Buffington Island, 234; at Corydon battlefield, 71
Covington (KY), 116
Covington Barracks, 116
Cowan, 1st Lt. Robert H., 23
Cowan, Sgt. William P., 180–181
Cowdry, Lydia, 252

Cox, Gen. Jacob Dolson, 39, 114, 128, 249
Crabs, R. Mitchell, 308, 312–313
Cravens, Lt. J.A., 127
Cravens, Col. James H., 96
Crawford, Henry, 332, 334
Crawford, Joseph, 334
Crawford, Rev. Thomas R., 295
Crawford County (IN), 41–42
Crawford family, 331
Creola (OH), 257
Crider, Mr. ? (farmer of Chapel Hill, OH), 264
Crider, Kitty, 263
Criss, James, 315
Crister, Ed, 311
Crittenden, Gen. George B., 96
Crittenden, Gen. Thomas L., 96, 220
Crossway, 2nd Lt. John N., 244
Crouch, James F., 336
Crouch, Robert, 51
Crow, 1st Lt. W.P., 243
Croxton, Lt. J.H., 336
Crubaugh, David, 331
Crubaugh family, 331, farm, C6
Crump, 2nd Lt. Edward H., 238
Crump, Sgt. John C., 238
Culbertson, James, 277
Cullers, Mr. ? (Union scout), 326
Cumberland (OH), 278, 280–281, 381
Cumberland County (KY), 19–21
Cumberland River: camping along, 15; crossing of, 13, 14, 15, 19–20; defense of, 194; recrossing of, 363; skirmish at, 379
Cunningham, Capt. S.P., 238–239
Current, 2nd Lt. Thomas J., 23
Currant, Lt. James H., 48, 67, 387
Curry, Cornelius, 327
Curry, Capt. James M., 324, 326, 328–329
Cutler, Julia, 241
Cutler, Samuel, 173, 175
Cutts, Capt. J.M., 252

Dailey, Pvt. Thomas Edward, 229
Daily, Jess, 326
Daily Cincinnati Enquirer, 104, 112, 114, 116–117, 122, 124, 149–150, 151, 159
Daily Richmond Enquirer, 366
Dalhgren guns, 218
Dana, Capt. ?, 189
Daniel, Pvt. Robert, 260
Daniels, Pvt. P.C., 29
Daugherty, Mr. ? (of Portland, OH), 209, 221
David, Col. James I., 27
Davidson, Bartlett, 294
Davidson, Celia, 308
Davis, Jefferson, xx, 9, 368, 376, B16
Davis, 2nd Lt. Sam, 203
Davis, Capt. William J., 40, 55–57, 193, A8
Day, Capt. D.W.H., 249

Dayton Guards, 110
de Steigner, Maj. ?, 189
Dearborn, Pvt. Samuel, 229
Dearborn County (IN), 98–104
Deavertown (OH), 265, 267
deBruin, Mrs. Jerome, 165
Deer Park (formerly East Sycamore, OH), 121, 124–125, 132–134
Deerwester, David, 140
defense, principles of: at Buffington Island, 235–236; at Corydon battlefield, 72–73
Denbo, Cynthia Booker, 67, 387
Denning, Capt. Benjamin F., 20
Dennison, William, 127
Denny, Sam, 57
Denton family (Brandenburg, KY), 40
Deputy (IN), 86–87, 90
Derby, Joseph, 336
Devine, Pat, 130
Devol, Delphine, 268, 270
Dexter (OH), 196
Dickerson, Joseph, 296
Dickerson, W.W., 296
Diedrich, George Franz, 80
Dill, Pvt. James, 230
Dill, Matthew, 103
Dillingham, Pvt. William R., 229
Dillonvale (OH), 299
Dillsboro (IN), 98
Dime (steamboat), 274
Dionysius Chenault Plantation, 376
disruption: at Buffington Island, 235–236; at Corydon battlefield, 73
diversionary raids, purpose of, 1
"Dixie" (song), 25, 228
Doke, Sgt. Charles F., 222
Donaldson, James, 325
Doolittle, Col. Jimmie, 367
Dorwart, William, 327
Dougherty, Margaret (a.k.a. Lizzie Duvall), 304
Douglas, Pvt. Reuben, 336
Douglas, Stephen, 252
Douglas Denbo and Co. (Corydon, IN), 67
Dover (IN), 101
Dow, Brig. Gen. Neal, 357
Dowd family, 257
Doyle, Carrie, 42
Doyle, Joseph C., 296
Dozier, Pvt. Peter, 225, 229
Duffer, Pvt. William Thomas, 238
Duke, Col. Basil Wilson: arrest of renegades by, 88; on arrival of Union gunboats, 48; autograph of, 351; on avoiding Union army, 99; bridges burned by, 97; at Buffington Island, 207, 209, 211, 215, 216, 217, 219, 221–222, 235; capture of, 6, 222–223, 224, 226, 229, 235, 247, 260; on capture of Salem (IN), 81; description of, 94; on difficulty of the march, 117,

121, 145; education of, 351–352; escape from prison by, 357; First Brigade under, 8, 19, 124; History of Morgan's Cavalry, x, xiv, xix, 10, 24, 202, 248, 335, 337, 377; injury of, 3; Morgan's Men Association formed by, 384; new command under, 375–376; plundered food eaten by, 142, 182–183; in prison, 347, 353, 354; procurement of horses by, 131–136; relationship to JHM, 16, 390; release of, 368; saving of John T. McCombs by, 51; scouting by, 5, 11, 43, 126; in Second Kentucky Cavalry, 7; on size of raider force, 106; on supply of fresh Union troops, 160; as tactician, 6, 7; in Wilkesville (OH), 188, A1, B6
Duke, Henrietta Hunt Morgan ("Tommie"), 351, 389, 390
Duke, Jesse, 342
Duley, William, 96
Dumble, Mrs. A.E., 228
Dumont, Gen. Ebenezer, 361
Dungan, D.D., 183
Dungannon (OH), 324
Dungan's Crossing (OH), 137
Dunkinsville (OH), 166
Dunlap, 1st Lt. W.T., 260
Dunn, George, 366
Dunn, Pvt. John, 61, 67
Dupont (IN), 90, 91, 92–94, 96, 97
Durham, Pvt. William Eli, 230
Durst, Mr. and Mrs.? (farmers of Meigs County, OH), 198
Dustin, Lt. William, 113, 181, 276
Duval, Pvt. John D., 336

Eagleport (OH), 264, 265, 267–273, 274, 381
East Springfield (OH), 306–307, 308, 382
Eastern (OH), 310
Echols, Brig. Gen. John C., 368
Eckert, W.H., 358
Eckmansville (OH), 156, 164
Edgar, 2nd Sgt. J.A., 229
Edgerly, Maj. ?, 219
Edwards, Pvt. Fredrick, 29
Edwards, Pvt. James W., 336
Edwards, Pvt. Jesse, 29
Eggleston, Benjamin, 258
Eggleston, Lavina, 258
Eighteenth Indiana Artillery ("Lilly Hoosier Battery"), 57–58
Eighteenth U.S. Infantry, 126, 129
Eighth Kentucky Cavalry (CSA), 8, 102; Company A, 40; Company B, 229; Company C, 229; Company E, 229; Company F, 229; Company I, 229; Company K, 229
Eighth Kentucky Cavalry (USA), 20, 33, 220

Eighth Michigan Cavalry, 27, 148, 153, 181, 217, 218, 338
Eighth Michigan (volunteer) Infantry, 22, 23
Eighty-first Indiana, 47
Eighty-sixth Ohio Volunteers (mounted infantry), 265, 267, 306, 316
Eison, Pvt. Charles, 229
Eleventh Kentucky Cavalry (CSA), 8, 23, 24, 50, 229, 235; Company B, 23, 229; Company C, 229
Eleventh Kentucky Cavalry (USA), 152, 215–216, 329, 330
Eleventh Michigan Artillery, 27, 148, 218
Eleventh Ohio Cavalry: First Battalion, 129; Second Battalion, 111, 128–129, 161–162; Second Battalion, Forty-third Company, 129
Elizabethtown (KY), 152
Elk (gunboat), 49, 208
Elkton (OH), 329
Ellis, Mr. ?(surveyor of Brown County, OH), 155
Ellsworth, George A. ("Lightning"), 37, 72, 85, 88, 89, 115, 120, 121, 237, A8
Ellsworth Rifles (Corydon), 63–64, 65, 71, 73
Eminence (KY), 78
Emma #2 (boat), 152
Emmitt, James, 177
Empire (formerly Shanghai Station, OH), 309
Enfield rifles, 10
Evans, Col. Peter, 182
Ewing, Elizabeth Morgan, 325, 326, 327–328
Ewing, Frank, 325
Ewing, Ida, 327
Ewing, Jim, 327
Ewing, Johnny, 325, 327, C7
Ewing, Nancy, 327
Ewing, Samuel, 325, 326
Ewington (OH), 195, 245, 254, 255, 381

Fairplay (tinclad), 192
Falls City (KY), 40
Farmer, "Widow" (of Salineville, OH), 320
Farmer's Bank of Kentucky (Mt. Sterling, KY), 368
Farmers Retreat (formerly Opptown, IN), 98
Farquar, Capt. William, 48, 63
Faulkner, William, xix
Faulkner, Pvt. William, 104
Fennell, Pvt. Jno. P., 260
Fergason, Pvt. John H., 244
Ferguson, Rev. ? (of Old Washington, OH), 285
Ferguson, Pvt. Hawkins, 29
Ferguson, 2nd Lt. James, 23

Ferguson, Pvt. Logwood, 29
Ferguson, Pvt. Sam, 29, 31
Ferguson, Pvt. Walter, 29
Ferree, Jacob, 66, 67, 387
Ferris, Rev. B.F., 99, home, A15
Fifteenth Indiana Artillery Battery, 153
Fifth Indiana, 152, 215–216
Fifth Kentucky Cavalry (CSA), 8, 23, 211, 216, 235, 244; Company D, 229
Fifth Kentucky Cavalry (USA), 78
Fifth North Carolina Mounted Infantry, 294
Fifth Tennessee, 293
Fincastle (OH), 159, 160
Finley, Dr. ? (a prisoner), 301
Finley, Mr. ? (of Rokeby, OH), 269
firearms. See weapons
First Brigade, x, 8, 19, 109, 121–122, 321
First Kentucky Cavalry (formerly infantry) (CSA), 7, 58
First Kentucky Cavalry (USA), 21, 33, 76, 218, 220, 245, 250, 316, 338, 361
First Louisiana, 293
Fishback, Capt. Brent, 21
Fisher (boat), 152
Fiske, Lt. ? (of Seventh Michigan Cavalry), 320
Fitch, Mr. ? (of Portland, OH), 209, 221
Fitch, Lt. Comm. Leroy, 49, 75, 191–193, 207–208, 214–215, 218–219, 237, 241–242, 249, B15
Fitch, Lester, 225
Fleeta, ? (aunt of Mrs. Harold Scatterday), 266
Fleming, John, 325, 326
Fletcher, Lydia Buckingham, 131
Fletcher, William W., 131–132
flexibility: at Buffington Island, 236; at Corydon battlefield, 73
Floyd County (IN), 57
Foraker, James, 267
Fordyce, John, 283
Fordyce, Lincoln, 56
Fordyce, Lt. S.W., 283
Fordyce, William, 56
Forgrave, Mr. ? (of Eagleport, OH), 268
Forker, James, 37
Forrest, Gen. Nathan Bedford, 9, 348
Forsyth, Dr. Alex, 390
Fort Ancient (OH), 126
Fort Laramie (Dakota Territory), 129
Fort Mitchell (KY), 360–361
Forty-fifth Ohio Cavalry, 33, 220, 244, 250
Forty-fifth Ohio Volunteer Infantry, 21, 181
Forty-fourth Ohio Mounted Infantry, 294
Forty-fourth Pennsylvania militia, 296
Foster's Crossing (OH), 126

Fourteenth Illinois Cavalry, 33, 211, 215, 250, 303, 316, 338
Fourteenth Kentucky Cavalry (CSA), 8, 20, 154
Fourth Kentucky Cavalry, 369
Fourth U.S. Cavalry, 27
Fouts, Johnny, 273
Frake's Mill (IN), 60
Frame, Thomas, 283
Franklin, Sgt. M.C., 29
Franks, Capt. Thomas B., 21, 45
Frazee, Mary Eleanor, 277–278
Frazee, Theodore March, 277
Freeman, James, 257
Freemasonry, 96, 165, 184, 277
French, John, 182
French Lick (IN), 44
Frew family, 270
Frow, Johnny, 165
Fry, James M., 370
Fugitive Slave Act, 125

Galbreth, Mr. ? (guide from Cheshire, OH), 244
Gallagher, Col. Thomas F., 303, 313, 315, 321
Gallia County (OH), 195, 243–246, 254, 255–256
Gallipolis (OH), 191, 195, 221, 228
Gammon, Pvt. James Riley, 244
Gardner, Lt. William, 29
Garfield, Brig. Gen. John A., 88, 389
Garnettsville (KY), 40, 41, 42
Garrard, Col. Israel, 217, 222
Garvin, Huston, 61
Gates, Alvira, 244
Gathright, Lt. Josiah B., 55
Gavers (OH), 325, 326, 382
Gavin, Col. James, 104
Georgetown (Brown County, OH), 154–155
Georgetown (Harrison County, OH), 296, 297
Gephard, Jacob, 101
Gerlach, Elmer, 275
Gettysburg, battle of, 15, 67
Gibson, Capt. Hart, 335
Gibson, Mrs. Hoch, 354
Gilbert, Col. ?, 186
Giles, James, 190
Giles, Joseph S., 198, 199, 203
Gill, Tom, 288
Gillem, Brigadier-General Alvan C., 370, 371, 372
Gilmore, Col. ?, 185
Giltner, Col. Henry L., 369, 374
Given, James, 130
Givens, Bill, 178
Givens Station (OH), 177
Glardon, William: son of, 101
Glendale (OH), 117, 118, 120–122, 124, 150
Glenn, Catherine, 61
Glenn, Charley, 61

Glenn, John, 61–62, 66
Glenn, Lizzie, 61
Glenn, Rev. Peter, 60–61, 67, 387
Glenn, Reuben, 61
Glenn, William, 62
Golden Era (steamboat), 247
Golden Lamb, 103, **A15**
Gooding, Pvt. David S., 104
Gorby, Benjamin, 196
Gordon, Geo. C., 51
Gordon, Sgt. John, 104
Goshen (OH), 139, 381
graffiti, preservation of, 146
Grafton, Capt. John J., 215
Graham, Maj. ?, 331
Graham, Edgar, 308
Graham, James, 301
Grant, Pvt. Francis H., 244
Grant, Gen. Ulysses S., 15–16, 123, 293, 338, **C9**
Gray, Jonathan, 174
Gray, Thomas L., 267
Gray, Tim, 252
Great Miami River, 103, 111
Green, Pvt. Elmore Harris, 245
Green, M.M., 264
Green, Sam, 174
Green River (KY), 21, 22–24, 33, 152
Green River Bridge, 22, 379
Greencastle (IN), 57
Greeneville (TN), 369–374
Greensburg (KY), 33
Gregg, Asst. Surgeon J.N., 24
Grenfell, Col. George St. Leger, 3
Grey Eagle (steamboat), 49
Grierson, Col. Benjamin H., 2, **A4**
Griffin, Velma, 335
Griffith, Capt. Micajah, 230
Grigsby, Col. J. Warren, 8, 97, 202, 211, 216, 238, **A14**
Grimes, Pvt. Robert D., 336
Grisard, W.H., 336
Grizzard, 3rd Sgt. Thomas T., 336
Grubbs, Hannah (Haas), 108
Guernsey County (OH), 277, 280–289
guerrilla tactics, xx
guides (pilots), use of, 109, 141, 147, 167, 190, 198–199, 203, 209, 224, 227, 237, 240, 244, 252, 267, 273, 281, 295, 296, 307, 309, 311, 312, 322, 323, 324, 329
Guise, Charles, 227
Gurley, Capt. Frank B., 230, 231
Guthridge, Richard, 223
Guthrie, Maj. ?, 189

Haas, Herman, 108
Haessly, Phillip, 323
Halleck, Gen. Henry Wager, 2, 115–116, 260–261, 292–294, 338, 346, **B3**
Hallett, Mr. and Mrs. Milton, 55
Hambleton, Mr. ?, 275
Hamby, Capt. John Hampton, 229
Hamby, Pvt. J.W., 229

Hamden (OH), 182, 185, 381
Hamer, Henry, 138
Hamilton, Lt. Col. ?, 8
Hamilton, Ida, 291
Hamilton (OH), 110, 115, 118, 181
Hamilton County (OH), 106–136, 149–153
Hammond, Capt. ?, 20
Hammondsville (OH), 314, 315–316
Haney, Pvt. Thomas, 336
Hannah, Mr. and Mrs. John, 302
Hanson, Lt. Col. Charles S., 27–28, 29–30
Hanson, Gen. Roger W., 27
Happs, John, 281–282
Harberry, James W., 336
Hardin, Calvin, 238
Hardin, Pvt. J.H., 238
Hardin, Pvt. Robert, 243
Hardin County (KY), 35
Hardintown (Hardinburg, IN), 104, 380
Hare, Capt. ?, 57
Harkness, Anthony, 120
Harney, Col. John H., 45
Harris, Lt. Charles W., 181
Harris, Capt. George, 146–147
Harris, Pvt. James A., 244
Harris, Len A., 114, 115, 149, **B1**
Harris, Pvt. Robert J., 244
Harrison, Benjamin, 388
Harrison, Pvt. William C., 230
Harrison, Gen. William Henry, 7
Harrison (OH), 101, 104, 106–109, 127, 225
Harrison County (IN), 48, 60–68, 74–78, 80
Harrison County (OH), 291–298
Harrison Guards (Corydon), 63
Harrison Mounted Hoosiers (Corydon), 48, 63
Harrisonville (OH), 189–190, 196, 252
Harrisville (OH), 297–298, 299, 382
Harrodsburg (KY), 35
Harshaville (OH), 166
Hart, Lt. William E., 104
Hartford (Buffalo, OH), 281
Hartleyville (OH), 263
Hartman, Mr. and Mrs. Nicholas, 99
Hartsuff, Gen. George Lucas, 74
Hatch, Col. Edward, 2
Hatch, Cpl. William P., 244
Hathaway, Lt. Leland, 64, 207, **B14**
Hawkins, Pvt. Thomas, 260
Hayden (formerly Hardenburg, IN), 90
Hayden Home Guards, 90
Hayes, Mr. and Mrs. Beezon, 82
Hayes, Col. Rutherford B., 179, 195, 201, 221, 388, **B10**
Hayford, Samuel, 148
Hazen, H., 350
Heath, William, 387
Hefner, Pvt. Ferdinand, 104
Helm, Capt. Neil, 239–240
Helmick, Joe, 267, 270

Hemlock (formerly Whipstown, OH), 262
Henry, Carlos, 254
Henry, 1st Lt. Charles, 253, 254
Henry, Mrs. Charles, 254
Henry, Jane Smith, 169–170
Henry, William, 169
Henry Logan (steamboat), 247
Henry repeating rifles, 58, 63–64
Henshaw, Capt. E., 212, 213, 216
Hensley, Pvt. G.W., 229
Hepner, John, 332
Herndon, J.F., 336
Heth, Capt. John T., 62, 63, **A6**
Heth, William, 66, 67
Hetzel, Margaret, 327
Hetzer, Sarah, 237
Hibbard, John, 189
Hickerson, Pvt. J.W., 243–244
Hieatt, Mr. ? (farmer from Hamilton Councty, OH), 135
High Hill (OH), 277
Highland County (OH), 161
Higley, Capt. ?, 206
Higley, Maj. Horace A., 335, 354
Hill, Adj. Gen. ?, 256
Hill, Gen. Ambrose P., 15, 390
Hill, Col. Joseph, 186, 265, 276
Hines, Capt.? (Union soldier trapped in Winchester, OH), 165
Hines, Capt. Thomas Henry, 5, 11, 43–45, 72, 147, 223, 356, 358–360, 362–364, **A4, C12**
Hisey, John, 325
Hisey, Mary, 325
Hisey, Willison, 67
historic markers and plaques: at Brandenburg crossing, 47; at Buffington Island, 386–387; at Corydon (IN), 62, 385; in Dearborn County (IN), 98, 101; at Lexington (IN), 86; near Dupont (IN), 93; near Mauckport (IN), 60; near Milan (IN), 97; at Rexville (IN), 96; at Salem (IN), 82; at Vernon (IN), 91; at Versailles (IN), 96; at Vienna (IN), 85; at Vinton (OH), 195. *See also* monuments
Hoback, J., 213
Hoback family, 209
Hobson, Brig. Gen. Edward Henry: in Mexican War, 16; pursuit of JHM led by, 16; pursuit of JHM through Indiana by, 59, 74, 75–76, 83, 84, 91, 94, 97, 102–103; pursuit of JHM through Kentucky by, 20, 33, 34–35, 38, 41, 50, 51; pursuit of JHM through Ohio by, 127, 146, 147–148, 155, 158, 162, 180, 185, 186, 194, 196, 202, 206, 207, 217, 218, 223, 224, 226–227, 234, 300; treatment of prisoners, 226; victory for, 241, **A3**

Hockersmith, Capt. Lorenzo Dow, 20, 97, 243, 245, 352, 356, 357, 358, 359; *Morgan's Escape,* 248, **C10**
Hocking County (OH), 257, 258–259, 264
Hocking County Sentinel, 258–259
Hocking Valley Rangers, 181
Hockingport (OH), 189, 250, 381
Hogan, Lt. M.A., 23
Holcomb, Anselm T., 195
Holden, Dr. William H., 263
Holloman, Whig, 143
Holloway, Lt. Col. ?, 20
Holloway, 1st Lt. George W., 23
Holmes, Emma, 348
Holt, Horace, 199
Holter, Daniel, 227
Holter, Washington, 227
home guards. *See* Indiana Legion
"Home Sweet Home" (song), 25
Hooker, Gen. Joseph, 252
Hoover's Gap (TN), battle at, 58–59
Hope, Pvt. John, 260
Hopper, Pvt. James C., 229
Horn and Newcomb Minstrel show, 151
horse-holders, appointment of, 6
horses: compensation for, 97, 131, 132, 176; convalescence of, 43; replenishment of, 35, 38–39, 53, 55–56, 82, 85, 101–102, 103, 107, 119, 122, 131–136, 143, 154–155, 176, 177, 198, 252, 257, 258, 259, 262, 263, 265, 280, 281, 295, 306, 308, 325; shoeing of, 156–157; shortage of, 76, 127, 180; supply of, 10–11
Horsley, Rev. ?, 97, 387
Hoskins, Col. William A., 20
hostages, 237, 252. *See also* guides (pilots), use of
Hostetter, Capt. William, Jr., 324, 342
Hoston, Capt. (of Meigs County Home Guards), 242
House, Cpl. John, 29
"How Are You? John Morgan" (song), **C14**
"How Are You, Telegraph?" (song), 366–367
Howell, 3rd Cpl. Nathan B., 229
howitzers, 33, 46–48, 109, 139, 152, 209, 215, 220
Howton, 1st Cpl. David H., 229
Hruby, Capt. J.F., 150
Hubbell, Abner, 197–198
Hubbles Corner (IN), 99
Hudson, 3rd Cpl. I.L., 229
Hudson, Dr. William N., 199, 387
Huffman, Lt. Col. J.M., 8, 224
Hughes, Edward L., 167–168
Hughes, 2nd Lt. John S., 243
Hugle, Pvt. John W., 238
Hull, Bill, 252
Hulse, David, 120–121
Hume, Coral Owens, 363

Humphrey, Elizabeth, xi, 136
Humphrey, Ella, xi
Humphrey, Louella, 136
Humphrey, Nathaniel, xi, 136
Hunsinger, Rufus, 184
Hunt, Catherine Grosh, 16
Hunt, John Wesley, 390
Hunter, Pvt. Nathan J., 229
Hunter, Pvt. William H., 229
Huntington Township (OH), 156
Huskroff, "Bill," 307
Hutchinson, "Hutty," 61
Hyde's Hill (OH), 287–288
Hysell, Holliday, 198–199, 388
Hysell, Mrs. James, 209

*I*da May (steamboat), 247
Ikirt, George P., 331
Imperial (steamboat), 191, 208, 241, 247
Indiana: battles and skirmishes in, 380; compensation by, 60, 83, 84, 92, 97, 384; description of Morgan's raid through, 55–104; path of Morgan's raid through, xii, 2, **54, 79, 95**; population of, 106; reaction to Morgan's raid in, 41; recruitment of militia in, 57, 75, 77, 96, 150; return of militiamen to, 151–152; scouting in, 43–44
Indiana Legion (home guard), 41, 44, 53, 60–61, 81, 83
Indiana Legion (home guard), 6th Regiment, 48, 55, 63
Indianapolis (IN), 57, 75, 76, 80
Indianapolis and Jeffersonville Railroad, 84
Indianapolis and Louisville Railroad, 83
Indianapolis Sentinel, 151
Ingerton, Lt. Col. William H., 370–371
Ingomar (steamboat), 247
Irene (letter writer from Owensville, OH), 141
Iron Valley Furnace (OH), 256
Irvin, Lt. Col. William J., 41, 47
Irwin, Lt. ?, 347
Irwin, Asbury, 202
Irwin, Henry, 202
Irwin, Rebecca, 320
Irwin, Sarah Wells, 202
Ivens, John, 122
Izetta (steamboat), 44

*J*ackson, Andrew, 366
Jackson, George, 56
Jackson, Pvt. Isaiah, 229
Jackson, Jerry, 56, 57
Jackson, Pvt. J.F., 238
Jackson, Pvt. Thomas W., 248
Jackson (OH), 158, 167–168, 180–184, 194, 255
Jackson County (IN), 84, 90
Jackson County (OH), 180, 182–186
Jackson County (OH) Express, 184

Jackson County (OH) *Standard,* 184
Jacksonville (Dunbarton, OH), 165, 166
Jacob, Col. Richard T., 20, 218, 220–221, 250
Jacobs' Hill (OH), 199, 228
James family, 178
Jasper, Sgt. William, 174
Jasper (OH), 172, 173, 174–176, 180
Jefferson County (IN), 86–90
Jefferson County (KY). *See* Louisville (KY)
Jefferson County (OH), 296, 298–316, 337
Jeffersonville (IN), 75
Jenkins, Gen. Albert Gallatin, 119
Jennings County (IN), 90–91
Jewett, 2nd Lt. Michael, 243
J.H. Done (steamboat), 247
Jimtown (KY), 21
John T. McCombs (packet), 40–41, 42, 45, 47, 51, 53, 59, 192
Johnson, Col. Adam R. ("Stovepipe"), 8, 15, 19–20, 28, 40, 65, 111, 122, 203, 204, 216, 217, 221, 235, 237, 238, 239–240, 365, **A5**
Johnson, Andrew, 370
Johnson, Hervey, 162
Johnson, John A., 252
Johnson, L. Claude, 371
Johnson, Col. Richard Mentor, 7
Johnson, Willis Washington, 238
Johnson's Island (prison), 248, 346
Johnston, Gen. Albert Sidney, 6
Johnston, Gen. Joseph E., 368
Johnston, William, 156, 388
Jonas Powell (steamboat), 265
Jones, Alonzo, 268
Jones, Ann, 270
Jones, Pvt. Ben, 260
Jones, Pvt. Oliver P., 104
Jones, Sarah Todd, 135
Jones, 3rd Sgt. William, 29
Jones, Capt. William H., 81
Jones' Station (OH), 118
Jordan, David, 66
Jordan, Col. Lewis, Sr., 48, 55, 60–63, 65, 66
Jordan, Capt. Wm. O., 8–9
Judah, Gen. Henry M., 1, 3; blunders made by, 20, 152, 211, 212–213, 261; in Mexican War, 16; pursuit of JHM by, 20, 74, 118, 149, 150, 152, 177–178, 179, 180, 186, 191, 202, 206, 207, 208, 211, 215–216, 217, 223, 224, 226–227, 234–235, 260; treatment of prisoners, 247; victory for, 241, **A3**
June, Jerusha, 135

*K*ain, John Wesley, 145
Kain's Tavern, **B7**
Kanawha River, 179, 191
Kane, John, Jr., 51
Kane, Martin, 305

Karn, Andrew Wolf, 257
Kautz, Col. August V., 148, 176, 180–181, 185, 206, 207, 216–217, 224, **B13**
Kaye, William, 102
Keefey, Alvin, 74
Keefey, Hazel, 74
Keefey, Joe, 74, **A12**
Keefey, Lola, 74
Keefey, Nobel, 74
Keefey, Rose Foster, 74
Keith, Maj. ?, 110
Keller, 1st Lt. J.E., 336, 352
Keller, Wm. H., 51
Kellison, Andrew, 176
Kelly, Harry (Henry), 271–272, 387
Kendall family, 169
Kent, Pvt. David, 336
Kentucky: authorization of Morgan's raids in, 3, 4, 6, 13, 14; battles and skirmishes in, 379; description of Morgan's raid through, 13–53; path of Morgan's raid through, xii, 2, **18, 26;** plundering in, 21; population of, 106; Union forts in, 119
"Kentucky Belle" (poem), xii–xiii
Kerr, John, 308
Kerr, Pat, 312
Key, Francis Scott, 16
Key, Pvt. William T., 230
Keystone Station (OH), 255
Kilgore, Andrew, 173, 175
Kindell, Jack, ix
King, Pvt. Dewitt, 230
King-Phillips Bank, 155
Kinney, Col. Peter, 255, 256
Kintner, Jacob W., 67
Kintner, Sallie, 67
Kirby, Lt. William, 111
Kirkpatrick, Capt. J.D., 212, 221
Kirkpatrick, Joseph, 296
Kirtley, 1st Lt. C.N., 23
Kise, Capt. R.C., 213
Kizer, Pvt. John Barnett, 245
Klee family, 99
Klump, Thomas and Kathy, 101
Knapp, Jacob, 267
Knight, Benjamin, 203
Knights of the Golden Circle, 43
Knouff, S.C., 288–289
Knox, Rev. ? (of Antrim, OH), 288
Knoxville (OH), 309, 313
Kyle, Pvt. Hugh B., 244

Ladd, Lt. ?, 32, 150
Lady Pike (boat), 41–42
LaFollette, Mr. and Mrs. William, 281–282
Lahue, Capt. George W., 63, 64, 73
Lamb, Pvt. Winfield Scott, 229
Landenburg, Mr. ? (farmer from Sharonville, OH), 133
Lang, Isaac, 65, 67, 387
Langsville (OH), 196, 197, 381

"Last Rose of Summer, The" (song), 25
Latrobe Furnace (OH), 255
Laughlin, Capt. John (James B.), 284–285, 286
Lawrence, Mr. ? (of Old Washington, OH), 285
Lawrence, Lt. Elias D., 47, 65, 209
Lawrenceburg (IN), 98, 99, 104
Lawrenceburg Democratic Register, 77
Lawson, Capt. Samuel, 63
Lawson Grey Rifles (Elizabeth), 63
Lea, Capt. N.M., 212
Leading Creek, 196–197
Leahy, James, 370
Leavenworth (IN), 41
Lebanon (KY), 27–28, 29–30, 33, 150, 379
Lebanon (TN), 7, 361
Lebanon Junction (KY), 33
Lee, Gen. Robert E., 3, 15, 377, **C9**
Leesburgh (OH), 162
Leffler, Robert, 67
Lemert, Col. ?, 265
Lena (letter writer from West Union, OH), 157
Leonard and Simonson (Dearborn County, IN), 103
Lewis, J.F., 92
Lewis, Dr. John A., 384
Lewis, Pvt. Thomas Sidney, 229
Lexington (IN), 86, 90
Lexington (KY): Alexander T. Hunt Civil War Museum, xi; Hunt-Morgan House, xi, 390; reunion at, 384–385; statue of JHM in, xiv; Transylvania College, xv, cemetery, **C14**
Lexington and Louisville Railroad, 78
Liberty (TN), 13
Lightning Brigade, 58–59
Lilly, Col. Eli, 57–59, **A9**
Lilly, Josiah, 57
Lincoln, Abraham, 80, 103, 168, 251–252, 292, **B16**
Lisbon (New Lisbon, OH), 324, 326, 328
"Listen to the Mockingbird" (song), 25
Litchfield (KY), 74, 152
Little Miami, Columbus and Xenia Railroad Co., 138, 358
Little Miami Railroad, 127–128, 134, 137–138, 345, 380
Little Miami River, 122, 129, 135–136, 137, 139
Lockwood, Daniel, 138
Lockwood, Nancy Burwell, 164
Locust Grove (OH), 166–167, 169, 178
Logan, Capt. M.D., 23
Logan, Capt. Robert D., 243, 244, 246
Logan (IN), 101
Logan (OH), 258, 271
Londonderry (OH), 289, 290
Long, Pvt. Joseph, 260

Long Bottom, 204, 254
Long Run Station (OH), 299
Longstreet, Gen. James, 338, 377
looting. *See* plundering
Lopp, Phillip R. ("Pete"), 60
"Lorena" (song), 24, 25
Loudon (KY), 294, 364
Louisiana Military Seminary, 123
Louisville, New Albany and Chicago Railroad, 81, 82–83
Louisville (KY), 37, 40, 55, 102, 152, 192
Louisville and Evansville Mail Company, 60
Louisville and Frankfort Railroad, 45
Louisville and Nashville (L&N) Railroad, 2, 37–38, 40, 194
Love, Brig. Gen. John, 90–91
Lovel, Pvt. William Anderson, 244
Loveland (formerly Paxton, OH), 110, 122, 124, 135, 138–139, **B5**
Ludlow, Mrs. ?, 360
Lynn, Pvt. Aaron Robert, 229
Lyons, Capt. G.W., 42, 47
Lytle, John (of Hockingport, OH), 250
Lytle, John (of Williamsburg, OH), 146
Lytle, Gen. William, 146

Madison (IN), 88–90, 193
Madison and Indianapolis Railroad, 90, 92
Madison *Courier,* 77
Madison Township (OH), 256
Magee, Gustavus S., 358
Magenis, Capt. ?, 34
Maginnis, T.J., 264
Magoffin, Beriah, 96
Manson, Brig. Gen. George L., 74, 78
Manson, Brig. Gen. John S., 113
Manson, Brig. Gen. Mahlon Dickerson, 156
Maple, Ezekel, 312
Maple, Mary, 312
Marietta (OH), 181, 186, 205, 256
Marietta and Cincinnati Railroad, 186, 256
Marion County (KY), 27–30, 33
Marion, Col. Francis, xx
Mark, Henry, 174
Markel, Dr. ?, 305
Marmora (steamboat), 247
Marquis, Crastilas K., 175
Marquis, Dr. David, 329
Marriner, Lt. R.G., 229
Marrowbone (KY), 20, 221
Marsh, Capt. ?, 265, 277
Marshall family, 322
Martin, Luther, 88–90
Martin family, 57
"Maryland, My Maryland" (song), 228
Mason, Brig. Gen. Jno. S., 344, 348
Mason, Robert, 369
Masonic Order. *See* Freemasonry

mass and concentration: at Buffington Island, 236; at Corydon battlefield, 73
Mast, Peter, 267
Mathews, Pvt. John, 260
Mathews family, 323
Matthews, Gen. ?, 150
Matthews, Lydia L., 195
Mauckport (IN), 41, 60
Maus, Lt. Charles D., 326, 328, 332, 333, 342–343
Maxwell, Thomas, 304, 305
Mayfield, Frank F., 92
Mayfield and Nichols (Dupont, IN), 92
Mayflower (steamboat), 276
Maynard, Pvt. G.W., 230
Maysville (OH), 156
McAdoo, Reeves, 267
McAfee, Banjamin, 252
McAllister, Cecelia, 324
McAllister, Daniel S., 324
McArthur (OH), 245, 256, 264
McCaleb, Dr. B.L., 178
McCall, Dr. James, 280
McCall, Dr. John, 277, 290
McCarty, Pvt. Eugene, 29
McCauley, Henry, 112, 122
McClain, Capt. ?, 238, 239
McClave, Stewart (Stuart), 308, 309, 310
McClellan, Gen. George B., 127
McClelland, Mr. ?, 315
McClelland, Mrs. Alexander, 280
McClelland, Alta, 280
McClelland, Mr. and Mrs. James, 280
McClelland, Mary, 280–281
McClelland family, 280–281
McClung, Calvin Morgan, 390
McColgen, Lt. ?, 222
McConaughey, Thomas, 310, 311
McConnellsville (OH), 181, 264–265, 269, 270, 276
McCook, Charles M., 230
McCook, Maj. Daniel, 230–231, 299, 322, 387, **B15**
McCook, Col. George W., 255, 299
McCook, Gen. Robert L., 230, 231
McCormick, Pvt. William E., 229
McCrea, John, 384
McCreary, Lt. Col. James Bennett, 28, 50, 98, 106–107, 171, 243, 246, 354, 384, 385, **A16**
McCullough, Jennie, 308
McCullough, J.N., 340
McCullough, Maggie, 308
McCurdy, Mr. ? (of Old Washington, OH), 285
McDill, Rev. David, 156
McDonald, Alice, 328
McDonald, John, 328
McDonald family, 326
McDougal, Elizabeth, 174, 175
McDougal, James, 387
McDougal, Joseph, 174–175, **B9**
McDowell, Maj. Malcolm, 114

McElhiney, Elizabeth, 272–273
McElhiney, Jim, 275
McElhiney, Richard, 272–273
McElhiney family, 269, 272, home, **C3**
McFarland, Lt. Col. R.W., 265, 267, 274, 277, 306
McGaughey, James D., 369
McGavran, Dr. S.B., 294
McGee, George, 133
McGee, Thomas S., 295
McGee, Pvt. Tommy (Thomas Milton), 269, 274–275, grave, **C1**
McGowan, Col. J.E., 224, 377
McGrain, Maj. Thomas, Jr., 63–64, 73
McIntire, Robert, 302
McIntosh, Mr. ? (prisoner), 310
McIntosh, Elizabeth, 313–314
McIntosh family, 319
McKee, Brian, 275
McKenzie, 2nd Cpl. Edward O., 229
McKinley, Jerry, 56
McKinley, 2nd Lt. William, Jr., 202, 388
McKinzie, Nathan, 65, 67, 387
McKnight, Capt. and Mrs. William, 197, **B12**
McKown, Eliza A., 135
McLain, Lt. John, 111–112
McMaster's mills (Rutland, OH), 196
McMillen (Miller), Mr. and Mrs. Robert, 314, 315
McMinnville (TN), x, 3, 13, 15
McMullin, Elizabeth, 284–286
McMurray, Pvt. James E., 229, **C1**
McVeigh, Albert, 383
Meacham, Elijah, 182
Meade County (KY), 35, 40–41
Mechanicstown (OH), 316, 382
Meglone, Pvt. W.W., 260
Meigs County (OH), 119, 179, 189, 195, 196–252
Meigs County Home Guards, 242
Merion, Nathaniel, 346, 347, 353, 354, 361–362, **C9**
Meriwether, Capt. H. Clay, 40, 45, **A9**
Mershon, Solomon, 143
Meter, Dr. Van, 156
Methews, Pvt. Daniel, 230
Mexican War, 16
Meyer family, 86
Meyers (Myers), Henry, 129, 388
Miamisville (OH), 127, 129, 380
Miamitown (OH), 110, 111, 117
Middleport (OH), 198, 199, 201, 228
Middleswart, Clayton, 209
Middleswart, Tunis, 204, 225
Middleswart family, 209
Milan (IN), 97
Milhous, Victor, 91
Miller, Mr. ? (of Sharon, OH), 120–121
Miller, Charles, 174
Miller, Cortez M., 47
Miller, Jim, 275

Miller, John (Confederate buried in OH), 319
Miller, Col. John K., 370, 371
Miller (or Mills), John K. (of East Springfield, OH), 307, 308, 310
Millertown (formerly Buchanan, OH), 263
Millport (OH), 322, 323, 329
Minersville (OH), 202
Mingo (OH), 303
Mingo Station (OH), 311
misinformation (false messages), 37
Mississippi Central Railroad, 2
Mitchell, Anita, 108
Mitchell, Pvt. D.A., 238
Mitchell, Pvt. David L., 336
Mitchell, Capt. James W., 174, **B9**
Mitchell, Lt. R.B., 336, 352
Mix, Maj. ?, 219, 222
Mobile and Ohio Railroad, 2
Monahan, Dr. I.T., 184
Moncrief, 1st Lt. Littleberry B., 244
Monroeville (formerly Croxton, OH), 311–316, 317, 320, 382
Montgomery, Pvt. Lemuel, 244
Montgomery (OH), 122, 131–136
Monticello (KY), 14
monuments: at Corydon (IN), 67; at Dillonvale (OH), 299; in Jefferson County (OH), 299, 300, 302, 304, 306, 307, 309, 316, 319; to Maj. Daniel McCook, 231, 387; at Moorefield (OH), 296; near Harrisville (OH), 298; near Pekin (IN), 57; at Rokeby Lock, 273; in Scott County (IN), 84. *See also* historic markers and plaques
Moody, Col. Granville, 114
Moore, Chaplain ?, 147
Moore, Amos, 318–319
Moore, Cecil, 275
Moore, Pvt. Columbus, 260
Moore, Cyrus, 318
Moore, Pvt. James W., 336
Moore, John, 319
Moore, Col. Orlando H., 22, 23, 24, **A5**
Moorefield (OH), 294, 295–296
Moose, USS (tinclad), 191, 192, 207–208, 214–215, 217, 218, 219, 221, 237, 240, 250
Morgan, Calvin Cogswell (John Hunt's father), 389, **C13**
Morgan, Capt. Calvin Cogswell, 6, 16, 28, 335, 354, 357, 389, **A2**
Morgan, Catherine Grosh, 389, 390
Morgan, Capt. Charlton Hunt, 16, 29–30, 224, 229, 346, 353, 354, 389, **A2**
Morgan, Pvt. Francis Key, 16, 389
Morgan, Henrietta Hunt (John Hunt's mother), 389, 390, **C13**
Morgan, Jane, 321
Morgan, Dr. John, 298

Morgan, Gen. John Hunt: authorization to conduct raids, 3, 4; background of, xi; birth of, xiv, 389; burial of, 374; capture of, x, 227, 329–330, 332–335, 339, 340–343; death of, 372–373; description of, 94, 345, 368, 390; discipline of men under, 170; education of, xv, 390; escape from Buffington Island, 220–221, 223–224, 236, 237–242, 247–248, 250–252; escape from prison, xiv, 356–364; held in Union prison, 344–349; last campaign by, 368–376; in Mexican War, 16, 336; personality of, xiv–xv, 7, 9, 38, 301, 321; photograph of, **frontispiece;** preparations for battle, 6, 11, 13; preparations for crossing Ohio River, 43; reward for recapture of, 362; statue of, xiv; support for slavery, xiv–xv; surrender of, 329–330, 332–335, 342–343, 348–349; as tactician, 6–7, 80, 142, 173; uniform of, 10, 38, **frontispiece, A1**
Morgan, Johnnie, 385, 390, 391, **C16**
Morgan, Martha Ready ("Mattie"), 4, 12, 16, 350–351, 356–357, 361, 365, 372, 389–390, 391, **C16**
Morgan, Nancy, 324, 327
Morgan, Rebecca Gratz Bruce, 30, 389, **C13**
Morgan, Col. Richard Curd, 8, 16, 31, 64, 83, 96, 154, 155–156, 157, 166, 169, 188, 217, 220–221, 389; capture and imprisonment of, 224, 226, 229, 346, 353, 356, 362, **A2**
Morgan, 1st Lt. Thomas Hunt, 16, 24–25, 28, 29, 389, **A2**
Morgan, Thomas Hunt (1866-1945), 391
Morgan, Capt. Thomas S., 335
Morgan Center (OH), 195
Morgan County (OH), 264–265, 266–276
Morgan family, genealogy of, 389–391
Morgan's Men Association, 384–385
Morris, Abraham, 188, 189
Morris, Pvt. James N., 244
Morrison, John I., 384
Morrow (OH), 126
Morse, Samuel F.B., 88
Morse code, 88
Morton, Frances Whitacre, 341
Morton, Oliver P., 44–45, 76–77, 110, 150, 151, **A13**
Morvin's Landing (IN), 42
Mosby, John Singleton, xx, xxi
Moss, Anna and Mr., 289
Moss, Cpl. Robert Barksdale, 212
Mount Auburn (OH), 118
Mount Notre Dame De Namur (Reading, OH), 123–124
Mount Orab (OH), 147, 159

Mount Pleasant (OH), 299
Mount Repose (OH), 139
Mount Vernon (KY), 294
Muldraugh Hill (KY), 31, 40
Mundy, Col. M., 102
Murfreesboro (TN), 1–4
Murphy, Capt. ?, 34
Murphy, Darius, 166
Murphy, Mary Ann Garmon, 166
Murray City (OH), 259
Murtaugh, James, 101
Museville (OH), 277
muskets, 47, 78, 110, 164, 256
Muskingum County (OH), 277–278
Muskingum River, 181, 264, 265, 267, 272–273, 276
muzzle-loading rifles, 10
Myers, John, 308
Myers, William, 326

Nantz, Georia (Jeremiah) T., 48, 67, 387, **A11**
Napoleon (IN), 97
Nash, 1st Lt. George C., 243
national anthem, 16
Naumkeag (tinclad), 208
Navigator (steamboat), 247
Navy, U.S.: at battle of Buffington Island, xvii, 208, 214–215; strategic use of, 191–193, 200, 241–242, 249–250
Neal family, 160
Neff, Lt. Col. George W., 113, 126, 128, 129, **B3**
Neff, Mrs. George W., 126–127
Nelson, Jas., 266
Nelson, Jerome, 327
Nelson, J.W., 266
Nelson, P.J., 266
Nelson, P.S., 266
Nelson, W., 266
Nelson County (KY), 27, 29, 31
Nelsonville (OH), 253, 258, 259, 261, 264, 265
Nessler, Mike, 176
New Albany (IN), 48, 49, 57, 64, 75
New Alexandria (OH), 300–301
New Alsace (IN), 99–101, 103
New Athens (OH), 296, 297
New Baltimore (OH), 111, 117, 118
New Burlington (OH), 117
New Haven (OH), 110, 117
New Haven Arms Company, 58
New Orleans, battle of, 366
New Philadelphia (IN), 84
New Plymouth (OH), 257
New Providence (IN), 56
New Salisbury (IN), 80
New Straitsville (OH), 262
New York City draft riots, 115
New York Herald correspondent, 38
Newberry (OH), 146
Newlon, Mr. and Mrs. ?, 265
Newlon, Anna, 265
Newport (KY), 360

Nichols, Pvt. William Murray, 229
Nineteenth Ohio Artillery Battery, 113, 118, 119, 181, 191, 276
Ninety-eighth Ohio Volunteer Infantry, Company I, 314
Ninth Corps, withheld, 293
Ninth Indiana Cavalry, 59
Ninth Indiana Legion, 86
Ninth Kentucky Cavalry (CSA), 4–5, 8, 11, 15, 43, 50, 229; Company A, 229; Company K, 43, 229
Ninth Kentucky Cavalry (USA), 33, 116, 153, 218, 220, 302, 315, 329
Ninth Michigan Cavalry, 27, 32, 148, 150, 181, 217, 302, 304, 305, 306, 311, 316, 338
Ninth Michigan Cavalry, Company H, 317
Ninth Tennessee Cavalry ("Ward's Ducks"), 7, 8, 45, 64, 65, 212, 221, 238, 336; Company A, 230, 238, 243–244; Company B, 244; Company C, 244, 245; Company D, 230, 244; Company E, 230, 238, 244; Company F, 244
Nolan, George, 241
Norristown (OH), 322
North Liberty (OH), 156
Northington, Capt. Samuel E., 371
Oakes, Capt. T.J., 191
Oasis (OH), 321, 322
observation. *See* scouting
obstacles, overcoming of: at Brandenburg crossing, 53; at Buffington Island, 234; at Corydon battlefield, 71
O'Connell, Charles B. (a.k.a. C.E. O'Donnell), 308
Odd Fellow (steamboat), 247
offense, principles of: at Buffington Island, 234–235; at Corydon battlefield, 72
Official Records of the Union and Confederate Armies, xii
O'Hair, Pvt. George, 230
Ohio: battles and skirmishes in, 380–383; compensations paid by, xi, xii, 131, 132, 138, 175–176, 177, 184, 188, 196, 198, 203, 266, 273, 277, 294, 301–302, 383–384; description of Morgan's raid through, 106–376; path of Morgan's raid through, xii, 2, **105, 163, 187, 279;** population of, 106; reaction to Morgan's raid in, 41; recruitment of militia in, 106, 113, 114, 149–150, 173
Ohio and Mississippi Railroad, 84, 97
Ohio National Guard, 173

Ohio River: bridges over, 112, 119, 360; crossing of, 34, 38, 45–46, 48–49, 50–51, 53; depth at Buffington Island, 191, 204–205, 208, 214; recrossing of, 112, 155–156, 191–192, 195, 198, 199, 204–205, 207, 212, 237, 250, 251; width of, 46

Ohio State Journal, 344

Ohio State Penitentiary (Columbus, OH), xiv, 346–348, 352–354, 362–363; escape from, xiv, 356–364, **C10**

Old Washington (OH), 283, 284–288, 382, **C3**

Oliver, Capt. ?, 324

Oliver family, 287

One Hundred Eighth Indiana, 57

One Hundred Eleventh Indiana, 57

One Hundred Eleventh Ohio, 152, 345

One Hundred Fifth Indiana, 57, 104

One Hundred Fourteenth Indiana, 57

One Hundred Fourth Indiana, 57, 104

One Hundred Ninth Indiana, 57

One Hundred Second Indiana, 57

One Hundred Seventh Illinois Mounted Infantry, 152

One Hundred Seventh Indiana, 57

One Hundred Sixth Indiana, 57

One Hundred Tenth Indiana, 57

One Hundred Third Indiana, 57

One Hundred Thirteenth Indiana, 57

One Hundred Twelfth Indiana, 57

O'Neil, Lt. John, 216

Orr, Ellie, 323

Osgood (IN), 97, 380

Overton, Mr. ?, 60

Overton, Pvt. John Waller, 336

Owen, Lt. Col. George Washington, 318

Owen, Capt. W.G., 8, 336

Owensville (formerly Boston, OH), 138, 141–142

Packwood, Jesse, 57

Packwood family, 56–57

Padgitt, Jim, 288

Page, W.G., 305

Paine, Capt. ?, 238

Palmyra (IN), 80, 380

Paoli (IN), 44

Paris Crossing (IN), 90

Parkinson, Jimmy, 197

Parkinson, Mr. and Mrs. J.L., 197

Parks, Henry L., 304

Parole of Honor, 32, 246, **A7**

Parrish, Capt. H.S., 30

Parrott guns (rifled cannon), 22, 27, 46, 47, 48, 49, 58, 65, 109, 139, 159, 192, 209, 216

Partisan Ranger Act of 1862, C.S.A., xx

Pasteur, Pvt. Francis A., 229

Patterson, Charles, 274

Patterson, Capt. John, 253

Patterson, Joshua, 333

Patterson, William, 176

Patton, Pvt. John F., 245

Paul, Gilbert, 164

Paxton, Lt. ? (of Loveland, OH, militia), 138

Paxton, Col. Thomas, 138

Payton, Pvt. James, 245

PC & StL Railroad, 301

Pearson, David F., 224

Peddicord, Lt. Kelion Franklin, 20, 137, **B6**

Peebles (OH), 166

Pekin (IN), 56

Peloponnesian War, 19

Pemberton, Lt. Gen. John C., 15

Pendleton, Capt. Virgil W., 273

Pennock, Capt. Alexander M., 50, 192

Pepper, Capt. James H., 41, 215

Pepper, Nathaniel, 215

Percifel, Judge ?, 49

Perry County (OH), 262–265

Peters, Pvt. John B., 336

Peters, Pvt. William R., 336

Peticolas, C.L., "Genl. Morgan's Grand March" (song), 366, **C14**

Pettet, Ann, 266

Pettet, George, 266

Pettet, Harriet, 266

Pettet, Jane Barron, 265–266

Pettet, Samuel, 266

Pettet, Thomas, 265–266

Pfrimmer, Maj. Jacob, 62

Phillips, J.F., 155

Pickaway Minute Men, 181

Pierceville (IN), 97

Pike County (OH), 169–181

Pike County Military Committee, 173

Piketon (OH), 167, 176, 185, 186

Pine, Lucy (Sister Mary), 123

Pineville (LA), 123

pistols, 10, **A6**

Platters family, 167

Pleasant View (OH), 203, 227

plundering: in Campbell's Station (OH), 283; in Corydon (IN), 67; in Cumberland (OH), 280; in Dupont (IN), 92; in Harrison (OH), 107–109, 225; in Hocking County (OH), 259; in Jackson (OH), 183; limits on, 87, 96, 165; in New Alexadnria (OH), 301; in New Alsace (IN), 100–101; in Pike County (OH), 170–172, 175, 178; reaction to, 21; in Salem (IN), 81; in Smyrna (OH), 294. *See also* compensation

Point Pleasant (Pleasant City) (OH), 281

Pomeroy (OH), 179, 186, 191, 194, 195, 199, 200, 202, 206, 207, 227, 261, 381, **B12**

Poplar Grove (OH), 169

Porter, Adm. David Dixon, 249

Porter, Attia, 68

Porter, Col. James R., 303

Porter, John, 159

Porter, Pvt. John, 104

Porter, John W., 159

Portland (OH): forces heading toward, 119, 179, 195, 199–200, 201, 202, 203, 204, 207; JHM's arrival at, 203, 204–205; location of, 208. *See also* Buffington Island, battle of

Portland (Rayland, OH), 299

Portsmouth (OH), 158, 177–178, 179, 191

Potersville (OH), 265

Potter, L.W., 342–343

Potter, Orville, 254

Potts, Bob, 312

Powell, 2nd Lt. Charles H., 243

Power, David, 274

Prather, Pvt. James S., 336

Prentiss, Capt. Frank, 296, 304

preparation: at Buffington Island, 235; at Corydon battlefield, 72–73

Preston, William, 384–385

Prewitt, 2nd Lt. David M., 243

Price, Anderson, 209, 231

Price, Charlie, 205

Price, Lt. Fred W., 213, 230, 231

Price, Marin, 225

Price, William, 268–269

prisoners: capture by Confederates, 21, 29–30, 31, 60, 65–66, 81–82, 92, 96, 110, 121, 129, 137–138, 173, 174, 182, 183, 197, 199, 203, 209, 213, 256, 266, 278, 308; capture by Union army and sympathizers, 24, 29, 32–33, 51, 55, 57, 64, 93, 111, 129, 140–141, 150, 175, 219, 221, 222–224, 228, 229–230, 242, 245–246, 246–249, 260, 274, 286, 316, 319, 320, 364; escape of, xiv, 165, 248–249, 300, 317; exchange of, 32, 231, 352, 365; parole of, 174–175; parole of, 30, 32–33, 41, 60, 66, 67, 82, 96, 110, 138, 161, 174, 256, 302, 319, 330, 333, 352; stealing from, 34, 266

Procter, Capt. ?, 126, 129

Pumphry and Irwin Warehouse (Salineville, OH), 320

Purseley, Pvt. Robert J.L., 230

Putnam, Col. W.R., 204

Pyncheon, Carrie, 390

Quakers, 80, 134, 161–162

Quirk, Capt. Thomas, 20, 45, **A5**

Quirk Scouts, 64

Racine (OH), 119, 202, 203, 227

Ragan, 1st Sgt. Isaac J., 336

Rager, 3rd Lt. John J., 29

raid claims. *See* compensation

raids, purpose of, 1

railroads, attacks on, 2

"Rally Round the Flag Boys" ("We'll Rally Round the Flag, Boys," song), 76, 228
Ramsey, Sgt. ? (of Loveland, OH, militia), 138
Ramsey (OH), 299
Randolph, Joseph, 237
Raney, Maj. Bill, 111
ransom note, **A7**
Ravenswood (WV), 209–210
Rawling, James C., 93, **A13**
Rawling, Margaret, 93
Ray, Capt. Dan E., 147
Raymor, 1st Cpl. Clay, 230
Reading (OH), 123–124
Ready, Col. Charles, 350
reconnaissance. *See* scouting
recruitment, of Morgan's raiders, 11
"Red, White and Blue" (song), 228
"Red, White and Red" (song), 228
Redman, John T., 137–138
Reed, Pvt. William B., 230
Reed's Mill (OH), 257
Reedsville (OH), 237, 240
Reese, Pvt. John A., 230
Regan, Thomas, 283
Reid, Whitelaw, 217
reimbursement. *See* compensation
Reindeer (tinclad), 192, 208
Report of the Commissioners of Morgan Raid Claims to the Governor of the State of Ohio, xii, 384
reunions, of Morgan's raiders, 384–385
revolvers, 6, **A6**
Rexville (IN), 96
Rice, Pvt. Grant, 336
Rice, Capt. H.M., 317, 318
Richards, Keene, 336
Richmond, Col. Lewis, 335, 349
Richmond (KY), 294
Richmond (OH), 303, 306
Richmond (VA), 365–366, 376
rifles, 10
Riley's Church (OH), 321–322
Ringer, John, 140
Ringo, Pete, 85
Rink, Fredrick, 107
Ripley (OH), 154, 155–156
Ripley County (IN), 96–97, 98
Rippy, 4th Sgt. James Wesley, 238
Rippy, Pvt. John M., 238
Rippy, Pvt. William Alfred, 244
Robbins, A., 183
Robbins, H.C., 313
Roberts, Wesley, 51
Roberts, W.H., 138
Robinson, John, 294
Robinson, "Aunt Julia," 87
Robinson, Middleton, 87
Robinson, Rebecca, 86
Robinson's Louisiana Artillery, 294
Rochester, AQM E.T., 243
Rock Haven (KY), 51
Rock Island (IL), 240

Rocksprings (OH), 202
Rodgers, Joseph, 263
Roebling Suspension Bridge, 112, 360
Roger, Julia, 266
Rogers, Pvt. ? (of Texas), 238, 239
Rogers, Frank, 312–313, 327
Rogers, Capt. James T., 371, 373
Rokeby (OH), 268, 269, 272–273, 274
Rolfe, Frederick (or John), 275
Rome (TN), 13
Rosch, J.M., 51
Rose, Thomas, 173
Rose, Dr. Thomas, 181
Rosecrans, Gen. William Starke, 1–2, 3, 58, 115–116, 127, 292, 337, 338, 377, **A3**
Ross, Lt. Col. ?, 244
Ross, 2nd Lt. John W., 49
Ross, Cpl. William Haywood, 244
Ross County (OH), 185
Roudebush, Emeline, 108–109, **B2**
Roudebush, Hamman Hersh, 108–109, **B2**
Roudebush, Henry, 108
Roudebush, Sarah, 108
Roush, 1st Lt. Dan, 203
Rue, Maj. George W., 116, 152–153, 190, 213, 227, 302, 306, 309, 310–311, 315, 316, 328–330, 331, 332, 333–334, 335, 342–343, 348–349, **C7**
Rumbough, Jacob, 370
Runkle, Col. Benjamin P., 181, 185–186, **B10**
Ruraldale (OH), 277
Rush Run (OH), 303
Russellville (OH), 158
Rutland (OH), 189–190, 196, 198, 202, 206, 207, 243, 252, **B13**
Ryan, S.B., 336
Ryan, W.B., 62–63

Sabers, 6
saddle, Morgan's, **A6**
Saffer, Levi G., 65
St. Louis (steamboat), 247
St. Paul (IN), 98–99
Salem (IN), 40, 55, 56, 80–84, 380
Salem Center (OH), 196
Salem Township (OH), 198
Saline (boat), 152
Salineville (OH), 312, 315, 316, 317, 320, 322, 324, 329, 339, 382
Sam (horse handler), 322
Sanders, Benjamin, 262, 263
Sanders, Camm, 263
Sanders, Spencer, 263
Sanders, Susannah, 262–263
Sanders, William, 263
Sanders, Col. William P., 14, 78, 148, 181, 185, 216, 217, 218, 223, **B15**
Sarchet, Col. Cyprus, 289–290
Sardinia (OH), 147, 159
Saufley, M.C., 384
Savage, Pvt. Moses, 29

Sawdon, John, 387
Scammon, Brig. Gen. E. Parker, 179, 191, 201, 202, 206, 209–210, 223
Schenck, Amelia, 124
Schenck, John, ix, 124–125, **B2**
Schooling, Sgt. Maj. James W., 243
Schreiber, Julius, 296
Schreiner, Capt. John, 201
Schultz, Mrs. ? (great-grandmother of Hannah Grubbs), 108
Schutte, D.A., 258
Scioto (boat), 152
Scioto County (OH), 177–178
Scioto River, 167, 176, 177, 180
Scott, Pvt. George R., 229
Scott, Pvt. Hubbard L., 229
Scott, 1st Sgt. James T., 229
Scott, Col. John S., 293–294
Scott, Gen. Winfield, 336
Scott County (IN), 84–86
Scott Guards (New Amsterdam), 63, 65
Scott's Landing (OH), 181
Scottsburg (IN), 85
scouting: by Confederates, 5, 11, 20, 43, 71, 72, 84, 90, 111–112, 155, 164, 199, 204, 217, 234, 317; by Union defenders, 62, 63, 86, 110, 138, 152, 189, 199, 208, 211, 234, 266, 297, 304, 317, 326, 329
Scriven (Scriver), Dr. D.K., 229
Seaton, William, 308
Second Brigade, x–xi, 8, 19, 109, 121–122, 173, 321, 322
Second Tennessee Mounted Infantry (USA), 33, 316, 338
Second Kentucky Cavalry (CSA), 3, 7–8, 10, 45, 51, 64, 65, 81, 216; Company A, 21, 229; Company C, 29, 31, 229, 320; Company D, 40; Company F, 212; Company I, 21; Company L, 81, 212; Company M, 20, 81
Second Kentucky Infantry (USA), 126
Second Ohio Cavalry, 148, 185, 217, 250
Second Ohio Volunteer Cavalry, 186; Company L, 180
Second Ohio Volunteer Infantry, 21; Company K, 308
Second Tennessee, 250, 293
Secrest, Harrison, 283
security: at Buffington Island, 235; at Corydon battlefield, 73
Seddon, James A., 368
Selfridge, Prov. Marshal C.W., 182
Selfridge, Ed, 182
Semple, Capt. A.C., 50
Senecaville (OH), 278, 282–283
Seppington, Pvt. H.T., 336
Sering, Col. Samuel B., 86
Serpent Mount (OH), 166
Settle, Pvt. Benjamin, 244
Seventeenth Indiana, 58

Seventh Division Hospital Corps (USA), 128
Seventh Kentucky Cavalry (CSA), 7, 8, 23; Company C, 229; Company I, 229
Seventh Michigan Cavalry, 217
Seventh Ohio Cavalry, 148, 180, 206, 217, 222
Seventh Ohio Mounted Infantry ("River Regiment"), 33
Seventy-first Indiana, 49, 77
Seventy-second Indiana, Company E, 58
Seymour (IN), 84, 90
Shackelford, Gen. James Murrell, 16; JHM's surrender to, 333–334, 336, 339, 342–343, 348–349; pursuit of escape raiders by, 243, 245; pursuit of JHM by, 20, 33, 35, 116, 130, 202, 207, 220–221, 224, 227, 250, 259, 260, 264, 273, 275, 286, 287, 289, 296, 297–298, 302, 303, 305, 310–311, 313–314, 316, 317, 321, 330, 333–334, B16
Shafer, John, 197
Shaffer, David, 74
Shaffer, Floyd, 74
Shaffer, Mary E., 74, A12
Shakertown (OH), 110
shako, A6
Shane, Capt. Washington C., 336
Shanks, Capt. T.H., 243
Sharon (Sharonville, OH), 120, 131
Sharp, Ethelbert, 320
Sharp, Sara A., 320
Sharp family, 319, 320, 322
Sharpe, Anna, 166
Sharpe, Charlie, 166
Sharpe, Nancy Wickerham, 166–167
Sharps rifles, 10, A6
Sheldon, Capt. Ralph, 29, 31, 309, 320, 322, 358, A5
Shelley, Mr. and Mrs. Benjamin, 306
Shepherd, Mr. ? (prisoner), 310
Sherman, Jacob, 60
Sherman, Maria Ewing ("Minnie"), 123
Sherman, Gen. William Tecumseh, 2, 123, B3
Shields, Joseph C., 181
Shilling, Jas., 275
Shiloh, battle of, 6, 128, 146
Shoemaker, Lina Silcott, 171–172
shotguns, 10
Shryock, Col. Kline G., 104
Siemmons, Abie, 68, 387
Silver Lake (tinclad), 192
Silver Moon (boat), 152
Simmonds, Mary, 107
Simmonds, Richard, 107
Simms, Charlie, 285
Simpson, Dr. Thomas R., 306
Sisson, Capt. John, 212, 221
Sixth Kentucky Cavalry (CSA), 8, 51, 97, 202, 211, 216, 217, 235, 244

Sixty-fifth Indiana Regiment, Company K, 20
Sixty-first Michigan, 91
Slain, Maj. ?, 255–256
Slaughter, 1st Sgt. Joseph, 29, 30
Slayton, 4th Cpl. Charles H., 230
Smith, Lt. ?, 129
Smith, Capt. ? (of Meigs County Home Guards), 242
Smith, Ben A., 165
Smith, Col. D. Howard, 8, 89, 211, 212, 213, 216, 221, 226, 235, 347–348, 369, 384, B14
Smith, Pvt. Daniel H., 245
Smith, Gen. Edmund Kirby, 119
Smith, Franklin, 243
Smith, James, 284, 285
Smith, Capt. Lot, 161
Smith, Mary Ann, 165
Smith, Lt. Robertson, 181
Smith, Samantha, 201
Smith, Capt. W.B., 218
Smith, Pvt. William, 336
Smithfield (OH), 299–300, 303, 382
Smyrna (OH), 294
Smyzer, Mr. ? (of Sharon, OH), 120–121
Snook, Harry H., 140
Snook, Josephine Mayfield, 140
Snow, Ike, 111
soldiers: naked, 19; substitutes for, 295–296
songs, 24–25. See also names of specific songs
Sons of Liberty, 43
Sontag, Lt. Col. ?, 255–256
Soper, 3rd Sgt. John, 230
Souder family, 57
Southern Mississippi Railroad, 2
Spangler, ? (blacksmith of Beaver, OH), 178
Sparta (TN), 13
Spencer Carbine Company, 58
Spencer Guards (Corydon), 63, 64, 71, 73
Spencer repeating rifles, 10, 58, 59, 218, 241
Spenser, B.F., 96
spies and spying: capture of spies, 122; by telegraph lines, 37, 85
Springdale (OH), 117
Springfield, Jackson and Pomeroy Railroad, 177
Springfield (KY), 30–31, 32–33
Springfield (tinclad), 48–49, 53, 55, 192, 193, 208
Stafford, James Madison, 156
Stalker, 1st Lt. John D., 244
Stanart, Nicholas, 189
Stanfield, N.B., 40
Stanton, Edwin M., 230, 343, 362
Starlight (steamboat), 210, 247
Starr (OH), 257, 258
Steedman, Col. J.B., 181
Steele, Maj. Theophilus, 332, 335, 352

Steele, William Asbury ("Berry"), 184
Steepleton, Harrison, 63, 67, 387
Stephens, Capt. Abraham M., 63
Stephenson, Harvey, 180
Stephenson, J.H., 183
Stephenson, Madison, 180
Sterling, Mr. ? (Union scout), 326
Sterling, Clarence R., xix
Sternberger, Sgt. Mark, 184
Steubenville (OH), 181, 190, 292, 296, 298, 302, 305, 306, 338, 382, C8
Steubenville and Indiana Railroad Company, 301, 338
Steubenville Daily Herald, 296, 355
Stevens, William, 197
Stinchcomb, Alex, 271
Stiversville (OH), 204
Stockport (OH), 265
Stone, Dr. ? (of Cumberland, OH), 280
Stone, E.H., 250
Stone, Sgt. Henry Lane, 5, 229, A4
Stone, Hermon, 144
Stones River, battle of, 1
Stoney Ridge (OH), 172
Stout, Mr. and Mrs. Thomas, 93
Streight, Col. Abel D., 346
Strong, Waldo, 198
Strother, 2nd Sgt. Richard, 230
Stuart, Charles, 259
Stumptown (OH), 296
Sturgis, Brig. Gen. Samuel D., 114
Sullivan, Lt. Thomas W., 27, 29, 31
Sullivan, 2nd Cpl. V.F., 229
Sunmansville (Sunman, IN), 97, 98, 99, 145
surprise: at Buffington Island, 235; at Corydon battlefield, 72
Swallow (boat), 152
Swaney, Capt. William, 322, 323
Swango, Pvt. George, 229
Swango, Pvt. J., 229
Swishes, Mr. ? (guide from Cheshire, OH), 244
swivel gun (cannon), 81
swords, Confederate, 84–85
Swytzer, George, 267
Syracuse (OH), 202, 203

tactics: of Brandenburg crossing, 53; for guerrilla fighting, xx; of JHM, 6–7
Tariscon (steamboat), 247
Tarr, Lt. ?, 153
Tate Township (OH), 144
Tatlock, Margaret Bloss, 84
Tatlock, Willis, 84
Tatman, Steve, 275
Taylor, Herdman, 309–310, 311
Taylor, Maria, 311
Taylor, Capt. Samuel B., 40, 45, 111–112, 357, 358, A9
Taylor County (KY), 22–25
Taylorsville (OH), 156
Tebb's Bend bridge (Green River), 21, 22, 240

Teeter, Dr. ? (of Pt. Pleasant, OH), 281
telegrams, 88–89
telegraph, 37, 85, 284, 329
tempo: of battle of Buffington Island, 235; of battle of Corydon, 72
Tennessee: authorization of Morgan's raids in, 6, 16; Union army activities in, 1–4
Tennyson (OH), 171
Tenth Confederate Cavalry, 293
Tenth Kentucky Cavalry (CSA), 8, 19, 40, 238; Company C, 229; Company F, 229; Company I, 175
terrain: at Brandenburg crossing, 53; at Buffington Island, 208, 214, 234; at Corydon battlefield, 62–63, 71–72; at Pomeroy (OH), 201
Third Kentucky Cavalry (USA), 20, 33, 220, 245, 287
Third Ohio Cavalry, 218
Thirteenth Tennessee Cavalry (USA), 370
Thirteenth Virginia (USA), 179
Thomas, Caleb, 66
Thomas, Gen. George H., 59, 88, 338
Thomas, Will, 361
Thomas, Dr. and Mrs. William Robinson, 360–361
Thompson, George, 263
Thompson, N.: family of, 125
Thompson, Sarah Elizabeth, 373–374
Thompson, Sylvanius H., 373
Thorpe, Pvt. Andrew, 64
Thorpe, Capt. Patrick Henry, 64, 221
Thorpe, 2nd Lt. Spencer Roane, 64
Thorpe, Capt. W.C., 298
"Three Cheers Jack Morgan! A Camp Song," 366
Thurman (OH), 179
Tiffany, Dr. Edward, 250
Tignor, Rachel, 87
Timberlake, Col. John, 47, 62
Tod, David, 113, 170, 171, 173, 186, 256, 258, 264, 278, 291, 297, 298, 335, 342–343, 344, 346, 354, 383, C9
Tod Scouts, 139, 152
Todd, Isaac, 131
Todd, James, 131
Todd, Nicholas, 131, B5
Towles, Pvt. J.S., 260
Tracewell, W.N., 65
treason, accusations of, 168
Tribble, Capt. Alex H., 23
Tridelphia (OH), 266
Triggs, Capt. John M., 336, 352
Trousdale, Sally, 92
Troutt, Pvt. Patton, 42–43
truces, requests for, 22–23, 27, 29, 31, 44, 61, 62, 66, 90, 245, 256, 305, 328, 330, 332
Truesdale, William F., 174
Tucker, Lt. Col. Joseph T., 8, 22, 229, 246
Tucker, Pvt. William Henry, 229

Tuppers Plains (OH), 243, 250, 252
Turkey-Neck Bend (Cumberland River), 15, 19–20
Turnage, Pvt. John Henry Alexander, 245
Turnage, Pvt. William, 245
Twelfth Kentucky Cavalry (USA), 33, 220
Twelfth Kentucky Infantry (USA), 20, 329
Twelfth Ohio Infantry, 247
Twelfth Rhode Island, 122
Twelve Mile Island (KY), 40, 55, 193, 379
Twentieth Kentucky (Federal), 27
Twenty-fifth Michigan (volunteer) Infantry, 22
Twenty-first Ohio Battery, 129
Twenty-second Indiana Battery, 20, 33
Twenty-third Indiana Artillery Battery, 49, 77
Twenty-third Michigan Mounted Infantry, 152
Twenty-third Ohio Volunteer Infantry, 179; Company D, 202
Twiss, Jimmy, 312, 317
Twiss, Samuel, 315
Two Ridges Presbyterian Church (OH), 304, 305, 382

Ulrey, Capt. William, 147
Underground Railroad, 125, 134, 170, 188, 198, 238, 258, 311, 325
Undine (boat), 152
uniforms: of common soldiers, 9–10, 289, 305; of JHM, 10, 38, frontispiece
Union (KY), 361
Union army: harrassment of Confederates by, 1–4; raids behind enemy lines, 2; size of, 1; uniform of, 10. See also Army of the Ohio
Union navy. See Navy, U.S.
United Methodist Church of Harrison (OH), 108

Vallandigham, Clement L., 103, 134, 328, A16
Vallile, Pirene, 93
Vance, William, 387
Vandiver, Frank, xix
Vanhise, Mr. ? (of Sharon, OH), 120–121
Vaughn, John C., 369
Vaughn's Ferry, 33
Vawter, Smith, 384
Venice (OH), 118
Vernon (IN), 90–91, 193, 380
Versailles (IN), 96–97, 380
Vevay (IN), 99
Vicksburg, surrender of, 15–16, 24, 67, 123
Victory (tinclad), 55, 192, 193, 208
Vienna (IN), 84, 85
Vienna (SC), 376

Viley, Warren, 361
Vinton (OH), 195
Vinton (OH) bridge, B11
Vinton County (OH), 188–194, 245, 256–257, 264
Vinton Furnace (OH), 256–257
Vinton Station (OH), 256, 257
Vogelsang, Elizabeth, 100
Vogelsang, Franz, A14
Vogelsang, George, 100
Vogelsang, Philomena, 100
von Doehn, Capt. William, 126
Vukelic, Robert Stephen, 362

Walden, Capt. ?, 296
Walker, Pvt. ? (of Deavertown, OH), 271
Walker, Charles E., 200
Walker, Dr. S.S., 147
Wallace, Maj. Gen. Lewis ("Lew"), 90–91, 99, 119, A13
Wallace, C.A., 301
Wallace, Col. Wm., 362
Walnut Hills (OH), 118
War of 1812, 7, 16
Ward, Capt. ? (of Third Kentucky Cavalry), 245, 287, 330
Ward, Helen, ix
Ward, Col. William Walker, 7, 8, 45, 48, 64, 217, 224
Warden, Frank A., 147
Warder, Capt. E.D., 336
Ward's Corner (OH), 138
Warren County (OH), 134–135
Warrenton (OH), 299, 303
Washington (OH). See Old Washington (OH)
Washington County (IN), 56, 80–84
Washington County (KY), 30–31, 32–33
Washington family, 227–228
Watson, Ens. Joseph, 48, 49, 192
Waverly (OH), 177
Way, Maj. W.B., 298, 301, 302, 304, 306, 311, 315, 316, 318, 321
Wayne Township (OH) Home Guards, 325
weapons: confiscation of, 30, 56, 96, 119; shortage of, 10, 77–78. See also ammunition; names of specific weapons
Weaver, John, 266, 267, farm, C2
Weaver, Nan, 266
Webber, Maj. Thomas B., 8, 48, 64, 81, 202, 251, 260, 352, 354, B16
Weber, Lib, 269–271
Weber, Mr. and Mrs. Theobold, 269
Weber family, 269
Webster, H.D.L., "Lorena" (song), 24
Weisburg (IN), 99
Welch, 1st Lt. A.S., 81
Welles, Gideon, 242, 249
Wells, Foster, 240
Wells, Harrison, 202
Wells family, 240

Wellsville (OH), 338, 339, 340
Wellsville River Museum (Wellsville, OH), 341
West, 1st Lt. Frank A., 23
West, Samuel, 295
West, William, 183
West Beaver Church, 325, **C5**
West Grove Cemetery, 318, 319, **C4**
West Harrison (IN), 101, 102
West Point (OH), capture of JHM near, x, 329–330, 331, 333, 382
West Union (OH), 156, 157–158
West Virginia: escape into, 151, 237–242; formation of, 151; raiders in, 119
Westport (KY), 78
Wharton, George L., 295
Wheat Ridge (OH), 166
Wheeler, Col. Joseph, 139
Wheeler, Maj. Gen. Joseph, 3, 4, 13, 14
Wheeling (WV), 285
Whitacre, Harve, 341
Whitacre, Thomas W., 340
Whitacre House, vi, 350, **C8**
White, Gen. Julius, 155
White, 2nd Lt. Benjamin, 229
White, Benjamin F., 189
White, Pvt. David, 229
White, David (farmer near Monroeville, OH), 311–312
White, Pvt. Elisha T., 230
White Oak (OH), 159
White Oak Station (OH), 159
Whitescarver, Pvt. George W., 244
Whitewater River, 104, 107, 108
Whitfield, Joseph W., 175
Wible, John, 387
Wickerham, Peter Noah, 166
Wilcox, Capt. Christopher C., 371, 372
Wilder, Col. John T., 58
Wiley, "Widow" (of Chapel Hill, OH), 264
Wilhite, Sgt. ?, 58
Wilkesville (OH), 188–189, 195
Willard, Elias, 324
Willard, John, 324
Willcox, Gen. Orlando Bolivar, 152
Williams, Col. ?, 90
Williams, Capt. ? (captured near Eagleport, OH), 267
Williams, Dr. Alexander, 369
Williams, Byron, 147, home, **B7**
Williams, Catherine, 369, 370, 371
Williams, Capt. D. Rufus, 336
Williams, Isaac, 329
Williams, Pvt. Joe, 141
Williams, John, 196
Williams, Joseph A., 374
Williams, Lucy, 369, 370, 373, 374
Williams, Thomas Lanier, 374
Williams, Maj. William Dickerson, 371, 374
Williamsburg (formerly Lytlestown, OH), 98, 139, 142, 145–148, 154

Williamsburg Omnibus, **B7**
Williamson, Capt. ? (of Loveland, OH, militia), 138
Williamson family, 209, 231
Williford, Pvt. Thomas R., 336
Wilson, N.L., 256
Wilson, Capt. R.B., 201
Wilson, Capt. W.H., 47
Winchell, Hiram, 270, 272
Winchester (OH), 148, 158, 159, 160, 164–166
Winchester (Winterset, OH), 286, 287
Winchester Company, 58
Winkler, Burbon, 90
Wintersville (OH), 303, 304, 306, 308, 382
Withers, Maj. C. Albert, 373
Withers, Pvt. William, 241
Withey, George, 252
W.L. & E.R.R., 299
Wolf, Harry, 227
Wolford, Col. Frank Lane: in charge of prisoners, 339, 340–341; as Mason, 96; in Mexican War, 16; prisoners brought in by, 224; pursuit of escape raiders by, 244, 245; pursuit of JHM by, 20, 21, 33, 35, 76, 207, 227, 250, 305, 333–334, 361, **A7**
Wolf's Bar, 119
Wolf's Crossing, 203
Womack, Pvt. Albert, 67
Womeldorff, George, 199
Wood, Capt. D.L., 204–205, 210, 242
Woodbury, Col. ?, 42
Woods, Jacob, 355
Woodson, Lt. Meade, xix, 238
Woodward, John F., 268
Woodward, "Lon," 268, 271, 275
Woolridge, Stephen H., 85–86
Woolson, Constance Fenimore: "Kentucky Belle" (poem), xii–xiii
Worley, Tom, 296
Wormer, Lt. Col. Grover S., 218, 223, 241
Worsham, Pvt. R.J., 29
wounded soldiers: removal of, 23; treatment of, 139, 250, 314, 320. See also Camp Dennison
Wren (boat), 152
Wright, Geo. W., 298
Wright, James, 387
Wright, Mr. and Mrs. John R., 121
Wright, Samuel J., 67
Wright and Brown's mill (Corydon), 67
W.W. Davidson and Co. (Dearborn County, IN), 102

Yaeger, Carl, 100, **A14**
Yaeger, Eva Margaretha, 100, **A14**
Yaeger, Henry, 100, **A14**
Yancey, Pvt. T.L., 260
"Yankee Doodle" (song), 345
Yankeetown (OH), 160

Yeagle, Pvt. C.H., 229
York Township (OH), 267
Young, Pvt. Bennett H., 336
Youree, 4th Cpl. Patrick E., 230

Zaleski (OH), 245, 256
Zanesville (OH), 141, 264, 265, 274
Zanesville City Times, 272
Zanesville Courier, 264, 275
Zeno (OH), 277, 280
Zouaves, 10